ALCOHOL AND THE FAMILY

ALCOHOL AND THE FAMILY

A Comprehensive Bibliography

Compiled by
Grace M. Barnes and Diane K. Augustino

Bibliographies and Indexes in Sociology, Number 9

Greenwood Press
New York • Westport, Connecticut • London

LIBRARY OF CONGRESS CATALOGING-IN-PUBLICATION DATA

Barnes, Grace M.
  Alcohol and the family.

  (Bibliographies and indexes in sociology, ISSN
0742-6895 ; no. 9)
  Includes index.
  1. Alcoholism—Bibliography. 2. Alcoholics—Family
relationships—Bibliography. I. Augustino, Diane K.,
1950-   . II. Title. III. Series.
Z7721.B364 1987   [HV5132] 016.3622'92   86-27112
ISBN 0-313-24782-X (lib. bdg. : alk. paper)

Library of Congress Catalog Card Number: 86-27112
ISBN: 0-313-24782-X
ISSN: 0742-6895

First published in 1987

Greenwood Press, Inc.
88 Post Road West, Westport, Connecticut 06881

Printed in the United States of America

The paper used in this book complies with the
Permanent Paper Standard issued by the National
Information Standards Organization (Z39.48-1984).

10 9 8 7 6 5 4 3 2 1

Contents

Preface

The family as the basic unit of society has the critical functions of procreation, socialization of children and stabilization of adult personalities. Alcohol use and abuse is related to each of these functions. The significance and scope of this area of investigation is evident in the present bibliography of over 6,000 citations directly linking alcohol and the family.

The intent of this work is to provide the most comprehensive and relevant listing of the literature on alcohol and the family available to date. This bibliography is the result of extensive searching from the following sources: the Journal of Studies on Alcohol Index, where over 50 family-related terms were searched from 1940-present; the International Bibliography of Studies on Alcohol from 1901-1950; numerous databases on the BRS Information Technologies system; the National Clearinghouse for Alcohol Information database; relevant journal titles in the field of alcohol; various fact sheets from the National Institute on Alcohol Abuse and Alcoholism; publication catalogs of publishers in the alcohol field; previous Greenwood Press bibliographies, <u>Alcohol and the Elderly</u> and <u>Alcohol and Youth;</u> selected bibliographies from Rutgers Center of Alcohol Studies; various national and private agencies such as National Clearinghouse on Child Abuse & Neglect, the Administration for Children, Youth & Families, Al-Anon Group Headquarters, Rutgers Center for Alcohol Studies; and the New York Times database which includes articles in the New York Times and 80 other major newspapers.

This bibliography has the advantage over database computer searches in that citations were included only after they had been checked for a direct relationship between alcohol and the family. Computer searches often contain many irrelevant citations, since a given work may have a reference to alcohol in one section and a reference to the family in another section without the two topics being related. References in this work were included after an informative abstract or the article itself was reviewed for its relevance to the topic of alcohol and the family.

References to literature published in languages other than English have also been included in this bibliography with the addition of an English translation of the title. Citations in the bibliography are listed alphabetically by the last name of the first author. In instances where no author is given, citations are listed alphabetically by the English title of the work. Complete journal titles are given without the use of abbreviations. A detailed subject index is provided at the end of the bibliography, with each entry indexed under a number of key topic areas using the citation's unique consecutive number from the bibliography.

The authors give special thanks to Carol Poveromo for carefully typing this bibliography. Special thanks is also given to Jeffrey Silberzweig and Paul Cascella for checking and verifying references and proofreading citations. The authors also gratefully acknowledge the assistance of Eliza Ferby, Robert Hamilton, Geraldine Talley and Barbara Smith for their contributions to this effort.

Introduction

Alcohol and the family is a broad-based topic of such great significance that it has been studied within the contexts of virtually all of the biological, clinical and social sciences. There are important reasons for examining alcohol use and abuse within the framework of the family and for using a variety of scientific approaches. It has long been observed that alcoholism runs in certain families. For example, it is now well accepted that children of alcoholics are a greater risk to develop alcoholism than are children of nonalcoholic parents. However, the reasons for this finding are frequently debated. There is evidence for a genetic predisposition to alcoholism among children of alcoholics. On the other hand, there is evidence for the importance of environmental influences in that alcoholic parents are often inadequate role models and inadequate agents of socialization for young children and adolescents.

Another important reason for examining alcohol use and abuse within the family context is that the vast majority of drinkers and problem drinkers do not live the isolated lives of the stereotyped "skid row" alcoholic. Rather, most people with alcohol problems live in families and have complex interactions with spouses, children, parents, and other family members. This fact provides a variety of areas for special study, including the effects of alcohol on family roles, marital interactions, and family violence. Alcohol may serve a positive role as part of family celebrations or family rituals. Alcohol also has the potential for abuse at every stage of the family life cycle -- from its relationship to fetal alcohol effects and child neglect to its relationship to various stresses of aging including widowhood and retirement. Thus, the vast literature on alcohol and the family indicates that alcohol abuse is a significant predictor of various family problems. In addition, various family characteristics have significant effects on the prevention, initiation, cessation and treatment of alcoholism and alcohol problems.

Genetic Transmission -

A review of the epidemiologic studies on the familial incidence of alcoholism clearly shows that alcoholics are much more likely than nonalcoholics to have fathers, mothers, and other relatives who are alcoholic. For example, most studies show that a third or more of alcoholic populations have at least one parent who was also an alcoholic, whereas approximately five percent of the general population have an alcoholic parent. This finding alone does not justify support for a genetic predisposition in the transmission of alcoholism. Many behaviors such as speaking English or Chinese run in families, but they are purely learned behaviors. There have been, however, twin and adoption studies which give support for the "inheritability" of alcoholism among some people.

Twin studies have relied on a naturally occurring experimental design; that is, identical (monozygotic) twins share all of their genes as well as the same environment, while fraternal (dizygotic) twins share only half of their genes but a similar family environment. Results from these twin studies show that the risk for alcoholism is twice as great for the identical twin of an alcoholic as it is for the fraternal twin of an alcoholic. This finding has given some support to the notion of a genetic factor in the transmission of alcoholism. Some researchers have criticized this finding by arguing that identical twins are treated more similarly than fraternal twins and therefore, identical twins have a more comparable environment than do fraternal twins.

Stronger evidence for the genetic theory of alcoholism comes from adoption studies. A major finding from these studies is that children of alcoholics who are adopted-away to an environment where there is no alcoholism in the adoptive parents are still four times more likely to develop alcoholism than are children of nonalcoholics raised by adoptive parents.

Currently, researchers are investigating how genetic predispositions for alcoholism might be transmitted. One approach has been to study high risk groups before the onset of alcoholism. For example, studies of preadolescent sons of alcoholics have revealed a significantly lower brain wave amplitude when compared with control groups-- even when no alcohol is present. Similar deficits have been found in adult alcoholics, indicating that there may be some cognitive or attention deficit in these high risk groups. This phenomenon may in turn be related to a decreased sensitivity to the effects of alcohol, leading to heavy and uncontrolled drinking patterns. Studies in which comparable doses of alcohol have been administered to high and low risk groups have shown that groups with a positive family history of alcoholism have less subjective intoxication than those with a negative family history of alcoholism.

Other work has suggested a possible genetic factor in the metabolism of alcohol. Nonalcoholic groups with a positive family history for alcoholism have been shown to metabolize alcohol differently than control groups. In particular, high risk groups accumulate the toxic breakdown product of ethanol, which is known as acetaldehyde, to a greater degree than do low risk groups. A great deal of research is presently in progress examining various genetic markers for the development of alcoholism. While there may be genetic factors which influence the development of alcoholism in some groups, there is a very significant amount of alcoholism and alcohol abuse which is left unexplained by genetic theories. Furthermore, most children of alcoholics are not adopted-away but rather grow up in the same families from which they inherit their genetic make-up. This indicates that in real life, the complex interaction of nature and nurture is critically important in the development of alcohol problems and alcoholism.

Environmental Transmission-Socialization of Children -

The family, as the primary unit of society, has as one of its major functions the socialization of children. During this process, children learn appropriate roles and behaviors based on their interactions with significant others--primarily parents. A child's first exposure to alcohol is likely to take place within the context of the family, where parents serve as role models for how to drink, on what occasions to do so, and for what reasons. In fact, it has been a consistent finding in surveys that the attitudes and behaviors of parents regarding alcohol are among the best predictors of an adolescent's own drinking behavior. Thus, not only are alcoholic parents likely to have children with alcohol problems, but also abstaining parents are more likely than other parents to have children who are also abstainers; similarly, moderate drinkers are likely to have children who drink moderately.

In addition to adolescents modeling their parents' patterns of alcohol use and abuse, other basic aspects of parental socialization are related to adolescent alcohol abuse and problem behavior. Parental nurturance (support) and parental discipline (control) are two key factors which are related to numerous childhood outcomes including alcohol-related behaviors. Where parental nurturance is high and parental discipline is administered in a moderate and consistent manner, adolescent problem behavior has been found to be low. On the other hand, where outward signs of affection and support are absent from the family and where discipline is either lax or very restrictive, adolescent alcohol abuse is likely to occur. Furthermore, adolescent alcohol abuse occurs within the context of a variety of other adolescent problem behaviors such as illicit drug abuse, poor school performance and delinquent behavior.

Examples of inadequate socialization are numerous in studies of alcoholic families. Retrospective studies of adult alcoholics have concluded that their socialization experiences within the family were grossly deficient as they were growing up. From a slightly different perspective, there have been case studies of the children of alcoholics. In these studies, the alcoholic parent has been found to be an inadequate role model for the developing child. Discipline is often inconsistent in the alcoholic family and the alcoholic home environment is often not conducive to the development of nurturant relationships between family members. Consequently, the child of an alcoholic parent is likely to have difficulties in developing a positive self-image, in learning socially acceptable roles for behavior, and in developing good interpersonal relationships.

Familial Psychiatric Disorders and Alcoholism -

Numerous studies have shown a significant association between having a family history of alcoholism and having a family history of other psychiatric disorders. In cases where parents have alcoholism, there is an increased risk of their children having psychiatric disorders as well as alcoholism. Similarly, there is an increased incidence of alcoholism among the family members of psychiatric clients as compared with clients seen for other medical conditions or individuals in the general population. Thus, alcoholism and other psychiatric illnesses occur as multiple syndromes in the same individuals and in members of the same families more often than would be expected by chance. Two psychiatric disorders which frequently occur with alcoholism are affective disorders (primarily depression) and sociopathy (antisocial personality disorders). Some investigators have shown that male first-degree relatives of alcoholics are likely to have alcoholism and sociopathy, whereas female first-degree relatives of alcoholics are likely to have depressive illness. The underlying reasons for the common occurrence of alcoholism and other psychiatric disorders in the same families are not known with certainty. There are theories that the disorders may share some genetic etiology and there are environmental theories which focus on the inadequate socialization process among families suffering from alcoholism and/or other psychiatric illnesses. Another explanation for this joint phenomenon is that one illness (either alcoholism or a psychiatric problem) may be primary and the other illness is a secondary result of the first. A significant conclusion from the various studies of the relationships between alcoholism and other psychiatric disorders is that children of alcoholics are not only at risk for developing alcoholism, but they are also more likely than children of non-alcoholics to develop related depression, sociopathy or other psychiatric disorders.

Marital Interactions -

Besides socialization of children, one of the other major functions of the family is the stabilization of adult personalities. This function is concentrated to a great extent within the marriage relationship where ideally the support and intimacy in the marital partnership provides emotional security and psychological stability for its members.

Problem drinking and alcoholism have been found to be a significant correlate of marital problems. It has been reported that the rate of separation and divorce among alcoholics and their spouses is seven times higher than it is in the general U.S. population. Furthermore, it is estimated that among intact alcoholic couples, a third or more have poor marital relationships. Other studies have shown that alcoholic couples, in comparison to non-alcoholic controls, have poorer communication skills, less affective attachments and less marital cohesiveness. It is not clear whether alcohol is the cause of marital difficulties or whether excessive drinking occurs as a response to pre-existing marital problems. There is evidence for both positions in that alcohol abuse is both a cause and an effect of marital conflict.

Family Violence -

It is commonly assumed that alcohol abuse and alcoholism are involved in family violence. Findings from studies examining this relationship are inconsistent. For example, in one study it was reported that alcohol was involved in as few as 6 percent of the cases involving marital violence, while other investigators report that alcohol is involved in as many as 50 percent of marital violence incidents. Similar discrepancies exist in the findings for the involvement of alcohol in cases of physical child abuse.

Where there is an observed relationship between family violence and alcohol abuse, a variety of explanations have been posed. One explanation is that alcohol has a disinhibiting effect which allows for the expression of underlying aggressive tendencies. Along a similar line of reasoning, alcohol impairs reasoning and judgement, and in the presence of interpersonal conflict, alcohol may facilitate violent behaviors. Other social theorists have suggested that alcohol provides a "time out" or an excuse for various deviant behaviors, including violent acts. Clearly more research is needed in this area to elucidate the relationships between alcohol abuse and family violence.

Family-Related Stresses of Aging –

In general, the prevalence of alcohol use among the elderly is lower than among other adults. However, it has been reported that alcohol abuse may increase significantly for certain elderly persons who are experiencing various stresses of aging. These stresses include the bereavement and loneliness of widowhood and its disruption to domestic life-styles. Some reports indicate that elderly widowers, for example, are a high risk group for alcohol abuse. In highly mobile societies, many older adults are physically removed from their children, grandchildren and other family members. This isolation, along with increased free time due to retirement and lack of activity, may contribute to stress and increased alcohol use and abuse. Most elderly people do not initiate a pattern of excessive drinking in their elderly years as a response to age-related stresses, but some reports indicate that among elderly alcohol abusers, approximately one-third can be characterized by this late-onset drinking which is a reaction to various stresses of the aging process. It is also important to note that even moderate amounts of alcohol may have deleterious effects for an older person because of numerous biological changes associated with aging. For example, an elderly person who has the same body weight as a younger person and who drinks the same amount of alcohol, will nonetheless have a higher blood alcohol level than the younger person. This is because older people have less body water and less lean body mass in relation to total body mass than do younger people. Furthermore, the elderly consume a disproportionate amount of prescription drugs and the drug interactions between alcohol and various medications can produce harmful consequences. Thus, family-related stresses which precipitate increased alcohol use can have particularly severe effects on the elderly person.

Family Therapy and the Treatment of Alcoholism –

Since the problem drinker usually lives with other family members, the whole family is affected by alcohol abuse and consequently, the whole family may have to be involved in the treatment and recovery process for a successful outcome. Family approaches to alcohol treatment are focused not only on the excessive drinking of the alcoholic family member, but also on the interactional and communication patterns of the other family members when the alcoholic is intoxicated and sober. The assumptions of family therapy are that the whole family is critical to the treatment outcome and that specific aspects of family behavior are associated with a positive recovery from alcoholism. Family cohesion (the emotional bonding that family members have toward one another) and adaptability (the family's ability to change in response to stress) have been found to be key factors in the family's ability to overcome alcohol-related problems. On the other hand, a poor prognosis of recovery has been associated with marital interaction which is characterized by conflict and lack of affection, a negative view of the alcoholic partner even when sober, and noninvolvement of the alcoholic spouse in family tasks and activities.

Even though there is strong support for the importance of family therapy, it is still not the predominant type of treatment for alcoholism. Individual therapy and group counseling are more frequently used than family treatment approaches, which are often more costly. Furthermore, well-controlled studies of the effectiveness of various family treatment approaches are still lacking.

A discussion of treatment approaches for families of alcoholics would not be complete without noting the importance of Al-Anon and Alateen as self-help groups with a large geographical network of outreach services. Al-Anon is for spouses and other relatives of alcoholics, while Alateen is

for teenagers who are predominantly the children of alcoholics. Both groups
provide a supportive context for working through the numerous problems of
dealing with an alcoholic family member.

Family Approaches in the Prevention of Alcohol Problems –

The family can play a major role in the prevention of alcohol problems.
Increased efforts in community education should be directed toward parents
who must recognize the importance of providing good role models in the use
(or nonuse) of alcoholic beverages. Primary prevention of alcohol abuse and
other problem behaviors also begins with effective parenting, which includes
a positive nurturant environment for the socialization of children as well
as reasonable guidance and discipline in directing the child's behavior.
Schools and other community organizations can work with the family in its
prevention efforts by assisting in the early detection of problems in
children and adolescents, and by providing referral for early intervention.
Special prevention efforts must continue to be directed at children of
alcoholics who are at a particularly high risk for alcoholism. Many alcohol
specialists feel that this group should be encouraged to totally avoid the
use of alcohol and thereby break the vicious cycle of family alcoholism.

ALCOHOL
AND THE
FAMILY

A

1. Aamark, C. Alkoholismens Forekomst Och Orsaker. (The Incidence and Causes of Alcoholism.) Nordisk Medicin, Helsinki, 60: 1003-1004, 1958.

2. Aamark, C. Alkoholismens Orsaker. (The Causes of Alcoholism.) Svenska Lakartidningen, Stockholm, 52: 2297-2314, 1955.

3. Aamark, C. Sociala och Konstitutionella Orsaksfaktorer Vid Alkoholism. (Social and Constitutional Factors in the Etiology of Alcoholism.) Tirfing, 41: 137-149, 1947.

4. Aamark, Curt. A Study in Alcoholism. Clinical Social-Psychiatric and Genetic Investigations. Acta Psychiatrica et Neurologica Scandinavica, Supplement 70, Copenhagen, 1951.

5. Aarens, Marc, Blau, Anne, Buckley, Stuart and Cameron, Tracy. Epidemiological Literature on Alcohol, Casualities and Crime: Systematic Quantitative Summaries. Report. Berkeley: University of California, School of Public Health, 1977.

6. Aarens, Marc, Cameron, Tracy and Roizen, Judy. Alcohol, Casualties and Crime. Report. Berkeley: University of California, School of Public Health, 1977.

7. Aasum, Bjarne. When--And Why--Can Stay in a Therapeutic Community Be Indicated As the Most Relevant Crisis Intervention. Acta Psychiatrica Scandinavica, Copenhagen, 265(16): 1976.

8. Abad, V. and Suarez, J. Cross-Cultural Aspects of Alcoholism Among Puerto Ricans. Proceedings of the Fourth Annual Alcoholism Conference of the National Institute on Alcohol Abuse and Alcoholism. Ed. Morris E. Chafetz. Rockville, MD: NIAAA, 1975, pages 282-294.

9. Abbott, S. Watch My Feet. Alcoholism: The National Magazine, 5(5): 1985.

10. Abbott, Stephanie. Don't Call Me "Sick". Alcoholism: The National Magazine, 5(1): 11, 1984.

11. Abbott, Stephanie. It's Nothing Personal. Alcoholism and Addiction: The National Magazine, 5(6): 11, 1985.

12. Abbott, Stephanie. On the First Day of Christmas My True Love Gave to Me. Alcoholism and Addiction, 6(2): 9, 1985.

13. Abe, K. Reactions to Coffee and Alcohol in Monozygotic Twins. Journal of Psychosomatic Research, 12: 199-203, 1968.

14. Abel, Ernest L. Characteristics of Mothers of Fetal Alcohol Syndrome Children. Neurobehavioral Toxicology and Teratology, 4(1): 3-4, 1982.

15. Abel, Ernest L. Fetal Alcohol Syndrome and Fetal Alcohol Effects.
    New York: Plenum Press, 1984.

16. Abel, Ernest L. Fetal Alcohol Syndrome, Volumes II and III.
    CRC Press, Inc., 1982.

17. Abel, Ernest L. Marihuana, Tobacco, Alcohol, and Reproduction.
    CRC Press, Inc., 1983.

18. Abel, Ernest L., Randall, Carrie L. and Riley, Edward P. Alcohol
    Consumption and Prenatal Development. In: Medical and Social
    Aspects of Alcohol Abuse. Eds. Boris Tabakoff, Patricia B.
    Sutker and Carrie L. Randall. New York: Plenum Press, 1983,
    pages 221-240.

19. Abelsohn, D.S. and Van Der Spuy, H.I.J. The Age Variable in
    Alcoholism. Journal of Studies on Alcohol, 39: 800-808, 1978.

20. Abittan, J. Essai de Prise en Charge d'alcooliques Chroniques
    et de Leurs Conjointes. (Attempt to Take Charge of Chronic
    Alcoholics and Their Spouses.) Doctoral Dissertation.
    Universite de Paris XII, 1973.

21. Ablon, J. The Significance of Cultural Patterning for the
    "Alcoholic Family." Family Process, 19: 127-144, 1980.

22. Ablon, Joan. Al-Anon Family Groups. American Journal of
    Psychotherapy, 29: 30-45, 1974.

23. Ablon, Joan. Al-Anon Family Groups. Impetus For Learning and
    Change Through the Presentation of Alternatives. American
    Journal of Psychotherapy, 28(1): 30-45, 1974.

24. Ablon, Joan. Family Behavior and Alcoholism. In: Cross-Cultural
    Approaches to the Study of Alcohol: An Interdisciplinary
    Perspective. Eds. Michael W. Everett, Jack O. Wadell and
    Dwight B. Heath. The Hague, Paris: Mounton, 1976, pages
    133-160.

25. Ablon, Joan. Family Research and Alcoholism. In: Recent
    Developments in Alcoholism, Volume 2. Learning and
    Social Models; Alcohol and the Liver; Aging and Alcoholism;
    Anthropology. Ed. M. Galanter. New York: Plenum Press,
    1984, pages 383-395.

26. Ablon, Joan. Family Structure and Behavior in Alcoholism: A Review
    of the Literature. In: The Biology of Alcoholism. Volume 4.
    Social Aspects of Alcoholism. Eds. B. Kissin and H. Begleiter.
    New York: Plenum Press, 1976, pages 205-242.

27. Ablon, Joan. Perspectives on Al-Anon Family Groups. In: Alcoholism:
    Development, Consequences and Interventions. Eds. N.J. Este
    and M.E. Heinemann. St. Louis, MO: C.V. Mosby Company, 1977,
    pages 274-282.

28. Ablon, Joan. Research Frontiers for Anthropologists in Family
    Studies. A Case in Point: Alcoholism and the Family.
    Human Organization, 38(2): 196-200, 1979.

29. Ablon, Joan, Ames, Genevieve and Cunningham, William. To All
    Appearances: The Ideal American Family. An Anthropological
    Case Study. In: Power to Change: Family Case Studies in
    the Treatment of Alcoholism. Ed. Edward Kaufman. New York:
    Gardner Press, 1984, pages 199-235.

30. Ablon, Joan and Cunningham, William. Implications of Cultural
    Patterning for the Delivery of Alcoholism Services Case
    Studies. Journal of Studies on Alcohol, 42(Supplement 9):
    185-206, 1981.

31. About Child Abuse. COA Review, 4: 4, 1983.

32. Abrams, Richard and Taylor, Michael Alan. Catatonia: Prediction of Response to Somatic Treatments. American Journal of Psychiatry, 134(1): 78-80, 1977.

33. Abrams, Richard and Taylor, Michael Alan. Mania and Schizo-Affective Disorder, Manic Type: A Comparison. American Journal of Psychiatry, 133: 1445-1447, 1976.

34. Abrams, Richard and Taylor, Michael Alan. Unipoloar Mania: A Preliminary Report. Archives of General Psychiatry, 30(4): 441-443, 1974.

35. Abu-Laban B. and Larsen, D.E. The Qualities and Sources of Norms and Definitions of Alcohol. Sociology and Social Research, 53: 34-43, 1968.

36. Abuse of Alcohol. In: Home Conditions; a Sociomedical Study of 1066 Hospitalized Patients with Skin and Venereal Diseases. Ed. E. Lomholt. Copenhagen: Rosenskilde and Bagger, 1958, pages 45-47.

37. Abused and Abuser: The Same, or Different. Downstate Reporter, Brooklyn, (Spring): 30-31, 1978.

38. Ackerman, J.M. Clinical Events Attending Father Loss in the Histories of V.A. Schizophrenic and Alcoholic Patients. Doctoral Dissertation. (University Microfilms No. 68-12386.) Denver: University of Colorado, 1968.

39. Ackerman, Robert J. Alcoholic Parents: Reducing the Impact. Focus on Family and Chemical Dependency, 7(1): 5-6, 1984.

40. Ackerman, Robert J. Alcoholism and the Family. In: Alcoholism: New Perspectives. Eds. H.K. Cleminshaw and E.B. Truitt. Akron: University of Akron, 1983, pages 79-94.

41. Ackerman, Robert J. Children of Alcoholics: A Guidebook for Educators, Therapists, and Parents. Holmes Beach, FL: Learning Publications, 1978; 2nd edition, 1983.

42. Ackerman, Robert J. Research Update: Alcoholic Mother, Alcoholic Father, Does the Gender Make a Difference? National Association for Children of Alcoholics (NACoA) Newsletter, 2(3): 6, 1985.

43. Ackerman, Robert J. Research Update: Mixed Messages, Identity and Adolescent Children of Alcoholics. National Association for Children of Alcoholics, 2(1): 1985.

44. Acres, Douglas I. Involvement With Alcoholism in General-Practice-Letter to Medical-Students From a Family Doctor British Journal on Alcohol and Alcoholism, 12(2): 52-56, 1977.

45. ACS Releases Dietary Guidelines Aimed at Reducing Cancer Risk. Medical World, March: 125-128, 1984.

46. Adams, C.C. The Cure. New York: Exposition Press, 1950.

47. Adams, David. Running. In: Having Been There. Ed. A. Luks. New York: Charles Scribner's Sons, 1979, pages 45-66.

48. Adams, Judith Karen. Familial Antecedents of Alcoholism and Gender Perception Among Alcoholics. Dissertation Abstracts International, 43(3): 860B, 1982.

49. Adams, Lucile Lauren. Blood Pressure Determinants in an Upwardly
    Mobile Population: Black College Freshmen. Dissertation
    Abstracts International, 45(2): 522B, 1983.

50. Addiction and the Family: A Bibliography with Notes.
    Washington, D.C.: Washington Area Council on Alcoholism
    and Drug Abuse, Inc., 1973.

51. Addiction to Drugs. Lancet, London, 7124: 587, 1960.

52. Adell, G. Psychiatric Examinations of Certain Male Vagrants and
    Alcoholics in Sweden in the Year 1938. Acta Psychiatrica
    et Neurologea, 13: 447-462, 1938.

53. Ades, J. and Lemperiere, T. Management of Alcoholics by the
    General Practitioner. Revue de L'Infirmiere, Paris,
    29(7): 40-43, 1979.

54. Ades, J. and Rouillon, F. Genetic Aspects of Alcoholic Behavior.
    Journal de Genetique Humaine, 29(Supplement 5): 583-592,
    1981.

55. Adis-Castro, G. Salud Mental y Alcoholismo. (Mental Health and
    Alcoholism.) Acta Psiquiatrica Y Psicologica De America
    Latina, Buenos Aires, 20: 142-146, 1974.

56. Adjustment of the Family to the Crisis of Alcoholism. Report.
    New Brunswick, NJ: Rutgers University Center of Alcohol
    Studies, 1971.

57. Adler, Israel and Kandel, Denise B. A Cross-Cultural Comparison
    of Sociopsychological Factors in Alcohol Use Among Adoles-
    cents in Israel, France, and the United States. Journal of
    Youth and Adolescence, 11(2): 89-113, 1982.

58. Adler, Peter T. and Lotecka, Lynn. Drug Use Among High School
    Students: Patterns and Correlates. International Journal
    of the Addictions, 8(3): 537-548, 1973.

59. Adler, Robert and Raphael, Beverly. Children of Alcoholics.
    Australian & New Zealand Journal of Psychiatry, 17(1):
    3-8, 1983.

60. Adolescent Fathers. ADAMHA News (Alcohol, Drug Abuse, and Mental
    Health Administration), 11(5): 3, 1985.

61. Adolescents and Alcoholic Parents. Al-Anon Family Group
    Headquarters. Pamphlet. New York: Al-Anon Family Group
    Headquarters, 1971.

62. Adoption of Children of Alcoholic Parents. Christian Science
    Monitor: page 6, column 1, December 22, 1975.

63. Adult Children of Alcoholics. Al-Anon Family Group Headquarters.
    Pamphlet. New York: Al-Anon Family Group Headquarters, 1979.

64. Adult Children of Alcoholics Inside Al-Anon: The Open Fold.
    Focus on Family and Chemical Dependency, 8(1): 6, 38,
    1985.

65. Adult COA. An Adult COA's Story: Three Days in October.
    COA Newsletter, 2(2): 4, 1984.

66. Adverse Social Consequences of Alcohol Use and Alcoholism. In:
    Alcohol and Health: Fifth Special Report to the United
    States Congress. Rockville, MD: National Institute on
    Alcohol Abuse and Alcoholism, 1983, 83-99.

67. Aetiology of Chronic Alcoholism. (Any Questions?) British Medical Journal, London, 1: 1015, 1958.

68. Aetiology of Chronic Alcoholism. (Notes and Comments.) British Medical Journal, London, 1: 1366, 1958.

69. Agahi, Cyrus and Spencer, Christopher. Beliefs and Opinions About Drugs and Their Users As Predictors of Drug-User Status of Adolescents in Post-Revolutionary Iran. Drug & Alcohol Dependence, 10(2-3): 99-110, 1982.

70. Agape, Key to Recovery Process; Success For Alcoholics, Families Found in Positive Attitudes. Focus on Alcohol and Drug Issues, 4(4): 7-8, 1981.

71. Agarwal, Dharam P., Harada, Shoji and Goedde, H.W. Racial Differences in Biological Sensitivity to Ethanol: The Role of Alcohol Dehydrogenase and Adelhyde Dehydrogenase Isozymes. Alcoholism: Clinical and Experimental Research, 5(1): 12-16, 1981.

72. Agarwal, Dharam P., Philippu, G., Milech, U., Goedde, H.W. and Schrappe, O. Platelet Monoamine Oxidase Activity in Alcoholics. Modern Problems of Pharmacopsychiatry, Basel, 19: 260-264, 1983.

73. Agencies Aid Victims of Domestic Violence. NIAAA Information and Feature Service (IFS No. 86): 7, July 30, 1981.

74. Agna, Mary A. The Literature of Medicine: Working With the Family in Primary Care: A Systems Approach to Health and Illness. Annals of Internal Medicine, 101(3): 414, 1984.

75. Agne, Charlene and Paolucci, Kristin. A Holistic Health Approach to an Alcoholic Treatment Program. Journal of Drug Education, 12(2): 137-144, 1982.

76. Aguzzi, O, Gattinoni, G. and Galli, T. Alcoolismo e Attivita Psico-Sociale nel Territorio. (Alcoholism and Psychosocial Activities in Outlying Districts. Rivista Sperimentale de Freniatria Medicina Legale delle Alienazioni: Mentali, 102: 991-1007, 1978.

77. Ahlfors, U.G. Alkoholpatienter i Oppen Vard. (Alcoholic Patients in Open Therapeutic Care.) Suom Laakarilehti, Finland, 20: 2485-2489, 1965.

78. Ahrens, E. Der Alkoholiker und Sein Soziales Umfeld aus der Sicht der Sozialberatung Eines Grossbetriebes. (The Alcoholic and His Social Environment from the Standpoint of the Social Service in a Large Enterprise.) Arbeitsmedizin, Sozialmedizin, Praventivmedizin, 13: 47-49, 1978.

79. Akhmina, N.I., Dyachenko, S.S., Korobova, L.I. and Pashchenkov, S.Z. Alkogolizm i Geneticheskiye Markery. (Alcoholism and Genetic Markers.) Zhurnal Nevropatologii I Psikhiatrii, Moscow, 75: 573-576, 1975.

80. Akiskal, Hagop Souren. Factors Associated with Incomplete Recovery in Primary Depressive Illness. Journal of Clinical Psychiatry, 43(7): 266-271, 1982.

81. Akiskal, Hagop Souren, King, Doug, Rosenthal, Ted, Robinson, Delbert and Scott-Strauss, Alice. Chronic Depressions 1. Clinical and Familial Characteristics in 137 Probands. Journal of Affective Disorders, Amsterdam, 3(3): 297-315, 1981.

82. Alani, A.A. The Battered Husband. _British Journal of Psychiatry_,
       London, _129_(96): 1976.

83. Al-Anon. _Journal of the American Medical Association_, _238_(10):
       1062-1063, 1977.

84. Al-Anon Family Group Headquarters. _Adult Children of Alcoholics_.
       Pamphlet. New York: Al-Anon Family Group Headquarters, no date.

85. Al-Anon Family Group Headquarters. Adult Children of Alcoholics
       Inside Al-Anon: The Open Fold. _Focus on Family and Chemical
       Dependency_, _8_(1): 6, 38, 1985.

86. Al-Anon Family Group Headquarters. _Al-Anon and Alateen, Groups
       at Work. The Basic Manual of Principles and Practices_.
       Pamphlet. New York, 1976.

87. Al-Anon Family Group Headquarters. _Al-Anon Faces Alcoholism_.
       2nd edition. New York, no date.

88. Al-Anon Family Group Headquarters. _Al-Anon Fact File_.
       Pamphlet. New York, 1969.

89. Al-Anon Family Group Headquarters. _Al-Anon Family Groups_.
       Pamphlet. New York, 1984.

90. Al-Anon Family Group Headquarters. _Al-Anon, Family Treatment
       Tool in Alcoholism_. Pamphlet. New York, 1971.

91. Al-Anon Family Group Headquarters. _Al-Anon Is for Adult Children
       of Alcoholics_. Pamphlet. New York, no date.

92. Al-Anon Family Group Headquarters. _Al-Anon Sharings From Adult
       Children_. Pamphlet. New York, no date.

93. Al-Anon Family Group Headquarters. _Al-Anon, You and the
       Alcoholic_. Pamphlet. New York, no date.

94. Al-Anon Family Group Headquarters. _Alateen -- A Day at a Time_.
       New York, no date.

95. Al-Anon Family Group Headquarters. _Alateen Do's and Don'ts_.
       Card. New York, 1970.

96. Al-Anon Family Group Headquarters. _Alateen: Hope for Children
       of Alcoholics_. New York, 1973.

97. Al-Anon Family Group Headquarters. _Alcoholism the Family Disease_.
       Pamphlet. New York, no date.

98. Al-Anon Family Group Headquarters. _Did You Grow Up With a Problem
       Drinker?_ Pamphlet. New York, no date.

99. Al-Anon Family Group Headquarters. _The Dilemma of the Alcoholic
       Marriage_. New York, 1971.

100. Al-Anon Family Group Headquarters. _Facts About Alateen_.
       Pamphlet. New York, 1969.

101. Al-Anon Family Group Headquarters. _For Teenagers with an
       Alcoholic Parent_. Pamphlet. New York, 1968.

102. Al-Anon Family Group Headquarters. _Forum Favorites_. New York,
       no date.

103. Al-Anon Family Group Headquarters. _A Guide for Sponsors of
       Alateen Groups_. Pamphlet. New York, 1968 (revised
       edition, 1974).

104. Al-Anon Family Group Headquarters. <u>How Can I Help My Children?</u>
      <u>Asks an Al-Anon Member</u>. Pamphlet. New York, 1973.

105. Al-Anon Family Group Headquarters. <u>If Your Parents Drink Too</u>
      <u>Much</u>. Pamphlet. New York, 1974.

106. Al-Anon Family Group Headquarters. <u>It's a Teenaged Affair</u>.
      Pamphlet. New York, 1964.

107. Al-Anon Family Group Headquarters. <u>Jane's Husband Drank Too</u>
      <u>Much</u>. Pamphlet. New York, no date.

108. Al-Anon Family Group Headquarters. <u>Living With an Alcoholic</u>.
      New York, 1960.

109. Al-Anon Family Group Headquarters. <u>Living With an Alcoholic,</u>
      <u>With the Help of Al-Anon</u> (revised edition). New York,
      1964. (Published in 1955 as: <u>The Al-Anon Family Group:</u>
      <u>A Guide for the Families of Problem Drinkers</u>.)

110. Al-Anon Family Group Headquarters. <u>Living With Sobriety:</u>
      <u>Another Beginning</u>. Pamphlet. New York, no date.

111. Al-Anon Family Group Headquarters. <u>Lois Remembers: Memoirs</u>
      <u>of the Co-Founder of Al-Anon and Wife of the Co-Founder</u>
      <u>of Alcoholics Anonymous</u>. New York, 1979.

112. Al-Anon Family Group Headquarters. <u>"My Wife Drinks Too Much"</u>.
      Pamphlet. New York, no date.

113. Al-Anon Family Group Headquarters. <u>One Day at a Time in</u>
      <u>Al-Anon</u>. New York, 1968.

114. Al-Anon Family Group Headquarters. <u>Operation Alateen</u>.
      Pamphlet. New York, 1962.

115. Al-Anon Family Group Headquarters. <u>Purposes and Suggestions</u>
      <u>for Al-Anon Family Groups</u>. Pamphlet. New York, 1962.

116. Al-Anon Family Group Headquarters. <u>A Teacher Finds Guidance in</u>
      <u>Al-Anon</u>. Pamphlet. New York, 1973.

117. Al-Anon Family Group Headquarters. <u>To the Mother and Father</u>
      <u>of an Alcoholic</u>. Pamphlet. New York, no date.

118. Al-Anon Family Group Headquarters. <u>Understanding Ourselves and</u>
      <u>Alcoholism</u>. Pamphlet. New York, 1979.

119. Al-Anon Family Group Headquarters. <u>What Do You Do About</u>
      <u>the Alcoholic's Drinking?</u>. Pamphlet. New York, 1966.

120. Al-Anon Family Group Headquarters. <u>"What's Next?" Asks the</u>
      <u>Husband of an Alcoholic</u>. Pamphlet. New York, 1972.

121. Al-Anon Family Group Headquarters. <u>Youth and the Alcoholic</u>
      <u>Parent: A Message to Young People</u>. Pamphlet. New York,
      1957 (revised 1966, 1972 and 1975).

122. Al-Anon Groups for Adult Children of Alcoholics. <u>ADAMHA</u>,
      <u>10</u>(1): 7A, January, 1984.

123. Alapin, Buieslaw. Trichlorethylene Addiction and Its Effects.
      <u>British Journal of Addiction</u>, Edinburgh, <u>68</u>(4): 331-335,
      1973.

124. Albaugh, Bernard and Albaugh, Patricia. Alcoholism and
     Substance Sniffing Among the Cheyenne and Arapaho Indians
     of Oklahoma. International Journal of the Addictions,
     Edinburgh, 14(7): 1001-1007, 1979.

125. Albert, W.G. and Simpson, R.I. Test Construction Procedures for
     Evaluating Alcohol Education: The "Decisions and Drinking"
     Program. International Journal of the Addictions, 18(7):
     1019-1027, 1983.

126. Albertson, Robert. Identifying Alcoholism as a Problem.
     In: Casework With Wives of Alcoholics. Eds. P.C. Cohen
     and M.S. Krause. New York: Family Service Association of
     America, 1971, pages 33-46.

127. Albornoz, C., Gonzalez, L. and Verdugo, M. Infantile Alcohol
     Consumption in 2 Urban Populations. Revista Chilena de
     Pediatria, Santiago, 55(1): 11-13, 1984.

128. Albrecht, Gary L. The Alcoholism Process: A Social Learning
     Viewpont. In: Alcoholism: Progress in Research and
     Treatment. Ed. Peter G. Bourne. New York: Academic
     Press, 1973, pages 11-42.

129. Albretsen, Carl S. and Vaglum, Per. The Alcoholic's Wife and
     Her Conflicting Roles. Scandinavian Journal of Social
     Medicine, Stockholm, 1: 7-12, 1973. (Also In: Alcohol
     Problems; Reviews, Research and Recommendations.
     Ed. D. Robinson. New York: Holmes and Meir, 1979, pages
     136-145.)

130. Albretsen, Carl S. and Vaglum, Per. The Alcoholic's Wife and
     Her Conflicting Roles - A Cause for Hospitalization.
     Acta Socio-Medica Scandinavica, 1: 41-50, 1971.

131. Albretsen, Carl S. and Vaglum, Per. The "Housewife Saver" --
     A Doubtful Helper. A Contribution to the Clarification
     of Helper Dynamics in Certain Marital Conflicts. Tidsskrift
     for den Norske Laegeforening, 92(7): 489-493, 1972.

132. ALCARE: When There is no Insurance. Alcoholism: The National
     Magazine, 5(1): 27, 72, 1984.

133. Alcohol. A Family Affair. Pamphlet. Chicago: National
     Parent-Teachers Association, no date.

134. Alcohol and Adolescents: A Problem of Use or Abuse. Keynote,
     3(4): 21-22, 1975.

135. Alcohol and Family Violence. Children of Alcoholics (COA) Review,
     4: 9, 1983.

136. Alcohol and Health. Bottom Line, Lansing, 4(3): 15, 1981.

137. Alcohol and Health: Fifth Special Report to the United States
     Congress. Rockville, MD: National Institute on Alcohol
     Abuse and Alcoholism, 1983.

138. Alcohol and the Family. Human Ecology, 9(3): 1-29, 1978.

139. Alcohol and the Family. St. Louis: Liguori Publications, 1978.

140. Alcohol and the Family. A Report on the New York State Conference
     on Alcoholism and Family Problems. Pamphlet. New York:
     National Council on Alcoholism, 1978.

141. Alcohol and the Family. Fact Sheet. Report. In: _Alcohol Topics in Brief_. Rockville, MD: National Institute on Alcohol Abuse and Alcoholism, 1980.

142. Alcohol, Heredity and Germ Damage. _Quarterly Journal of Studies on Alcohol_, (Supplement No. 5), 1947.

143. Alcohol in Perspective. _Comsumer Reports_, 40(7): 351-352, 354, 378, 1983.

144. Alcoholic and Family. _Journal of Alcoholism_, 7(1): 27-28, 1972.

145. _Alcoholic in the Family_? Pamphlet. New York: National Council on Alcoholism, 1978.

146. Alcoholic Patients' Children Get Assistance. _National Institute on Alcohol Abuse and Alcoholism Information and Feature Service_ (IFS No. 49), 4, July 11, 1978.

147. Alcoholic Wife is Grateful for Al-Anon. _Department of State Newsletter_, 167(39): 1975.

148. An Alcoholic Wife. Letter. _British Medical Journal_, London, 2: 1160, 1951.

149. Alcoholics Anonymous. _Alcoholics Anonymous_. Alcoholics Anonymous World Services, 1955.

150. Alcoholism -- A Family Disease. _Australian Nurses Journal_, 4(8): 34-35, 42, 1975.

151. _Alcoholism: A Family Illness_. New York: Christopher D. Smithers, 1972.

152. _Alcoholism. A Family Illness_. Pamphlet. New York: National Council on Alcoholism, 1974.

153. Alcoholism: A Family Illness. Fourth Annual Conference on Alcoholism. _Pharmacology Biochemistry and Behavior_, 12(2): 323-330, 1980.

154. _Alcoholism: A Family Matter_. Hollywood, FL: Health Communications, Inc., 1984.

155. Alcoholism: An Inherited Disease? _British Medical Journal_, London, 281(6251): 1301-1302, 1980.

156. Alcoholism and Heredity. (Queries and Minor Notes.) _The Journal of the American Medical Association_, 136: 849, 1948.

157. _Alcoholism and the Family_. Boston: Massachusetts Department of Public Health, Division of Alcoholism, 1971.

158. Alcoholism and the Family: Putting the Pieces Together. _Alcoholism: The National Magazine_, 1(3): 19-22, 1981.

159. _Alcoholism and the Family: Thirteenth Annual Report_. Liverpool: Merseyside Lancashire and Cheshire Council on Alcoholism. 1976.

160. Alcoholism and Women. _Alcohol Health and Research World_, (Summer): 2-7, 1974.

161. Alcoholism and Youth. _New Jersey Educational Review_, 50(8): 20-21, 1977.

162. Alcoholism As It Affects the Moral and Social Condition of the
      Child, the Home, and the Nation. International Congress
      Against Alcoholism, 12: 114, 138-142, 1909.

163. Alcoholism: Diagnosis. Maryland State Medical Journal,
      19(10): 99-100, 1970.

164. Alcoholism: Heredity and Congenital Effects. In: United States.
      Department of Health, Education, and Welfare National Institute
      on Alcohol Abuse and Alcoholism. 2nd Special Report to the
      U.S. Congress on Alcohol and Health from the Secretary of Health,
      Education and Welfare. Washington, D.C.: U.S. Government Printing
      Office, 1974, pages 45-50.

165. Alcoholism in Childhood: Is It a New Problem? Pediatrics, 58(2):
      176, 1976.

166. Alcoholism in Industry and Family. Lancet, 2(7579): 1179, 1968.

167. Alcoholism in Women. Journal of the American Medical Association,
      225(8): 988, 1973.

168. Alcoholism is a Family Disease. Nursing Mirror, 144(25): 23, 1977.

169. Alcoholism: New Understanding of an Ancient Illness. Human Ecology,
      5(2): 1-31, 1974.

170. Alcoholism Research and Training, Inc. Stages in Family Adjustment
      to an Alcoholic Member. Pamphlet. Durango, CO: San Juan
      Basin Health Department, 1971.

171. Alcoholism. Resources for Helping the Problem Drinker. Industrial
      Medicine, 39(7): 280-294, 1970.

172. Alcoholism Treatment Services for Children of Alcoholics.
      In: U.S. Dept. of Health and Human Services. National
      Institute on Alcohol Abuse and Alcoholism. Services for
      Children of Alcoholics. Washington, D.C.: U.S. Government
      Printing Office, 1979, pages 102-109.

173. Aldoory, Shirley. Research Into Family Factors. Alcohol Health
      and Research World, 3(4): 2-6, 1979.

174. Alexander, C.N. Jr. Alcohol and Adolescent Rebellion. Social
      Forces, 45: 542-550, 1967.

175. Alexander, C.N. Jr. and Campbell, E.Q. Balance Forces and
      Environmental Effects; Factors Influencing the Cohesiveness
      of Adolescent Drinking Groups. Social Forces, 46:
      367-374, 1968.

176. Alexander, C. Norman and Campbell, Ernest Q. Peer Influences
      on Adolescent Drinking. Quarterly Journal of Studies on
      Alcohol, 28(3): 444-454, 1967.

177. Alexander, Ludmilla. One Man's Commitment to Alcoholics.
      Listen, 32(8): 16-17, 1979.

178. Alexopoulos, George S., Brescia, Robert A., Frances, Richard J.
      and Seixas, Frank A. Managing Alcoholic Medical Patients:
      The Psychiatrist's Role. Psychosomatics, 22(7): 598,
      603-605, 1981.

179. Alexopoulos, George S., Lieberman, Kenneth W. and Frances,
      Richard J. Platelet MAO Activity in Alcoholic Patients
      and Their First-Degree Relatives. American Journal of
      Psychiatry, 140(11): 1501-1504, 1983.

180. Alford, Geary S. Alcoholics Anonymous: An Empirical Outcome
     Study. Addictive Behaviors, 5(4): 359-370, 1980.

181. Alkon, D.L. Parental Deprivation. Acta Psychiatrica
     Scandinavica, Supplement 223, Copenhagen, 1-48, 1971.

182. All in the Family -- Understanding How We Teach and Influence
     Children About Alcohol. Operation Threshold, 1975.

183. All in the Family: Understanding How We Teach and Influence
     Children About Alcohol. Participant's Workbook and
     Chairman's Guide. Rockville, MD: National Institute on
     Alcohol Abuse and Alcoholism, 1975. (Eric Document Number
     ED116063).

184. Allen, Darrel L., Petersen, Dennis R., Wilson, James R.,
     McClearn, Gerald E. and Nishimoto, Teresa K. Selective
     Breeding for a Multi Variate Index of Ethanol Dependence
     in Mice: Results from the First Five Generations. Alcohol:
     Clinical and Experimental Research, 7(4): 443-447, 1983.

185. Allen, Donald M. Young Male Prostitutes: A Psychosocial Study.
     Archives of Sexual Behavior, 9(5): 399-426, 1980.

186. Allen, L.R. Note on the Position of the Alcoholic in the
     Therapeutic Programme. Psychological Reports, 24(3):
     695-697, 1969.

187. Allen, Nancy H. Homicide Followed by Suicide: Los Angeles,
     1970-1979. Suicide and Life-Threatening Behavior,
     13(3): 155-165, 1983.

188. Alltop, L.B., Lemley, D. and Williams, T. Do Children Seen in
     Mental Health Clinics Come From "Problem Drinking" Households?
     Inventory, 19(4): 9-11, 20, 1970.

189. Almy, F. and Bent, R.A. Symposium: What We do When the Breadwinner
     is Intemperate. Proceedings of the National Conference on
     Charities and Corrections, 43: 121-127, 1916.

190. Alonzi, James, and Faigel, Harris C. A Structured Therapeutic
     Approach to Drug Abuse. Pediatrics, 50(5): 754-759,
     1972.

191. Altemeier, William A. III, O'Connor, Susan, Vietze, Peter M.,
     Sandler, Howard M. and Sherrod, Kathryn B. Antecedents
     of Child Abuse. Journal de Pediatria, Rio de Janeiro,
     100(5): 823-829, 1982.

192. Alterman, A.I., Bridges, K.R. and Tarter, R.E. Influence of
     Drinking and Familial Risk on Cognitive-Functioning.
     Alcoholism: Clinical and Experimental Research, 10(1):
     92, 1986.

193. Alterman, A.I., Gottheil, E., Skoloda, T.E. and Thornton, C.C.
     Consequences of Social Modification of Drinking Behavior.
     Journal of Studies on Alcohol, 38: 1032-1035, 1977.

194. Alterman, A.I., Petrarulo, E., Tarter, R. and McGowan, J.R.
     Hyperactivity and Alcoholism: Familial and Behavioral
     Correlates. Addictive Behaviors, 7(4): 413-421, 1982.

195. Alterman, A.I. and Tarter, R.E. Relationship Between Familial
     Alcoholism and Head Injury. Journal of Studies on Alcohol,
     46(3): 256-258, 1985.

196. Alterman, A.I., Tarter, R.E., Baughman, T.G., Bober, B.A. and
      Fabian, S.A. Differentiation of Alcoholics High and Low
      in Childhood Hyperactivity. Drug and Alcohol Dependence,
      15(1-2): 111-121, 1985.

197. Alterman, Arthur I. and Tarter, Ralph E. The Transmission of
      Psychological Vulnerability. Implications for Alcoholism
      Etiology. Journal of Nervous and Mental Disease, 171(3):
      147-154, 1983.

198. Altman, H., Evenson, R. and Cho, D.W. Predicting Length of Stay
      by Patients Hospitalized for Alcoholism or Drug Dependence.
      Journal of Studies on Alcohol, 39: 197-201, 1978.

199. Altman, H., Sletten, I.W. and Evenson, R.C. Childhood and
      Adolescent Problems of Adult Psychiatric Inpatients.
      Comprehensive Psychiatry, 16: 479-484, 1975.

200. Altman, M., Crocker, R.W. and Gaines, D. Female Alcoholics:
      The Men They Marry. Forum on Women: Journal of Addictions
      and Health, 1(1): 33-41, 1980.

201. Altman, Marjorie and Crocker, Ruth (Eds.). Social Groupwork and
      Alcoholism. New York: Haworth Press, 1982.

202. Alvan, G., Bergstrom, K., Borga, O., Iselius, L. and Pederson, N.
      Family Study of Genetic and Environmental Factors Determining
      the Protein Binding of Propranolol. European Journal of
      Clinical Pharmacology, Berlin, 25(4): 437-441, 1983.

203. Alvarez, W.C. The Medical Complaints of the Relatives of
      the Psychotic, the Alcoholic and the Epileptic. Eugenics
      Quarterly, 3: 143-147, 1956.

204. Aman, A. Studium Av Utvecklingen Av Alkoholistklientelets
      Sammansattning Under 1950-Talet. (Studies on the Development
      of the Composition of the Alcoholic Clientele During the
      1950s'.) Stockholm: Institutet for Maltdrycksforskning
      (Publication Number 11), 1963.

205. Ambrozik, Wieslaw. Sytuacja Spoleczna Dziecka Rodziny
      Alkoholicznej W Kulturowo Zaniedbanym Rejonie Wielkiego
      Miasta. (The Social Situation of a Child in an Alcoholic
      Family in a Culturally Neglected Quarter of a Big Town.)
      Uniwersytet Im. Adama Mickiewicza W Poznaniu: Seria
      Psychologia I Pedagogika, No. 56, 1983.

206. Ames, G. Family Ethnography: A New Approach to Alcohol Studies.
      Drinking and Drug Practices Surveyor, 20: 49-50, 1985.

207. Ames, G.M.W. Maternal Alcoholism and Family Life: A Cultural
      Model for Research and Intervention. Dissertation Abstracts
      International, 44(09): 2612A, 1984.

208. Amini, Fariborz and Burke, Edward. Acting Out and Its Role in
      the Treatment of Adolescents. Bulletin of the Menninger
      Clinic, 43(3): 249-259, 1979.

209. Amir, M. and Eldar P. An Experiment in the Treatment of
      Alcoholics in Israel. Drug Forum, 7: 105-119, 1978-79.

210. Amoateng, Acheampong Yaw and Bahr, Stephen J. Religion, Family,
      and Adolescent Drug Use. Sociological Perspectives,
      29(1): 53-76, 1986.

211. AMSA on Alcohol Leading Articles. Medical Journal of Australia,
      Sydney, 2: 410-411, 1980.

212. Anderson, Barbara Gallatin. How French Children Learn to Drink.
     Trans-Action, _5_(7): 20-22, 1968.

213. Anderson, C., McElfresh, O. and Filstead, W.J. Comparison of
     Alcoholics Perceptions of Family-Life Pre and Post Treatment.
     Alcoholism: Clinical and Experimental Research, _3_(2):
     166, 1979.

214. Anderson, Carl L. Control of Alcoholism. In: _Alcohol and_
     Alcoholism. Toronto: University of Toronto Press, 1970,
     pages 346-349.

215. Anderson, Carol, Hogarty, Gerard E. and Jacob, Theodore. A
     Comparative Study of the Social Support Networks of Families
     of Alcoholics, Depressives, Schizophrenics, and Normals.
     Research Report, NIMH Grant 5R01-MH-30750, 1978.

216. Anderson, D. and Cooper, P. _The Other Side of the Bottle_.
     New York: A.A. Wyn, 1950.

217. Anderson, Daniel J. Delivery of Essential Services to
     Alcoholics Through the "Continuum of Care". _Cancer_
     Research, _39_(7): 2855-2858, 1979.

218. Anderson, Daniel J. and Burns, John P. Hazelden Foundation: Part
     of the Caring Community. In: _Alcoholism Rehabilitation:_
     Methods and Experiences of Private Rehabilitation Centers.
     Ed. Vincent Groupe. New Brunswick, NJ: Rutgers University
     Center of Alcohol Studies, 1978, pages 39-55.

219. Anderson, Daniel J., Mills, Wilbur, Crosby, Gary and Greene, S.
     Progression. In: _Courage to Change_. Boston: Houghton
     Mifflin Company, 1984, pages 45-69.

220. Anderson, E.E. and Quast, W. Young Children in Alcoholic
     Families: A Mental Health Needs-Assessment and an
     Intervention/Prevention Strategy. _Journal of Primary_
     Prevention, _3_(3): 174-187, 1983.

221. Anderson, E.W. Strindberg's Illness. _Psychological Medicine_,
     London, _1_(2): 104-117, 1971.

222. Anderson, Gary W. Candid Concern: The Church's Ministry to the
     Chemically Dependent Person. _E/SA_, _10_: 15-19, 1982.

223. Anderson, Lorna M. and Shafer, Gretchen. The Character-
     Disordered Family: A Community Treatment Model for Family
     Sexual Abuse. _American Journal of Orthopsychiatry_,
     _49_(3): 436-445, 1979.

224. Anderson, Paul. The Outpatient Alternative. _EAP Digest_,
     _4_(2): 18-21, 23, 1984.

225. Anderson, Peter. Alcohol. _British Medical Journal_, London,
     _284_(6331): 1758-1760, 1982.

226. Anderson, S.C. Alcoholic Women: Sex-Role Identification and
     Perceptions of Parental Personality Characteristics.
     Sex Roles, _11_(3-4): 277-287, 1984.

227. Anderson, S.E. Early Recovery for the Chemically Addicted
     Co-Dependent. _Focus on Family and Chemical Dependency_,
     _8_(2): 23, 27, 30, 1985.

228. Anderson, Sandra C. and Henderson, Donna C. Family Therapy in
     the Treatment of Alcoholism. _Social Work in Health Care_,
     _8_(4): 79-94, 1983.

229. Anderson, Wayne P. and Holcomb, William R. Accused Murderers:
      Five MMPI Personality Types. Journal of Clinical
      Psychology, 39(5): 761-768, 1983.

230. Ando, Haruhiko and Hasegawa, Etsuko. Drinking Patterns and
      Attitudes of Alcoholics and Nonalcoholics in Japan.
      Quarterly Journal of Studies on Alcohol, 31(1-A):
      153-161, 1970.

231. Andreasen, N.C. and Winokur, G. Secondary Depression: Familial,
      Clinical, and Research Perspectives. American Journal of
      Psychiatry, 136: 62-66, 1979.

232. Andreichikov, S.N. Opyt Organizatsii I Raboty Narkologicheskogo
      Dispansera. (Experience in the Organization and Work of
      a Narcological Dispensary.) Zhurnal Nevropatologii I
      Psikhiatrii Imeni S.S. Korsakova, 59: 761-763, 1959.

233. Andreini, M. and Green, S. Statistical Description of Cases
      Followed by the Anchorage Child Abuse Board, Inc., October,
      1972 - March, 1975. Alaska: Anchorage Child Abuse Board,
      Inc., 1975.

234. Andres, Francis D. Alcoholism: A Family Affair. Paper presented
      at the AMA Conference on "Medical Complications of Alcohol
      Abuse," Washington, D.C., October, 1973.

235. Andrieux, Le Guirriec J., Laouabdia, S. and Maisondieu, J.
      Para-Incestuous Filiations. (Incestuous Relations.)
      Annales Medico Psychologiques, 139(7): 833-837, 1981.

236. Andriezen, W.L. The Problems of Heredity with Special Reference
      to Pre-Embryonic Life. Journal of Mental Science, London,
      51: 33-43, 1905.

237. Andruzzi, Ellen A. Nursing Care for the Alcoholic. Maryland
      State Medical Journal, 19(2): 93-94, 1970.

238. Angel, P., Taleghani, M., Choquet, M. and Cortecuisse, N. Abord
      Epidemiologique De La Tentative De Suicide De L'Adolescent:
      Quelques Reponses De L'Environnement. (An Epidemiological
      Approach to Suicide Attempts in Adolescence: Some Responses
      of the Environment.) Evolution Psychiatrique, 43(2):
      351-367, 1978.

239. Angermeyer, M.C. and Bock, B. Das Soziale Netzwerk
      Alkoholkranker. (Social Network of Alcoholics.)
      Psychotherapie Psychosomatik Medizinische Psychologie,
      1(34): 1-9, 1984.

240. Angst, J., Baumann, U., Muller, Ursula and Ruppen, R.
      Epidemiology of Drug Consumption in the Canton of Zurich
      (Switzerland): Inquiry in a Group of 6315 Young Men and
      1381 Young Women All Aged 19. Archiv Fur Psychiatrie Und
      Nervenkrankheiten, Berlin, 217(1): 11-24, 1973.

241. Anhalt, Herbert S. and Klein, Mark. Drug Abuse in Junior High
      School Populations. American Journal of Drug & Alcohol
      Abuse, 3(4): 589-603, 1976.

242. Annis, Helen M. Adolescent Drug Use: The Role of Peer Groups
      and Parental Example. The Ontario Psychologst, 7(4):
      7-9, 1975.

243. Annis, Helen M. Pattern of Intra-Familial Drug Use. British
      Journal of Addiction, 69: 361-369, 1974.

244. Ansoms, Stan. Detoxication Cure: Some Points for Discussion.
      Acta Psychiatrica Belgica, 80(2): 183-190, 1980.

245. Anthony, M. Al-Anon. Journal of the American Medical
      Association, 238(10): 1062-1063, 1977.

246. Antonijevic, M. Some Social Aspects of Drug Addiction in Youth.
      Alcoholism, Zagreb, 6(2): 82-86, 1970.

247. Apgar, Fred M. Our Children Are Going to Pot: Comments From
      a Health Educator. Journal of School Health, 50(1):
      40-41, 1980.

248. Apgar, Ruth and Fuller, Robert. Functions and Scope of an
      Alcoholism Out-Patient Program. Journal of Perth Amboy
      General Hospital, 3(4): 12-14, 1974.

249. Aponte, Harry J. and VanDeusen, John M. Structural Family
      Therapy. In: Handbook of Family Therapy. Eds. A.S.
      Gurman and D.P. Kniskern. New York: Brunner/Mazel,
      1981, pages 310-360.

250. Apperson, L.B. Childhood Experiences of Schizophrenics and
      Alcoholics. Journal of Genetic Psychology, 106:
      301-313, 1965.

251. Apperson, L.B. and McAdoo, W.G. Jr. Paternal Reactions in
      Childhood as Described by Schizophrenics and Alcoholics.
      Journal of Clinical Psychology, 21(4): 369-373, 1965.

252. Apperson, L.B. and Stinnett, P.W. Parental Factors as Reported
      by Patient Groups. Journal of Clinical Psychology,
      31(3): 419-425, 1975.

253. Appleton, W. The Battered Woman Syndrome. Annals of Emergency
      Medicine, 9: 84-91, 1980.

254. Apsler, Robert and Blackman, Camilla. Adults' Drug Use:
      Relationship to Perceived Drug Use of Parents, Friends,
      While Growing Up, and Present Friends. The American
      Journal of Drug and Alcohol Abuse, 6(3): 291-300, 1979.

255. APTP From Several Perspectives. Journal of Iowa Medical Society,
      71(10): 426-427, 1981.

256. Arafat, I. Drinking Behavior In High School, College and Adult
      Groups. Free Inquiry, 7: 87-91, 1979.

257. Arana, George W. The Impaired Physician: A Medical and Social
      Dilemma. General Hospital Psychiatry, 4(2): 147-153,
      1982.

258. Archambault, J.C. Alcohol and Anguish: Apropos of a Case Report.
      Soins. Psychiatrie, 8: 28-30, 1981.

259. Archer, N. Sidney. Perceptions and Attitudes of Family Members
      (Co-Dependents): Pre-and Post-Treatment. Labor-Management
      Alcoholism Journal, 9(2): 75-80, 1979.

260. Arentzen, W.P. Impact of Alcohol Misuse on Family Life.
      Alcoholism: Clinical and Experimental Research, 2(4):
      349-351, 1978.

261. Arevalo, Rodolfo and Minor, Marianne. (Eds.). Chicanas and
      Alcoholism: A Socio-Cultural Perspective of Women.
      San Jose: San Jose State University, School of Social
      Work, 1982.

262. Argeriou, M. Refusal to Take Breathalyzer Test-Rebutting
      Adverse Persumption. Criminal Law Bulletin, 11:
      350-355, 1975.

263. Argeriou, Milton and Paulino, Donna. Women Arrested for Drunken
      Driving in Boston. Social Characteristics and Circumstances
      of Arrest. Journal of Studies on Alcohol, 37(5):
      648-658, 1976.

264. Arieli, A. Multicouple Group Therapy of Alcoholics. International
      Journal of the Addictions, 16: 773-782, 1981.

265. Arikawa, K. and Inanaga, K. The Therapeutic Mechanism of the
      Double Medication Technique with Cyanamide for Alcoholism.
      Folia Psychiatrica et Neurologica Japonica, 27: 9-15, 1973.

266. Arikawa, K., Itai, S. and Akiyama, T. The Changes in Wives'
      Expectation and Evaluation Toward The Role of Alcoholic
      Husbands Thereof During Treatment Processes. Japanese
      Journal of Studies on Alcohol, Kyoto, 13: 17-27, 1978.

267. Arikawa, Katsuyoshi, Naganuma, Rokuichi and Ohshima, Masachika.
      The Change of Behavior Pattern of Alcohol Addicts Treated
      with Cyanamide Double Medication -- Observations by Their
      Families. Clinical Psychiatry, Tokyo, 14(5): 447-455,
      1972.

268. Arlet, P., Cousergues, C., Gaillemin, C., Botreau, Y., Duffaut,
      M. and LeTallec, Y. A Medical Investigation of 160 Chronic
      Alcoholic Patients Hospitalized in a Department of Internal
      Medicine. Nature and Pathological Consequences of the
      Intoxication. Semaine Des Hopitaux de Paris, 57(43-44):
      1858-1863, 1981.

269. Arlitt, A.H. The Effect of Alcohol on the Intelligent Behavior of
      the White Rat and its Progeny. Psychological Monographs,
      26(115): 1-50, 1919.

270. Armand-Delille, P.F. La Sante Des Enfants De La Population
      Rurale Nees Pendant La Periode Des Restrictions D'Alcool.
      (The Health of Children in the Rural Population Born During
      the Period of Restriction of Alcohol.) Bulletin de
      L'Academic Nationale De Medicine, Paris, 131: 691-692,
      1947.

271. Armstrong, A.L. Self-Concept, Locus of Control and Family
      Representation of Daughters of Alcoholic and Non-Alcoholic
      Parents. Doctoral Dissertation. Los Angeles: International
      College, 1983.

272. Armstrong-Jones, Robert. Alcoholism and Eugenics. British
      Journal of Inebriety, 13: 72-75, 1915.

273. Arnold, Marie Agnes and Braband, Henning. (Soziale Situation,
      Einstellung und Persolichkeitsaspekte von Jugendlichen
      Obdachlosen.) Social Situation, Attitudes and Personality
      Aspects of Homeless Youth. Zeitschrift fur Klinische
      Psychologie und Psychotherapie, 25(3): 246-255, 1977.

274. Arocas-Estelles, A., Gomez-Moya, P. and Frutos-Lopez, C. Help for
      the Alcoholic Patient in the Community. Drogalcohol, 3:
      107-113, 1978.

275. Aron, William S. Family Background and Personal Trauma Among Drug
      Addicts in the United States: Implications for Treatment.
      British Journal of Addiction, 70: 295-305, 1975.

276. Aronson, H. and Gilbert, A. Preadolescent Sons of Male Alcoholics.
      An Experimental Study of Personality Patterning. Archives of
      General Psychiatry, 8(3): 235-241, 1963.

277. Aronson, M., Kyllerman, M., Sabel, K.G., Sandin, B. and Olegard, R.
      Children of Alcoholic Mothers. Developmental, Perceptual and
      Behavioural Characteristics as Compared to Matched Controls.
      Acta Paediatrica Scandinavica, 74: 27-35, 1985.

278. Aronson, M., Larsson, G. and Olega'rd, R. Konsekvenserna Av
      Alkohol Som Miljofaktor For Det Vaxande Fostret Och Barnet.
      (Consequences of Alcohol for the Growing Fetus and the
      Child.) Lakartidningen, Stockholm, 78: 789-792, 1981.

279. Arrowood, Nina R.F. Problem: The Use/Abuse of Drugs as an
      Indicator of the Bilingual/Bicultural Assimilation
      Difficulties Encountered by Mexican-Americans Coping
      with the Anglo-American Mainstream -- A Literature Review.
      1979. (Eric Document Number 186184.)

280. Arthaud, P. Aspects et Role Defensif Des Conduites Alcooliques.
      (Aspects and Defensiveness of Alcoholic Behavior). Doctoral
      Dissertation. France: Universite De Grenoble, 1972.

281. As a Family You Should Know These Facts About Alcoholism.
      Pamphlet. Burlington: Vermont Alcoholic Rehabilitation
      Board, 1971.

282. Asander, H. A Field Investigation of Homeless Men in Stockholm.
      A Sociopsychiatric and Clinical Follow-Up Study. Acta
      Psychiatrica Scandinavica, Copenhagen, 61(Supplement 281),
      1980.

283. Ascher, J. and Delahousse, J. Psychopathological Approach of a
      Population on Non-Psychotic Suicides. Annales Medico-
      Psychologiques, Paris, 2(5): 615-650, 1969.

284. Ashby, Howard B. and Crowe, Raymond R. Unipolar Depression:
      A Family of a Large Kindred. Comprehensive Psychiatry,
      19(5): 415-417, 1978.

285. Ashley-Miller, M. The Chief Scientist Reports...the Problems
      of Alcohol. Health Bulletin, Edinburgh, 34: 299-300,
      1976.

286. Asma, Fern E., Eggert, Raymond L. and Hilker, Robert R.J.
      Long-Term Experience with Rehabilitation of Alcoholic
      Employees. Journal of Occupational Medicine, 13(12):
      581-585, 1971.

287. Asnes, Daniel P. and Shulman, Helen. Florid Psychosis after
      Retirement in a 68-Year-Old Man: A Case Report. Journal of
      Geriatric Psychiatry, 9(2): 237-253, 1976.

288. Aso, S. A Genealogical Study of One Family with Doubt of the
      Influence of Excessive Drinking to the Next Generation.
      Japanese Journal of Alcohol Studies and Drug Dependence,
      Kyoto, 18(1): 125-137, 1983.

289. Asper, Samuel P. Self-Regulation in the Use of Alcohol.
      Maryland State Medical Journal, 23(12): 24-25, 1974.

290. Assaultiveness and Alcohol Use in Family Disputes -- Police
      Perceptions. Criminology, 12(3): 281-292, 1974.

291. Association of Labor-Management Administrators and Consultants
      on Alcoholism, Inc. -- Seventh Annual Meeting. Arlington,
      VA, October, 1978.

292. **Assorted Pamphlets.** Waterbury, CT: Central Naugatuck Valley
     Consortium for Alcoholism Services, 1979.

293. Atkins, Merrilee. Family Approach to the Treatment of Alcoholism.
     Paper presented at the National Conference on Social Welfare.
     Dallas, May, 1971.

294. Attkisson, C. Clifford. Suicide in San Francisco's Skid Row.
     Archives of General Psychiatry, 23(2): 149-157, 1970.

295. Attneave, Carolyn. American Indians and Alaska Native Families:
     Emigrants in their Own Homeland. In: _Ethnicity and Family_.
     Eds. Monica McGoldrick, John K. Pearce and Joseph Giordano.
     New York: Guilford Press, 1982, pages 55-83.

296. Aubertin, Claire. A Pilot Project for Treatment of Alcoholics:
     The Familial Dimension. _Toxicomanies_, 1(2): 217-219, 1968.

297. August, G.J. The Use of Family History to Produce Homogeneous
     Subgroups of Childhood Hyperactivity. _Behavior Genetics_,
     12(6): 576-577, 1982.

298. August, Gerald J. and Stewart, Mark A. Familial Subtypes of
     Childhood Hyperactivity. _Journal of Nervous and Mental
     Disease_, 171(6): 362-368, 1983.

299. Aujaleu, E., Derobert, L. and Pequignot, H. Enquete Sur
     L'Evolution Et Le Cout De L'Alcoolisme En France De 1938
     a 1948. (Inquiry on the Evolution and the Cost of
     Alcoholism in France Between 1938 and 1948.) _Archives de
     Medecine Sociale_, Paris, 6: 67-115, 1950.

300. Aumack, Lisa. Drinking Decisions: Evaluation of A Short-Term
     Behavioral Self-Assessment Program for Problem Drinkers.
     Doctoral Dissertation. University of Oregon. _Dissertation
     Abstracts International_, 42(5): 2040B, 1981.

301. Aurelius, G. Adjustment and Behavior of Finnish Immigrant
     Children in Stockholm, Sweden. 2. Parent Assessment.
     Scandinavian Journal of Social Medicine, Stockholm,
     8: 43-48, 1980.

302. Austin, Katherine Biddle, Manak, Joseph J. and Horwitz, Robert.
     A Workshop for Introducing Adolescents to Mental Health
     Services. _Social Casework_, 62(6): 368-372, 1981.

303. Avendano, A., Avendano, P., Almonte, C., Sepulveda, G. and
     Valenzuela, C. Characteristics of the Psychosocial
     Development in Adolescents from 12 to 15. Northern Santiago.
     Revista Chilena de Pediatria, Santiago, 54(4): 273-281,
     1983.

304. Awad, George A. Father-Son Incest: A Case Report. _Journal of
     Nervous and Mental Disease_, 162(2): 135-139, 1976.

305. Ayars, Albert L. and Milgram, Gail Gleason. Alcohol and Life.
     In: _The Teenager and Alcoholism_. Eds. Albert L. Ayars and
     Gail Gleason Milgram. New York: Richards Rosen Press, 1970,
     pages 44-51.

306. Ayars, Albert L. and Milgram, Gail Gleason. Alcoholism -- A Major
     Health and Social Problem. In: _The Teenager and Alcoholism_.
     Eds. Albert L. Ayars and Gail Gleason Milgram. New York:
     Richard Rosens Press, 1970, pages 52-62.

307. Ayars, Albert L. and Milgram, Gail Gleason. Alcoholism-Information
     and Treatment Services. In: _The Teenager and Alcoholism_.
     Eds. Albert L. Ayars and Gail Gleason Milgram. New York:
     Richard Rosens Press, 1970, pages 63-73.

308. Ayers, J., Ruff, C.F. and Templer, D.I. Essential Alcoholism and
      Family History of Alcoholism. Quarterly Journal of Studies
      on Alcohol, 35: 655-657, 1974.

309. Ayres, H.P. Family of the Physician Alcoholic. In: Alcoholism:
      A Modern Perspective. Ed. P. Golding. Lancaster: MTP Press,
      1982, pages 353-354.

310. Azrin, N.H. Improvements in the Community Reinforcement Approach
      to Alcoholism. Behavior Research and Therapy, Oxford,
      14(5): 339-348, 1976.

B

311. Babadzhanova, G. Yu., Mazovetskiy, A.G., Kurayeva, T.L. and
     Mukhamedov, Kh. A. Khlorpropamid-Alkosol' Naya Proba Pri
     Sakharnom Diabete. (Chlorpropamide-Alcohol Test in Diabetes
     Mellitus. Sovetskaya Meditsina, 7: 101-103, 1984.

312. Babow, Irving, Bassett, Sylvia and Matteoli, Ralph. A Study
     of Suicidal Patients Admitted to a State Mental Hospital.
     California Mental Health Research Digest, 7(2): 79-81, 1969.

313. Babow, Irving and Kridle, Robin. Problems and Encounters of a
     Suicidal Adolescent Girl. Adolescence, 7(28): 459-478, 1972.

314. Babst, D.V., Dembo, R. and Burgos, W. Measuring Consequences of Drug
     and Alcohol Abuse among Junior High School Students. Journal of
     Alcohol and Drug Education, 25(1): 11-19, 1979.

315. Babst, D.V., Deren, S., Schmeidler, J., Lipton, D.S. and Dembo, R.
     A Study of Family Affinity and Substance Use. Journal of Drug
     Education, 8: 29-40, 1978.

316. Babst, D.V., Uppal, G.S. and Schmeidler, J. Relationship of
     Youths' Attitudes to Substance Use in New York State.
     Journal of Alcohol and Drug Education, 23: 24-37, 1978.

317. Babst, Dean V., Miran, Michael and Koval, Mary. The Relationship
     Between Friends' Marijuana Use, Family Cohesion, School Interest
     and Drug Abuse Prevention. Journal of Drug Education, 6(1):
     23-41, 1976.

318. Bach, O. Prinzipien Psychiatrischer Rehabilitation. (Principles
     of Psychiatric Rehabilitation.) Zeitschrift fur Arztliche
     Fortbildung, Jena, 73: 851-855, 1979.

319. Bach, O., Feldes, D. and Gruss, U. Vyznam Rodinne Terapie V
     Psychiatricke Lecbe. (Effect of Family Therapy in Psychiatric
     Treatment). Ceskoslovenska Psychiatrie, 68(4): 193-198, 1972.

320. Bach, Otto, Feldes, Dieter, Kriegel, Annegret and Smolinsky, Bernhard.
     Gruppen Therapie Mit Ehepaaren. (Group Therapy With Married
     Couples.) Psychiatrie, Neurologie und Medizinische Psychologie,
     24(2): 90-97, 1972.

321. Bach, Y. Rita George, Lion, John R., Climent, Carlos E. and Ervin,
     Frank R. Episodic Dyscontrol: A Study of 130 Violent Patients.
     American Journal of Psychiatry, 127(11): 1473-1478, 1971.

322. Bachman, Jerald, Johnston, Lloyd, and O'Malley, Patrick. Smoking,
     Drinking, and Drug Use Among American High School Students:
     Correlates and Trends, 1975-1979. American Journal of
     Public Health, 71(1): 59-69, 1981.

323. Bachman, Jerald G., O'Malley, Patrick M. and Johnston, Lloyd D.
     Correlates of Drug Use, Part 1: Selected Measures of
     Background, Recent Experiences, and Lifestyle Orientations.
     Monitoring the Future Occasional Paper Series No. 8.
     Ann Arbor, MI: University of Michigan, Institute for Social
     Research, 1980.

324. Bachrach, L.L. Characteristics of Diagnosed and Missed Alcoholic
     Male Admissions to State and County Mental Hospitals, 1972.
     Mental Health Statistical Note, 124: 1-12, 1976.

325. Bacon, M.F. Male Pride and the Alcoholic Wife. Maryland State
     Medical Journal, 14(10): 69-70, 1965.

326. Bacon, Selden D. Abstinence, Alcohol Use and Related Problems.
     Address presented at the Semi-Annual Meeting of the North
     Conway Institute held at the Old South Church, Copley Square,
     Boston, MA, November, 1979.

327. Bacon, Selden D. Alcohol, Alcoholism, and Crime. Crime and
     Delinquency, 9(1): 1-14, 1963.

328. Bacon, Selden D. Alcoholism and Social Isolation. In: Cooperation
     in Crime Control. Ed. M. Bell. New York: National Probation
     Association, 1945, pages 209-234.

329. Bacon, Selden D. Excessive Drinking and the Institution of the
     Family. In: Alcohol, Science and Society. Westport, CT:
     Greenwood Press, 1945, pages 233-238.

330. Bacon, Selden D. Inebriety, Social Integration, and Marriage.
     Quarterly Journal of Studies on Alcohol, 5: 86-125, 1944.

331. Bacon, Selden, D. Meeting the Problems of Alcoholism in the
     United States. In: World Dialogue on Alcohol and Drug
     Dependence. Boston, MA: Beacon Press, 1970, pages 134-145.

332. Bacon, Selden D. and Roth, Frances L. Drunkenness in Wartime
     Connecticut. Hartford, Connecticut: Connecticut War
     Council, 1943.

333. Badonnel. Defaut de Soins et Mauvais Traitement des Enfants.
     (Neglect and Maltreatment of Children.) Revue Droit Penal
     et de Criminologie, Brussels, 86(1): 39-42, 1962.

334. Baekeland, Frederick and Lundwall, Lawrence K. Engaging the Alcoholic
     in Treatment and Keeping Him There. In: Treatment and
     Rehabilitation of the Chronic Alcoholic. Eds. B. Kissin and
     H. Begleiter. New York: Plenum Press, 1977, pages 161-195.

335. Baekeland, Frederick, Lundwall, Lawrence and Shanahan, Thomas J.
     Correlates of Patient Attrition in the Outpatient Treatment
     of Alcoholism. Journal of Nervous & Mental Disease,
     157(2): 99-107, 1973.

336. Baer, Paul E., Morin, Karen and Gaitz, Charles M. Familial
     Resources of Elderly Psychiatric Patients: Attitude,
     Capability, and Service Components. Archives of General
     Psychiatry, 22(4): 343-350, 1970.

337. Bahr, Howard M. Birth Order and Failure; the Evidence from Skid Row.
     Quarterly Journal of Studies on Alcohol, 32: 669-686, 1971.

338. Bahr, Howard M. Family Size and Stability as Antecedents of
     Homelessness and Excessive Drinking. Journal of Marriage
     and the Family, 31(3): 477-483, 1969.

339. Bahr, Howard M. Lifetime Affiliation Patterns of Early- and Late-
      Onset Heavy Drinkers on Skid Row. Quarterly Journal of Studies
      on Alcohol, 30(3): 645-656, 1969.

340. Bahr, Howard M. and Caplow, Theodore. Old Men, Drunk and Sober.
      New York: New York University Press, 1973.

341. Bahr, Howard M. and Langfur, Stephen J. Social Attachment and
      Drinking in Skid-Row Life Histories. Social Problems,
      14(4): 464-472, 1967.

342. Bailey, Katherine G. Impact of Family Alcoholism on the Job
      Performance of a Non-Alcoholic. Labor-Management Alcoholism
      Journal, 6(1): 8-10, 1976.

343. Bailey, M.B. Psychophysiological Impairment in Wives of Alcoholics
      as Related to Their Husband's Drinking and Sobriety. In:
      Alcoholism; Behavioural Research, Therapeutic Approaches.
      Ed. R. Fox. New York: Springer, 1967, pages 134-144.

344. Bailey, M.B. Research on Alcoholism and Marriage. In: Social
      Work Practice. New York: Columbia University Press,
      1963, pages 19-30.

345. Bailey, Margaret B. Alcoholism and Family Casework: Theory
      and Practice. New York: Community Council of Greater
      New York, 1968.

346. Bailey, Margaret B. Alcoholism and Family Casework Theory
      Practice. Pamphlet. New York: National Council on
      Alcoholism, 1970.

347. Bailey, Margaret B. Alcoholism and Marriage. A Review of
      Research and Professional Literature. Quarterly Journal
      of Studies on Alcohol, 22: 81-97, 1961.

348. Bailey, Margaret B. Alcoholism and the Family. In: Nurse Care
      Planning on Alcoholism. Eds. J. Lotterhos and M. McGuire.
      Greenville, NC: East Carolina University, 1974, pages
      107-115. (Also in: Alcoholism and Family Casework: Theory
      and Practice. Ed. M.B. Bailey. New York: Community
      Council of Greater New York, 1968, pages 56-66.)

349. Bailey, Margaret B. Alcoholism Treatment in Family Casework.
      Alcohol Health and Research World, Summer: 25-28, 1973.

350. Bailey, Margaret B. Attitudes Toward Alcoholism Before and
      After a Training Program for Social Caseworkers.
      Quarterly Journal of Studies on Alcohol, 31(3):
      669-683, 1970.

351. Bailey, Margaret B. The Family Agency's Role in Treating the Wife of
      an Alcoholic. Social Casework, 44: 273-279, 1963.

352. Bailey, Margaret B. The Family Agency's Role in Treating the Wife
      of an Alcoholic. Pamphlet. New York: National Council on
      Alcoholism, no date.

353. Bailey, Margaret Burton. Al-Anon Family Groups as an Aid to Wives
      of Alcoholics. Social Work, 10(1): 68-74, 1965.

354. Bailey, Margaret B., Haberman, Paul and Alksne, Harold. Outcomes
      of Alcoholic Marriages: Endurance, Termination or Recovery.
      Quarterly Journal of Studies on Alcohol, 23: 610-623, 1962.

355. Bailey, Margaret B., Haberman, Paul W. and Alksne, Harold. The
      Epidemiology of Alcoholism in an Urban Residential Area.
      Quarterly Journal of Studies on Alcohol, 26(1): 19-40, 1965.

356. Bailey, Margaret B., Haberman, Paul W., and Sheinberg, Jill.
      Dinstinctive Characteristics of the Alcoholic Family.
      New York, NY: National Council on Alcoholism, 1965. (Also in:
      Journal of Alcohol and Drug Education, 29(1): 1-11, 1983.)

357. Baird, Kathy. Special Unit Treats Problems of Teenagers.
      Hospitals, 54(3): 50-53, 1980.

358. Baither, Richard C. Family Therapy with Adolescent Drug Abusers:
      A Review. Journal of Drug Education, 8: 337-343, 1978.

359. Bakan, David. The Relationship Between Alcoholism and Birth Rank.
      Quarterly Journal of Studies on Alcohol, 10: 434-440, 1949.

360. Bakdash, Diane. Essentials the Nurse Should Know About Chemical
      Dependency. Journal of Psychiatric Nursing and Mental Health
      Services, 16(10): 33-37, 1978.

361. Baker, Max, Dorzab, Joe, Winokur, George and Cadoret, Remi.
      Depressive Disease: Evidence Favoring Polygenic Inheritance
      Based on an Analysis of Ancestral Cases. Archives of
      General Psychiatry, 27(3): 320-337, 1972.

362. Baker, S.M. Social Case Work with Inebriates. In: Alcohol,
      Science and Society; Twenty-Nine Lectures with Discussions
      as Given at the Yale Summer School Alcohol Studies.
      Lecture 27. New Haven, Connecticut: Quarterly Journal of
      Studies on Alcohol, 1943, pages 419-435.

363. Baker, Timothy B. Halfway Houses for Alcoholics: Shelters or
      Shackles. International Journal of Social Psychiatry,
      London, 18(3): 201-211, 1972.

364. Balak, K.J. Genetic and Developmental Regulation of Mouse Alcohol
      Dehydrogenase Genes. Dissertation Abstracts International,
      44(4): 1005B, 1983.

365. Balandiuk, Opalalinskaia. Social-Hygienic Factors of Morbidity
      of Textile Workers With Loss of Work Time. Sovetskoe
      Zdravookhranenie, 31(9): 25-29, 1972.

366. Balcerzak, Ann M. Hope for Young People with Alcoholic Parents.
      Pamphlet. Center City, Minnesota: Hazelden, no date.

367. Balcerzak, J.G. Children of Alcoholics: A Review and Clinical
      Observations. The Catalyst, 1(1): 38-43, 1979.

368. Baldwin, D.S. Effectiveness of Casework in Marital Discord with
      Alcoholism. Smith College Studies in Social Work, 18:
      69-122, 1947.

369. Bales, F. Types of Social Structure as Factors in "Cures" for
      Alcohol Addiction. Applied Anthropology, 1: 1-13, 1942.

370. Balint, I. Signs Referring to Deviant Behaviour in the Cases of
      Alcoholic Parents of the Children Drawn into the Research
      of Environmental and Genetical Harms. Paper presented at
      the 21st International Institute on the Prevention and
      Treatment of Alcoholism, Helsinki, Finland, June, 1975,
      pages 201-203.

371. Balis, S.A. Illusions That Affect Treatment for ACOAs. Focus on
      Family and Chemical Dependency, 8(3): 16-17, 33, 1985.

372. Balis, Susan and Zirpoli, Edith. Four Plus Four: A Short-Term
      Family Group for Relatives of Alcoholics. In: Social
      Groupwork and Alcoholism. Eds. Marjorie Altman and Ruth
      Crocker. New York, NY: Haworth Press, 1982, pages 49-55.
      (Also in: Social Work with Groups, 5(1): 49-55, 1982.)

373. Ballantyne, J.W. Alcohol as a Beverage in its Relation to
     Infantile Mortality. British Medical Journal, 2: 252-255.

374. Ballard, R.G. The Interrelatedness of Alcoholism and Marital
     Conflict. Symposium, 1958. 3. The Interaction Between
     Marital Conflict and Alcoholism as Seen Through MMPI's of
     Marriage Partners. American Journal of Orthopsychiatry,
     29: 528-546, 1959.

375. Bammer, G. Australian High and Low Avoidance Rat Strains:
     Differential Effects of Ethanol and Alpha-Methyl-P-Tyrosine.
     Behavioural Brain Research, 8(3): 317-333, 1983.

376. Banagale, Raul C. and McIntire, Matilda S. Child Abuse and
     Neglect: A Study of Cases Reported to Douglas County Child
     Protective Service from 1967-1973. Part II. Nebraska
     Medical Journal, 60(10): 393-396, 1975.

377. Bander, Karen W., Stilwell, Nancy A., Fein, Edith and Bishop,
     Gerrie. Relaionship of Patient Characteristics to Program
     Attendance by Women Alcoholics. Journal of Studies on
     Alcohol, 44(2): 318-327, 1983.

378. Bank, Barbara J., Biddle, Bruce J., Anderson, Don S., Hauge,
     Ragnar, Keats, Daphne M., Keats, John A., Marlin, Majorie
     M. and Valantin, Simone. Comparative Research on the
     Social Determinants of Adolescent Drinking. Social
     Psychology Quarterly, 48(2): 164-177, 1985.

379. Banks, Ellen and Smith Michael R. Attitudes and Background
     Factors Related to Alcohol Use Among College Students.
     Psychological Reports, 46(2): 571-577, 1980.

380. Bannerman, Robin M., Marinello, Michelle J., Cohen, Maimon M.
     and Lockwood, Clara. A Family with an Inherited Marker
     Chromosome (46,D-, Mar15+). American Journal of Human
     Genetics, 23(3): 281-288, 1971.

381. Bano, N., Gabelic, I., Milakovic, I., Prazic, B., Rugelj, J.,
     Rupena, Osolnik M., Smajkic, A. and Ulemek, L. Health
     Education of Patients in the Field of Social Psychiatry,
     Notably Alcoholics. International Journal of Social
     Psychiatry, 18(3): 157-170, 1973.

382. Baraga, D.J. Self-Concept in Children of Alcoholics.
     Doctoral Dissertation (University Microfilms No. 7810312).
     North Dakota: University of North Dakota, 1977.

383. Baranowski, M.D. Adolescents' Attempted Influence on Parental
     Behaviors. Adolescence, 13: 585-604, 1978.

384. Baranton, P. Les Difficultes Du Depistage Precoce De L'Alcoolisme
     Et De La Mise En Route Du Traitement. (The Difficulties of
     the Early Detection of Alcoholism and the Commencement of the
     Treatment.) Revue De L'Alcoolisme, Paris, 16(1): 32-36, 1970.

385. Baraona, E., Guerra, M. and Lieber, C.S. Cytogenetic Damage of
     Bone Marrow Cells Produced by Chronic Alcohol Consumption.
     Life Sciences, 29(17): 1797-1802, 1981.

386. Barchasz, M. Effects of Alcoholism on the Family. Revue de
     L'Infirmiere, 23(3): 221-229, 1973.

387. Bard, Morton and Zacker, Joseph. Assaultiveness and Alcohol
     Use in Family Disputes; Police Perceptions. Criminology,
     12(3): 281-292, 1974.

388. Barefoot, Earl F. A Theological Reflection: Families of Faith
     Confront Rapid Change. E/SA, 10: 29-35, 1982.

389. Barensten, P. Child Mortality, Alcoholism, and Criminality in
     Northeast Brabant. Nederlandsch Tijdschrift Voor
     Geneeskunde, 67(2): 268-275, 1923.

390. Barilyak, I.R. and Kozachuk, S. Yu. Vliyaniye Etanola Na
     Geneticheskiy Apparat Polovykh Kletok Mlekopitayushchikh.
     (Effect of Ethanol on the Genetic Apparatus of Mammalian
     Reproductive Cells.) Tsitologiya i Genetika, Kiev,
     15(6): 29-32, 1981.

391. Barker, D. Carrier Clinic: Concealed Repetitive Therapy
     Techniques. In: Alcoholism Rehabilitation: Methods and
     Experiences of Private Rehabilitation Centers. Ed. Vincent
     Groupe. New Brunswick, NJ: Rutgers University Center of
     Alcohol Studies, 1978, pages 7-17.

392. Barnard, C.P. Alcoholism and Incest -- Improving Diagnostic
     Comprehensiveness. International Journal of Family
     Therapy, 5(2): 136-144, 1983.

393. Barnard, C.P. Alcoholism and Incest. Part I: Similar Traits,
     Common Dynamics. Focus on Family and Chemical Dependency,
     7(1): 27, 29, 1984.

394. Barnard, C.P. Alcoholism and Incest. Part II: Issues in
     Treatment. Focus on Family and Chemical Dependency,
     7(2): 29-32, 1984.

395. Barnard, C.P. Families, Alcoholism and Therapy. Springfield,
     Illinois: Charles C. Thomas, 1981.

396. Barnard, George W., Holzer, Charles and Vera, Hernan. A
     Comparison of Alcoholics and Non-Alcoholics Charged with
     Rape. Bulletin of the American Academy of Psychiatry and
     the Law, 7(4): 432-440, 1979.

397. Barnard, George W., Vera, Hernan, Vera, Maria I. and Newman,
     Gustave. Till Death Do Us Part: A Study of Spouse Murder.
     Bulletin of the American Academy of Psychiatry & The Law,
     10(4): 271-280, 1982.

398. Barnes, F.H. Heredity in Alcoholism. Long Island Medical
     Journal, 9: 337-341, 1915.

399. Barnes, Grace M. Adolescent Alcohol Abuse and Other Problem
     Behaviors: Their Relationships and Common Parental Influences
     Journal of Youth and Adolescence, 13(4): 329-348, 1984.

400. Barnes, Grace M. Adolescent and Adult Drinking Patterns: A
     Comparison of Values and Behavior Associated with Alcohol Use.
     Master's Thesis. Buffalo, NY: State University of New York
     at Buffalo and Research Institute on Alcoholism, 1976.

401. Barnes, Grace M. Adolescent Drinking and the Family Socialization
     Process. Ph.D. Dissertation. (Ann Arbor, MI: University
     Microfilms.) Buffalo, NY: State University of New York at
     Buffalo, 1984.

402. Barnes, Grace M. Alcohol and Youth: A Comprehensive Bibliography.
     Westport, Connecticut: Greenwood Press, 1982.

403. Barnes, Grace M. Alcohol Use Among Older Persons: Findings from a
     Western New York State General Population Survey. Journal of
     the American Geriatrics Society, 27(6): 244-250, 1979.

404. Barnes, Grace M. The Development of Adolescent Drinking Behavior:
     An Evaluative Review of the Impact of the Socialization Process
     within the Family. Adolescence, 12(48): 571-591, 1977.

405. Barnes, Grace M. Drinking Among Adolescents: A Subcultural
     Phenomenon or a Model of Adult Behaviors. Adolescence,
     16(61): 211-229, 1981.

406. Barnes, Grace M. Evaluation of Alcohol Education -- A Reassessment
     Using Socialization Theory. Journal of Drug Education,
     14(2): 133-150, 1984.

407. Barnes, Grace M. and Cairns, Allen L. The Development of a New
     Methodological Approach for Determining Family Influences
     on Adolescent Drinking. Abstract. Alcoholism: Clinical
     and Experimental Research, 6(1): 136, 1982.

408. Barnes, Grace M., Farrell, Michael P. and Cairns, Allen. Parental
     Socialization Factors and Adolescent Drinking Behaviors.
     Journal of Marriage and the Family, 48: 27-36, 1986.

409. Barnes, Judith L., Benson, Carole S., and Wilsnack, Sharon C.
     Psychosocial Characteristics of Women with Alcoholic Fathers.
     In: Currents in Alcoholism. Volume 6. Treatment and
     Rehabilitation and Epidemiology. Ed. M. Galanter. New York:
     Grune and Stratton, 1979, pages 209-222.

410. Barnes, Paul D. Attributions by Observers in a Recreated Incident
     of Spouse Abuse. Dissertation Abstracts International,
     44(10-B): 3238, 1984.

411. Barnhill, L.R. Clinical Assessment of Intrafamilial Violence.
     Hospital and Community Psychiatry, 31(8): 543-547, 1980.

412. Barnhill, Lawrence. Clinical Approaches to Family Violence.
     (Family Therapy Collection 3.) Rockville, MD: Aspen Systems
     Corporation, 1982.

413. Barraclough, B., Bunch, J., Nelson, B. and Sainsbury P. A Hundred
     Cases of Suicide: Clinical Aspects. British Journal of
     Psychiatry, 125: 355-373, 1974.

414. Barrett, Thomas M. Chronic Alcoholism in Veterans. Quarterly
     Journal of Studies on Alcohol, 4: 68-78, 1943.

415. Barron, Frank. Family Relationships, Problem Drinking and
     Antisocial Behavior Among Adolescent Males. Master's
     Thesis. East Lansing, MI: Michigan State University,
     Department of Psychology, 1970.

416. de Barros, M. Consideracoes Sobre Eugenia A Proposito Da
     Esquizofrenia E Do Alcoolismo Cronico. (Considerations
     on Eugenics in Connection with Schizophrenia and Chronic
     Alcoholism.) Journal do Medico, 44: 217-221, 1961.

417. Barrucand, D. Les Inegalites Biologiques Devant l'Alcoolisation.
     (Biological Differences in Alcohol Use.) Alcool ou Sante,
     Paris, April: 6-15, 1983.

418. Barry, Herbert. Childhood Family Influences on Risk of Alcoholism.
     Progress in Neuro-Psychopharmacology, 3(6): 601-612, 1979.

419. Barry, Herbert. Cross-Cultural Evidence That Dependency Conflict
     Motivates Drunkenness. In: Cross-Cultural Approaches to
     the Study of Alcohol: An Interdisciplinary Perspective.
     Eds. Michael W. Everett, Jack O. Waddell and Dwight B. Heath.
     Paris: Mouton Publishers, 1976, pages 249-263.

420. Barry, Herbert. A Psychological Perspective on Development of
      Alcoholism. In: Encyclopedic Handbook of Alcoholism.
      Eds. E. Mansell Pattison & Edward Kaufman. New York, NY:
      Gardner Press, 1982, pages 529-539.

421. Barry, Herbert Jr., Barry, Herbert III and Blane, Howard T.
      Birth Order of Delinquent Boys with Alcohol Involvement.
      Quarterly Journal of Studies on Alcohol, 30(2): 408-413,
      1969.

422. Barry, Herbert III. Contribution to Understanding and Treating
      Alcoholics. Annals of the New York Academy of Sciences,
      273: 453-457, 1976.

423. Barry, Herbert III and Blane, Howard T. Birth Order as a Method of
      Studying Environmental Influences in Alcoholism. Annals of
      the New York Academy of Sciences, 197: 172-178, 1972.

424. Barry, Herbert III and Blane, Howard T. Birth Positions of
      Alcoholics. Journal of Individual Psychology, 33(1):
      62-69, 1977.

425. Barry, J.R., Anderson, H.E. Jr. and Thomason, O.B. MMPI
      Characteristics of Alcoholic Males Who are Well and Poorly
      Adjusted in Marriage. Journal of Clinical Psychology,
      23(3): 355-360, 1967.

426. Barry, Steven Patrick. Washington State Professionals' Response to
      Incidents of Child Abuse: A Preliminary Study. Dissertation
      Abstracts International, 41(8): 3167B, 1980.

427. Bartemeier, L.H. Treatment of the Spouse of the Alcoholic.
      Modern Treatment, 3: 542-547, 1966.

428. Bartholomew, A A. The Social Implications of Alcoholism.
      The Medical Journal of Australia, Sydney, 2(13):
      742-743, 1972.

429. Bartlett, Sylvan and Tapia, Fernando. Glue and Gasoline "Sniffing,"
      The Addiction of Youth. Case Report. Missouri Medicine,
      63: 270-272, 1966.

430. Barton, R. and Whitehead, J.A. The Gas Light Phenomenon. The
      Lancet, London, 1(608): 1258-1260, 1969.

431. Bartz, Karen W. Selected Childrearing Tasks and Problems of
      Mothers and Fathers. Family Coordinator, 27(3): 209-214,
      1978.

432. Barwick, P. Alcoholism and Leisure Time. People, Raleigh,
      North Carolina, 1(1): 16-17, 1973.

433. Baselga, Eduardo. Young Drug Users: Sociological Study of One
      Sample. Bulletin on Narcotics, 24(3): 17-22, 1972.

434. Bateman, Mildred E. Engaging the Alcoholic Man and His Wife in
      Casework Treatment. In: Casework with Wives of Alcoholics.
      Eds. Pauline C. Cohen and Merton S. Krause. New York: Family
      Service Association of America, 1971, pages 59-78.

435. Bateman, N.I. and Petersen, D.M. Variables Related to Outcome
      of Treatment for Hospitalized Alcoholics. International
      Journal of the Addictions, 6(2): 215-224, 1971.

436. Bates, Mildred. Using the Environment to Help the Male Skid Row
      Alcoholic. Social Casework, 64(5): 276-282, 1983.

437. Bates, Richard C. An Alcoholic Treatment Unit in a General
      Hospital. Hospital Progress, 51(6): 30-36, 1970.

438. Batizy, G.A. Social Psychiatry in Hungary. The International
      Journal of Social Psychiatry, London, 22(1): 47-52, 1976.

439. Battegay, R. Alkoholismus: Aus Psychiatrischer Sicht. (Alcoholism
      from the Psychiatric Point of View.) Suchtgefahren, Hamburg,
      19: 52-58, 1973.

440. Battegay, R. Psychotherapy of Drug Dependents and Alcoholics.
      In: Drug Dependence: Current Problems and Issues.
      Ed. M.M. Glatt. Baltimore: University Park Press, 1977,
      pages 169-193.

441. Battegay, R. and Bergdol, A.-M. Psychiatrische Aspekte des
      Alkoholismus: Ursachen und Entstehungsbedingungen.
      (Psychiatric Aspects of Alcoholism: Causes and Development.)
      In: Prophylaxe des Alkoholismus. (Prevention of
      Alcoholism.) Eds. R. Battegay and M. Wieser. Bern:
      Verlag Hans Huber, 1979, pages 94-111.

442. Battegay, R., Bergdol, A.-M. and Raillard, U. Das Alkoholproblem:
      Medizinisch-Psychiatrische Aspekte Und Behandlungskonzepte.
      (The Alcohol Problem: Medicopsychiatric Aspects and
      Treatment Concepts.) Drogalkohol, 5(1): 17-25, 1981.

443. Battegay, R., Ladewig, D., Muhlemann, R. and Weidemann, M.
      The Culture of Youth and Drug Abuse in Some European
      Countries. The International Journal of the Addictions,
      11: 245-261, 1976.

444. Battegay, R. and Muhlemann, R. Drogen, Alkohol und Familienplanung;
      Sozialpsychiatrische Gesichtspunkte. (Drugs, Alcohol and Family
      Planning; Sociopsychiatric Aspects.) Praxis, 63: 1143-1148,
      1974.

445. Battegay, R. and Muhlemann, R. Pilot Study at a Military Recruit
      School on Alcohol Consumption, Drug Use and Smoking Habits.
      Schweizer Archiv Fur Neurologie, Neurochirurgie Und
      Psychiatrie, 113(1): 109-135, 1973.

446. Battegay, R., Muhlemann, R., Hell, D., Zehnder, R., Hoch, P. and
      Dillinger, A. Alcohol, Tobacco and Drugs in the Lives of
      Young Men. Studies of Drug Abuse in 4082 Swiss Recruits in
      Private Life and During Military Training. Sozialmedizinische
      und Padagogische Jugendkunde, Basel, 14: 1-149, 1977.

447. Battegay, R., Muhlemann, R. and Zehnder, R. Comparative
      Investigations of the Abuse of Alcohol, Drugs, and Nicotine
      for a Representative Group of 4082 Men of Age 20.
      Comprehensive Psychiatry, 16(3): 247-254, 1975.

448. Battenberg, Beverly Harju. A Home Study of Sober, Drinking, and
      Recovered Alcoholic Family Systems. Doctoral Dissertation.
      (University Microfilms No. 7822113.) San Diego, CA:
      California School of Professional Psychology, 1978.

449. Battered Wives: Now They're Fighting Back. U.S. News & World
      Report, 81(12): 47-48, 1976.

450. The Battered Woman: Family Violence in America. Behavioral
      Medicine, 6(10): 38-41, 1979.

451. Battered Women: Issues of Public Policy. Washington, D.C.:
      United States Commission on Civil Rights, 1978.

452. Bauer, H. and Bauer, H. Confronting Physicians with the Problem
     of Aging. Paper presented at the Annual Session of the
     American Public Health Association. Montreal, November, 1982.

453. Baumann, P. and Ligeti, R. Psychopathologisch Bewertete
     Beobachtungen bei Kindern von Trunksuchtigen Eltern.
     (Psychopathologically Evaluated Observations of Children
     of Alcoholics.) Alcoholism, Zagreb, 5: 63-68, 1969.

454. Bavoux, R. and Robert, A. Alcohol, Challenge or Defeat. The
     Alcoholic and His Family: Systematic Approach. Soins
     Psychiatrie, 38: 37-40, 1983.

455. Bayer, Gready A. and Bayer, Marilyn A. Identifying Alcoholism
     in Families Seeking Mental Health Treatment. Annual
     Convention of the American Personnel and Guidance
     Association. Atlanta, GA, March, 1980.

456. Bazelon, David L., Tyce, Francis A.J., Usdin, Gene L. and
     Farnsworth, Dana L. Rehabilitating the Street Criminal:
     Panel Discussion. Psychiatric Annals, 7(6): 71, 74-75,
     79-81, 84-86, 1977.

457. Beamer, Brenda and Collins, Betty R. Intervention as a
     Therapeutic Process for the Families of Alcoholics. Paper
     presented at the National Council on Alcoholism Forum,
     New Orleans, LA, April, 1981. (Also in: Journal of Applied
     Sciences, 7(2): 187-202, 1983.)

458. Bean, Margaret H. Denial and the Psychological Complications
     of Alcoholism. In: Dynamic Approaches to the Understanding
     and Treatment of Alcoholism. Eds. Margaret H. Bean and
     Norman E. Zinberg. New York, NY: The Free Press, 1981.

459. Bean, Margaret H. and Zinberg, Norman E. (Eds.) Dynamic Approaches
     to the Understanding and Treatment of Alcoholism. New York:
     The Free Press, 1981.

460. Bean, Philip. Social Aspects of Drug Abuse: A Study of London
     Drug Offenders. Journal of Criminal Law, Criminology &
     Police Science, 62(1): 80-86, 1971.

461. Beardslee, William R. and Vaillant, George E. Prospective
     Prediction of Alcoholism and Psychopathology. Journal of
     Studies on Alcohol, 45(6): 500-503, 1984.

462. Beaton, William. Community Psychiatric Nursing: An Alcoholic
     Patient. Nursing Times, London, 72(44): 1710-1711, 1976.

463. Beaubrun, M.H. Treatment of Alcoholism in Trinidad and Tobago,
     1956-65. British Journal of Psychiatry, 113(499):
     643-658, 1967.

464. Beauvais, Fred. Preventing Drug Abuse Among American Indian
     Young People. Washington, D.C.: National Science
     Foundation, 1980. (Eric Document Number ED196630.)

465. Beaven, W.H. Abstinence in the Family. Paper presented at the
     Fourth World Congress for the Prevention of Alcoholism and
     Drug Dependency, Nairobi, Kenya, 1982, pages 407-414.

466. Beavers, W. Robert. Indications and Contraindications for Couples
     Therapy. Psychiatric Clinics of North America, 5(3):
     469-478, 1982.

467. Beck, M.N. Twenty-Five and Thirty-Five Year Follow Up of First
     Admissions to Mental Hospital. Canadain Psychiatric
     Association Journal, Ottawa, 13(3): 219-229, 1968.

468. Becker, A., Wylan, L. and McCourt, W. Primary Prevention --
     Whose Responsibility? The American Journal of Psychiatry,
     128(4): 412-417, 1971.

469. Becker, J.V. and Miller, P.M. Verbal and Nonverbal Marital
     Interaction Patterns of Alcoholics and Nonalcoholics.
     Journal of Studies on Alcohol, 37(11): 1616-1624, 1976.

470. Becker, Judith V. Analysis and Comparison of Verbal and
     Nonverbal Behaviors in Alcoholics and Their Wives and
     Nonalcoholics and Their Wives. Doctoral Dissertation.
     (Ann Arbor, MI: University Microfilms No. 75-22488.)
     Hattiesburg: University of Southern Mississippi, 1975.

471. Beckman, L.J., Day, T., Bardsley, P. and Seeman, A.Z. The
     Personality Characteristics and Family Backgrounds of Women
     Alcoholics. International Journal of the Addictions,
     15(1): 147-154, 1980.

472. Beckman, Linda J. Alcoholism Problems and Women: An Overview.
     In: Alcoholism Problems in Women and Children. Eds.
     M. Greenblatt and M.A. Schuckit. New York: Grune and
     Stratton, 1976, pages 65-96.

473. Beckman, Linda J. Women Alcoholics: A Review of Social and
     Psychological Studies. Journal of Studies on Alcohol,
     36(7): 797-824, 1975.

474. Beckman, Linda J. and Amaro, Hortensia. Patterns of Women's
     Use of Alcohol Treatment Agencies. In: Alcohol Problems
     in Women: Antecedents, Consequences, and Intervention.
     Eds. Sharon C. Wilsnack and Linda J. Beckman. New York:
     The Guilford Press, 1984, pages 319-348. (Also in: Alcohol
     Health and Research World, 9(2): 14-25, 1985.)

475. Beckmann, M. Situation Und Behandlungsmoglichkeiten Der
     Suchtkranken Frau. (The Position and Therapeutic
     Possibilities of the Woman Addict.) Gesundheitsfursorge,
     Stuttgart, 14: 95-99, 1964.

476. Bedate-Vilar, J. Psicodrama Con Alcoholicos. (Psychodrama with
     Alcoholics.) Drogalcohol, 5: 25-33, 1980.

477. Bedi, Ashok R. Demographic Correlates of Admissions to an
     Alcoholism Screening Program. Journal of Studies on
     Alcohol, 43(9): 956-963, 1982.

478. Bedrosian, Richard C. and Kagel, Steven A. A Woman Under the
     Influence: An Example of Multiple Victimization within a
     Family. American Journal of Family Therapy, 7(3):
     51-58, 1979.

479. Beecham, William Michael. Effects of a History of Paternal
     Alcoholism on the Appraisal of Drinking Behavior. Doctoral
     Dissertation. Tuscaloosa, AL: University of Alabama, 1982.
     (Dissertation Abstracts International, 44(2): 600B-601B,
     1983.)

480. Begleiter, H. Brain Potentials in Boys and Alcoholism.
     Biomedicine and Pharmacotherapy, 39(3): 159, 1985.

481. Begleiter, H. and Porjesz, B. Brain Electrophysiology and
     Alcoholism In: Pharmacological Treatments for Alcoholism.
     New York: Methuen, 1984, pages 351-362.

482. Begleiter, H., Projesz, B., Bihari, B. and Kissin, B. Event-
     Related Brain Potentials in Boys at Risk for Alcoholism.
     Science, 225(4669): 1493-1496, 1984.

483. Begleiter, H., Porjesz, B. and Kissin, B. Brain-Dysfunction in
      Alcoholics with and without a Family History of Alcoholism.
      Alcoholism: Clinical and Experimental Research, 6(1):
      136, 1982.

484. Behar, D., Winokur, G., Van-Valkenburg, C. and Lowry, M.
      Familial Subtypes of Depression: A Clinical View.
      Journal of Clinical Psychiatry, 41: 52-56, 1980.

485. Behar, D., Winokur, G., VanValkenburg, C., Lowry, M. and
      Lachenbruch, P.A. Clinical Overlap Among Familial
      Subtypes of Unipolar Depression. Neuropsychobiology,
      Basel 7: 179-184, 1981.

486. Behar, David, Berg, Carol J., Rapoport, Judith L., Nelson,
      William, Linnoila, Markku, Cohen, Martin, Bozevich, Clara
      and Marshall, Toni. Behavioral and Physiological Effects
      of Ethanol in High-Risk and Control Children: A Pilot
      Study. Alcoholism: Clinical and Experimental Research,
      7(4): 404-410, 1983.

487. Behavioral Therapy Used By Parents in the Home. NIAAA Information
      and Feature Service, (IFS No. 24): 6, May 25, 1976.

488. Behling, D.W. Alcohol Abuse as Encountered in 51 Instances of
      Reported Child Abuse. Clinical Pediatrics, 18(2): 87-88,
      90-91, 1979.

489. Beigel, Allan and Ghertner, Stuart. Toward a Social Model: An
      Assessment of Social Factors Which Influence Problem Drinking
      and Its Treatment. In: Treatment and Rehabilitation of
      the Chronic Alcoholic. Volume 5. The Biology of
      Alcoholism. Eds. Benjamin Kissin and Henri Begleiter.
      New York: Plenum Press, 1977, pages 197-233.

490. Beitelman, M.S. Role of the Family in Preventing Recurrence of
      Chronic Alcoholism. Feldsher I Akusherka, 38(10): 46-49,
      1973.

491. Bejerot, N. En Ha'rd Dom Over En Oformogen Samhallsapparat.
      (Harsh Judgement on an Inept Social Establishment.) Alkohol
      Och Narkotika, 75(3): 16, 18, 1981.

492. Belasco, James A. The Criterion Question Revisited. The British
      Journal of Addiction, 66(1): 39-44, 1971.

493. Beletsis, S.G. and Brown, S. Developmental Framework for
      Understanding the Adult Children of Alcoholics. Focus on
      Women: Journal of Addictions and Health, 2(4): 187-203,
      1981.

494. Belfer, Myron L. and Shader, Richard I. Premenstrual Factors
      as Determinants of Alcoholism in Women. In: Alcoholism
      Problems in Women and Children. Eds. Milton Greenblatt
      and Marc A. Schuckit. New York: Grune and Stratton, 1976,
      pages 97-102.

495. Belic, J. and Lalic, D. Loss of Parents During Childhood or
      Adolescence in Male Alcoholics. Medicinski Pregled,
      Novi Sad, 34(7-8): 317-321, 1981.

496. Belkin, Gary S. and Goodman, Norman. Crises in the Family:
      Violence, Alcoholism, Divorce. In: Marriage, Family and
      Intimate Relationships. Gary S. Belkin and Norman Goodman.
      Chicago: Rand McNally College Publishing Co., 1980, pages
      409-441.

497. Bell, B. and Cohen, R. Bristol Social Adjustment Guide: Comparison
      Between the Offspring of Alcoholic and Nonalcoholic Mothers.
      The British Journal of Clinical Psychology, 20(2): 93-95, 1981.

498. Bell, Catherine S. and Battjes, Robert. Prevention Research:
      Deterring Drug Abuse Among Children and Adolescents.
      Rockville, MD: National Institute on Drug Abuse, 1985.

499. Bell, D.S. and Champion, R.A. Deviancy, Delinquency and Drug Use.
      British Journal of Psychiatry, London, 134: 269-276, 1979.

500. Bell, David S. Review of Alcoholism: A Handbook by N.R.H.
      Drew, J.R. Moon and F.H. Buchanan. Australian Journal of
      Alcoholism and Drug Dependence, 1(4): 136-137, 1974.

501. Bell, R.G. Treatment and Rehabilitation of Alcohol Addicts.
      Ontario Medical Review, Toronto, 18(10): 23-25, 38, 1951.

502. Bell, R. Gordon. Role of Alcohol in Community Life. Paper
      presented at the 2nd Conference on Alcohol Education,
      Stowe, VT, October, 1961, pages 9-15.

503. Bell, Roger A., Keeley, Kim A., Clements, Ray D., Warheit, George
      J. and Holzer, Charles E. Alcoholism, Life Events, and
      Psychiatric Impairment. Annals of the New York Academy of
      Sciences, 273: 467-480, 1976.

504. Bello, Sergio and Salinas, M. Judith. Evaluacion De Un Programa
      De Prevencion Secundaria Del Alcoholismo. (Evaluation of a
      Program for Secondary Prevention of Alcoholism.) Revista
      Medica de Chile, 106(8): 636-640, 1978.

505. Beltrame, T.F. Meeting the Special Needs of Appalachian
      Alcoholics. Hospital & Community Psychiatry, 29(12):
      792-794, 1978.

506. Benda, P. and Taleghani, M. L'alcoolique Dangereux Et Les Siens;
      Aspects Semeiologiques Et Therapeutiques Des Visites A Domicile.
      (The Dangerous Alcoholic and His Family; Semeiological and
      Therapeutic Aspects of House Visits.) Annales Medico-
      Psychologiques, Paris, 124(1): 193-226, 1966.

507. Bender, Robert B. Perceived Parental Attitudes and Their
      Relationship to Chronic Alcoholism in a Veterans
      Administration Hospital Patient Population: An Empirical
      Test of McCord and McCord's Theory of the Origins of
      Alcoholism. Doctoral Dissertation. (Ann Arbor, MI:
      University Microfilms No. 74-28315). Tucson: University
      of Arizona, 1974.

508. Bendia, M.T., Giaquinto, S., Massi, G., Ricolfi, A. and Vitali, S.
      Indagine Catamnestica su Alcoolisti Svezzati. (A Follow-Up
      Study of Treated Alcoholics.) Minerva Medica, Torino, 70:
      1503-1506, 1979.

509. Bene-Kociemba, Alice, Cotton, Paul G. and Frank, Arlene. Predictors
      of Community Tenure of Discharged State Hospital Patients.
      American Journal of Psychiatry, 136: 1556-1561, 1979.

510. Benincasa-Stagni, E. and Citterio, C. Psicogenesi e Sociogenesi
      Dell'alcoolismo Femminile. (Psychogenesis and Sociogenesis of
      Alcoholism in Women.) Lavoro Neuropsichiatrico, Rome, 27:
      331-412, 1960.

511. Benjamin, David M. Problems of Polypharmacy. Archives of the
      Foundation of Thanatology, New York, 7(1): 11, 1978.

512. Benjamin, Rommel and Benjamin, Mary. Sociocultural Correlates
      of Black Drinking: Implications for Research and Treatment.
      Journal of Studies on Alcohol, (Supplement 9), 241-245, 1981.

513. Benjamin, Rommel and Rao, V. Prakasa. Alcohol-Related Problems
      and Intra-Familial Management Among Blacks. Paper presented
      at the Southwestern Sociological Association (SWSA), 1977.

514. Bennett, A.N. and Pethybridge, R. A Study of Abused Children on
      the Gosport (Hampshire) Peninsula. Journal of the Royal
      Society of Medicine, 72(10): 743-747, 1979.

515. Bennett, Gerald and Woolf, Donna S. Current Approaches to Substance
      Abuse Therapy. In: Substance Abuse: Pharmacologic,
      Developmental, and Clinical Perspectives. Eds. Gerald Bennett,
      Christine Vourakis and Donna S. Wolf. New York: John Wiley &
      Sons, 1983, pages 341-369.

516. Bennett, L.A. Combining Qualitative and Quantitative Methods in
      Studies of Familial Alcoholism. Drinking and Drug Practices
      Surveyor, 20: 51-52, 1985.

517. Bennett, L.A. Family Environment and Inter-Generational Transmission
      of Alcoholism. Alcoholism, Zagreb, 16(1-2): 56-58, 1980.

518. Bennett, L.A. and Ames, G.M. (Eds.) American Experience with
      Alcohol: Contrasting Cultural Perspectives. New York, NY:
      Plenum Press, 1985.

519. Bennett, L.A. and Wolin, S.J. Cross-Generational Transmission of
      Alcoholism in Families. The Alcoholism and Family Heritage
      Study. Anali Klinicke Bolnice. Dr. M. Stojanovic,
      23(2): 207-214, 1984.

520. Bennett, L.A., Wolin, S.J. and Noonan, D.L. Family Identity and
      Intergenerational Recurrence of Alcoholism. Alcoholism:
      Journal on Alcoholism and Related Addictions, Zagreb, 13:
      100-108, 1977.

521. Bennett, Linda A. and Wolin, Steven J. A Comparison of Children
      from Alcoholic and Non-Alcoholic Families: Cognitive and
      Psychosocial Functioning. Paper presented to the National
      Council on Alcoholism Forum, Washington, D.C., April, 1985.

522. Bennett, Michael. An Investigation of Factors Related to Burnout
      in Mothers of Handicapped and Non-Handicapped Children.
      Dissertation Abstracts International, 45(2): 660B, 1983.

523. Bennun, I. Two Approaches to Family Therapy with Alcoholics:
      Problem-Solving and Systemic Therapy. Journal of Substance
      Abuse Treatment, 2(1): 19-26, 1985.

524. Benoit, J.-C., Daigremont, A. Guitton, C., Porot, D. and Rabeau, B.
      Les Entretiens Collectifs Pour Le Couple, en Psychiatrie de
      Secteur. (Conjoint Marital Counseling in a Sector of Psychiatry.)
      Annales Medico-Psychologiques, Paris, 136: 901-908, 1978.

525. Benowitz, S.I. Studies Help Scientists Home in on Genetics of
      Alcoholism. Science News, 126(13): 196, 1984.

526. Bensinger, A. and Lazuk, A.J. Systems Approach to Counseling
      Supervisors. Labor-Management Alcoholism Journal, 11(2):
      66-72, 1981.

527. Bensinger, A. and Pilkington, C F. An Alternative Method in the
      Treatment of Alcoholism: The United Technologies Corporation
      Day Treatment Program. Journal of Occupational Medicine,
      25(4): 300-303, 1983.

528. Benson, C.S. Coping and Support Among Daughters of Alcoholics. Doctoral Dissertation. (University Microfilms No. 8029210.) Indiana: Indiana University, 1980.

529. Bensoussan, P.A. Quelques Caracteres Particuliers Des Familles d'Alcooliques Et Leur Consequences Therapeutiques. (Some Special Characteristics of the Families of Alcoholics and Their Therapeutic Implications.) Revue de Medecine Pratique, 4: 489-495, 1958.

530. Bentinck, Catherine A., Miller, Bryon, A. and Pokorny, Alex D. Relatives as Informants in Mental Health Research. Mental Hygiene, 53(3): 446-450, 1969.

531. Bentler, P.M. and Newcomb, Michael D. Longitudinal Study of Marital Success and Failure. Journal of Consulting and Clinical Psychology, 46(5): 1053-1070, 1978.

532. Berenson, David. Alcohol and the Family System. In: Family Therapy: Theory and Practice. Ed. Philip J. Guerin, Jr. New York: John Wiley, 1976, pages 284-297.

533. Berenson, David. A Family Approach to Alcoholism. Psychiatric Opinion, 13(1): 33-38, 1976.

534. Berenson, David. Sexual Counseling with Alcoholics. In: Workshop on Sexual Counseling for Persons with Alcohol Problems. Pittsburgh, PA, January, 1976, pages 48-65.

535. Berenson, David. The Therapist's Relationship with Couples with an Alcoholic Member. In: Family Therapy of Drug and Alcohol Abuse. Eds. E. Kaufman and P.N. Kaufmann. New York: Gardner Press, 1979, pages 233-242.

536. Berest, Joseph J. Medico-Legal Aspects of Incest. Journal of Sex Research, 4(3): 195-205, 1968.

537. Berger, A. Family Involvement and Alcoholics' Completion of a Multiphase Treatment Program. Journal of Studies on Alcohol, 42: 517-521, 1981.

538. Berger, Fred. Alcoholism Rehabilitation: A Supportive Approach. Hospital and Community Psychiatry, 34(11): 1040-1043, 1983.

539. Berger, J. and Stojiljkovic, C. Comparative Analysis of Psychosomatic Development of Children of Alcoholics and Nonalcoholic Parents in Two Different Areas. Paper Presented at the 3rd International Congress of Social Psychiatry, Zagreb, September, 1970.

540. Berger, M.E. Investigation of the MMPI Scores of College Freshmen who Married Those Who Were or Subsequently Became Alcoholic. Dissertation Abstracts International, 44(2): 431A, 1983.

541. Bergler, Edmund. Contributions to the Psychogenesis of Alcohol Addiction. Quarterly Journal of Studies on Alcohol, 5: 434-449, 1944.

542. Berk, R.A. and Newton, P.J. Does Arrest Really Deter Wife Battery? An Effort to Replicate the Findings of the Minneapolis Spouse Abuse Experiment. American Sociological Review, 50(2): 253-262, 1985.

543. Berkel, V. Aspects et Problemes de L'Intemperance Critique. (Aspects and Problems of Critical Intemperance.) Revue de l'Alcoolisme, Paris, 16: 62-65, 1970.

544. Berkstresser, Gordon Abbott III. The Impact of Abnormal
     Conditions on Family Consumption Behavior: A Comparison
     of Purchasing Behavior of Family Units Containing an
     Alcoholic Husband and a Non-Alcoholic Husband. Dissertation
     Abstracts International, 38(11): 6811A, 1978.

545. Berman, Alan L. Dyadic Death: Murder-Suicide. Suicide and
     Life-Threatening Behavior, 9(1): 15-23, 1979.

546. Berman, Kenneth K. Multiple Conjoint Family Groups in the
     Treatment of Alcoholism. The Journal of the Medical Society
     of New Jersey, 65(1): 6-8, 1968.

547. Bernard, C.P. Families, Alcoholism and Therapy. Springfield,
     Illinois: Charles C. Thomas, 1981.

548. Bernard, J.G. Enfants de Peres Alcooliques. (Children of Alcoholic
     Fathers.) Bulletin d'Information sur l'Alcoolisme, 148:
     31-34, 1982.

549. Bernard, J.G. Juvenile Alcoholism and Its Prevention. Revue
     International De Services De Sante, 54(5): 383-393, 1981.

550. Bernard, P., Lecuyer, R. and Bles, G. Alcooliques Traites Dans
     Un Hopital Psychiatrique. (Three Hundred Alcoholics Treated
     in a Psychiatric Hospital.) Semaine Medicale Professionelle
     et Medico-Sociale, (Semaine des Hopitaux), Paris, 33:
     45-49, 1957.

551. Bernardin, Joseph L. International Synod Targets Four Family-
     Centered Health Care Concerns. Hospital Progress,
     61(10): 46-48, 1980.

552. Berner, P. and Solms, W. Alkoholismus Bei Frauen. (Alcoholism
     in Women.) Weiner Zeitschrift fur Nervenheilkunde und Deren
     Girenzgebiete, Vienna, 6: 275-301, 1953.

553. Bernstein, Joel S. The Autistic Character. Psychoanalytic
     Review, 62(4): 537-555, 1975-76.

554. Berry, J.C. Antecedents of Schizophrenia, Impulsive Character,
     and Alcoholism in Males. Doctoral Dissertation (University
     Microfilms No. 67-14,025; Dissertation Abstracts
     International, 28: 2134B, 1967.) New York: Columbia
     University, 1967.

555. Bertini, Franco. Quelques Aspects Psycho-Sociaux De
     L'Intoxication Alcoolique En Piemont. (Some Psychosocial
     Aspects of Alcoholic Intoxication in Piedmont.) Alcool Ou
     Sante, Paris, 131(4): 44-49, 1975.

556. Bertolino, A., Quinto, A. and La-Mura, G. L'alcoolismo E Una
     Tossicomania; Rilievi Clinico-Statistici Nell'ospedale
     Psichiatrico Di Bisceglie. (Alcoholism is an Addiction;
     Remarks on Clinical Statistics of Patients at the
     Psychiatric Hospital of Bisceglie.) Acta Neurologica,
     Napoli, 27: 68-97, 1972.

557. Beschner, George and Brotman, Richard (Eds.). National Institute
     on Drug Abuse Symposium on Comprehensive Health Care for
     Addicted Families and Their Children: May 20 & 21, 1976,
     New York, New York. Washington, D.C.: U.S. Government
     Printing Office, 1977.

558. Bespali, De Consens Y. Some Aspects of Alcoholism in Uruguay.
     Alcoholism, Zagreb, 8(1): 51-55, 1972.

559. Betros, Emeel S., Lang, Irving, Garcia, Robert, Brill, Henry, Dunne, John R., Galiber, Joseph L., Hardt, Chester R., Hevesi, Alan G. and Lombardi, Tarki. Drug Abuse Prevention: Report of the Temporary State Commission to Evaluate the Drug Laws. New York State Legislative Document #11. Albany, New York: New York State Legislature, 1974. (Eric Document Number ED091312.)

560. Bevia, F.J.O. The Families of Alcoholic Women. Actas Luso-Espanolas De Neurologia, Psiquiatria Y Ciencias Afines, Madrid, 4(4): 227-238, 1976.

561. Bezdicek, J. and Slavik, V. Navrh Systemu Socialni Pece O Alkoholiky A Jejich Rodiny. (A Proposal for the System of Social Care of Alcoholics and Their Families.) Protialkoholicky Obzor, Bratislava, 6: 168-177, 1969.

562. Beznosiuk, E.V. and Evstigneev, A.I. Incidence and Several Features of Chronic Alcoholic Patient Detection. Zhurnal Nevropatologii I Psikhiatrii, 78(9): 1369-1374, 1978.

563. Bezzola. A Statistical Investigation Into the Role of Alcohol in the Origin of Innate Imbecility. Quarterly Journal of Inebriety, Hartford, 23: 346-354, 1901.

564. Bhatia, Pritam S. Multiphasic Matrix for the Diagnosis of Alcoholism. Alcohol Health and Research World, 3(4): 24-30, 1979.

565. Bianco, Dorothy M. Adolescent Female Drug Abusers and Their Families: Some Variables Associated with Successful Treatment Outcome. Dissertation Abstracts International, 45(3): 1005B, 1984.

566. Bibb, Richard E. The Outpatient Treatment of the Alcoholic. The Ohio State Medical Journal, 66: 686-689, 1970.

567. Bidder, T. George and Jaeger, Patricia D. Malondialdehyde Production by Erythrocytes from Alcoholic and Nonalcoholic Subjects. Life Sciences, 30(12): 1021-1027, 1982.

568. Biddle, Bruce J., Bank, Barbara J., Anderson, Don S., Hauge, Ragnar, Keats, Daphne M., Keats, John A., Marlin, Marjorie M. and Valantin, Simone. Comparative Research on Social Determinants of Adolescent Drinking. Social Psychology Quarterly, 48(2): 164-177, 1985.

569. Biddle, Bruce J., Bank, Barbara J. and Marlin, Marjorie M. Parental and Peer Influence on Adolescents. Social Forces, 58(4): 1057-1080, 1980.

570. Biddle, Bruce J., Bank, Barbara J. and Marlin, Marjorie M. Social Determinants of Adolescent Drinking: What They Think, What They Do and What I Think and Do. Journal of Studies on Alcohol, 41: 215-241, 1980.

571. Bieder, J. and Agababa, P. The Adoptee Method in Psychiatry. Annales Medico-Psychologiques, Paris, 141(1): 1-23, 1983.

572. Biek, J.E. Screening Test for Identifying Adolescents Adversely Affected by a Parental Drinking Problem. Journal of Adolescent Health Care, 2(2): 107-114, 1981.

573. Biennial Report of the New Hampshire Division of Alcoholism. Quarterly Journal of Studies on Alcohol, 12: 666-675, 1951.

574. Bigus, Odis E. Some Secondary Deviance Aspects of the Alcoholic Career. Free Inquiry, 5(2): 48-58, 1977.

575. Bihari, Bernard. Alcoholism in M.M.T.P. Patients: Etiological
     Factors and Treatment Approaches. Paper presented at the
     National Conference on Methadone Treatment, 1973, pages
     288-295.

576. Billings, A.G., Gomberg, C.A., Nash, B.H., Kessler, M. and
     Weiner, S. Synchronized Sipping in Alcoholics and Social
     Drinkers; A Preliminary Investigation. Journal of Studies
     on Alcohol, 39: 554-559, 1978.

577. Billings, Andrew G., Kessler, M., Gomberg, C.A. and Weiner, S.
     Marital Conflict Resolution of Alcoholic and Nonalcoholic
     Couples During Drinking and Nondrinking Sessions.
     Journal of Studies on Alcohol, 40: 183-195, 1979.

578. Billings, Andrew G. and Moos, Rudolf H. Psychosocial Processes
     of Recovery Among Alcoholics and Their Families:
     Implications for Clinicians and Program Evaluators.
     Addictive Behaviors, Oxford, 8(3): 205-218, 1983.

579. Billings, Andrew G. and Moos, Rudolf H. Social Support and
     Functioning Among Community and Clinical Groups: A Panel Model.
     Journal of Behavioral Medicine, 5(3): 295-311, 1982.

580. Binder, S. New Approaches to the Treatment of Alcoholics.
     Zeitschrift Fur Psychotherapie Und Medizinische Psychologie,
     21(6): 239-247, 1971.

581. Bingol, N., Schuster, C., Fuchs, M., Iosub, S. and George, G.
     Influence of Socioeconomic Factors on the Occurrence of
     Fetal Alcohol Syndrome. Paper presented at the National
     Council on Alcoholism Forum, Washington, D.C., April, 1985.

582. Binion, Victoria J. A Descriptive Comparison of the Families
     of Origin of Women Heroin Users and Nonusers. In: United
     States Department of Health, Education and Welfare, National
     Institute on Drug Abuse. Addicted Women, Family Dynamics,
     Self Perceptions, and Support Systems. Washington, D.C.:
     U.S. Government Printing Office, 1979, pages 77-113.

583. Binion, Victoria Jackson. Sex Differences in Socialization
     and Family Dynamics of Female and Male Heroin Users.
     The Journal of Social Issues, 38(2): 43-57, 1982.

584. Binkiewicz, A., Robinson, M.J. and Senior, B. Pseudo-Cushing
     Syndrome Caused by Alcohol in Breast Milk. Journal of
     Pediatrics, 93: 965-967, 1978.

585. Biomedical Consequences of Alcohol Use and Abuse. In: Alcohol
     and Health: Third Special Report to the United States
     Congress. Ed. Ernest P. Noble. Rockville, MD: National
     Institute on Alcohol Abuse and Alcoholism, 1978, pages 25-37.

586. Birkasova, M., Rehan, V. and Skula, E. Trilete Zkusenosti S
     Letnim Manzelskym Taborem. (The 3-year Performance of
     a Summer Camp for Married Couples.) Protialkoholicky
     Obzor, Bratislava, 13: 217-220, 1978.

587. Birke, S. and Mayer, K. Learning to Make Choices: Breaking the
     Family Circle of Alcoholism. Focus on Family and Chemical
     Dependency, 7(6): 5, 38, 43, 1984.

588. Birrell, R G. and Birrell, J.H. The Maltreatment Syndrome in
     Children: A Hospital Survey. The Medical Journal of
     Australia, Sydney, 2(23): 1023-1029, 1968.

589. Birtchnell, J. Sibship Size and Mental Illness. British Journal
     of Psychiatry, 117(538): 303-308, 1970.

590. Birtchnell, John. Early Parent Death and Mental Illness.
      British Journal of Psychiatry, 116(532): 281-288, 1970.

591. Bishop, F.I. Education of the Community. In: Symposium:
      Alcohol and Drugs -- A Challenge for Education. Melbourne,
      Australia, January, 1971, pages 15-22.

592. Bissell, D., Paton, A. and Ritson, Bruce. ABC of Alcohol.
      Help: Referral. British Medical Journal, (Clinical
      Research Edition), London, 284(6314): 495-497, 1982.

593. Bissell, L. Alcoholism in Physicians. Tactics to Improve the
      Salvage Rate. Postgraduate Medicine, 74(1): 177-187, 1983.

594. Bissell, L. Some Perspectives on Alcoholism: A Professional
      Guide. Pamphlet. Minneapolis, MN: Johnson Institute, 1982.

595. Bissell, L. and Haberman, P.W. Alcoholism in the Professions.
      New York: Oxford University Press, 1984.

596. Bissell, LeClair. Diagnosis and Recognition. In: Alcoholism: A
      Practical Treatment Guide. Eds. Stanley E. Gitglow and Herbert
      S. Peyser. New York: Grune and Stratton, 1980, pages 23-45.

597. Bissell, LeClair and Deakins, Susan M. Smithers Alcoholism
      Center: A Comprehensive Alcoholism Program in an Urban
      Voluntary Hospital. In: Alcoholism Rehabilitation:
      Methods and Experiences of Private Rehabilitation Centers.
      Ed. Vincent Groupe. New Brunswick, NJ: Rutgers University
      Center on Alcohol Studies, 1978, pages 95-105.

598. Black, Claudia. Alcohol Education: Children of Alcoholics.
      Prairie Rose, 59(2): 15, 1980.

599. Black, Claudia. Alcohol Education: Children of Alcoholics,
      Part I. Oklahoma Nurse, 25(3): 2, 1980.

600. Black, Claudia. Alcohol Education: Children of Alcoholics,
      Part II. Oklahoma Nurse, 25(4): 2, 1980.

601. Black, Claudia. Alcoholism and Family Violence. Alcoholism:
      The National Magazine, 6(3): 46-47, 1986.

602. Black, Claudia. Children of Alcoholic Families: Community
      Must Accept Responsibility. Focus on Alcohol and Drug
      Issues, 6(2): 13, 25, 1983.

603. Black, Claudia. Children of Alcoholics. Alcohol Health and
      Research World, 4(1): 23-27, 1979. (Also in: The
      Catalyst, 1(3): 15-21, 1980; Recovery Newsletter in
      Alcoholism: The National Magazine, 5(4): R4, 1985.)

604. Black, Claudia. Children of Alcoholics -- The Clinical Profile.
      In: Changing Legacies: Growing Up in an Alcoholic Home.
      Pompano Beach, FL: Health Communications, 1984, pages 73-75.

605. Black, Claudia. Children of Alcoholics -- The Need to Believe.
      Recovery Newsletter in Alcoholism: The National Magazine,
      Feb: 4, 1985.

606. Black, Claudia. Dear Santa. Alcoholism: The National
      Magazine, 5(2): R3, 1984.

607. Black, Claudia. Don't Let It Happen to You. Recovery Newsletter
      in Alcoholism: The National Magazine, 5(7): R7, 1985.

608. Black, Claudia. Don't Talk -- The Family Law. Focus on
      Alcohol and Drug Issues, 6(4): 6-7, 1981.

609. Black Claudia. The Family Law in Alcoholic Homes -- Don't Talk.
In: Changing Legacies: Growing Up in an Alcoholic Home.
Pompano Beach, FL: Health Communications, 1984, pages 39-42.

610. Black, Claudia. Innocent Bystanders at Risk: The Children of
Alcoholics. Alcoholism: The National Magazine, 1(3):
22-26, 1981.

611. Black, Claudia. It Will Never Happen to Me! Denver, CO:
M.A.C. Printing and Publications Division, 1982.

612. Black, Claudia. Learning to Enjoy Success. Recovery Newsletter
in Alcoholism: The National Magazine, 5(6): R3, 1985.

613. Black, Claudia. My Dad Loves Me, My Dad Has a Disease;
A Workbook for Children of Alcoholics. Newport Beach, CA:
Alcoholism Children Therapy (ACT), 1979.

614. Black, Claudia. A New Concept in Working With Children of
Alcoholics. In: Proceedings of the Eighth Annual Meeting
of ALMACA, Detroit, MI, October 1-5, 1979. Association
of Labor-Management Administrators and Consultants on
Alcoholism, Inc. Arlington, VA: ALMACA, 1980, pages 75-102.

615. Black, Claudia. Process of Recovery: Al-Anon and the Adult Child.
Pamphlet. New York: Al-Anon Family Group Headquarters, 1985.

616. Black, Claudia. Repeat After Me. Denver, CO: M.A.C. Printing
and Publications, 1985.

617. Black, Claudia. Teaching, Talking, Touching. Alcoholism:
The National Magazine, 5(2): 26-28, 1984.

618. Black, Marvin A. What's a Parent to Do. Pamphlet. New York:
National Council on Alcoholism, no date.

619. Black, Rebecca. Conflict and Crisis Typify Life for Children
from Alcoholic Families. In: Changing Legacies: Growing
Up in an Alcoholic Home. Pompano Beach, FL: Health
Communications, 1984, pages 37-38.

620. Black, Rebecca and Mayer, Joseph. An Investigation of the
Relationship Between Substance Abuse and Child Abuse and
Neglect. Boston: Washington Center for Addictions,
1979. (Eric Document Number ED175228.)

621. Black, Rebecca and Mayer, Joseph. Parents with Special
Problems: Alcoholism and Opiate Addiction. In: The
Battered Child. Eds. C.H. Kempe and R.E. Helfer.
Chicago, IL: University of Chicago, 1980, pages 104-113.
(Also in: Child Abuse and Neglect, 4: 45-54, 1980.)

622. Black, Rebecca M., Mayer, Joseph and Zaklan, A. The Relationship
between Opiate Abuse and Child Abuse and Neglect. In:
Critical Concerns in the Field of Drug Abuse: Proceedings
of the Third National Drug Abuse Conference, Inc., New York,
1976. Eds. A. Schecter, H. Alksne and E. Kaufman. New York:
Marcel Dekker, 1978, pages 755-758.

623. Blackburn, Nancy Elizabeth West. Problems Employees Take to a
Marriage and Family Counselor. Dissertation Abstracts
International, 44(10): 3229B, 1983.

624. Blackwell, B. Physician Lifestyle and Medical Marriages.
Wisconsin Medical Journal, 81(4): 23-25, 1982.

625. Blackwell, Rebecca. Genie in the Bottle. In: Having Been There.
      Ed. A. Luks. New York: Charles Scribner's Sons, 1979, pages
      30-35.

626. Blanchard, Joan Marie. Self-Concept and Leisure Attitude.
      Dissertation Abstracts International, 45(3A): 961A, 1984.

627. Blane, H.T. Sex of Siblings of Male Alcoholics. Journal of
      the American Medical Association, 234(8): 879, 1975.

628. Blane, H.T. and Barry, H. III. Sex of Siblings of Male Alcoholics.
      Archives of General Psychiatry, 32: 1403-1405, 1975.

629. Blane, Howard T. Trends in the Prevention of Alcoholism.
      Psychiatric Research Reports, 24: 1-9, 1968.

630. Blane, Howard T. and Barry, Herbert. Birth Order and Alcoholism:
      A Review. Quarterly Journal of Studies on Alcohol,
      34(3): 837-852, 1973.

631. Blane, Howard T., Barry, Herbert III, and Barry Herbert Jr.
      Sex Differences in Birth Order of Alcoholics. British
      Journal of Psychiatry, London, 119(553): 657-661, 1971.

632. Blane, Howard T. and Hewitt, L.E. Alcohol and Youth: An
      Analysis of the Literature, 1960-1975. Prepared for
      the National Institute on Alcohol Abuse and Alcoholism.
      Springfield, Virginia: U.S. National Technical Infor-
      mation Service, 1977. (National Technical Information
      Service No. PB-268-698.)

633. Blane, Howard T. and Hill, Marjorie J. Public Health Nurses Speak
      Up About Alcoholism. Nursing Outlook, 12: 34-37, 1964.

634. Blangiardo, John and Gold, Judith. Alternatives Drug and Alcohol
      Prevention Program. Self Evaluation, 1981-82. Brooklyn,
      NY: Community School District 22, 1982. (Eric Document
      Number ED234286.)

635. Blass, J.P. and Gibson, G.E. Genetic Factors in Wernicke-
      Korsakoff Syndrome. Alcoholism: Clinical and Experimental
      Research, 3: 126-134, 1979.

636. Blass, John P. and Omenn, Gilbert S. Molecular Neurogenetics.
      Neurology, 31(2): 172-173, 1981.

637. Blath, R.A., McClure, J.N. Jr. and Wetzel, R.D. Familial
      Factors in Suicide. Diseases of the Nervous System,
      34(2): 90-93, 1973.

638. Blechman, Elaine A., Berberian, Rosalie M. and Thompson, W.
      Douglas. How Well Does Number of Parents Explain Unique
      Variance in Self-Reported Drug Use? Journal of Consulting
      and Clinical Psychology, 45(6): 1182-1183, 1977.
      (Also in: Drugs and the Family. Ed. Thomas J. Glynn.
      Washington, D.C.: U.S. Government Printing Office, 1981.)

639. Blek, J.E. Screening Test for Identifying Adolescents Adversely
      Affected by a Parental Drinking Problem. Paper presented
      at a Conference, Madison, WI, February, 1983. (Also in:
      Working with Adolescent Alcohol/Drug Problems: Assessment,
      Intervention and Treatment. Madison, WI: Department of
      Public Instruction, pages 23-31.)

640. Bleuler, M. A Comparative Study of the Constitutions of Swiss
      and American Alcoholic Patients. In: Etiology of Chronic
      Alcoholism. Ed. O. Diethelm. Springfield, IL: Thomas,
      1955, pages 167-178.

641. Bleuler, M. Familial and Personal Background of Chronic Alcoholics.
     In: Etiology of Chronic Alcoholism. Ed. O. Diethelm.
     Springfield, IL: Thomas, 1955, pages 110-166.

642. Block, M.A. Alcoholism. Journal of the American Medical
     Association, 176: 891, 1961.

643. Block, Marvin A. Alcohol -- A Family Problem. Material presented at
     an Information Forum on Family Health presented for community
     members in April, 1984 in Atlantic City, NJ.

644. Block, Marvin A. Motivating the Alcoholic Patient. In:
     Alcoholism: A Practical Treatment Guide. Eds. Stanley E.
     Gitglow and Herbert S. Peyser. New York: Grune and
     Stratton, 1980, pages 47-71.

645. Block, Marvin A. Rehabilitation of the Alcoholic. Journal of
     the American Medical Association, 188: 84-86, 1964.

646. deBlois, C.S. and Stewart, M.A. Marital Histories of Women Whose
     First Husbands were Alcoholic or Antisocial. British Journal
     of Addiction, Edinburgh, 78(2): 205-213, 1983.

647. Blom, G.E., Cheney, B.D. and Snoddy, J.E. MSU Program Cork
     Drinking/Nondrinking Curriculum for Growing Up in America.
     Curriculum Guide. East Lansing, MI: Michigan State
     University, College of Education, 1982.

648. Blom, G.E., Cheney, B.D. and Snoddy, J.E. MSU Program Cork
     Drinking/Nondrinking Curriculum for Teaching Socialization
     Issues. Curriculum Guide. East Lansing, MI: Michigan
     State University, College of Education, 1982.

649. Bloom, B.L. and Hodges, W.F. Predicament of the Newly Separated.
     Community Mental Health Journal, 17(4): 277-293, 1981.

650. Bloom, Patricia J. Alcoholism After 60. American Family
     Physician, 28(2): 111-113, 1983.

651. Blout, William R. and Dembo, Richard. Personal Drug Use and
     Attitudes Toward Prevention Among Youth Living in a High
     Risk Environment. Journal of Drug Education, 14(3):
     207-225, 1984.

652. Blue Book Volume 36: Proceedings From the 36th Annual Symposium
     at Cherry Hill, NJ, June, 1984. Washington, D.C.: National
     Clergy Council on Alcoholism and Related Drug Problems, 1984.

653. Bluglass, R. Current Developments in Forensic Psychiatry in the
     United Kingdom. Psychiatric Journal of the University of
     Ottawa, 2(2): 53-62, 1977.

654. Bluglass, Robert. Incest. British Journal of Hospital
     Medicine, London, 22(2): 152, 154-157, 1979.

655. Bluhm, A. Alcohol and Heredity. An Answer to the Article by
     C. Gyllensward. Tirfing, 25: 129-139, 1931.

656. Blum, Arthur and Singer, Mark. Substance Abuse and Social
     Deviance: A Youth Assessment Framework. In: Adolescent
     Substance Abuse: A Guide to Prevention and Treatment.
     Eds. Richard Isralowitz and Mark Singer. New York: The
     Haworth Press, 1983, pages 7-21.

657. Blum, K. Alcohol and Central Nervous System Peptides. Substance
     and Alcohol Actions/Misuse, 4(2/3): 73-87, 1983.

658. Blum, Richard H. An Argument for Family Research. In: Drug
     Abuse from the Family Perspective. Ed. Barbara Gray
     Ellis. Washington, D.C.: U.S. Government Printing Office,
     1980, pages 104-116.

659. Blum, Richard H. and Associates. Horatio Alger's Children: The
     Role of the Family in the Origin and Prevention of Drug
     Risk. San Francisco, CA: Jossey-Bass, 1972.

660. Blum, Richard H. and Blum, Eva M. Alcoholism in Greece.
     A Cultural Case Study: Temperate Achilles. In: Society
     and Drugs. San Francisco: Jossey-Bass, 1970, pages
     189-227.

661. Blumberg, B.S. Genetic and Environmental Effects on Disease:
     On "Association" in the Study of Disease Etiology.
     Annals of the New York Academy of Sciences, 197:
     152-159, 1972.

662. Blumberg, Neil H. Arson Update: A Review of the Literature on
     Firesetting. Bulletin of the American Academy of Psychiatry
     & the Law, 9(4): 255-265, 1981.

663. Blume, Sheila B. Alcohol Problems in Women. New York State
     Journal of Medicine, 82(8): 1222-1224, 1982.

664. Blume, Sheila B. Diagnosis, Casefinding, and Treatment of Alcohol
     Problems in Women. Alcohol Health and Research World,
     3(1): 10-22, 1978.

665. Blume, Sheila B. Preventing Alcohol-Related Violence: The
     Physician's Role. New York State Journal of Medicine,
     85(2): 56-57, 1985.

666. Blumenfield, M., Riester, A.E., Serrano, A.C. and Adams, R L.
     Marijuana Use in High School Students. Diseases of the
     Nervous System, 33(9): 603-610, 1972.

667. Bobley, R. (Ed.). The Family Guide to Good Living: A
     Practical Book of Often-Sought Advice on Common Personal
     Problems. Woodbury, New York: Bobley, 1977.

668. Bocaud, M. de and Gachie, J.P. L'action du Psychiatre Dans un
     Service Hospitalo-Universitaire de Phtisiologie. (The Work
     of the Psychiatrist in a Phthisiology Section of a University
     Hospital.) Revue de l'Alcoolisme, Paris, 14: 125-131,
     1968.

669. Boche, H. Leonard. Alcohol and Drug Abuse Services. In: Handbook
     of the Social Services. Eds. Neil Gilbert and Harry Specht.
     Englewood Cliffs, NJ: Prentice-Hall, 1981, pages 202-214.

670. Bodine, George E. Family Crisis: A Broad Spectrum Bibliography.
     1979. (Eric Document Number ED183148.)

671. Bodnyanskaya, N.N., Barinova, N.G., Zamarayeva, T.D. and
     Lozovskaya, N.M. Deti Bol'nykh Alkoholizmon. (Children
     of Alcoholic Patients.) In: Tretii Vseros. S'yezd
     Nevropatologov I Psikhiatrov, Kazan'. Tom 3. Tezisy I
     Doklady. (Symposium of the Third All-Russian Conference
     of Neuropathologists and Psychiatrist, Kazan'. Volume 3.
     Theses and Proceedings.) Moscow, 1974.

672. Bogg, Richard A. and Hughes, J. Wesley. Correlates of Marijuana
     Usage at a Canadian Technological Institute. The International
     Journal of the Addictions, 8(3): 489-504, 1973.

673. Boggs, M.H. The Role of Social Work in the Treatment of
     Inebriates. Quarterly Journal of Studies on Alcohol,
     4: 557-567, 1944.

674. Bohlke, J.U., Singh, S. and Goedde, H.W. Cytogenetic Effects
     of Acetaldehyde in Lymphocytes of Germans and Japanese:
     SCE, Clastogenic Activity, and Cell Cycle Delay. Human
     Genetics, Berlin, 63(3): 285-289, 1983.

675. Bohman, M. Genetic Aspects of Alcoholism and Criminality in the
     Light of an Adoption Series. Lakartidningen, 73(34):
     2734-2738, 1976.

676. Bohman, M. Some Genetic Aspects of Alcoholism: An Adoptee
     Study. Alcoholism: Clinical and Experimental Research,
     New York, 5: 441-442, 1981.

677. Bohman, M., Cloninger, C.R., Sigvardsson, S. and von-Knorring,
     A.L. Predisposition to Petty Criminality in Swedish Adoptees.
     Genetic and Environmental Heterogeneity. Archives of General
     Psychiatry, 39(11): 1233-1241, 1982.

678. Bohman, M., Cloninger, C.R., von-Knorring, A.L. and Sigvardsson, S.
     An Adoption Study of Somatoform Disorders. III. Cross-Fostering
     Analysis and Genetic Relationship to Alcoholism and Criminality.
     Archives of General Psychiatry, 41(9): 872-878, 1984.

679. Bohman, M. and Sigvardsson, S. Variationer I Formagan Att Omsatta
     Alkohol Genetiskt Bestamd. (Variations in Alcohol-Metabolizing
     Capacity are Genetically Determined.) Lakartidningen, 77:
     85-87, 1980.

680. Bohman, M., Sigvardsson, S. and Cloninger, C.R. Maternal
     Inheritance of Alcohol Abuse; Cross-Fostering Analysis
     of Adopted Women. Archives of General Psychiatry,
     38: 965-969, 1981.

681. Bohman, M. and von-Knorring, A.L. Psychiatric Illness Among
     Adults Adopted as Infants. Acta Psychiatrica Scandinavica,
     Copenhagen, 60(1): 106-112, 1979.

682. Bohman, Michael. Alcoholism and Crime: Studies of Adoptees.
     Substance and Alcohol Actions/Misuse, 4(2/3): 137-147,
     1983.

683. Bohman, Michael. Early Prevention of Social Maladjustment:
     A Study of the Adopted Offspring of Parents with Severe
     Criminality or Alcohol Abuse. Acta Psychiatrica
     Scandinavica, (Supplement), Copenhagen, 265: 38, 1976.

684. Bohman, Michael. The Interaction of Heredity and Childhood
     Environment: Some Adoption Studies. Journal of Child
     Psychology and Psychiatry and Allied Disciplines, 22(2):
     195-200, 1981.

685. Bohman, Micheal. Some Genetic Aspects of Alcoholism and
     Criminality. A Population of Adoptees. Archives of
     General Psychiatry, 35(3): 269-276, 1978.

686. Bolin, Robert K., Wright, Robert E., Wilkinson, Mary N. and
     Linder, Clare K. Survey of Suicide Among Patients on Home
     Leave from a Mental Hospital. Psychiatric Quarterly,
     Utica, NY, 42(1): 81-89, 1968.

687. Bonals, A. Influencia Del Alcoholismo Paterno En El Desarrollo
     Psiquico Del Nino. (Influence of Paternal Alcoholism on
     the Psychological Development of the Child.) Communicacion
     Psiquiatria, 77(1): 369-382, 1978.

688. Bonassi, E., Sperone Bona, P. and Trevisio, A. L'alcoolismo Del
     Padre Quale Fattore Rischio Nello Suiluppo Psico-Affettive
     Del Bambino. (Paternal Alcoholism as a Risk Factor in the
     Psychoaffective Development of the Child.) Minerva
     Pediatrica, Torino, 26(36): 1801-1809, 1974.

689. Bond, Richard A. Early Predictors of Alcohol Aubse: A Study of
     Relationships Between Interests, Values and Personality
     Variables from the 1960 TALENT Data Base and Alcohol Abuse
     in Later Life. Final Report. Bethesda, MD: National
     Institutes of Health (DHEW), 1977. (Eric Document Number
     ED195900.)

690. Bonfiglio, G. Attuali Problemi Dell'assistenza Agli Alcoolisti.
     (Curent Problems Concerning the Care of Alcoholics.)
     Minerva Medica, Torino, 61: 1446-1448, 1970.

691. Bonk, J.R. Perceptions of Psychodynamics During a Transitional
     Period as Reported in Families Affected by Alcoholism.
     Dissertation Abstracts International, 46(2): 634B, 1985.

692. Bonn, R., De-Vanna, M., Ottolenghi, F. and Verrienti, P.
     Correlation between T.B. and Alcoholism. Alcoholism,
     Zagreb, 14: 107-111, 1978.

693. Bonney, M.E. Parents as the Makers of Social Deviates.
     Social Forces, 20: 77-87, 1942.

694. Booth, Bramwell. Alcohol in Relation to the Home. British
     Journal of Inebriety, no volume number, 188-193, no date.
     (Availability: Drug Information Services, College of
     Pharmacy, University of Minnesota, Minneapolis.)

695. Booth, L. Spirituality for the Family and Adult Children of
     Alcoholics. Focus on Family, 8(5): 31-32, 1985.

696. Boothryod, Wilfred E. Nature and Development of Alcoholism in
     Women. In: Research Advances in Alcohol and Drug Problems,
     Volume 5: Alcohol and Drug Problems in Women. Ed. Oriana
     Josseau Kalant. New York: Plenum Press, 1980, pages 299-329.

697. Booz-Allen and Hamilton, Inc. An Assessment of the Needs of and
     Resources for Children of Alcoholic Parents. Prepared for
     the National Institute on Alcohol Abuse and Alcoholism.
     (Rep. No. PB-241-119; NIAAA/NCALI-75/13; Eric Document Number
     ED113634.) Springfield, VA: U.S. National Technical Information
     Service, 1974.

698. Booz-Allen and Hamilton, Inc. Development of a New Alcoholism
     Treatment Concept and Test of Its Economic Feasibility;
     Final Report. (Rep. No. PB-243-425; NIAAA/NCALI-75/23).
     Springfield, VA: U.S. National Technical Information Service,
     1974.

699. Borg, S. Hemlosa Man; En Socialpsykiatrisk Och Klinisk Undersokning.
     (Homeless Men; A Sociopsychiatric and Clinical Study.) Alkohol
     och Narkotika, 69: 66-69, 1975.

700. Borg, S. Homeless Men. A Clinical and Social Study with Special
     Reference to Alcohol Abuse. Acta Psychiatrica Scandinavica
     Supplement, Copenhagen, 276: 1-90, 1978.

701. Borg, Stefan, Fyro, Bengt and Myrhed, Marten. Psychosocial Factors
     in Alcohol-Discordant Twins. British Journal of Addiction,
     Edinburgh, 74: 189-198, 1979.

702. Borg, Stefan and Hagglov, Erik. Vard I Storfamilj Och
      Gruppkollektive. (Treatment in Large Family Groups and
      Collectives.) Alkoholfragan, Stockholm, 66(2): 50-56,
      1972.

703. Borg, V. Klinikkbehandling av alkoholskadede. (Clinical
      Treatment of Alcoholics.) Tidsskrift For Den Norske
      Laegeforening, Oslo, 84: 1117-1120, 1964.

704. Borjeson, G. Tva' Sokarljus Borde Ha Anvants. (Two Approaches
      Should Have Been Used in Rydelius' Study on Children of
      Alcoholic Fathers.) Alkohol Och Narkotika, 75(3): 14-15,
      1981.

705. Borkman, Thomasina. Children of Alcoholics: A Critical Review.
      Paper presented at the National Council on Alcoholism Forum.
      Washington, D.C., April, 1985.

706. Borkowska, U. Liczba Puw Wsrod Dzieci Powiatu Pultuskiego.
      (DMF Index in Children in the County of Pultusk.)
      Czasopismo Stomatologiczne, Warsaw, 32: 449-452, 1979.

707. Bornstein, S., Martel, J., Ruat, A. and Harlay, A. Perpetrators
      of Child Abuse. Annales Medico-Psychologiques, Paris,
      138(8): 939-952, 1980.

708. Born to Drink? Science Digest, 92: 16, 1984.

709. Born to Drink? (Editorial) Lancet, 1: 24-25, 1979.

710. Borowitz, G.H. Some Ego Aspects of Alcoholism. British Journal
      of Medical Psychology, Letchworth, England, 37: 257-263,
      1964.

711. Borrero, I. Michael. Psychological and Emotional Impact of
      Unemployment. Journal of Sociology and Social Welfare,
      7(6): 916-934, 1980.

712. Borsch, H., Bickel, P. and Uchtenhagen, A. Familiare
      Verhaltnisse Von Drogenhabhangigen Und Hope Beziehung
      Zer Aktuelben Situation. (Family Circumstances of Drug
      Addicts and the Influence on Their Current Situation.)
      Social Psychiatry, Berlin, 14: 41-47, 1979.

713. Borsetti, G. Some Preliminary Considerations for a Psycho
      Therapeutic Intervention in Juvenile Toxicomanias.
      Alcoholism, Zagreb, 13(1-2): 109-113, 1977.

714. Bort, R.F. Threats to the President Revisited. Forensic
      Science, Lausanne, 9(3): 173-178, 1977.

715. Bort, Robert F. Ambulatory Management in Alcoholism. American
      Family Physician, 16(5): 131-134, 1977.

716. Borzova, Eva. Problems of Mental Development of Children in the
      Alcoholic Family. Psychologia A Patopsychologia Dietata,
      3(2): 153-160, 1967-68.

717. Bosma, W.G. Alcoholism and Teenages. Maryland State Medical
      Journal, 24(6): 62-68, 1975.

718. Bosma, Willem G.A. Alcoholism and the Family. Addictions,
      2(5): 14-16, 1973.

719. Bosma, Willem G.A. Alcoholism and the Family. Addictions,
      Toronto, 5(2): 11-12, 1976.

720. Bosma, Willem G.A. Alkoholizam I Porodica: Zanemaren Problem.
      (Alcoholism and the Family: A Neglected Problem.)
      Alkoholizam, Beograd, 13(3-4): 43-47, 1973.

721. Bosma, Willem G.A. Children of Alcoholics--A Hidden Tragedy.
      Maryland State Medical Journal, 21(1): 34-36, 1972.

722. Bosron, W.F. and Li, T.-K. Genetic Determinants of Alcohol
      and Aldehyde Dehydrogenases and Alcohol Metabolism.
      Seminars in Liver Disease, 1(3): 179-188, 1981.

723. Bosron, W.F., Magnes, L.J. and Li, T.K. Human Liver Alcohol
      Dehydrogenase: ADH Indianapolis Results from Genetic
      Polymorphism at the ADH 2 Gene Locus. Biomedical Genetics,
      21(7-8): 735-744, 1983.

724. Bosworth, Kris, Gustafson, David H., Hawkins, Robert P., Chewning,
      Betty and Day, Trish. Adolescents, Health Education, and
      Computers: The Body Awareness Resource Network (BARN).
      Health Education, 14(6): 58-60, 1983.

725. Bottom, W. and Lancaster, J. Ecological Orientation Toward Human
      Abuse. Family and Community Mental Health, 4(2): 1-10,
      1981.

726. Boucaud, M. De. and Gachie, J.P. L'action du Psychiatre Dans Un
      Service Hospitalo-Universitaire De Phtisiologie. (The Work
      of a Psychiatrist in a Phthisiology Section of a University
      Hospital.) Revue de L'Alcoolisme, Paris, 14: 125-131,
      1968.

727. Boudreau, Richard J. Alcohol Abuse and the Family System.
      Canada's Mental Health, Ottawa, 30(2): 17-18, 1982.

728. Boulin, B. Children and Drugs. Australian Journal of Alcoholism
      and Drug Dependence, 6(1): 7-11, 1979.

729. Boulougouris, John, Liakos, Aris, Madianou, Demitra and Stefanis,
      Costas. Characteristics of Hashish Users and Controls:
      Social, Family, and Personal. In: Hashish: Studies of
      Long-Term Use. Ed. C. Stefanis. New York: Raven Press,
      1977, pages 33-38.

730. Bourg, M., Vanhoove, D., Barreau, A. and Faidherbe, D. The Wife
      of the Alcoholic Sailor. An Attempt at an Ethno-Socio-
      Psychiatric Understanding of Alcoholism in a Breton Marine
      Environment. Annales Medico Psychologiques, Paris,
      139(9): 1014-1023, 1981.

731. Bourgeois, M., Levigneron, M. and Delage, H. Les Enfants
      D'Alcooliques; Une Enquete Sur 66 Enfants D'Alcooliques
      D'un Service Pedopsychiatrique. (Children of Alcoholics;
      A Study of 66 Children of Alcoholics in a Child Psychiatry
      Service.) Annales Medico-Psychologiques, Paris, 133(2):
      592-609, 1975.

732. Bourgeois, M., Michelet, X., Favarel, G. and Morel, H. Severe
      Disfiguration in Suicide by Fire Arms. Annales Medico-
      Psychologiques, Paris, 2(2): 323-332, 1974.

733. Bourgeois, M. and Penaud, F. Alcoolisme et Depression Enquete
      Statistique sur les Antecedents Familiaux de Depression
      Et D'Alcoolisme Dans Une Serie d'Hommes Alcooliques Et
      De Femmes Depressives. (Alcoholism and Depression:
      Statistical Study on Familial Antecedents of Depression
      and Alcoholism in a Series of Men Alcoholics and Women
      Depressives.) Annales Medico-Psychologiques, Paris, 2:
      686-699, 1976.

734. Bourne, P.G. and Fox, R. (Eds.). Alcoholism; Progress in
      Research and Treatment. New York: Academic, 1973.

735. Bourne, Peter G. Alcoholism in the Urban Negro Population.
      In: Alcoholism: Progress in Research and Treatment.
      Ed. Peter G. Bourne. New York: Academic Press, 1973,
      pages 211-226.

736. Bourne, Peter G. and Light, Enid. Alcohol Problems in Blacks
      and Women. In: The Diagnosis and Treatment of Alcoholism.
      Eds. Jack H. Mendelson and Nancy K. Mello. New York:
      McGraw Hill, 1979, pages 84-123.

737. Bourneville, D.M. and Noir, J. Idiotie Congenitale-Atrophie
      Cerebraletics Nombreux: Recherches Cliniques Et
      Therapeutiques Sur L'epilepsie, L'hysterie Et L'idiotisme.
      (Congenital-Atrophic Idiocy with Numerous Cerebral Tics:
      Clinical and Therapeutic Research on Epilepsy, Hysteria and
      Idiocy.) Information Psychiatrique, 54: 797-802, 1978.

738. Bourrat, M.L. Les Acces Delirants Chez Les Alcooliques de la
      Seconde Generation. (Occurrences of Delirium in Alcoholics
      of the Second Generation.) Lyon Medical, 166: 729-732,
      1941.

739. Bovet, L. Psychiatric Aspects of Juvenile Delinquency.
      (World Health Organization Monograph Series No. 1).
      Geneva: World Health Organization, 1951.

740. Bowden, Marie. Astonish the Public Mind. Drugs, Alcohol and
      Women; A National Forum Source Book. Ed. M. Ellis.
      Sponsored by the National Institute on Drug Abuse, Program
      for Women's Concerns, October 24-26, 1975, Miami Beach,
      Florida. Washington, D.C: National Research and
      Communications Associates, Inc., 1976.

741. Bowden, Paul. The Relationship Between Different Evaluations
      of Drinking Behavior. Psychological Medicine, 6(1):
      139-142, 1976.

742. Bowen, M. Alcoholism and the Family. In: Family Therapy in
      Clinical Practice. Ed. M. Bowen. New York, NY: Aronson
      Publishers, 1978, pages 259-268.

743. Bowen, Murray. Alcoholism As Viewed Through Family Systems Theory
      and Family Psychotherapy. Annals of the New York Academy
      of Sciences, 233: 115-120, 1974.

744. Bowen, Murray. Behavioral Problems in Children of Alcoholics.
      Addictions, Toronto, 4(6): 4-6, 1975.

745. Bowen, Murray. A Family Systems Approach to Alcoholism.
      Addictions, Toronto, 21(2): 28-39, 1974. (Also as:
      A Family Systems Approach to Alcoholism. Pamphlet.
      New York: National Council on Alcoholism, 1974.)

746. Bowen, William T. and Twemlow, Stuart W. People Who Accompany
      Alcoholics to the Hospital as a Predictor of Patient Dropout.
      Hospital and Community Psychiatry, 28(12): 880-881, 1977.

747. Bowker, L.H. The Influence of the Perceived Home Drug
      Environment on College Student Drug Use. Addictive
      Behaviors, Oxford, 1: 293-298, 1976.

748. Bowles, C. Children of Alcoholic Parents. American Journal
      of Nursing, 68: 1062-1064, 1968.

749. Box, Sally. Alcoholism as a Family Illness. *International Social Work*, Bombay, 18(3): 43-49, 1975.

750. Boyatzis, Richard E. *Implementation of Power Motivation Training as a Rehabilitation Countermeasure for DWI's*. Boston, MA: McBer and Co., 1976.

751. Boyd, B.W. Will Alabama's Children Survive the 80's? *Journal of the Medical Association of the State of Alabama*, 51(1): 29-32, 1981.

752. Boyko, V.V. and Sytinsky, I.A. The Study of Socio-Psychological Aspects of Drunkenness and Alcoholism. *Addictive Behaviors*, 5(2): 159-170, 1980.

753. Boyson, M.A. Helping the Alcoholic Cope with Sobriety. *RN*, 38(7): 37, 1975.

754. Bozhanov, A. Tobacco Smoking Alcohol and Drug Use and Abuse Among High School Students. *Khig Zdraveopaz*, 23(4): 343-348, 1980.

755. Bozyk, Z. Alcoholism and the Health State of Alcoholics and Their Family Members as Compared with the General Health State in the Province of Warsaw Poland Pilot Study. *Zdrow Publiczne*, Warsaw, 87(8): 597-600, 1976.

756. Bradfer, J. Comparative Study of the Therapeutic Results and of Clinical and Psychosocial Data From a Medico-Social Guidance Center For Alcoholics. *Acta Psychiatrica Belgica*, Brussels, 74(6): 617-629, 1974.

757. Bradley, Nelson J., Keller, John E. and McElfresh, Orville. Lutheran General Hospital: An Alcoholism Rehabilitation Center for Treatment, Training and Research. In: *Alcoholism Rehabilitation; Methods and Experiences of Private Rehabilitation Centers*. Ed. V. Groupe. New Brunswick, NJ: Rutgers Center of Alcohol Studies, 1978.

758. Bragg, T.L. Teen-Age Alcohol Abuse. *Journal of Psychiatric-Nursing and Mental Health Services*, 14(12): 10-18, 1976.

759. Braithwaite, J. and Braithwaite, V. An Exploratory Study of Delinquency and the Nature of Schooling. *Australian and New Zealand Journal of Sociology*, 14: 25-32, 1978.

760. Brajsa, Pavao. Einige Soziopsychodynamische Aspekten Der Familie Des Chronischen Alkoholikers. (Some Sociopsychodynamic Aspects in the Family of Chronic Alcoholics.) *Alcoholism*, Zagreb, 5(1): 21-30, 1969.

761. Brajsa, Pavao. Obiteljska Patologija Kod Kronicnih Alkoholicara. (Family Pathology in Chronic Alcoholics.) *Alkoholizam*, Beograd, 8(2/3): 32-49, 1968.

762. Brajsa, Pavao and Kisic, T. Agresivitet Unutar Obiteljske Grupe. (Aggression Within the Family Group.) *Lijecnicki Vjesnik*, Zagreb, 91: 1265-1272, 1969.

763. Bratfos, O. Attempted Suicide. A Comparative Study of Patients Who Have Attempted Suicide and Psychiatric Patients in General. *Acta Psychiatrica Scandinavica*, Copenhagen, 47(1): 38-56, 1971.

764. Bratfos, O. The Course of Narco Mania in Adolescence: A Comparison of Young Psychiatric In-patients With and Without Drug Abuse. *Acta Psychiatrica Scandinavica*, Copenhagen, 61(2): 157-168, 1980.

765. Bratfos, O., Ettinger, L. and Tau, T. Mental Illness and Crime
      in Adopted Children and Adoptive Parents. Acta Psychiatrica
      Scandinavica, Copenhagen, 44(4): 376-384, 1968.

766. Bratter, Thomas Edward. The Psychotherapist as a Twelfth Step
      Worker in the Treatment of Alcoholism. Family and Community
      Health, 2(2): 31-58, 1979.

767. Braucht, G.N. How Environments and Persons Combine to Influence
      Problem Drinking: Current Research Issues. In: Recent
      Developments in Alcoholism, Volume 1, Genetics, Behavioral
      Treatment, Social Mediators and Prevention, Current Concepts
      in Diagnosis. Ed. Marc Galanter. New York: Plenum Press,
      1983, pages 79-103.

768. Braucht, G.N., Brakarsh, D., Follingstad, D. and Berry, K.L.
      Deviant Drug Use in Adolescence: A Review of Psychosocial
      Correlates. Psychological Bulletin, 79(2): 92-106.

769. Brautigam, W. Neuere Erfahrungen bei der Behandlung des
      Alkoholikers. (Recent Experience in the Treatment of
      the Alcoholic.) Munchener Medizinische Wochenschrift,
      109: 2698-2701, 1967.

770. Breese, Edward. Love You in My Fashion. In: Having Been There.
      Ed. A. Luks. New York: Charles Scribner's Sons, 1979, pages
      170-184.

771. Brenk, E., Dominicus, R.D., Hauer, I. and Jochinke, C.
      Kommunikationstraining In Der Ehepaartherapie
      Alkoholkranker. (Communication Training Involving
      Alcoholics and Their Spouses.) Psychiatrische
      Praxis, Stuttgart, 5: 159-166, 1978.

772. Brennenstuhl, W. and Wielguszewski, J. Psychoterapia Rodzinna W
      Poradni Odwykowej. (Family Psychotherapy in Clinics for
      Outpatient Alcoholism Treatment.) Problemy Alkoholizmu,
      Warsaw, 27(10): 5-6, 1980.

773. Breslau, Barbara Ellen. An Exploration of Boundary Phenomena
      in Alcoholic and Non-Alcoholic Marriage: Intrapsychic
      and Interpersonal Aspects. Dissertation Abstracts
      International, 77-11354, 1977.

774. Bresnahan, M.T. and Bresnahan, J.P. Too Much, Not Enough Contact:
      Family Boundary Systems. Focus on Family and Chemical
      Dependency, 8(1): 26-27, 1985.

775. Bressler, Bernard. Suicide and Drug Abuse in the Medical
      Community. Suicide and Life-Threatening Behavior, 6(3):
      169-178, 1976.

776. Brewster, D.J. Genetic Analysis of Ethanol Preference in Rats
      Selected for Emotional Reactivity. Journal of Heredity,
      59(5): 283-286, 1968.

777. Bridges Between Theory and Therapy of Alcoholism: Sustaining a
      Therapeutic Alliance. Boston, MA: Conference Proceedings
      at the Boston University School of Medicine, November, 1983.

778. Brigance, R.S. Family and Religious Factors in Problem Drinking
      Among High School Students. Master's Thesis. Mississippi
      State University, 1968.

779. Briggs, Robert Arthur. Combat Level and Family Support:
      Correlates of Post-Vietnam Adjustment (PTSD, Stress).
      Dissertation Abstracts International, 45(3): 1005B,
      1984.

780. Brigham, Steven L., Rekers, George A., Rosen, Alexander C., Swihart, Judson J., Pfrimmer, Gene and Ferguson, Larry N. Contingency Management in the Treatment of Adolescent Alcohol Drinking Problems. Journal of Psychology, 109(1): 73-85, 1981.

781. Briley, M. Deadly Deception. Dynamic Years, 20(2): 40-44, 1985.

782. Briley, M. Family Saves Itself. Dynamic Years, 20(3): 40-44, 1985.

783. Brill, Leon. Family Therapy. In: The Clinical Treatment of Substance Abusers. New York: The Free Press, 1981, pages 133-150.

784. Brisbane, F.L. Understanding the Female Child's Role of Family Hero in Black Alcoholic Families: The Significance of Race, Culture and Gender. Bulletin of the New York State Chapter of the National Black Alcoholism Council, Inc., 4(1): 5-8, 1985.

785. Brisbane, F.L. and Stuart, B.L. Self-Help Model for Working with Black Women of Alcoholic Parents. Alcoholism Treatment Quarterly, 2(3/4): 199-219, 1985.

786. Brisbane, F.L. and Womble, M. Afterthoughts and Recommendations. Alcoholism Treatment Quarterly, 2(3/4): 249-270, 1985.

787. Brisbane, Frances. The Causes and Consequences of Alcohol Abuse Among Black Youth. Journal of Afro-American Issues, 4(1): 241-254, 1976.

788. Brisbane, Frances. Minority Family Attitudes, Social Forces and Culture as Factors in the Causation and Treatment of Alcoholism. Paper presented at the National Council on Alcoholism. Milwaukee, Wisconsin, April, 1985.

789. Briscoe, C.W. and Smith, J.B. Depression and Marital Turmoil. Archives of General Psychiatry, 29(6): 811-817, 1973.

790. Briscoe, C.W. and Smith, J.B. Psychiatric Illness--Marital Units and Divorce. The Journal of Nervous and Mental Disease, 158(6): 440-445, 1974.

791. Brissett, D., Laundergan, J.C., Kammeier, M.L. and Biele, M. Drinkers and Nondrinkers at Three and a Half Years After Treatment; Attitudes and Growth. Journal of Studies on Alcohol, 41(9): 945-952, 1980.

792. Brock, C.P. Our Theory and Practice of Intervention. Digest of Alcoholism Theory and Application, 1(4): 17-19, 1982.

793. Brodbelt, Samuel. College Dating and Aggression. College Student Journal, 17(3): 273-277, 1983.

794. Brodsky, Carroll M. Medical Roles in Family Treatment. Psychosomatics, 8(4): 227-234, 1967.

795. Brodzki, J. Alkohol-Rodzina-Wymiar Sprawiedliwosci. (Alcohol, Family and the Administration of Justice.) Problemy Alkoholizmu, Warsaw, 25(10): 12-16, 1978.

796. Broken Hearts. British Medical Journal, London, 5570: 2-3, 1967.

797. Bromet, Evelyn and Moos, Rudolf H. Environmental Resources and the Posttreatment Functioning of Alcoholic Patients. Journal of Health and Social Behavior, 18: 326-338, 1977.

798. Bromet, Evelyn and Moos, Rudolf H. Sex and Marital Status in
      Relation to the Characteristics of Alcoholics. Journal
      of Studies on Alcohol, 37(9): 1302-1312, 1976.

799. Bron, B. Aktuelle Probleme des Alkoholmissbrauchs Bei Kindern Und
      Jugendlichen. (Current Problems of Alcohol Misuse in Children
      and Adolescents.) Zeitschrift Fur Allgemeinmedizin, 52:
      505-511, 1976.

800. Bron, B. Alkoholmissbrauch bei Kindern und Jugendlichen.
      (Alcohol Misuse Among Children and Adolescents.)
      Suchtgefahren, Hamburg, 22: 41-52, 1976.

801. Brook, David W. and Brook, Judith S. Adolescent Alcohol Use.
      Alcohol and Alcoholism, 20(3): 259-262, 1985.

802. Brook, Judith S., Lukoff, Irving and Whiteman, Martin. Peer,
      Family and Personality Domains as Related to Adolescents' Drug
      Behavior. Psychological Reports, 41: 1095-1102, 1977.

803. Brooks, B. Intervention Helps Alcoholics. EAP Digest, 4(1):
      12, 1983.

804. Brooks, C. Secret Everyone Knows. San Diego, CA: Kroc
      Foundation, 1981.

805. Brooks, K.F. Adult Children of Alcoholics... Psychosocial Stages
      of Development. Focus on Family and Chemical Dependency,
      6(5): 34-36, 1983.

806. Brotman, R. A Functional Approach. International Journal of
      Psychiatry, 9: 349-354, 1970-1971.

807. Brow, Judy and Cripps, Rosalie. Austin Family House Program.
      Journal of Substance Abuse Treatment, 2(1): 63-67, 1985.

808. Brown, A. Sorrows of Gin: Art Imitates Life. Magazine of
      the Texas Commission on Alcoholism, 6(3): 15-16, 1980.

809. Brown, K-A., and Sunshine, J. Group Treatment of Children from
      Alcoholic Families. In: Social Groupwork and Alcoholism.
      Eds. M. Altman and R. Crocker. New York: Haworth Press,
      1982, pages 65-72.

810. Brown, P. and Renaud, N.W. Continuum of Care Essentials. Focus
      on Family and Chemical Dependency, 6(5): 31-32, 1983.

811. Browne-Mayers, A.N., Seelye, E.E. and Sillman, L. Psychosocial
      Study of Hospitalized Middle-Class Women. Annals of the
      New York Academy of Sciences, 273: 593-604, 1976.

812. Browne-Mayers, Albert, Seelye, Edward E. and Brown, David E.
      Reorganized Alcoholism Service: Two Years After. Journal
      of the American Medical Association, 224(2): 233-235,
      1973.

813. Browne, William J. and Palmer, Anthony J. A Preliminary Study of
      Schizophrenic Women Who Murdered Their Children. Hospital
      and Community Psychiatry, 26(2): 71, 75, 1975.

814. Brownell, S.M. The Navy Alcoholism Prevention Program.
      Alcoholism: Clinical and Experimental Research, 2(4):
      362-365, 1978.

815. Browning, D.H. and Boatman, B. Incest: Children at Risk.
      American Journal of Psychiatry, 134: 69-72, 1977.

816. Browning, Diane H. Follow-Up Study of Twenty Narcotics Addicts. Psychiatry in Medicine, 1(3): 223-232, 1970.

817. Brozovsky, Morris and Winkler, Emil G. Glue Sniffing in Children and Adolescents. New York State Journal of Medicine, 65(15): 1984-1989, 1965.

818. Bruder, Ernest E. The Clergyman's Contribution to Community Mental Health. Hospital and Community Psychiatry, 22(7): 207-210, 1971.

819. Brugger, C. Untersuchungen an Kindern, Neffen, Nichten, und Enkeln von Chronischen Trinkern. (Investigations on Children, Nephews, Nieces, and Grandchildren of Chronic Alcoholics.) Zeitschrift fur die Gesamte Neurologie und Psychiatrie, Berlin, 154: 223-241, 1935.

820. Brumback, Roger A., Dietz-Schmidt, Susan G. and Weinberg, Warren A. Depression in Children Referred to an Educational Diagnostic Center: Diagnosis and Treatment and Analysis of Criteria and Literature Review. Diseases of the Nervous System, 38(7): 529-535, 1977.

821. Brun, M. Studies of the Genealogies of the Families of Alcoholics. Rocznik Psychiatrische, 13: 125-162, 1930.

822. Brunkow, Katherine A. Families Countering the Alienating Society (Alcoholism, Drug Abuse). E/SA, 10: 10-14, 1982.

823. Brunner-Orne, Martha. The Role of a General Hospital in the Treatment and Rehabilitation of Alcoholics. Quarterly Journal of Studies on Alcohol, 19: 108-117, 1958.

824. Bruno, V., Truppi, M.C. and Zugaro, M. Preliminari Su Alcoolismo Terapia Familiare. (Preliminary Data on Alcoholism and Familial Treatment.) Minerva Medica, 73(21): 1473-1480, 1982.

825. Brunswick, A.F. and Tarica, C. Drinking and Health: A Study of Urban Black Adolescents. Addictive Diseases, 1: 21-42, 1974.

826. Bruun, K. Saation Tutkimusohjelma. (The Research Program of the Foundation.) Alkoholipolitiikka, Helsinki, 6: 199-203, 1957.

827. Bruun, K. Stiftelsens Forskningsprogram. (The Research Program of the Foundation.) Alkoholipolitiikka, Helsinki, 4: 107-111, 1957.

828. Bruun, Kettil and Hauge, Ragnar. Drinking Habits Among Northern Youth. Helsinki: Finnish Foundation for Alcohol Studies. 1963.

829. Bry, Brennah. Empirical Foundations of Family-Based Approaches to Adolescent Substance Abuse. In: Preventing Adolescent Drug Abuse: Intervention Strategies. (National Institute on Drug Abuse Research, Monograph Number 47. A Rous Review Report.) Eds. Thomas J. Glynn, Carol G. Leukefeld and Jacqueline P. Ludford. Rockville, MD: National Institute on Drug Abuse, 1983, pages 154-171.

830. Buchan, I.C., Buckley, E.G., Deacon, G.L., Irvine, R. and Ryan, M.P. Problem Drinkers and Their Problems. Journal of the Royal College of General Practitioners, 31(224): 151-153, 1981.

831. Buchbinder, D. Growing Up Alcoholic. Paper presented at the
      National Council on Alcoholism Forum. New Orleans, LA, 1981.

832. Buckley, Timothy J., McCarthy, John J., Norman, Elaine and
      Quaranta, Mary Ann (Eds.) New Directions in Family Therapy
      Therapy. Oceanside, NY: Dabor Science Publications, 1977.

833. Bucky, Steven F., Bunn, Jere, Jacobs, David, Czescik, Barbara,
      DelNuovo, Anthony and Boyatzis, Richard. Treatment.
      In: The Impact of Alcoholism. Ed. Steven F. Bucky.
      Center City, MN: Hazelden, 1978, pages 75-112.

834. Buda, B. A Csalad Szerepe a Devians Magatartasformak
      Kialakitasaban; Kulonos Tekintettel az Alkoholizmusra.
      (The Role of the Family in the Development of Deviant
      Behavior, with Special Reference to Alcoholism.)
      Alkohologia, Budapest, 3: 81-87, 1972.

835. Bufano, Douglas Lawrence. An Investigation into Background and
      Current Status -- Variables Associated with Dependency Types
      in Male Alcoholics. Dissertation Abstracts International,
      37(2): 689-690B, 1976.

836. Buffington, Veronica, Martin, Donald C. and Becker, Joseph.
      Ver Similarity Between Alcoholic Probands and Their
      First-Degree Relations. Psychophysiology, 18(5):
      529-533, 1981.

837. Buglass, D. and Horton, J. The Repetition of Parasuicide:
      A Comparison of Three Cohorts. British Journal of
      Psychiaty, London, 125(0): 168-174, 1974.

838. Buglass, D. and McCulloch, J.W. Further Suicidal Behaviour:
      The Development of Validation of Predictive Scales.
      The British Journal of Psychiatry, London, 116(534):
      483-491, 1970.

839. Buhler, Charlotte and Lefever, D. Welty. A Rorschach Study on
      the Psychological Characteristics of Alcoholics. Quarterly
      Journal of Studies on Alcohol, 8: 197-260, 1947.

840. Buhler, D. Influence of Social Learning on Alcohol Consumption.
      Sozial Praeventivmedizin, 22(4): 178-179, 1977.

841. Building Trust in ACOA Counseling Groups. Paper presented at the
      National Council on Alcoholism Forum. Washington, D.C., 1985.

842. Bukelic, Jovan. Asocial Adolescent Behavior and Possibilities for
      Preventive Actions. Psihijatrija Danas, 11(2): 279-287,
      1979.

843. Bullard, Ida D. Maternal and Child Nursing. In: Substance
      Abuse; Pharmacologic, Developmental and Clinical
      Perspectives. Eds. Gerald Bennett, Christine Vourakis
      and Donald S. Woolf. New York: John Wiley & Sons, 1983,
      pages 240-251.

844. Bullock, S.C. and Mudd, E.H. The Interrelatedness of Alcoholism
      and Marital Conflict. American Journal of Orthopsychiatry,
      29: 519-527, 1959.

845. Bunn, G.A. Continuum of Care: Treatment, Training, Prevention.
      Paper presented at the International Conference on
      Alcoholism, Oxford, England, 1982.

846. Burch, Claire. Alcoholics. In: Stranger in the Family: A Guide
      to Living with the Emotionally Disturbed. Indianapolis,
      Indiana: Bobbs-Merrill Co., 1972, pages 169-180.

847. Bureau of Alcoholic Rehabilitation. For Troubled Teens With Problem Parents. Center City, Minnesota: Hazelden, no date.

848. Bureau of Alcoholism and Drug Abuse. Family Alcoholism Out-Patient Program. Dayton, OH: Montgomery County Combined General Health District, no date.

849. Burgess, Mary M. Alcohol: America's Most Widely Misused Drug. Journal of Drug Education, 1(1): 25-31, 1971.

850. Burgin, J.E. Guidebook for the Family with Alcohol Problems. Center City, Minnesota: Hazelden Foundation, 1982.

851. Burgin, James E. Help for the Marriage Partner of an Alcoholic. Pamphlet. Center City, Minnesota: Hazelden, no date.

852. Burk, E. David. Some Contemporary Issues in Child Development and the Children of Alcoholic Parents. Annals of the New York Academy of Sciences, 197: 189-197, 1972.

853. Burke, R.J. and Weir, T. Patterns In Husbands' and Wives' Coping Behaviors. Psychological Reports, 44: 951-956, 1979.

854. Burkett, Steven R. Religion, Parental Influence, and Adolescent Alcohol and Marijuana Use. Journal of Drug Issues, 7(3): 263-273, 1977.

855. Burkett, Steven R. and Carrithers, William T. Adolescents' Drinking and Perception of Legal and Information Sanctions: A Test of Four Hypotheses. Journal of Studies on Alcohol, 41(9): 839-853, 1980.

856. Burnett, M.M. Toward a Model for Counseling the Wives of Alcoholics: A Feminist Approach. Alcoholism Treatment Quarterly, 1(2): 51-60, 1984.

857. Burns, C. Alcoholism--The Family Disease. New Zealand Medical Journal, 79: 748-755, 1974.

858. Burns, L. Fathers and Daughters: A Hidden Hangover. Magazine of the Texas Commission on Alcoholism, 8(3-4): 8-9, 1982.

859. Burrow, Betty, Meyers, Robert and Wacker, Jean. The Dilemma of the Alcoholic Female in Treatment. In: Currents in Alcoholism, Volume B, Treatment and Rehabilitation and Epidemiology. Ed. Marc Galanter. New York: Grune and Stratton, 1979, pages 223-227.

860. Burrows, Graham D. Stress and Distress in Middle Age -- The Mental Health of Doctors. Australian Family Physician, 5(9): 1203, 1205-1206, 1209-1210, 1976.

861. Burtle, Vasanti (Ed.). Developmental/Learning Correlates of Alcoholism in Women. In: Women Who Drink; Alcoholic Experience and Psychotherapy. Springfield, IL: Charles C. Thomas, 1979, pages 145-174.

862. Burtle, Vasanti (Ed.). Women Who Drink: Alcoholic Experience and Psychotherapy. Springfield, IL: Charles C. Thomas, 1979.

863. Burton, Genevieve. Group Counseling with Alcoholic Husbands and Their Nonalcoholic Wives. Journal of Marriage and the Family, 24(1): 56-61, 1962.

864. Burton, Genevieve and Kaplan, Howard M. Group Counseling
     in Conflicted Marriages where Alcoholism is Present:
     Clients' Evaluation of Effectiveness. Journal of
     Marriage and the Family, 30: 74-79, 1968.

865. Burton, Genevieve and Kaplan, Howard M. Marriage Counseling
     with Alcoholics and Their Spouses. II. The Correlation
     of Excessive Drinking Behavior with Family Pathology and
     Social Deterioration. British Journal of Addiction,
     Edinburgh, 63: 161-170, 1968.

866. Burton, Genevieve and Kaplan, Howard M. Sexual Behavior and
     Adjustment of Married Alcoholics. Quarterly Journal of
     Studies on Alcohol, 29: 603-609, 1968.

867. Burton, Genevieve, Kaplan, Howard M. and Mudd, E.H. Marriage
     Counseling with Alcoholics and Their Spouses. I. A
     Critique of the Methodology of a Follow-Up Study.
     British Journal of Addiction, Edinburgh, 63(3):
     151-160, 1968.

868. Burton, M. An Alcoholic in the Family. New York: J.B.
     Lippincott, 1974.

869. Bury, C. Qu'en Est-il De Nous-Meme Dans Notre Relation A
     L'alcoolique? (Where Do We Stand in Our Relationship
     with the Alcoholic?) Psychologie Medicale, Paris, 9:
     1853-1859, 1977.

870. Busch, Edwin J. Developing an Employee Assistance Program.
     Personnel Journal, 60(9): 708-711, 1981.

871. Busch, H. and Feuerlein, W. Sozialpsychologische Aspekte in
     Ehen von Alkoholikerinnen. (Socio-Psychological Aspects
     in Marriages of Alcoholic Women.) Schweizer Archiv Fur
     Neurologie, Neurochirurgie, Und Psychiatrie, Zurich,
     116(2): 329-341, 1975.

872. Busch, H., Kormendy, E. and Feuerlein, W. Partners of Female
     Alcoholics. British Journal of Addiction, 68(3):
     179-184, 1973.

873. Bustamante, M. Psychodynamics of Alcoholism in Women. Archivos
     de Neurobiologia, Madrid, 34(3): 267-286, 1971.

874. Butler, F.O. The Defective Delinquent. American Journal of
     Mental Deficiency, 47: 7-13, 1942.

875. Butler, Frank S. Alcoholism: Control of the Uncontrolled
     Alcoholic. Journal of the American Geriatrics Society,
     15(9): 848-851, 1967.

876. Butler, J.R., Reid, B.E. and Peek, L.A. Prediction of Drug Use
     Using Life History Antecedents with College Populations.
     Proceedings of the 81st Annual Convention of the American
     Psychological Association, 8: 303-304, 1973.

877. Butler, M.G., Sanger, W.G. and Veomett, G.E. Increased
     Frequency of Sister-chromatid Exchanges in Alcoholics.
     Mutation Research, Amsterdam, 85(2): 71-76, 1981.

878. Butorina, N.E., Movchan, N.G., Kazakov, V.S. and Rybakova, L.P.
     Initial Manifestations of Alcoholism in Adolescents (Social-
     Psychological and Clinical Aspects). Zhurnal Nevropatologii
     i Psikhiatrii, 78(10): 1569-1572, 1978.

879.   Button, Alan D.   The Psychodynamics of Alcoholism: A Survey of
       87 Cases.   Quarterly Journal of Studies on Alcohol, 17:
       443-460, 1956.

880.   Buzzo, A., Agostini De Munoz, A. and Calabrese, A.   La Aversion
       Del Lactante Al Seno Maternal.   (Aversion of the Infant to
       the Maternal Breast.)   Pediatria de las Americas, 1:
       254-256, 1943.

881.   Byles, J.A.   Violence, Alcohol Problems and Other Problems in
       Disintegrating Families.   Journal of Studies on Alcohol,
       39: 551-553, 1978.   (Also as: Family Violence in Hamilton.
       Canada's Mental Health, 28(1): 4-6.)

882.   Byram, O. Wayne and Fly, Jerry W.   Family Structure, Race and
       Adolescents' Alcohol Use: A Research Note.   The American
       Journal of Drug and Alcohol Abuse, 10(3): 467-478, 1984.

883.   Byrne, Margaret M. and Holes, James H.   "Co-Alcoholic" Syndrome.
       The Labor-Management Alcoholism Journal, 9(2): 68-74, 1979.

C

884. C., Anne. Tough Love. *Alcoholism: The National Magazine*,
     3(3): 30, 1983.

885. Cabanis, D. and Phillip, E. The Paedophile-Homosexual Incest in
     Court. *Deutsche Zeitschrift fuer die Gesamte Gerichtliche
     Medizin*, 66(2): 46-74, 1969.

886. Cadogan, D.A. Family Approach to Problem Drinking -- 4 Week
     Family Forum. *Journal of Studies on Alcohol*, 39(1):
     235-236, 1978.

887. Cadogan, Donald A. Alcohol is Destroying Our Marriage: A Couple
     in Mixed Marital Group Therapy. In: *Power to Change:
     Family Case Studies in the Treatment of Alcoholism*.
     New York: Gardner Press, 1984, pages 177-197.

888. Cadogan, Donald A. Marital Group Therapy in Alcoholism
     Treatment. In: *Family Therapy of Drug & Alcohol Abuse*.
     Eds. E. Kaufman and P. Kaufman. New York: Gardner Press,
     1979, pages 187-200. (Also in: *Quarterly Journal of
     Studies on Alcohol*, 34(4): 1187-1194, 1973.)

889. Cadoret, R.J. Adoption Studies -- Historical and Methodological
     Critique. *Psychiatric Developments*, 4(1): 45-64, 1986.

890. Cadoret, Remi J. Discussion On: Genetic Studies in Man and in
     Animals. *Alcoholism: Clinical and Experimental Research*,
     5: 442-443, 1981.

891. Cadoret, Remi J. Genetic Determinants of Alcoholism. In:
     *Alcoholism. Interdisciplinary Approaches to an Enduring
     Problem*. Eds. R.E. Tarter and A. Arthur Sugerman.
     Reading, MA: Addison-Wesley Publishing Company, 1976,
     page 225.

892. Cadoret, Remi J. The Genetics of Affective Disorder and Genetic
     Counseling. *Social Biology*, 23: 116-122, 1976.

893. Cadoret, Remi J., Baker, Max, Dorzab, Joe and Winokur, George.
     Depressive Disease: Personality Factors in Patients and
     Their Relatives. *Biological Psychiatry*, 3(1): 85-93, 1971.

894. Cadoret, Remi J. and Cain, Colleen A. Sex Differences in
     Predictors of Antisocial Behavior in Adoptees. *Archives
     of General Psychiatry*, 37(10): 1171-1175, 1980.

895. Cadoret, Remi J., Cain, Colleen A. and Crowe, R.R. Evidence
     for Gene-Environment Interaction in the Development of
     Adolescent Antisocial Behavior. *Behavior Genetics*,
     13(3): 301-310, 1983.

896. Cadoret, Remi J., Cain, Colleen A. and Grove, William M.
         Development of Alcoholism in Adoptees Raised Apart from
         Alcoholic Biologic Relatives. Archives of General
         Psychiatry, 37: 561-563, 1980.

897. Cadoret, Remi J. and Gath, A. Inheritance of Alcoholism in
         Adoptees. British Journal of Psychiatry, London, 132:
         252-258, 1978.

898. Cadoret, Remi J., O'Gorman, Thomas W., Troughton, Ed and
         Heywood, Ellen. Alcoholism and Antisocial Personality -
         Interrelationships, Genetic and Environmental Factors.
         Archives of General Psychiatry, 42(2): 161-167, 1985.

899. Cadoret, Remi J. and Winokur, George. Genetic Principles in
         the Classification of Affective Illness. International
         Journal of Mental Health, 1(1-2): 159-175, 1972.

900. Cadoret, Remi J., Woolson, Robert and Winokur, George.
         The Relationship of Age of Onset in Unipolar Affective
         Disorder to Risk of Alcoholism and Depression in
         Parents. Journal of Psychiatric Research, Oxford,
         13: 137-142, 1977.

901. Caeser, P.L. Wife Beater: Personality and Psychosocial
         Characteristics. Dissertation Abstracts International,
         46(8): 2797B, 1986.

902. Caffentzis, Peter S. A Four-Generation Scan of an Alcoholic
         Family System. Paper presented at the Third Annual
         Alcoholism Conference of the National Institute on Alcohol
         Abuse and Alcoholism, Washington, D.C., June, 1973. (Also
         in: Alcoholism: A Multilevel Problem -- Treatment:
         Organization and Management. Ed. M.E. Chafetz.
         Washington, DC: U.S. Government Printing Office, 1974,
         pages 27-32; Also as: DHEW Publication No. ADM 75-137.)

903. Cahalan, D. Correlates of Change in Drinking Behavior in an
         Urban Community Sample Over a Three-Year Period. Doctoral
         Dissertation. (Universtiy Microfilms No. 69-689.)
         Washington, D.C.: George Washington University, 1968.
         (Also in: Dissertation Abstracts, 29: 2355-2356A, 1968.)

904. Cahalan, Dan and Cisin, Ira H. American Drinking Practices:
         Summary of Findings From a National Probability Sample.
         In: Alcoholism: Introduction to Theory and Treatment.
         Ed. David A. Ward. Dubuque, IA: Kendall/Hunt, 1980, pages
         101-118.

905. Cahalan, Don, Cisin, Ira H. and Crossley, Helen M. American
         Drinking Practices: A National Study of Drinking Behavior
         and Attitudes. New Haven, CT: College and University
         Press, 1969.

906. Cahill, M.H. and Volicer, B.J. Male and Female Differences in
         Severity of Problems with Alcohol at the Workplace. Drug
         and Alcohol Dependence, Lausanne, 8: 143-156, 1981.

907. Cahill, Mary H., Volicer, Beverly J. and Neuburger, Evelyn.
         Female Referral to Employees Assistance Programs: The
         Impact of Specialized Intervention. Drug and Alcohol
         Dependence, 10(2-3): 223-233, 1982.

908. Caine, Edwin. Two Contemporary Tragedies: Adolescent Suicide/
         Adolescent Alcoholism. Journal of the National Association
         of Private Psychiatric Hospitals, 9(3): 4-11, 1978.

909. Calanca, A. Alcoholism in the Young. Bulletin der
     Schweizerischen Akademie der Medizinischen Wissenschaften,
     35(1-3): 221-225, 1979.

910. Caldwell, Bernice. Assistance Programs Stress Individual Needs.
     Employee Benefit Plan Review, 38(6): 76, 78, 1983.

911. Caleekal, John Anuppa and Goodstadt, Michael S. Alcohol Use
     and Its Consequences Among Canadian University Students.
     Canadian Journal of Higher Education, 13(2): 59-69, 1983.

912. Calef, Victor. Alcoholism and Ornithophobia in Women. The
     Psychoanalytic Quarterly, 36(4): 584-587, 1967.

913. Calhoun, James F. An Examination of Patterns of Drug Use in
     Six Suburban Groups. The International Journal of the
     Addictions, 10(3): 521-538, 1975.

914. Calhoun, James F. Perceptions of the Use of Drugs -- A Cross-
     Sectional Analysis. Adolescence, 11(41): 143-152, 1976.

915. Callaghan, K.A. and Fotheringham, B.J. Practical Management of
     the Battered Baby Syndrome. Medical Journal of Australia,
     Sydney, 1(26): 1282-1284, 1970.

916. Callan, D., Garrison, J. and Zerger, F. Working with the
     Families and Social Networks of Drug Abusers. Journal of
     Psychedelic Drugs, 7(1): 19, 1975.

917. Callan, Victor J. and Jackson, Debra. Children of Alcoholic
     Fathers and Recovered Alcoholic Fathers: Personal and Family
     Functioning. Journal of Studies on Alcohol, 47: 180-182,
     1986.

918. Calobrisi, Arcangelo. Treatment Programs for Alcoholic Women.
     In: Alcoholism Problems in Women and Children. Eds.
     M. Greenblatt and M.A. Schuckit. New York: Grune and
     Stratton, 1976, pages 155-162.

919. Calton, Elaine. Nursing Care Study. Alcoholism: Drinking to
     Death -- By the Age of 39. Nursing Mirror, 147(20):
     39-40, 1978.

920. Camberwell Council on Alcoholism. Women and Alcohol. New York:
     Tavistock Publications, 1980.

921. Cameron, D. A Pilot Controlled Drinking Out-Patient Group.
     In: Alcoholism and Drug Dependence; A Multidisciplinary
     Approach. Eds. J.S. Madden, R. Walker and W.H. Kenyon.
     New York: Plenum Press, 1977, pages 199-207.

922. Cameron, D. and Spence, M.T. Lessons From an Out-Patient
     Controlled Drinking Group. Journal of Alcoholism, London,
     11: 44-55, 1976.

923. Cameron, Julia. If Your Parents Drank Too Much. Mademoiselle,
     89: 180, 1983.

924. Cameron, Lyle. St. Croix: An Outpatient Family Treatment
     Approach. Alcohol Health and Research World, 3(4):
     16-17, 1979.

925. Campailla, G. Genetique et Alcoolisme. (Genetics and
     Alcoholism.) Actualites Psychiatriques, Breuillet,
     10(2): 16-20, 1980.

926. Campbell, Harry. Alcoholism and Eugenics. The British Journal
     of Inebriety, 13: 68-70, 1915.

927. Camps, F.E. Genetics and Alcoholism. Annals of the New York
        Academy of Sciences, 197: 134-137, 1972.

928. Cancrini, Luigi and Cancrini, Coletti Grazia. Alcool E Droga
        Nella Famiglia: Implicazioni Pratiche Per L'Adozione Di
        Una Prospettiva Relazionale. (Alcohol and Drugs in the
        Family: Practical Implications for the Adoption of a
        Possible Prospective). Rivista Di Psichiatria, Rome,
        11(2): 158-174, 1976.

929. Cannon, Dale S., Baker, Timothy B. and Ward, Nadine O.
        Characteristics of Volunteers for a Controlled Drinking
        Training Program. Journal of Studies on Alcohol, 38(9):
        1799-1803, 1977.

930. Canter, F.M. Treatment Participation Related to Hospitalization
        Goals of Alcoholic Patients and Their Families. Psychiatric
        Quarterly, 46: 81-94, 1972.

931. Cantwell, D.P. Genetic Studies of Hyperactive Children;
        Psychiatric Illness in Biologic and Adopting Parents.
        In: Genetic Research in Psychiatry. Eds. R.R. Fieve,
        D. Rosenthal and H. Brill. Baltimore: John Hopkins
        University Press, 1975, pages 273-280.

932. Cantwell, Dennis P. Genetic Factors in the Hyperkinetic Syndrome.
        Journal of the American Academy of Child Psychiatry,
        15(2): 214-223, 1976.

933. Cantwell, Dennis P. Parents of Hyperactive Children: Cause or
        Effect? Medical Insight, 5(11): 24-28, 1973.

934. Cantwell, Dennis P. Psychiatric Illness in the Families of
        Hyperactive Children. Archives of General Psychiatry,
        27: 414-417, 1972.

935. Caplan, R.B. Dependency and Dependency Conflict in Offspring
        of Problem Drinking Parents. Doctoral Dissertation.
        University of Michigan. Dissertation Abstracts
        International, 44(6): 1953B, 1983.

936. Capuzzi, Dave and Lecoq, Lindy Low. Social and Personal
        Determinants of Adolescent Use and Abuse of Alcohol
        and Marijuana. Personnel & Guidance Journal, 62(4):
        199-205, 1984.

937. Cara, Alcoholism Counselor. Women and Alcohol: A Close-Up.
        In: Women Who Drink: Alcoholic Experience and
        Psychotherapy. Ed. Vasanti Burtle. Springfield, IL:
        Charles C. Thomas, 1979, pages 12-25.

938. Carde, Mary Deborah. An Interpersonal Perception Study of
        Twenty Alcoholic Families. Doctoral Dissertation.
        University of Southern California. Dissertation Abstracts
        International, 38(7): 3385B, 1978.

939. Carder, J.H. Families in Trouble. Paper presented at the 24th
        International Institute on the Prevention and Treatment of
        Alcoholism, Zurich, June-July, 1978, pages 296-301.

940. Carducci, Bernardo J. and McNeely, Judith A. Attribution of
        Blame for Wife Abuse by Alcoholics and Nonalcoholics.
        Paper presented at the Annual Convention of the American
        Psychological Association, Los Angeles, CA, August, 1981.
        (Eric Document Number ED209593.)

941. The C.A.R.E. Center. COA Newsletter, 3(2): 1+, 1985.

942. Carey, P. and Feinstein, B.B. "It Will Never Happen to Me":
     The Grown-Up Employed Child of the Alcoholic, Implications
     for the Industrial Alcoholism Field. Paper presented at the
     National Meeting of the ALMACA, Detroit, MI, October, 1979.

943. Carithers, R.L. Jr. Alcoholic Hepatitis. In: Current
     Hepatology: Volume 5. Ed. Gary Gitnick. Chicago:
     Year Book Medical Publishers, 1985, pages 87-112.

944. Carlson, Bonnie E. Battered Women and Their Assailants. Social
     Work, 22(6): 455-465, 1977.

945. Carman, Roderick S. Drinking Behavior as Related to Personality
     and Sociocultural Factors. Doctoral Dissertation.
     (University Microfilms No. 69-4316). Denver: University of
     Colorado, 1968.

946. Carman, Roderick S. Expectations and Socialization Experiences
     Related to Drinking Among U.S. Servicemen. Quarterly
     Journal of Studies on Alcohol, 32: 1040-1047, 1971.

947. Carman, Roderick S. Family Disorganization and Problem Drinking
     in a Rural Population. International Journal of Social
     Psychiatry, 27: 253-256, 1981.

948. Carmen, E.H., Rieker, P.P. and Mills, T. Victims of Violence
     and Psychiatric Illness. American Journal of Psychiatry,
     141(3): 378-383, 1984.

949. Carnes, Patrick James. Educating Interactionally Impaired Adults:
     An Analysis of Curriculum Impact on Family Environment.
     Dissertation Abstracts International, 41(5-A): 1967-1968,
     1980.

950. Carney, M.W.P. and Laws, T.G.G. The Etiology of Alcoholism in
     the English Upper Social Classes. Quarterly Journal of
     Studies on Alcohol, 28(1): 59-69, 1967.

951. Carney, P.A., Timms, M.W.H. and Stevenson, R.D. The Social and
     Psychological Background of Young Drug Abusers in Dublin.
     British Journal of Addiction, 67(3): 199-207, 1972.

952. Carone, Pasquale A. and Krinsky, Leonard W. A Program Geared
     Specifically to Industry by the Private Psychiatric Hospital.
     Psychiatric Hospital, 13(3): 84-87, 1982.

953. Carpenter, G.H. Alcohol, Heredity, and Environment.
     International Congress Against Alcoholism, 20:
     215-218, 1934.

954. Carrasco, Joaquin Santo-Domingo, Carrasco, Gomez J. Jose and
     Alonso, Adela. Suicide Attempts: A Study of a Group of
     94 Attempted Suicides. Archivos De Neurobiologia, 33(2):
     131-169, 1970.

955. Carrere, J. The Drinker's Environment. Annales Medico-
     Psychologiques, 2(1): 106-114, 1972.

956. Carrere, J. and Baron, J.-C. Vers Une Therapie Dynamique Au
     Long Cours De L'alcoolisme Chronique. (Toward a Dynamic
     Long-term Therapy of Chronic Alcoholism.) Annales Medico-
     Psychologiques, Paris, 126(1): 258-262, 1968.

957. Carrere, J. and Seguier, R. Interet de la Dynamisation des
     Psychotherapies de Groupes de Buveurs Par la Participation
     d'Alcooliques Anonymes et de Leurs Epouses. (Activation of
     Psychotherapy of Groups of Alcoholics Through Participation
     of Alcoholics Anonymous Members and Their Wives.) Annales
     Medico-Psychologiques, Paris, 123(2): 87-92, 1965.

958. Carrigan, Zoe Henderson. Research Issues: Women and Alcohol
     Abuse. Alcohol Health and Research World, 3(1): 2-9, 1978.

959. Carter, Elizabeth A. Generation After Generation: The Long-Term
     Treatment of an Irish Family with Widespread Alcoholism Over
     Multiple Generations. In: Family Therapy: Full Length Case
     Studies. Ed. Peggy Papp. New York: Gardner Press, 1977,
     pages 47-67.

960. Carter, W. Alcohol and Child Mortality. Medical Temperance
     Review, 11: 36-46, 1908.

961. Cartwright, A.K.J., Shaw, S.J. and Spratley, T.A. Designing a
     Comprehensive Community Response to Problems of Alcohol
     Abuse. (Report to the Department of Health and Social
     Security by the Maudsley Alcohol Pilot Project.) London:
     Maudsley Alcohol Pilot Project, 1975.

962. Caruana, S. and O'Hagen, Mary. Social Aspects of Alcohol and
     Alcoholism. London: B. Edsall and Co. Ltd., 1976.

963. Carver, V., Huneault, N. and Pinder, L. Characteristics, Service
     Patterns and Needs of Female Alcoholics in Ottawa-Carleton.
     Paper presented at the 11th Annual Conference: Canadian
     Foundation on Alcohol & Drug Dependencies. Toronto, June,
     1976.

964. Casework with Family of Alcoholic. Social Work, 17(5):
     79-84, 1972.

965. Casework with the Family of the Alcoholic. Pamphlet.
     St. Louis, MO: Alcoholism Treatment Center, Malcolm Bliss
     Mental Health Center, 1971.

966. Casner, C.A. Co-Dependent Style: A Gender and Professional
     Liability? Paper presented at the Ninth Annual California
     Conference on Alcohol Problems: New Waves of Knowledge '84,
     San Mateo, CA, September, 1984, pages 2-8.

967. Cassady, John L. Use of Parents and Contract Therapy in
     Rehabilitating Delinquent Adolescents Involved in Drug
     and Alcohol Abuse. Paper presented to the Alcohol and Drug
     Problems Association of North America, Chicago, September,
     1975.

968. Cassata, Donald M. and Kirkman, Liff Bradford L. Mental Health
     Activities of Family Physicians. The Journal of Family
     Practice, 12(4): 683-692, 1981.

969. Casselman, J. and Solms, H. Le Milieu Familial De L'alcoolique;
     Presentation Bibliographique. (The Family Environment of
     Alcoholics; A Bibliographic Review.) Information
     Psychiatrique, Paris, 47: 39-47, 1971. (Also as: Az
     Alkoholistak Csaladi Kornyezete; Bibliografiai Szemle.
     Alkohologia, Budapest, 3: 33-40, 1972.)

970. Casswell, S. Alcohol Use by Auckland High School Students.
     New Zealand Medical Journal, 95(721): 856-858, 1982.

971. Casswell, Sally, Gilmore, Lynette and Silva, Phil. Early
     Experiences with Alcohol: A Survey of an Eight and Nine
     Year Old Sample. New Zealand Medical Journal, Dunedin,
     96(745): 1001-1003, 1983.

972. Caste, C.A., Blodgett, J., Glover, J. and Mojica, M.I. Alcohol
     Abuse and Parental Drinking Patterns Among Puerto Ricans.
     In: Report on CSSMHO's National Hispanic Conference on
     Families. Washington, D.C., 1979.

973. Castro, Gonzalo Adis. Salud Mental Y Alcoholismo. (Mental Health
and Alcoholism.) Acta Psiquiatria Y Psicologia De Americana
Latina, Buenos Aires, 20: 142-146, 1974.

974. Castro, Laura. Program Planning for Hispanic Women: One Ideal
Model. In: Chicanas and Alcoholism: A Socio-Cultural
Perspective of Women. Eds. Rodolfo Arevalo and Marianne
Minor. San Jose, CA: San Jose State University, School of
Social Work, 1981, pages 17-22.

975. Castro, M. Elena, Valencia, Marcelo and Smart, Reginald G. Drug
and Alcohol Use, Problems and Availability Among Students
in Mexico and Canada. Bulletin on Narcotics, 31(1):
41-48, 1979.

976. Catanzaro, R.J. Evolution of Family Treatment. Focus on
Alcohol and Drug Issues, 6(4): 2-3, 1983.

977. Catanzaro, R.J. Evolution of Substance Abuse: Challenge for
the Family. Voices: Valuing the Alcoholic, 20(1):
48-51, 1984.

978. Catanzaro, R.J., Pisani, V.D., Fox, R. and Kennedy, E.R.
Familization Therapy: An Alternative to Traditional Mental
Health Care. In: Drugs and the Family. Ed. Thomas J.
Glynn. Washington, D.C.: U.S. Government Printing Office,
1981, pages 204-205.

979. Catanzaro, Ronald J. Combined Treatment of Alcoholics, Drug
Abusers, and Related Problems in a "Family Residential
Center." Toxicomanies, Quebec, 6(2): 179-188, 1973.
(Also in: Drug Forum, 2(2): 203-212, 1973.)

980. Catanzaro, Ronald J. and Pisani, Vincent D. Familization
Therapy -- An Alternative to Traditional Mental Health
Care. Paper presented at the ADPA Conference.
San Francisco, December, 1974.

981. Catanzaro, Ronald J. and Pisani, Vincent D. Familization Therapy:
With Alcoholics and Drug Abusers. Paper presented at the
Twenty Third Annual Meeting of Alcohol and Drug Problems
Association, Atlanta, GA, 1972, pages 55-58.

982. Cater, Christie. Alcoholism: The Whole Family Pays the Price.
In: Broken By the Bottle: A Report on Alcohol and Its
Effects. Lincoln: University of Nebraska, School of
Journalism, 1975, pages 35-36.

983. Caudill, Barry D. and Marlatt, G. Alan. Modeling Influences in
Social Drinking: An Experimental Analogue. Journal of
Consulting and Clinical Psychology, 43(3): 405-415, 1975.

984. Cavenar, J.O., Jr. and Caudill, L.H. Isakower Phenomenon
Variant in an Initial Dream. Journal of Clinical
Psychiatry, 40: 437-439, 1979.

985. Cekiera, Czesaw. Psychologiczne I Srodowiskowe Determinanty
Alkoholizmu Modziezy. (Psychological and Environmental
Causes of Juvenile Alcoholism.) Problemy Alkoholizmu,
Warsaw, 20(12): 9-10, 1973.

986. Cermak, T.L. Adult Children of Alcoholics as Chemical Dependency
Therapists. Paper presented at the National Council on
Alcoholism Forum, Washington, D.C., April, 1985.

987. Cermak, T.L. Parallels in the Recovery Process for Alcoholics
and Adult Children of Alcoholics. Paper presented at the
National Council on Alcoholism Forum, Houston, April, 1983.

988. Cermak, T.L. Readers Exchange: Children of Alcoholics and the
        Case for a New Diagnostic Category of Codependency. Alcohol
        Health and Research World, 8(4): 38-42, 1984.

989. Cermak, T.L. and Brown, S. Interactional Group Therapy with
        the Adult Children of Alcoholics. International Journal
        of Group Psychotherapy, 32(3): 375-389, 1982.

990. Cermak, Timmen L. Children of Alcoholics and the Case for a New
        Diagnostic Category of Codependency. Alcohol Health and
        Research World, 8(4): 38-42, 1984.

991. Cermak, Timmen L. A Primer on Adult Children of Alcoholics.
        Pompano Beach, Florida: Health Communications, Inc., 1985.

992. Cerny, L. and Cerna, M. Deti Z Rodin Alkoholiku. (Children from
        Families of Alcoholics.) Ceskoslovenska Pediatrie, Praha,
        29(10): 548-551, 1974.

993. Cervantes, L.L. Not for Women Only: FAS. Alcoholism:
        The National Magazine, 5(2): 30-31, 1984.

994. Chafetz, M.E. The Problem of Alcoholism in the United States.
        Alcoholism, Zagreb, 8(1): 71-74, 1972.

995. Chafetz, Morris E. Alcoholism. In: A Concise Handbook of
        Community Psychiatry. Ed. L. Bellak. New York: Grune and
        Stratton, 1974, pages 163-182.

996. Chafetz, Morris E. Children of Alcoholics. New York University
        Education Quarterly, 10(3): 23-29, 1979.

997. Chafetz, Morris E. Consumption of Alcohol in the Far and Middle
        East. New England Journal of Medicine, 271(6): 297-301,
        1964.

998. Chafetz, Morris E. International Studies on Alcohol Abuse and
        Alcoholism. In: International Collaboration in Mental
        Health. Washington, D.C.: DHEW, National Institute on
        Alcohol Abuse and Alcoholism, 1973, pages 271-284.

999. Chafetz, Morris E. New Perspectives on an Old Problem. The
        American Journal Of Drug and Alcohol Abuse, 1(2):
        141-145, 1974.

1000. Chafetz, Morris E. A Procedure for Establishing Therapeutic
        Contact with the Alcoholic. Quarterly Journal of Studies
        on Alcohol, 22(2): 325-328, 1961.

1001. Chafetz, Morris E., Blane, Howard T. and Hill, Marjorie J.
        Children of Alcoholics: Observations in a Child Guidance
        Clinic. Quarterly Journal of Studies on Alcohol,
        32(3): 687-698, 1971. (Also in: Drug Use and Social
        Policy. Ed. J. Susman. New York: AMS Press, 1972,
        pages 223-232; Also in: Mental Health Digest, 4(2):
        35-38, 1972.)

1002. Chafetz, Morris E. and Demone, Harold W. Al-Anon Groups.
        In: Alcoholism and Society. New York: Oxford University
        Press, 1962, pages 166-171.

1003. Chafetz, Morris E. and Demone, Harold W. Causes of Alcoholism.
        In: Alcoholism and Society. New York: Oxford University
        Press, 1962, pages 17-29.

1004. Chafetz, Morris E. and Demone, Harold W. Our Method of
        Prevention. In: Alcoholism & Society. New York:
        Oxford University Press, 1962, pages 233-235.

1005. Chafetz, Morris E. and Demone, Harold W. Secondary Prevention.
       In: Alcoholism & Society. New York: Oxford University
       Press, 1962, pages 192-203.

1006. Chafetz, Morris E. and Hill, Marjorie J. Alcoholic in Society.
       In: The Practice of Community Mental Health. Ed. Henry
       Grunebaum. Boston, MA: Little, Brown, 1970, pages 145-169.

1007. Chafetz, Morris E. and Lemone, Harold W. Jr. Al-Anon Family
       Groups. In: Deviance. Ed. S. Dinitz. New York: Oxford
       University Press, 1969, pages 272-276.

1008. Chalfant, H.P. Alcohol Use and Labeling of the Alcoholic: Factors
       in the Classification of Deviance. British Journal on Alcohol
       and Alcoholism, London, 14: 90-99, 1979.

1009. Chalfant, H. Paul. The Alcoholic in Magazines for Women.
       Sociological Focus, 6(4): 19-26, 1973.

1010. Chalfant, H. Paul and Beckley, Robert E. Beguiling and Betraying:
       The Image of Alcohol Use in Country Music. Journal of
       Studies on Alcohol, 38(7): 1428-1433, 1977.

1011. Chambers, Carl D., Inciardi, James A. and Siegal, Harvey A. The
       Use and Abuse of Licit Drugs in Rural Families. Chemical
       Dependencies: Behavioral & Biomedical Issues, 4(3):
       153-165, 1982.

1012. Chamow, Larry. Some Thoughts on the Difficulty Men Have
       Initiating Individual Psychotherapy. Family Therapy,
       5(1): 67-71, 1978.

1013. Chandler, H.M. Family Crisis Intervention: Point and Counterpoint
       in the Psychosocial Revolution. Journal of the National
       Medical Association, 64(3): 211-216, 224, 1972.

1014. Chanfreau, Diana, Furhmann, Irge, Lokare, Vaman G. and Montoya,
       Carlos. Drinking Behavior of Children in Santiago Chile.
       Journal of Studies on Alcohol, 40(9): 918-922, 1979.

1015. Changes: For and About Children of Alcoholics. Volume 1.
       Pompano Beach, FL, 1986.

1016. Changing Legacies: Growing Up in an Alcoholic Home. Pompano
       Beach, FL: Health Communications, 1984.

1017. Channabasavanna, S.M., Isaac, Mohan K. and Bhaskar, M.S.
       Juvenile Delinquency: A Socio-Demographic Study. Indian
       Journal of Criminology and Criminalistics, 1(1): 47-49,
       1981.

1018. Channing, A. Alcoholism Among Parents of Juvenile Delinquents.
       Social Service Review, 1: 357-383, 1927.

1019. Chans Caviglia, J.C. La Labor Del Servicio Medico Social
       Antialcoholista En El Hogar. (The Work of the Medicosocial
       Antialcoholic Service in the Home.) Revista de Psiquiatria
       del Uruguay, 15(86): 11-15, 1950.

1020. Chapa, D., Smith, P.L., Rendon, F.V., Valdez, R. and Yost, M.
       The Relationship Between Child Abuse and Substance Abuse
       in a Predominantly Mexican-American Population. In:
       Child Abuse and Neglect: Issues on Innovation and
       Implementation. Proceedings of the Second National
       Conference on Child Abuse and Neglect, April 17-20, 1977.
       Vol. 1. Eds. M.L. Lauderdale, R.N. Anderson and S.E.
       Cramer. Washington, D.C.: National Center on Child Abuse
       and Neglect, 1978, pages 116-125. (DHEW Publication No.
       OHDS 78-30147).

1021. Chapel, James L. and Taylor, Daniel W. Glue Sniffing. Missouri Medicine, 65(4): 288-292, 296, 1968.

1022. Chapman, Marsha, Cobb, Jeremy and Lee, Richard. Two Families: Family Therapy with Alcoholics and Their Families. Paper presented at the Boston University School of Medicine, November, 1973.

1023. Chappell, M.N., Goldberg, H.D. and Campbell, W.J. Use of Alcoholic Beverages by High School Students in Nassau County Related to Parental Permissiveness. New York: The Mrs. John S. Sheppard Foundation, 1954.

1024. Characteristics of the Drug Addict. American Journal of Psychiatry, 95(5): 1233-1235, 1938/1939.

1025. Chassin, Laurie. Adolescent Substance Use and Abuse. Advances in Child Behavioral Analysis & Therapy, 3: 99-152, 1984.

1026. Chatham, L.R. State-of-the-Art Treatment Research. Paper presented at the First Annual Wisconsin AODA Research Conference: "Critical Issues in Alcoholism Research and Treatment," Milwaukee, University of Wisconsin, April, 1983, pages 13-21.

1027. Chazaud, J. Roudil, C. Schmidt, F.A. and Meuly, J.P. Troubles Psychiques Chez Un Enfant Presentant Un Syndrome De Silverman. (Psychic Disturbances in a Child Presenting With Silverman's Syndrome). Revue De Neuropsychiatrie Infantile, 20(5): 411-415, 1972.

1028. Cheek, F.E. Family Socialization Techniques and Deviant Behavior. Family Process, 5: 199-217, 1966.

1029. Cheek, F.E., Burtle, V. and Laucius, J. Behavior Modification Training Program for Alcoholics and Their Wives. Report. Princeton, NJ: New Jersey Neuropsychiatric Institute, 1971.

1030. Cheek, Frances E., Franks, Cyril M., Laucius, Joan and Burtle, Vasanti. Behavior-Modification Training for Wives of Alcoholics. In: Alcoholism: Introduction to Theory and Treatment. Ed. David A. Ward. Dubuque, Iowa: Kendall/ Hunt Publishing Co., 1980, pages 344-349. (Also in: Quarterly Journal of Studies on Alcohol, 32: 456-461, 1971.)

1031. Cheek, F.E. and Mendelson, M. Developing Behavior Modification Programs With Emphasis on Self-Control. Hospital and Community Psychiatry, 24(6): 410-415, 1973.

1032. Cheek, F.E., Tomarchio, T., Burtle, V., Moss, H. and McConnell, D. A Behavior Modification Training Program for Staff Working with Drug Addicts. The International Journal of the Addictions, 10: 1073-1101, 1975.

1033. Chegwidden, M.J. The Management of Alcoholism in General Practice. Medical Journal of Australia, Sydney, 55-2(10): 445-446, 1968.

1034. Chessick, Richard D. The Psychotherapy of Borderland Patients. American Journal of Psychotherapy, 20(4): 600-614, 1966.

1035. The Child and the Adolescent in Society. Report on a WHO Conference. EURO Reports and Studies - 3. Copenhagen, Denmark: World Health Organization, September, 1978. (Eric Document Number ED178160.)

1036. Children of Alcoholic Parents. Bibliography. Alcohol Health and Research World, Summer: 31-32, 1975.

1037. Children of Alcoholic Parents Assisted. NIAAA Information and Feature Service, (IFS No. 27): 2, August 27, 1976.

1038. Children of Alcoholic Parents Need Professional Evaluation. NIAAA Information and Feature Service, (IFS No. 17): 4, October 10, 1975.

1039. Children of Alcoholics. Professional, 10(1), 1964.

1040. Children of Alcoholics. Freedom Fighter Wyoming State, 1(1): 16-17, 1985.

1041. Children of Alcoholics. (Alcohol Resources: Update.) Rockville, MD: National Institute on Alcohol Abuse and Alcoholism, National Clearinghouse for Alcohol Information, October, 1985.

1042. Children of Alcoholics. (Directory.) Rockville, Maryland: National Clearinghouse for Alcohol Information, 1985.

1043. Children of Alcoholics: A Review of the Literature. COA Newsletter, 3(1): 1, 1985.

1044. Children of Alcoholics: A Special Report. ADAMHA News, 10(1): 1A-8A, 1984.

1045. Children of Alcoholics: An Interview with the NIAAA Director. Alcohol Health and Research World, 8(4): 3-5, 1984.

1046. Children of Alcoholics: Critical Population, Powerful Movement. U.S. Journal of Drug and Alcohol Dependence, 7(10): 6, 1983.

1047. Children of Alcoholics Target of Prevention. NIAAA Information and Feature Service, (IFS No. 69): 1, February 19, 1980.

1048. Children of Military Prevention Focus. NIAAA Information and Feature Service, (IFS No. 70): 5, March 19, 1980.

1049. Children's Behavior Problems Often Alcohol Related. NIAAA Information and Feature Service, (IFS No. 14): 3, August 4, 1975.

1050. Children's Feelings Groups Aid Family Recovery. NIAAA Information and Feature Service, (IFS No. 84): 5, June 1, 1981.

1051. Children's Groups Affect Related Family Services. NIAAA Information and Feature Service, (IFS No. 67): 6, December 31, 1979.

1052. Child's Perception May Determine Behavior. NIAAA Information and Feature Service, (IFS No. 62): 1; August 6, 1979.

1053. Childs, B. Human Behavioural Genetics. Postgraduate Medical Journal, Oxford, 52(Supplement 2): 45-53, 55-56, 1976.

1054. Chiles, John A., Miller, Michael L. and Cox, Gary B. Depression in an Adolescent Delinquent Population. Archives of General Psychiatry, 37(10): 1179-1184, 1980.

1055. Chiles, John A., Stauss, F.S. and Benjamin, L.S. Marital Conflict and Sexual Dysfunction in Alcoholic and Non-alcoholic Couples. British Journal of Psychiatry, London, 137: 266-273, 1980.

1056. Chimbos, Peter D. Marital Violence: A Study of Interspouse Homicide. San Francisco, CA: R & E Research Associates, 1978.

1057. Chira, Susan. New York Times, 14 January 1982, B1, B4.
       (Students Who Skip School Tell of Family Problems and a
       Search for Identity.) (Also in: COA Review, 1: 4,
       1983.)

1058. Choi, Sei Young. Dreams as a Prognostic Factor in Alcoholism.
       The American Journal of Psychiatry, 130(6): 699-702,
       1973.

1059. Christiaens, L., Mizon, J.P. and Delmarle, G. Sur La Descendance
       Des Alcooliques. (On the Offspring of Alcoholics.) Annales
       de Pediatrie, Paris, (La Semaine Des Hospitaux, Paris),
       36: 37-42, 1960.

1060. Christian Education Materials for Youth & Families. Alcohol &
       Drugs. Center City, MN: Hazelden, 1983.

1061. Christmas, June J. Alcoholism Services for Minorities: Training
       Issues and Concerns. Alcohol Health and Research World,
       2(3): 20-27, 1978.

1062. Christmas, June Jackson. Shall We Abandon Need? Paper presented
       at the National Institute on Drug Abuse, Program for Women's
       Concerns, Miami Beach, October, 1975. (Also in: Drugs,
       Alcohol and Women; A National Forum Source Book. Ed. M.
       Nellis. Washington, D.C.: National Research and
       Communications Associates, Inc., 1976, pages 152-156.)

1063. Chruszczow, R. Niektore Prawne Srodki Ochrony Rodziny. III.
       (Some Legal Safeguards for the Protection of Families.
       Part III.) Problemy Alkoholizmu, Warsaw, 26(1):
       9-10, 1979.

1064. Church, M.W., Gerkin, K.P. and McPherson, E.W. The Incidence
       of Sudden Infant Death Syndrome (SIDS) Amongst the Older
       Siblings of Children with Fetal Alcohol Syndrome.
       Alcoholism: Clinical and Experimental Research, 10(1):
       93, 1986.

1065. Cisin, I.H. and Cahalan, D. Comparison of Abstainers and Heavy
       Drinkers in a National Survey. Psychiatric Research
       Reports, 24: 10-21, 1968.

1066. Citron, P. Group Work with Alcoholic, Polydrug-Involved
       Adolescents with Deviant Behavior Syndrome. Social Work
       Groups, 1: 39-52, 1978.

1067. Ciucci, Mirella, Scamperle, Susanna and Cancrini, Luigi. Bere
       E Non Bere. Analisi Delle Modalita E Del Significato Di
       Un Intervento "Strategico" Nel Corso Di Una Terapia Di
       Coppia. (To Drink and Not To Drink: Analysis of the Use
       and Meaning of "Strategic" Assistance in Couples Therapy.)
       Rivista Di Psichiatria, Roma, 11(3): 263-289, 1976.

1068. Clair, D.J. and Genest, M. Variables Associated with the
       Adjustment of Offspring of Alcoholic Fathers. Paper
       presented at the 92nd Annual Convention of the American
       Psychological Association, Toronto, August, 1984.

1069. Clare, A.W. The Causes of Alcoholism. In: Alcoholism in
       Perspective. Eds. M. Grant and P. Gwinner. Baltimore:
       University Park Press, 1979, pages 64-76.

1070. Clare, A.W. Diazepam, Alcohol, and Barbiturate Abuse. British
       Medical Journal, London, 4(5783): 340, 1971.

1071. Clark, Austen and Friedman, Matthew J. Nine Standardized Scales
       for Evaluating Treatment Outcome in a Mental Health Clinic.
       Joural of Clinical Psychology, 39(6): 939-950, 1983.

1072. Clark, N.H. Deliver Us From Evil; An Interpretation of American
         Prohibition. New York: Norton, 1976.

1073. Clark, Walter B. Conceptions of Alcoholism: Consequences for
         Research. Addictive Diseases, 1(4): 395-430, 1975.

1074. Clark, Walter B. Loss of Control, Heavy Drinking and Drinking
         Problems in a Longitudinal Study. Journal of Studies
         on Alcohol, 37: 1256-1290, 1976.

1075. Clark, William. Sex Roles and Alcoholic Beverage Usage.
         Berkeley, CA: Mental Research Institute, 1964.

1076. Clausen, J. and Runck, B. Mentally Ill at Home: A Family Matter.
         In: Families Today. Volume II. Ed. E. Corfman.
         Washington, D.C.: U.S. Government Printing Office, 1979,
         pages 633-695.

1077. Claypool, J. Alcohol and You. New York: Franklin Watts, 1981.

1078. Clayton, P.J. The Clinical Morbidity of the First Year of
         Bereavement: A Review. Comprehensvie Psychiatry, 14(2):
         151-157, 1973.

1079. Clayton, P.J. and Winokur, G. Family History Studies IV:
         Comparison of Male and Female Alcoholics. Quarterly
         Journal of Studies on Alcohol, 29: 885-891, 1968.

1080. Clayton, P.J. and Winokur, G. Family History Studies II: Sex
         Differences and Alcoholism in Primary Affective Illness.
         British Journal of Psychiatry, 113: 973-979, 1967.

1081. Clayton, Paula J. and Lewis, Collins E. The Significance of
         Secondary Depression. Journal of Affective Disorders,
         Amsterdam, 3(1): 25-36, 1981.

1082. Clayton, Richard R. The Delinquency and Drug Use Relationship
         Among Adolescents: A Critical Review. In: Drug Abuse
         and the American Adolescent. Eds. Dan J. Lettieri and
         Jacqueline P. Ludford. Rockville, MD: National Institute
         on Drug Abuse, 1981.

1083. Clayton, Richard R. The Family and Federal Drug Abuse Policies--
         Programs: Toward Making the Invisible Family Visible.
         Journal of Marriage and the Family, 637-647, 1979.

1084. Clayton, Richard R. The Family Drug Abuse Relationship.
         In: Drug Abuse from the Family Perspective. Ed. B.G.
         Ellis. Washington, D.C.: U.S. Government Printing Office,
         1980, pages 86-103.

1085. Clayton, Richard R. and Lacy, William B. Interpersonal Influences
         on Male Drug Use and Drug Use Intentions. International
         Journal of the Addictions, 17(4): 655-666, 1982.

1086. Clement, J.A. and Boylan, S.R. Actualizing Theory in Practice.
         Perspectives in Psychiatric Care, 20(3): 126-133, 1982.

1087. Clement, J.A. and Notaro, C. Nursing Intervention in the Alcohol
         Detoxification Process. Alcohol Health and Research World,
         Summer: 27-28, 33, 1975.

1088. Clements, C. and Bofenkamp, B. Adolescent Co-Dependency: From
         Discouragement to Empowerment. Focus on Family and Chemical
         Dependency, 7(6): 21-22, 29, 32, 1984.

1089. Cleminshaw, H.K. and Truitt, E.B. (Eds.) Alcoholism: New
         Perspectives. Akron, OH: University of Akron Center for
         Urban Studies, 1983.

1090. Clemmons, Penny. A Comprehensive Psychoanalytic Approach to
       Alcoholism Treatment. In: Women Who Drink: Alcoholic
       Experience and Psychotherapy. Ed. Vasanti Burtle.
       Springfield, IL: Charles C. Thomas, 1979, pages 217-228.

1091. Clemmons, Penny. Issues in Marriage, Family and Child Counseling
       in Alcoholism. In: Women Who Drink: Alcoholic Experience
       and Psychotherapy. Ed. Vasanti Burtle. Springfield,
       IL: Charles C. Thomas, 1979, pages 127-144.

1092. Clifford, Bernard J. A Study of the Wives of Rehabilitated and
       Unrehabilitated Alcoholics. Social Casework, 41:
       457-460, 1960.

1093. Clifford, C.A., Fulker, D.W. and Murray, R. Genetic and
       Environmental Influences on Drinking Patterns in Normal
       Twins. In: Alcohol Related Problems: Room for Manoeuvre.
       New York: John Wiley and Sons, 1984, pages 115-126.

1094. Climent, Carlos E. and Ervin, Frank R. Historical Data in the
       Evaluation of Violent Subjects. A Hypothesis Generating
       Study. Archives of General Psychiatry, 27(5): 621-624,
       1972.

1095. Clinebell, H.J. American Protestantism and the Problem of
       Alcoholism. Journal of Clinical Pastoral Work, 2:
       199-215, 1949.

1096. Clinebell, H.J., Jr. The Agony of the Family of the Alcoholic.
       Pastoral Psychology, 13(123): 5-7, 1962.

1097. Clinebell, H.J., Jr. Pastoral Care of the Alcoholic's Family
       Before Sobriety. Pastoral Psychology, 13(123): 19-29,
       1962.

1098. Clinebell, Howard J. Helping the Family of the Alcoholic.
       In: Understanding and Counseling the Alcoholic.
       Nashville: Abingdon Press, 1968, pages 266-293.

1099. Clinebell, Howard J. Jr. Pastoral Counseling of the Alcoholic
       and His Family. In: Alcoholism: The Total Treatment
       Approach. Ed. Ronald J. Catanzaro. Springfield, IL:
       Charles C. Thomas, 1968, pages 189-207. (Also as: Pastoral
       Counseling of the Alcoholic and His Family. Springfield,
       IL: Charles C. Thomas, 1974.)

1100. Clinic Aids Children of Alcoholic Patients. NIAAA Information
       and Feature Service, (IFS No. 45): 6, March 3, 1978.

1101. Cloninger, C.R. Genetic and Environmental Factors in the
       Development of Alcoholism. Journal of Psychiatric Treatment
       and Evaluation, 5(6): 487-496, 1983.

1102. Cloninger, C.R., Bohman, M. and Sigvardsson, S. Inheritance
       of Alcohol Abuse; Cross-Fostering Analysis of Adopted Men.
       Archives of General Psychiatry, 38: 861-868, 1981.

1103. Cloninger, C.R., Bohman, Michael, Sigvardsson, Soren and
       von Knorring, Anne-Liis. Psychopathology in Adopted-Out
       Children of Alcoholics: The Stockholm Adoption Study.
       In: Recent Developments in Alcoholism, Volume 3, High-Risk
       Studies, Prostaglandins and Leukotrienes, Cardiovascular
       Effects, Cerebral Function in Social Drinkers. New York:
       Plenum Press, 1985, pages 37-51.

1104. Cloninger, C.R., Christiansen, K.O., Reich, T. and Gottesman, I.I. Implications of Sex Differences in the Prevalences of Antisocial Personality, Alcoholism, and Criminality for Familial Transmission. Archives of General Psychiatry, 35: 941-951, 1978.

1105. Cloninger, C.R. and Guze, S.B. Psychiatric Illnesses in the Families of Female Criminals: A Study of 288 First-Degree Relatives. British Journal of Psychiatry, London, 122: 697-703, 1973.

1106. Cloninger, C.R., Reich, T. and Guze, S.B. The Multifactorial Model of Disease Transmission: II. Sex Differences in the Familial Transmission of Sociopathy (Antisocial Personality). The British Journal of Psychiatry, 127: 11-22, 1975.

1107. Cloninger, C.R., Reich, T. and Wetzel, R. Alcoholism and Affective Disorders: Familial Associations and Genetic Models. In: Alcoholism and Affective Disorders; Clinical, Genetic, and Biochemical Studies. Eds. D.W. Goodwin and C.K. Erickson. New York: SP Medical & Scientific Books, 1979, pages 57-86.

1108. Cloninger, C.R., von Knorring, A.L, Sigvardsson, S. and Bohman, M. Gene-Environment Interaction in the Familial Relationship of Alcoholism, Depression, and Antisocial Personality. In: Pharmacological Treatments for Alcoholism. New York: Methuen, 1984, pages 417-444.

1109. Cloninger, C. Robert and Reich, Theodore. Genetic Heterogeneity in Alcoholism and Sociopathy. Research Publications Association for Research in Nervous and Mental Disease, 60: 145-166, 1983.

1110. Clopton, J.R. Alcoholism and the MMPI. A Review. Journal of Studies on Alcohol, 39(9): 1540-1558, 1978.

1111. Clute, J.E. Aiding the "Other Victims" on the Job. Occupational Health and Safety, 49(2): 34-35, 38, 1980.

1112. Cmelic, Stojan and Brankovic, Miodrag. Da Li Je Alkoholizam Hereditarno Oboljenje? (Is Alcoholism a Hereditary Disease?) Socijalna Psihijatrija, 10(1): 57-60, 1982.

1113. COA (Children of Alcoholics) Newsletter. Volume 1. Hempstead: New York State Coalition for the Children of Alcoholic Families, Inc., 1983.

1114. COA Review: The Newsletter About Children of Alcoholics. Number 1. Rutherford, NJ: Thomas W. Perrin, Inc., 1983.

1115. Coates, M. and Paech, G. Alcohol and Your Patient: A Nurse's Handbook. Pamphlet. Toronto: Addiction Research Foundation, 1979.

1116. Cobb, John. Morbid Jealousy. Journal of Hospital Medicine, London, 21(5): 511-518, 1979.

1117. Cobbs, Leonard W. Family-Therapy of Drug and Alcohol Abuse. Psychosomatics, 22(3): 267, 1981.

1118. Cody, Thomas. Outcast State. In: Having Been There: The Personal Drama of Alcoholism. New York: Charles Scribner's Sons, 1979, pages 105-111.

1119. Coffey, C.W. Alcoholism in Industry; A $100-Million Hangover for Texas. Texas Business Review, 57: 161-168, 1969.

1120. Cohen, Arie and Barr, Harriet L.   Should We Treat All Addicted People in the Same Way.   Contemporary Drug Problems, 7(2): 211-214, 1978.

1121. Cohen, B.M. and Zubenko, G.S.   Relevance of Genetic Variability to Clinical Psychopharmacology.   Psychopharmacology Bulletin, 21(3): 641-650, 1985.

1122. Cohen, Frederick S. and Densen, Gerber Judianne.   A Study of the Relationship Between Child and Drug Addiction in 178 Patients: Preliminary Results.   Child Abuse and Neglect, Oxford, 6(4): 383-387, 1982.

1123. Cohen, P.T.   A New Approach to the Treatment of Male Alcoholics and their Families.   American Journal of Orthopsychiatry, 36: 247-248, 1966.

1124. Cohen, Pauline.   How to Help the Alcoholic.   Pamphlet. New York: National Council on Alcoholism, 1970.

1125. Cohen, Pauline C.   Outcomes of the Project and Next Steps. In: Casework with Wives of Alcoholics.   Eds. P.C. Cohen and M.S. Krause.   New York: Family Service Association of America, 1971, pages 113-117.

1126. Cohen, Pauline C.   Overview of the Project.   In: Casework with Wives of Alcoholics.   Eds. P.C. Cohen and M.S. Krause. New York: Family Service Association of America, 1971, pages 3-16.

1127. Cohen, Pauline C. and Krause, Merton S.   Casework with Wives of Alcoholics.   New York: Family Service Association of America, 1971.

1128. Cohen, Sidney.   Adolescence and Drug Abuse: Biomedical Consequence.   In: Drug Abuse and the American Adolescent. Eds. Dan J. Lettieri and Jacqueline P. Ludford.   Rockville, MD: National Institute on Drug Abuse, 1981.

1129. Cohen, Sidney.   Teenage Drinking: The Bottle Babies.   Drug Abuse & Alcoholism Newsletter, 4(7): 1-4, 1975.

1130. Cohen, Sidney.   The Youthful Lush.   Paper presented at the National Institute on Drug Abuse, Program for Women's Concerns, Miami Beach, October, 1975.   (Also in: Drugs, Alcohol and Women; A National Forum Source Book. Washington, D.C.:   National Research and Communications Associates, Inc., 1976.)

1131. Cohen, Sidney, Custer, Robert L., Goodwin, Donald, Henningfield, Jack, Kleher, Herbert D., O'Brien, Charles P., Jaginsler, Donald, Taylor, Irving J. and Taylor, Bruce T.   Panel Discussion.   Journal of Clinical Psychiatry, 45(12-2): 39-44, 1984.

1132. Cohen-Holmes, S.   Patients in Their Own Right, Families of Alcoholics Deserve Equal Attention in Treatment.   Focus on Alcohol and Drug Issues, 4(4): 5-6, 25, 1981.

1133. Cohen-Holmes, S. and Land, D.R.   Nutrition and the Dysfunctional Family.   Focus on Family and Chemical Dependency, 7(2): 10-12, 1984.

1134. Cohn, Anne H.   Family Violence and Service Delivery: Some Thoughts Based on Experiences Evaluating Child Abuse Treatment Programs.   Berkeley, CA: National Center for Health Services Research, 1978.

1135. Cohn, Lucille. Counselor Solves Personnel Problems, Promotes
        Harmony. Modern Hospital, 113(2): 70, 72, 1969.

1136. Cole, K.E., Fisher, Gary and Cole, Shirley S. Women Who Kill:
        A Sociopsychological Study. Archives of General
        Psychiatry, 19(1): 1-8, 1968.

1137. Coleman, Alice F. How To Enlist Family as an Ally. American
        Journal of Drug and Alcohol Abuse, 3(1): 167-173, 1976.

1138. Coleman, D.H. and Strauss, M.A. Alcohol Abuse and Family
        Violence. In: Alcohol, Drug Abuse and Aggression.
        Ed. E. Gottheil. Springfield, IL: Charles C. Thomas,
        1983, pages 104-124.

1139. Coleman, E. Family Intimacy and Chemical Abuse: The
        Connection. Journal of Psychoactive Drugs, 14(1-2):
        153-158, 1982.

1140. Coleman, E. and Colgan, P. Boundary Inadequacy in Drug
        Dependent Families. Journal of Psychoactive Drugs,
        18(1): 21-30, 1986.

1141. Coleman, John C. Who Leads Who Astray? Causes of Anti-Social
        Behaviour in Adolescence. Journal of Adolescence, 2(3):
        179-185, 1979.

1142. Coleman, K.H., Weinman, M.L. and Bartholomew, P. Factors
        Affecting Conjugal Violence. Journal of Psychology,
        105(2): 197-202, 1980.

1143. Coleman, Karen Howes. Conjugal Violence: What 33 Men Report.
        Journal of Marital and Family Therapy, 6(2): 207-213,
        1980.

1144. Coleman, N.J. Marital Adjustment and Work Adjustment in the
        Alcoholic Marriage. Dissertation Abstracts International,
        45(10): 3331B, 1985.

1145. Coleman, Sandra B. Cross-Cultural Approaches to Addict Families.
        In: Drugs and the Family. Ed. Thomas J. Glynn.
        Washington, D.C.: U.S. Government Printing Office, 1981.

1146. Coleman, Sandra B. An Endangered Species: The Female as Addict
        or Member of an Addict Family. In: Drugs and the Family.
        Ed. Thomas J. Glynn. Washington, D.C.: U.S. Government
        Printing Office, 1981.

1147. Coleman, Sandra B. The Family as a Vehicle For Confronting
        Drug/ Alcohol Crises. Paper presented at the 11th Annual
        Eagleville Conference. Eagleville, PA, May, 1978. (Also
        in: Treating Mixed Psychiatric-Drug Addicted and Alcohol
        Patients. Eds. D.J. Ottenberg, J.F.X. Carrol and C.
        Bolognese. Eagleville, PA: Eagleville Hospital and
        Rehabilitation Center, 1979, pages 33-35.)

1148. Coleman, Sandra B. Incomplete Mourning and Addict/Family
        Transactions: A Theory for Understanding Heroin Abuse.
        In: Theories on Drug Abuse: Selected Contemporary
        Perspectives. (NIDA Research Monograph Series 30.)
        Eds. Dan J. Lettieri, Mollie Sayers and Helen Wallenstein
        Pearson. Washington, D.C.: U.S. Government Printing Office,
        1980, pages 83-89.

1149. Coleman, Sandra B. Incomplete Mourning in Substance-Abusing
        Families: Theory, Research and Practice. In: Group
        and Family Therapy. Eds. L.R. Wolberg and M.L. Aronson.
        New York: Brunner/Mazel Publishers, 1981, pages 269-283.

1150. Coleman, Sandra B. Sib Group Therapy: A Prevention Program for
      Siblings from Drug-Addicted Families. The International
      Journal of the Addictions, 13(1): 115-127, 1978.

1151. Coleman, Sandra B. Siblings in Session. In: Family Therapy
      of Drug and Alcohol Abuse. Eds. E. Kaufman and P.N.
      Kaufman. New York: Gardner Press, 1979, pages 131-143.

1152. Coleman, Sandra B. and Davis, D.I. Family Therapy and Drug
      Abuse: A National Survey. Family Process, Basel, 17:
      21-29, 1978.

1153. Collier, Walter V. and Hijazi, Yusse A. A Follow-Up Study
      of Former Residents of a Therapeutic Community.
      The International Journal of the Addictions, 9(6):
      805-826, 1974.

1154. Collins, Gregroy B. Treatment of Alcoholism: The Role of the
      Primary Care Physician. Postgraduate Medicine, 69(1):
      145-149, 1981.

1155. Collins, Gregory B., Kotz, Margaret, Janesz, Joseph W., Messina,
      Matthew and Ferguson, Thomas. Alcoholism in the Families
      of Bulimic Anorexics. Cleveland Clinic Quarterly, 52(1):
      65-67, 1985.

1156. Collins, J. Some Thoughts on Care and Aftercare of Alcoholics
      and Their Families. The Journal of Alcoholism, London,
      5: 152-155, 1970.

1157. Collins, J. and Carson, N. Trauma Resolution Therapy (TRT):
      An Experiential Model for Working with Victimization.
      Focus on Family and Chemical Dependency, 8(2): 26, 31,
      36, 1985.

1158. Collins, R. Lorraine and Marlatt, G. Alan. Psychological
      Correlates and Explanations of Alcohol Use and Abuse.
      In: Medical and Social Aspects of Alcohol Abuse.
      Eds. Boris Tabakoff, Patricia B. Sutker and Carrie L.
      Randall. New York: Plenum Press, 1983, pages 273-303.

1159. Collins, R. Lorraine and Marlatt, G. Alan. Social Modeling as
      a Determinant of Drinking Behavior: Implications for
      Prevention and Treatment. Addictive Behaviors, Oxford,
      6: 233-239, 1981.

1160. Collins, Thomas Peter. An Analysis of the Degree of Internal-
      ization of Selected Attitudes and Their Relationship with
      Locus of Control and Sex of Children of Alcoholics and a
      Comparison Group. Dissertation Abstracts International,
      43(6): 1886A, 1982.

1161. Colorado Group Studies Alcohol, Family Violence. NIAAA
      Information and Feature Service, (IFS No. 88): 6,
      September 29, 1981.

1162. Coltoff, Philip and Luks, Allan. Preventing Child Maltreatment:
      Begin with the Parent. New York: National Council on
      Alcoholism, 1978.

1163. Comer, James P. If Your Child Is Drinking. Parents, 58: 93,
      1983.

1164. Compilation of Papers Presented to the 3rd School of Alcohol
      Studies at Massey University of Manawatu, New Zealand.
      Auckland, New Zealand: National Society on Alcoholism,
      1968.

1165. Confidentiality of Alcohol and Drug Abuse Patient Records and
        Child Abuse and Neglect Reporting. Alcohol Health and
        Research World, 4(1): 31-35, 1979.

1166. Conley, J.J. Family Configuration as an Etiological Factor
        in Alcoholism. Journal of Abnormal Psychology, 89:
        670-673, 1980.

1167. Conley, James Joseph. Ordinal Position, Personality and
        Alcoholism. Dissertation Abstracts International,
        39(10): 5059B, 1979. (University Microfilms No. 7907050.)

1168. The Connecticut Commission on Alcoholism Report, 1949-1950, to
        the Governor. In: Reports on Government-Sponsored Programs.
        Ed. Ernest A. Shepard. Quarterly Journal of Studies on
        Alcohol, 11(4): 677-694, 1950.

1169. Connelly, John C. The Alcoholic Physician: An Overview.
        Journal of the Kansas Medical Society, 79(11): 601-604,
        1978.

1170. Connelly, John C. Alcoholism: Clinical and Research Perspectives.
        Journal of the National Association of Private Psychiatric
        Hospitals, 9(4): 37-40, 1978.

1171. Connolly, Thomas E. The Importance of Mental Health in the Modern
        Family. In: Marital Counseling: Psychology, Ideology,
        Science. Ed. Hirsch Lazaar Silverman. Springfield, IL:
        Charles C. Thomas, 1967, pages 254-260.

1172. Connor, Bernadette and Babcock, Marguerite L. The Impact of
        Feminist Psychotherapy on the Treatment of Women Alcoholics.
        Focus on Women, 1: 77-92, 1980.

1173. Connor, R. An Investigation of Parental Attitudes Toward
        Drinking and Five Additional Factors in the Childhood
        Environment of Alcoholics. Master's Thesis. University
        of Washington, 1953.

1174. Conway, J. Significant Others Need Help Too: Alcoholism Treat-
        ment Just as Important to Rest of Family. Focus on Alcohol
        and Drug Issues, 4(3): 17-19, 1981.

1175. Conway, J.P. Treatment of the Non-Alcoholic Significant Other
        Person. Paper presented at the National Council on
        Alcoholism Forum, New Orleans, April, 1981.

1176. Conway, M. Recovery: A Way of Life. In: Alcoholism:
        Treatment and Recovery. Ed. Marshall Goby. St. Louis,
        MO: Catholic Health Association, 1984, pages 117-121.

1177. Cook, Brian and Winokur, George. Separate Heritability of
        Alcoholism and Psychotic Symptoms. American Journal of
        Psychiatry, 142(3): 360-361, 1985.

1178. Cook, Brian L. and Winokur, George. A Family Study of Familial
        Positive vs. Familial Negative Alcoholics. The Journal of
        Nervous and Mental Disease, 173(3): 175-178, 1985.

1179. Cook, D., Fewell, C. and Riolo, J. (Eds.) Social Work Treatment
        of Alcohol Problems. New Brunswick, NJ: Rutgers Center
        of Alcohol Studies, 1983.

1180. Cook, Richard S. Alcoholic Treatment: The Group Experience.
        Illinois Medical Journal, 139(5): 514-518, 1971.

1181. Cooke, S.E. Project Rehab: A Progress Report. Maryland State
        Medical Journal, 21(6): 82-87, 1972.

1182. Cooklin, Alan, Miller, Ann C. and McHugh, Brenda. An
        Institution for Change: Developing a Family Day Unit.
        Family Process, 22(4): 453-468, 1983.

1183. Cooley, H.K. Case Report: Winning the Person with Alcoholism to
        Counseling. Individual Psychology, 40(4): 484-496, 1984.

1184. Coombs, R.H. and Dickson, K.M. Generational Continuity in the
        Use of Alcohol and Other Substances: A Literature Review.
        Abstracts and Reviews in Alcohol and Driving, 2(4): 1-7,
        1981.

1185. Coombs, Robert H., Wellisch, David K. and Fawzy, Fawzy I.
        Drinking Patterns and Problems Among Female Children and
        Adolescents: A Comparison of Abstainers, Past Users, and
        Current Users. American Journal of Drug and Alcohol Abuse,
        11(3&4): 315-348, 1985.

1186. Cooney, John G. Rehabilitation of the Alcoholic. Journal of the
        Irish Medical Association, 63: 219-222, 1970.

1187. Corder, B.F., Corder, Robert F. and Laidlaw, Nancy D. An
        Intensive Treatment Program for Alcoholics and Their Wives.
        Quarterly Journal of Studies on Alcohol, 33(4):
        1144-1146, 1972.

1188. Corder, B.F., Hendricks, A. and Corder, R.F. An MMPI Study of
        a Group of Wives of Alcoholics. In: Quarterly Journal of
        Studies on Alcohol, 25: 551-554, 1964.

1189. Corder, B.F., McRee, C. and Rohrer, H. Brief Review of Literature
        on Daughters of Alcoholic Fathers. North Carolina Journal
        of Mental Health, 10(20): 37-43, 1984.

1190. Corder, Billie F., Ball, Brenda C., Haizlip, Thomas M., Rollins,
        Robert and Beaumont, Ralph. Adolescent Parricide: A
        Comparison with Other Adolescent Murder. American Journal
        of Psychiatry, 133(8): 957-961, 1976.

1191. Corenblum, B. Reactions to Alcohol-related Marital Violence:
        Effects of One's Own Abuse Experience and Alcohol Problems
        on Causal Attributions. Journal of Studies on Alcohol,
        44(4): 665-674, 1983.

1192. Corenblum, B. and Fischer, Donald G. Some Correlates of Al-Anon
        Group Membership. Journal of Studies on Alcohol, 36(5):
        675-677, 1975.

1193. Corfman, E. (Ed.). Families Today: Volume II. A Research
        Sampler on Families and Children. Washington, D.C.:
        U.S. Government Printing Office, 1979.

1194. Cork, R. Margaret. Case Work in a Group Setting with Wives of
        Alcoholics. Social Worker, Ottawa, 24(3): 1-6, 1956.

1195. Cork, R. Margaret. The Forgotten Children. Toronto:
        Addiction Research Foundation, 1969.

1196. Cork, R. Margaret. The Forgotten Children: A Study of Children
        with Alcoholic Parents. In: The Forgotten Child. Ed.
        R. Margaret Cork. Toronto: Addiction Research Foundation,
        1969, pages 19-41.

1197. Cork, R. Margaret. Forgotten Children: Who Are They? In:
        Nurse Care Planning on Alcoholism. Eds. J. Lotterhos
        and M. McGuire. Greenville, NC: East Carolina University,
        1974, pages 116-129.

1198. Cornsweet, A.C. and Locke, B.   Alcohol as a Factor in Naval
      Delinquencies.   Naval Medical Bulletin, 46: 1690-1695,
      1946.

1199. Cornu, F.   Katamnesen Bei Kastrierten Sittlichkeitsdelinquenten
      Aus Forensisch - Psychiatrischer Sicht.   (Case Histories
      of Castrated Sex Offenders from a Forensic Psychiatric
      Viewpoint).   Bibliotheca Psychiatrica, 149: 1-132, 1973.

1200. Cornwell, Georgia.   Factors in Interpersonal and Family
      Relationships and Alcoholism.   Journal of Psychiatric
      Nursing & Mental Health Services, 6(5): 274-278, 1968.

1201. Corrigan, E.M.   Alcoholic Women in Treatment.   New York:
      Oxford University Press, 1980.

1202. Corrigan, E.M. and Anderson, S.C.   Homeless Alcoholic Women on
      Skid Row.   American Journal of Drug and Alcohol Abuse,
      10(4): 535-549, 1984.

1203. Corrigan, Eileen M.   Alcoholic Women in Treatment: A Summary of
      Findings.   In: Social Work Treatment of Alcohol Problems.
      Eds. David Cook, Christine Fewell and John Riolo.   New
      Brunswick, NJ: Rutgers Center on Alcohol Studies, 1983,
      pages 109-118.

1204. Cosper, Ronald and Mozersky, Kenneth.   Social Correlates of
      Drinking and Driving.   Quarterly Journal of Studies on
      Alcohol, (Supplement 4): 58-117, 1968.

1205. Cosqueric, Jean Pierre and Gueguen, Anne Marie.   Approche
      Indirecte De L'alcoolisme Parental Dans Une Famille d'A.
      E.M.O.   (An Indirect Approach to Parental Alcoholism in a
      Family Treated at Home).   Sauvegarde De l'Enfance,
      35(3): 404-414, 1980.

1206. Costello, R.M.   Alcoholism Treatment and Evaluation: In Search
      of Methods.   International Journal of the Addictions, 10:
      251-275, 1975.

1207. Costello, Raymond M.   "Chicana Liberation" and the Mexican-
      American Marriage.   Psychiatric Annals, 7(12): 64, 67-69,
      73, 1977.

1208. Cotroneo, Margaret and Krasner, Barbara R.   Addiction, Alienation
      and Parenting.   In: Drugs and the Family.   Ed. Thomas J.
      Glynn.   Washington, D.C.:   U.S. Government Printing Office,
      1981, pages 88-89.   (Also in: Nursing Clinics of North
      America, 11(3): 517-525, 1976.)

1209. Cottington, Eric Malcolm.   Occupational Stress, Psychosocial
      Modifiers, and Blood Pressure in a Blue-Collar Population.
      Dissertation Abstracts International, 44(8): 2387B, 1983.

1210. Cottle, T.J.   Children's Secrets.   Garden City, NJ: Anchor
      Press, 1980.

1211. Cotton, Nancy S.   The Familial Incidence of Alcoholism; A Review.
      Journal of Studies on Alcohol, 40: 89-116, 1979.

1212. Cotugno, H.E.   Dr. Harry E. Cotugno: Gallup Organization, Inc.
      Paper presented at the Family Awareness Conference,
      Washington, D.C., 1984, pages 22-25.

1213. Coudret, N.A. and Huffman, B.   Relationship of Locus of Control
      to Successful Alcoholism Treatment. Paper presented at the
      Second Spring Conference for Nurse Educators in Alcohol and
      Drug Abuse Nursing, Colorado Springs, May, 1982, pages
      243-255.

1214. Counselors Should Study Own Family System. *NIAAA Information and Feature Service*, (IFS No. 62): 4, August 6, 1979.

1215. Count Ellen. *Twenty Eight Million Forgotten Children. Help for Young Victims of Alcoholic Homes*. Pamphlet. New York: National Council on Alcoholism, 1976.

1216. Course Outline: *Alcoholism and Family Systems*. *Curriculum Guide*. Baltimore, MD: University of Maryland, Graduate School of Nursing, 1982.

1217. Coursey, Robert D., Buchsbaum, Monte S. and Murphy, Dennis L. Platelet MAO Activity and Evoked Potentials in the Identification of Subjects Biologically at Risk for Psychiatric Disorders. *British Journal of Psychiatry*, London, 134: 372-381, 1979.

1218. Coursey, Robert D., Buchsbaum, Monte S. and Murphy, Dennis L. Two Year Follow-up of Subjects and their Families Defined as at Risk for Psychopathology on the Basis of Platelet Mono Amine Oxidase Activities. Two Year Follow-up of Low Platelet Mono Amine Oxidase. *Neuropsychobiology*, 8(1): 51-56, 1982.

1219. Couture, Josie Balaban. Employed Wife of the Alcoholic. *Labor-Management Alcoholism Journal*, 6(1): 11-13, 1976.

1220. Couture, Josie Balaban. *Statement Before the United States Subcommittee on Alcoholism and Narcotics, September 29, 1976*. New York: The Other Victims of Alcoholism, Inc., 1976.

1221. Couzigou, P. and Fleury, B. Is Alcoholism Hereditary? *Nouvelle Presse Medicale*, Paris, 10(39): 3237-3240, 1981.

1222. Covington, S.S. *Women and Addiction*. La Jolla, CA, 1985.

1223. Covington, Stephanie Stewart. Alcohol and Family Violence. Paper presented at the 29th International Institute on the Prevention and Treatment of Alcoholism. Zagreb, 1983.

1224. Covner, Bernard J. Screening Volunteer Alcoholism Counselors. *Quarterly Journal of Studies on Alcohol*, 30: 420-425, 1969.

1225. Cowdery, Marcia Ann. A Comparison of Alcoholism Beliefs Between Two Different Type Problem Drinkers. *Dissertation Abstracts International*, 43(8): 2703B, 1982.

1226. Cowie, John, Cowie, Valerie and Slater, Eliot. Early Studies of Delinquency in Girls. In: *Delinquency in Girls*. New York: Humanities Press, 1968, pages 1-24.

1227. Cowper, Smith Frances. Case Studies on the Dependence of Alcohol. I Thought Excess Gave Me Credit Until... *Nursing Times*, London, 74(29): 1191-1192, 1978.

1228. Coyle, P. Vulnerability and Power in Group Therapy for ACOAs. *Focus on Family and Chemical Dependency*, 8(4): 21, 27, 35, 1985.

1229. Crabbe, J.C. Sensitivity to Ethanol in Inbred Mice: Genotypic Correlations Among Several Behavioral Responses. *Behavioral Neuroscience*, 97(2): 280-289, 1983.

1230. Crabbe, J.C., Janowsky, J.S., Young, E.R., Kosobud, A., Stack, J. and Rigter, H. Tolerance to Ethanol Hypothermia in Inbred Mice: Genotypic Correlations with Behavioral Responses. Alcoholism: Clinical and Experimental Research, 6: 446-458, 1982.

1231. Crabbe, J.C., Kosobud, A. and Young, E.R. Genetic Selection for Ethanol Withdrawal Severity: Differences in Replicate Mouse Lines. Life Sciences, 33(10): 955-962, 1983.

1232. Crabbe, J.C., Kosobud, A. and Young, E.R. Peak Ethanol Withdrawal Convulsions in Genetically Selected Mice. Proceedings of the Western Pharmacology Society, 26: 201-204, 1983.

1233. Crabbe, J.C. Jr. Hypophyseal Hormones and Ethanol: Genetic Studies in Mice. In: Ethanol Tolerance and Dependence: Endocrinological Aspects. Rockville, MD: National Institute on Alcohol Abuse and Alcoholism, 1983, pages 89-101.

1234. Craddick, R.A., Leipold, V. and Leipold, W.D. Effect of Role Empathy on Human Figures Drawn by Women Alcoholics. Journal of Studies on Alcohol, 37: 90-97, 1976.

1235. Crafoord, C. Put the Booze on the Table - Some Thoughts About Family - Therapy and Alcoholism. Journal of Family Therapy, 2(1): 71-81, 1980.

1236. Craig, R.J. Treating Drug Addicts and Alcoholics in Combined Treatment Settings: Issues and Perspectives. Journal of Psychiatric Treatment and Evaluation, 3(1): 87-94, 1981.

1237. Craig, R.J. and Baker, S.L. (Eds.). Drug Dependent Patients: Treatment and Research. Springfield, IL: Charles C. Thomas, 1982.

1238. Craig, Sara. Help for Women Alcoholics. Opportunity, 2(5): 18-23, 1972.

1239. Cramer, James A. Parental Alcohol Abuse and Social Adjustment of Offspring: A Preliminary Model. Report. Richmond: Virginia Commonwealth University, no date.

1240. Cramer, Patrice A. An Educational Strategy to Impact the Children of Alcoholic Parents: A Feasibility Report. Arlington, VA: National Center for Alcohol Education, 1977.

1241. Cranford, V. and Seliger, R.V. Alcohol Psychopathology in a Family Constellation. Journal of Criminal Psychopathology, 5: 571-583, 1944.

1242. Craven, Allen B. and Lloyd, Stephanie. Co-Counseling With the Dual-Suffering Family: Chemical Dependency and Sexual Trauma. Focus on Family and Chemical Dependency, 8(4): 28-29, 35, 1985.

1243. Crawford, Gail A., Washington, Melvin C. and Senay, Edward C. Socio Familial Characteristics of Black Male Heroin Addicts and Their Nonaddicted Friends. Drug and Alcohol Dependence, Lausanne, 6(6): 383-390, 1980.

1244. Crawford, Jack J., Carris, William and McCoy, Colleen. Competency Training for Alcoholism Counselors. 1977. (Eric Document Number ED151655.)

1245. Crawford, R.J.M. Spouses of Alcoholics. New Zealand Medical Journal, Dunedin, 96(734): 545, 1983.

1246. Cretcher, Dorothy. Steering Clear. Helping Your Child Through the High-Risk Drug Years. Center City, Minnesota: Hazelden, no date.

1247. Criteria for the Diagnosis of Alcoholism by the Criteria Committee, National Council on Alcoholism. The American Journal of Psychiatry, 129(2): 127-135, 1972. (Also in: Alcoholism: Introduction to Theory and Treatment. Ed. David A. Ward. Dubuque, IA: Kendall/Hunt, 1980, pages 230-241.)

1248. Critical Concerns in the Field of Drug Abuse. New York: Marcel Dekker, 1978.

1249. Cronkite, R.C. and Moos, R.H. Sex and Marital Status in Relation to the Treatment and Outcome of Alcoholic Patients. Sex Roles, 11(1-2): 93-112, 1984.

1250. Cronkite, Ruth C. and Moos, Rudolf H. Determinants of the Posttreatment Functioning of Alcoholic Patients: A Conceptual Framework. Journal of Consulting & Clinical Psychology, 48(3): 305-316, 1980.

1251. A Cross-Section of Ideas, Opinions, and Approaches: Family Program Profiles. Alcoholism: The National Magazine, 1(3): 39-47, 1981.

1252. Cross, Wilbur. Housewife. In: Having Been There. Ed. A. Luks. New York: Charles Scribner's, 1979, pages 79-87.

1253. Crothers, T.D. The Influence of Alcoholic Heredity in Diseases of Children. Medical News, New York, 81: 1023-1024, 1902.

1254. Croughan, J.L. Contribution of Family Studies to Understanding Drug Abuse. In: Series in Psychosocial Epidemiology. Ed. Lee N. Robins. New Brunswick, NJ: Rutgers University Press, 1985, pages 93-116.

1255. Crowe, R.R. Adoption Studies in Psychiatry. Biological Psychiatry, 10: 353-372, 1975.

1256. Crowe, R.R., Noyes, R., Pauls, D.L. and Slymen, D. Family Study of Panic Disorder. Archives of General Psychiatry, 40(10): 1065-1069, 1983.

1257. Crowe, Raymond R., Namboodiri, Kadambari K., Ashby, Howard B. and Elston, Robert C. Segregation and Linkage Analysis of a Large Kindred of Unipolar Depression. Neuropsychobiology, 7(1): 20-25, 1981.

1258. Crowley, James F. Alliance for Change: A Plan for Community Action on Adolescent Drug Abuse. Minneapolis, Minnesota: Community Intervention, Inc., 1984.

1259. Crowley, T.J. Alcoholism Identification, Evaluation and Early Treatment. Western Journal of Medicine, 140(3): 461-464, 1984.

1260. Cruz-Coke, R. Asociacion Entre La Oportunidad Para La Seleccion Natural, Los Defectos de Vision de Colores Y el Alcoholismo Cronico, En Diversas Poblaciones Humanas. (Association Between Opportunity for Natural Selection, Color Blindness and Chronic Alcoholism in Different Human Populations.) Archivos de Biologia Y Medicina Experimentales, Santiago, 3: 21-26, 1966.

1261. Cruz-Coke, R. Colour-Blindness and Cirrhosis of the Liver. Lancet, 2: 1064-1065, 1964. (Also in: Lancet, 1: 1131-1133, 1965.)

1262. Cruz-Coke, R. Genetics and Alcoholism. Neurobehavioral
        Toxicology and Teratology, 5(2): 179-180, 1983. (Also
        as: Paper presented at the 5th Annual Conference on
        Alcoholism: Genetics and Alcoholism, El Paso, Texas,
        February, 1981.)

1263. Cruz-Coke, R. Heterogeneidad Genetica De La Dependencia Al
        Alcohol. (Genetic Heterogeneity in Alcohol Dependence.)
        Revista Medica de Chile, Santiago, 107: 534-539, 1979.

1264. Cruz-Coke, R., Rivera, L., Kattan, L. and Mardones, J. Defectos
        de Vision de Colores En Mujeres Alcoholicas Y Sus Parientes.
        (Color Vision Defects in Women Alcoholics and Their
        Relatives.) Revista Medica de Chile, Santiago, 99:
        118-124, 1977.

1265. Cruz-Coke, R., Rivera, L., Varela, A. and Mardones, J.
        Correlation Between Colour Vision Disturbance and Appetite
        for Alcohol. Clinical Genetics, Copenhagen, 3: 404-410,
        1972.

1266. Cruz-Coke, R. and Varela, A. Colour-Blindness and Alcohol
        Addiction. Lancet, 2: 1348, 1965.

1267. Cruz-Coke, R. and Varela, A. Inheritance of Alcoholism; Its
        Association with Colour-Blindness. Lancet, 2:
        1282-1284, 1966.

1268. Cseh, Szombathy Laszlo. The Internalization of Deviant
        Behavior Patterns During Socialization in the Family.
        The Sociological Review Monograph, 17: 207-216, 1972.

1269. Cureton, Louise Witmer. Parents' Police Records for Drunkenness
        and Behavior Problems of Their Children. Paper presented at
        the 1st Annual Alcoholism Conference of NIAAA, Rockville, MD:
        June, 1971, pages 262-275.

1270. Cureton, Witmer. Project Talent: Arrests for Drunkenness of
        Young Adults and Their Parents and Adolescent Behavior
        Problems. Palo Alto, CA: American Institutes for
        Research, 1973.

1271. Curlee, J. Alcoholism and the "Empty Nest." Bulletin of the
        Menninger Clinic, 33: 165-171, 1969.

1272. Curlee, J. Women Alcoholics. Federal Probation, 32(10):
        16-20, 1968.

1273. Curlee, Joan. A Comparison of Male and Female Patients at an
        Alcoholism Treatment Center. Journal of Psychology,
        74(2): 239-247, 1970.

1274. Curlee-Salisbury, Joan. When the Woman You Love is an
        Alcoholic. St. Meinrad, IN: Abbey Press, 1978.

1275. Curtis, Charlotte. The New York Times, 27 November 1984,
        sec. 3, p. 12, col. 4. (History of Counselor/Survivor
        of Alcoholism, Incest and Abuse.)

1276. Curtis, John H. Alcohol and Teenagers -- 4 Case Studies. Family
        Relations, 31(3): 467-468, 1982.

1277. Cushman, S.B. Relationship of Role Strain, Role Conflict,
        Self-Esteem and Mastery to the Level of Alcohol Use
        Among Married Working Women. Dissertation Abstracts
        International, 44(7): 2239B, 1984.

1278. Cushner, I.M. Maternal-Behavior and Perinatal Risks - Alcohol,
Smoking and Drugs. Annual Review of Public Health, 2:
201-218, 1981.

1279. Cutland, E. Helping the Whole Family: Family Program at Broadway
Lodge. In: Alcoholism: A Modern Perspective. Lancaster,
England: MTP Press, 1982, pages 191-197.

1280. Cutland, E. Intervening in Alcoholism. In: Alcoholism:
A Modern Perspective. Ed. P. Golding. Lancaster, England:
MTP Press, 1982, pages 185-190.

1281. Cutland, E.A. Family Program at Broadway Lodge, England.
In: Association of Labor-Management Administrators and
Consultants on Alcoholism, Inc. Arlington, VA: ALMACA,
1980, pages 65-74.

1282. Cutland, L. Children of Alcoholics: Victims and Survivors.
Paper presented at the International Council on Alcohol
and Addictions, Vienna, 1981.

1283. Cutler, Charles Michael. Relational Communication in the Marriage
of the Alcoholic. Doctoral Dissertation. (University
Microfilms No. 77-7437.) 1976.

1284. Cutter, H.S.G. and O'Farrell, T.J. Effects of Adding a Behavioral
or an Interactional Couples Group to Individual Outpatient
Alcoholism Counseling. Paper presented at the Sixteenth
Annual Convention of the Association for the Advancement of
Behavior Therapy, Los Angeles, 1982.

1285. Cutter, H.S.G. and O'Farrell, T.J. Evaluating Behavioral
Marital Therapy for Male Alcoholics. Paper presented at
the Annual Meeting of the American Psychological Association,
Washington, D.C., August, 1982.

1286. Cutter, Henry S.G. and Fisher, Joseph C. Family Experience and
the Motives for Drinking. The International Journal of
the Addictions, 15(3): 339-358, 1980.

1287. Cutting, Allan R. and Prosser, Frank J. Family Oriented Mental
Health Consultation to a Naval Research Group. Social
Casework, 60(4): 236-242, 1979.

1288. Cvitkovic, Joseph Francis. Alcohol Use and Communication
Congruence in Alcoholic and Nonalcoholic Marriages.
Doctoral Dissertation. (University Microfilms No. 7816784.)
Pittsburgh: University of Pittsburgh, 1978.

D

1289. Dahlgren, L. and Myrhed, M. Ways of Admission of the Alcohol Patient; A Study with Special Reference to the Alcoholic Female. *Acta Psychiatrica Scandinavica*, Copenhagen, 56: 39-49, 1977.

1290. Dahlgren, Lena. Female Alcoholics. III. Development and Pattern of Problem Drinking. *Acta Psychiatrica Scandinavica*, Copenhagen, 57: 325-335, 1978.

1291. Dahlgren, Lena. Female Alcoholics. IV. Marital Situation and Husbands. *Acta Psychiatrica Scandinavica*, Copenhagen, 59: 59-69, 1979.

1292. Daikuhara, H. Instructions Given to the Families of Local Alcohol-Dependent Patients. *Kango Gijutsu*, Tokyo, 26(16): 2173-2178, 1980.

1293. Daille, Roger. Alcoolisme et Violence. (Alcoholism and Violence.) *Instantanes Criminologiques*, Lyon, 28: 17-18, 1976.

1294. Daley, D.C. Relapse Prevention: Individual and Family Cornerstone for Recovery. *Focus on Family and Chemical Dependency*, 8(6): 19, 28-29, 1985.

1295. Dalla Volta, A. Alcoolismo Infantile e Influenza Dell'Ambiente Familiare. (Alcoholism in Children and the Influence of the Family Environment.) *Neuropsichiatria*, Genoa, 10: 1-8, 1954.

1296. Dallos, Vera. Iatrogenic Epilepsy Due to Antidepressant Drugs. *British Medical Journal*, 4(5675): 80-82, 1969.

1297. Dalton, M.S.; Chewidden, M.J. and Duncan D. Wistaria House: Results of Transition of Alcoholics From Treatment Unit to Community House. *International Journal of Social Psychiatry*, 18(3): 212-216, 1972.

1298. Daly, Emmet. A Report on the Pilot Plan Alcoholism Rehabilitation Clinic at San Francisco. In: Reports on Government-Sponsored Programs. Ed. Ernest A. Shepherd. *Quarterly Journal of Studies on Alcohol*, 13(2): 345-355, 1952.

1299. Damato, F. Colucci. Rapporti Scuola, Famiglia ed Igiene Mentale. (School Relations, Family and Mental Hygiene.) *L'ospedale Psichiatrico Provinciale*, Napoli, 38(1-2): 264-268, 1970.

1300. Damkot, David K. and Meyer, Elizabeth. Alcohol and Social Policy: An Historical Perspective on Evolving Intervention Strategies. *Journal of Drug Issues*, 14(3): 479-490, 1984.

1301. Damorim, Maria Alice. Estudo Comparativo da Percepcao da Doenca
       Mental Pela Comunidade. (Comparative Study of the Perception
       of Mental Illness by the Community.) Arquivos Brasileiros de
       Psicologia, 33(1-2): 75-83, 1981.

1302. Damour, M., Shahani, B.T. and Young, R.R. Tremor in Alcoholic
       Patients. Electroencephalography and Clinical
       Neurophysiology, Amsterdam, 43(1): 147, 1977.

1303. Dancey, Travis, E. Constructive Coercion Technique in Alcoholism
       and Drug-Dependency Programs. In: Drug Abuse in Industry.
       Ed. J.M. Scher. Springfield, IL: Charles C. Thomas, 1973,
       pages 243-257.

1304. Daniels, Robert S. Brief Psychotherapeutic Technic for the Treat-
       ment of Severe Alcoholism by the Family Physician. New York
       State Journal of Medicine, 58: 397-401, 1958.

1305. Danilevskii, V.F. Nevrotiziruyushcheye Vliyaniye Bol'nykh
       Khronicheskim Alkogolizmom na Blizhaishikh Rodstvennikov.
       (Neurotogenic Effect of Chronic Alcoholism on Close Relatives.)
       Vrachebnoe Delo, 10: 119-120, 1975.

1306. Danilova, E.A. O Roli Alkogolizma v Formirovanii Patologii
       Povedeniya u Detei i Podrostkov. (On the Role of Alcoholism
       in the Development of Pathological Behavior in Children and
       Juveniles.) In: Ttretii Vseros. S'Yezd Nevropatologov i
       Psikhiatrov, Kazan Tom 3. Tezisy i Doklady. (The Third
       All-Russian Conference of Neuropathologists and
       Psychiatrists, Kazan'. Vol. 3 Theses are Proceedings).
       Moscow, 1974, 164-167.

1307. Dank, Barry M. Six Homosexual Siblings. Archives of Sexual
       Behavior, 1(3): 193-204, 1971.

1308. D'Arcy, A.J. Alcoholic Parents: Raped Children. Cycles in and
       Causes of Incest Child Abuse. Pamphlet. Cincinnati, OH: Pamplet
       Publications, 1978.

1309. D'Argenio, L. Sull'Alcoolismo Infantile. (On Alcoholism in Children.)
       Rassegna di Studi Psichiatrici, Siena, 48: 879-898, 1959.

1310. Darity, William A. Alcohol and Other Drugs as Cripplers: A Crucial
       Problem in the Black Community. Urban League Review, 4(1):
       36-46, 1979.

1311. Darnaud, J., Denard, Y., and Darnaud, CH. Diabetes in the Course of
       Alcoholic Cirrhosis. Revue Francaise D' Endocrinologie Clinique,
       Nutrition et Metabolisme, Paris, 22(1): 35-42, 1981.

1312. Darshan, Salilesh, Neki, J.S., and Mohan D. Drug Abuse in a Farm
       Community: A Brief Appraisal of Research Work. Drug and
       Alcohol Dependence, Lausanne, 7(4): 347-366, 1981.

1313. Darwin, Leonard. Alcoholism and Eugenics. British Journal of
       Inebriety, 13: 55-66, 1915.

1314. Darwin, Leonard. A Note on the Study of Alcoholism and Eugenics.
       British Journal of Inebriety, 13: 211-214, 1916.

1315. D'Augelli, Judith Frankel. Communication and Parenting Skills:
       Leader Guide and Parent Workbook. Rockville, MD: National
       Institute on Drug Abuse, 1979. (Eric Document Number
       ED176153).

1316. D'Augelli, Judith Frankel. Parenting Skills for Alcohol Abuse
       Prevention: A Programmatic Approach. Pamphlet.
       University Park, PA: Pennsylvannia State University, no date.

1317. D'Augelli, Judith Frankel, and Weener, Joan M. Development of a
       Parent Education Program as a Drug Abuse Prevention Strategy.
       University Park, PA: Pennsylvania State University, 1977.

1318. Dauteuil, R. and Dauteuil, C. Les Tables Rondes du Comite de
       Paris Contre L'Alcoholisme. (Round Tables of the Paris
       Committee on Alcoholism Prevention. Paper presented at the
       21st International Institute on the Prevention & Treatment
       of Alcoholism, Helsinki, Finland, 1975, pages 248-255.

1319. Dauteuil, R. and Dauteuil C. Le Conjoint Du Malade Alcoolique.
       (Spouse of an Alcoholic Patient). Alcool Ou Sante,
       163(4): 9-12, 1982.

1320. Davenport, C.B. Effects of Alcohol on Animal Offspring. In:
       Ed. H. Emerson. Alcohol and Man. New York: Macmillan,
       1932, 120-125.

1321. Davenport, Yolande B., Zahn-Waxler, Carolyn, Adland, Marvin L.,
       and Mayfield, Anne. Early Child-Rearing Practices in
       Families with a Manic-Depressive Parent. American Journal
       of Psychiatry, 141(2): 230, 1984.

1322. David, K. An Alcoholic--Married To Me. Nursing Times,
       67(11): 332, 1971.

1323. Davidson, A.F. An Evaluation of the Treatment and After-Care
       of a Hundred Alcoholics. British Journal of Addicton,
       Edinburgh, 71: 217-224, 1976.

1324. Davidson, F. and Choquet, M. Etude Epidemiologique du Suicide
       de L'adolescent: Comparaison Entre Suicidants Primaires
       et Suicidants Recidivistes. (An Epidemiological Study of
       Adolescent Suicide: Comparison between Primary Suicide
       Attempts and Repeaters.) Revue d Epidemiologie, Medecine
       Sociale et Sante Publique, Paris, 24: 11-26, 1976.

1325. Davidson, Francoise, Defrance, Jacques, and Facy, Francoise.
       Typology of Young Drug Addicts. Psychiatrie de L'Enfant,
       25(2): 295-318, 1982.

1326. Davidson, R.S. and Stein, S. Reliability of Self-Report of
       Alcoholics. Behavior Modification, 6(1): 107-119, 1982.

1327. Davidson, Sharon V. The Assessment of Alcoholism. Family &
       Community Health, 2(1): 1-32, 1979.

1328. Davies, D.L. Alcoholism and the Family. Maternal and Child
       Health, 7(8): 316, 318, 1982.

1329. Davies, J.B. Transmission of Alcohol Problems in the Family.
       In: Alcohol and the Family. Eds. J. Orford and J.
       Harwin. New York: St. Martin's Press, 1982, pages 73-87.

1330. Davies, J.L. Role of Alcohol in Family Violence. Dissertation
       Abstracts International, 45(12): 3770B, 1985.

1331. Davies, John and Stacey, Barrie. Teenagers and Alcohol-A
       Developmental Study in Glasgow. Scotland: Health
       Education Unit, Scottish Home and Health Department,
       no date.

1332. Davies, John B. Children's and Adolescent's Attitudes Towards
       Alcohol and Alcohol-Dependence. In: Alcohol and Youth.
       (Child Health and Development, Volume 2). Ed. O. Jeanneret.
       Basel: S. Karger, 1983, pages 42-53.

1333. Davies-Osterkamp, S. Alkoholismus bei Frauen. (Alcoholism in
        Women.) Drug and Alcohol Dependence, Lausanne, 1:
        191-213, 1976.

1334. Davis, A. and Lipson A. A Challenge in Managing a Family with the
        Fetal Alcohol Syndrome. Letter. Clinical Pediatrics,
        23(5): 304, 1984.

1335. Davis, C.N. Early Warning Signs of Alcoholism. Comprehensive
        Therapy, 4(9): 58-62, 1978.

1336. Davis, D.M., Gonzalez, V., and Piat, J. Follow-Up of Adolescent
        Inpatients. Southern Medical Journal, 73(9): 1215-1217,
        1980.

1337. Davis, Donald I. Alcoholics Anonymous and Family Therapy.
        Journal of Marital and Family Therapy, 6(1): 65-73, 1980.

1338. Davis, Donald I. Alcoholism and the Family: Why Family Therapy
        Should be Seen as Complementary and Not as a Threat to AA and
        Al-Anon. Paper presented at the National Conference on
        Alcoholism Meeting, St. Louis, 1978.

1339. Davis, Donald I. Changing Perceptions of Self and Spouse from
        Sober to Intoxicated State: Implications for Research Into
        Family Factors that Maintain Alcohol Abuse. Annals of the
        New York Academy of Sciences, 273: 497-506, 1976.

1340. Davis, Donald I. Family in Alcoholism. In: Phenomenology and
        Treatment of Alcoholism. Eds. William E. Fann, Ismet
        Daracan, Alex D. Pokorny and Robert L. William. Jamaica, NY:
        Spectrum Publishers, 1980, pages 111-125.

1341. Davis, Donald I. Family Therapy for Alcoholism: The State of the
        Art in the U.S. Papers presented at the 24th International
        Institute on the Prevention and Treatment of Alcoholism. Ed.
        E.J. Tongue. Lausanne: International Council on Alcohol and
        Addictions, 1978, 375-381.

1342. Davis, Donald I. I Need Help to Stop Drinking: An Integrative
        Family Therapy Approach to the Management of a Family in
        Early Recovery. In: Power to Change: Family Case Studies
        in the Treatment of Alcoholism. Ed. Edward Kaufman.
        New York: Gardner Press, 1984, pages 1-24.

1343. Davis, Donald I. Review of Alcoholic Marriage -- Alternative
        Perspectives, by T.J. Paolino and B.S. McCrady. American
        Journal of Family Therapy, 7(3): 86-87, 1979.

1344. Davis, Donald I. Special Problems in Family Therapy Posed
        by Alcohol Abuse. In: Family Therapy and Major
        Psychopathology. Ed. M.R. Lansky. New York: Grune
        and Stratton, 1981, pages 231-245.

1345. Davis, Donald I. Why Family Therapy for Drug Abuse? From the
        Clinical Perspective. In: Drug Abuse from the Family
        Perspective. Ed. Barbara Gray Ellis. Washington, D.C.:
        U.S. Government Printing Office, 1980, pages 63-70.

1346. Davis, Donald I., Berenson, David, Steinglass, Peter and Davis,
        Susan. The Adaptive Consequences of Drinking. Psychiatry,
        37(3): 209-215, 1974.

1347. Davis, Donald I. and Steinglass, Peter. Therapeutic Strategies
        in Conjoint Hospitalization for the Treatment of Alcoholism.
        In: Family Therapy of Drug & Alcohol Abuse. Eds. E.
        Kaufman and P. Kaufman. New York: Gardner Press, 1979,
        pages 215-232.

1348. Davis, Fred T.   Alcoholism and the Disavantaged Pupil, Arlington,
      VA : National Center for Alcohol Education, no date.

1349. Davis, P., Stern, D.R. and Van Deusen, J.M. Enmeshment-
      Disengagement in the Alcoholic Family. Paper presented at
      the National Council on Alcoholism, San Diego, April-May,
      1977. (Also in: Currents in Alcoholism, Vol. IV.
      Psychiatric, Psychological, Social and Epidemiological
      Studies. Ed. F.A. Seixas. New York: Grune and Stratton,
      1978, pages 15-28.)

1350. Davis, Ruth Bresnihan. Adolescents From Alcoholic Families: An
      Investigation of Self-Esteem, Locus of Control, and Know-
      ledge and Attitudes Toward Alcohol. Dissertation Abstracts
      International, 43(10): 3346B, 1983.

1351. Davis, T.S. and Hagood, L.A. In-Home Support for Recovering
      Alcoholic Mothers and Their Families; The Family
      Rehabilitation Coordinator Project. Journal of Studies
      on Alcohol, 40: 313-317, 1979.

1352. Davis, Terry S. and Hagood, Linda A. Family Rehabilitation
      Coordinator Training for In-Home Recovery Assistance
      Services to Alcoholic Mothers, Their Children and Families.
      Curriculum Guide. Los Angeles: University of California,
      Department of Continuing Education in Health Sciences, 1977.

1353. Davis, Terry S., Shanahan, Patricia, Majchrzak, Shirley M., and
      Hagood, Linda. Recovery for the Alcoholic Mother and Family
      Through Home-Based Intervention. Paper presented at the
      American Psychological Association, Washington, DC,
      September, 1976.

1354. Davis, W.W. Practical Experience with an Alcoholism Program in
      Industry. Ohio State Medical Journal, 66: 814-816, 1970.

1355. Dawkins, Marvin P. Alcohol Information on Black Americans: Current
      Status and Future Needs. Journal of Alcohol and Drug Education,
      25(3): 28-40, 1980.

1356. Dax, E. Cunningham. Suicide in Today's Society. Medical Journal
      of Australia, Sydney, 2(26): 1197-1200, 1968.

1357. Day, B.R. Alcoholics and the Family. Journal of Marriage and
      Family, 23: 253-258, 1961.

1358. Deakins, S.M., Seif, N.N. and Weinstein, D.L. Support of Routine
      Screening for Alcoholism. In: Social Work Treatment of
      Alcohol Problems. Eds. D. Cook, C. Fewell and J. Riolo.
      New Brunswick, NJ: Rutgers Center of Alcohol Studies, 1983,
      pages 16-22.

1359. Dealing With The Drinking Problem. Manpower, 2(12): 2-7, 1970.

1360. Dealmeida, Steven Craig. Relationship of Antisocial Personality
      Syndrome in Boys to Parental Alcohol/Drug Dependency.
      Dissertation Abstracts International, 43(1): 104B, 1981.

1361. Debray, Q. La Place du Facteur Genetique Dans le Risque Psychia-
      trique Familial. (Situation of the Genetic Factor in the
      Family Psychiatric Risk.) Psychologie Medicale, 14(10):
      1575-1579, 1982.

1362. Deckman, Joanne and Downs, Bill. A Group Treatment Approach for
      Adolescent Children of Alcoholic Parents. Social Work With
      Groups, 5(1): 73-77, 1982. (Also in: Social Groupwork
      and Alcoholism. Eds. M. Altman and R. Crocker. New York:
      Haworth Press, 1982, pages 73-77.)

1363. Dee, B. Identifying the Family With an Alcoholism Problem. Paper presented to the Victorian Foundation on Alcoholism and Drug Dependence, Counseling and Referral Service, Melbourne, March, 1976. (Also in: Alcoholism and the Social Worker, pages A1.1.-A1.5., 1976.)

1364. DeForest, John William, Roberts, Thomm Kevin and Hays, J. Ray. Drug Abuse: A Family Affair? Journal of Drug Issues, 4: 130-134, 1974.

1365. DeFries, J.C. and Plomin, Robert. Behavioral Genetics. Annual Review of Psychology, 29: 473-515, 1978.

1366. Dehlin, Ore, Enerback, Lennart and Lundvall, Ore. Porphyria Cutanea Tarda-A Genetic Disease? A Biochemical and Fluorescence Microscopical Study in 4 Families. Acta Medica Scandinavica, Stockholm, 194(4): 265-270, 1973.

1367. Deitrich, R.A. and McClearn, G.E. Neurobiological and Genetic Aspects of the Etiology of Alcoholism. Federation Proceedings, 40(7): 2051-2055, 1981.

1368. Deitrich, Richard A. and Spuhler, Karen. Genetics of Alcoholism and Alcoholism Actions. In: Research Advances in Alcohol and Drug Problems, Vol. 8. Eds. Reginald G. Smart, Howard, D. Cappell and Fredick B. Gaser. New York, NY: Plenum Press, 1984, pages 47-98.

1369. Dekoning, Hoag A. Gold Rings. In: Having Been There. Ed. A. Luks. New York: Charles Scribner's Sons, 1979, pages 13-22.

1370. Delahousse, J. and Vaneecloo, M. La Femme du Jaloux Pathologique. (The Wife of the Pathologic Jealous Man.) Annales Medico-Psychologiques, Paris, 1(1): 127-138, 1972.

1371. Delaine, John K. Who's Raising the Family? A Workbook for Parents and Children, Wisconsin State Department of Health and Social Services, 1981. (Eric Document Number ED220770.)

1372. Delaney, Geraldine O. Litte Hill-Alena Lodge: Nonpermissive Treatment of Alcoholics and Polyaddicts. In: Alcoholism Rehabilitation; Methods and Experiences of Private Rehabilitation Centers. (NIAAA-RUCAS Alcoholism Treatment Series No. 3.) Ed. Vincent Groupe. New Brunswick, NJ: Rutgers Center of Alcohol Studies, 1978, pages 64-74.

1373. Delaware Court Aids Families with Alcohol Problems. NIAAA Information and Feature Service, (IFS No. 52): 3, November 2, 1978.

1374. Del Castillo, Guillermo and Gralnick, Alexander. The Inpatient Treatment of a Child Drug-Abuser in a Mixed Age Group. Psychiatric Quarterly, 45(4): 593-602, 1971.

1375. Delevic, Z., Konstantinovic, D. and Lazarevic, G. A Comparative Analysis of Some Disorders in the Social Relations of Young Alcoholics and Drug Addicts. Alcoholism, Zagreb, 11(2): 128-135, 1975.

1376. Delevic, Z. and Stankovic, I. La Presentation Comme Un Acces Psichotherapeutique Vise Dans La Psichotherapie De Groupe Des Alcooliques. (Self-Presentation As a Psychotherapeutic Method Used in the Group Psychotherapy of Alcoholics.) Alcoholism, Zagreb, 14: 140-145, 1978.

1377. DeLint, J., Blane, H.T., and Barry, H. III. Birth Order and Alcoholism. Quarterly Journal of Studies on Alcohol, 35(1): 292-295, 1974.

1378. DeLint Jan E. Alcoholism, Birth Rank, and Parental Deprivation.
      American Journal of Psychiatry, 120: 1062-1065, 1964.

1379. DeLint Jan E. The Position of Early Parental Loss in the Etiology
      Alcoholism. Alcoholism, Zagreb, 2(1): 56-64, 1966.

1380. Della Corte, Betty. Shelter From the Storm. Center City, MN:
      Hazelden, no date.

1381. Dell-Orto, Arthur E. The Role and Resources of the Family During
      the Drug Rehabilitation Process. Journal of Psychedelic
      Drugs, 6(4): 435-445, 1974.

1382. Delong, G.R. Lithium Carbonate Treatment of Select Behavior
      Disorders in Children Suggesting Manic-Depressive Illness.
      Journal of Pediatrics, 93: 689-694, 1978.

1383. Delorme, M.F. Aspects Etiopathogeniques de L'Acloolisation
      et de L'Alcoolisme. (Etiopathogenetic Aspects of Alcohol
      Intoxication and Alcoholism). In: Alcoologie. Riom,
      Cedex, France: Riom Laboratories, 1984, pages 123-130.

1384. Delorme, M.F. and Barrucand, D. Aspects Genetiques de
      L'Alcoolisme. (Genetic Aspects of Alcoholism.) In:
      Alcoologie. Riom, Cedex, France: Riom Laboratories,
      1984, pages 131-140.

1385. Delorme, M.F. and Barrucand, D. Genetics and Alcoholism. Revue
      de L'Alcoolisme, Paris, 27(4): 166-182, 1981.

1386. Deluca, John R. Women and Crisis Conference: Remarks. Paper
      presented at the National Institute on Alcohol Abuse and
      Alcoholism, New York, May, 1979.

1387. DeMahy, Michael Douglas. Power, Support and Conflict Resolution
      in the Marriages of Male Alcoholics. Doctoral Dissertation.
      (University Microfilms No. 8111816.) Kansas: Kansas State
      University, 1980. (Also in: Dissertation Abstracts,
      42(2): 547A, 1980.)

1388. Demay, Demay-Laulan and Ortas. Difficultes de Relations de
      L'Alcoolique avec ses Enfants. (Difficulties of the
      Alcoholic's Relationship with his Children.) Scapel,
      Brussels, 118: 1029, 1965.

1389. Dembo, Richard, Burgos, William, Des-Jarlais, Don, and Schmeidler,
      James. Ethnicity and Drug Use Among Urban Junior High School
      Youths. International Journal of the Addictions, 14:
      557-568, 1979.

1390. Demel, I. Die Rolle Des Partners Und Der Familie in Der Behandlung
      Von Abhangigkeitsprozessen, Insbesondere bei suchterkrankung
      der Frau. (The Role of Spouse and Family in the Treatment of
      Addiction Processes, Especially of Addiction Disease of Women.)
      Suchtgefahren, Hamburg, 23: 10-22, 1977.

1391. Demerdash, A.M., Mizaal, H., El-Farouki, S., and El-Mossalem, H.
      Some Behavioral and Psychosocial Aspects of Alcohol and
      Drug Dependence in Kuwait Psychiatric Hospital. Acta
      Psychiatrica Scandinavica, Copenhagen, 63(2): 173-185, 1981.

1392. Demogeot, C. Psychosociologie. (Psychosociology.) In: Alcoologie.
      Riom, Cedex, France: Riom Laboratories, 1984, pages 185-193.

1393. Demone, H.W., Hoffman, H.J. and Hoffman, L.W. Alcoholism: An
      Evaluation of Intervention Strategy in Family Agencies.
      Final Report. Boston, MA: United Community Planning Corp., 1974.

1394. Demone, Harold W. Jr. and Wechsler, Henry. Changing Drinking
      Patterns of Adolescents Since the 1960's. In: Alcoholism
      Problems in Women and Children. Eds. M. Greenblatt and
      M.A. Schuckit. New York: Grune and Stratton, 1976, pages
      197-210.

1395. Demone, Harold Wellinton Jr. Drinking Attitudes and Practices of
      Male Adolescents. Doctoral Dissertation (University Microfilms
      No. 66-13637). Massachusetts: Brandeis University, 1966.

1396. Demone, Harold Wellinton Jr.; and Cleary, Paul D. Health and Other
      Service Needs in a Metropolitan Area. Health & Social Work,
      8(3): 165-173, 1983.

1397. Dendy, M. Correspondence on Environment and Heredity. British
      Medical Journal, London, 2: 50-51, 348-349, 1910.

1398. Denk, D. and Van Dyke, M. Investigation of the Relationship
      Between Alcoholism and Battering. Paper presented at
      the National Council on Alcoholism Annual Convention,
      New Orelans, April, 1981.

1399. Dennehy, C.M. Childhood Bereavement and Psychiatric Illness.
      British Journal of Psychiatry, London, 112: 1049-1069, 1966.

1400. Dennison, Darwin. The Effects of Selected Field Experiences
      Upon the Drinking Behavior of University Students.
      The Journal of School Health, 47(1): 38-41, 1977.

1401. Densen-Gerber, Judianne. Drug-Related Child Abuse and Other
      Antisocial Behavior. In: Substance Abuse: Clinical Problems
      and Perspectives. Eds. J.H. Lowinson and P. Ruiz. Baltimore,
      MD: Williams and Wilkins, 1981, pages 770-780.

1402. Densen-Gerber, Judianne and Hutchinson, Stephen F. Medical-Legal and
      Societal Problems Involving Children -- Child Prostitution, Child
      Pornography and Drug-Related Abuse; Recommended Legislation.
      In: The Maltreatment of Children. Ed. S.M. Smith. Baltimore,
      MD: University Park Press, 1978, pages 317-350.

1403. Densen-Gerber, Judianne, Hutchinson, Stephen F. and Levine, Ruth M.
      Incest and Drug-Related Child Abuse-Systematic Neglect by the
      Medical and Legal Professions. Contemporary Drug Problems,
      6(2): 135-172, 1977.

1404. Dent, J.Y. Apomorphine Treatment of Addiction. Some Recent
      Developments. British Journal of Addiction, Edinburgh,
      46: 15-28, 1949.

1405. Dent, J.Y. Editorial. British Journal of Addiction, Edinburgh,
      46: 1-3, 1949.

1406. De-Ortiz, Shelia Archilla. Alcoholism: Puerto Rican Male and
      Female Social Context of Drinking Patterns and Their Familistic
      Ambience. Doctoral Dissertration. (University Microfilms No.
      82-07239). Columbus: Ohio State University. (Also in:
      Dissertation Abstracts International, 42(10): 4587-4588A,
      1982.)

1407. DeParades, B. Le Boire et la Fete Bretonne. (Drinking and the
      Breton Feast.) In: Proceedings of the International Meeting
      on "Cultures, Drinking Habits and Alcoholism". Eds. Guy Caro
      and Jean-Francois Lemoine. Rennes, France, 1984, Pages 81-85.

1408. Deschamps, J.P. Les Enfants de Parents Alcooliques. (Children of
      Alcoholic Parents.) In: Alcoologie. Riom, Cedex, France:
      Riom Laboratories, 1984, pages 194-196.

1409. Deschamps, J.P., Pertuy, J., Delorme, M.F., and Barrucand, D.
Relations Entre un Centre d'examens de Sante et un Centre
d'Hygiene Alimentaire. (Relationship Between a Medical
Examination Center and a Nutritional Hygiene Center.)
Bulletin de La Societe Francaise d'Alcoologie, 4(3):
72-75, 1982.

1410. Descombey, J.P., Moury, R. and Lerebouillet, L. Les Alcooliques
et la Psychiatrie. (Alcoholics and Psychiatry). La Revue
de L'Alcoolisme, Paris, 18(1): 37-48, 1972.

1411. Deshaies, G. L'Alcoolisme Hereditaire. (Hereditary Alcoholism.)
Encephale, Paris, 34(2): 446-468, 1941.

1412. Deshaies, G. Les Problemes Psychologiques de la Femme de
L'alcoolique. (The Psychological Problems of the Alcoholic's
Wife.) Vie Medicale, Paris, 46: 1731-1736, 1965.

1413. Despotovic, A. Alkoholizam, Narkomaniji i Porodica. (Alcoholism, Drug
Addictions and the Family.) Anali Zavoda za Mentalno Zdravje,
Beograd, 6(2-3): 191-202, 1974. (Also in: Journal of Studies
on Alcohol, 37(10): 1456, 1976.)

1414. Desrosiers, Norman A. The Psychiatric Treatment of Alcoholism.
Journal of the South Carolina Medical Association, 76(2):
53-57, 1980.

1415. Deutsch, C. Children of Alcoholics: Understanding and Helping.
Hollywood, FL: Health Communications, 1983.

1416. Deutsch, C. Planning Community-based Services. Focus on Alcohol
and Drug Issues, 6(2): 5-7, 1983.

1417. Deutsch, C., DiCicco, L. and Mills, D. Reaching Children from
Families with Alcoholism: Some Innovative Techniques.
Paper presented at the Twenty-Ninth Annual Meeting of the
Alcohol and Drug Problems Association of North America,
Seattle, September, 1978, pages 54-58.

1418. Deutsch, C., DiCicco, L., and Mills, D.J. Services for Children
of Alcoholic Parents. In: Prevention, Intervention and
Treatment: Concerns and Models. Washington, D.C.: U.S.
Government Printing Office, 1982, pages 147-174.

1419. Deutsch, Charles. Broken Bottles, Broken Dreams: Understanding and
Helping the Children of Alcoholics. New York: Teachers
College Press, 1982.

1420. Deutsch, Charles. Understanding and Helping Children of Alcoholics.
In: Changing Legacies: Growing Up in an Alcoholic Home.
Pompano Beach, FL: Health Communications, 1984, pages 43-52.

1421. De-Vanna, M. Struttura e Dinamica Familiare Negli Alcoolisti,
con Elaborazione Elettronica Dei Dati: nota Preventiva.
(Structure and Dynamics of Families of Alcoholics: With a
Preliminary Report on the Electronic Processing of Data.)
Minerva Psichiatrica e Psicologica, Turin, 15: 72-102, 1974.

1422. DeVanna, M. and Fracasso, G. Il Rischio Di Morbilita Specifico
in Figli Di Psicotici Alcoolisti: Inchiesta Su 4,725 Probandi.
(The Risk of Specific Morbidity in Children of Alcoholic
Psychotics: Inquiry of 4,725 Subjects.) Minerva Psichiatrica,
Torino, 20(3): 165-168, 1979.

1423. DeVanna, M. and Malannino, S. Suicide Among Alcoholics. Minerva
Psichiatrica, Torino, 21(1): 1-6, 1980.

1424. Devereaux, M.M. and Spain, J.L. Jr. Case Studies: Learning from
      the Recovering Co-Alcoholic. Paper presented at the 8th Annual
      Meeting of the Association of Labor-Management Administrators
      and Consultants on Alcoholism, Detroit, October, 1979. (Also in:
      ALMACA. Compiled by Marcia Moran-Sackett, pages 103-116.)

1425. DeVito, R.A., Flaherty, L.A. and Mozdzierz, G.J. New Dimensions
      in the Treatment of Alcoholism. Illinois Medical Journal,
      135: 389-392, 1969.

1426. Devrient, Pierre and Lolli, Giorgio. Choice of Alcoholic
      Beverage among 240 Alcoholics in Switzerland. Quarterly
      Journal of Studies on Alcohol, 23: 459-467, 1962.

1427. Dewhurst, K. Personality Disorder in Huntington's Disease.
      Psychiatrica Clinica, 3(4): 221-229, 1970.

1428. Dewhurst, K. and McKnight, A.L. Psychiatric Aspects of Mental
      Health Legislation. Medicine Science and the Law, 9(3):
      183-187, 1969.

1429. Dewitt, Karen. New York Times, 13 February 1978, p. 16, col. 3.
      (Increase in Hispanic-Population and Rising Problems of
      Family Disintegration, Alcohlism, and Child and Wife Abuse.)

1430. Dhadphale, M. and Acuda, S.W. Attitude of Private Practitioners
      in Nairobi Towards Alcoholism and Alcohol-Related Problems.
      East African Medical Journal, 62(1): 32-37, 1985.

1431. Diaz, P. and Slotwinski, J. Helping Children to Help Themselves.
      Focus on Family and Chemical Dependency, 7(2): 36-37, 1984.

1432. Dibartolomeo, Joseph John. A Descriptive Study of the Problem
      Drinking Behavior Among Spanish-Speaking Youth of Puerto
      Rican Heritage. Doctoral Dissertation. (University
      Microfilms No. 81-16468.) Adelphi: University of Maryland, 1980.

1433. DiCicco, Lena. Children of Alcoholic Parents: Issues in
      Identification. Paper presented to the NIAAA, Silver Spring,
      MD. September, 1979. (Also in: Services for Children of
      Alcoholics, NIAAA Research Monograph No. 4. Washington, DC:
      U.S. Government Printing Office, 1981, pages 44-59.

1434. DiCicco, Lena, Biron, Ronald, Carifio, James, Deutsch, Charles,
      Mills, Dixie J., Orenstein, Alan, Re, Andrea, Unterberger,
      Hilma and White, Robert E. Evaluation of the Caspar
      Alcohol Education Curriculum. Journal of Studies on
      Alcohol, 45(2): 160-169, 1984.

1435. DiCicco, Lena, Davis, Ruth B., Hogan, James, MacLean, Annette
      and Orenstein, Alan. Group Experiences for Children of
      Alcoholics. Alcohol Health and Research World, 8(4):
      20-24, 37, 1984.

1436. DiCicco, Lena, Davis, Ruth B. and Orenstein, Alan. Identifying
      the Children of Alcoholic Parents from Survey Responses.
      Journal of Alcohol and Drug Education, 30(1): 1-17, 1984.

1437. DiCicco, Lena, Davis, Ruth B., Travis, Joseph and Orenstein, Alan.
      Recruiting Children From Alcoholic Families into a Peer
      Education Program. Alcohol Health and Research World, 8(2):
      28-34, 1984.

1438. DiCicco, Lena, Unterberger, Hilma and Mack, John E. Confronting
      Denial: An Alcoholism Intervention Strategy. Psychiatric
      Annals, 8(11): 54-64, 1978.

1439. DiCicco-Bloom, Barbara, Space, Sharon and Zahourek, Rothlyn P.
The Homebound Alcoholic. _American Journal of Nursing_,
February, 167-169, 1986.

1440. Dickson, M. Involvement of the Spouse in the Treatment of the
Alcoholic. _Nursing Mirror and Midwives Journal_, London,
_139_(4): 77-79, 1974.

1441. DiClemente, Carlo C. and Gordon, Jack R. Aging, Alcoholism, and
Addictive Behavior Change: Diagnostic Treatment Models. In:
_Aging Volume 25: Alcoholism in the Elderly: Social and Bio-
medical Issues_. Eds. James T. Hartford and T. Samorajski.
New York: Raven Press, 1984, Pages 263-275.

1442. Dida, Ali. Socioloski Aspekti Alkoholizma S Posebnim Osvrtom
Na Alkoholizam Maloletnih Migranata. (Social Aspect of
Alcoholism with Special Review of Alcoholism Between Under
Age Migrants. _Revija Za Socijologiju_, Zagreb, _5_(3):
37-45, 1975.

1443. Diehm, A.P. Alcohol, Drugs and Adolescents. _Australian Journal
of Alcoholism and Drug Dependence_, _6_: 52-58, 1979.

1444. Diesenhaus, Herman. Current Trends in Treatment Programming
for Problem Drinkers and Alcoholics. In: _Prevention,
Intervention and Treatment: Concerns and Models_.
Washington, DC: U.S. Government Printing Office, 1982,
pages 219-290.

1445. Dietrich, H. and Herle, L. Uber Alter, Sozialschicht, Mobilitat
und Wohnort Chronischer Alkoholiker. (On Age, Social Status,
Mobility and Place of Residence of Chronic Alcoholics.)
Kolner Zeitschrift fur Soziologie und Sozial-Psychologie,
_15_: 277-294, 1963.

1446. Diffendale, David C. Correlates of Continuation in Aftercare
Following Inpatient Treatment of Alcoholics. _Dissertation
Abstracts International_, _36_: 1428B, 1975.

1447. _Dilemma of the Alcoholic Marriage_. New York: Al-Anon Family
Group Headquarters, 1971.

1448. Diller, Julie. The Psychological Autopsy in Equivocal Deaths.
Perspectives in Psychiatric Care, _17_(4): 156-161, 1979.

1449. Dimensions of Alcoholism Treatment: Special Issue of Social Casework.
New York: Family Service Association of America, 1978.

1450. Dimitrijevic, D.T. Alkoholizam Roditelja u Patogenezi Decijih
Neuroza. (Alcoholism of the Parents in the Pathogenesis of
Neuroses in Children.) _Medicinski Archiv_, Sarajevo, _12_(1):
81-85, 1958.

1451. Dimitrov, K.H.R. and Aleksiev, A. Nyakoi Semeyni Vliyaniya
Osobenosti i Klinichni Proyavi Pri Narkomanite (Alkoholisum i
Morfinisium). (On Some Family Influences, Personality
Characteristics and Clinical Aspects in Narcomania [Alcoholism
and Morphine Addiction].) _Nevrologia, Psikhiatria i
Nevrokhirurgia_, Sofia, _8_(6): 432-440, 1969.

1452. Dinaburg, Daniel, Glick, Ira D. and Feigenbaum, Elliot. Marital
Therapy of Women Alcoholics. _Journal of Studies on
Alcohol_, _38_(7): 1247-1258, 1977.

1453. DiNapoli, R.J. Marital Interactions of Alcoholic Couples and
Non-Alcoholic, Non-Conflicted Couples: A Comparative Study.
MA: Boston University School of Education. _Dissertation
Abstract International_, _44_(5): 1384A, 1983.

1454. Discussion -- Question, Answer, and Comment Period. Presented at
      the National Institute on Drug Abuse, Program for Women's
      Concerns, Miami Beach, October, 1975. (Also in: Drugs
      Alcohol and Women. Ed. M. Nellis. Washington, DC: National
      Research and Communications Associates. Inc., 1976, pages 55-60.)

1455. Dishion, Thomas J. and Loeber, Rolf. Adolescent Marijuana and Alcohol
      Use: The Role of Parents and Peers Revisited. American Journal
      of Drug and Alcohol Abuse, 11(1-2): 11-25, 1985.

1456. District's Outpatient Clinic for Alcoholics. Washington, DC:
      Adams Mill Alcoholism Center, no date.

1457. Dittrich, Joan E. and Trapold, Milton A. Wives of Alcoholics:
      A Treatment Program and Outcome Study, 1983. (Eric Document
      No. ED234318.)

1458. Ditzler, J. Alcoholism: A Family Illness. Nursing Times,
      London, 76(25): 1103-1105, 1980.

1459. Divine, T. Infantile Mortality and Alcohol. Medical Temperance
      Review, 9: 264-270, 1906.

1460. Dixon, Katharine N., Arnold, L. Eugene and Calestro, Kenneth.
      Father-Son Incest: Underreported Psychiatric Problem?
      American Journal of Psychiatry, 135(7): 835-838, 1978.

1461. Dixon, Tom. Enabling: The No-Win Game of Addiction. EAP Digest,
      5(6): 40-45, 1985.

1462. Dixon, William T. Current Alcohol Treatment in Minnesota.
      A Visit to Minneapolis. Maryland State Medical Journal,
      25(11): 74-75, 1976.

1463. Djukanovic, B. Porodica i Alkoholizam. (Alcoholism and the
      Family.) Alkoholizam, Beograd, 16(3-4): 83-108, 1976.

1464. Djukanovic, B., Fridman, V., Milosavljevic, V., Vasev, C. and
      Ljububratic, D. Les Familles Parentales des Alcooliques et de
      Leuirs Epouses. (Family History of Alcoholics and Their
      Spouses.) La Revue De L' Alcoolisme, 24(4): 245-250, 1978.

1465. Djukanovic, B., Milosavcevic, V. and Drakic, S. Poremecaji
      Navika i Ponasanja Dece iz Porodica Alkoholicara. (Habit
      and Behavior Disorders of Children from Alcoholic Families.)
      Alkoholizam, Beograd, 19(1-2): 19-30, 1979.

1466. Djukanovic, B., Milosavcevic, V. and Jovanovic, R. Drustveni
      Zivot Alkoholicara i Njihovih Supruga. (The Social Life
      of Alcoholics and Their Wives.) Alkoholizam, Beograd,
      16 (3-4): 67-75, 1976.

1467. Dobson, S. and Allen, K.B. Who are They? Alcoholism the National
      Magazine, 5(2): 52-53, 1984.

1468. Dodshon, Derrick. The Pathology of Marriage. Medical Journal
      of Australia, 2(1): 27-30, 1979.

1469. Dodson, Mary Elizabeth. Major Components of the Casework
      Process. In: Casework with Wives of Alcoholics.
      Eds. Pauline C. Cohen and Merton S. Krause. New York:
      Family Service Association of America, 1971, pages 47-57.

1470. Dogliani, P. and Micheletti, V. Sull'influsso Della Intossi-
      cazione Alcoolica Acute Nell'Incesto e Nella Zoofilia.
      (On the Influence of Acute Alcoholic Intoxication on Incest
      and Zoophilia.) Rivista Sperimentale di Freniatria e
      Medicina Legale Delle Alienazioni Mentali, Italy, 82:
      485-499, 1958.

1471. Dolan, J.S. All in the Family: Understanding How We Teach and
      Influence Children About Alcohol. Paper Presented at the
      Annual Meeting of the Alcohol and Drug Problems Association,
      Chicago, September 15, 1975.

1472. Dolan, Kathryn J., Tuchfeld, Barry S. and Lipton, Wendy L.
      Alcoholic Persons and Their Families: Assessing the
      Relationship of Home Environment to Recovery. Society for
      Study of Social Problems, 1853, 1982.

1473. Dolmierski, R., Walden, Galuszko K. and Nitka, J. Alcoholism
      vrs. Work Ability in Polish Merchant Marine. Roczniki
      Pomorskiej Akademii Medyczneg w Szczecinie, Supplement 10,
      95-100, 1974.

1474. Dominian, J. Management: Basic Counselling. British Medical
      Journal, 6195: 915-916, 1979.

1475. Dominian, J. Marital Pathology. A Review. Postgraduate Medical
      Journal, 48(563): 517-528, 1972.

1476. Dominian, J. Marriage and Psychiatric Illness. British Medical
      Journal, London, 2: 854-855, 1979.

1477. Donahue, Jack. A Halfway-House Program for Alcoholics. Quarterly
      Journal of Studies on Alcohol, 32(2): 468-472, 1971.

1478. Donath, G. Is the Effect of Alcohol on the Offspring a Heredity
      or a Degeneration? Gyogyaszat, 64: 828-829, 1924.

1479. Donnelly, Patrick G. Alcohol Problems and Sales in the Counties
      of Pennsylvania: A Social Area Investigation. Journal of
      Studies on Alcohol, 39(5): 848-858, 1978.

1480. Donnelly, Paul Albert. The Psychological and Sociological Factors
      that Predict Recidivism of Criminal Offenders. Doctoral
      Dissertation. (University Microfilms No. 80-24091.) Boston:
      Boston Univerisity School of Education, 1980. (Also in:
      Dissertation Abstracts International, 41(5): 1970B.)

1481. Donovan, Bruce E. A Collegiate Group for the Sons and Daughters
      of Alcoholics. Journal of the American College Health
      Association, 30(2): 83-86, 1981.

1482. Donovan, Maruth and Cutler, Robert. Volunteers Who've Been There
      Support Recovering Alcoholics. Volunteer Leader, 21(3):
      6-7, 1980.

1483. Dooley, William H. Self-Perceptions and Perceptions of Male and
      Female Parental Figures Among Alcoholics and Reconstructed
      Alcoholics. Doctoral Dissertation. (University Microfilms
      No. 73-07308.) Tempe: Arizona State University, 1973.

1484. Dordevic-Bankovic, V. and Sedmak, T. Supruge Alkoholicara i
      Njihovo Sudelovanje u Lecenju. (Alcoholic's Wives and Their
      Participation in Treatment.) In: Socijalna Psihijatrija,
      Ed. N. Persic. Zagreb: Pliva, 1971, pages 609-612.

1485. Dordevic-Bankovic, V. and Sedmak, T. Primary Family and the
      Process of Socialization of Alcohol-Sociopaths. Alcoholism,
      Zagreb, 8: 120-125, 1972.

1486. Dordevic, Milka and Dukanovic, Borislav. Uticaj Alkoholizma Na
      Emotivne Odnose U Porodici. (Impact of Alcoholism on
      Emotional Relationships in the Family.) Sociologija,
      Belgrade, 16(3-4): 473-488, 1974.

1487. Dorfman, Elaine. Content-Free Study of Marital Resemblances in
       Group Therapy. Journal of Abnormal Psychology, 73(1):
       78-80, 1968.

1488. Dorfman, Wilfred. Recognition and Management of Masked Depression
       in Clinical Practice. New York State Journal of Medicine,
       74(2): 373-375, 1974.

1489. Dorn, Nick. Standing Their Ground: Teenage Drinking and the
       Transition to Work. London: Croom Helm, 1982.

1490. Dornfeld, Clinton Alvin. Dimensions of Personality in Alcoholic
       Patients and Prediction of Treatment Outcome. Doctoral
       Dissertation. (University Microfilms No. 81-16370.) San Diego,
       CA: United States International University, 1981. (Also in:
       Dissertation Abstracts International, 42(2): 763B, 1982.)

1491. Doroff, David R. Group Psychotherapy in Alcoholism. In: Biology
       of Alcoholism, Vol. 5, Treatment and Rehabilitation of the
       Chronic Alcoholic. Eds. Benjamin Kissin and Henri Begleiter.
       New York: Plenum Press, 1977, pages 235-258.

1492. Dorsch, Graydon; Talley, Ruth; and Bynder, Herbert. Response to
       Alcoholics by the Helping Professions and Community Agencies
       in Denver. Quarterly Journal of Studies on Alcohol, 30(4):
       905-919, 1969.

1493. Do's and Dont's for the Spouses of Alcoholics. Pamphlet.
       Willmar, MN: Alcohol and Drug Dependency Services, 1971.

1494. Do's -- Dont's for the Wives of Alcoholics. Pamphlet.
       New York: National Council on Alcoholism, 1971.

1495. Doss, M., Von Tiepermann, R. and Look, D. Hereditary and
       Non-Hereditary Form of Chronic Hepatic Porphyria: Different
       Behavior of Uroporphyrinogen Decarboxylase in Liver and
       Erythrocytes. Klinische Wochenschrift, 58(24): 1347-1356,
       1980.

1496. Doucette, S.R. and McCullah, R.D. Domestic Violence: The
       Alcohol Relationship. U.S. Navy Medicine, 71: 4-8, 1980.

1497. Dougherty, Ed. Intervention Counseling. In: Alcoholism and
       the Family. Eds. Sharon Wegscheider-Cruse and Richard
       W. Esterly. Wernersville, PA: The Caron Institute, 1985,
       pages 45-48.

1498. Douglas, Donald B. Who is a Real Alcoholic? Practical Help in
       Managing Alcoholism. New York State Journal of Medicine,
       76(4): 603-607, 1976.

1499. Douglas, R. Aged Alcoholic Widows in the Nursing Home. Focus on
       Women-Journal of Addictions And Health, 1(4): 258-265, 1980.

1500. Douglass, Richard L. Opportunities for Prevention of Domestic
       Neglect and Abuse of the Elderly. Prevention in Human
       Services, 3(1): 135-150, 1983.

1501. Dourdil, F. Problematica Psicologica de la Esposa del Enfermo
       Alcoholico. (Psychological Problems of Spouses of
       Alcoholics.) Communicacion Psiquiatrica, 77(1):
       384-390, 1978.

1502. Dowling, Glenda. Houston Chronicle, 2 July 1984, Section 5,
       P. 1 Col. 2. (Blood Test for Genetic Tendency Toward
       Alcoholism.)

1503. Downey, Gregg W. Alcoholism. Modern Healthcare, 5(4):
       20-26, 1976.

1504. Downing, Robert W., Rickels, Karl, McNair, Douglas M., Lipman, Ronald S., Kahn, Richard J., Fisher, Seymour, Covi, Lino and Smith, Virginia K. Description Sample Comparison of Anxious and Depressed Groups and Attrition Rates. Psychopharmacology Bulletin, 17(3): 94-96, 1981.

1505. Downs, W.R. Alcoholism as a Developing Family Crisis. Family Relations, 31(1): 5-12, 1982.

1506. Downstate Medical Center Seeks COA's for Brain Wave Research. COA Review, 5: 8, 1983.

1507. Dowsling, J.L. Sex Therapy for Recovering Alcoholics: An Essential Part of Family Therapy. International Journal of the Addictions, 15(8): 1179-1190, 1980.

1508. Drane, R. Stephen. Drug Abuse: The Need for Professional Cooperation. Journal of the Maine Medical Association, 62(4): 83-84, 1971.

1509. Drew, L.R.H. Alcoholic Offenders in a Victorian Prison. Medical Journal of Australia, Sydney, 48(2): 575-578, 1961.

1510. Drew, L.R.H., Moon, J.R., Buchanan, F.H. and Thomas, B.B. Counseling the Family of the Alcoholic. Australian Journal of Alcoholism and Drug Dependence, 1(3): 76-78, 1974.

1511. Drewek, K.J. Inherited Drinking and its Behavioural Correlates. In: Animal Models in Alcohol Research. Eds. K. Erriksson, J.D. Sinclair, and K. Kiianmaa. Papers Presented at the International Conference on Animal Models in Alcohol Research, Helsinki, Finland, 4-8 June, 1979. New York: Academic Press, 1980, pages 35-49.

1512. Drewek, K.J. and Broadhurst, P.L. More on the Heritability of Alcohol Preference in Laboratory Mice and Rats. Behavior Genetics, 13: 123-125, 1983.

1513. Drewery, J. and Rae, J.B. A Group Comparison of Alcoholic and Non-Alcoholic Marriages Using the Interpersonal Perception Technique. British Journal of Psychiatry, 115(520): 287-300, 1969.

1514. Drewery, J. and Rae, J.B. Interpersonal Patterns in Alcoholic Marriages. British Journal of Psychiatry, 120: 615-621, 1972.

1515. Drews, Toby Rice. Getting Them Sober Volume 1. Center City, MN: Hazelden, 1980.

1516. Drews, Toby Rice. Getting Them Sober Volume 2. Center City, MN: Hazelden, no date.

1517. Drews, Toby Rice. If Your Parent is Alcoholic, Here's What To Do. Listen, 32(7): 14-16, 1979.

1518. Driscoll, Esther. Chemical Abuse Programs: Flexible Program Seen as Key. Hospitals: Journal of American Hospital Association, 48(20): 63-64, 1974.

1519. Drug Abuse. The Nova Scotia Medical Bulletin, 49(4): 102-103, 1970.

1520. Drug Abuse Prevention for Your Family. Rockville, MD: National Institute on Drug Abuse, 1977; Revised edition, 1980.

1521. Drugs and Addiction. Medical Journal of Australia, Sydney, 55-62(23): 1057-1958, 1968.

1522. Drummond, Terry. The Alcoholic and the Church: A Pastoral Response. International Journal of Offender Therapy & Comparative Criminology, 26(3): 275-280, 1982.

1523. Dubanoski, Richard A. Child Maltreatment in European and Hawaiian-Americans. Child Abuse and Neglect, 5(4): 457-465, 1981.

1524. Dube, K.C., Kumar, A., Kumar, N. and Gupta, S.P. Prevalence and Pattern of Drug Use Among College Students. Acta Psychiatrica Scandinavica, Copenhagen, 57(4): 336-356, 1978.

1525. Dublineau, J. and Angelergues, R. Sur Quelques Problemes Socio-Economiques de L'Alcoolisme. Resultats d'un Questionnaire Soumis a 200 Buveurs Internes. (On Some Socioeconomic Problems of Alcoholism. Results of a Questionnaire Submitted to 200 Interned Alcoholics.) Archives de Medecine Sociale, Paris, 6: 250-278, 1950.

1526. Dubourg, G.O. After-Care for Alcoholics -- A Follow-Up Study. British Journal of Addiction, Edinburgh, 64: 155-163, 1969.

1527. Duby, J. and Schuckit, M.A. Acute Subjective Feelings after a Single Drink of Alcohol. Alcoholism: Clinical and Experimental Research, 5: 147, 1981.

1528. Duckert, Fanny. Behavioral Analysis of the Drinking Pattern of Alcoholics--With Special Focus on Degree of Control in Various Situations. Scandinavian Journal of Behavior Therapy, 10(3): 121-133, 1981.

1529. Ducote, D. The Role of Femininity in the Recovered Alcoholic Female. Paper presented at the International Symposium on the Psychobiology of Alcoholism. Beverly Hills, January, 1983. (Also in: Substance and Alcohol Actions/Misuse, 4(2-3): 238, 1983.)

1530. Ducote, D'Ann and Koch, Alberta. Alcoholism, Sobriety, & Family Therapy. Proceedings of the National Council on Family Relations Annual Meeting Held at St. Paul, MN, October, 1983.

1531. Dudley, D.L., Roszell, D.K., Mules, J.E. and Hague, W.H. Heroin vs. Alcohol Addiction -- Quantifiable Psychosocial Similarities and Differences. Journal of Psychosomatic Research, London, 18(5): 327-335, 1974.

1532. Duester, G., Hatfield, G.W. and Smith M. Molecular Genetic Analysis of Human Alcohol Dehydrogenase. Alcohol, 2(1): 53-56, 1985.

1533. Duhamel, Thomas Roland. The Interpersonal Perceptions, Interactions, and Marital Adjustment of Hospitalized Alcoholic Males and Their Wives. Doctoral Dissertation. (University Microfilms No. 71-8010.) Amherst: University of Massachusetts, 1970.

1534. Dukanovic, B. Alkoholizam Porodica i Porodicni Odnosi; u Svetlu Jednog Istrazivanja. (Alcoholism in the Family and Family Relationships; In the Light of One Investigation.) Alkoholizam, Beograd, 12(1): 65-87, 1972.

1535. Dukanovic, B. Znacaj Porodice u Etiologiji Alkoholizma. (Importance of Family Life in the Etiology of Alcoholism.) In: Socijalna Psihijatrija. Ed. N. Persic. Zagreb: Pliva, 1971, pages 97-101.

1536. Dukanovic, B. Distribucija Uloga u Porodicama Alkoholicara. (Role Distributions in Alcoholic Families.) Alkoholizam, Beograd, 19(3-4): 100-108, 1979.

1537. Dukanovic, Borislav. Porodice I Porodicni Odnosi Kod Jedne Grupe Alkoholicara. (Family and Family Relations in One Group of Alcoholics). Sociologica, Olomuoc, 12(2): 209-226, 1970.

1538. Dukanovic, Borislav. Bracno Porodicnakriza Alkoholicara. (The Marital-Family Crisis of Alcoholics.) Socioloski Pregled, 11(2-3): 21-49, 1977.

1539. Dukanovic, Borislav. Dve Grupe Alkoholicara i Dve Vrste Alkoholizma. (Two Groups of Alcoholics and Two Kinds of Alcohlism.) Sociologija, Beograd, 20(2-3): 323-335, 1978.

1540. Dulfano, Celia. Alcoholism in the Family System. In: New Directions in Family Therapy. Ed. T. Buckley. Oceanside, NY: Dabor Science Publications, 1977, pages 77-89. (Also as: Paper presented at the National Alcoholism Forum, Milwaukee, April-May, 1975.)

1541. Dulfano, Celia. Families, Alcoholism, and Recovery: Ten Stories. Center City, MN: Hazelden Educational Services, 1982.

1542. Dulfano, Celia. Family Therapy of Alcoholism. In: Practical Approaches to Alcoholism Psychotherapy. Eds. S. Zimberg, J. Wallace and S.B. Blume. New York: Plenum, 1978, pages 119-136.

1543. Dulfano, Celia. History of a Group of Women Affected by Alcoholism. In: Alcoholism: A Modern Perspective. Ed. P. Golding. Lancaster, England: MTP Press, 1982, pages 319-331.

1544. Dulfano, Celia. The Impact of Alcoholism on Jewish Family Life. In: Alcoholism and the Jewish Community. Ed. A. Blaine. New York: Commission on Synagogue Relations, Federation Jewish Philantropies of New York, Inc., 1980, pages 231-237.

1545. Dulfano, Celia. Observations on Alcohol Problems Among Immigrants From Puerto Rico. In: Proceedings of Puerto Rican Conferences on Human Services. Editor-in-Chief, D.J. Curren, Associate Editors, J. Julian Rivera and R.B.Sanchez. Washington, DC: National Coalition of Spanish-Speaking Mental Health Organizations, 1975, pages 103-106.

1546. Dulfano, Celia. Recovery: Rebuilding the Family. Alcoholism: The National Magazine, 1(3): 33-36, 1981.

1547. Dul'nev, V.D. K Voprosu o Roli Alkogolizma Ottsa v Etiologii Umstvennoi Nedostatochnosti u Potomstva. (On the Role of Paternal Alcoholism in the Etiology of Mental Deficiency in Offspring.) Pediatriya, 44(1): 68-69, 1965.

1548. Dumont, Matthew P. Is Mental Health Possible Under Our Economic System? No. Psychiatric Opinion, 14(3): 9-11, 32-33, 44-45, 1977.

1549. Dun, E. My Experience in Working with Substance Abuse in the United Kingdom. Paper presented at the Second Pan Pacific Conference on Drugs and Alcohol. Hong Kong: November - December, 1983.

1550. Dunlop, J., Skorney, B. and Polefka, D. Family Involvement in the Treatment of Older Alcoholics. Paper Presented at National Council on Alcoholism. New Orleans, April, 1981.

1551. Dunlop, Jean, Skorney, Barbara and Hamilton, James. Group Treatment for Elderly Alcoholics and Their Families. In: Social Groupwork and Alcoholism. Eds. Marjorie Altman and Ruth Crocker. New York: Haworth Press, 1982, pages 87-92.

1552. Dunn, M.M., Buckwalter, K.C., Weinstein, L.B. and Palti, H. Spousal
      Concordance for High-Rish Behaviors Among Expectant Parents in
      Jerusalem. Family and Community Health, 8(3): 83-87, 1985.

1553. Dunn, N.J. Patterns of Alcohol Abuse and Marital Stabilty.
      Doctoral Dissertation. (University Microfilms No. 85-04402.)
      Pittsburgh: University of Pittsburgh, 1985. (Also in:
      Dissertation Abstracts International, 43(12): 3935B, 1981.)

1554. Dunn, Robert B. and Hedberg, Allan G. Treating the Two Faces
      of Alcoholism: A Medical-Behavioral Approach. Asian Journal
      of Modern Medicine, Hong Kong, 10(8): 282-287, 1974.

1555. Dunner, D.L. and Fieve, R.R. Psychiatric Illness in Fathers of
      Men With Bipolar Primary Affective Disorder. Archives of
      General Psychiatry, 32(9): 1134-1137, 1975.

1556. Dunner, D.L., Fleiss, J.L., Addonizio, G. and Fieve, R.R.
      Assortative Mating in Primary Affective Disorder.
      Biological Psychiatry, 11(1): 43-51, 1976.

1557. Dunner, D.L., Hensel, B.M. and Fieve, R.R. Bipolar Illness:
      Factors in Drinking Behavior. American Journal of
      Psychiatry, 136: 583-585, 1979.

1558. Dunner, David L. The Implication of Family History in Depression.
      Continuing Medical Education: Syllabus and Proceedings
      in Summary Form. Washington, D.C.: American Psychiatric
      Association, 1971.

1559. Dunovsky, J. and Sucha, M. Social Conditions of Children in
      Weekly and Residential Nurseries in Czechoslovakia.
      Social Science & Medicine, Oxford, 7(4): 267-279, 1973.

1560. DuPont, Robert L. Getting Tough on Gateway Drugs. Center City,
      MN: Hazelden, no date.

1561. DuPont, Robert L. New Perceptions. Paper presented at the National
      Institute on Drug Abuse, Program for Women's Concerns, Miami
      Beach, October, 1975. (Also in: Drugs, Alcohol and Women; A
      National Forum Source Book. Ed. M. Nellis. Washington, DC:
      National Research and Communications Associates, Inc., 1976,
      pages 7-13.

1562. DuPont, Robert L. Parents and Kids: Kids Can Be Kids Only If
      Parents are Parents. In: Getting Tough on Gateway Drugs:
      A Guide for the Family. Ed. Robert Dupont. Washington, D.C.:
      American Psychiatric Press, 1984, pages 181-236.

1563. Dupree, R. and Rodriquez, T. Challenge: Minorites Alcoholism,
      and Programs in Topeka, Kansas. In: El Uso De Alcohol;
      A Resource Book For Spanish Speaking Communites. Atlanta:
      Southern Area Alcohol Education and Training Program, Inc., 1977.

1564. Dupuis, C., Dehaene, P., Deroubaix-Tella, P., Blanc-Garin, A.P.,
      Rey, C. and Carpentier-Courault, C. Les Cardiopathies des
      Infants nes de Mere Alcoholique. (Cardiopathy in Children
      Born of Alcoholic Mothers.) Archives des Maladies du Coeur
      et des Vaisseaux, Paris, 71: 565-572, 1978.

1565. Durig, K. Robert. Group Counseling Project in Clark County,
      Indiana. Jeffersonville, IN: Indiana University (Southeast),
      no date.

1566. DuToit, A.E., Johnson S. and Coster, M.E. Functions of a Health
      Centre. South African Medical Journal, 45(12): 307-319,
      1971.

1567. Dvoskin, Joel Alan. Battered Women -- An Epidemiological Study
       of Spousal Violence. Doctoral Dissertation. (University
       Microfilms No. 81-26175.) Tuscon: The University of Arizona,
       1981. (Also in: Dissertation Abstracts International,
       42(6): 2525B, 1981.)

1568. Dwinell, L. Working Through Grief: The Essential Elements.
       Focus on Family and Chemical Dependency, 8(3): 18-19, 1985.

1569. Dymek, Danuta. Wplyw Domu Rodzinnego na Proces Wykolejania Sie
       Dzieci i Mlodziezy. (Influence of Family Home on the Process
       of Children and Juveniles Going Astray.) Przeglad
       Socjologiczny, 29: 249-273, 1977.

E

1570. Earls, Felton. Parenting in Urban America. Journal of the National Medical Association, 73(2): 99-100, 1981.

1571. Eberle, Patricia A. Alcohol Abusers and Non-Users: A Discriminant Analysis of Differences Between Two Subgroups of Batterers. Journal of Health and Social Behavior, 23(3): 260-271, 1982.

1572. Eccles, W.M. Alcohol as a Factor in the Causation of Deterioration in the Individual and the Race. British Journal of Inebriety, 2: 146-155, 1905.

1573. Eccles, W.M. Alcohol as Affecting Wages and Infantile Mortality. Medical Temperance Review, 11: 91-94, 1908.

1574. Eckardt, Michael J., Harford, Thomas C., Kaelber, Charles T., Parker, Elizabeth S., Rosenthal, Laura S., Ryback, Ralph S., Salmoiraghi, Gian C., Vanderveen, Ernestine and Warren, Kenneth R. Health Hazards Associated with Alcohol Consumption. Journal of the American Medical Association, 246(6): 648-666, 1981.

1575. Ecke, Shirley Ann. The Role of the Significant Other in Alcoholism. Doctoral Dissertation. (University Microfilms No. 8023573.) San Diego, CA: United States International University, 1980. (Also in: Dissertation Abstracts International, 41(4): 1499-1500B, 1980.)

1576. Eckerd, Marcia Bogdanoff. Psychiatric Illness in the Families of Patients With DSM III Antisocial Personality Disorder. Doctoral Dissertation. (University Microfilms No. 83-02495.) New York: City University of New York, 1982. (Also in: Dissertation Abstracts International, 43(9): 3026B, 1982.)

1577. Edelbrock, Craig. Running Away From Home: Incidence and Correlates Among Children and Youth Referred for Mental Health Services. Journal of Family Issues, 1(2): 210-228, 1980.

1578. Edmunds, Evelyn P. Outline-Alphabet of 26 Marital Problems and Techniques for Dealing With Them. 1974. (Eric Document Number ED141709.)

1579. Edmundson, W.F., Davies, J.E., Acker, J.D. and Myer, B. Patterns of Drug Abuse Epidemiology in Prisoners. Industrial Medicine, 41(1): 15-19, 1972.

1580. Educating Young People About Drugs. (Notes and News.) WHO (World Health Organization) Chronicle, 30: 208-209, 1976.

1581. Edwards, Carolyn. The Relationship Between Driving Behavior and
       Behavioral and Personal Characteristics of Problem Drinkers.
       Doctoral Dissertation. (University Microfilms No. 82-16921.)
       San Diego, CA: United States International University, 1982.
       (Also in: Dissertation Abstracts International, 43(3): 851B,
       1982.)

1582. Edwards, D.W. and Letman, S.T. Alcoholism in the Urban Community.
       Chicago, IL: Loyola University, 1982.

1583. Edwards, Dan W. Spouse Participation in the Treatment of
       Alcoholism: Completion of Treatment and Recidivism.
       In: Social Groupwork and Alcoholism. Eds. Marjorie
       Altman and Ruth Crocker. New York: Haworth Press, 1982,
       pages 41-48.

1584. Edwards, G. Review of Alcohol and the Family, by J. Orford and
       J. Harwin. British Journal of Addiction, 77(4): 439, 1982.

1585. Edwards, G. Review of Drinking Problems, Family Problems, by
       M.L. Meyer. British Journal of Addiction, 78(1): 105, 1983.

1586. Edwards, G. A Doubtful Prognosis. International Journal of
       Psychiatry, 9: 354-358, 1970-71.

1587. Edwards, G. The Meaning and Treatment of Alcohol Dependence.
       British Journal of Psychiatry, Special Publication, 9:
       239-251, 1975.

1588. Edwards, G., Fisher, M.K., Hawker, A. and Hensman, C. Clients of
       Alcoholism Information Centres. British Medical Journal,
       London, 4(575): 346-349, 1967.

1589. Edwards, G. and Orford J. Management of Alcoholism. The Lancet,
       London, 2(8050): 1233-1234, 1977.

1590. Edwards, G. and Orford, Jim. A Plain Treatment for Alcoholism.
       Proceedings of the Royal Society of Medicine, London,
       70(5): 344-348, 1977.

1591. Edwards, Griffith. Alternative Strategies for Minimizing Alcohol
       Problems; Coming Out of the Doldrums. The Journal of
       Alcoholism, London, 10: 45-66, 1975.

1592. Edwards, Griffith. A Community as Case Study: Alcoholism Treatment
       in Antiquity and Utopia. In: Proceedings of the Second Annual
       Alcoholism Conference of the NIAAA. Ed. Morris Chafetz.
       Rockville, MD: National Institute on Alcohol Abuse and
       Alcoholism, 1973, pages 116-136.

1593. Edwards, Griffith, Chandler, Jane and Hensman, Celia. Drinking in a
       London Suburb. 1. Correlates of Normal Drinking. Quarterly
       Journal of Studies on Alcohol, (Supplement 6): 69-93, 1972.

1594. Edwards, Griffith, Duckitt, Anita, Oppenheimer, Edna, Sheehan,
       Margaret and Taylor, Colin. What Happens to Alcoholics?
       The Lancet, London, 2(8344): 269-271, 1983.

1595. Edwards, Griffith and Grant, Marcus. Alcoholism: New Knowledge
       and New Responses. London: Croom Helm, 1977.

1596. Edwards, Griffith, Hawker, A., Williamson, V. and Hensman, C.
       London's Skid Row. The Lancet, London, 1: 249-252, 1966.

1597. Edwards, Griffith, Orford, Jim, Egert, S., Guthrie, S., Hawker, A.,
       Hensman, C., Mitcheson, M., Oppenheimer, E. and Taylor, C.
       Alcoholism; A Controlled Trial of "Treatment" and "Advice."
       Journal of Studies on Alcohol, 38: 1004-1031, 1977.

1598. Edwards, J.E. and Whitlock, F.A. Suicide and Attempted Suicide
      in Brisbane. 1. The Medical Journal of Australia, Sydney,
      1(22): 932-938, 1968.

1599. Edwards, J.E. and Whitlock, F.A. Suicide and Attempted Suicide
      in Brisbane. 2. The Medical Journal of Australia, Sydney,
      1(23): 989-995, 1968.

1600. Edwards, Patricia, Harvey, Cheryl and Whitehead, Paul C. Wives
      of Alcoholics: A Critical Review and Analysis. Quarterly
      Journal of Studies on Alcohol, 34(1): 112-132, 1973.

1601. Edwards, W.N. The Influence of Parental Alcoholism on the
      Physique and Ability of the Offspring. A Bibliography of
      the Controversy Between Professor Karl Pearson and His
      Critics. National Temperance Quarterly, London, 2:
      233-240, 1911.

1602. Edwing, J.A. and Fox, R.E. Family Therapy in Alcoholism.
      In: Current Psychiatric Therapies, 8: 86-91, 1968.

1603. Eels, M.A.W. Multigenerational Transmission of Alcoholism: Using the
      Concept in Clinical Practice With Families. Paper presented at
      the Third Annual National Conference for Nurse Educators on Alcohol
      and Drug Abuse, Washington, D.C., May, 1983. (Also in: Current
      Issues in Alcohol and Drug Abuse Nursing: Research, Education,
      and Clinical Practice, pages 222-224.)

1604. The Effect of Alcohol on Feelings. COA Review, 4: 8, 1983.

1605. Effects of Drinking on Marriage Stressed. NIAAA Information and
      Feature Service, (IFS No. 44): 3, January 17, 1978.

1606. Egger, Garry J., Webb, R.A.J. and Reynolds, Ingrid. Early
      Adolescent Antecedents of Narcotic Abuse. The International
      Journal of the Addictions, 13(5): 773-781, 1978.

1607. Ehline, D. and Tighe, P.O. Alcoholism: Early Identification and
      Intervention in the Social Service Agency. Child Welfare,
      56: 584-592, 1977.

1608. Ehrmann, G. Der "Morbus Pringle," Eine Scheinbar Benigne
      Missbildung Als Ausdruck Einer Anlagegebundenen Schadigung Des
      Ektodermen Keimblattes. ("Morbus Pringle, a Benign Malformation
      as Expression of Blastophthoria of the Ectodermal Germinal Layer.)
      Wiener Medizinische Wochenschrift, Wien, 104: 697-698, 1954.

1609. Eiduson, Samuel and Groshong, Regina. Effect of Maternal Alcohol
      Ingestion on Developing Rat Brain MAO. In: Biological Genetic
      Factors in Alcoholism. (NIAAA Research Monograph No. 9.)
      Eds. Victor M. Hesselbrock, Edward G. Shaskan and Roger E. Meyer.
      Washington, D.C.: U.S. Government Printing Office, 1983.

1610. Eilryyr, J.-A.L. Family Socialization and High School Social Climate
      Effects on Adolescent Alcohol and Marijuana Use. Doctoral
      Dissertation. (University Microfilms No. 78-12895.) University
      of Maryland, 1977.

1611. Eimerl, T.S. General Practice in New Zealand Today. The New
      Zealand Medical Journal, Dunedin, 68(434): 9-20, 1968.

1612. Einstein, Stanley and Quinones, Mark A. Drugs as a Smoke Screen.
      Drug Forum, 1(2): 99-100, 1972.

1613. Eisenberg, M. Michael. How to Recognize the Ulcer-Prone Patient.
      Behavioral Medicine, 7(2): 26-32, 1980.

1614. Eisler, Richard M., Miller, Peter M. and Hersen, Michel. Effects
       of Assertive Training on Marital Interaction. Archives of
       General Psychiatry, 30: 643-649, 1974.

1615. Eisterhold, M.J., Murphy, P., Beneke, W. and Scott, G. Multiple-
       Drug Use Among High School Students. Psychological Reports,
       44: 1099-1106, 1979.

1616. Ekberg, Linda L. Outpatient Support Groups: Their Role in
       Recovery from Alcoholism. In: Perspectives on Treatment
       of Alcoholism. Eds. M.J. Goby and J.E. Keller, 1978,
       pages 97-101.

1617. Ekenstein, G. and Larsson, G. Institutional Care of Infants
       in Sweden; Criteria for Admission in 1970, 1975 and 1980.
       Child Abuse and Neglect, 7(1): 11-16, 1983.

1618. Eklund, L. and Nylander, I. Risken For Aterfall I Fylleri Bland
       Stockholmspojkar. (Risk of Repeated Intoxication in Stockholm
       Boys.) Social-Medicinsk Tidskrift, 42: 201-205, 1965.

1619. Eldar, P. An Israeli Experiment in the Treatment of Alcoholism.
       Ed. A. Lavine. Jerusalem: State of Israel, Ministry of
       Social Welfare, Department of International Relations, 1976.

1620. Elder, G.H. Porphyria Cutanea Tarda and Hla-Linked Hemochromatosis.
       Gastroenterology, 88(5-1): 1276-1279, 1985.

1621. Elderton, E.M. and Pearson, K. First Study of Influence of Parental
       Alcoholism on Physique and Ability of Offspring. Eugenics
       Laboratory Memoirs, London, 10: 1-46, 1910.

1622. Electroencephalograph Readings May Spot Men With a Genetic
       Predisposition to Alcoholism, According to HJ Neville of
       Salk Inst. Medical World. Issue 11/22/82, pages 38 and 40.

1623. Elejalde, B.R. Marihuana and Genetic Studies on Columbia: The
       Problem in the City and in the Country. In: Cannabis and
       Culture. Ed. Vera Rubin. The Hague, Paris: Mouton
       Publishers, 1975, pages 327-343.

1624. de Elejalde, Fernando. Inadequate Mothering: Patterns and Treatment.
       Bulletin of the Menninger Clinic, 35(3): 182-198, 1971.

1625. El-Guebaly, Nady. Children of Alcoholics. Paper presented at the
       11th Annual Conference: Canadian Foundation on Alcohol & Drug
       Dependencies, Toronto, June, 1976. (Also as: Paper presented
       at the Alcohol and Aquatics Symposium, Winnipeg, May, 1977,
       pages 35-36.)

1626. El-Guebaly, Nady. The Offspring of Alcoholics: Outcome
       Predictors. In: Children of Exceptional Parents.
       Ed. Mary Frank. New York: Haworth Press, 1983, pages 3-12.
       (Also in: Journal of Children in Contemporary Society,
       15(1): 3-12, 1982.)

1627. El-Guebaly, Nady and Offord, David R. The Offspring of Alcoholics:
       A Critical Review. American Journal of Psychiatry, 134(4):
       357-365, 1977.

1628. El-Guebaly, Nady and Offord, David R. On Being the Offspring
       of an Alcoholic: An Update. Alcoholism: Clinical and
       Experimental Research, 3: 148-157, 1979.

1629. El-Guebaly, Nady, Offord, David R., Sullivan, K.T. and Lynch, G.W.
       Psychosocial Adjustment of the Offspring of Psychiatric
       Inpatients: The Effect of Alcoholic, Depressive and
       Schizophrenic Parentage. Canadian Psychiatric Association
       Journal, Ottawa, 23: 281-290, 1978.

1630. Elkin, Michael. Families Under the Influence: Changing Alcoholic Patterns. New York: W.W. Norton & Co., 1984.

1631. Ellekjaer, Erik F. and Andersen, Lund Bjorg M. Social Conditions and Use of Drugs in a Group of Young Addicts in Oslo. Tidsskrift for den Norske Laegeforening, Oslo, 93(28): 2081-2086, 1973.

1632. Ellermann, M. Social and Clinical Features of Chronic Alcoholism. (Based on a Study of 231 Male Patients.) Journal of Nervous and Mental Disease, 107: 556-568, 1948.

1633. Elliott, David J. and Johnson, Norbert. Fetal Alcohol Syndrome: Implications and Counseling Considerations. Personnel and Guidance Journal, 62(2): 67-69, 1983.

1634. Elliott, Juanita J. What You Should Know About Alcoholism. Family Coordinator, 25(3): 323-324, 1976.

1635. Elliott, William J. Intemperance and the N.S.P.C.C. British Journal of Inebriety, 26: 226-228, 1929.

1636. Ellis, B.G. Drug Abuse from the Family Perspective: Coping is a Family Affair. Rockville, MD: National Institute on Drug Abuse, 1980.

1637. Ellis, Barbara Gray (Ed.). Perspectives on Family Research. Report of a Workshop. 1982. (Eric Document Number ED234290.)

1638. Ellis, Barbara Gray. Report of a Workshop on Reinforcing the Family System as the Major Resource in the Primary Prevention of Drug Abuse. In: Drug Abuse from the Family Perspective. Ed. B.G. Ellis. Washington, D.C.: U.S. Government Printing Office, 1980, pages 127-140.

1639. Ellis, D.C. Parents As Participants, Potential Agents of Change: Treatment for Adolescent Chemical Dependency. Focus on Family and Chemical Dependency, 7(5): 13-15, 37-38, 1984.

1640. Ellis, Godfrey J. and Stone, Lorene H. Marijuana Use in College: An Evaluation of a Modeling Explanation. Youth and Society, 10(4): 323-334, 1979.

1641. Ellwood, L.C. Effects of Alcoholism as a Family Illness on Child Behavior and Development. Military Medicine, 145: 188-192, 1980.

1642. Elmasian, R., Neville, H., Woods, D., Schuckit, Marc A. and Bloom, F. Event-Related Brain Potentials are Different in Individuals at High and Low Risk for Developing Alcoholism. Proceedings of the National Academy of Sciences of the United States of America, 79(241): 7900-7903, 1982.

1643. Elton, Martin and Hornquist, Jan Olof. Grounds for Disability Pension. The Younger Abuser as Compared with Older Abusers of Alcohol. Scandinavian Journal of Social Medicine, 11(2): 53-58, 1983.

1644. Emerson, Charles D. Family Violence: A Study by the Los Angeles County Sheriff's Department. Police Chief, 46(6): 48-50, 1979.

1645. Emrick, C.D. A Review of Psychologically Oriented Treatment of Alcoholism. I. The Use and Interrelationships of Outcome Criteria and Drinking Behavior Following Treatment. Quarterly Journal of Studies on Alcohol, 35: 523-549, 1974.

1646. Emslie, Graham J. and Rosenfeld, Alvin. Incest Reported by Children
       and Adolescents Hospitalized for Severe Psychiatric Problems.
       American Journal of Psychiatry, 140(6): 708-711, 1983.

1647. Encel, S., Kotowicz, K.C. and Resler, H.E. Drinking Practices
       and Attitudes in an Australian Metropolitan Area. Social
       Science and Medicine, Oxford, 5(5): 469-482, 1971.

1648. Engage/Social Action Forum. Preventing Chemical Dependency:
       The Family Role. E/SA, 10: 9-40, 1982.

1649. Engel, Margaret. Washington Post, 24 February 1983, sec. 1, p. 1,
       col. 2. (Increase of Battered Women, Child Abuse, and
       Alcoholism Due to Financial Pressures.)

1650. Engelbrecht, G.K. Alcohol as a Possible Variable in Suicide.
       Humanitas: Journal for Research in the Human Sciences,
       Pretoria, 9(1): 61-68, 1983.

1651. Engeset, A. and Idsoe, R. Alkoholmisbrukeres Foreldre og
       Brode. Sammenhenqen Mellom Foreldrenes Alkoholvaner oq
       Alkoholmisbruk Blant Sonnene. (Misuse of Alcohol in Parents
       and Brothers. Connection Between the Drinking Habits of
       Parents and the Incidence of Alcohol Misuse Among Their
       Sons.) Quarterly Journal of Studies on Alcohol, 20(3):
       684, 1959.

1652. Ennis, J. Self-harm: Part 2. Deliberate Nonfatal Self-Harm.
       Canadian Medical Association Journal, Ottawa, 129(2):
       121-125, 1983.

1653. Enslein, K. and Rose, C.L. Computer Based Analysis in Longevity
       Research. Computers and Biomedical Research, 3(4):
       289-329, 1970.

1654. Ensminger, Margaret E., Brown, C. Hendricks and Kellam, Sheppard G.
       Sex Differences in Antecedents of Substance Use Among Adolescents.
       Journal of Social Issues, 38(2): 25-42, 1982.

1655. Entin, G.M. and Novak, V.M. Reabilitatsiya Bol'nykh Alkogolizmom
       Putem Sozdaniya Ustoichivykh Psikhoterapevticheskikh Kollektivov.
       (Rehabilitation of Alcoholics Through Long-Term Psychotherapeutic
       Groups. Trudy Leningradskogo Psykhonevrologicheskoi Instituta,
       Bekhtereva, 84: 44-50, 1977.

1656. Erikson, Robert C. and Carducci, Judith. Assertiveness Training
       Interventions and the Alcoholic Family System. Brecksville, OH:
       Cleveland VA Medical Center, Alcoholism Treatment Program, no date.

1657. Eriksson, C.J.P. and Schuckit, M.A. Elevated Blood Acetaldehyde
       Levels in Alcoholics and Their Relatives: A Reevaluation.
       Science, 207: 1383-1384, 1980.

1658. Eriksson, K. Inherited Metabolism and Behavior Towards Alcohol:
       Critical Evaluation of Human and Animal Research.
       In: Animal Models in Research. Eds. K. Eriksson, J.D.
       Sinclair and K. Kiianmaa. New York: Academic Press, 1980.
       (Also as: Paper presented at the International Conference on
       Animal Models in Alcohol Research, Helsinki, June, 1979.)

1659. Eriksson, K. Alkoholin Nauttiminen Periytyvana Ilmiona. (The Use
       of Alcohol as a Hereditary Phenomenon.) Alkoholikysymys,
       41: 8-12, 1973.

1660. Eriksson, M., Larsson, G. and Zetterstrom, R. Abuse of Alcohol,
       Drugs and Tobacco During Pregnancy-Consequences for the
       Child. Paediatrician, 8: 228-242, 1979.

1661. Erler, F. Schlussfolgerungen Fur Die Gesundheitserziehung Aus
       Untersuchungen Uber Einstellung Und Alkoholverhalten
       Jugendlicher. (End Results of the Health Education Program
       Based on Research on Attitudes and Alcohol Associated Behavior
       of Adolescents.) Deutsche Gesundheitswesen, 33: 89-92, 1978.

1662. Erne, H., Bruppacher, R. and Ritzel, G. Familiare Faktoren Und
       Alkoholkonsum Bei 14- Bis 15Jahrigen Basler Schulern. (Family
       Factors and Alcohol Consumption in 14-15 Year Old Basel
       Schoolchildren.) Sozial- Und Praventivmedizin, Bern, 20(5):
       234-235, 1975.

1663. Ernst, Ann R. The Relationship of Abdominal Pain in Children
       to Somatization Disorder (Briquet's Syndrome) in Adults.
       Dissertation Abstracts International, 43(4): 1250B, 1982.

1664. Ervin, Cynthia S., Little, Ruth E., Streissguth, Ann and Beck,
       Don E. Alcoholic Fathering and Its Relation to Child's
       Intellectual Development: A Pilot Investigation.
       Alcoholism: Clinical and Experimental Research, 8(4):
       362-365, 1984.

1665. Erwin, V.G., Wilson, J.R. and Petersen, D.R. Methodological
       Considerations in Studies of Physical Dependence on or
       Tolerance to Ethanol. In: Ethanol Tolerance and
       Dependence: Endocrinological Aspects. Rockville, MD:
       National Institute on Alcohol Abuse and Alcoholism, 1983,
       pages 33-46.

1666. Erwin, V. Gene and McClearn, Gerald E. Genetic Influences on
       Alcohol Consumption and Actions of Alcohol. In: Currents
       in Alcoholism, Volume 8: Recent Advances in Research and
       Treatment. Ed. Marc Galanter. New York: Grune and
       Stratton, 1981, pages 405-420.

1667. Espada, F. Family Treatment of Alcoholics; An Overview.
       Alcoholism and Alcohol Education, 7(3): 8-9, 1977.

1668. Espada-Baya, J.L., Chappa, H.J. and Corsico, R. Habito
       Infantil y Alcoholismo; Bases Para Una Clasificacion
       Tipologica Del Alcoholista Cronico. (Habits in Children,
       and Alcoholism; Bases for a Typological Classification of
       Chronic Alcoholics.) Revista Argentina De Neurologia Y
       Psiquiatria, Buenos Aires, 1: 124-129, 1964.

1669. Esselstrom, J. and Nieminen, I. Vaasan Nuorisotutkimus 1954.
       (A Social Study of Youth in the City of Vaasa in 1954.)
       Alkoholikysymys, Helsinki, 25: 12-62, 1957.

1670. Esser, P.H. Conjoint Family Therapy for Alcoholics. British
       Journal of Addiction, Edinburgh, 63: 177-182, 1968.

1671. Esser, P.H. Conjoint Family Therapy with Alcoholics -- A New
       Approach. British Journal of Addiction, Edinburgh, 64:
       275-286, 1970.

1672. Esser, P.H. Evaluation of Family Therapy with Alcoholics.
       British Journal of Addiction, Edinburgh, 66: 251-255, 1971.

1673. Esser, P.H. Group Psychotherapy with Alcoholics. British Journal
       of Addiction, Edinburgh, 57: 105-114, 1961. (Also in:
       Psychiatria, Neurologia, Neurochirurgia, Amsterdam, 64:
       365-372, 1961.)

1674. Esterly, R.W. Alcoholism and the Family: Overview. In: Alcoholism
       and the Family: A Book of Readings. Eds. Sharon Wegscheider-
       Cruse and Richard Esterly. Wernersville, PA: Caron Institute,
       1985, pages 4-6.

1675. Esterly, R.W. Model Drug and Alcohol Insurance Benefits and the
       Family. Paper presented at the National Council on Alcoholism
       Forum, New Orleans, April, 1981.

1676. Estes, N.J. and Hanson, K.J. Alcoholism in the Family: Perspectives
       for the Nurse Practitioner. Nurse Practitioner, 1(3): 125-131,
       1976.

1677. Estes, N.J., Smith-DiJulio, K. and Heinemann, M.E. (Eds.) Family
       Members of the Alcoholic Person. In: Nursing Diagnosis of the
       Alcoholic Person. St. Louis: The C.V. Mosby Company, 1980,
       pages 214-241.

1678. Estes, Nada J. Counseling the Wife of an Alcoholic Spouse.
       American Journal of Nursing, 74(7): 1251-1255, 1974.
       (Also in: Alcoholism: Introduction to Theory and
       Treatment. Ed. David A. Ward. Dubuque, IA: Kendall/Hunt
       Publishing Co., 1980, pages 366-372. Also in: Alcoholism:
       Development, Consequences, and Interventions. Eds. Nada J.
       Estes and M. Edith Heinemann. St. Louis: The C.V. Mosby
       Company, 1977, pages 259-265.)

1679. Estes, Nada J. and Baker, Joan M. Spouses of Alcoholic Women.
       In: Alcoholism: Development, Consequences, and
       Interventions. Eds. Nada J. Estes and M. Edith Heinemann.
       St. Louis, MO: C.V. Mosby Company, 1977, pages 186-193.

1680. Estes, Nada J. and Hanson, Kathye J. Sobriety: Problems,
       Challenges, and Solutions. American Journal of Psychotherapy,
       30: 256-266, 1976. (Also in: Alcoholism: Development,
       Consequences, and Interventions. Eds. Nada J. Estes and
       M. Edith Heinemann. Saint Louis: The C.V. Mosby Company, 1977,
       pages 311-318.)

1681. Estrada, Antonio, Rabow, Jerome and Watts, Ronald K. Alcohol Use
       Among Hispanic Adolescents: A Preliminary Report. Hispanic
       Journal of Behavioral Sciences, 4(3): 339-351, 1982.

1682. Etchegoyen, R.H., Gabay, J. and Quiroga, N. Imagen Del Padre En
       Un Grupo De Alcoholicos. (The Father Image in a Group of
       Alcoholics.) Acta Psiquiatrica Y Psicologica De America
       Latina, Buenos Aires, 11: 277-280, 1965.

1683. Evaluating the Effectiveness of Conjoint Treatment of Alcohol --
       Complicated Marriages -- Clinical and Methodological Issues.
       Journal of Marital and Family Therapy, 9(1): 61-72, 1983.

1684. Evaluation of Family Therapy with Alcoholics. British Journal
       of Addiction, 66(4): 251, 1971.

1685. Evans, D.G. Alcoholism, Domestic Violence and the Law. Focus on
       Family, 8(5): 10-11, 42-43, 1985.

1686. Evans, David G. How to Handle the Client with an Alcohol
       Problem. New Jersey State Bar Journal, 85: 1-5, 1978.

1687. Evans, David G. Kids, Drugs, and the Law. Center City, MN:
       Hazelden, no date.

1688. Evans, David G. A Practitioner's Guide to Alcoholism & the Law.
       Center City, MN: Hazelden, 1983.

1689. Evans, M. and Avril, M. Alcoholism--A Family Disease. Health
       Visitor, London, 42: 459-461, 1969.

1690. Evans, M., Fine, E.W. and Phillips, W.P. Community Care for
       Alcoholics and Their Families. British Medical Journal,
       5502: 1531-1532, 1966.

1691. Evans, Marion and Collins, Joan. A Welsh Survey. 1. Nursing
       Time in an Alcoholic Unit. In: Nursing Times, London,
       63(43): 1441-1443, 1967.

1692. Evans, O.N. The Wife of the Alcoholic-Villain or Victim?
       Military Medicine, 131: 1422-1430, 1966.

1693. Evans, W.B. and Fortin, M.T. Correlates of Loss of Control
       Over Drinking in Women Alcoholics. Journal of Studies on
       Alcohol, 44(5): 787-796, 1983.

1694. Eve, S.I. Defining Boundaries: The Basis of Individuality.
       Focus on Family and Chemical Dependency, 8(2): 18, 34,
       1985.

1695. Evenson, Richard C., Altman, Harold, Sletten, Ivan W. and Knowles,
       Raymond R. Factors in the Description and Grouping of
       Alcoholics. American Journal of Psychiatry, 130(1):
       49-54, 1973.

1696. Evenson, Richard C., Sletten, Ivan W., Altman, Harold and Brown,
       Marjorie, L. Disturbing Behavior: A Study of Incident
       Reports. Psychiatric Quarterly, 48(2): 266-275, 1974.

1697. Everett, Michael W., Waddell, Jack O. and Heath, Dwight B. (Eds.).
       Cross-Cultural Approaches to the Study of Alcohol; An
       Interdisciplinary Perspective. Paris: Mouton, 1976.

1698. Evseeff, G.S. and Wisniewski, E.M. A Psychiatric Study of a
       Violent Mass Murderer. Journal of Forensic Sciences,
       17(3): 371-376, 1972.

1699. Ewing, J.A. Family Therapy of Alcoholism. In: 28th
       International Congress on Alcohol and Alcoholism, Volume 1,
       Abstracts. Eds. Mark Keller and Maria Majchrowicz.
       Lausanne: International Council on Alcohol and Addictions, 1968,
       pages 15-20.

1700. Ewing, John A. Biopsychosocial Approaches to Drinking and
       Alcoholism. In: Phenomenology and Treatment of
       Alcoholism. Eds. William E. Fann, Ismet Karacan, Alex D.
       Pokorny and Robert L. Williams. Jamaica, New York:
       Scientific and Medical Books, 1980, pages 1-19.

1701. Ewing, John A. Counseling Help for the Alcoholic Marriage.
       In: Marriage Counseling in Medical Practice. Eds. Ethel
       M. Nash, Lucie Jessner and D. Wilfred Abse. Chapel Hill, NC:
       University of North Carolina Press, 1964, pages 92-116.

1702. Ewing, John A. Different Approaches to the Treatment of
       Alcoholism. In: Recent Advances in the Study of
       Alcoholism. Ed. C-M. Idestrom. Amsterdam: Excerpta
       Medica, 1977, pages 23-31.

1703. Ewing, John A. The Etiology of Alcoholism: Current Research
       Issues. Journal: National Association of Private
       Psychiatric Hospitals, 12(3): 109-112, 1981.

1704. Ewing, John A., Long, Virginia and Wenzel, Gustave G. Concurrent
       Group Psychotherapy of Alcoholic Patients and Their Wives.
       International Journal of Psychotherapy, 11: 329-338, 1961.

1705. Ewing, John A., Rouse, Beatrice A. and Pellizzari, E.D. Alcohol
       Sensitivity and Ethnic Background. American Journal of
       Psychiatry, 131(2): 206-210, 1974.

1706. Extended Family Ties Among Alcoholics - Neglected Area of Research.
       Quarterly Journal of Studies on Alcohol, 33(2): 513, 1972.

1707. Eyden, Pamela. Crisis Intervention for Troubled Children. <u>Community Intervention</u>, Winter: 1, 10, 1985.

1708. Eyden, Pamela. A School-Based Program for Children of Alcoholics. <u>Community Intervention</u>, Winter: 1, 12-13, 1985.

F

1709. Facts for Planning 11: Cost and Utilization of Alcoholism
      Treatment Under Health Insurance: A Review of Three Studies.
      Alcohol Health and Research World, 9(2): 45-52, 72, 1985.

1710. Fahlberg, E., Nordlund, R. and Perris, C. Gruppverksamhet Och
      Gruppterapi Med Alkoholisthustrur; Nagra Teoretiska Och
      Methodologiska Reflektioner Samt Praktiska Erfarenheter.
      (Group Activity and Group Therapy for Wives of Alcoholics;
      Some Theoretical and Methodological Reflections and Practical
      Experiences.) Nordisk Psykiatrisk Tidsskrift, Huddinge,
      19: 11-22, 1965.

1711. Faigel, Harris C. Commentary: Why Our Children Drink. Clinical
      Pediatrics, 15(6): 509, 1976.

1712. Fairchild, D.M. Teen Group I: A Pilot Project in Group Therapy
      with Adolescent Children of Alcoholic Patients. Journal of
      Fort Logan Mental Health Center, 2: 71-75, 1964.

1713. Fairfax Hospital Association. Alcoholism: A Family Affair.
      Fax: Fairfax Hospital Association, Winter: 1-15, 1985.

1714. Fakhruddin, A.K.M. Identification and Alcoholism. Psychiatric
      Quarterly, 41(2): 307-310, 1967.

1715. Falicov, Celia Jaes. Mexican Families. In: Ethnicity and
      Family Therapy. Eds. Monica McGoldrick, John K. Pearce
      and Joseph Giordano. New York: The Guilford Press, 1982,
      pages 134-163.

1716. Falk, M. Kombiniert Stationare Und Ambulante Entwohnungsbehandlungen
      Fur Alkoholabhangige In Der Rochet Klinik, Heidelberg. (Combined
      Ward and Ambulatory Withdrawal Treatment for Alcohol Dependency
      in the Rochet Clinic, Heidelberg.) Suchtgefahren, 29(1):
      45-46, 1983.

1717. Fallon, Donald and Cunningham, John P. Parish Priest and Alcohol
      Problems of Parishioners. In: The Blue Book, Volume 24.
      Scottsdale, AZ: Franciscan Renewal Center, 1972, pages 45-60.

1718. Falstein, E.I. Juvenile Alcoholism: A Psychodynamic Case Study
      of Addiction. American Journal of Orthopsychiatry, 23:
      530-551, 1953.

1719. Families Anonymous Aids Parents of Addicted Youths. NIAAA Information
      and Feature Service, (IFS No. 59): 2, May 4, 1979.

1720. Families Deeply Involved in Treatment of Youths. NIAAA Information
      and Feature Service, (IFS No. 49): 6, July 11, 1978.

1721. Family Abuse and Alcohol. Pamphlet. Lincoln: Nebraska Alcohol
      Information Clearinghouse, 1980.

1722. Family Action: Anti-Drug Movement Sweeps Nation. Focus on
         Alcohol and Drug Issues, 5(1): 3, 10, 1982.

1723. Family Agency's Role in Treating the Wife of an Alcoholic. Pamphlet.
         Frankfort: Kentucky Department of Mental Health, Office of
         Alcoholism, 1971.

1724. The Family and the Alcoholic. South African Medical Journal,
         Cape Town, 38: 946, 1964.

1725. Family Assistance. All Hands, August-September: 67-73, 1980.

1726. Family Assistance Program. Pamphlet. Lincoln, NE: State
         Department of Institutions, Division of Alcoholism, 1973.

1727. The Family Assistance Program; Leader's Guide and Participant
         Material. Curriculum Guide. Milwaukee, WI: DePaul
         Rehabilitation Hospital, no date.

1728. Family Dysfunction Tied to Adolescent Alcohol Problems. NIAAA
         Information and Feature Service, (IFS No. 86): 10, July 30,
         1981.

1729. Family Enablers. Minneapolis, MN: Johnson Institute, 1982.

1730. Family, Friends Target of Early Intervention. NIAAA Information
         and Feature Service, (IFS No. 62): 5, August 6, 1979.

1731. Family House Treats Mothers and Children. Innovations, 5(3):
         29-30, 1978.

1732. Family Medicine Curriculum Guide to Alcoholism and Other Chemical
         Dependence. Pamphlet. Kansas City: Society of Teachers of
         Family Medicine, 1983.

1733. Family Members Focus of Kemper EAP. Alcohol Health and Research
         World, 8(4): 52-53, 1984.

1734. Family Pedigree of Alcohol and Control Patients. International
         Journal of the Addictions, 18(3): 351-356, 1983.

1735. Family Playhouse: Romance to Recovery. Pamphlet. Los Angeles:
         FMS Productions, no date.

1736. Family Problems, Social Adaptation and Sources of Help for Children
         of Alcoholic and Nonalcoholic Parents. San Francisco:
         Scientific Analysis Corporation, 1976.

1737. Family Program Profiles; A Cross-Section of Ideas, Opinions, and
         Approaches. Alcoholism: The National Magazine, 1(3):
         39-47, 1980.

1738. A Family Response to the Drug Problem; A Family Program for the
         Prevention of Chemical Dependence with Group Facilitator
         Guidelines. Rockville, MD: National Institute on Drug
         Abuse (DHEW/PHS), 1976. (Eric Document Number ED153097.)

1739. Family Role "Cornerstone" of Inpatient Program. NIAAA Information
         and Feature Service, (IFS No. 46): 2, April 3, 1978.

1740. Family Secret: Tips on Counseling. Pamphlet. Avon Park:
         The State of Florida Bureau of Alcoholic Rehabilitation, 1971.

1741. Family Therapy with Alcohol Abusers. Family Therapy:
         A Summary of Selected Literature. Washington, D.C.:
         U.S. Government Printing Office, 1980.

1742. Family Therapy of Alcoholism. COA Review, 3: 3, 1983.

1743. Family Therapy Approaches Studied. NIAAA Information and Feature Service, (IFS No. 23): 2, April 12, 1976.

1744. Family Therapy in Cases of Drug-Addiction and Alcoholism. Eds. E. Kaufman and P. Kaufmann. Caritas, 84(4): 221-222, 1983.

1745. Family Therapy Helpful, Social Workers Say. NIAAA Information and Feature Service, (IFS No. 10): 3, April 1, 1975.

1746. Family Therapy Helps Addict. Journal of the American Medical Association, 241(6): 546-551, 1979.

1747. Family Therapy is Primary Treatment for Children and Their Alcoholic Parents. NIAAA Information and Feature Service, (IFS No. 19): 5, January 7, 1976.

1748. Family Therapy Seen Complementary to Alcoholics Anonymous, Al-Anon. NIAAA Information and Feature Service, (IFS No. 49): 1, July 11, 1978.

1749. Family Violence (Association Between Alcoholism and All Kinds of Domestic Violence). Alcohol Health and Research World, 4: 2-35, 1979.

1750. Family Violence Program: Law Enforcement Assistance Administration Guide for Discretionary Grant Programs. Report. Washington, D.C.: Law Enforcement Assistance Administration, 1977.

1751. Family Violence Research Program. Report. Durham: University of New Hampshire, Department of Sociology, 1979.

1752. Fanai, F. Progress and Prognosis of Degeneration: Catamnesis of Adolescents with Disturbed Social Behavior. Psychiatria Clinica, 2(1): 1-13, 1969.

1753. Fandetti, Donald V. and Gelfand, Donald E. Attitudes Toward Symptoms and Services in the Ethnic Family and Neighborhood. American Journal of Orthopsychiatry, 48(3): 477-486, 1978.

1754. Fanshel, David. The Pediatrician and Children in Foster Care. Pediatrics, 60(2): 255-257, 1977.

1755. Farber, D. Families May Mask Alcoholism but Workers Can Be Trained to Spot Real Problem. Focus on Alcohol and Drug Issues, 4(3): 25, 1981.

1756. Farber, D.S. Family Service Agency Approach to the Alcoholic Family. Report. MI: Plymouth Family Service, 1981.

1757. Farber, M.L. Suicide in France: Some Hypotheses. Suicide and Life-Threatening Behavior, 9(3): 154-162, 1979.

1758. Farberow, N.L. and Simon, M.D. Suicides in Los Angeles and Vienna. An Intercultural Study of Two Cities. Public Health Report, 84(5): 389-403, 1969.

1759. Farberow, Norman L. and Reynolds, David K. Sources of Suicide and Schizophrenia within the Family. Psychiatria Fennica, 41-51, 1981.

1760. Farid, B., ElSherbini, M. and Raistrick, D. Cognitive Group Therapy for Wives of Alcoholics: A Pilot Study. Paper Presented at the Society for the Study of Addiction to Alcohol and Other Drugs, London, November, 1985.

1761. Faris, Ruth, Paolino, Thomas J. Jr. and McCrady, Barbara, S. Clinical and Administrative Aspects of Joint Hospital Admissions for Alcoholic Couples. International Journal of Family Psychiatry, 1(3): 295-307, 1980.

1762. Farkasinszky, T., Simon, A., Wagner, A. and Szilard, I.
Entwicklungsstorungen der Personlichkeit bei Kindern
Alkoholiker. (Development of Personality Disturbances
in Children of Alcoholics.) Alcoholism, Zagreb, 9:
3-8, 1973.

1763. Farkasinszky, T., Simon, A., Wagner, A. and Szilard, I. Neuropsychiatric and Sociologic Study of Children from Alcoholic
Families. Ideggyogyaszati Szemke i Budapest, 27: 433-443,
1974. (Also in: Excerpta Medica Psychiatry, Amsterdam,
32(3032): 1975.)

1764. Farnsworth, Dana L. Introduction: Pressures on Adolescents.
Psychiatric Annals, 8(8): 11-12, 15-18, 1978.

1765. Farr, V. and Rehfeldt, N. Alcohol: A Factor in Child Sexual
Abuse. Paper presented at the First Pan-Pacific Conference
on Drugs and Alcohol, Australia, 1980, pages 191-192.

1766. Father-Daughter Incest Linked with Alcoholism. NIAAA Information and
Feature Service, (IFS No. 80): 9, January 30, 1981.

1767. Fau, M.R., Boucharlat, J. and Salomon, C. Dangerous State in
Confirmed Delirium Tremens: Apropos of 414 Observations.
Annales Medico-Psychologiques, Paris, 2(5): 761-767, 1967.

1768. Faulk, M. A Psychiatric Study of Men Serving a Sentence in
Winchester Prison. Medicine, Science and the Law,
London, 16: 244-251, 1976.

1769. Fauman, M.A. and Fauman, B.J. Chronic Phencyclidine (PCP) Abuse:
A Psychiatric Perspective. Journal of Psychedelic Drugs,
12(3-4): 307-315, 1980.

1770. Favazza, A.R. and Thompson, J.J. Psychosocial Network Approach
to Alcoholism. In: Psychosocial Treatment of Alcoholism.
Eds. Marc Galanter and E. Mansell Pattison. Washington,
D.C.: American Psychiatric Press, 1984, pages 45-55.

1771. Favazza, A.R. and Thompson, J.J. Social Networks of Alcoholics:
Some Early Findings. Alcoholism: Clinical and Experimental
Research, 8(1): 9-15, 1984.

1772. Favazza, Armando R. and Oman, Mary. Overview: Foundations of
Cultural Psychiatry. American Journal of Psychiatry, 135(3):
293-303, 1978.

1773. Fawcett, J. Suicidal Depression and Physical Illness. The
Journal of the American Medical Association, 219(10):
1303-1306, 1972.

1774. Fawzy, F.I., Coombs, Robert H. and Gerber, Barry. Generational
Continuity in the Use of Substances: The Impact of Parental
Substance Use on Adolescent Substance Use. Addictive
Behaviors, Oxford, 8: 109-114, 1983.

1775. Federal Laws Create Substance Abuse Programs. Mental Disability
Law Reporter, 4(2): 113, 1980.

1776. Feeney, D.J. Jr. and Dranger, P. Alcoholics View Group Therapy;
Process and Goals. Journal of Studies on Alcohol, 37:
611-618, 1976.

1777. Feeney, Don J. Jr. and Silverman, Manuel S. Paradox in
Alcoholism. American Journal of Drug and Alcohol Abuse,
8(4): 513-532, 1981-82.

1778. Feinglass, S.J. and Lappin, M. Alcoholism, Drug Abuse and
       Pregnancy: Causative Factors in Child Abuse and Neglect?
       In: Child Abuse and Neglect: Issues on Innovation and
       Implementation. Proceedings of the Second National
       Conference on Child Abuse and Neglect, April 17-20, 1977.
       Volume II. Eds. M.L. Lauderdale, R.N. Anderson and
       S.E. Cramer. Washington, D.C.: National Center on Child
       Abuse and Neglect, 1978, pages 301-303.

1779. Feingold, K.R. and Siperstein, M.D. Normalization of Fasting
       Blood Glucose Levels in Insulin-Requiring Diabetes: The
       Role of Ethanol Abstention. Diabetes Care, 6(2):
       186-188, 1983.

1780. Feinstein, B.B. and O'Brien, D.R. A Partnership Approach to
       Alcoholism Treatment with the Family. Paper presented at the
       Seventh Annual Meeting of the Association of Labor-Management
       Administrators and Consultants on Alcoholism, San Francisco,
       October, 1978, pages 209-216.

1781. Feit, Marvin D. Effect of Length of Time and Different Treatment
       Modalities on the Social Functioning of Alcoholics.
       Doctoral Dissertation. (University Microfilms No. 75-21753.)
       Pittsburgh: University of Pittsburgh, School of Social Work, 1975.

1782. Feldberg, M., Sacirbey, N., Blackmon, W.D. and McGowan, J.C.
       Manic-Depressive Illness in Three Generations of One Family:
       A Case Study. Psychiatria Clinica, Basel, 12: 1-8, 1979.

1783. Feldman, Ben H. and Rosendrantz, Arthur L. Drug Use by College
       Students and Their Parents. Addictive Diseases, 3(2):
       235-242, 1977.

1784. Feldman, D.J. Alcoholism: A Problem in Environment.
       Rehabilitation Record, 5: 22-24, 1964.

1785. Feldman, D.J., Pattison, E.M., Sobell, L.C., Graham, T. and
       Sobell, M.B. Outpatient Alcohol Detoxification: Initial
       Findings on 564 Patients. American Journal of Psychiatry,
       132(4): 407-412, 1975.

1786. Feldman, Rosalind Brodofsky. A Study of the Relationship Between
       Adolescent Use of Psychoactive Substances and Perceived
       Communication with Parents. Dissertation Abstracts
       International, 43(4): 1053B, 1982.

1787. Felice, Marianne and Offord, D.R. Three Developmental Pathways
       to Delinquency in Girls. British Journal of Criminology,
       12(4): 375-389, 1972.

1788. Ferguson, Frances N. Similarities and Differences Among a Heavily
       Arrested Group of Navajo Indian Drinkers in a Southwestern
       American Town. In: Cross-Cultural Approaches to the Study
       of Alcohol; An Interdisciplinary Perspective. Eds. Michael
       W. Everett, Jack O. Waddell and Dwight B. Heath. Paris: Mouton,
       1976, pages 161-174.

1789. Ferguson, Frances N. Stake Theory as an Explanatory Device in
       Navajo Alcoholism Treatment Response. Human Organization,
       35(1): 65-78, 1976.

1790. Ferguson, Frances N. A Treatment Program for Navaho Alcoholics.
       Results after Four Years. Quarterly Journal of Studies on
       Alcohol, 31: 898-919, 1970.

1791. Ferkovic, M., Bilalbegovic, Z., Lazic, N. and Banusic, Z.
       Ponasanje Djece Iz Obitelji Alkoholicara Nakon Izdvajanja
       Iz Obiteljske Sredine. (Behavior of Children of Alcoholics
       During Evacuation after an Earthquake.) In: Socijalna
       Psihijatrija. Ed. N. Persic. Zagreb: Pliva, 1971, pages
       405-413.

1792. Fernandez, F.A. The State of Alcoholism in Spain Covering Its
       Epidemiological and Aetiological Aspects. British Journal
       of Addiction, Edinburgh, 71: 235-242, 1976.

1793. Fernando, Robert J. An Exploratory Study of Alcohol Misuse
       and Acting-Out Behavior Among College Youth. Dissertation
       Abstracts International, 43(1): 230B, 1982.

1794. Ferrant, J.P., Benard, J.Y., Laudier, J., Gauto, C. and Martinay,
       C. L'Hospitalisation de L'Alcoolique. (Hospitalization of
       Alcoholics.) La Revue De Medecine, Paris, 23(17):
       901-905, 1982.

1795. Ferrant, J.P., Bernot, J.L. and Heinrich, C.H. Therapeutique de
       Groupe Appliquee a l'Alcoolisme. (Group Therapy Application
       to Alcoholism.) La Revue De l'Alcoolisme, 22(3): 221-227,
       1976.

1796. Ferreira, Antonio J. Family Therapy in Alcoholism. Psychotherapy &
       Psychosomatics, 15(1): 20, 1967.

1797. Ferrey, G., Breton, J. and Agman, G. 2 Patients with 47, XYY
       Karyotype. Mental Disorders and Chromosome Abnormalities.
       Revue de Medicine Psychosomatique, 14(4): 399-414, 1972.

1798. Ferrier, P.E. and Stettler, M. Child as a Victim of Abuse
       and Negligence. Plea for a Pluridisciplinary Approach
       and for Public Education. Schweizerische Medizinische
       Wochenschrift, 107(39): 1349-1354, 1977.

1799. Ferro, Frank, Deluca, John R. and Pollin, William. Confidenti-
       ality of Alcohol and Drug Abuse Patient Records and Child
       Abuse and Neglect Reporting. Alcohol Health and Research
       World, 4(1): 31-35, 1979.

1800. Feuer, B. Association of Flight Attendants Employee Assistance
       Program: Peer Referral Model. Report. Washington, D.C.:
       Association of Flight Attendants, Employee Assistance Program,
       1982.

1801. Feuerlein, W. Treatment of Alcoholics in Medical Practice.
       Social Psychiatry, 7(1): 36-46, 1972.

1802. Feuerlein, W. and Busch, H. Partnership of the Chronic Female
       Alcoholic. Paper presented at the 31st International Congress on
       Alcoholism and Drug Dependence, Bangkok, 1975, pages 659-662.

1803. Feuerlein, W. and Dittmar, F. Wenn Alkohol zum Problem wird;
       ein Ratgeber fur Betroffene und Interessierte. (When
       Alcohol Becomes A Problem; Advice for the Affected and the
       Interested.) Stuttgart: Georg Thieme Verlag, 1978.

1804. Feuerlein, Wilhelm. Der Alkoholismus in Sozialpsychiatrischer
       Sicht. (Alcoholism from a Sociopsychiatric Viewpoint.)
       Medizinische Klinik, Munich, 62: 922-926, 1967.

1805. Feuerlein, Wilhelm. Zur Soziologie des Alkoholdelir-Patienten.
       (On the Sociology of Patients with Alcoholic Delirium.)
       Social Psychiatry, Berlin, 4: 95-100, 1969.

1806. Feuerlein, Wilhelm. Sozialpsychiatrische Aspekte und Probleme
       bei Alkoholikern. (Sociopsychiatric Aspects and Problems
       Concerning Alcoholics.) Munchener Medizinische
       Wochenschrift, Munich, 107(49): 2482-2487, 1965.

1807. Fewell, Christine. The Social Work Role in an Inpatient
       Alcoholism Treatment Team. Social Work in Health Care,
       1(2): 155-166, 1976.

1808. Fewell, Christine Huff and Bissell, LeClair. The Alcoholic
       Denial Syndrome: An Alcohol-Focused Approach. Social
       Casework, 59(1): 6-13, 1978.

1809. Fialkov, M.J. Alcoholics and the Emergency Ward. Part 1.
       Clinical Characteristics. South African Medical Journal,
       Cape Town, 52(15): 613-616, 1977.

1810. Fialkow, P.J., Thuline, H.C. and Fenster, F. Lack of Association
       Between Cirrhosis and the Common Types of Color Blindness.
       New England Journal of Medicine, 275: 584-587, 1966.

1811. Ficker, F. Junge Suizidpatienten und das Emotionale Klima der
       Familie. (Young Suicide Patients and the Emotional Climate
       in the Family.) Psychiatrie, Neurologie und Medizinische
       Psychologie, Leipzig, 29: 39-45, 1977.

1812. Fiddes, Dorothy O. Scotland in the Seventies--Adolescents in
       Care and Custody. A Survey of Adolescent Murder in Scotland.
       Journal of Adolescence, 4(1): 47-65, 1981.

1813. Fielding, Jonathan E. Preventive Medicine and the Bottom Line.
       Journal of Occupational Medicine, 21(2): 79-88, 1979.

1814. Fields, Bessie L. Adolescent Alcoholism: Treatment and
       Rehabilitation. Family and Community Health, 2(1):
       61-90, 1979.

1815. Fierstein, Robert Fred. Social Correlates of Child Abusing
       Families. Dissertation Abstracts International, 41(7):
       3039-3040, 1980.

1816. The Fight Against Alcoholism. Retail, Wholesale and Department
       Store Union, AFL-CIO, 16(22): 13, 1969.

1817. Figley, Charles R. and Sprenkle, Douglas H. Delayed Stress
       Response Syndrome: Family Therapy Indications. Journal
       of Marriage and Family Counseling, 4(3): 53-60, 1978.

1818. Figuerido, C.A. Los Llamados Males Germinales Y Los Descendientes
       de Toxicomanos. (So-Called Germ Damage and the Offspring of
       Addicts.) Revista de Sanidod e Higiene Publica, Madrid,
       21: 1215-1221, 1947.

1819. Fike, D., Ostrowsky E., Nuehring, E., Brady, D. and Abrams, H.
       Personal and Family Aspects. In: Impact Analysis of Alcohol
       Abuse in Dade County, Florida. Miami: Dade-Monroe Mental
       Health Board, 1982, pages 114-166.

1820. Fillmore, K.M. Abstinence, Drinking and Problem Drinking Among
       Adolescents as Related to Apparent Parental Drinking
       Practices. Master's Thesis. Amherst: University of
       Massachusetts, 1970.

1821. Fillmore, K.M. Relationships between Specific Drinking Problems
       in Early Adulthood and Middle Age; An Exploratory 20-Year
       Follow-Up Study. Journal of Studies on Alcohol, 36:
       882-907, 1975.

1822. Filstead, W., McElfresh, O. and Anderson, C. Alcoholism and
      Family Life Research Project at Luthern General Hospital:
      A Summary of the Findings and Their Implications. Paper
      presented at the National Council on Alcoholism's Annual
      Meeting, The Family and Alcoholism Symposium, 1979.

1823. Filstead, W.J. Substance Abuse and Family Life; A Selected
      Bibliography. San Diego: Operation Cork, no date.

1824. Filstead, W.J., Anderson, C. and McElfresh, O. An Examination
      of Male and Female Alcoholics' Perceptions of Their
      Present and Ideal Family Environments. Ed. M. Galanter.
      In: Currents in Alcoholism. Volume 7. Recent Advances
      in Research and Treatment. New York: Grune and Stratton,
      1980, pages 435-445.

1825. Filstead, William J. Alcohol Misuse, the Family and Alcoholism
      Programs: Some Suggested Strategies of Intervention.
      Journal of Studies on Alcohol, 42(1): 172-179, 1981.

1826. Filstead, William J. The Family, Alcohol Misuse and Alcoholism:
      Priorities and Proposals for Intervention. Journal of
      Studies on Alcohol, 38(7): 1447-1454, 1977.

1827. Filstead, William J. and Anderson, Carl L. Conceptual and
      Clinical Issues in the Treatment of Adolescent Alcohol
      and Substance Misusers. In: Adolescent Substance Abuse:
      A Guide to Prevention and Treatment. Eds. Richard
      Isralowitz and Mark Singer. New York: The Haworth Press,
      1983, pages 103-116.

1828. Filstead, William J., McElfresh, Oru and Anderson, Carl. Comparing
      the Family Environments of Alcoholic and "Normal" Families.
      Journal of Alcohol and Drug Education, 26(2): 24-31, 1981.

1829. Final Report: An Assessment of the Needs of and Resources for
      Children of Alcoholic Parents. Rockville, MD: NIAAA, 1974.

1830. Finch, Jefferson Ross. A Study of College Students' Patterns and
      Problems of Alcohol Consumption. Dissertation Abstracts
      International, 45(3): 750A, 1983.

1831. Fine, E. Observations of Young Children from Alcoholic Homes.
      Philadelphia: West Philadelphia Community Mental Health
      Consortium, 1975.

1832. Fine, E.W. Alcoholic Family Dynamics and Their Effect on the
      Children. Alcoholism Digest, 4(7): 6-9, 1975.

1833. Fine, E.W., Scoles, P. and Mulligan, M. Under the Influence;
      Characteristics and Drinking Practices of Persons Arrested
      the First Time for Drunk Driving, with Treatment Implications.
      Public Health Reports, 90: 424-429, 1975.

1834. Fine, Eric W. Alcoholism and Forensic Psychiatry. American
      Journal of Forensic Psychiatry, 4(3): 113-118, 1983.

1835. Fine, Eric W., Yudin, Lee W., Holmes, Jan and Heinemann, Shirley.
      Behavior Disorders in Children with Parental Alcoholism.
      Paper Presented at the Annual Conference of the National
      Council on Alcoholism, Milwaukee, April-May, 1975. (Also as:
      Behavioral Disorders in Children with Parental Alcoholism.
      Annals of the New York Academy of Sciences, 273: 507-517,
      1976.)

1836. Fine, Stuart. Adolescent Somatic Symptoms: Masks for Individual
      and Family Psychopathology. Comprehensive Psychiatry,
      18(2): 135-140, 1977.

1837. Fineman, S. Disintegration Through Substance Abuse: The Family in Crisis. Training Module 10 -- Summary. Paper presented at the 13th Annual Eagleville Conference on Substance Abuse: The Family in Trouble, Eagleville, PA, May, 1980, pages 288-292.

1838. Fink, R. and Chroman, P. Parental Drinking and Its Impact on Adult Drinking Behavior. Report. In: Drinking Practices Study. Berkeley, CA: Mental Research Institute, 1966.

1839. Fink, R., Chroman, P. and Clark, W. Parental Drinking and Its Impact on Adult Drinkers. Berkeley, CA: Social Research Group, 1962.

1840. Finkelstein, Norma, Brown Kendra-Ann N. and Laham, Cheryl Qamar. Alcoholic Mothers and Guilt: Issues for Caregivers. Alcohol Health and Research World, 6(1): 45-49, 1981.

1841. Finlay, D. Alcoholism: Illness or Problem in Interaction. Social Work, 19(4): 398-405, 1974.

1842. Finlay, Donald G. Alcoholism and Systems Theory: Building a Better Mousetrap. Psychiatry: Journal for the Study of Interpersonal Processes, 41(3): 272-278, 1978.

1843. Finlay, Donald G. Anxiety and the Alcoholic. Social Work, 17: 29-33, 1972.

1844. Finley, B. Nursing Interventions Into Domestic Violence. Paper presented at the National Council on Alcoholism Forum, Seattle, 1980.

1845. Finley, Britt G. Family and Substance Abuse. In: Substance Abuse; Pharmacologic, Developmental, and Clinical Perspectives. Eds. Gerald Bennett, Christine Vourakis, and Donna S. Woolf. New York: John Wiley & Sons, 1983, pages 119-134.

1846. Finn, J. Stresses and Coping Behavior of Battered Women. Social Casework, 66(6): 341-349, 1985.

1847. Finn, Peter. Alcohol: You Can Help Your Kids Cope. Instructor, 85(3): 76-78, 83-84, 1975.

1848. Finney, J.W. and Moos, R.H. Characteristics and Prognoses of Alcoholics Who Become Moderate Drinkers and Abstainers After Treatment. Journal of Studies on Alcohol, 42: 94-105, 1981.

1849. Finney, J.W., Moos, R.H., Cronkite, R.C. and Gamble, W. Conceptual Model of the Functioning of Married Persons with Impaired Partners: Spouses of Alcoholic Patients. Journal of Marriage and the Family, 45(1): 23-34, 1983.

1850. Finney, John W. and Moos, Rudolf H. Life Stressors and Problem Drinking Among Older Adults. In: Recent Developments in Alcoholism: Volume 2: Learning and Social Models, Alcohol and the Liver, Aging and Alcoholism, Anthropology. Ed. M. Galanter. New York: Plenum Press, 1984, pages 267-288.

1851. Finney, John W. and Moos, Rudolf H. Treatment and Outcome for Empirical Subtypes of Alcoholic Patients. Journal of Consulting and Clinical Psychology, 47(1): 25-38, 1979.

1852. Finney, John W., Moos, Rudolf H. and Mewborn, C. Ronald. Posttreatment Experiences and Treatment Outcome of Alcoholic Patients Six Months and Two Years After Hospitalization. Journal of Consulting & Clinical Psychology, 48(1): 17-29, 1980.

1853. Fisch, Marcia. Homeostasis: A Key Concept in Working with Alcoholic
       Families. Paper presented at the Alcohol and Drug Problems
       Association Conference, San Francisco, December, 1974. (Also in:
       Family Therapy, 3(2): 133-139, 1976.)

1854. Fischer, Arlene. The New Alcoholics. Glamour, 81: 250-258, 1983.

1855. Fischer, E. Beitrag zur Wirkung des Chron. Alkoholkonsums auf
       die Entwicklung des Kindes. (Contribution on the Effect of
       Chronic Alcohol Consumption in Child Development.) Archiv
       fuer Kinderheilkunde, Stuttgart, 138: 199-211, 1950.

1856. Fischer, J. Psychotherapy of Adolescent Alcohol Abusers.
       In: Practical Approaches to Alcoholism Psychotherapy.
       Eds. Sheldon Zimberg, John Wallace and Sheila B. Blume.
       New York: Plenum, 1978, pages 219-235.

1857. Fischer, M. and Gottesman, I.I. Study of Offspring of Parents
       Both Hospitalized for Psychiatric Disorders. In: Social
       Consequences of Psych. Illness. Ed. L.N. Robins.
       New York: Brunner/Mazel, 1980, pages 75-90.

1858. Fischer, Margaret. Components of Adolescent Depression in a Cross-
       Cultural Setting, 1981. (Eric Document Number ED212942.)

1859. Fischler, Ronald S. Child Abuse and Neglect in American Indians,
       1983. (Eric Document Number ED233849.)

1860. Fishbain, David A., D'Achille, Linda, Barsky, Steve and Aldrich,
       Tim E. A Controlled Study of Suicide Pacts. The Journal
       of Clinical Psychiatry, 45(4): 154-157, 1984.

1861. Fisher, D. and Weiner, H. Substance Abuse: A Family Tradition
       Through Three Generations. Paper presented at the 7th World
       Conference of Therapeutic Communities, Chicago, May 1983,
       pages 49-52.

1862. Fisher, Joseph V. Family Physicians: Alcohol and Drug Education
       in Family Medicine Training Programs. Alcohol Health and
       Research World, 8(1): 17-18, 1983.

1863. Fishman, R. and Kuver, J.M. Family Dysfunction: A Driving Force in
       Adolescent Alcohol Abuse. In: Alcohol Related Problems: Room
       for Manoeuvre. Eds. N. Drasner, J.S. Madden, and R.J. Walker.
       New York: John Wiley & Sons, 1984, pages 91-96.

1864. Fitch, F.J. and Papantonio, A. Men Who Batter: Some Pertinent
       Characteristics. Journal of Nervous and Mental Disease,
       171(3): 190-192, 1983.

1865. Fitz, Gerald Stephen Kendall. Value Differences of Spouses in
       Families with and without Alcohol-Abusing Members.
       Dissertation Abstracts International, 45(5): 338B, 1984.

1866. Fitze, F., Pescia, G. and Spahr, A. Alcoholic Embryopath --
       A Study of a Family. Helvetica Paediatrica Acta,
       1978(S40): 17, 1978.

1867. Fitzgerald, J.L. and Mulford, H.A. Alcoholics in the Family?
       The International Journal of the Addictions, 16: 349-357,
       1981.

1868. Fitzgerald, J.L. and Mulford, H.A. Factors Related to Problem-
       Drinking Rates. Journal of Studies on Alcohol, 45(5):
       424-432, 1984.

1869. Fitzgerald, Mary Catherine. Correlates of Alcoholism Among Roman
       Catholic Nuns: Psychological and Attitudinal Variables.
       Dissertation Abstracts International, 43(1): 246B, 1982.

1870.   Flach, Frederic F.   Community Hospitals Psychiatry and Illness
        Prevention.   Psychiatry in Medicine, 3(2): 99-100, 1972.

1871.   Flanzer, J.   Alcohol Abuse and Family Violence: The Domestic
        Chemical Connection.   Focus on Family and Chemical
        Dependency, 7(4): 5-6, 1984.

1872.   Flanzer, J.   Alcohol and Family Violence.   Part II. Treatment:
        How to Work with Tough Families.   Focus on Family and
        Chemical Dependency, 7(5): 24-25, 40, 1984.

1873.   Flanzer, J.P.   Alcohol and Family Violence: The Treatment of
        Abusing Families.   Paper presented at the International
        Congress on Drugs and Alcohol, Jerusalem, September, 1981.

1874.   Flanzer, J.P.   Families that Abuse: Adolescent and Alcohol Abuse.
        Paper presented at the 32nd Annual Meeting of the American
        Association of Psychiatric Services for Children, New Orleans,
        November, 1980.

1875.   Flanzer, J.P.   The Stress Factor.   The Alcohol Abusing Single
        Parent and Their Battered Adolescents.   Paper presented at
        the National Council on Alcoholism Forum, Seattle, May, 1980.
        (Also in: Alcoholism: Clinical and Experimental Research,
        4: 214, 1980.)

1876.   Flanzer, J.P.   Theoretical Connections Between Substance Abuse
        and Domestic Violence.   Paper presented at the Fourth National
        Conference on Child Abuse and Neglect, Los Angeles, October, 1979.

1877.   Flanzer, J.P.   Treating Abused Teenage Alcoholics.   Paper presented
        at the 59th Annual Meeting of the American Orthopsychiatric
        Association, Inc., San Francisco, 1982.

1878.   Flanzer, J.P.   Treating the Combination of Alcohol and Family Violence.
        Paper presented at the 40th Annual Conference of the American
        Association for Marriage and Family Therapy.   October, 1982.

1879.   Flanzer, J.P., Seidenschnur, P.-P.T. and Sturkie, D.K.   Treatment
        and Research Issues Relating to Alcohol and Adolescent
        Abusing Families.   Paper presented at the 57th Annual Meeting
        of the American Orthopsychiatric Association, Toronto, 1980.

1880.   Flanzer, Jerry P.   Alcohol Abusing Parents and Their Battered
        Adolescents.   In: Currents in Alcoholism: Recent Advances
        in Research and Treatment.   Volume 7.   Ed. M. Galanter.
        New York: Grune and Stratton, 1980, pages 529-538.   (Also
        in: Alcoholism: Clinical and Experimental Research,
        3(2): 175, 1979.   Also as :   Alcohol Abusing Parents and
        Their Battered Adolescents.   Little Rock, AR: University
        of Arkansas, Graduate School of Social Work, 1979.)

1881.   Flanzer, Jerry P.   Alcohol and Family Violence.   In: The Many
        Faces of Family Violence.   Ed. J.P. Flanzer.   Springfield,
        IL: Charles C. Thomas, 1982, pages 34-50.

1882.   Flanzer, Jerry P.   Alcohol Use Among Jewish Adolescents: A 1977
        Sample.   In: Currents in Alcoholism, Volume 6, Treatment
        and Rehabilitation and Epidemiology.   Ed. Marc Galanter.
        New York: Grune and Stratton, 1979, pages 257-268.

1883.   Flanzer, Jerry P.   Family-Focused Management: Treatment of Choice
        for Deviant and Dependent Families.   International Journal
        of Family Counseling, 6(2): 25-31, 1978.

1884.   Flanzer, Jerry P.   Family Management, Not Family Therapy for the
        Treatment of Alcoholics.   Paper presented at the National
        Council on Alcoholism Forum, San Diego, 1977.

1885. Flanzer, Jerry P. Family Management in the Treatment of
       Alcoholism. British Journal on Alcohol and Alcoholism,
       London, 13: 45-49, 1978.

1886. Flanzer, Jerry P. (Ed.) The Many Faces of Family Violence.
       Springfield, IL: Charles C. Thomas, 1982.

1887. Flanzer, Jerry P. The Vicious Circle of Alcoholism and Family
       Violence. Alcoholism: The National Magazine, 1(3):
       30-32, 1981.

1888. Flanzer, Jerry P. and O'Brien, Gregory M. St. L. Family Focused
       Treatment and Management: A Multi-Discipline Training
       Approach. In: Alcoholism and Drug Dependence; A Multi-
       disciplinary Approach. Proceedings of the Third
       International Conference on Alcoholism and Drug Dependence,
       Liverpool, April, 1976. Eds. J.S. Madden, R. Walker and
       W.H. Kenyon. New York: Plenum Press, 1977, pages 239-261.

1889. Flanzer, Jerry P. and Sturkie, D.K. Arkansas Alcohol/Child Abuse
       Demonstration Project. Report. Little Rock: University of
       Arkansas Graduate School of Social Work, 1982.

1890. Flanzer, Jerry P. and Sturkie, D.K. The Effect of Drinking Level
       on Masking Self-perception and the Problem of Evaluating
       Family Treatment. Alcoholism: Clinical and Experimental
       Research, 5: 149, 1981.

1891. Fleming, J.B. Stopping Wife Abuse: A Guide to the Emotional,
       Psychological, and Legal Implications for the Abused Woman
       and Those Helping Her. Garden City, NY: Anchor Books, 1979.

1892. Fleming, Jan E., Extein, Irl, Sternbach, Harvey A., Pottash, A.L.C.
       and Gold, Mark S. The Thyrotropin-Releasing Hormone and
       Dexamethasone Suppression Tests in the Familial Classification
       of Depression. Psychiatry Research, 9(1): 53-58, 1983.

1893. Fleming, T.C. Violence: The Role of Chemical Agents. Postgraduate
       Medicine, 69(6): 27-28, 30, 1981.

1894. Fligic, M. Teskoce Angazovanja Clanova Porodice u Lecenju
       Alkoholicara. (The Difficulties of Involving the Family
       in the Treatment of Alcoholics.) Alkoholizam, Beograd,
       18 (3-4): 51-55, 1978.

1895. Floch, Maurice. Imprisoned Abnormal Drinkers: Application of the
       Bowman-Jellinek Classification Schedule to an Institutional
       Sample. Part I. Review and Analysis of Data. Quarterly
       Journal of Studies on Alcohol, 7: 518-566, 1947.

1896. Floch, Maurice. Imprisoned Abnormal Drinkers: Application
       of the Bowman-Jellinek Classification Schedule to an
       Institutional Sample. Part II. Illustrative Case Histories
       and Conclusions. Quarterly Journal of Studies on Alcohol,
       8: 61-120, 1947.

1897. Flohr, Rinna B. Promoting Community Investment. Paper presented
       at the National Institute on Drug Abuse, Program for Women's
       Concerns, Miami Beach, October, 1975. (Also in: Drugs,
       Alcohol and Women; A National Forum Source Book. Washington,
       D.C.: National Research and Communications Associates, Inc.,
       1976, pages 67-70.)

1898. Florenzano-Ursua, R., Molina, O.F., Figueroa, C., Hinrichsen, M.,
       Jimenez, K. and Nunez, R. Alcoholismo y Depression: Estudio
       Epidemiologico de su Asociacion. (Alcoholism and Depression:
       Epidemiological Correlations.) Revista Medica de Chile,
       Santiago, 107: 799-806, 1979.

1899. Flynn, John P. Recent Findings Related to Wife Abuse. _Social Casework_, 58(1): 13-20, 1977.

1900. Flynn, William, Chafetz, Morris E., Lisansky, Ephram T. and McCambridge-Mercedes, Bowen. Alcoholism: Early Diagnosis and Referral. _Georgetown Medical Bulletin_, 27(1): 7-23, 1973.

1901. Focus on Children of Alcoholic Patients. _ADAMHA News_, 9(6): 5, 1983.

1902. Foinitskii, I. Ya. On the Question of the Care of the Children of Convict-Alcoholics. _Trudy Komissii Po Voprosu Ob Al'kogolizme_, 7/8(1): 466, 1905.

1903. Foley, Charles Patrick. _An Understanding: Alcoholism and the Family for General Ministry_. Newton Centre, MA: Andover Newton Theological School, 1982.

1904. Foley, Vincent D. Alcoholism: A Family System Approach. _Journal of Family Counseling_, 4(2): 12-18, 1976.

1905. Foley, Vincent D. Structural Family Therapy: One Approach to the Treatment of the Alcoholic Family. In: _Family Treatment Methods in Alcohol Abuse and Alcoholism_. Pittsburgh, PA: University of Pittsburgh, 1976, pages 53-75.

1906. Fontaine, C.M. International Relocation: A Comprehensive Psychosocial Approach. _EAP Digest_, 3(3): 27-31, 1983.

1907. Fontana, Alan F. and Dowds, Barbara Noel. Assessing Treatment Outcome. I. Adjustment in the Community. _The Journal of Nervous and Mental Disease_, 161(4): 221-230, 1975.

1908. Fontana, V.J. Child Abuse: Prevention in Teenage Parent. _New York State Journal of Medicine_, 80(1): 53-56, 1980.

1909. Fontana, Vincent J. Social Manifestations. In: _The Maltreated Child_. 2nd Edition. Ed. V. Fontana. Springfield, IL: Charles C. Thomas, 1971, pages 17-21.

1910. Fontana, Vincent J. _Somewhere a Child is Crying: Maltreatment - Causes and Prevention_. New York: Macmillan, 1973.

1911. Fontane, Patrick E. and Layne, Norman R., Jr. The Family as a Context for Developing Youthful Drinking Patterns. _Journal of Alcohol and Drug Education_, 24(3): 19-29, 1979.

1912. Forbes, A.R. and Rae, J.B. Clinical and Psychometric Characteristics of the Wives of Alcoholics. _British Journal of Psychiatry_, 112: 197-200, 1966.

1913. Ford, Howard L. Marriage Counseling a Prevention of Alcoholism. _California State Marriage Counseling Association_, 6(1): 1-5, 1970.

1914. Forel, A. L'heredite Alcoolique. _Schweizerische Medizinische Wochenschrift_, 55: 873-874, 1925.

1915. _Forgotten Children_. Toronto: Addiction Research Foundation of Ontario, 1971.

1916. Fornari, Ugo, Miano, Mario, and Offidani, Maria Luisa. Considerations on Some Clinical and Psychopedagogic Aspects of a Group of Antisocial Minor Children of Alcoholics. _Minerva Medicolegale_, 88(3): 147-172, 1968.

1917. Forney, Mary Ann. The Effect of Sociocultural Factors on the
         Knowledge, Attitudes, and Behaviors Toward the Use of Alcohol
         Among Middle School Students. Dissertation Abstracts
         International, 44(4): 984A, 1983.

1918. Forney, Mary Ann, Forney, Paul D., Davis, Harry, Van Hosse, John,
         Cafferty, Thomas and Allen, Harvey. A Discriminant Analysis
         of Adolescent Problem Drinking. Journal of Drug Education,
         14(4): 347-355, 1984.

1919. Forrest, G.G. The Diagnosis and Treatment of Alcoholism.
         Springfield, IL: Charles C. Thomas, 1975.

1920. Forrest, G.G. The Diagnosis and Treatment of Alcoholism,
         Second Edition. Springfield, IL: Charles C. Thomas, 1978.

1921. Forrest, Gary G. Alcoholism, Narcissism and Psychopathology.
         Springfield, IL: Charles C. Thomas, 1983.

1922. Forrest, Gary G. How to Cope with a Teenage Drinker. New
         Alternatives & Hope for Parents & Families. New York:
         Antheneum Publications, 1983.

1923. Forrest, Gary G. How to Live with a Problem Drinker and Survive.
         New York: Atheneum Publications, 1980.

1924. Forrest, Gary G. Treatment II: Group Psychotherapy. In: The
         Diagnosis and Treatment of Alcoholism. Springfield, IL:
         Charles C. Thomas, 1975, pages 93-109.

1925. Forrest, Gary G. Treatment II: Group Psychotherapy. In: The
         Diagnosis and Treatment of Alcoholism, 2nd Edition.
         Springfield, IL: Charles C. Thomas, 1978, pages 95-111.

1926. Forrest, Gary G. Treatment III: Alcoholics Anonymous. In: The
         Diagnosis and Treatment of Alcoholism. Springfield, IL:
         Charles C. Thomas, 1975, pages 110-124.

1927. Forrest, Gary G. Treatment III: Alcoholics Anonymous. In: The
         Diagnosis and Treatment of Alcoholism, 2nd Edition.
         Springfield, IL: Charles C. Thomas, 1978, pages 112-125.

1928. Forrest, Gary G. Treatment VI: Marital and Family Therapy.
         In: The Diagnosis and Treatment of Alcoholism, 2nd Edition.
         Springfield, IL: Charles C. Thomas, 1978, pages 168-210.

1929. Forrest, Gary G. Treatment VI: The Recovery Issue. In: The
         Diagnosis and Treatment of Alcoholism. Springfield, IL:
         Charles C. Thomas, 1975, pages 149-154.

1930. Forrest, Gary G. Treatment VII: Toward a Causative Theory of
         Alcohol Addiction. In: The Diagnosis and Treatment of
         Alcoholism. Springfield, IL: Charles C. Thomas, 1975,
         pages 155-166.

1931. Forrest, Gary G. Treatment VIII: Toward a Causative Theory of
         Alcohol Addiction. In: The Diagnosis and Treatment of
         Alcoholism, 2nd Edition. Springfield, IL: Charles C.
         Thomas, 1978, pages 217-229.

1932. Forslund, M.A. and Gustafson, T.J. Influence of Peers and Parents
         and Sex Differences in Drinking by High-School Students.
         Quarterly Journal of Studies on Alcohol, 31(4): 868-875,
         1970.

1933. Forslund, M.A. and Gustafson, T.J. Relative Influence of Peers
         and Parents on Drinking by High-School Seniors. Albuquerque:
         Department of Sociology, The University of New Mexico, no date.

1934. Forssman, H. and Thuwe I. Continued Follow-up Study of 120 Persons Born After Refusal of Application for Therapeutic Abortion. Acta Psychiatrica Scandinavica, Copenhagen, 64(2): 142-149, 1981.

1935. Forssman, H., Thuwe, I. and Eriksson, B. Children with Supernumerary X-Chromosome; A Ten-Year Follow-Up Study of School Children in Special Classes. Journal of Mental Deficiency Research, 23: 189-193, 1979.

1936. For Teenagers with an Alcoholic Parent. Pamphlet. New York: Al-Anon Family Group Headquarters, 1971.

1937. Fortin, M.T. and Evans, S.B. Correlates of Loss of Control Over Drinking in Women Alcoholics. Journal of Studies on Alcohol, 44(5): 787-796, 1983.

1938. Fortin, Mary Lynch. Community Health Nursing. In: Substance Abuse: Pharmacologic, Developmental, and Clinical Perspectives. Eds. Gerald Bennett, Christine Vouvakis and Donna S. Wolf. New York: John Wiley & Sons, 1983, pages 209-222.

1939. Fortin, Mary Lynch. Detoxification, Then What? A Community Nursing Course in Alcoholism. American Journal of Nursing, 80(1): 113-114, 1980.

1940. Foster, Tiah Ann. Why Patients Decide to Discontinue Renal Dialysis. Journal of the American Medical Women's Association, 31(6): 234-235, 1976.

1941. Foster, W. Let's Include the Child in Family Therapy. Alcoholism: The National Magazine, 1(4): 14, 1981.

1942. Foster, Euphesenia W. Viewing "Corrections" Inside Out. Paper presented at the National Institute on Drug Abuse, Program for Women's Concerns, Miami Beach, October, 1975. (Also in: Drugs, Alcohol and Women; A National Forum Source Book. Washington, D.C.: National Research and Communications Associates, 1976, pages 82-84.)

1943. Foster, Willard O. Jr. and Fay, William A.J. Children of Alcoholic Parents: Their Needs and the Response. NIAAA Discussion Paper. Rockville: National Institute on Alcohol Abuse and Alcoholism, 1978.

1944. Foulds, G.A. and Hassall, C. The Significance of Age of Onset of Excessive Drinking in Male Alcoholics. The British Journal of Psychiatry: The Journal of Mental Science, London, 115(526): 1027-1032, 1969.

1945. Fowler, R.C. and Tsuang, M.T. Schizophrenics' Families. British Journal of Psychiatry, 128: 100-101, 1976.

1946. Fowler, R.C., Tsuang, M.T. and Cadoret, R.J. Parental Psychiatric Illness Associated with Schizophrenia in the Siblings of Schizophrenics. Comprehensive Psychiatry, 18: 271-275, 1977.

1947. Fowler, R.C., Tsuang, M.T. and Cadoret, R.J. Psychiatric Illness in the Offspring of Schizophrenics. Comprehensive Psychiatry, 18: 127-134, 1977.

1948. Fowler, R.C., Tsuang, M.T., Cadoret, R.J. and Monnelly, E. Non-Psychotic Disorders in the Families of Process Schizophrenics. Acta Psychiatrica Scandinavica, Copenhagen, 51: 153-160, 1975.

1949. Fowler, R.C., Tsuang, M.T., Cadoret, R.J., Monnelly, E. and McCabe, M. A Clinical and Family Comparison of Paranoid and Non-Paranoid Schizophrenics. The British Journal of Psychiatry: The Journal of Mental Science, London, 124(0): 346-351, 1974.

1950. Fowler, Richard C. and Tsuang, Ming T. Spouses of Schizophrenics:
      A Blind Comparative Study. Comprehensive Psychiatry,
      16(4): 339-342, 1975.

1951. Fox, Ruth. The Alcoholic Spouse. In: Neurotic Interaction in
      Marriage. Ed. V.W. Eisenstein. New York: Basic Books, 1956.

1952. Fox, Ruth. Alcoholism as a Form of Acting Out. In: Acting Out:
      Theoretical and Clinical Aspects. Eds. Lawrence Edwin Apt
      and Stuart L. Weissman. New York: Grune and Stratton, 1965,
      pages 119-128.

1953. Fox, Ruth. Children in the Alcoholic Family. In: Problems in
      Addiction: Alcoholism and Narcotics. Ed. W.C. Bier. New
      York: Fordham University Press, 1962, pages 71-96.

1954. Fox, Ruth. The Effect of Alcoholism on Children. In: Progress
      in Child Psychiatry. Proceedings of the Fifth International
      Congress of Psychotherapy, Vienna, 1961. Ed. B. Stokvis. Basel:
      Karger, 1963, pages 55-65. (Also as: The Effect of Alcoholism
      on Children. New York: National Council on Alcoholism, 1972.)

1955. Fox, Ruth. A Multidisciplinary Approach to the Treatment of
      Alcoholism. The American Journal of Psychiatry, 123(7):
      769-778, 1967. (Also in: Maryland State Medical Journal,
      16(3): 100-117, 1967; Also in: International Journal of
      Psychiatry, 5(1): 34-44, 1968.)

1956. Fox, Ruth. Treating the Alcoholic's Family. In: Alcoholism;
      the Total Treatment Approach. Ed. R.J. Catanzaro.
      Springfield, IL: Charles C. Thomas, 1968, pages 105-115.
      (Also in: Nurse Care Planning on Alcoholism. Eds. J.
      Lotterhos and M. Mcguire. Greenville, NC: East Carolina
      University, 1974, pages 130-139.)

1957. Fox, Vernelie. Alcoholism in Adolescence. Journal of School
      Health, 43(1): 32-35, 1973.

1958. Fox, Vernelle and Lowe, George D. II. Day-Hospital Treatment of
      the Alcoholic Patient. Quarterly Journal of Studies on
      Alcohol, 29(3): 634-641, 1968.

1959. Fox, Vernelle and Raines, Florence. Day Hosptial as a Treatment
      Modality for Alcoholism. Paper presented at the North American
      Congress on Alcohol and Drug Problems. San Francisco, December,
      1974.

1960. Fox, Vernelle and Smith, Marguerite A. Evaluation of a
      Chemopsychotherapeutic Program for the Rehabilitation
      of Alcoholics. Quarterly Journal of Studies on Alcohol,
      20: 767-780, 1959.

1961. Fraillon, J.M. Alcohol and its Effect on the Family. Australian
      Family Physician, Sydney, 6: 1391-1398, 1977.

1962. France, R. From a Casebook of Behaviour Therapy in General
      Practice (2). Practitioner, 226(1368): 1128-1133, 1982.

1963. Frances, Allen and Frances, Richard. Detoxifying and Treating
      a Woman Who Has Been Unable to Stop Drinking. Hospital and
      Community Psychiatry, 35(7): 675-676, 678, 1984.

1964. Frances, Mary Brown. Identification of Alcohol Problems Among
      Health Maintenance Organization Patients, Using the MacAndrew
      Alcoholism Scale. Dissertation Abstracts International,
      42(8): 3418B, 1981.

1965. Frances, Richard. Application of Psychoanalytic Concepts in
       Alcoholism Treatment. In: Social Work Treatment of
       Alcohol Problems. Ed. D. Cook. New Brunswick, NJ:
       Rutgers Center of Alcohol Studies, 1983, pages 81-87.

1966. Frances, Richard J., Bucky, Steven and Alexopoulos, George S.
       Outcome Study of Familial and Nonfamilial Alcoholism.
       American Journal of Psychiatry, 141(11): 1469-1471, 1984.

1967. Frances, Richard J., Timm, Stephen and Bucky, Steven. Studies of
       Familial and Nonfamilial Alcoholism. I. Demographic Studies.
       Archives of General Psychiatry, 37: 564-566, 1980.

1968. Frank, P. Alcohol & the Family. Three Sure Ways to Solve the
       Problem. Liguori, MO: Liguori Publications, 1978.

1969. Frank, P. El Alcohol Y La Familia. Liguori, MO: Liguori
       Publications, 1981.

1970. Frankel, Barbara. On Participant-Observation as a Component of
       Evaluation: Strategies, Constraints and Issues. Evaluation
       & Program Planning, 5(3): 239-246, 1982.

1971. Frankenstein, W. and Wilson, G.T. Alcohol's Effects on Self-
       Awareness. Addictive Behaviors, 9(4): 323-328, 1984.

1972. Frankenstein, William, Hay, William M. and Nathan, Peter E.
       Effects of Intoxication on Alcoholics' Marital Communication
       and Problem Solving. Journal of Studies on Alcohol,
       46(1): 1-6, 1985.

1973. Franklin, J.L., Kittredge, L.D. and Thrasher, J.H. A Survey of
       Factors Related to Mental Hospital Readmissions. Hospital
       & Community Psychiatry, 26(11): 749-751, 1975.

1974. Franks, D.D. and Thacker, B.T. Assessing Familial Factors in
       Alcoholism from MMPI Profiles. American Journal of
       Psychiatry, 136: 1084-1085, 1979.

1975. Fraser, Judy. The Female Alcoholic. Addictions, 20(3): 64-80,
       1973.

1976. Freed, A.H. Educating Doctors in Health-Related Problems of
       Alcohol: A Paper Based on Working Group on the Role of the
       Family Physician in Helping with Alcohol Related Problems.
       Paper presented at the National Drug Institute, Brisbane,
       May, 1983, pages 89-91.

1977. Freed, E.X. Characteristics of Male Alcoholics. The Journal
       of the Medical Society of New Jersey, 68(12): 1011-1013,
       1971.

1978. Freed, Earl X. Alcoholism: Comprehensive Rehabilitation Needed.
       American Archives of Rehabilitation Therapy, 16(3-4):
       74-75, 1969.

1979. Freed, Earl X. Alcoholism and Schizophrenia: The Search for
       Perspectives. A Review. Journal of Studies on Alcohol,
       36(7): 853-881, 1975.

1980. Freedberg, Edmund J. and Johnston, William E. Effects of Various
       Sources of Coercion on Outcome of Treatment of Alcoholism.
       Psychological Reports, 43(3): 1271-1278, 1978.

1981. Freedberg, Edmund J. and Scherer and Shawn E. The Ontario Problem
       Assessment Battery for Alcoholics. Psychological Reports,
       40(3): 743-746, 1977.

1982. Freedman, Alfred M. and Brotman, Richard E. Multiple Drug Use
        Among Teenagers: Plans for Action -- Research. In: Drugs
        and Youth. Ed. J. Wittenborn. Springfield, IL: Charles
        C. Thomas, 1969, pages 335-344.

1983. Freedman, R.P. and Williams, T. Hazelden Community Education
        Program: Alcohol Drugs and Family Health. "Implementation
        of an Innovative Community Education Program for Prevention."
        Report. Minneapolis: University of Minnesota, School of
        Public Health, 1981.

1984. Freeman, T. and Hopwood, S.E. Characteristics and Response to
        Treatment of an Unselected Group of Alcoholics. Scottish
        Medical Journal, Glasgow, 13(7): 237-241, 1967.

1985. Freiova, E. Alkoholismus Rodicu a Mravni Narusenost Mladeze
        Skolniho Veku. (Alcoholism in Parents and the Moral
        Impairment of School-Age Children.) Ceskoslovenska
        Psychiatrie, 62: 188-192, 1966.

1986. French, J.M. A Study of the Hereditary Effects of Alcohol.
        Medicine, 8: 20-24, 1902.

1987. French, Laurence. Social Problems Among Cherokee Females:
        A Study of Cultural Ambivalence and Role Identity. American
        Journal of Psychoanalysis, 36(2): 163-169, 1976.

1988. Freour, M. Paul. From Alcoholism to the Alcoholic Patient.
        Acta Psychiatrica, Belgica, 80(2): 131-137, 1980.

1989. Freour, P. The Fight Against Alcoholism and Its Consequences
        in General Practice. Semaine des Hopitaux de Paris,
        55(15-16): 757-761, 1979.

1990. Frequency, Causes, Social and Economic Consequences, and Prevention
        of Alcoholism in Families with Low Incomes. Springfield, VA:
        National Technical Information Service, 1969.

1991. Freston, Margie S. Development of a Survey Instrument for
        Assessing Selected Risk Factors Related to Cardiovascular
        Health. Dissertation Abstracts International, 42(6):
        2318B, 1981.

1992. Frets, G.P. Alcohol and Heredity. Mensch en Maatschappij, 2:
        444-446, 1926.

1993. Frets, G.P. Alcohol and Offspring. Wegwijzer, Hoenderloo, 32:
        101-109, 1931.

1994. Frets, G.P. Delirium Tremens En De Erfelijkheid Van Alcoholisme.
        (Delirium Tremens and the Heredity of Alcoholism.)
        Geneeskundige Gids, (The Hague), 20: 679-686, 693-698,
        1942.

1995. Freudenberger, H.J. Burnout and Job Dissatisfaction: Impact on
        the Family. In: Perspectives on Work and the Family.
        Volume 2. Eds. James C. Hansen and Stanley H. Cramer. 1984,
        pages 95-105.

1996. Freudenberger, Herbert J. The Issues of Re-entry for the Resident
        and Staff in Therapeutic Communities. Journal of Psychedelic
        Drugs, 12(1): 65-69, 1980.

1997. Freund, Kurt, Heasman, Gerald A. and Roper, Vincent. Results
        of the Main Studies on Sexual Offences Against Children and
        Pubescents: A Review. Canadian Journal of Criminology,
        24(4): 387-397, 1982.

1998. Freund, P.J. Armenian American Drinking Patterns. <u>Alcohol Health and Research World</u>, <u>5</u>(1): 47-50, 1980.

1999. Freund, P.J. Armenian American Drinking Patterns Ethnicity Family and Religion. <u>Alcoholism</u>, Zagreb, <u>16</u>(1-2): 9-25, 1981.

2000. Fried, J. Emerging Trends: Treatment Approaches of Alcoholism and Domestic Violence Programs. <u>National Council on Alcoholism Forum</u>, New Orleans, April, 1981.

2001. Fried, P.A., Watkinson, B., Grant, A. and Knights, R.M. Changing Patterns of Soft Drug Use Prior to and During Pregnancy: A Prospective Study. <u>Drug and Alcohol Dependence</u>, Lausanne, <u>6</u>(5): 323-343, 1980.

2002. Friedman, Alfred S., Pomerance, Errol, Sanders, Richard, Santo, Yoav and Utada, Arlene. The Substance and Problems of Families of Adolescent Drug Abusers. <u>Contemporary Drug Problems</u>, <u>1</u>(3): 327-356, 1981.

2003. Friedman, C. Jack, Mann, Frederica and Friedman, Alfred S. A Profile of Juvenile Street Gang Members. <u>Adolescence</u>, <u>10</u>(40): 563-607, 1975.

2004. Friedman, Lisa Adrian. Differential Family Recovery in Alcoholism. Doctoral Dissertation. (University Microfilms No. 8110154.) Berkeley, CA: California School of Professional Psychology, 1980. (Also in: <u>Dissertation Abstracts International</u>, <u>41</u>(12): 4661B, 1981.)

2005. Friedman, R.C. DSM-III and Affective Pathology in Hospitalized Adolescents. <u>Journal of Nervous and Mental Disease</u>, <u>170</u>(9): 511-521, 1982.

2006. Friedrich, W.N. and Loftsgard, S.O. Comparison of Two Alcoholism Scales with Alcoholics and Their Wives. <u>Journal of Clinical Psychology</u>, <u>34</u>: 784-786, 1978.

2007. Frieze, I.H. and Schafer, P.C. Alcohol Use and Marital Violence: Female and Male Differences in Reactions to Alcohol. In: <u>Alcohol Problems in Women: Antecedents, Consequences, and Intervention</u>. Eds. Sharon C. Wilsnack and Linda J. Beckman. New York: Guilford Press, 1984, pages 260-279.

2008. Frieze, Irene Hanson and Knoble, Jaime. The Effects of Alcohol on Marital Violence. Paper presented at the American Psychological Association Annual Meeting. Montreal, 1980.

2009. Frigo, Daniel Callistus. Relapse in Alcoholism Treatment: Supportive Families and Posttreatment Therapy. <u>Dissertation Abstracts International</u>, <u>43</u>(12): 4044A, 1983.

2010. Frisone, L. Ricerca Sull'ereditarieta Delle Psicosi Alcooliche. (Research on the Inheritance of Alcoholic Psychoses. <u>Giornale di Psichiatria e Neuropatologia</u>, Ferrara, <u>94</u>: 417-430, 1966.

2011. Frost, M. and Fahrlander, R.S. <u>Evaluation of the Children from Alcoholic Families Project</u>. Report. Omaha: University of Nebraska, 1983.

2012. Frost, Nicholas R. and Clayton, Paula J. Bereavement and Psychiatric Hospitalization. <u>Archives of General Psychiatry</u>, <u>34</u>(10): 1172-1175, 1977.

2013. Fujisawa, S. Rehabilitation of a Husband's Alcoholism with the Aid of His Family's Independence. <u>Kango</u>, <u>30</u>(3): 77-81, 1978.

2014. Fuller, R.K. and Roth, H.P. Disulfiram for the Treatment of
       Alcoholism. An Evaluation in 28 Men. Annals of the
       Internal Medicine, 90(6): 901-904, 1979.

2015. Furman, Leola E. and Selbyg, Arne. Rural Alcoholic Women: Study
       and Treatment. Human Services in the Rural Environment,
       7(2): 15-23, 1982.

2016. Furnham, Adrian and Lowick, Victoria. Lay Theories of the Causes
       of Alcoholism. British Journal of Medical Psychology,
       57: 319-332, 1984.

2017. Furumoto, Laurel. Responses to Alcohol, Smoking, Drug Related
       and Neutral Words by Sons of Alcoholics. Final Report.
       NIMH Grant, MH-20536, 1972.

2018. Futterman, S. Personality Trends in Wives of Alcoholics. Journal
       of Psychiatric Social Work, 23: 37-41, 1953.

G

2019. Gabriel, E. Beitrage Zur Frage der Erworbenen Vorbedingungen
       des Alkoholismus. (The Acquired Prerequisites for
       Alcoholism.) Allgemeine Zeitschrift fur Psychiatrie and
       Psychischgerichtliche Medizin, Berlin, 101: 411-485, 1934.

2020. Gabrielli, W.F. and Mednick, S.A. Intellectual Performance in
       Children of Alcoholics. Journal of Nervous and Mental
       Disease, 171(7): 444-447, 1983.

2021. Gabrielli, W.F. Jr. and Plomin, R. Drinking Behavior in the
       Colorado Adoptee and Twin Sample. Journal of Studies on
       Alcohol, 46(1): 24-31, 1985.

2022. Gabrielli, W.F. Jr. and Plomin, R. Individual Differences in
       Anticipation of Alcohol Sensitivity. Journal of Nervous
       and Mental Disease, 173(2): 111-114, 1985.

2023. Gachot, H. Alcohol and Eugenics. International Congress Against
       Alcoholism, 20: 210-215, 1934.

2024. Gacic, B. Alcoholism and the Family. Psihijatrija Danas,
       Beograd, 6(4): 21-34, 1974.

2025. Gacic, B. Family - Therapy for Alcohol - %Combined Intensive
       Family - Therapy for Alcoholism. Revue De L'Alcoolisme,
       23(4): 242-254, 1977.

2026. Gacic, B. Hazaspari Csoportterapia Az Alkoholistak Kezeleseben.
       (Group Therapy for Married Couples in the Treatment of
       Alcoholics.) Alkohologia, Budapest, 7: 185-188, 1976.

2027. Gacic, B. Importance of the Family and Social Network in the
       Treatment of Alcoholism. Paper presented at the 27th
       International Institute on the Prevention and Treatment of
       Alcoholism, Vienna, June, 1981, pages 475-484.

2028. Gacic, B. Intenzivna Kombinovana Porodicna Terapija Alkoholizma.
       (Intensive Combined Family Therapy in Alcoholism.)
       Alkoholizam, Belgrade, 18(1): 35-68, 1978.

2029. Gacic, B., Arezina, O., Gardinovacki, I., Gacic, R. and Ivanovic,
       M. Komunikacije Bracnih Partnera u Toku Intenzivne Porodicne
       Terapije Alkoholizma. (Communication of Marital Couples
       During Intensive Family Therapy of Alcoholism.)
       Psihijatrija Danas, 9: 109-120, 1977.

2030. Gacic, B., Ivanovic, M. and Sedmak, T. Kompenzovana I Dekompenzovana
       Kriza Porodicnog Sistema U Razvoju I Lecenju Alkoholizma.
       (Compensation and Decompensation Crisis of the Family System
       in Developing and Treated Alcoholism. Psihijatrija Danas,
       Belgrade, 13(3): 229-237, 1981.

2031.   Gacic, B. and Kastel, P.   La Maladie Alcoolique a Belgrade.
        (Alcoholic Malady in Belgrade.)   Revue De L'Alcoolisme,
        Paris, 21(3): 171-184, 1975.

2032.   Gacic, B. and Kastel, P.   Savrememo Lecenje Alkoholizma.
        (Modern Alcoholism Treatment.)   Alkoholizam,
        Beograd, 16(3-4): 22-36, 1976.

2033.   Gacic, B., Sedmak, T. and Ivanovic, M.   Familial Treatment
        of Alcoholism as a Modality of Community Psychiatry.
        Toxicomanies, Quebec, 13(3-4): 217-224, 1980.

2034.   Gacic, Branko.   General System Theory and Alcoholism.
        Psihijatrija Danas, Beograd, 10(3-4): 309-316, 1978.

2035.   Gade, E.M. and Goodman, R.E.   Vocational Preference of Daughters of
        Alcoholics.   Vocational Guidance Quarterly, 24: 41-47, 1975.

2036.   Gad-Luther, I.   Types of Marital Interaction in Alcoholic Family
        Systems and their Relationships with Existing Patterns of
        Sexual Difficulties.   Doctoral Dissertation.   San Francisco
        Institute for the Advanced Study in Human Sexuality, 1979.

2037.   Gad-Luther, I. and Dickman, D.   Psychosexual Therapy with
        Recovering Alcoholics, a Pilot Study.   Journal of Sex
        Education and Therapy, 1(5): 11-16, 1979.

2038.   Gad-Luther, I. and Laube, H.   Types of Interaction in Alcoholism
        Complicated Marriages and Their Relationship with Existing
        Patterns of Sexual Difficulties.   I. Preliminary Data and
        Methodological Considerations.   In: Drug Dependence and
        Alcoholism   Volume 1: Biomedical Issues.   Ed. A.J.
        Schecter.   New York: Plenum Press, 1981, pages 719-728.

2039.   Gaertner, Miriam Luise.   The Alcoholic Marriage. A Study Based
        on 15 Case Records and Pertinent Psychoanalytical
        Writings.   New York: New York School of Social Work, 1939.

2040.   Gaines, Josephine.   The Right to Quality Life: A Challenge for
        Parenting Education.   Health Education, 12(2): 18-20, 1981.

2041.   Gaitz, C.M. and Baer, Paul E.   Characteristics of Elderly Patients
        with Alcoholism.   Archives of General Psychiatry, 24(4):
        372-378, 1971.

2042.   Galanter, M.   Use of Social Networks in Office Management of the
        Substance Abuser.   In: Psychosocial Treatment of Alcoholism.
        Eds. M. Galanter and E.M. Pattison.   Washington, DC: American
        Psychiatric Press, 1984, pages 97-144.

2043.   Galanter, Marc (Ed.)   Recent Developments in Alcoholism.   Volume 1.
        Genetics, Behavioral Treatment, Social Mediators, and Prevention:
        Current Conceps in Diagnosis.   New York: Plenum Press, 1983.

2044.   Galanter, Marc, Gleaton, Thomas, Marcus, Carol E. and McMillen, Jean.
        Self-Help Groups for Parents of Young Drug and Alcohol Abusers.
        American Journal of Psychiatry, 141(7): 889-891, 1984.

2045.   Galanter, Marc and Pattison, E. Mansell.   Alcoholism Treatment
        Through Systems Intervention: A Perspective -- Part I.
        Introduction to a Symposium.   Alcoholism: Clinical and
        Experimental Research, 8(1): 1-3, 1984.

2046.   Galdi, Z. and Koczkas, I   Alkoholista Betegek Utogondozasanak
        Szervezesi Kerdesei.   (Organizational Problems in the
        Aftercare of Alcoholic Patients.)   Alkohologia, Budapest,
        3: 8-9, 1972.

2047.   Galdston, R. Disorders of Early Parenthood: Neglect,
        Deprivation, Exploitation, and Abuse of Little Children.
        In: Basic Handbook of Child Psychiatry, Vol. 2. Ed.
        J.D. Noshpitz. New York: Basic Books, 1979, pages 581-593.

2048.   Gale, Fay and Bennett, J.H. Huntington's Chorea in a South
        Australian Community of Aboriginal Descent. Medical Journal
        of Australia, Sydney, 2(10): 482-484, 1969.

2049.   Gallant, D.M. New Information on Genetics and Alcoholism.
        Alcoholism: Clinical and Experimental Research 6(1):
        130-131, 1982.

2050.   Gallant, D.M., Rich, A., Bey, E. and Terranova, L. Group Psychotherapy
        with Married Couples: A Successful Technique in New Orleans
        Alcoholism Clinic Patients. Journal of the Louisiana State
        Medical Society, 122(2): 41-44, 1970.

2051.   Gallimberti, L. Le Mari de la Femme Alcoolique: Etude Effectuee
        sur 34 Sujets au Moyen du Test de Rorschach. (Husband of the
        Woman Alcoholic: A Study of 34 Subjects, Using the Rorschach
        Test.) Paper presented at the 25th International Institute on
        the Prevention and Treatment of Alcoholism. Tours, June, 1979.

2052.   Gallimberti, L., Benussi, G., Orlandini, D. and Gasparini, V.
        Studio Socio-psicologico Caso-Controllo su 50 Soggetti con
        Sindrome di Dipendenza Alcolica (S.D.A.). (Psychosocial Case
        Control Study of 50 Subjects with Alcohol Dependence Syndrome
        (ADS). Minerva Psichiatrica, Torino, 24(1): 25-32, 1983.

2053.   Gallup, George. Liquor: A Cause of Family Problems. Pamphlet.
        Princeton: Gallup Corp., 1978.

2054.   Gantman, Carol A. Family Interaction Patterns Among Families With
        Normal, Disturbed and Drug-Abusing Adolescents. Journal of
        Youth and Adolescence, 7(4): 429-440, 1978.

2055.   Garcia, Prieto A. and Cabenzudo, Fernandez A. Patologia Psiquiatrica
        Infantil en Hijos de Alcoholicos: Estudio de 56 Casos Comparados
        Con un Grupo de Control. (Childhood Psychiatric Pathology in
        Children of Alcoholics: Study of 56 Cases Compared to a Control
        Group.) Actas Luso-Espanolas de Neurologia, Psiquiatriay Ciencias
        Afines, 2(6): 507-516, 1974.

2056.   Garcia-Preto, Nydia. Puerto Rican Families. In: Ethnicity and
        Family Therapy. Eds. Monica McGoldrick, John K. Pearce
        and Joseph Giordano. New York: The Guilford Press, 1982,
        pages 164-186.

2057.   Garcica, B. and Djukanovic, B. Modifikacije Bracnih Odnosa U Toku
        Intenzivne Porodicne Terapije Alkoholizma. (Changes in
        Marital Relationships in the Course of Intensive Family
        Therapy of Alcoholism.) Alkoholizam, Beograd, 15(3):
        178-184, 1975.

2058.   Gardner, A.W. Identifying and Helping Problem Drinkers at Work.
        Journal of the Society of Occupational Medicine. 32(4):
        171-179, 1982.

2059.   Gardner, Yvelin. Counseling the Alcoholic and the Family.
        NCALI Report. New York: National Council on Alcoholism, 1971.

2060.   Gardner, Yvelin. The Pastor's Use of Community Resources (in
        Helping the Family of an Alcoholic). Pastoral Psychology,
        13(123): 39-44, 1962.

2061.   Garfinkel, Barry D., Froese, Art and Hood, Jane. Suicide Attempts in
        Children and Adolescents. American Journal of Psychiatry,
        139(10): 1257-1261, 1982.

2062. Gargani, Judith K. and Stiles, Colleen L. Treating Chemical
      Dependency in the Adolescent (Resecrance Chemical Dependency
      Treatment Program). E/SA, 10: 20-23, 1982.

2063. Garlie, N.W. Characteristics of Teenagers with Alcohol Related
      Problems. Dissertation Abstracts International, 31(9):
      4544A, 1971.

2064. Garner, Gerald W. Police Role in Alcohol-Related Crises.
      Springfield, IL: Charles C. Thomas, 1979.

2065. Garrett, G.R. and Bahr, H.M. The Family Backgrounds of Skid
      Row Women. Signs; Journal of Women in Culture and
      Society, 2:369-381, 1976.

2066. Gartner, Alan. Self-Help and Mental Health. Social Policy,
      7: 28-40, 1976.

2067. Garvey, M.J., Tuason, V.B., Hoffman, N. and Chastek, J. Suicide
      Attempters, Nonattempters, and Neurotransmitters.
      Comprehensive Psychiatry, 24(4): 332-336, 1983.

2068. Gary, J.D. Sex Differences in Selected Psychological
      Characteristics in the Alcoholic. Doctoral Dissertation.
      Dissertation Abstracts International, 44(1): 307-308B,
      1983.

2069. Garzon, Sally. Book Review of The Forgotten Children by R. Margaret
      Cork. Alcohol Health and Research World, 1969.

2070. Gavaghan, P. Paul Gavaghan: Distilled Spirits Council of the
      United States. Paper presented at the Family Awareness
      Conference, Washington, D.C., December, 1984, pages 17-19.

2071. Gavanski, N. Principi Porodicne Terapije Alkoholizma i Faktori
      Recidivizma. (Principles of Family Therapy in Alcoholism
      and Factors of Relapse.) Alkoholizam, Beograd, 19(3-4):
      36-44, 1979.

2072. Gavornikova, M. K Problemu Sebahodnotenia A Interpersonalnych
      Vzt'ahov U Alkoholikov. (On the Problem of Self-Evaluation
      and Interpersonal Relations of Alcoholics.)
      Protialkoholicky Obzur, Bratislava, 8: 87-93, 1973.

2073. Gay Family Systems Seen as Treatment Factor. NIAAA Information
      and Feature Service, (IFS No. 86): 7, July 30, 1981.

2074. Gayda, M. and Vacola, G. Famille et Alcoolisme. (Family and
      Alcoholism.) Bulletin de la Societe Francaise d'Alcoologie,
      6(3): 38-44, 1984.

2075. Gayford, J.J. Battered Wives. British Journal of Hospital
      Medicine, 22(5): 496, 498, 500-503, 1979. (Also in:
      Violence and the Family. Ed. J.P. Martin. New York:
      Wiley, 1978, pages 19-39.)

2076. Gayford, J.J. Treatment of Young Alcoholics. Royal Society of
      Health Journal, London, 97(1): 21-26, 1977.

2077. Gayford, J.J. Wife Battering: A Preliminary Survey of 100 Cases.
      British Medical Journal, London, 1(5951): 194-197, 1975.

2078. Gazikova, J. Vyskyt Depresie u Alkoholikov. (Depression Among
      Alcoholics.) Protialkoholicky Obzor, Bratislava, 7: 24-30,
      1972.

2079. Geismar, Ludwig L. and Krisberg, Jane. The People. In: The
      Forgotten Neighborhood. Ed. L. Geismar. Metuchen, NJ:
      Scarecrow Press, 1967, pages 23-50.

2080.   Geiss, S.K. and O'Leary, K.D. Therapist Ratings of Frequency and
        Severity of Marital Problems: Implications for Research.
        Journal of Marital and Family Therapy, 7(4): 515-520, 1981.

2081.   Gelb, L. Decision-Making Skills Help. ADAMHA News (Alcohol,
        Drug Abuse, and Mental Health Administration), 11(5):
        3, 1985.

2082.   Gelder, M.G. The Future of Psychiatry in Britain. Australian
        and New Zealand Journal of Psychiatry, Melbourne, 13(2):
        103-108, 1979.

2083.   Gelfand, M. Alcoholism in Contemporary African Society.
        Central African Journal of Medicine, Salisbury,
        12: 12-13, 1966.

2084.   Gelles, R.J. Violent Home: A Study of Physical Aggression
        Between Husbands and Wives. Beverly Hills: Sage Publication,
        1972.

2085.   Gelles, R.J. and Straus, M.A. Determinants of Violence in the
        Family: Toward a Theoretical Integration. Ed. W. Burr.
        In: Contemporary Theories About the Families. Vol. I.
        New York: Free Press, 1979, pages 549-581.

2086.   Gendreau, Paul and Ross, Bob. Effective Correctional Treatment:
        Bibliotherapy for Cynics. Crime and Delinquency, 25(4):
        463-489, 1979.

2087.   Genetic Component in Alcoholism. New York Times, Section 3,
        Page 2, Column 2, June, 1980.

2088.   Genetic and Family Factors Relating to Alcoholism. In: Alcohol
        and Health: Third Special Report to the United States
        Congress. Ed. Ernest P. Noble. Rockville, MD: National
        Institute on Alcohol Abuse and Alcoholism, 1978, pages 57-60.

2089.   Genetics and Alcoholism. In: Alcohol and Health: Fifth Special
        Report to the United States Congress. Rockville, MD:
        National Institute on Alcohol Abuse and Alcoholism, 1983,
        pages 15-24.

2090.   Gennett, S.D. Daughters of Alcoholic Fathers: An Investigation
        of Personality Traits. Dissertation Abstracts
        International, 44(4): 1236-1237B, 1983.

2091.   Georgia Commission on Alcoholism. Spotlight on Alcoholism.
        Pamphlet. Atlanta: Georgia Commission on Alcoholism, 1953.

2092.   Gerald, D.L. and Saegner, G. Out-Patient Treatment of
        Alcoholism; A Study of Outcome and Its Determinants.
        (Brookside Monograph of the Addiction Research Foundation,
        No. 4.) Toronto: Toronto Press, 1966.

2093.   Gerald, F. and Kendall, S. Value Differences of Spouses in
        Families with and without Alcohol-Abusing Members.
        Dissertation Abstracts International, 45(1): 338-339B,
        1984.

2094.   Gerchow, Joachim. Alcohol Use and Juvenile Delinquency.
        In: Alcohol and Youth. (Child Health and Development,
        Volume 2.) Ed. O. Jeanneret. Basel: S. Karger, 1983,
        pages 127-135.

2095.   Gerkowicz, T. Wplyw Alkoholizmu Rodzicow Na Zdrowie Dziecka.
        (The Influence of Parental Alcoholism on the Health of Their
        Children.) Problemy Alkoholizmu, Warsaw, 23(4): 7-8, 1976.

2096. Gershon E.S., Dunner, D.L. and Goodwin, F.K. Toward a Biology
       of Affective Disorders. Genetic Contributions. Archives of
       General Psychiatry, 25 1(1): 1-15, 1971.

2097. Gershon, E.S. and Hamovit, J.R. Genetic Methods and Preventive
       Psychiatry. Progress in Neuro-Psychopharmacology, 3
       (5-6): 565-573, 1979.

2098. Gershon, Elliot S., Hamovit, Joel, Guroff, Juliet J., Dibble,
       Eleanor, Leckman, James F., Sceery, Walter, Targum, Steven
       D., Nurnberger, John I., Goldin, Lynn R. and Bunney, William
       E. A Family Study of Schizoaffective, Bipolar-I, Bipolar-II,
       Unipolar, and Normal Control Probands. Archives of General
       Psychiatry, 39(10): 1157-1167, 1982.

2099. Gesue, A., Pavan, F. and Betta, F. The Treatment Group and the
       "Acute" Alcoholic in Psychiatric Hospital Undergoing
       Reform. Minerva Psichiatrica, 21(2): 139-153, 1980.

2100. Ghadirian, A.M. Adolescent Alcoholism: Motives and Alternatives.
       Comprehensive Psychiatry, 20(5): 469-474, 1979.

2101. Ghinger, C. and Grant M. Alcohol and the Family in Literature.
       In: Alcohol and the Family. Eds. J. Orford and J. Harwin.
       New York: St. Martin's Press, 1982, pages 25-55.

2102. Ghinger, Carol and Grant, Marcus. Alcohol and the Family.
       In: Alcohol and the Family. Eds. Jim Orford and Judith
       Harwin. London: Croom Helm, 1982, pages 9-24.

2103. Ghodse, A.H. Living with an Alcoholic. Postgraduate Medical
       Journal, Oxford, 58(684): 636-640, 1982.

2104. Giannini, A. Considerazioni sulle psicosi alcooliche
       osservate presso la Clinica Neuro Psichiatrica
       di Pisa nel decennio 1945-1955. Studio statistico.
       (Considerations on Alcoholic Psychoses Observed at
       the Clinica Neuro Psichiatrica di Pisa During the
       Decade 1945-1955. A Statistical Study.)
       Neopsichiatria, Pisa, 22: 86-110, 1956.

2105. Gibbens, T.C. and Silberman, M. Alcoholism Among Prisoners.
       Psychological Medicine, London, 1(1): 73-78, 1970.

2106. Gibbs, Leonard and Flanagan, John. Prognostic Indicators of
       Alcoholism Treatment Outcome. The International Journal
       of the Addictions, 12(8): 1097-1141, 1977.

2107. Gibbs, W.F. The Wife of the Alcoholic. Virginia Medical
       Monthly, 88: 379-380, 1961.

2108. Gideon, W.L. Training for Certification of Alcoholism Counselors.
       Doctoral Dissertation. Houston: University of Texas, Health
       Science Center, 1975.

2109. Gil, David, G. Violence Against Children: Physical Child Abuse
       in the United States. Cambridge: Harvard University Press,
       1973.

2110. Gilbert, J. Family Process in the Alcohol System: The
       Uncontrolled Generation. The Family, 8(1): 46, 1980.

2111. Gilbert, J.G. After the Drinking Stops: Working with the
       "Sober" Family. The Family, 9(1): 11-14, 1981.

2112. Gilbert, S. Trouble at Home. New York: Lothrop, Lee &
       Shepard Books, 1981.

2113. Giles, Sims Jean Grindell. Stability and Changes in Patterns
       of Wife-Beating: A Systems Theory Approach. Doctoral
       Dissertation. (University Microfilms Number 8027790.)
       Durham: University of New Hampshire, 1979. (Also in:
       Dissertation Abstracts International, 41(6): 2781A,
       1980.)

2114. Gilgun, John. King, My Father. In: Having Been There.
       Ed. A. Luks. New York: Charles Scribner's Sons, 1979,
       pages 23-29.

2115. Gillespie, C. Nurses Help Combat Alcoholism. American Journal
       of Nursing, 69: 1938-1941, 1969.

2116. Gillis, L.S. and Keet, M. Prognostic Factors and Treatment
       Results in Hospitalized Alcoholics. Quarterly Journal of
       Studies on Alcohol, 30: 426-437, 1969.

2117. Giora, Shoham S., Rahav, G., Esformes, Y., Markovski, R., Chard,
       F. and Kaplinsky, N. Some Parameters of the Use of Alcohol
       by Israeli Youth and Its Relationship to Their Involvement
       with Cannabis and Tobacco. Drug and Alcohol Dependence,
       Lausanne, 6: 263-272, 1980.

2118. Giovannoni, Jeanne M. and Becerra, Rosina M. Professionals View
       Child Mistreatment. In: Defining Child Abuse. New York:
       Free Press, 1979, pages 77-156.

2119. Giusti, G., Ruggiero, G., Galanti, B., Piccinino, F., Nardiello,
       S., Russo, M., Galante, D. and Aloisio, V. Etiological,
       Clinical and Laboratory Data of a Series of Chronic Liver
       Diseases from a Southern Italy Area. Acta Hepato-
       Gastroenterologica, Stuttgart, 25(6): 431-437, 1978.

2120. Glade, Eldon M. and Goodman, Ronald E. Vocational Preferences
       of Daughters of Alcoholics. Vocational Guidance
       Quarterly, 24(1): 41-47, 1975.

2121. Glashagel, Jerry and Glashagel, Char. Valuing Families.
       Activity Guide. Rockville, MD: National Institute on
       Alcohol Abuse and Alcoholism (DHEW/PHS), 1975. (Eric
       Document Number ED107551.)

2122. Glass, G.S. Multiple Couples Treatment of Alcoholics and Their
       Spouses. In: Currents in Alcoholism. Vol 2. Psychiatric,
       Psychological, Social and Epidemiological Studies.
       Ed. F.A. Seixas. New York: Grune and Stratton, 1977,
       pages 95-102.

2123. Glassco, K. Drinking Habits of Seniors in a Southern University.
       Journal of Alcohol & Drug Education, 21(1): 25-29, 1975.

2124. Glasser, Sidney M. Alcoholism. American Family Physician,
       28(1): 48-50, 1983.

2125. Glasser, W. Take Effective Control of Your Life. New York:
       Harper and Row, 1984.

2126. Glatt, M.M. The Alcoholic and Controlled Drinking. British
       Journal on Alcohol and Alcoholism, 15(2): 48-55, 1980.

2127. Glatt, M.M. Complications of Alcoholism in the Social Sphere.
       British Journal of Addiction, 62: 35-44, 1967.

2128. Glatt, M.M. Jewish Alcoholics and Addicts in the London Area.
       Mental Health and Society, Basel, 2(3-6): 168-174, 1975.

2129.   Glatt, Max M.   The Alcoholic and the Help He Needs.   London:
        Priory Press, 1969.   (Reprinted, Priory Press, 1972.)

2130.   Glatt, Max M.   Alcoholism, Crime and Juvenile Delinquency.
        The British Journal of Delinquency, 9: 84-93, 1958.

2131.   Glatt, Max M.   Alcoholism in Industry and Family.   Lancet, 1:
        203, 1969.

2132.   Glatt, Max M.   Psychodynamic Aspects of Various Treatment Methods
        in Alcoholism.   Paper presented at the 15th International
        Institute on the Prevention and Treatment of Alcoholism,
        Budapest, Hungary, 1969.

2133.   Glatt, Max M.   Public Attitude and Influence Towards the
        Rehabilitation of Alcoholics.   Rehabilitation, Bonn,
        24(4): 49-56, 1971.

2134.   Glatt, Max M.   Reflections on the Treatment of Alcoholism in
        Women.   British Journal on Alcohol and Alcoholism,
        London, 14: 77-83, 1979.

2135.   Glatt, Max M.   Treatment of Alcohol Dependence: Long-Term
        Treatment of the Psychological Effects.   British
        Medical Bulletin, London, 38(1): 106-108, 1982.

2136.   Glatt, Max M.   Twenty-Five Years of Alcoholism Units.   British
        Journal on Alcohol and Alcoholism, 13: 11-20, 1978.

2137.   Glatt, Max M. and Hills, D.R.   Alcohol Abuse and Alcoholism
        in the Young.   British Journal of the Addictions,
        63: 183-191, 1968.

2138.   Gleason, M.G.   Alcoholism in the Family: Implications for the
        School.   Grassrotts/Education-Prevention: 3-6, 1982.

2139.   Gliedman, L.H.   Concurrent and Combined Group Treatment of Chronic
        Alcoholics and Their Wives.   International Journal of Group
        Psychotherapy, 7: 414-424, 1957.

2140.   Gliedman, L.H., Rosenthal, D., Frank, J.D. and Nash, H.T.   Group
        Therapy of Alcoholics with Concurrent Group Meetings of Their
        Wives.   Quarterly Journal of Studies on Alcohol, 17:
        655-670, 1956.

2141.   Globetti, G.   Alcohol: A Family Affair.   Paper presented at the
        National Congress of Parents and Teachers.   St. Louis, 1973.

2142.   Globetti, G.   Problem and Non-Problem Drinking Among High School
        Students in Abstinence Communities.   International Journal
        of the Addictions, 7(3): 511-523, 1972.

2143.   Globetti, G.   Social Adjustment of High School Students and
        Problem Drinking.   Journal of Alcohol Education, 13(2):
        21-29, 1967.

2144.   Globetti, G.   The Use of Beverage Alcohol by Youth in an
        Abstinence Setting.   Journal of School Health, 39:
        179-183, 1969.

2145.   Globetti, Gerald.   A Comparative Study of White and Negro Teenage
        Drinking in Two Mississippi Communities.   Phylon, 28(2):
        131-138, 1967.

2146.   Globetti, Gerald.   General Considerations on Prevention of Alcohol
        Abuse and Alcohol Problems in Children and Adolescents.
        In: Alcohol and Youth.   Ed. O. Jeanneret.   (Child Health
        and Development, Volume 2.)   Basel: S. Karger, 1983, pages
        95-107.

2147.   Globetti, Gerald. Teenage Drinking in an Abstinence Setting.
        The Kansas Journal of Sociology, 3(3): 124-132, 1967.

2148.   Globetti, Gerald and Brigance, Roy S. The Use and Nonuse of
        Drugs Among High School Students in a Small Rural Community.
        Journal of Drug Education, 1(4): 317-322, 1971.

2149.   Globetti, Gerald and Windham, Gerald. The Social Adjustment
        of High School Students and the Use of Beverage Alcohol.
        Sociology and Social Research, 51(2): 148-158, 1967.

2150.   Glynn, Thomas J. (Ed.). Drugs and the Family. National Institute
        of Drug Abuse. Research Issue No. 29. Washington, DC: U.S.
        Government Printing Office, 1981. (DHHS Publication No. ADM
        81-1151.)

2151.   Glynn, Thomas J. Families and Drugs: A Life-Span Research
        Approach. American Journal of Drug and Alcohol Abuse,
        9(4): 397-412, 1983.

2152.   Glynn, Thomas J. From Family to Peer: A Review of Transitions
        of Influence Among Drug-Using Youth. In: Drugs and the
        Family. Ed. Thomas J. Glynn. Washington, D.C.: U.S.
        Government Printing Office, 1981, pages 42-43. (Also in:
        Journal of Youth and Adolescence, 10: 363-383, 1981.)

2153.   Glynn, Thomas J. From Family to Peer: Transitions of Influence
        Among Drug-Using Youth. In: Drug Abuse and the American
        Adolescent. Eds. Dan J. Lettieri and Jacqueline P. Ludford.
        Department of Health, Education and Welfare, Public Health
        Service, ADM 81/1166, Research Monograph Series 38, 1981,
        pages 57-81.

2154.   God Love the Children. Expo Magazine, 1(4): 54, 1979.

2155.   Godwod-Sikorska, C., Kiejlan, G., Mlodzik, B., Pankowska-
        Jurkowska, M. and Piekarska-Ekiert, A. Problemy Alkoholizmu
        Wsrod Mlodziezy z Wielodzietnych r Alkoholikow na Podstawie
        Dziesiecioletnich Danych Katamnestycznych. (Problems of
        Alcoholism in Youngsters from Alcoholic Familes with Many
        Children, Based on Data Spanning a 10-Year Follow-up Period.)
        In: Alkohol, Alkoholizm i Inne Uzaleznienia. Przejawy,
        Profilaktyka, Terapia, 2. (Alcohol, Alcoholism and Other
        Addicions. Symptomatology, Prophylaxis and Therapy.
        Volume 2.) Ed. J. Morawski. Warsaw: Wydawnictwo
        Prawnicze, 1977, pages 7-27.

2156.   Godycka, Z.C. Alcoholism and Its Treatment in Poland.
        International Journal of Offender Therapy and Comparative
        Criminology, 18(1): 106-108, 1974.

2157.   Goedde, H.W. and Agarwal, D.P. Alcohol Metabolizing Enzymes:
        Biochemical Properties, Genetic Heterogeneity and Their
        Possible Role in Alcohol Metabolism in Humans. Journal
        of Clinical Chemistry and Clinical Biochemistry, Berlin,
        19(4): 179-189, 1981.

2158.   Goedde, H.W., Agarwal, D.P., Eckey, R. and Harada S. Population
        Genetic and Family Studies on Aldehyde Dehydrogenase
        Deficiency and Alcohol Sensitivity. Alcohol, 2(3):
        383-390, 1985.

2159.   Goedde, H.W., Agarwal, D.P. and Harada, S. Genetic Studies on
        Alcohol-Metabolizing Enzymes: Detection of Isozymes in
        Human Hair Roots. Enzyme, Basel, 25(4): 281-286, 1980.

2160.   Goedde, H.W., Agarwal, D.P. and Harada, S. Pharmacogenetics
        of Alcohol Sensitivity. Pharmacology Biochemistry and
        Behavior, 18(Supplement 1): 161-166, 1983.

2161. Goedde, H.W., Meier-Tackmann, D., Agarwal, D.P. and Harada, S.
       Physiological Role of Aldehyde Dehydrogenase Isozymes. In:
       Enzymology of Carbonyl Metabolism: Aldehyde Dehydrogenase
       and Aldo/Keto Reductase. New York: Alan R. Liss, Inc.,
       1982, pages 347-362.

2162. Goetzl, U., Green, R., Whybrow, P. and Jackson, R.   X Linkage
       Revisited. A Further Family study of Manic-Depressive
       Illness. Archives of General Psychiatry, 31(5): 665-
       672, 1974.

2163. Gold, S. and Sherry, L. Hyperactivity, Learning Disabilities,
       and Alcohol. Journal of Learning Disabilities, 17(1):
       3-6, 1984.

2164. Goldberg, D.A., Posakony, J.W. and Maniatis, T. Correct
       Developmental Expression of a Cloned Alcohol Dehydrogenase
       Gene Transduced into the Drosophila Germ Line. Cell, 34(1):
       59-73, 1983.

2165. Goldenberg, Herbert. Alcoholism and Drug Dependence. In: Abnormal
       Psychology: A Social/Community Approach. Monterey, CA:
       Brooks/Cole Publishing Co., 1977, pages 523-561.

2166. Goldenberg, M., Korn, F., Sluzki, C.E. and Tarnopolsky, A.
       Attitudes Towards Alcohol, Alcoholism, and the Alcoholic -
       An Exploratory Study. Social Science Medicine, Oxford,
       2: 29-39, 1968.

2167. Golder, G.M. The Alcoholic, His Family and His Nurse. Nursing
       Outlook, 3: 528-530, 1955.

2168. Goldfarb, A.I. and Berman, S. Alcoholism as a Psychosomatic
       Disorder. 1. Endocrine Pathology of Animals and Man
       Excessively Exposed to Alcohol; Its Possible Relation to
       Behavioral Pathology. Quarterly Journal of Studies on
       Alcohol, 10: 415-429, 1949.

2169. Goldfarb, C. Patients Nobody Wants -- Skid Row Alcoholics.
       Diseases of the Nervous System, 31(4): 274-281, 1970.

2170. Goldfried, M.R. Prediction of Improvement in an Alcoholism Out-
       patient Clinic. Quarterly Journal of Studies on Alcohol.
       30(1): 129-139, 1969.

2171. Goldman, A.P. Relationship of Alcoholic Mothers and Their
       Children: Description and Evaluation. Dissertation
       Abstracts International, 46(5): 1685B, 1985.

2172. Goldman, L. Alcoholism - A Challenge to the Family Practitioner.
       Australian Family Physician, Sydney, 7(Supplement): 8-9,
       1978.

2173. Goldmeier, D., Hollander, D. and Sheehan, M.J. Relatives and
       Friends Group in a Psychiatric Ward. British Medical
       Journal, London, 1(6168): 932-934, 1979.

2174. Goldney, R.D. and Temme, P.B. Case Report: Manic Depressive
       Psychosis Following Infectious Mononucleosis. Journal of
       Clinical Psychiatry, 41(9): 322-323, 1980.

2175. Goldshtein, L.M. and Baldashov, E. Ectodermal. Sluchay
       Ektodermal'noy Displazii. (Case of Ectodermal Dysplasia.)
       Vestnik Dermatologii I Venerologii, 10: 55-56, 1976.

2176. Goldstein, M.S. Mixed Models of Alcoholism. Definitions,
       Etiology, Treatment and Prognosis in Health Education
       Textbooks. Journal of Studies on Alcohol, 36(7):
       925-937, 1975.

2177. Goldwater, E. Practical Ways to Help Your Alcohol Abusers.
       Medical Times, 103(6): 31-35, 1975.

2178. Gollnick, H., Tsambaos, D. and Orfanos, C.E. Risk Factors Promote
       Elevations of Serum Lipids in Acne Patients Under Oral 13-CIS
       Retinoic-Acid Iso Tretinoin. Archives of Dermatological
       Research, Berlin, 271(2): 189-196, 1981.

2179. Gomberg, Christopher A. and Billings, Andrew G. Family Treatment
       Approaches to Alcoholism: Assessing the "Alcoholic Family",
       1982. (Eric Document Number ED221792.)

2180. Gomberg, E.M. A Study of the Relationship Between Physical Child
       Abuse and Alcohol. Master's Thesis. (University Microfilms
       No. 1315191.) Long Beach: California State University, 1980.

2181. Gomberg, E.S. Drinking Patterns of Women Alcoholics. In: Women
       Who Drink: Alcoholic Experience and Psychotherapy. Ed.
       Vasanti Bertle. Springfield, IL: Charles C. Thomas, 1979,
       pages 26-48.

2182. Gomberg, E.S. Problems with Alcohol and Other Drugs. In:
       Gender and Disordered Behavior; Sex Differences in
       Psychopathology. Eds. E.S. Gomberg and V. Franks.
       New York: Brunner/Mazel, 1979, pages 204-240.

2183. Gomberg, E.S. Women and Alcoholism. In: Women in Therapy; New
       Psychotherapies for a Changing Society. Eds. V. Franks and
       V. Burtle. New York: Brunnell-Mazel, 1974, pages 169-190.

2184. Gomberg, E.S. Women, Sex Roles, and Alcohol Problems.
       Professional Psychology, 12(1): 146-155, 1981.

2185. Gomberg, E.S. The Young Male Alcoholic. A Pilot Study.
       Journal of Studies on Alcohol, 43(7): 683-701, 1982.

2186. Gomberg, E.S. Lisansky, and Lisansky, J.M. Antecedents of
       Alcohol Problems in Women. In: Alcohol Probems in Women:
       Antecedents, Consequences, and Intervention. Eds. S.C.
       Wilsnack and L.J. Beckman. New York: The Guilford Press,
       1984, pages 233-259.

2187. Gomberg, Edith S. The Female Alcoholic. In: Alcoholism:
       Interdisciplinary Approaches to an Enduring Problem.
       Eds. Ralph E. Tarter and Arthur A. Sugerman. Reading, MA:
       Addison-Wesley, 1976, pages 603-636.

2188. Gomez, J. Learning to Drink: The Influence of Impaired
       Psychosexual Development. Journal of Psychosomatic
       Research, 28(5): 403-410, 1984.

2189. Gomez, J. and Dally P. Psychologically Mediated Abdominal Pain
       in Surgical and Medical Outpatients Clinics. British
       Medical Journal, 1(6074): 1451-1453.

2190. Gonin, D. Violences Intra-Familiales et Crise Alcoolique.
       (Intrafamily Violence and Drinking Bouts.) Alcool
       ou Sante, Paris, 165(2): 5-12, 1983.

2191. Gonzalez, M., Yamhure, A., Garcia, R., Pardo, F. and
       Betancourth, E. Epidemiology of Mental Disorders in Bogota.
       The 1st Step. Results of the Survey on Psychiatric
       Symptomatology. Acta Psiquiatrica y Psicologica de
       America Latina, 24(2): 93-99, 1978.

2192. Good News: You Can Lick Liquor. Harper's Bazaar, 3262: 1983.

2193. Goode, E. Cigarette Smoking and Drug Use on a College Campus.
       International Journal of the Addictions, 7(1): 133-140,
       1972.

2194. Gooderham, M.E.W. Clinical Approach to Alcoholism. Canadian
       Family Physician, 23(943): 79-82, 1977.

2195. Gooderham, Melville. The Therapy of Relationships. Addictions,
       Toronto, 19(4): 58-63, 1972.

2196. Goodman, H.T. Jr. D.D.T. -- The Drinker's Dilemma and Treatment:
       A Psychiatrist's View. Ohio State Medical Journal, 66(7):
       684-686, 1970.

2197. Goodman, James Arthur. Study of Group Therapy with Spouses
       of Alcoholic Patients in an Outpatient Clinic. Doctoral
       Dissertation. Georgia: Atlanta University, 1958.

2198. Goodman, L.M. Support for the Family of the Person with Alcohol-
       Related Problems. In: The Community Health Nurse and
       Alcohol-Related Problems. Rockville, MD: National Institute
       on Alcohol Abuse and Alcoholism, 1978, pages 83-106.

2199. Goodrich, James R. Alcohol Addiction: Hope for Understanding
       and Recovery. Alcoholism: The National Magazine, 3(4):
       53-55, 1983.

2200. Goodrich, M.F. and Blair, B.R. Developing New Employee
       Assistance Programs Through Family Service Agencies. In:
       Proceedings of the Seventh Annual Meeting, San Francisco,
       October 3, Vol 4. Arlington, VA: 1978, pages 27-38.

2201. Goodrick, J.H. Clues for Early Identification of Sexual Abuse of
       Children in Alcohol Abusing Families. Paper presented in
       Madison, WI, February, 1983. (Also in: Working with
       Adolescent Alcohol/Drug Problems: Assessment, Intervention
       and Treatment. pages 37-43.)

2202. Goodstein, Richard K. and Page, Ann W. Battered Wife Syndrome:
       Overview of Dynamics and Treatment. American
       Journal of Psychiatry, 138(8): 1036-1044, 1981.

2203. Goodwin, D.W. Alcohol Problems in Adoptees Raised Apart from
       Alcoholic Biological Parents. Pamphlet. New York:
       National Council on Alcoholism, no date.

2204. Goodwin, D.W. Bad-Habit Theory of Drug Use. In: Theories on Drug
       Abuse: Selected Contemporary Perspectives. Eds. Dan J.
       Lettieri, Mollie Sayers and Helen Wallenstein Pearson.
       Washington, D.C.: U.S. Government Printing Office, National
       Institute on Drug Abuse Research Monograph Series 30, 1980,
       pages 12-17.

2205. Goodwin, D.W. Clinical Science Review: The Genetics of
       Alcoholism. Substance and Alcohol Actions/Misuse, 1:
       101-117, 1980.

2206. Goodwin, D.W. Family Histories of Male and Female Alcoholics.
       Conference Paper, Farmington, CT, October, 1979. (Also in:
       Evaluation of the Alcoholic Conference. pages 109-128.)

2207. Goodwin, D.W. Genetic Aspects of Alcoholism. Paper presented to
       the Non-Medical Use of Drug Directorate, National Health and
       Welfare, Halifax, August, 1974. (Also in: Biomedical
       Research in Alcohol Abuse Problem. pages 214-245.)

2208. Goodwin, D.W. Genetic Determinants of Alcohol Addiction. Advances
       in Experimental Medicine and Biology, 56: 339-355, 1975.

2209.   Goodwin, D.W.   Genetic Determinants of Alcoholism.   In: The
        Diagnosis and Treatment of Alcoholism.   Eds. J.H. Mendelson
        and N.K. Mello.   New York: McGraw-Hill, 1979, pages 59-82.

2210.   Goodwin, D.W.   Genetic Factors in Alcoholism.   In: Advances in
        Substance Abuse Vol. 1.   Ed. N.K. Melb.   Greenwich, CT:
        JAI Press, 1980, pages 305-326.

2211.   Goodwin, D.W.   High Risk Studies of Alcoholism: Overview.
        In: Recent Developments in Alcoholism: Volume 3.
        New York: Plenum Press, 1985, pages 3-10.

2212.   Goodwin, D.W.   Introduction "To Clinical and Genetic Studies."
        In: Alcoholism and Affective Disorders; Clinical, Genetic,
        and Biochemical Studies.   Ed. D.W. Goodwin and C.K. Erickson.
        New York: SP Medical and Scientific Books, 1979, pages 5-8.

2213.   Goodwin, D.W.   Is Alcoholism Hereditary?   A Review and Critique.
        Archives of General Psychiatry, 25(6): 545-549, 1971.

2214.   Goodwin, D.W.   Overview of Treatment and Rehabilitation.
        In: Currents in Alcoholism; Volume 6:   Treatment and
        Rehabilitation and Epidemiology.   New York: Grune
        and Stratton, 1979, pages 1-5.

2215.   Goodwin, D.W.   Studies of Familial Alcoholism: A Growth
        Industry.   In: Longitudinal Research in Alcoholism.
        Eds. D.W. Goodwin, K.T. Van Dusen and S.A. Mednick.
        Boston: Kluwer Academic Publishers, 1984, pages 97-105.

2216.   Goodwin, D.W. and Erickson, C.K. (Eds.).   Alcoholism and Affective
        Disorders; Clinical, Genetic, and Biochemical Studies.
        New York: SP Medical and Scientific Books, 1979.

2217.   Goodwin, D.W., Van Dusen, K.T. and Mednick, S.A. (Eds.)
        Longitudinal Research in Alcoholism.   Boston: Kluwer
        Academic Publishers, 1984.

2218.   Goodwin, Donald W.   Adoption Studies of Alcoholism.   In: The Bases
        of Addiction.   Ed. J. Fishman.   Berlin: Abakon, 1978.   (Also
        in: Journal of Operational Psychiatry, 7(1): 54-63, 1976;
        Progress in Clinical and Biological Research, 69 Pt.C: 71-76,
        1981;   Acta Geneticae Medicae et Gemellologiae, Rome, 29: 76,
        1980.)

2219.   Goodwin, Donald W.   Alcoholism and Affective Disorders: The Basic
        Questions.   In: Alcoholism and Clinical Psychiatry.
        Ed. Joel Solomon.   New York: Plenum Medical Book Company,
        1982, pages 87-95.

2220.   Goodwin, Donald W.   Alcoholism and Genetics.   The Sins of the Fathers.
        Archives of General Psychiatry, 42(2): 171-174, 1985.

2221.   Goodwin, Donald W.   Alcoholism and Heredity; A Review and Hypothesis.
        Archives of General Psychiatry, 36: 57-61, 1979.

2222.   Goodwin, Donald W.   Alcoholism and Heredity: Update on the Implacable
        Fate.   In: Alcohol, Science and Society Revisited.   Ed. E.L.
        Gomberg.   Ann Arbor: University of Michigan Press, 1982, pages
        162-170.

2223.   Goodwin, Donald W.   The Cause of Alcoholism and Why It Runs in
        Families.   British Journal of Addiction, Edinburgh, 74:
        161-164, 1979.

2224.   Goodwin, Donald W.   Familial Alcoholism: A Diagnostic Entity.
        In: Critical Issues in Psychiatric Diagnosis.   Ed. R. Spitzer.
        New York: Raven Press, 1978, pages 225-235.

2225.   Goodwin, Donald W. Familial Alcoholism: A Separate Entity?
        Substance & Alcohol Actions/Misuse, 4(2-3): 129-136, 1983.

2226.   Goodwin, Donald W. Family and Adoption Studies of Alcoholism.
        In: Biosocial Bases of Criminal Behavior. Eds. Sarnoff A.
        Mednick and Karl O. Christiansen. New York: Gardner Press,
        1977, pages 143-157.

2227.   Goodwin, Donald W. Family Studies of Alcoholism. Journal of
        Studies on Alcoholism, 42: 156-162, 1981.

2228.   Goodwin, Donald W. Follow-Up Study of Children from Alcoholic
        Parents Who Live in Foster Homes. In: Alcohol and Youth.
        Volume 2. Child Health and Development. Ed. O.
        Jeanneret. Basel: S. Karger, 1983, pages 86-94.

2229.   Goodwin, Donald W. Genetic Aspects of Alcohol Addiction.
        Addictions, 4(6): 21-23, 1975.

2230.   Goodwin, Donald W. Genetic Component of Alcoholism. Annual
        Review of Medicine, 32: 93-99, 1981.

2231.   Goodwin, Donald W. Genetic Determinants of Alcoholism. In: The
        Diagnosis and Treatment of Alcoholism. Eds. Jack H.
        Mendelson and Nancy K. Mello. New York: McGraw Hill, 1979,
        pages 60-82.

2232.   Goodwin, Donald W. Genetic and Experiential Antecedents of
        Alcoholism: A Prospective Study. Alcoholism: Clinical and
        Experimental Research, 1(3): 259-265, 1977.

2233.   Goodwin, Donald W. Genetics of Alcoholism. Hospital and
        Community Psychiatry, 34(11): 1031-1034, 1983. (Also
        in: Alcohol Technical Report, 12-13: 7-11, 1983-84.)

2234.   Goodwin, Donald W. The Genetics of Alcoholism. Substance and Alcohol
        Actions/Misuse, 1: 101-117, 1980. (Also in: Etiologic
        Aspects of Alcohol and Drug Abuse. Eds. E. Gottheil, K.A.
        Druley, T.E. Skoloda and H.M. Waxman. Springfield, IL: Charles C.
        Thomas, 1983, pages 5-13; Alcohol Health and Research World,
        2(3): 2-12, 1978.)

2235.   Goodwin, Donald W. The Genetics of Alcoholism: Implications for
        Youth. Alcohol Health and Research World, 7(4): 58-63, 1983.

2236.   Goodwin, Donald W. Heredity Factors in Alcoholism. Hospital
        Practice, 13(5): 121-124, 127-130, 1978.

2237.   Goodwin, Donald W. Is Alcoholism a Familial Disease. Concours
        Medical, Paris, 103(37): 5863-5881, 1981.

2238.   Goodwin, Donald W. Is Alcoholism Hereditary? New York:
        Oxford University Press, 1976.

2239.   Goodwin, Donald W. Is Alcoholism Hereditary? In: Alcoholism:
        Introduction to Theory and Treatment. Ed. David A. Ward.
        Dubuque, IA: Kendall/Hunt, 1980, pages 132-139.

2240.   Goodwin, Donald W. Is Alcoholism Inherited? Paper presented at the
        Third Annual Alcoholism Conference of the National Institute
        on Alcohol Abuse and Alcoholism. Ed. Morris E. Chafetz.
        Washington, D.C., June, 1973.

2241.   Goodwin, Donald W. The Management of Depression in Alcoholism.
        Journal of Psychiatric Treatment and Evaluation, 5(5):
        445-450, 1983.

2242. Goodwin, Donald W. Overview. Section 1: High Risk Studies of
      Alcoholism. In: Recent Developments in Alcoholism, Volume 3,
      High-Risk Studies, Prostaglandins and Leukotrienes, Cardiovascular
      Effects, Cerebral Function in Social Drinkers. Ed. Marc
      Galanter. New York: Plenum Press, 1985, pages 3-10.

2243. Goodwin, Donald W. Overview. Section 1: The Role of Genetics
      in the Expression of Alcohol. In: Recent Developments in
      Alcoholism, Volume 1, Genetics, Behavioral Treatment, Social
      Mediators and Prevention, Current Concepts in Diagnosis.
      Ed. Marc Galanter. New York: Plenum Press, 1983, pages 3-8.

2244. Goodwin, Donald W. Studies of Familial Alcoholism: A Review.
      Journal of Clinical Psychiatry, 45(12): 14-17, 1984.

2245. Goodwin, Donald W., Crane, Bruce J. and Guze, Samuel B. Felons
      Who Drink; An 8-year Follow-Up. Quarterly Journal of
      Studies on Alcohol, 32: 136-147, 1971.

2246. Goodwin, Donald W., Davis, D.H. and Robins, L.N. Drinking Amid
      Abundant Illicit Drugs; the Vietnam Case. Archives of
      General Psychiatry, 32: 230-233, 1975.

2247. Goodwin, Donald W. and Guze, Samuel B. Heredity and Alcoholism.
      In: The Biology of Alcoholism, Volume 3. Clinical
      Pathology. Eds. Benjamin Kissin and Henri Begleiter.
      New York: Plenum Press, 1974, pages 37-52.

2248. Goodwin, Donald W., Johnson, J., Maher, C., Rappaport, A. and
      Guze, Samuel B. Why People Do Not Drink; A Study of
      Teetotalers. Comprehensive Psychiatry, 10: 209-214, 1969.

2249. Goodwin, Donald W., Schulsinger, Fini, Hermansen, Leif, Guze,
      Samuel B. and Winokur, George. Alcohol Problems in Adoptees
      Raised Apart From Alcoholic Biological Parents. Archives of
      General Psychiatry, 28(2): 238-243, 1973. (Also in:
      Alcoholism: Introduction to Theory and Treatment.
      Dubuque, IA: Kendall/Hunt, 1980, pages 140-152.)

2250. Goodwin, Donald W., Schulsinger, Fini, Hermansen, Leif, Guze,
      Samuel B. and Winokur, George. Alcoholism and the
      Hyperactive Child Syndrome. The Journal of Nervous and
      Mental Disease, 160(5): 349-353, 1975.

2251. Goodwin, Donald W., Schulsinger, Fini, Knop, Joachim, Mednick,
      Sarnoff and Guze, Samuel B. Psychopathology in Adopted and
      Nonadopted Daughters of Alcoholics. In: Alcoholism &
      Affective Disorders - Clinical, Genetic & Biochemical
      Studies. Eds. Donald W. Goodwin and Carlton K. Erikson.
      New York: SP Medical & Scientific Books, 1979, pages 87-98.
      (Also in: Archives of General Psychiatry, 34: 1005-
      1009, 1977).

2252. Goodwin, Donald W., Schulsinger, Fini, Knop, L. and Guze, Samuel B.
      Alcoholism and Depression in Adopted-Out Daughters of Alcoholics.
      Archives of General Psychiatry, 34: 751-755, 1977.

2253. Goodwin, Donald W., Schulsinger, Fini, Moller, Niels, Hermansen, Leif,
      Winokur, George and Guze, Samuel. Drinking Problems in Adopted
      and Nonadopted Sons of Alcoholics. St. Louis: Washington
      University School of Medicine, Department of Psychiatry, no date.
      (Also in: Archives of General Psychiatry, 31(2): 164-169,
      1974.)

2254. Goodwin, Jean. Common Psychiatric Disorders in Elderly Persons.
      Western Journal of Medicine, 139(4): 502-506, 1983.

2255.   Gopaldas, Tara, Gupta, Ajali and Saxena, Kalpna. The Impact of
        Sanskritization in a Forest-Dwelling Tribe of Gujarat, India.
        Ecology, Food Consumption Patterns, Nutrient Intake,
        Anthropometric, Clinical and Hematological Status.
        Ecology of Food and Nutrition, 12(4): 217-228, 1983.

2256.   Gorad, Stephen Lee. Alcoholic and His Wife: Their Personal Styles
        of Communication and Interaction. Doctoral Dissertation.
        (University Microfilms No. 71-26417). MA: Boston University,
        1971. (Also in: Dissertation Abstracts International, 32(4):
        2395-2396B, 1971.)

2257.   Gorad, Stephen Lee. Communicational Styles and Interaction of
        Alcoholics and Their Wives. Family Process, 10(4):
        475-489, 1971.

2258.   Gorad, Stephen Lee, McCourt, William F. and Cobb, Jeremy C.
        A Communications Approach to Alcoholism. Quarterly
        Journal of Studies on Alcohol, 32: 651-668, 1971.

2259.   Gordon, A. Parental Alcoholism as a Factor in the Mental
        Deficiency of Children: A Statistical Study of 117 Families.
        Monthly Cyclopedia and Medical Bulletin, Philadelphia, 5:
        9-15, 1912. (Also in: Journal of Inebriety, 33: 90-99,
        1911 and 35: 58-65, 1913.)

2260.   Gordon, David A., Gibson, Gordon and Werner, John L. Treatment
        of Alcoholism in a Community Based Alcohol Rehabilitation
        Programme. British Journal of Addiction, 72(3): 217-222,
        1977.

2261.   Gordon, Jack D. The Civilian General Hospital. In: Alcoholism:
        The Total Treatment Approach. Springfield, IL: Charles C.
        Thomas, 1968, pages 383-386.

2262.   Gordon, L. Alcoholism and Heredity. British Journal of Inebriety,
        1: 202-209, 1904.

2263.   Gordon, M.E. Children of Alcoholics: The Forgotten Ones.
        Young Miss Magazine, 33(6): 62-64, 66, 69, 91, 1985.

2264.   Gordon, Mary Ebitt. If One of Your Parents Drinks Too Much What
        Are Your Problems Going to Be? Pamphlet. New York:
        National Council on Alcoholism, no date.

2265.   Gordon, Richard, Ogburn, Benjamin, Bellino, Robert, and Williams,
        Robert. Problems of the Military Retiree. Journal of the
        Florida Medical Association, 56(4): 245-248, 1969.

2266.   Gorman, Edward. Dancers. In: Having Been There. Ed. A. Luks.
        New York: Charles Scribner's Sons, 1979, pages 67-86.

2267.   Gorman, J.M. and Rooney, J.F. Delay in Seeking Help and Onset of
        Crisis Among Al-Anon Wives. American Journal of Drug and
        Alcohol Abuse, New York, 6: 223-233, 1979.

2268.   Gorman, J.M. and Rooney, J.F. Influence of Al-Anon on the Coping
        Behavior of Wives of Alcoholics. Journal of Studies on
        Alcohol, 40: 1030-1038, 1979.

2269.   Gorrell, G.J. A Study of Defective Colour Vision with the Ishihara
        Test Plates. Annals of Human Genetics, 31(1): 39-44, 1967.

2270.   Gorrell, G.J., Thuline, H.C. and Cruz-Coke, R. Inheritance of
        Alcoholism. Lancet, 1: 274-275, 1967.

2271.   Gorski, T. and Miller, M. Relapse: The Family's Involvement.
        Focus on Family and Chemical Dependency, 6(5): 17-18, 1983.

2272. Gorski, T. and Miller, M. Relapse: The Family's Involvement.
       Part Two: Co-Alcoholism and Relapse. Focus on Family and
       Chemical Depedency, 6(6): 10-11, 1983.

2273. Gorski, T. and Miller M. Relapse: The Family's Involvement.
       Part Three: Protocol for Long-Term Recovery. Focus on
       Family and Chemical Dependency, 7(1): 13, 36, 1984.

2274. Gorst, J. and Kirk, J. Communications on Mrs. Mary Scharlieb's Paper,
       "Alcohol and the Children of the Nation." British Journal of
       Inebriety, 5: 71-82.

2275. Gorwitz, Kurt, Bahn, Anita, Warthen, Frances Jean and Cooper,
       Myles. Some Epidemiological Data on Alcoholism in Maryland:
       Based on Admissions to Psychiatric Facilities. Quarterly
       Journal of Studies on Alcohol, 31(2): 423-443, 1970.

2276. Goshen, Charles E. Transcultural Studies: A State Prison
       Population of Youthful Offenders. Adolescence, 4(15):
       401-430, 1969.

2277. Gossner, K.J. Alcoholism and its Treatment: Medical and
       Non-Medical Model. Alcoholism: Journal of Alcoholism
       and Related Addictions, Zagreb, 13(2-3): 69-77, 1977.

2278. Gostomzyk, J.G. Kindesmisshandlung. (Child Abuse.) Offentliche
       Gesundheitswesen, Stuttgart, 39: 279-288, 1977.

2279. Gotestam, K. Gunnar and Eriksen, Lasse. Behaviour Therapy in
       Alcoholism. Lakartidningen, 78(23): 2293-2294, 1981.

2280. Gotteheil, E., Druley, K.A., Skoloda, T.E. and Waxman, H.M.
       Alcohol, Drug Abuse and Aggression. Springfield, IL:
       Charles C. Thomas, 1983.

2281. Gottesfeld, Benjamin H. and Yager, H. Leon. Psychotherapy of the
       Problem Drinker. Quarterly Journal of Studies on Alcohol,
       11: 222-229, 1950.

2282. Gottieb, Nancy. What Happen to the "Forgotten Children"?
       Focus: on Alcohol and Drug Issues, 6(4): 17, 19, 1981.

2283. Gould, Alfred Pearce, Woodhead, German Sims, Clouston, T.S., Mott,
       F.W., Jones, Robert, Price, G. Basil, Taylor, Claude E.,
       Saleeby, C.W., Sullivan, W.C., Campbell, Harry, Shaw, T. Claye,
       Neild, Theodore, Leslie, R. Murray, Shuttleworth, G.E.,
       Scharlieb, Mary, Gregory, Arthur E., Edwards, Walter N. and
       Hercod, R. Communications on the Influence of Parental
       Alcoholism on the Physique and Ability of Offspring.
       British Journal of Inebriety, 8: 184-215, 1911.

2284. Goya, Savitri. Educational Aspects of Alcoholism for Wives.
       Social Welfare, New Delhi, 19(1): 26-27, 1972.

2285. Grady, Virginia. How the Family Concept Fits Existing
       Programs. Labor-Management Alcoholism Journal , 7(1):
       3-11, 1977.

2286. Graeven, David B. and Schaef, Robin D. Family Life and Levels of
       Involvement in an Adolescent Heroin Epidemic. International
       Journal of the Addictions, 13(5): 747-771, 1978.

2287. Graham, A.V., Sedlacek, D., Reeb, K.G., and Thompson, J.S.
       Early Diagnosis and Treatment of Alcoholism. Journal
       of Family Practice, 19(3): 297-313, 1984.

2288. Graham, Philip J. Intergenerational Influences on Psychosocial
       Development. International Journal of Mental Health,
       6(3): 73-89, 1977.

2289. Gram, William H. Breaking Up: A Study of Fifty-Nine Case
        Histories of Marital Collapse. Dissertation Abstracts
        International, 43(6): 2118A, 1982.

2290. Grandguillaume, P., Guidoux, L. and Bula, J.J. Consumption
        of Tobacco and Alcohol, Sedentariness, Family Milieu and
        Health in the School Milieu. Revue Medicale de al Suisse
        Romande, 102(7): 693-706, 1982.

2291. Grandguillaume, P. Guidoux, L. and Bula J.J. The Lausanne Study.
        IV. Smoking, Consumption of Alcohol, Inactivity, Family
        Environment and School Health Environment. Revue Medicale
        de la Suisse Romande, Lausanne, 102(7): 693-706, 1982.

2292. Grant, Igor, Gerst, Marvin, and Yager, Joel. Scaling of Life
        Events by Psychiatric Patients and Normals. Journal of
        Psychosomatic Research, 20(2): 141-149, 1976.

2293. Grant, Marcus and Ginner, Paul (Eds.). Alcoholism in Perspective.
        Baltimore: University Park Press, 1979.

2294. Graven, D.B. and Schaef, R.D. Family Life and Levels of
        Involvement in an Adolescent Heroin Epidemic. Chemical
        Dependencies, 4(3): 187-208, 1982.

2295. Graves, J.R. Orem's Self-Care Concept of Nursing Practice:
        Use with Recovering Alcoholics and Coalcoholics. Paper
        presented at the National Council on Alcoholism Forum.
        Washington, D.C., 1982.

2296. Graves, Theodore D., Graves, Nancy B., Semu, Vineta N. and Ah Sam,
        Iulai. Patterns of Public Drinking in a Multiethnic Society:
        A Systematic Observational Study. Journal of Studies on
        Alcohol, 43(9): 990-1009, 1982.

2297. Gravitz, Herbert L. and Bowden, Julie D. Guide to Recovery: A
        Book for Adult Children of Alcoholics. Holmes Beach, FL:
        Learning Publication, 1985.

2298. Gravitz, Herbert L. and Bowden, Julie D. Recovery Continuum for
        Adult Children of Alcoholics: Insights to Treatment.
        Focus on Family and Chemical Dependency, 8(3): 6-7,
        39-40, 1985.

2299. Gravitz, Herbert L., and Bowden, Julie D. Therapeutic Issues of
        Adult Children of Alcoholics. Alcohol Health and Research
        World, 8(4): 25-29, 36, 1984.

2300. Gray, Lucy. Diary of Hope. Grand Rapids, MI: Baker Book
        House, 1970.

2301. Grcic, Radmila, Kastel, Pavle, Bonevic, Kristina and Kacarevic,
        Radmila. Terapija Bolesti Zavisnosti -- Alkoholizam
        Adolescenata. (Therapy of Dependent Diseases: Adolescent
        Alcoholism.) Psihijatrija Danas, Beograd, 13(1-2):
        117-123, 1981.

2302. Greeley, A.M. and McCready, W.C. A Preliminary Reconnaissance
        Into the Persistence and Explanation of Ethnic Subcultural
        Drinking Patterns. Medical Anthropology, 2(4): 31-51, 1978.

2303. Green, A.H. Child-Abusing Fathers. Journal of the American
        Academy of Child Psychiatry, 18: 270-282, 1979.

2304. Green, Arthur H. Child Abuse. In: Handbook of Treatment of
        Mental Disorders in Childhood and Adolescence. Eds.
        Benjamin B. Wolman, James Egan and Alan O. Ross. Englewood
        Cliffs, NJ: Prentice Hall, 1978, pages 430-455.

2305. Green, Shep. Boy Who Drank Too Much. New York: Viking Press, 1979.

2306. Greenberg, B.H., Blackwelder, W.C. and Levy, R.I. Primary Type 5
       Hyper Lipo Proteinemia. A Descriptive Study in 32 Families.
       Annals of Internal Medicine, 87(5): 526-534, 1977.

2307. Greenberg, L.A. Is Alcoholism Inherited? Inventory, 7(2):
       13-17, 1957.

2308. Greenberger, Ellen, Steinberg, Laurence D. and Vaux, Alan.
       Person-Environment Congruence as a Predictor of Adolescent
       Health and Behavioral Problems. American Journal of
       Community Psychology, 10(5): 511-526, 1982.

2309. Greenblatt, Milton and Schuckit, Marc A. (Eds.) Alcoholism
       Problems in Women and Children. New York: Grune and
       Stratton, 1976.

2310. Greene, D.R. and Cole, L. Foster Homes for Older Adults: An
       Attitudinal Study. Gerontologist, 15(5): 94, 1975.

2311. Greenleaf, J. Co-alcoholic...Para-alcoholic...Who's Who...and
       What's the Difference? Alcoholism: The National Magazine,
       3(5): 24-25, 1983. (Also as: Paper presented at the National
       Council on Alcoholism Forum. New Orleans, April, 1981.)

2312. Greenleaf, J. What We Don't Know Can Hurt Us... and Others.
       Focus on Alcohol and Drug Issues, 6(2): 14-15, 31, 1983.

2313. Greenleaf, Jael. Emotional Caretaking, Parental Roles and Self-
       Esteem: Three Personal Stories. In: Changing Legacies:
       Growing Up in an Alcoholic Home. Pompano Beach, FL:
       Health Communications, 1984, pages 65-71.

2314. Greenwald, Shayna G., Carter, Joan S. and Stein, Elliott, M.
       Differences Between the Background, Attitude, Functioning,
       and Mood of Drug Addicts, Alcoholics, and Orthopedic Patients.
       International Journal of the Addictions, 8(5): 865-874, 1973.

2315. Greer, B.G. Role of Alcohol Abuse in Perpetrators of Child Abuse
       and Neglect. Paper presented at the National Conference
       of the Natonal Council on Alcoholism, Houston, April, 1983.

2316. Greer, H. Steven. Suicidal Patients. Nursing Mirror and
       Midwives Journal, London, 130(3): 36-37, 1970.

2317. Gregory, I. Alcoholism, Family Size and Ordinal Position. Canadian
       Psychiatric Association Journal, Ottawa, 10: 134-140, 1965.

2318. Gregory, I. Family Data Concerning the Hypothesis of Hereditary
       Predisposition Toward Alcoholism. Journal of Mental
       Science, London, 106: 1068-1072, 1960.

2319. Gregory, Ian. Alcoholism and Drug Addiction. Minnesota
       Medicine, 44(11): 445-453, 1961.

2320. Griffee, C. Arkansas Gazette, 30 June 1982. (Family Center Ends
       Study of Drinking and Abuse; Releases Early Findings.)

2321. Griffin, John B. Jr. Introduction to Alcohol Abuse in Adolescents
       and Young Adults. In: Currents in Alcoholism, Volume 6,
       Treatment and Rehabilitation and Epidemiology. Ed. Marc
       Galanter. New York: Grune and Stratton, 1979, pages 229-231.

2322. Griffith, H.E. Family Counseling and Its Importance in the
       Recovery of the Alcoholic. Paper presented at the Seventh
       Annual Meeting of the Association of Labor-Management
       Administrators and Consultants on Alcoholism, Inc., San
       Francisco, October 1978, pages 45-52.

2323. Griggs, D. and Winting, G. Model for the Treatment of the Alcoholic
       and Spouse During Outpatient Treatment and the Resulting Impacts
       on Recovery. In: Alcoholism: A Modern Perspective. Ed. P.
       Golding. Lancaster, England: MTP Press, 1982, pages 225-232.

2324. Grimmett, J.O. Understanding and Treating the Alcoholic.
       Inventory, 20(1): 9-12, 26-27, 1970.

2325. Grislain, J.R., Mainard, R., Berranger, P. de, Ferron, C. de, and
       Brelet, G. Les Sevices Commis Sut Les Enfants; Problemes
       Sociaux et Juridiques. (Child Abuse; Social and Legal Problems.)
       Annales de Pediatrie, Paris, 15(6): 440-448, 1968.

2326. Griswold, D. Addiction and Maryland's Medical Families.
       Maryland State Medical Journal, 31(6): 30-31, 1982.

2327. Gritz, E.R. The Female Smoker Research and Intervention Targets.
       In: Psychosocial Aspects of Cancer. Eds. J. Cohen, J.W. Cullen
       and L.R. Martin. New York: Raven Press, 1982, pages 39-50.

2328. Groman, V. Alcohol and Other Drug Abuse Prevention and the Family:
       Together You Can Make it Work. Grassroots/Education-Prevention:
       1-2, 1982.

2329. Groop, L., Koskimies, S., and Tolppanen, E.M. Characterization
       of Patients with Chlorpropamide-Alcohol Flush. Acta Medica
       Scandinavica, 215(2): 141-149, 1984.

2330. Gross, Meir. Incest and Hysterical Seizures. Medical Hypoanalysis,
       3(4): 146-152, 1982.

2331. Gross, Meir. Incestuous Rape: A Cause for Hysterical Seizures in Four
       Adolescent Girls. American Journal of Orthopsychiatry, 49(4):
       704-708, 1979.

2332. Group Experiences for Children of Alcoholics. NCALI. 1984.

2333. The Group Psychotherapy Literature: 1977. International Journal of
       Group Psychotherapy, 28(4): 509-555, 1978.

2334. Group Therapy with Adolescent Children of Alcoholics. Pamphlet.
       Rochester, NY: National Council on Alcoholism -- Rochester Area,
       Health Association of Rochester and Monroe County, 1971.

2335. Group Therapy with Alcoholics and Their Spouses. Report. Frankfort:
       Kentucky Department of Mental Health, Office of Alcoholism, 1971.

2336. Groupe, Vincent. Alcoholism Rehabilitation: Methods and Experiences
       of Private Rehabilitation Centers. New Brunswick, NJ: Rutgers
       University Center of Alcohol Studies, 1978.

2337. Grove, O. and Lynge J. Suicide and Attempted Suicide in Greenland:
       A Controlled Study in Nuuk (Godthaab). Acta Psychiatrica
       Scandinavica, Copenhagen, 60(4): 375-391, 1979.

2338. Grove, William M. and Cadoret, Remi J. Genetic Factors in Alcoholism.
       In: The Biology of Alcoholism, Volume 7. The Pathogenesis of
       Alcoholism: Biological Factors. Eds. Benjamin Kissin and
       Henri Begleiter. New York: Plenum Press, 1983, pages 31-56.

2339. Grubbauer, H.M. and Schwarz, R. Peritoneal Dialysis in Alcohol
       Intoxication in a Child. Archives of Toxicology, Berlin,
       43: 317-320, 1980.

2340. Gruner, W. The Problem of Juvenile Alcoholism. An Analysis of
       the Literature. Fortschritte der Neurologie-Psychiatrie und
       Ihrer Grenzgebiete, Stuttgart, 45(2): 77-97, 1977.

2341. Gruss, U. and Kreyssig, M. Therapie des Alkoholismus Unter Den
      Bedingungen Der Sektorisierten Psychiatrischen Versorgung Zu
      Atiopathogenese, Diagnostischen Systemen und Prognose Des
      Alkoholismus. (Therapy of Alcoholism Based on Compartmental-
      ized Psychiatric Care. Etiopathogenesis, Diagnostic Systems
      and Prognosis of Alcoholism.) Zeitschrift fur Arztliche
      Fortbildung, 74: 71-77, 1980.

2342. Gualtiere, C.T. and Koriath U. Family History of Alcoholism in
      Hyperactive and Behavior Disordered Children. Alcoholism:
      Clinical and Experimental Research, 5(2): 350, 1981.

2343. Gualtruzzi, A.E. El Alcoholismo. (Alcoholism.) Semana Medica,
      Buenos Aires, 48: 413-418, 1941.

2344. Guide for the Family of the Alcoholic. Pamphlet. Chicago:
      Public Relations Department, Kemper Insurance Group, 1971.

2345. Guide for the Family of the Alcoholic. Al-Anon Family Groups.
      Pamphlet. New York: Al-Anon Family Group Headquarters, 1971.

2346. Guidelines for the Family to Help the Alcoholics. Pamphlet.
      Spokane, WA: Raleigh Hills Hospitals, no date.

2347. Guidelines for School-Based Alcohol and Drug Abuse Prevention
      Programs. California State Department of Education, 1981.
      (Eric Document Number ED208315.)

2348. Gumpel, J.M. and Mason, A.M. Self-Administered Clinical
      Questionnaire for Outpatients. British Medical Journal,
      London, 2(912): 209-212, 1974.

2349. Gunderson, E.K. and Schuckit, M.A. Hospitalalization Rates for
      Alcoholism in the Navy and Marine Corps. Diseases of the
      Nervous System, 36(12): 681-684, 1975.

2350. Gunderson, Ingrid. Incest and Alcoholism. Catalyst, 1(3):
      22-25, 1980.

2351. Gundlach, R.H. Data on the Relation of Birth Order and Sex of
      Sibling of Lesbians Oppose the Hypothesis that Homosexuality
      in Genetic. Annals of the New York Academy of Science,
      197: 179-181, 1972.

2352. Gunn, Alexander D.G. Vulnerable Groups. 1. Lives of Loneliness:
      The Medical-Social Problems of Divorce and Widowhood.
      Nursing Times, London, 64(12): 391-392, 1968.

2353. Gunn, J. Social Factors and Epileptics in Prison. The British
      Journal of Psychiatry: The Journal of Mental Science,
      London, 124: 509-517, 1974.

2354. Gurling, H.M.D., Grant, S. and Dangl, J. The Genetic and Cultural
      Transmission of Alcohol Use, Alcoholism, Cigarette Smoking and
      Coffee Drinking: A Review and an Example Using a Log Linear
      Cultural Transmission Model. British Journal of Addiction,
      80: 269-279, 1985.

2355. Gurling, H.M.D. and Murray, R.M. Alcoholism and Genetics: Old and
      New Evidence. In: Alcohol Related Problems: Room for
      Manoeuvre. Eds. N. Krasner, J.S. Madden, and R.J. Walker.
      New York: John Wiley and Sons Ltd, 1984, pages 127-136.

2356. Gurling, H.M.D., Murray, R.M. and Clifford, C.A. Psychological
      Deficit, Brain Damage, and the Genetic Predisposition to
      Alcoholism: A Twin Study. Acta Geneticae Medicae et
      Gemellologiae, Rome, 29: 64-65, 1980.

2357. Gurling, H.M.D., Oppenheim, B.E. and Murray, R.M. Depression,
       Criminality and Psychopathology Associated with Alcoholism:
       Evidence from a Twin Study. Acta Geneticae Medicae et
       Gemellologiae, 33(2): 333-339, 1984.

2358. Gurmeet, S. and Agarwal, M.L. A Family and Genetic Study of
       Primary Affective Disorders. Indian Journal of Psychiatry,
       22(1): 39-50, 1980.

2359. Gusfield, Joseph R. The Structural Context of College Drinking.
       Quarterly Journal of Studies on Alcohol, 22(3): 428-443, 1961.

2360. Gust, D. Face to Face with Alcoholism. Center City, MN:
       Hazelden, 1979.

2361. Gustav, Jahoda. Children and Alcohol: A Developmental Study in
       Glasgow. London: Her Majesty's Stationery Office, 1972.

2362. Guyette, Susan. Selected Characteristics of American Indian
       Substance Abusers. International Journal of the Addictions,
       17(6): 1001-1014, 1982.

2363. Guze, Samuel B. Criminality and Psychiatric Illness: The Role
       of Alcoholism. Paper presented at the Joint Conference on
       Alcohol Abuse and Alcoholism, Washington, D.C., February,
       1972, pages 13-23.

2364. Guze, Samuel B. Psychiatric Illness in Adopted Children of
       Alcoholics. Annals of the New York Academy of Sciences,
       197: 188, 1972.

2365. Guze, Samuel B. Studies in Hysteria. Canadian Journal of
       Psychiatry, Ottawa, 28(6): 434-437, 1983.

2366. Guze, Samuel B., Goodwin, Donald W. and Crane, J. Bruce.
       A Psychiatric Study of the Wives of Convicted Felons:
       An Example of Assortative Mating. American Journal
       of Psychiatry, 126(12): 1773-1776, 1970.

2367. Guze, Samuel B., Tuason, Vicente B., Gatfield, P.D., Stewart,
       Mark A. and Picken, Bruce. Psychiatric Illness and Crime,
       with Particular Reference to Alcoholism: A Study of 223
       Criminals. Journal of Nervous and Mental Disease, 134:
       512-521, 1962.

2368. Guze, Samuel B., Tuason, Vicente B., Stewart, Mark A. and Picken,
       Bruce. The Drinking History: A Comparison of Reports by
       Subjects and their Relatives. Quarterly Journal of Studies
       on Alcohol, 24: 249-260, 1963.

2369. Guze, Samuel B., Wolfgram, E.D., McKinney, J.K. and Cantwell, D.P.
       Delinquency, Social Maladjustment and Crime: The Role of
       Alcoholism: A Study of First-Degree Relatives of Convicted
       Criminals. Diseases of the Nervous System, 29: 238-243,
       1968.

2370. Guze, Samuel B., Wolfgram, E.D., McKinney, J.K. and Cantwell, D.P.
       Psychiatric Illness in the Families of Convicted Criminals:
       A Study of 519 First-degree Relatives. Diseases of the
       Nervous System, 28(10): 651-659, 1967.

2371. Gwirtsman, Harry E. and Gerner, Robert H. Neurochemical
       Abnormalities in Anorexia Nervosa: Similarities to Affective
       Disorders. Biological Psychiatry, 16(10): 991-996, 1981.

2372. Gyllensward, C. Alcohol and Heredity. Tirfing, 25: 24-31,
       170-176, 1931.

2373. Gyllensward, C. *Contribution to the Question of the Effect of Alcohol on Heredity*. Stokholm: Norstedt, 1923.

2374. Gynther, M.D., Altman, H., Warbin, R.W. and Sletten, I.W. A New Empirical Automated MMPI Interpretive Program: The 1-2--2-1 Code Type. *Journal of Clinical Psychology*, 29(1): 54-57, 1973.

2375. Gynther, M.D. and Brilliant, P.J. Marital Status, Readmission to Hospital and Intrapersonal and Interpersonal Perceptions of Alcoholics. *Quarterly Journal of Studies on Alcohol*, 28(1): 52-58, 1967.

2376. Gynther, Malcolm D., Presher, Charles H. and McDonald, Robert L. Personal and Interpersonal Factors Associated with Alcoholism. *Quarterly Journal of Studies on Alcohol*, 20: 321-333, 1959.

H

2377. H., Mary. My Mother is an Alcoholic. Leaflet. Carmel, NY:
       Guideposts Associates, 1960.

2378. Haastrup, S. and Thomsen, K. The Social Backgrounds of Young
       Addicts as Elicited in Interviews with Their Parents. Acta
       Psychiatrica Scandinavica, Copenhagen, 48: 146-173, 1972.

2379. Haastrup, Soren and Thomsen, Kirsten. The Adolescence Conditions
       of Young Drug Addicts Elucidated by Patient-Interviews.
       Acta Psychiatrica Scandinavica, Copenhagen, 217: 61, 1970.

2380. Haber, S., Paley, A. and Block, A.S. Treatment of Problem
       Drinkers at Winter Veterans Administration Hospital.
       Bulletin of the Menninger Clinic, 13: 24-30, 1949.

2381. Haberman, Paul W. Childhood Symptoms in Children of Alcoholics
       and Comparison Group Parents. Journal of Marriage and the
       Family, 28: 152-154, 1966.

2382. Haberman, Paul W. Differences Between Families Admitting and
       Denying an Existing Drinking Problem. Journal of Health
       and Human Behavior, 4: 141-145, 1963.

2383. Haberman, Paul W. Psychological Test Score Changes for Wives
       of Alcoholics During Periods of Drinking and Sobriety.
       Journal of Clinical Psychology, 20(2): 230-232, 1964.

2384. Haberman, Paul W. Psycho-Physiologic and Childhood Symptoms
       in Alcoholics and Their Children. Milbank Memorial Fund
       Quarterly, 47(1): Part 2, 175-180, 1969.

2385. Haberman, Paul W. Some Characteristics of Alcoholic Marriages
       Differentiated by Level of Deviance. Journal of Marriage
       and the Family, 27(1): 34-36, 1965.

2386. Haberman, Paul W. and Baden, Michael M. Drinking, Drugs, and
       Death. The International Journal of the Addictions,
       9(6): 761-773, 1974.

2387. Hadden, S.B. Editorial: Our Most Serious Health Problem.
       Pennsylvania Medicine, 78(6): 30-31, 1975.

2388. Haer, John L. Drinking Patterns and the Influence of Friends and
       Family. Quarterly Journal of Studies on Alcohol, 16:
       175-185, 1955.

2389. Haertzen, C.A., Monroe, J.J., Hill, H.E. and Hooks, N.T., Jr.
       Manual for Alcoholic Scales of the Inventory of Habits and
       Attitudes. Psychological Reports, 25(3): 947-973, 1969.

2390. Hagenhoff, R. and Lang, W. Stabilisierung der Alkoholabstinenz: Fallbeispiele Aus Einer Therapiegruppe. (Stabilization of Abstinence in Alcoholics Case Studies from a Therapy Group.) In: Alkoholkonsum und Alkoholabhangigkeit. (Alcohol Consumption and Alcohol Dependence.) Eds. H. Berger, A. Legnaro, and K.H. Reuband. Stuttgart: W. Kohlhammer, 1979, pages 170-182.

2391. Hagger, Rona and Dax, E. Cunningham. Driving Records of Multiproblem Families. Social Science and Medicine, Oxford, 11: 121-127, 1977.

2392. Hagglund T.B. and Pylkkanen, K. Nvorten Huumeidenkayttajien Depressiotausta. (The Depressive Background of Adolescent Drug Abusers.) Duodecim, 92(4): 166-176, 1976.

2393. Hagnell, O., Kreitman, N. and Duffy, J. Mental Illness in Married Pairs in a Total Population. British Journal of Psychiatry, 125: 293-302, 1974.

2394. Hagnell, O. and Wretmark, G. Peptic Ulcer and Alcoholism. A Statistical Study in Frequency, Behavior, Personality Traits, and Family Occurrence. Journal of Psychosomatic Research, Oxford, 2: 35-44, 1957.

2395. Hagood, Linda A., Majchrzak, Shirley S., Davis, Terry S. and Shanahan, Patricia. Intervention in Alcoholic Families. Family Rehabilitation Coordinator: A Paraprofessional in the Home. Marriage & Family Counselors Quarterly, 11(4): 22-28, 1977.

2396. Halberstam, M. Ist Alkoholismus Erblich? (Is Alcoholism Hereditary?) Fursorger, 47: 74-75, 1979.

2397. Halikas, James A. A Clinical Prognostic Scale for Skid Row Male Alcoholics. In: Currents in Alcoholism, Vol. 7, Recent Advances in Research and Treatment. Ed. Marc Galanter. New York: Grune & Stratton, 1980, pages 321-330.

2398. Halikas, James A., Darvish, Harriet S. and Rimmer, John D. The Black Addict: I. Methodology, Chronology of Addiction, and Overview of the Population. American Journal of Drug and Alcohol Abuse, 3(4): 529-543, 1976.

2399. Halikas, James A. and Lyttle, Marvin D. Alcohol Abuse Patterns Among Juvenile Delinquents. Paper presented at the 13th Annual Medical-Scientific Conference of the National Alcoholism Forum on Progress in Alcoholism Research and Treatment, Washington, D.C., April, 1985. (Also in: Alcoholism: Clinical and Experimental Research, 6(1): 144, 1982.)

2400. Hall, C. Assessment and Treatment of Adolescent Alcoholism: Unit 2. Curriculum Guide. Springfield: Illinois Alcoholism Counselor Certification Board, Inc., 1983.

2401. Hall, C. Assessment and Treatment of Polydrug Abuse: Unit 2. Curriculum Guide. Springfield: Illinois Alcoholism Counselor Certification Board, Inc., 1983.

2402. Hall, Nancy L. True Story of a Drunken Mother. Plainfield, VT: Daughters, Inc., 1974.

2403. Hall, R.L. Assortative Mating in the Families of Alcoholics. Annals of Human Biology, 10(1): 84, 1983.

2404. Hall, R.L., Hesselbrock, V.M. and Stabenau, J.R. Familial Distribution of Alcohol Use. Part II: Assortative Mating of Alcoholic Probands. Behavior Genetics, 13(4): 373-382, 1983.

2405. Hall, Richard W. An Alternative to the Criminality of Driving While
       Intoxicated. Journal of Police Science & Administration, 5(2):
       138-144, 1977.

2406. Hall, Roberta L., Hesselbrock, Victor M. and Stabenau, James R.
       Familial Distribution of Alcohol Use. Part I: Assortative
       Mating in the Parents of Alcoholics. Behavior Genetics,
       13(4): 361-372, 1983.

2407. Halleck, S.L. Psychodynamic Aspects of Violence. Bulletin of the
       American Academy of Psychiatry and the Law, 4(4): 328-335, 1976.

2408. Haller, Scot. The Sad Ballad of Bing and His Boys. People Weekly,
       19: 88-94, 1983.

2409. Halmi, K.A. and Loney, J. Familial Alcoholism in Anorexia Nervosa.
       British Journal of Psychiatry, London, 123(572): 53-54, 1973.

2410. Halpern, F. Alcoholic "Potentials." Alcohol Hygiene, 1(7): 18-22,
       1945.

2411. Hambrecht, M. Inappropriate Helping Behavior and Its Impact on
       the Identified Patient. Psychotherapy: Theory, Research and
       Practice, 20(4): 494-502, 1983.

2412. Hamburg, B.A., Kraemer, H.C. and Jahnke, W. A Hierarchy of Drug
       Use in Adolescence: Behavioral and Attitudinal Correlates of
       Substantial Drug Use. American Journal of Psychiatry, 132:
       1155-1163, 1975.

2413. Hamer, J. and Steinbring, J. (Eds.) Alcohol and Native Peoples of
       the North. Lanham, MD: University Press of America, 1980.

2414. Hamer, J.H. Guardian Spirits, Alcohol and Cultural Defense
       Mechanisms. Anthropologica, 11: 215-241, 1969.

2415. Hames, L.N. The Case for Having the Public Schools Teach Our
       Youngsters How to Drink. Clinical Toxicology, 11(4):
       473-478, 1977.

2416. Hamilton, C.J. and Collins, J.J. Role of Alcohol in Wife Beating and
       Child Abuse: A Review of the Literature. In: Drinking and
       Crime. Ed. J.J. Collins. New York: Guilford Press, 1981,
       pages 253-287.

2417. Hamilton, Gayle R. Taking Needs Seriously. Paper presented at the
       National Institute on Drug Abuse, Program for Women's Concerns,
       Miami Beach, October, 1975. (Also in: Drugs, Alcohol and Women:
       A National Forum Source Book. Washington, D.C.: National
       Research and Communications Associates, 1976, pages 186-188.)

2418. Hamilton, Lyn. Ostracized from Childhood: The Child of the
       Alcoholic. Young Family, 1(1): 41-44, 48-50, 1975.

2419. Hamlin, Diane E., Hurwitz, Dorothy B. and Spieker, Gisela.
       Perspectives: Family Violence. Alcohol Health and
       Research World, 4(1): 17-22, 1979.

2420. Hammen, C.L. Depression in College Students: Beyond the Beck
       Depression Inventory. Journal of Consulting and Clinical
       Psychology, 48: 126-128, 1980.

2421. Hammerschlag, Carl A. Identity Groups with American Indian
       Adolescents. 1974. (Eric Document Number ED098451.)

2422. Hammond, Isaac William. An Epidemiological Study of Coronary
       Bypass Surgery Among Airmen. Dissertation Abstracts
       International, 43(4): 1053B, 1982.

2423. Hanak, K. Alkoholista Szulok--Allami Gondozott Gyerekek.
       (Alcoholic Parents -- Children as Wards of the State.)
       Alkohologia, Budapest, 3: 98-107, 1972.

2424. Hancock, Betsy Ledbetter. Alcohol and Drug Use by Teen-Age Youth.
       In: School Social Work. Ed. Betsy L. Hancock. Englewood
       Cliffs, NJ: Prentice-Hall, Inc., 1982, pages 182-198.

2425. Hancock, Betsy Ledbetter. Child Abuse and Neglect. In: School
       Social Work. Ed. Betsy L. Hancock. Englewood Cliffs, NJ:
       Prentice-Hall, Inc., 1982, pages 146-162.

2426. Handbook for the Alcoholism Counselor. Rockville, MD:
       National Institute on Alcohol Abuse and Alcoholism
       (DHEW/PHS), 1972. (Eric Document Number ED145296.)

2427. Hanks, Susan E. and Rosenbaum, C.P. Battered Women: A Study of
       Women Who Live With Violent Alcohol-Abusing Men. American
       Journal of Orthopsychiatry, 47(2): 291-306, 1977.

2428. Hanna, Joel M. Ethnic Groups, Human Variation, and Alcohol Use.
       In: Cross-Cultural Approaches to the Study of Alcohol:
       An Interdisciplinary Perspective. Eds. Michael W. Everett,
       Jack O. Waddell and Dwight B. Heath. Paris: Mouton
       Publishers, 1976, pages 235-242.

2429. Hanngren, A. and Reizenstein, P. Studies in Dumping Syndrome. V.
       Tuberculosis in Gastrectomized Patients. The American
       Journal of Digestive Diseases, 14(10): 700-710, 1969.

2430. Hanrahan, M.E. Miami Herald, 31 July 1983, page 3.
       (Involuntary Treatment: Godsend for Alcoholics.)

2431. Hansen, Constance Collinge. An Extended Home Visit with Conjoint
       Family Therapy. Family Process, 7(1): 67-87, 1968.

2432. Hansen, P.L. The Development of an Alcoholism Unit in a Private
       General Hospital. Minnesota Medicine, 55: 577-579, 1972.

2433. Hansen, S.E. Review of Treatment - Family - Therapy for Alcoholic
       Parents by B. Borjeson. Nordisk Psykologi, 30(3): 272-274,
       1978.

2434. Hanson, David J. A Note on Parental Attitudes and the Incidence
       of Drinking. Drinking and Drug Practices Surveyor, 8:
       12-14, 1973.

2435. Hanson, F.B. The Effect of Administration of Alcohol Fumes to 5
       Successive Generations of Albino Rats. Anatomical Record,
       26: 392, 1923.

2436. Hanson, F.B. and Cooper, Z.K. The Effects of 10 Generations of
       Alcoholic Ancestry Upon Learning Ability in the Albino Rat.
       Journal of Experimental Zoology, 56: 369-392, 1930.

2437. Hanson, Kathye J. and Estes, Nada J. Dynamics of Alcoholic
       Families. In: Alcoholism: Development, Consequences and
       Interventions. Eds. Nada J. Estes and M. Edith Heinemann.
       St. Louis: C.V. Mosby Company, 1977, pages 67-75.

2438. Hanson, P.G., Sands, P.M. and Sheldon R.B. Patterns of
       Communication in Alcoholic Marital Couples. Psychiatric
       Quarterly, 42(3): 538-547, 1968.

2439. Harada, S., Agarwal, D.P., Goedde, H.W. and Ishikawa, B. Aldehyde
       Dehydrogenase Isozyme Variation and Alcoholism in Japan.
       Pharmacology, Biochemistry and Behavior, 18(Supplement 1):
       151-153, 1983.

2440. Harada, S., Misawa, S. and Agarwal, D.P. Liver Alcohol
       Dehydrogenase and Aldehyde Dehydrogenase in the Japanese:
       Isozyme Variation and its Possible Role in Alcohol
       Intoxication. American Journal of Human Genetics, 32:
       8-15, 1980.

2441. Haraway, Kay. Guide for the Family of the Alcoholic. Denver:
       National Council on Alcoholism, 1979.

2442. Harbison, Raymond D. (Ed.) Perinatal Addiction. New York:
       Halsted Press, 1975.

2443. Harburg, Ernest, Davis, Deborah R. and Caplan, Roberta. Parent
       and Offspring Alcohol Use: Imitative and Aversive
       Transmission. Journal of Studies on Alcohol, 43(5):
       497-516, 1982.

2444. Hardin, Kay. Treating Intoxicated Patients in the Emergency
       Department. Journal of Emergency Nursing, 5(1): 11-14,
       1979.

2445. Hardy, Richard E. and Cull, John G. Group Counseling and Therapy
       Techniques in Special Settings. Springfield, IL: Charles C.
       Thomas, 301-327, 1974.

2446. Harford, T.C. Beverage Specific Drinking Contexts. International
       Journal of the Addictions, 14(2): 197-205, 1979.

2447. Harford, T.C. Teenage Alcohol Use. Postgraduate Medicine,
       60(1): 73-76, 1976.

2448. Harju, E. and Vaisanen, E. Parents and Children in Oral Acting
       and Dietary Habits. Proceedings of the Nutrition Society,
       38(3): 109A, 1979.

2449. Harley, Roy A. Child Abuse and Its Relationship to Alcoholism:
       A Statement of Problems and Needs for Study. Report. Urbana:
       University of Illinois, Department of Anthropology, 1979.

2450. Harmsworth, Harry C. A Survey of the Alcohol and Narcotics
       Problem in Idaho. Moscow: University of Idaho, 1954.

2451. Harper, Frederick D. Alcohol Use and Alcoholism Among Black Americans:
       A Review. In: Black Alcoholism: Toward a Comprehensive
       Understanding. Eds. Thomas D. Watts and Roosevelt Wright, Jr.
       Springfield, IL: Charles C. Thomas, 1983, pages 19-36, 1983.

2452. Harper, Frederick D. Research and Treatment with Black Alcoholics.
       Alcohol Health and Research World, 4(4): 10-16, 1980.

2453. Harrell, L. Frank. The Residue of Alcoholism: A Case Study of
       the Succeeding Generation of an Alcoholic Marriage. Family
       Therapy, 10(3): 239-251, 1983.

2454. Harrington, Virginia Clarke. A Family Disease. Momentum,
       14(3): 28-30, 1983.

2455. Harris, E.L., Noyes, R., Crowe, R.R. and Chaudhry, D.R. Family
       Study of Agoraphobia. Report of a Pilot Study. Archives of
       General Psychiatry, 40(10): 1061-1064, 1983.

2456. Harris, Hiawatha. Addiction and Family Disintegration. Paper
       presented at the National Institute on Drug Abuse, Program
       for Women's Concerns, Miami Beach, October, 1975. (Also in:
       Drugs, Alcohol and Women; A National Forum Source Book.
       Washington, D.C.: National Research and Communications
       Associates, 1976, pages 75-76.)

2457. Harris, James R. and Myers, J. Martin. Hospital Management of the Suicidal Patient. In: Suicidal Behaviors: Diagnosis and Management. Boston: Little Brown, 1968, pages 297-305.

2458. Harris, Thomas A. Counseling the Serviceman and His Family. Englewood Cliffs, NJ: Prentice Hall, 1964.

2459. Harrison, D.E. Emerging Drinking Patterns of Pre-Adolescents: A Study of the Influence of Significant Others. Doctoral Dissertation. (University Microfilms No. 71-8837.) Mississippi State University, 1970.

2460. Harrison, D.E., Bennett, W.H. and Globetti, G. Factors Related to Alcohol Use Among Pre-Adolescents. Journal of Alcohol Education, 15(2): 3-10, 1970.

2461. Harrison, T.W. Medical Role in the Treatment of Alcoholism. Paper presented at Queen Mary Hospital, Hanmer Springs, New Zealand. In: Dependency. Christchurch: Canterbury University, 1974, pages 102-107.

2462. Hart, G. Social Aspects of Venereal Disease. II. Relationship of Personality to Other Sociological Determinants of Venereal Disease. British Journal of Veneral Diseases, London, 49(6): 548-552, 1973.

2463. Hart, Larry. Rehabilitation Need Patterns of Men Alcoholics. Journal of Studies on Alcohol, 38(3): 494-451, 1977.

2464. Hart, Larry, S. and Stueland, Dean. An Application of the Multidimensional Model of Alcoholism. Differentiation of Alcoholics by Mode Analysis. Journal of Studies on Alcohol, 40(3): 283-290, 1979.

2465. Hart, Larry S. and Stueland, Dean. The Relationship Between Changes in Drinking Behavior and Psychological Need Satisfaction. Journal of Studies on Alcohol, 43(3): 393-396, 1982.

2466. Hart, Larry S. and Stueland, Dean. Relationship of Sociodemographic and Drinking Variables to Differentiated Subgroups of Alcoholics. Community Mental Health Journal, 15(1): 47-57, 1979.

2467. Hartford, James T. and Thienhaus, Ole J. Psychiatric Aspects of Alcoholism in Geriatric Patients. In: Aging, Volume 25: Alcoholism in the Elderly: Social and Biomedical Issues. Eds. James T. Hartford and T. Samorajski. New York: Raven Press, 1984, pages 253-262.

2468. Hartie, M. Nursing Care Study - Alcoholism: The Sins of the Father. Nursing Mirror, 151(7): 38-41, 1980.

2469. Hartley, T.R. Families Need to Get Tough: Make Alcoholics Responsible. Freedom Fighter, 2(2): 101, 1984.

2470. Hartocollis, P. Denial of Illness in Alcoholism. Bulletin of the Menninger Clinic, 32: 47-53, 1968.

2471. Hartocollis, Pitsa-Calliope. Personality Characteristics in Adolescent Problem Drinkers. A Comparative Study. Journal of the American Academy of Child Psychiatry, 21(4): 348-353, 1982.

2472. Harvey, A.F. The Economic Effects of Alcoholism in Relation to Family Life. International Congress Against Alcoholism, 14: 147-166.

2473. Harvey, Elinor B., Gazay, Louis and Samuels, Bennett. Utilization of a Psychiatric-Social Work Team in an Alaskan Native Secondary Boarding School. Annual Progress in Child Psychiatry & Child Development, 693-710, 1977.

2474. Harvey, M.L. and Brown, J.H. Psychiatric Patients in the General Hospital Casualty Service. Report of a Study. Canadian Psychiatric Association Journal, 16(2): 129-135, 1971.

2475. Harwin, J. Excessive Drinker and the Family: Approaches to Treatment. In: Alcohol and the Family. Eds. J. Orford and J. Harwin. New York: St. Martin's Press, 1982, pages 201-240.

2476. Harwin, J. and Orford, J. Overview: Problems in Establishing a Family Perspective. In: Alcohol and the Family. Eds. J. Orford and J. Harwin. New York: St. Martin's Press, 1982, pages 260-265.

2477. Hasleton, S. The Incidence and Correlates of Marihuana Use in an Australian Undergraduate Population. The Medical Journal of Australia, Sydney, 2,(6): 302-308, 1971.

2478. Hassall, Christine. A Controlled Study of the Characteristics of Young Male Alcoholics. The British Journal of Addiction. 63(3): 193-201, 1968.

2479. Hassall, Christine and Foulds, G.A. Hostility Among Young Alcoholics. The British Journal of Addiction, 63(3): 203-208, 1968.

2480. Hassett, Carol Alice. The Relationship of Gender, Alcoholic Parentage and Intervention to Mental Abilities, Locus of Control and Zinc Level. Dissertation Abstracts International, 42(5): 2110B, 1981.

2481. Hassett, D.G. Family Alcoholism and Child Abuse: Where Do You Start? Focus on Family and Chemical Dependency, 8(4): 14-15, 31, 1985.

2482. Hastings, J. and Typpo, M.H. Elephant in the Living Room: A Leader's Guide for Helping Children of Alcoholics. Minneapolis: CompCare Publications, 1984.

2483. Hathaway, Jane and Dennison, Andrea. Family Treatment; Changing Concepts in Healing. Focus on Alcohol and Drug Issues, 6(4): 6-7, 30, 1983.

2484. Hatsukami, Dorothy K. and Owen, Patricia. The Relationship of Social Roles to the Treatment Outcome in Female Alcoholics. Minneapolis: Hazelden Research Services, 1980.

2485. Hatsukami, Dorothy K. and Owen, Patricia. Social Roles and Treatment Outcome in Women with Alcohol of Drug Abuse Problems. Focus on Women: Journal of Addictions and Health, 3(2): 118-123, 1982.

2486. Hatsukami, Dorothy K. and Owen, Patricia. Treatment Outcome in Female Alcoholics: A New Perspective. Minneapolis: Hazelden Research Services, 1979.

2487. Haumonte, M.T. and Levy, M. L'image de la Femme Dans un Groupe Therapeutique d'alcooliques et de Nevrotiques. (Image of the Woman in a Therapeutic Group of Alcoholics and Neurotics.) Annales Medico-Psychologiques, Paris, 142(1): 47-60, 1984.

2488. Hausfeld, R.G. Social, Ethnic and Cultural Aspects of Aboriginal Health. Australian Family Physician, 6(10): 1301-1307, 1977.

2489. Havighurst, Robert J. The Extent and Significance of Suicide Among American Indians Today. Mental Hygiene, 55(2): 174-177, 1971.

2490. Havlik, R.J., Garrison, R.J. and Feinleib, M. Evidence for Additional Blood Pressure Correlates in Adults 20-56 Years Old. Circulation, 61: 710-715, 1980.

2491. Hawker, A. Adolescents and Alcohol. Report of an Enquiry Into Adolescent Drinking Patterns Carried Out from October 1975 to June 1976. London: Edsall, 1978.

2492. Hawkins, H.N. Some Effects of Alcoholism of Parents on Children in the Home. St. Louis: Salvation Army, Midland Division, 1950.

2493. Hawkins, James L. Lesbianism and Alcoholism. In: Alcoholism Problems in Women and Children. Eds. Milton Greenblatt and Marc A. Schuckit. New York: Grune and Stratton, 1976, pages 137-153.

2494. Hawks, D., Mitcheson, M., Ogborne, A. and Edwards, G. Abuse of Methylamphetamine. British Medical Journal, London, 1(659): 715-721, 1969.

2495. Hawley, N.P. and Brown, E.L. Use of Group Treatment with Children of Alcoholics. Social Casework, 62(1): 40-46, 1981.

2496. Hawthorne, T. Children Teaching Grown-Ups: A Kid's View of the National Convention. Focus on Family and Chemical Dependency, 8(2): 12-13, 1985.

2497. Hay, W.M. Behavioral Assessment and Treatment of an Alcoholic Marriage. In: Clinical Case Studies in the Behavioral Treatment. Eds. W. Hay and P. Nathan. New York: Plenum Press, 1982, pages 157-182.

2498. Hayashi, S. Alcoholism and Marriage; Family Court Divorce Conciliation. Japanese Journal of Studies on Alcohol, Kyoto, 13: 177-190, 1978.

2499. Hayashid, M., Dorus, W. Schaefer, M. and Collins, J. Alcoholics Family History of Psychiatric-Illness and Severity of Alcoholism and Depression. Alcoholism: Clinical and Experimental Research, 10(1): 96, 1986.

2500. Hayaski, N. and Zamami, M. Paternal Loss and Birth Order of Alcoholics: From the Investigation of Alcoholics and Schizophrenics. Japanese Journal of Alcohol Studies and Drug Dependence, Kyoto, 18(3): 316-324, 1983.

2501. Hayden, Joyce. Wife Battering: One Perspective. 1978. (Eric Document Number ED183978.)

2502. Hayek, M.A. Recovered Alcoholic Women With and Without Incest Experience: A Comparative Study. Doctoral Dissertation. Portland, Oregon: Reed University, 1980.

2503. Haykin, Martin D. Transactional Analysis and the Treatment of Alcoholism. In: Alcoholism: Development, Consequences, and Interventions. Eds. Nada J. Estes and M. Edith Heinemann. St. Louis: The C.V. Mosby Company, 1977, pages 303-310.

2504. Hayman, Max. Alcoholics Anonymous and Religious Groups. In: Alcoholism: Mechanism and Management. Ed. M. Hayman. Springfield, IL: Charles C. Thomas, 1966, pages 171-194.

2505. Hayman, Max. History and Examination of the Alcoholic. In: Alcoholism: Mechanism and Management. Ed. M. Hayman. Springfield, IL: Charles C. Thomas, 1966, pages 91-104.

2506. Hayman, Max. Institutions in Alcoholism. In: Alcoholism: Mechanism and Management. Ed. M. Hayman. Springfield, IL: Charles C. Thomas, 1966, pages 130-144.

2507. Hayman, Max. Ministrants to the Alcoholic. In: <u>Alcoholism:</u>
      <u>Mechanism and Management</u>. Ed. M. Hayman. Springfield, IL:
      Charles C. Thomas, 1966, pages 76-90.

2508. Hayman, Max. Psychopathology of the Alcoholic. In: <u>Alcoholism:</u>
      <u>Mechanism and Management</u>. Ed. M. Hayman. Springfield, IL:
      Charles C. Thomas, 1966, pages 43-59.

2509. Hayman, Max. Psychotherapy of Alcoholism. In: <u>Alcoholism:</u>
      <u>Mechanism and Management</u>. Ed. M. Hayman. Springfield, IL:
      Charles C. Thomas, 1966, pages 195-231.

2510. Hayman, Max. Viewpoints on Alcoholism. In: <u>Alcoholism:</u>
      <u>Mechanism and Management</u>. Ed. M. Hayman. Springfield, IL:
      Charles C. Thomas, 1966, pages 27-42.

2511. Hazel, Nancy and Kalvesten, A.L. Fostering Disturbed Adolescents:
      The Pioneering Work of the Stockholm Youth Office.
      <u>International Social Work</u>, Bombay, <u>17</u>(3): 8-13, 1974.

2512. Hazelden Family Program & Research Services. <u>Families in Crisis:</u>
      <u>A Study of the Hazelden Family Program</u>. Minneapolis:
      Hazelden Research Services, 1981.

2513. Hazelden Foundation. <u>The Family and Social Change: Alcoholism</u>
      <u>and the Family Academic Unit VII</u>. Center City: Hazelden,
      no date.

2514. Headlam, H.K., Goldsmith, R.J., Hanenson, I.B. and Rauh, J.L.
      Demographic Characteristics of Adolescents With Self-
      Poisoning; a Survey of 235 Instances in Cincinnati, Ohio.
      <u>Clinical Pediatrics</u>, <u>18</u>: 147, 151, 154, 1979.

2515. Health Education of Children and Young People. <u>World Health</u>
      <u>Organization Chronicle</u>, Geneva, <u>32</u>(9): 333-334, 1978.

2516. Health Insurance Should Pay for Alcoholism Treatment in Order to
      Reduce Costs of Treating Related Illnesses, According to
      the National Institute on Alcohol Abuse & Alcoholism.
      <u>Medical World</u>, (November): 36, 38, 1982.

2517. Health Promotion: Alcohol and Drug Misuse Prevention. <u>Public Health</u>
      <u>Reports</u>, September-October(Supplement): 116-132, 1983.

2518. Health Visitor and "A Family Disease". <u>Journal of Alcoholism</u>,
      <u>8</u>(4): 129-132, 1973.

2519. Heard, David B. Death as a Motivator: Using Crisis Induction to
      Break Through the Denial System. In: <u>The Family Therapy of</u>
      <u>Drug Abuse and Addiction</u>. Eds. M. Duncan Stanton and Thomas
      C. Todd. New York: The Guilford Press, 1982, pages 203-234.

2520. Hebblethwaite, David. Reflections on Healing Alcohol Abuse. <u>Royal</u>
      <u>Society of Health Journal</u>, London, <u>96</u>(4): 189-192, 1976.

2521. Hebe, Serrano. Family Psychotherapy in Medical Institutions of the
      Instituto del Servicio de Segurida Social de los Trabajadores
      del Estado. <u>Neurologia-Neurocirugia-Psiquiatria</u>, Mexico,
      <u>18</u>(2-3): 173-177, 1977.

2522. Hecht, Murray. Children of Alcoholics Are Children at Risk.
      <u>American Journal of Nursing</u>, <u>73</u>(10): 1764-1767, 1973.

2523. Hecht, Murray. A Cooperative Approach Toward Children from Alcoholic
      Families. <u>Elementary School Guidance & Counseling</u>, <u>11</u>(3):
      197-203, 1977.

2524. Heckler, J. <u>Fragile Peace</u>. New York: G.P. Putnam's Sons, 1986.

2525. Hedberg, Allan G. and Campbell, Lowell. A Comparison of Four
        Behavioral Treatments of Alcoholism. _Journal of Behavior
        Therapy and Experimental Psychiatry_, 5(3/4): 251-256, 1974.

2526. Hedge, H.R. Recovering Addicted Dentists: A Preliminary Survey.
        Iowa Dental Journal, 68: 41-42, 1982.

2527. Hegedus, A.M., Alterman, A.I. and Tarter, R.E. Learning Achievement
        in Sons of Alcoholics. _Alcoholism: Clinical and Experimental
        Research_, 8(3): 330-333, 1984.

2528. Hegedus, A.M., Tarter, R.E., Hill, S.Y., Jacob, T. and Winsten, N.E.
        Static Ataxia: A Possible Marker for Alcoholism. _Alcoholism:
        Clinical and Experimental Research_, 8(6): 580-582, 1984.

2529. Heilman, R.O., Amit, Z., Erwin, V.G. and Deitrich, R.A. Prevention
        Through Early Detection of the Genetic Predisposition to
        Chemical Dependency: An Overview of Current Scientific Research
        Projects on Genetic Markers. Paper presented at the National
        Alcoholism Forum, Washington, D.C., April, 1985.

2530. Heinemann, E. Alcohol and Drug Abuse: A Challenge for Nurse
        Educators. Paper presented at the _Second Spring Conference
        for Nurse Educators in Alcohol and Drug Abuse Nursing_.
        Colorado Springs, May, 1982, pages 2-11.

2531. Heinemann, M. Edith and Smith-DiJulio, Kathleen. Assessment and
        Care of the Chronically Ill Alcoholic Person. In: _Alcoholism:
        Development, Consequences, and Interventions_. Eds. Nada J.
        Estes and M. Edith Heinemann. St. Louis: The C.V. Mosby Company,
        1977, pages 239-248.

2532. Heinemeyer, F. _Aufgaben und Moglichkeiten Kirchlichen Handelns
        an Alkoholkranken_. (The Problems and Possibilities of
        Pastoral Care of Alcoholics.) Berlin: Siemensstadter Press,
        1974.

2533. Heins, Terence J. and Yelland, John H. Validity Studies on the
        Ryle Marital Patterns Test. _British Journal of Medical
        Psychology_, London, 54(part 1): 51-58, 1981.

2534. Held, Barbara S. and Heller, Linda. Symptom Prescription as Metaphor:
        A Systemic Approach to the Psychosomatic-Alcoholic Family.
        Family Therapy, 9(2): 133-145, 1982.

2535. Helgason, Thomas and Asmundsson, Gylfi. Behaviour and Social
        Characteristics of Young Asocial Alcohol Abusers.
        Neuropsychobiology, Basel, 1(2): 109-120, 1975.

2536. Hell, D., Battegay, R., Muhlemann, R. and Dillinger, A. Personal
        Motivation, Environmental Factors, and the Extent of Drug
        Comsumption of Adolescents. _Nervenarzt_, 47(6): 402-406, 1976.

2537. Hell, D., Battegay, R., Muhlemann, R. and Dillinger, A. Die
        Selbstdarstellung von Alkohol- und Drogen-Konsumenten in
        Personlicher und Sozialer Hinsicht. (Self-Assessment of
        Alcohol and Drug Users: A Personal and Social Self-
        Assessment.) _Archiv fur Psychiatrie und Nervenkrankheiten_,
        Berlin, 221(4): 345-360, 1976.

2538. Heller, K., Sher, K.J. and Benson, C.S. Problems Associated With
        Risk Overprediction in Studies of Offspring of Alcoholics:
        Implications for Prevention. _Clinical Psychology Review_,
        2(2): 183-200, 1982.

2539. Helm, Stanley T. Predisposition of Alcoholism. In: _Resource
        Book for Drug Abuse Education_. American Association for
        Health, Physical Education and Recreation. Washington, D.C.:
        U.S. Government Printing Office, 1969, pages 87-88.

2540.   Helmchen, Von Hanfried. Findings and Anamneses of Hospitalized
        Alcoholics. Deutsch e Medizinische Journal, 23(8):
        505-509, 1972.

2541.   Helms, D.J. A Guide to the New Federal Rules Governing the
        Confidentiality of Alcohol and Drug Abuse Patient Records.
        Medical Record News, 47(4): 7, 12-20, 1976.

2542.   Helms, E. Women at Work. EAP Digest, 1(5): 9-10, 1981.

2543.   Help for Families of Problems Drinkers. Nursing Times, 76(50):
        2198, 1980.

2544.   Helzer, J.E. Bipolar Affective Disorder in Black and White Men;
        A Comparison of Symptoms and Familial Illness. Archives of
        General Psychiatry, 32(9): 1140-1143, 1975.

2545.   Helzer, John E., Robins, Lee N. and Davis, Darlene, H.
        Depressive Disorders in Vietnam Returnees. The Journal of
        Nervous and Mental Disease, 163(3): 177-185, 1976.

2546.   Helzer, John E. and Winokur, George. A Family Interview Study of
        Male Manic Depressives. Archives of General Psychiatry,
        31(1): 73-77, 1974.

2547.   Hemminki, E. Tobacco, Alcohol, Medicines and Illegal Drug
        Taking. Adolescence, 9(35): 421-424, 1974.

2548.   Henderson, C.D. Countering Resistance to Acceptance of Denial
        and the Disease Concept in Alcoholism Families: Two
        Examples of Experiential Teaching. Alcoholism Treatment
        Quarterly, 1(4): 117-121, 1984.

2549.   Henderson, George I., Patwardham, Rashmi V., Hoyumpa, Jr.,
        Anastacio, M. and Schenker, Steven. Pathogenesis of the
        Fetal Alcohol Syndrome. In: Biological Approach to
        Alcoholism. Ed. Charles S. Sieber. Research Monograph
        No. 11. Washington, D.C.: U.S. Government Printing Office,
        1983, pages 46-62.

2550.   Henle, Llse. Die Tragodie der Labdakiden: Unentrinnbares Schicksal
        einer Alkoholikerfamilie. (The Tragedy of the Descendants of
        Labdacus: Inescapable Fate of the Alcoholic's Family?) Praxis
        der Kinderpsychologie und Kinderpsychiatrie, Gottingen, 26(2):
        46-52, 1977. Dissertation Thesis. (Ann Arbor, MI: University
        Microfilms No. 75-22546).

2551.   Hennecke, L. Stimulus Augmenting and Field Dependence in Children
        of Alcoholic Fathers. Journal of Studies on Alcohol,
        45(6): 486-492, 1984.

2552.   Hennecke, Lynne, Gitlow, Stanley, E. Alcohol Use and Alcoholism
        in Adolescence. New York State Journal of Medicine,
        83(7): 936-940, 1983.

2553.   Hennessy, B.L., Bruen, W.J. and Cullen, J. The Canberra Mental
        Health Survey: Preliminary Results. Medical Journal of
        Australia, Sydney, 1(15): 721-728, 1973.

2554.   Henry, J.D. and Zastowny, T.R. Perceptual Differences: Alcoholics
        and Significant Others. Alcohol Health and Research World,
        3(1): 36-39, 1978.

2555.   Hensel, B., Dunner, D.L. and Fieve, R.R. The Relationship of
        Family History of Alcoholism to Primary Affective Disorders.
        Journal of Affective Disorders, (1): 105-113, 1979.

2556.   Hentel, Nat H.   Memorandum -- Decision in the Matter of the
        Application of Spence Chapin Services to Families and
        Children.   Contemporary Drug Problems, 6(2): 173-197, 1977.

2557.   Heppner, Mary J.   Counseling the Battered Wife: Myths, Facts, and
        Decisions.   Personnel and Guidance Journal, 56(9): 522-525,
        1978.

2558.   Herjanic, Barbara M., Barredo, Victor H., Herjanic, Marijan and
        Tomelleri, Carlos J.   Children of Heroin Addicts.   The
        International Journal of the Addictions, 14(7): 919-931, 1979.

2559.   Herjanic, Barbara M., Herjanic, Marijan, Penick, Elizabeth,
        Tomelleri, Carlos and Armbruster, Robert B.   Children of
        Alcoholics.   Paper Presented at the 7th Annual Medical-Scientific
        Session of the National Alcoholism Forum, Washington, D.C., May
        1976. (Also in: Currents in Alcoholism.   Volume 2.
        Psychiatric, Psychological, Social and Epidemiological Studies.
        Ed. F.A. Seixas.   New York: Grune and Stratton, 1977, pages
        445-456.)

2560.   Herjanic, Barbara, Herjanic, Marijan, Wetzel, R. and Tomelleri,
        Carlos.   Substance Abuse: Its Effect on Offspring.   Research
        Communications in Psychology, Psychiatry and Behavior, 3:
        65-75, 1978.

2561.   Herjanic, Barbara and Welner, Zila.   Adolescent Suicide.
        Advances in Behavioral Pediatrics, 1: 195-223, 1980.

2562.   Herman, C.S., Kirchner, G.L., Streissguth, A.P. and Little, R.E.
        Vigilance Paradigm for Preschool Children Used to Relate
        Vigilance Behavior to IQ and Prenatal Exposure to Alcohol.
        Perceptual and Motor Skills, 50: 863-867, 1980.

2563.   Herman, C.S., Little, R.E., Streissguth, A.P. and Beck, D.E.
        Alcoholic Fathering and its Relation to Child's Intellectual
        Development.   Alcoholism: Clinical and Experimental
        Research, 4: 217, 1980.

2564.   Herman, Judith and Hirschman, Lisa.   Families at Risk for Father-
        Daughter Incest.   American Journal of Psychiatry, 138(7):
        967-970, 1981.

2565.   Herman, William W.   Fathers: What Are You?   Who Are You.
        Adolescence, 8(29): 139-144, 1973.

2566.   Herrenkohl, Roy C., Herrenkohl, Ellen C. and Egolf, Brenda P.
        Circumstances Surrounding the Occurrence of Child Maltreatment.
        Journal of Consulting and Clinical Psychology, 51(3): 424-431,
        1983.

2567.   Herrera-Hernandez, M.   El Problema del Alcoholismo en la Infancia.
        (The Problem of Alcoholism in Childhood.)   Acta Pediatrica
        Espanola, 23: 497-504, 1965.

2568.   Herrington, Roland E.   Impaired Physician-Recognition, Diagnosis,
        and Treatment.   Wisconsin Medical Journal, 78:21-23, 1979.

2569.   Herrington, Roland E., Riordan, Patrick R. and Jacobson, George R.
        Alcohol and Other Drug Dependence in Adolescence:
        Characteristics of Those Who Seek Treatment, and Outcome of
        Treatment.   In: Currents in Alcoholism, Volume 8:   Recent
        Advances in Research and Treatment.   Ed. Marc Galanter.
        New York: Grune and Stratton, 1981, pages 253-268.

2570.   Herrmann, Dagmar and Lotz, Jurgen.   Drug Consumption Among School
        Children of a Small Town in Northern Germany.   Report on a
        Pilot Study.   Muenchener Medizinische Wochenschrift, 114(9):
        393-397, 1972.

2571.   Hersen, M. and Luber, R.F.   Use of Group Psychotherapy in a Partial
        Hospitalization Service: The Remediation of Basic Skill
        Deficits.   International Journal of Group Psychotherapy,
        27: 361-376, 1977.

2572.   Hersen, Michel, Miller, Peter and Eisler, Richard.   Interactions
        Between Alcoholics and Their Wives: A Descriptive Analysis
        of Verbal and Nonverbal Behavior.   Quarterly Journal of
        Studies on Alcohol, 34(2): 516-520, 1973.

2573.   Hersh, Stephen, P.   Manpower Issues Related to Alcohol, Drug
        Abuse and Mental Health Services for Children, Youth and
        Families.   Report of the ADMAHA Manpower Policy Analysis
        Task Force, 2: 261-280, 1978.

2574.   Hertzman, M., Balsley, E., Davis, D.I. and Richmond, R.   Alcohol
        and Other Drug-Abuse by Psychiatric Inpatients: Treatment
        Pursuant to a Family Contract.   In: Drugs and the Family.
        Washington, D.C.:   U.S. Government Printing Office, 1981,
        pages 230-231.   (Also in: Contemporary Drug Problems,
        8(1): 73-85, 1979.)

2575.   Hertzman, M. and Hertzman, R.Z.   Marital Conflicts Caused by
        Alcoholism.   Medical Aspects of Human Sexuality, 15(7):
        69-83, 1981.

2576.   Hertzman, Marc.   Family Contracts - For Treatment: One Year's
        Experience.   Paper presented at the National Council on
        Alcoholism Annual Conference, Washington, D.C., April, 1979.

2577.   Hertzman, Marc.   Getting Alcoholics Out of Your Office, Into
        Treatment, and Back to Your Office.   Primary Care, 6(2):
        403-416, 1979.

2578.   Herzog, Elizabeth, Sudia, Cecelia E. and Harwood, Jane.   Drug
        Use Among the Young: As Teenagers See it.   Children Today,
        17(6): 207-212, 1970.

2579.   Hes, Jozef P.   Drinking in a Yemenite Rural Settlement in Israel.
        British Journal of Addiction, Edinburgh, 65(4): 293-296,
        1970.

2580.   Hesselbrock, M., Hesselbrock, V., Weidenman, M., Szymanski, K.
        and Goldschneider, K.   Psychopathology and Family History
        of Alcoholics Who Attempted Suicide.   Alcoholism: Clinical
        and Experimental Research, 10(1): 96, 1986.

2581.   Hesselbrock, M.N., Meyer, M.D., Babor, T.F. and Hesselbrock, V.M.
        An Examination of Genetic/Familial Factors in the Alcohol
        Dependence Syndrome and Its Consequences.   Paper presented
        at the 13th Annual Medical-Scientific Conference of the
        National Alcoholism Forum on Progress in Alcoholism Research
        and Treatment, Washington, D.C., April, 1982.   (Also in:
        Alcoholism: Clinical and Experimental Research, 6(1):
        145, 1982.)

2582.   Hesselbrock, V.M., Hesselbrock, M.N. and Stabenau, J.R.
        Alcoholism in Men Patients Subtyped by Family History and
        Antisocial Personality.   Journal of Studies on Alcohol,
        46(1): 59-64, 1985.

2583.   Hesselbrock, V.M., O'Connor, S.J. and Tasman A.   Neuropsycho-
        logical and EVP Performance in Young Men at Risk for
        Alcoholism.   Alcoholism: Clinical and Experimental
        Research, 10(1): 96, 1986.

2584. Hesselbrock, V.M., Shaskan, Edward G. and Meyer, Roger E. (Eds.) Introduction. In: Biological/Genetic Factors in Alcoholism. Washington, D.C.: U.S. Government Printing Office, 1983, pages viii-xii. DHHS Publication No. (ADM) 83-1199.

2585. Hesselbrock, V.M., Shaskan, Edward G. and Meyer, Roger E. Biological/Genetic Factors in Alcoholism. National Institute on Alcohol Abuse and Alcoholism Research Monograph Series No. 9. Washington, D.C.: U.S. Government Printing Office, 1983. DHHS Publication No. (ADM) 83-1199.

2586. Hesselbrock, V.M. and Stabenau, J.R. Varieties of Psychopathology in Alcoholics and Their Family Members. Paper presented at the 13th Annual Medical-Scientific Conference of the National Alcoholism Forum on Progress in Alcoholism Research and Treatment. Washington, D.C., April, 1982. (Also in: Alcoholism: Clinical and Experimental Research, 6(1): 145, 1982.)

2587. Hesselbrock, V.M., Stabenau, J.R. and Hall, Roberta. Drinking Style of Parents of Alcoholic and Control Probands. Alcohol: An International Biomedical Journal, 2(3): 525-528, 1985.

2588. Hesselbrock, V.M., Stabenau, J.R. and Hesselbrock, M.N. Minimal Brain Dysfunction and Neuropsychological Test Performance in Offspring of Alcoholics. In: Recent Developments in Alcoholism, Volume 3, High Risk Studies, Prostaglandins and Leukotrienes, Cardiovascular Effects, Cerebral Function in Social Drinkers. Ed. Marc Galanter. New York: Plenum Press, 1985, pages 65-82.

2589. Hesselbrock, V.M., Stabenau, J.R., Hesselbrock, M.N., Meyer, R.E. and Babor, T.F. The Nature of Alcoholism in Patients with Different Family Histories for Alcoholism. Progress in Neuropsychopharmacology and Biological Psychiatry, Oxford, 6(4-6): 607-614, 1982.

2590. Hesselbrock, V.M., Tennen, Howard, Stabenau, J.R. and Hesselbrock, M.N. Affective Disorder in Alcoholism. The International Journal of the Addictions, 18(4): 435-444, 1983.

2591. Hetherington, R. Drugs and Disabled Task Force Group Therapy for the Deaf Substance Abuser. Paper presented at the 1st Annual Meeting of the National Drug Conference, Washington, D.C., August, 1979.

2592. Heuer, Marti. Family Treatment for Adolescents: Building the Foundations. Focus on Family and Chemical Dependency, 8(5): 28-29, 1985.

2593. Heuyer, G., Mises, R. and Dereux, J.-F. La Descendance des Alcooliques. (Offspring of Alcoholics.) Prensa Medica, Argentina, 65: 657-658, 1957.

2594. Heyman, Margaret M. Alcoholism Programs in Industry -- The Patient's View. New Brunswick, NJ: Rutgers University Press, Center of Alcohol Studies, 1978, pages 35-46.

2595. Heyman, Margaret M. Referral to Alcoholism Programs in Industry Coercion, Confrontation and Choice. Journal of Studies on Alcohol, 37(7): 900-907, 1976.

2596. Hicks, Carolyn Faye. Family and Cultural Factors in the Development of Eating Disorders: A Study of Feminine Identity in Twenty-Four Bulimic Women. Dissertation Abstracts International, 43(4): 1255B, 1982.

2597. Higgins, Paul C., Albrecht, Gary L. and Albrecht, Maryann H. Black-White Adolescent Drinking: The Myth and the Reality. Social Problems, 25(2): 215-224, 1977.

2598. Higier, H. Congenital Syphilis, Alcoholism and Psychopathy in
       Children. Polska Gazeta Lekarska, 5: 810-813, 1926.

2599. Higuchi, S., Yamada, K., Muraoka, H., Shigemori, K., Saito, S.
       and Kono, H. A Study of Young Alcoholics. Japanese Journal
       of Alcohol Studies and Drug Dependence, Kyoto, 18(4):
       422-436, 1983.

2600. Hilberman, Elaine. Overview: The "Wife-Beater's Wife" Reconsidered.
       American Journal of Psychiatry, 137: 1336-1347, 1980.

2601. Hilberman, Elaine and Munson, Kit. Sixty Battered Women.
       Victimology: An International Journal, 2(3-4): 460-471,
       1977-1978.

2602. Hildek, D. Alcohol Abuse and the Battered Wife Syndrome:
       Implications for Research. Report. Minneapolis: University
       of Minnesota, Division of School Health Education, 1979.

2603. Hilgard, J.R. and Newman, M.F. Early Parental Deprivation as
       a Functional Factor in the Etiology of Schizophrenia and
       Alcoholism. American Journal of Orthopsychiatry, 33:
       409-420, 1963.

2604. Hilgard, J.R. and Newman, M.F. Parental Loss by Death in Childhood
       as an Etiological Factor Among Schizophrenic and Alcoholic
       Patients Compared with a Non-Patient Community Sample. Journal
       of Nervous and Mental Disease, 137: 14-28, 1963.

2605. Hilker, R.R., Asma, F.E. and Eggert, R.L. A Company-Sponsored
       Alcoholic Rehabilitation Program. Ten Year Evaluation.
       Journal of Occupational Medicine, 14(10): 769-772, 1972.

2606. Hill, Archie. Closed World of Love. New York: Simon and
       Schuster, 1976.

2607. Hill, Harris E. The Social Deviant and Initial Addiction to
       Narcotics and Alcohol. National Institute on Drug Abuse
       Research Monograph Series, 30: 90-94, 1980.

2608. Hill, Paul S. Alcoholism: Images, Impairments, Interventions.
       Postgraduate Medicine, 74(5): 87-91, 95, 99, 1983.

2609. Hill, R.W., Langevin, R. and Paitich, D. Is Arson an Aggressive
       Act or a Property Offence? A Controlled Study of Psychiatric
       Referrals. Canadian Journal of Psychiatry, Ottawa, 27(8):
       648-654, 1982.

2610. Hill, Shirley Y. Vulnerability Model for Alcoholism in Women.
       Focus on Women, 2(2): 68-91, 1981.

2611. Hill, Shirley Y. Vulnerability to the Biomedical Consequences
       of Alcoholism and Alcohol-Related Problems Among Women.
       In: Alcohol Problems in Women: Antecedents, Consequences,
       and Intervention. Eds. Sharon C. Wilsnack and Linda J.
       Beckman. New York: The Guilford Press, 1984, pages 121-154.

2612. Hill, Shirley Y., Cloninger, C. Robert and Ayre, Frederick R.
       Independent Familial Transmission of Alcoholism and Opiate
       Abuse. Alcoholism: Clinical and Experimental Research,
       1(4): 335-342, 1977.

2613. Hill, Shirley Y., Goodwin, D.W., Cadoret, R., Osterland, C.K. and
       Doner, S.M. Association and Linkage Between Alcoholism and
       Eleven Serological Markers. Journal of Studies on Alcohol,
       36: 981-992, 1975.

2614. Hille, J. Principles of Classification and Nomenclature in
           Families with Striking Social Peculiarities Shown by an
           Example of the District of Osterburg. Aerztliche
           Jugendkunde, East Germany, 69(5): 327-336, 1978.

2615. Hiltner, Seward. Helping Alcoholics. A Guide for Pastors in
           Counseling Relationships with Alcoholics and Their Families.
           Philadelphia: Division of Social Education and Action,
           Board of Christian Education, Presbyterian Church, 1948.

2616. Hiltner, Seward. Pastoral Counseling. New York: Abingdon-
           Cokesbury Press, 1949.

2617. Hindman, Margaret. Child Abuse and Alcohol Abuse: Knowledge
           Building. Paper presented at the University of Arkansas
           Graduate School of Social Work Symposium, Hot Springs, July,
           1978.

2618. Hindman, Margaret. Child Abuse and Neglect: The Alcohol
           Connection. Alcohol Health and Research World, 1(3):
           2-7, 1977. (Also in: Lifelines, 19(3): 5-12, 1977.)

2619. Hindman, Margaret. Child Abuse Demonstration Project. ADAMHA,
           10(1): 1A-end, 1984.

2620. Hindman, Margaret. Children of Alcoholic Parents. Alcohol Health
           and Research World, 1(3): 2-6, 1975.

2621. Hindman, Margaret. Children of Alcoholic Parents: An Overview.
           Paper presented at the 11th Annual Conference of the Canadian
           Foundation on Alcohol & Drug Dependencies, Toronto, June, 1976.

2622. Hindman, Margaret. Children of Alcoholics Learn to Make Choices.
           ADAMHA News, 10(1): 4A, 1984.

2623. Hindman, Margaret. Family Therapy in Alcoholism. Alcohol Health
           and Research World, 1(1): 2-9, 1976.

2624. Hindman, Margaret. Family Violence and Alcohol Problems. Police
           Chief, 49(12): 39-41, 1982.

2625. Hindman, Margaret. Family Violence: An Overview. Alcohol Health
           and Research World, 4(1): 2-11, 1979.

2626. Hindman, Margaret. Research on Children of Alcoholics: Expanding the
           Knowledge. Child Abuse Projects Reveal Need for Treatment.
           Alcohol Health and Research World, 8(4): 7, 12-13, 37, 1984.

2627. Hindman, Margaret. Symposium Targets Needs of Children of
           Alcoholics. NIAAA Information and Feature Service,
           (IFS No. 67): 3, December 31, 1979.

2628. Hindman, Margaret, Williams, M. Vejnoska, J. and Samll, J.
           Children of Alcoholics: A Special Report. ADAMHA News,
           10(1): 1A-8A, 1984.

2629. Hinga, J.A. Comparative Study of Alcoholic and Nonalcoholic
           Women's Perception of Their Relationship with Their Father.
           Dissertation Abstracts International, 46(6): 2064B, 1985.

2630. Hingson, Ralph, Scotch, Norman and Barrett, Jane. Life Satisfaction
           and Drinking Practices in the Boston Metropolitan Area.
           Journal of Studies on Alcohol, 42(1): 24-37, 1981.

2631. Hinkle, L.M. Treatment of the Family System Damaged by Alcoholism.
           Paper presented at the Alcohol and Drug Problems Association
           of North America, Washington, D.C., August, 1983.

2632.   Hinkle, Lorraine M. Treatment of the Family System with a
        Recovering Alcoholic. Paper Presented at the 101st Annual
        Forum of the National Conference on Social Welfare.
        Cincinnati, May, 1974.

2633.   Hipple, J. Suicide and the Alcoholic Family. Focus on Family
        and Chemical Dependency, 8(3): 9-10, 32, 1985.

2634.   Hipple, John and Rekers, Gail. Crisis Intervention with the
        Family System. Focus on Family and Chemical Dependency,
        8(5): 19-21, 38, 1985.

2635.   Hirsch, Robert and Imhof, John E. A Family Therapy Approach to
        the Treatment of Drug Abuse and Addiction. Journal of
        Psychedelic Drugs, 7(2): 181-185, 1975.

2636.   Hirschberg, Besse. Alcoholism in the Case Load of the New York
        City Welfare Department. Quarterly Journal of Studies on
        Alcohol, 15: 402-412, 1954.

2637.   Hislop, I.G. Childhood Deprivation: An Antecedent of the
        Irritable Bowel Syndrome. Medical Journal of Australia,
        Sydney, 2: 372-374, 1979.

2638.   Hispanic Program Stresses Importance of Home, Family. NIAAA
        Information and Feature Service, (IFS No. 83): 1, April 30,
        1981.

2639.   Hittel, Zelda Z. Perceptual Differentiation Among Subtypes of
        Alcoholics. Doctoral Dissertation. (University Microfilms
        No. 75-22546). Tempe: Arizona State University, 1975.

2640.   Hjortzberg-Nordlund, H. Abuse of Alcohol in Middle-Aged Men
        in Goteborg; A Social-Psychiatric Investigation. Acta
        Psychiatrica Scandinavica, Copenhagen, 44(Supplement
        199): 1-127, 1968.

2641.   Hoar, C.H. Children of Alcoholic Mothers and Their Daughters:
        Adolescents Together. Focus on Family and Chemical
        Dependency, 8(6): 10-11, 38-39, 1985.

2642.   Hochenegg, L. and Kuhnert, K. Alcoholism and Suicide. Wiener
        Medizinische Wochenschrift, 130(13-14): 468-471, 1980.

2643.   Hochhauser, Mark, Needle, Richard and McCubbin, Hamilton.
        Contextual Factors in Adolescent Substance Use. Rockville,
        MD: National Institute on Drug Abuse (DHHS), 1981. (Eric
        Document Number ED212951.)

2644.   Hocking, R.B. Problems Arising from Alcohol in the New Hebrides.
        The Medical Journal of Australia, Sydney, 2(20): 908-910,
        1970.

2645.   Hodge, James R. How to Handle a Psychiatric Emergency. Medical
        Times, 101(10): 167-169, 1973.

2646.   Hodosi, R. and Konig, E. Az Alkoholizmus Jelentosege a Gyermek-
        Ideggondozas Teruleten. (The Importance of Alcoholism in
        the Area of Child Psychiatry.) In: Tanulmanyok az
        Alkoholizmus Pszichiatriai Kovetkezmenyeirol. (Results
        of Psychiatric Study of Alcoholism.) Eds. I. Tarisika,
        G. Gereby and G. Kardos. Budapest: Alkohilizmus
        Elleni Orszagos Bizottsag, 1969, pages 131-136.

2647.   Hoeft, H. and Obe, G. SCE-inducing Congeners in Alcoholic
        Beverages. Mutation Research, 121(3-4): 247-251, 1983.

2648. Hofeller, Kathleen Hartsough. Social, Psychological, and
         Situational Factors in Wife Abuse. Dissertation Abstracts
         International, 41(1): 408B, 1980. (University Microfilms
         No. 80-15604.)

2649. Hoff, E.C. Alcoholism: The Hidden Addiction. New York:
         Seabury Press, 1974.

2650. Hoff, E.C. A Multidisciplinary Approach to Rehabilitation of
         Alcoholics and Their Families. Psychiatry Digest, 27(9):
         33-43, 1966.

2651. Hoff, E.C. A New Plan for the Study and Comprehensive Treatment
         of Alcoholics in Virginia. Virginia Medical Monthly, 94:
         515-518, 1967.

2652. Hoff, E.C. Special Techniques in the Treatment of Alcoholism.
         Paper presented at the Interagency Development and Coordination
         of Services for Alcoholics and Their Families Conference.
         Damphin Island, AL, 1962, pages 14-20.

2653. Hoffer, A. A Vitamin B3 Dependent Family. Schizophrenia,
         3(1): 41-46, 1971.

2654. Hoffer, Abram and Osmond, Humphry. New Hope for Alcoholics.
         New Hyde Park, NY: University Books, 1968.

2655. Hoffmann, Helmut and Noem, Avis A. Adjustment of Chippewa Indian
         Alcoholics to a Predominantly White Treatment Program.
         Psychological Reports, 37(3): 1284-1286, 1975.

2656. Hoffmann, Helmut and Noem, Avis A. Alcoholism Among Parents
         of Male and Female Alcoholics. Psychological Reports,
         36(1): 322, 1975.

2657. Hoffmann, Helmut and Noem, Avis A. Alcoholism and Abstinence
         Among Relatives of American Indian Alcoholics. Journal
         of Studies on Alcohol, 36(1): 165, 1975.

2658. Hoffmann, Helmut and Noem, Avis A. Social Background Variables,
         Referral Sources and Life Events of Male and Female Alcoholics.
         Psychological Reports, 37: 1087-1092, 1975.

2659. Hoffmann, Helmut, Noem, Avis A. and Petersen, D. Treatment
         Effectivenes as Judged by Successfully and Unsuccessfully
         Treated Alcoholics. Drug and Alcohol Dependence,
         Lausanne, 1(4): 241-246, 1976.

2660. Hoffman, Herbert J. and Hoffman, Ludmila W. Alcoholism: An
         Evaluation of Intervention Strategy in Family Agencies.
         Final Report. Rockville, MD: National Institute on
         Alcohol Abuse and Alcoholism (DHEW/PHS), 1974. (Eric
         Document Number ED126416.)

2661. Hofstra College Research Bureau, Psychological Division. Use of
         Alcoholic Beverages by High School Students in Nassau County
         Related to Parental Permissiveness. New York: Sheppard
         Foundation, 1954.

2662. Hogan, Robert A., Kirchner, John H., Hogan, Kathleen A. and
         Fox, Anne N. The Only Child Factor in Homosexual
         Development. Psychology: A Quarterly Journal of Human
         Behavior, 17(1): 19-33, 1980.

2663. Hojat, Mohammad Reza. Loneliness as a Function of Selected
         Personality, Psychosocial and Demographic Variables in
         Iranian Students. Dissertation Abstracts International,
         42(3): 1149B, 1981.

2664. Holden, C. Genes, Personality and Alcoholism: Some People May
       Inherit A Vulnerability to a Severe Form of Alcoholism.
       Psychology Today, 19(1): 38-39, 42-44, 1985.

2665. Holden, M. Treatability of Children of Alcoholic Parents.
       Smith College Studies in Social Work, 16 : 44-61, 1945.

2666. Holden, Peter H. Psychiatric Aspects of Alcoholism.
       North Carolina Medical Journal, 30(3): 83-88, 1969.

2667. Holder, Harold D. and Hallan, J. Systems Approach to Planning
       Alcoholism Programs in North Carolina. American Journal
       of Public Health and the Nation's Health, 62(10):
       1415-1421, 1972.

2668. Holding, T.A., Buglass, D., Duffy J.C. and Kreitman, N.
       Parasuicide in Edinburgh -- A Seven-Year Review 1968-1974.
       The British Journal of Psychiatry: The Journal of Mental
       Science, London, 130: 534-543, 1977.

2669. Holistic Therapy with Alcoholic Families. Rockville, MD:
       NCALI, 1982.

2670. Holland, I. Heads You Win, Tails I Lose. Philadelphia:
       Lippincott, 1973.

2671. Holland, S. and Griffin, A. Adolescent and Adult Drug Treatment
       Clients: Patterns and Consequences of Use. Journal of
       Psychoactive Drugs, 16(1): 79-89, 1984.

2672. Hollin, Clive R. Young Offenders and Alcohol: A Survey of the
       Drinking Behaviour of a Borstal Population. Journal of
       Adolescence, 6(2): 161-174, 1983.

2673. Hollis, Judy. Treating the Family System for Alcoholism. Report.
       San Pedro: San Pedro and Peninsula Hospital Alcoholism
       Recovery Services, 1977.

2674. Holloway, I. Behavioral Modification of Excessive Drinking in
       the Environmental Setting. Alcoholism, Zagreb, 9(2):
       44-56, 1973.

2675. Hollstedt, C., Olsson, O. and Rydberg, U. The Effect of Alcohol
       on the Developing Organism: Genetical, Teratological and
       Physiological Aspects. Medical Biology, 55(1): 1-14, 1977.

2676. Holmgren, S. Alkoholmissbruk och Atgarder i Japan. (Alcohol Misuse
       and Countermeasures in Japan.) Alkohol och Narkotika,
       70(5): 1-9, 1976.

2677. Holsaple, R. and White, M. Model School-Based Comprehensive
       Alcohol/Drug Abuse Prevention Program. Journal of the
       Florida Medical Association, 71(4): 233-234, 1984.

2678. Holser, M.A. A Socialization Program for Chronic Alcoholics.
       Alcoholism, Zagreb, 13(1-2): 56-63, 1977.

2679. Holser, Mary Ann. The Support System of the Alcoholic: Responses
       and Interventions. In: Drug Dependence & Alcoholism
       Volume 2: Social and Behavioral Issues. Ed. Arnold J.
       Schecter. New York: Plenum Press, 1981, pages 47-70. (Also
       in: Alcoholism: Journal of Alcoholism and Related Addictions,
       13(1-2): 23-33, 1979.)

2680. Holst, P. Alcoholism: The Double-Edged Sword. Paper presented at
       the National Council on Alcoholism Forum, Washington, D.C.,
       April, 1982.

2681. Holter, James Allan. A Comparison of Selected Family-of-Origin Perceptions Within the Alcohol-Distressed Marital Dyad and the Non-Alcohol-Distressed Marital Dyad. Doctoral Dissertation. (University Microfilms No. 82-25391.) East Texas State University, 1982. (Also in: Dissertation Abstracts International, 43(6): 2100A, 1982.)

2682. Holzgreve, W. 75 Jahre Deutscher Frauenbund fur Alkoholfreie Kultur. (Seventy-five Years of the German Women's Union for an Alcohol-Free Culture.) Suchtgefahren, Hamburg, 21: 146-147, 1975.

2683. Holzhauer, Robert A. The Addiction Syndrome -- A Model Training Program for Counselors. Alcohol Health and Research World, 4(1): 28-30, 1979.

2684. Homer, Monica M. Teacher's Processing Discussion Guide for Use with Alcohol Trigger Films for Junior High Schools. Falls Church, VA: AAA Foundation for Traffic Safety, 1978.

2685. Homiller, Jonica D. Alcoholism Among Women. Chemical Dependencies: Behavioral and Biomedical Issues, 4(1): 1-31, 1980.

2686. Homma, T., Kubo, K. and Sato, T. HLA Antigen and Chronic Pancreatitis in Japan. Digestion, Basel, 21(5): 267-272, 1981.

2687. Homonoff, Emeline and Stephen, Arville. Alcohol Education for Children of Alcoholics in a Boston Neighborhood. Journal of Studies on Alcohol, 40: 923-926, 1979.

2688. Honest Answers to Questions Teenagers Ask About Drinking. Pamphlet. West Des Moines, IA: Preferred Risk Insurance Companies, 1978.

2689. Hoobler, Raymond Leslie. Drug Use by Male and Female High School Students as Related to Sex-Role, Locus of Control, and Perceptions of Their Parents. Doctoral Dissertation. (University Microfilms No. 77-6475.) Boston: University of Massachusetts, 1976.

2690. Hood, Jane. Suicide Attempts in Children and Adolescents. American Journal of Psychiatry, 139(10): 1257-1261, 1982.

2691. Hoover, Eleanor Links. Far Out: Violence and Pleasure. Human Behavior, 5(1): 10-11, 1976.

2692. Hope for Children of Alcoholics: Alateen. (Esperanza Para Hijos de Alcoholicos: Alateen.) New York: Al-Anon Family Group, 1977.

2693. Hope, E.H. A Study of Some Students' Opinions and Knowledge of Smoking and Drinking. The Journal of the American College Health Association, 20(3): 219-227, 1972.

2694. Hope, K. The Study of Hostility in the Temperaments of Spouses: Definitions and Methods. The British Journal of Mathematical and Statistical Psychology, 22(1): 67-95, 1969.

2695. Hopkins, Anthony. Community Care: Practical Help. The Lancet, 1(8391): 1393-1396, 1984.

2696. Hore, B.D. The Etiology of Drinking Problems. In: Medical Consequences of Alcohol Abuse. Ed. P.M.S. Clark and L.J. Kricka. New York: Halsted Press, John Wiley and Sons, 1980, pages 39-49.

2697.   Horn, J.L., Wanberg, K.W. and Adams, G. Diagnosis of Alcoholism:
        Factors of Drinking, Background and Current Conditions in
        Alcoholics. Quarterly Journal of Studies on Alcohol, 35:
        147-175, 1974.

2698.   Horn, John L. and Wanberg, Kenneth W. Dimensions of Perception
        of Background and Current Situation of Alcoholic Patients.
        Quarterly Journal of Studies on Alcohol, 31(3): 633-658, 1970.

2699.   Hornik, Edith Lynn. You and Your Alcoholic Parent. New York:
        Association Press, 1974. (Also as: Pamphlet. New York:
        Public Affairs Committee, 1974.)

2700.   Hornik-Beer, Edith Lynn. A Teenager's Guide to Living with an
        Alcoholic Parent. Center City, MN: Hazelden, no date.

2701.   Hornstra, R.K. and Udell, B. Psychiatric Services and Alcoholics.
        Missouri Medicine: Journal of the Missouri State Medical
        Association, 70(2): 103-107, 1973.

2702.   Horowitz, B. and Wolock, I. Material Deprivation, Child
        Maltreatment, and Agency Interventions Among Poor Families.
        In: The Social Context of Child Abuse and Neglect.
        Ed. Larry H. Pelton. New York: Human Sciences Press, 1981,
        pages 137-184.

2703.   Horowitz, Ronald N. and North, Ronald. The Treatment of Drug
        Abuse by the Family Physician. Journal of Drug Issues,
        3(1): 91-95, 1973.

2704.   Horowitz, S.H. Fetal Alcohol Effects in Children: Cognitive,
        Educational, and Behavioral Considerations. Dissertation
        Abstracts International, 45(8): 2482A-2483A, 1985.

2705.   Horvat, D. Chromosome Damages in Chronic Alcohol Consumers. Collegium
        Antropologicum, Zagreb, 7(1): 71-77, 1983.

2706.   Horwitz, J., Naveillan, P., Marambio, C., Cordua, M. and Gonzalez, H.
        Evaluacion de los Resultados del Tratamieto del Alcoholismo.
        (Evaluation of the Results of Alcoholism Treatment.) Archivos
        de Biologia y Medicina Experimentales, Chile, Supplement (3):
        161-175, 1969. (Also in: Alcohol and Alcoholism. Ed. R.E.
        Popham. Toronto: University of Toronto Press, 1970, pages
        179-192.)

2707.   Hosek, K., Hoskova, V. and Voracova, J. Deti Z Rodin Alkoholiku.
        (Children from Alcoholic Families.) Protialkoholicky Obzur,
        Bratislava, 14: 43-47, 1979.

2708.   Hotch, D.F., Sherin, K.M., Harding, P.N. and Zitter, R.E. Use
        of the Self-Administered Michigan Alcoholism Screening Test
        in a Family Practice Center. Journal of Family Practice,
        17(6): 1021-1026, 1983.

2709.   Houghton, A.B. I Don't Drink Cocktails Anymore. Reader's
        Digest, 125(748): 173, 1984.

2710.   Housden, Leslie George. The Prevention of Cruelty to Children.
        New York: Philosophical Library, 1956.

2711.   How Does Family Environment Influence Drug Use in Young. Journal
        of Alcohol and Drug Education, 19(3): 31, 1974.

2712.   How Drinking Affected A Foreign Service Marriage. Department of
        State Newsletter, 226: 29-32, 1980.

2713.   How to Help an Alcoholic Who Insists He Doesn't Need Any Help.
        Bakersfield, CA: Kehn County Department of Mental Health
        Services, no date.

2714. How to Help Families of Alcoholics. Lancet, 1(8067): 783, 1978.

2715. How Important are Genetic Influences on Alcohol Dependence?
      British Medical Journal, London, 2: 1371-1372, 1977.

2716. How to Live With an Alcoholic. New York: Simon and Schuster,
      Inc., 1971.

2717. How to Talk with Children About Drinking. Pamphlet. Chicago:
      National Parent-Teachers Association, no date.

2718. How You Can Help Your Child Make Responsible Decisions About
      Drinking. PTA Today, 7(4): 6-8, 1981-1982.

2719. Howard, Don and Howard, Nancy. A Family Approach to Problem
      Drinking; The Four Week Family Forum. Report. Columbia,
      MO: Family Training Center, 1976. (Eric Document Number
      ED147731.)

2720. Howard, Don and Howard, Nancy. The Family Counseling Model: An
      Early Intervention Approach to Problem Drinking. 1976.
      (Eric Document Number ED149224.)

2721. Howard, Donald and Howard, Nancy. Touching Me, Touching You.
      Columbia, MO: Family Training Center, 1977.

2722. Howard, Donald and Howard, Nancy. Treatment of the Significant Other.
      In: Practical Approaches to Alcoholism Psychotherapy.
      Eds. S. Zimberg, J. Wallace and S.B. Blume. New York:
      Plenum, 1978, pages 137-162.

2723. Howard, M. Teenage Drinking: Did I Have a Good Time? New York:
      Continuum Publishing, 1980.

2724. Howerton, Gary W. Cooperative Occupational Programs for Small
      Companies in a Rural Area: Making it Work. Paper presented
      at the Labor-Management Conference, NCA Annual Forum, Washington,
      D.C., May, 1979.

2725. Hoyt, Charles N. Alcoholism; A Review and Overview of the Problem.
      The Ohio State Medical Journal, 66: 674-680, 1970.

2726. Hsu, L.K., Holder, D., Hindmarsh, D. and Phelps, C. Bipolar
      Illness Preceded by Anorexia Nervosa in Identical Twins.
      Journal of Clinical Psychiatry, 45(6): 262-266, 1984.

2727. Huang, Lucy J., Kloepper, Howard W. and Leonard, Wilbert M. A
      Comparison of the "Only Child" and the Siblings' Perceptions
      of Parental Norms and Sanctions. Adolescence, 16(63):
      641-655, 1981.

2728. Huba, George J. and Bentler, Peter M. The Role of Peer and Adult Models
      for Drug Taking at Different Stages in Adolescence. Journal
      of Youth and Adolescence, 9(5): 449-465, 1980.

2729. Huba, George J., Wingard, Joseph A. and Bentler, Peter M. Beginning
      Adolescent Drug Use and Peer and Adult Interaction Patterns.
      Journal of Consulting and Clinical Psychology, 47: 265-276,
      1979.

2730. Huba, George J., Wingard, Joseph A. and Bentler, Peter M.
      Framework for an Interactive Theory of Drug Use. National
      Institute on Drug Abuse Research Monograph Series, 30:
      95-101, 1980.

2731. Hubbard, Richard W., Santos, John F. and Santos, Mary Alice.
      Alcohol and Older Adults: Overt and Covert Influences.
      Social Casework, 60(3): 166-170, 1979.

2732. Huber, C.B. Attitudes of Adolescent Offspring of Male
       Alcoholics: A Comparative Study. Doctoral Dissertation.
       (University Microfilms No. 78-01684.) San Francisco:
       California School of Professional Psychology, 1977.

2733. Huber, J. and Gain. Enfance en Danger Moral et Alcoolisme.
       (Children in Moral Danger and Alcoholism.) Bulletin de
       L'Academie Nationale de Medecine, Paris, 137: 377-378,
       1953.

2734. Huber, K.E. Comparison of Adolescents from Alcoholic and
       Non-Alcoholic Families. Dissertation Abstracts International,
       45(10): 3321B, 1985.

2735. Huberty, Catherine E. and Huberty, David J. Treating the Parents of
       Adolescent Drug Abusers. Contemporary Drug Problems, 5(4):
       573-592, 1975. (Also as: Treating the Parents of Adolescent
       Drug Abusers: The Necessity for Marriage Counseling. The
       Alcoholism Digest Annual, 5: 1-10, 1976-77.)

2736. Huberty, David J. Treating the Young Drug User. In: Drugs and
       the Youth Culture. Eds. F.R. Scarpitti and S.K. Datesman.
       Beverly Hills: Sage Publications, 1980, pages 283-315.

2737. Huberty, David J. and Huberty, Catherine E. Helping the Parents to
       Survive: A Family Systems Approach to Adolescent Alcoholism.
       In: Power to Change: Family Case Studies in the Treatment of
       Alcoholism. Ed. Edward Kaufman. New York: Gardner Press,
       1984, pages 131-176.

2738. Huberty, David J. and Malmquist, Jeffrey D. Adolescent Chemical
       Dependency. Perspectives in Psychiatric Care, 16(1):
       21-27, 1978.

2739. Hudgens, R.W., DeCastro, M.I. and DeZuniga, E.A. Psychiatric
       Illness in a Developing Country: A Clinical Study.
       American Journal of Public Health, 60: 1788-1805, 1970.

2740. Hudolin, Vladimir. The Control of Alcoholism. International
       Journal of Mental Health, 5(1): 85-105, 1976.

2741. Hudolin, V. Familie Und Alkoholismus. (The Family and
       Alcoholism.) Hamburg: Neuland-Verlagsgesellschaft, 1975.

2742. Hudolin, V. Die Stellung der Familie in der Pravention und
       Behandlung der Suchtkrankheit. (The Role of the Family in
       the Prevention and Treatment of Addiction.) Suchtgefahren,
       Hamburg, 24: 9-27, 1978. (Also in: Alkoholizam, Beograd,
       17(3-4): 104-122, 1977.)

2743. Hudolin, Vladimir, Bano, N., Milakovic, I., Prazic, B., Rugelj,
       J., Rupena, Osolnik, M., Smajkic, A. and Ulemek, L. Health
       Education of Patients in the Field of Social Psychiatry,
       Notably Alcoholics. International Journal of Social
       Psychiatry, London, 18(3): 157-170, 1972.

2744. Hudson, Ann and Lovintosse, Lee. Commonalities Among Female Alcoholics.
       In: Chicanas and Alcoholism: A Socio-Cultural Perspective of
       Women. Eds. Rodolfo Arevalo and Marriane Minor. San Jose:
       School of Social Work, San Jose State University, 1981, pages
       23-30.

2745. Hudson, J.I., Pope, H.G. Jr., Jonas, J.M. and Yurgelun, Todd D.
       Phenomenologic Relationship of Eating Disorders to Major
       Affective Disorder. Psychiatry Research, 9(4): 345-354, 1983.

2746. Huessy, H.R. Genetics of Alcoholism. Hospital and Community
       Psychiatry, 35(6): 620-621, 1984.

2747. Huff-Fewell, Christine and Bissell, LeClair. The Alcoholic Denial Syndrome: An Alcohol-Focused Approach. Social Casework, 59(1): 6-13, 1978.

2748. Hughes, E.M. Problem Alcoholics in a State Mental Hospital and on Parole. Journal of Clinical Psychopathology, 6: 551-570, 1945.

2749. Hughes, J.P.W. Identifying Alcoholism and Dealing with the Problem. Transactions of the Society of Occupational Medicine, London, 19: 58-59, 1969.

2750. Hughes, Judith M. Adolescent Children of Alcoholic Parents and the Relationship of Alateen to these Children. Journal of Consulting and Clinical Psychology, 45(5): 946-947, 1977.

2751. Hughes, R. Conclusions Based on Results of a Statistical Inquiry on the Prevalence of Alcoholic Intemperance in the Families of Mentally Defective School-Children. British Journal of Inebriety, 19: 56-59, 1921.

2752. Hughes, Stella P. and Dodder, Richard A. Alcohol-Related Problems and Collegiate Drinking Patterns. Journal of Youth and Adolescence, 12(1): 65-76, 1983.

2753. Humphrey, John A., Puccio, Dominick, Niswander, G. Donald and Casey, Thomas M. An Analysis of the Sequence of Selected Events in the Lives of a Suicidal Population: A Preliminary Report. Journal of Nervous & Mental Disease, 154(2): 137-140, 1972.

2754. Hun, N. and Vertes, L. Az Idopercent Alkoholbetegek Rehabilitacioja. (Rehabilitation of Aged Alcoholics.) Alkohologia, Budapest, 11: 199-200, 1980.

2755. Hundleby, John D. and Girard, Suzanne. Home and Family Correlates of Prior Drug Involvement Among Institutionalized Male Adolescents. The International Journal of the Addictions, 15(5): 689-699, 1980.

2756. Hunt, Arthur. My Dad Drinks Too Much (There's Hope for Your Family Too.) In: Your Family. A Love and Maintenance Manual for People with Parents and Other Relatives. Downers Grove, IL: Inter Varsity Press, 1982.

2757. Hunt, George and Azrin, N.H. A Community-Reinforcement Approach to Alcoholism. Behaviour Research and Therapy, Oxford, 11: 91-104, 1973. (Also in: Alcoholism -- Introduction to Theory and Treatment. Dubuque, IA: Kendall/Hunt, 1980, pages 330-343.)

2758. Hunt, L. Review of Alcohol and the Family by J. Orford and J. Harwin. British Journal of Social Work, 13(2): 235-237, 1983.

2759. Hunt, R.D., Cohen, D.J., Shaywitz, S.E. and Shaywitz, B.A. Strategies for Study of the Neurochemistry of Attention Deficit Disorder in Children. Schizophrenia Bulletin, 8(2): 236-252, 1982.

2760. Hunt, S.C. and Delmastro, R.A. Body Cries; Medical Consequences of Growing Up in an Alcoholic Family. Focus on Family and Chemical Dependency, 8(4): 24-25, 1985.

2761. Hunter, C., Bonnell, L., Falwell, J. and Steiger, R. Families of Alcoholics. In: Courage to Change. Ed. D. Wholey. Boston: Houghton Mifflin Company, 1984, pages 205-223.

2762. Hunter, Edna and Nice, D. Military Families: Adaptation to Change. New York: Praeger Publishers, 1978.

2763. Hunter, George. Alcoholism and the Family Agency; With Particular Reference to Early Phase and Hidden Types. Quarterly Journal of Studies on Alcohol, 24: 61-79, 1963.

2764. Hunter, S. and Moberg, P. PICADA's Family Education Program: An Evaluation Paper. Paper presented in Madison, WI, February, 1983. (Also in: Working with Adolescent Alcohol/Drug Problems: Assessment, Intervention and Treatment, pages 55-65.)

2765. Huppert, S. The Role of Al-Anon Groups in the Treatment Program of a VA Alcoholism Unit. Hospital and Community Psychiatry, 27: 693, 697, 1976.

2766. Hurwitz, Dorothy B. Violence in Families. Paper presented at the University of Arkansas Graduate School of Social Work, 1978.

2767. Hurwitz, Dorothy B., Hamlin, Diane and Spieker, Gisela. Perspectives: Family Violence. Alcohol Health and Research World, 4(1): 17-22, 1979.

2768. Hurwitz, Jacob I. and Daya, Dalpat K. Non-Help-Seeking Wives of Employed Alcoholics: A Multilevel Interpersonal Profile. Journal of Studies of Alcohol, 38: 1730-1739, 1977.

2769. Husain, A., Anasseril, D.E. and Harris, P.W. Study of Young-Age and Mid-life Homicidal Women Admitted to a Psychiatric Hospital for Pre-trial Evaluation. Canadian Journal of Psychiatry, Ottawa, 28(2): 109-113, 1983.

2770. Husni-Palacios, May and Scheur, Philip. The High School Student: A Personality Profile, 1972. (Eric Document Number ED071001.)

2771. Huss, Stephen F. The Alcohol Related Traffic Offenders Program: Initiating Alcoholism Treatment. Federal Probation, 40(3): 13-16, 1976.

2772. Hyman, Merton M. Accident Vulnerability and Blood Alcohol Concentrations of Drivers by Demographic Characteristics. Quarterly Journal of Studies on Alcohol, 4: 34-57, 1968.

2773. Hyman, Merton M. Alcoholics 15 Years Later. Annals of the New York Academy of Sciences, 273: 613-623, 1976.

2774. Hyman, Merton M. Extended Family Ties Among Alcoholics: A Neglected Area of Research. Quarterly Journal of Studies on Alcohol, 33: 513-516, 1972.

2775. Hyman, Merton M. The Social Characteristics of Persons Arrested for Driving While Intoxicated. Quarterly Journal of Studies on Alcohol, 4: 138-177, 1968.

2776. Hymes, H., Fritz, S., Driemen, P., Freeman, J., Tillson, S., George, G. and Holt, G. Family Approach to the Treatment of Chemical Addiction. Paper presented at the 8th Annual ALMACA Meeting, Detroit, October, 1979, pages 117-131.

2777. Hyslop, T.B. The Influence of Parental Alcoholism on the Physique and Ability of Offspring. British Journal of Inebriety, 8: 175-183, 1911. (Also in: Lancet, 180: 77-78, 1911; International Congress on Alcoholism and Drug Dependence, 13: 195-222, 1912.)

I

2778. Ida Mae, D. Problem Children. Journal of the American Medical
      Association, 241: 167-168, 1979.

2779. Idol, Maestas Lorna. Behavior Patterns in Families of Boys
      with Learning and Behavior Problems. Journal of Learning
      Disabilities, 14(6): 347-349, 1981.

2780. If He Meets These Standards, He's An Alcoholic. Medical World
      News, 13(31): 5, 1972.

2781. If There's an Alcoholic in the Family. Pamphlet. Buffalo:
      Marvin A. and Lillian K. Block Foundation, 1971. (Also
      available through: Edmonton: The Alberta Alcoholism and
      Drug Abuse Commission, Administrative Centre.)

2782. Igersheimer, Walter W. Group Psychotherapy for Nonalcoholic
      Wives of Alcoholics. Quarterly Journal of Studies on
      Alcohol, 20: 77-85, 1959.

2783. Iglesiasi-Rodriguez, L. Factores Sociales en el Alcoholismo.
      (Social Factors in Alcoholism.) Actas Luso-Espanolas de
      Neurologia y Psiquiatria, Madrid, 25: 26-32, 1966.

2784. Igra, Amnon and Moos, Rudolf H. Alcohol Use Among College
      Students: Some Competing Hypotheses. Journal of Youth
      and Adolescence, 8(4): 393-405, 1979.

2785. Imbrogno, S. and Imbrogno, N.I. Changes Are Emerging. Social
      Casework, 67(2): 90-100, 1986.

2786. Improving Alcohol/Drug Education in Illinois Schools. Illinois
      State Board of Education. 1982. (Eric Document Number
      ED222822.)

2787. Imre, Paul D. Drinking Habits of Church-Affiliated Teenagers.
      Quarterly Journal of Studies on Alcohol, 24(2): 320, 1963.

2788. In Touch with Your Child. Pamphlet. Staunton, VA: The Chemical
      People, 1984.

2789. Inborn Alcoholism? Lancet, 1(8443): 1427-1428, 1985.

2790. Inborn Biochemical Traits and Tendency Toward Alcoholism.
      New York Times, page 65, 6 September 1978.

2791. Incidence of Alcohol Related Domestic Violence: An Assessment.
      Rockville, MD: National Clearinghouse for Alcohol Information,
      1984.

2792.   Indian Health Training Center, Training Course TC-70-3 (February 9-27, 1970): A Descriptive Study of the Academic Achievement, Delinquency, and Alcohol Usage of the Teenage Population of the Reno-Sparks Indian Colony. Washington, D.C.: Public Health Service (DHEW), 1970. (Eric Document Number ED154971.)

2793.   Indian Teenage Suicides Shock Investigators. Roche Medical Image and Commentary, 12(6): 11-13, 1970.

2794.   Influence Decisive Des Parents Et Des Copoeins. (Decisive Influence of Parents and Friends.) Points De Vue, page 5, 23 June 1979.

2795.   The Influence of Parental Alcoholism on the Physique and Ability of Offspring. British Medical Journal, 1: 94-97, 1911.

2796.   Ingersoll, Richard L. Socialization, Inconsistencies and Alcoholism: A Study of Attitudes. Doctoral Dissertation. (University Microfilms No. 65-6695.) Iowa City: University of Iowa, 1965.

2797.   Inghe, M.-B. and Inghe, G. Children of Poor Families in the Welfare State. Acta Socio-Medica Scandinavica, Stockholm, 1(2): 117-128, 1969.

2798.   Inghe, M.-B. and Olin, R. Wives of Alcohol Abusers. Acta Socio-Medica Scandinavica (Supplement), Stockholm, 4: 3-104, 1972.

2799.   Inghe, M.-B. and Olin, R. Alkoholisthustrur. (Wives of Alcoholics.) Jonkoping, Sweden: Tiden/Folksam, 1970.

2800.   Inter-Agency Cooperation Optimizes Help. COA Newsletter, 3(2): 1-2, 1985.

2801.   International Conference on the Family. Alcool Ou Sante, 149(2): 29-32, 1979.

2802.   Intervention. In: United States. Department of Health and Human Services. National Institute on Alcohol Abuse and Alcoholism. Fourth Special Report to the U.S. Congress on Alcohol and Health from the Secretary of Health and Human Services. Washingon, D.C.: U.S. Government Printing Office, 1981, pages 122-135. (Also in: Alcohol Health and Research World, 5(3): 41-47, 1981.

2803.   Iosub, S., Fuchs, M. and Bingol, N. Long-Term Follow-Up of Three Siblings with Fetal Alcohol Syndrome. Alcoholism: Clinical and Experimental Research, 5(4): 523-527, 1981.

2804.   Iosub, S., Fuchs, M., Bingol, N., Rich, H., Stone, R.K., Gromisch, D.S. and Wasserman, E. Familial Fetal Alcohol Syndrome: Incidence in Blacks and Hispanics. Alcoholism: Clinical and Experimental Research, 9(2): 185, 1985.

2805.   Irle, G. Resozialisation des Suchtkranken. (Resocialisation of the Addict.) Medizinische Klinik, 67(41): 1318-1322, 1972.

2806.   Irrgang, Gloria K. and Unkovic, Charles M. The Double Alcoholic Marriage. Free Inquiry in Creative Sociology, 11(1): 89-94, 100, 1983.

2807.   Irwell, L. Influence of Parental Alcoholism Upon the Human Family. Medical Times, 41: 114, 1913.

2808.   Irwell, Lawrence. Alcohol as a Factor in the Evolution of the Human Race. Denver Medical Times, 33: 131-134, 1913.

2809. Is Alcoholism Hereditary? Revue de l'Alcoolisme, Paris, 21:
       249-259, 1975.

2810. Is the Doctor Failing the Alcoholic. Journal of the Medical
       Society of New Jersey, 69(6): 506, 1972. (Also in:
       Journal of the Indiana State Medical Association, 65(8):
       848, 1972.)

2811. Is There an Alcoholic in Your Life? Pamphlet. New York:
       Alcoholics Anonymous World Services, no date.

2812. Ishikawa, B., Asaka, A. Takemura, S. and Hemmi, T. Mono Zygotic
       Twins Concordant for Alcoholism and Discordant for Criminality.
       Proceedings of the 26th Annual Meeting of the Japan Society of
       Human Genetics. 1981. (Also in: Japanese Journal of Human
       Genetics, 27(2): 198-199, 1982.)

2813. Israel, L., Couadau, A. and Ritter, M. Apropos of Wives of
       Alcoholics. Annales Medico-Psychologiques, 2(5): 685, 1966.

2814. Issues in Child Protection and Substance Abuse: Summary and
       Recommendations from the Wingspread Conference, December 6-8,
       1979. The Catalyst, 1(3): 8-13, 1980.

2815. Itoh, N. Alcohol Dependence and Withdrawal in Two Different Strains
       of Mice. I. Behavioral and Electroencephalographic Changes.
       Japanese Journal of Alcohol Studies and Drug Dependence,
       Kyoto, 18(2): 184-202, 1983.

2816. Itoh, N. Alcohol Dependence and Withdrawal in Two Different
       Strains of Mice. II. Changes in Brain Monoamine Concentrations.
       Japanese Journal of Alcohol Studies and Drug Dependence,
       Kyoto, 18(2): 203-210, 1983.

2817. Itoh, N. Alcohol Dependence and Withdrawal in Two Different Strains
       of Mice. III. Changes in Gamma-Glutamyltranspeptidase Activities.
       Japanese Journal of Alcohol Studies and Drug Dependence, Kyoto,
       18(2): 211-217, 1983.

2818. Ivanets, N.N. and Igonin, A.L. Significance of Several Factors for
       Actualization of the Pathologic Drive to Alcohol in Chronic
       Alcoholism. Zhurnal Nevropatologii I Psikhiatrii, 79(6):
       758-763, 1979.

2819. Izikowitz, S. Om Alkoholismens Medicinska Terapi Och Profylax,
       Nagra Synpunkter Och Erfarenheter. (On the Medical Therapy
       and Prophylaxis of Alcoholism; Some Viewpoints and Experiences.)
       Nordisk Medicin, Sweden, 31: 2039-2048, 1946.

J

2820. J., Linda and L., David. <u>Alcoholism: The Horror and the Pity</u>.
      Pamphlet. Pleasantville, NY: Reader's Digest, 1974.

2821. Jackson, J.G. Personality Characteristics of Adult Daughters of
      Alcoholic Fathers as Compared with Adult Daughters of Non-
      Alcoholic Fathers. <u>Dissertation Abstracts International</u>,
      <u>46</u>(1): 338B, 1985.

2822. Jackson, Joan K. Adjustment of the Family to Alcoholism.
      In: <u>Social Problems Today: Dilemmas and Dissensus</u>.
      Ed. Clifton D. Bryant. Philadelphia: J.B. Lippincott Co.,
      1971, pages 358-370. (Also in: <u>Marriage and Family</u>, <u>18</u>:
      361-369, 1956.)

2823. Jackson, Joan K. The Adjustment of the Family to the Crisis of
      Alcoholism. <u>Quarterly Journal of Studies on Alcohol</u>, <u>15</u>:
      562-586, 1954. (Also in: <u>Sourcebook in Abnormal Psychology</u>.
      Eds. L.Y. Rabkin and J.E. Carr. Boston: Houghton, Mifflin,
      1967, pages 312-325; <u>Deviance: The Interactionsist Perspective</u>.
      Eds. E. Rubington and M.S. Weinberg. New York: Macmillan, 1968,
      pages 50-66; <u>Alcoholism: Introduction to Theory and Treatment</u>.
      Ed. David A. Ward. Dubuque, IA: Kendall/Hunt, 1980, pages
      351-365.)

2824. Jackson, Joan K. Alcoholism and the Family. In: <u>Society,</u>
      <u>Culture, and Drinking Patterns</u>. Eds. David J. Pittman
      and Charles R. Snyder. New York: John Wiley & Sons, 1962,
      pages 472-492. (Also in: <u>The Annals of the American Academy</u>
      <u>of Political and Social Science</u>, <u>315</u>: 90-98, 1958.)

2825. Jackson, Joan K. Alcoholism as a Family Crisis. <u>Pastoral</u>
      <u>Psychology</u>, <u>13</u>(123): 8-18, 1962.

2826. Jackson, Joan K. Drinking, Drunkenness and the Family.
      In: <u>Alcohol Education for the Classroom and Community:</u>
      <u>A Source Book for Educators</u>. Ed. R.G. McCarthy.
      New York: McGraw-Hill, 1964, pages 155-166.

2827. Jackson, Joan K. Family Structure and Alcoholism. <u>Mental</u>
      <u>Hygiene</u>, <u>43</u>: 403-406, 1959.

2828. Jackson, Joan K. <u>Social Adjustment Preceding, During and</u>
      <u>Following the Onset of Alcoholism</u>. Doctoral Dissertation.
      University of Washington, 1955.

2829. Jackson, Joan K. and Connor, Ralph. Attitudes of the Parents of
      Alcoholics, Moderate Drinkers and Nondrinkers Toward Drinking.
      <u>Quarterly Journal of Studies on Alcohol</u>, <u>14</u>: 596-613, 1953.

2830. Jackson, Joan K. and Kogan, Kate L. The Search for Solutions:
       Help-Seeking Patterns of Families of Active and Inactive
       Alcoholics. Quarterly Journal of Studies on Alcohol, 24:
       449-472, 1963.

2831. Jackson, Joan K., Mykut, Margaret, Burr, Roscoe C. and Fagan,
       Ronald J. The Alcoholism Training Program at the University
       of Washington School of Medicine. Quarterly Journal of
       Studies on Alcohol, 21: 298-313, 1960.

2832. Jackson, Marvin A., Kovi, Joseph J., Heshmat, Martin Y., Jones,
       George W., Rao, Mamidanna S. and Ahluwalia, Balwant S.
       Factors Involved in the High Incidence of Prostatic Cancer
       Among American Blacks. In: Progress in Clinical and
       Biological Research, Volume 53. Cancer Among Black
       Populations. Eds. C. Mettlin and G.P. Murphy. New York:
       Alan R. Liss, Inc., 1981, pages 111-132.

2833. Jacob, Theodore. The Alcoholic's Spouse, Children and Family
       Interactions: Substantive Findings and Methodological Issues.
       Journal of Studies on Alcohol, 39: 1231-1251, 1978.

2834. Jacob, Theodore. Alcoholism and Family Interaction. 1982.
       (Eric Document Number ED227402.)

2835. Jacob, Theodore. An Introduction to the Alcoholic's Family.
       In: Currents in Alcoholism. Volume 7. Recent
       Advances in Research and Treatment. Ed. Marc Galanter.
       New York: Grune and Stratton, 1980, pages 505-515.

2836. Jacob, Theodore, Dunn, Nancy Jo and Leonard, Kenneth. Patterns
       of Alcohol Abuse and Family Stability. Alcoholism:
       Clinical and Experimental Research, 7(4): 382-385, 1983.

2837. Jacob, Theodore, Favorini, Alison, Meisel, Susan S. and Anderson,
       Carol M. The Alcoholic's Spouse, Children and Family
       Interactions: Substantive Findings and Methodological Issues.
       Journal of Studies on Alcohol, 39(7): 1231-1251, 1978.

2838. Jacob, Theodore, Ritchey, Diane, Cvitkovic, Joseph F. and Blane,
       Howard T. Communication Styles of Alcohol and Nonalcoholic
       Families When Drinking and Not Drinking. Journal of Studies
       on Alcohol, 42(5): 466-482, 1981.

2839. Jacob, Theodore and Seilhamer, R.A. Impact on Spouses and How They
       Cope. In: Alcohol and the Family. Eds. J. Orford and
       J. Harwin. New York: St. Martin's Press, 1982, pages 114-126.

2840. Jacobsen, K. Alkoholproblemet Og Abortus Provocatus. (The Alcohol
       Problems and Induced Abortion.) Ugeskrift for Laeger,
       Copenhagen, 126: 409-412, 1964.

2841. Jacobsen, R. Impact of Parental Alcoholism on Adolescent Psychosocial
       Development. Paper presented at the Third Annual National
       Conference for Nurse Educators on Alcohol and Drug Abuse,
       Washington, D.C., May, 1983. (Also in: Current Issues in Alcohol
       and Drug Abuse Nursing: Research, Education and Clinical
       Practice, pages 175-180.)

2842. Jacobsson, L., Perris, C., Roman, G. and Roman, O. A Social-
       Psychiatric Comparison of 399 Women Requesting Abortion and
       118 Pregnant Women Intending to Deliver. Acta Psychiatrica
       Scandinavica, Copenhagen, 255: 279-290, 1974.

2843. Jacoby, M.G. Alcoholism and Colour-Blindness. Lancet, 1:
       113, 1967.

2844. Jahoda, G., Davies, J.B. and Tagg, S. Parents' Alcohol Consumption and Children's Knowledge of Drinks and Usage Patterns. British Journal of Addiction, Edinburgh, 75(3): 297-303, 1980.

2845. Jalali, Behnaz, Jalali, Mehroad, Crocetti, Guido and Turner, Floyd. Adolescents and Drug Use: Toward a More Comprehensive Approach. American Journal of Orthopsychiatry, 51(1): 120-130, 1981.

2846. James, C. Family Involvement -- A Key to Program Success. Labor-Management Alcoholism Journal, 9: 192-195, 1980.

2847. James, Jane E. Symptoms of Alcoholism in Women: A Preliminary Survey of A.A. Members. Journal of Studies on Alcohol, 36(11): 1564-1569, 1975.

2848. James, Jane E. and Goldman, Morton. Behavior Trends of Wives of Alcoholics. Quarterly Journal of Studies on Alcohol, 32: 373-381, 1971.

2849. James, N. and Chapman, C.J. A Genetic Study of Bipolar Affective Disorder. British Journal of Psychiatry, 126: 449-456, 1975.

2850. Jamieson, H.S. Follow-Up Program for Treated Alcohol and Drug Addicts. Paper presented at the 24th Annual Meeting of the ADPA. Bloomington, MN, September, 1973, pages 75-77.

2851. Janes, Cynthia L., Hesselbrock, Victor M., Myers, Darcy G. and Penniman, Janet H. Problem Boys in Young Adulthood: Teacher's Ratings and Twelve-Year Follow-Up. Journal of Youth and Adolescence, 8(4): 453-472, 1979.

2852. Jansen, Donald J. Ministering to the Alcoholic Family in the Military. Decatur, GA: Columbia Theological Seminary, 1979.

2853. Janzen, Curtis. Families in the Treatment of Alcoholism. Journal of Studies on Alcohol, 38(1): 114-130, 1977.

2854. Janzen, Curtis. Family Treatment for Alcoholism: A Review. Social Work, 23(2): 135-141, 1978.

2855. Janzen, Curtis. Reader's Exchange: Use of Family Treatment Methods by Alcoholism Treatment Services. Alcohol Health & Research World, 10(2): 44-45, 60, 1985/86.

2856. Japenga, Ann. Los Angeles Times, 14 December 1984, p. 1, 34. (Pop Star's Song Fuels Anti-Drunk Driving Campaign.)

2857. Jasinsky, M. Alcoholism in School-Age Children. Fortschritte der Medizin, 93(31): 1511-1514, 1975.

2858. Jasso, Ricardo. Chicano Alcohol Abuse and Alcoholism in the Barrio. 1977. (Eric Document Number ED171436.)

2859. Jedlovsky, A. and Lucova, A. Familial Incidence of Pancreatitis. Ceskoslovenska Gastrventerologie a Vyziva, 30(2): 100-106, 1976.

2860. Jeffries, L.M.B. Marriage in Relation to Alcohol and Drug Addiction. British Journal of Inebriety, 35: 49-55, 1937.

2861. Jelemensky, Linda Marlene Craig. A Descriptive Study of the Factors Associated with Depression Spectrum Disease Among Young Women. Dissertation Abstracts International, 45(3): 1060B, 1983.

2862. Jellinek, E.M. Heredity of the Alcoholic. Lecture 9 in Alcohol, Science and Society. Journal of Studies on Alcohol, 1945.

2863. Jellinek, E.M. Notes of the First Half Year's Experience at the
       Yale Plan Clinics. Quarterly Journal of Studies on Alcohol,
       5: 279-302, 1944.

2864. Jenkins, Richard L. Varieties of Children's Behavioral Problems
       and Family Dynamics. American Journal of Psychiatry,
       124(10): 1440-1445, 1968.

2865. Jenner, C. Die Heutige Daseinssituation als Herausforderung an
       Die Alkoholerziehung. (The Current Existential Situation
       as Challenge to Alcohol Education.) In: Papers Presented
       at the 24th International Institute on the Prevention and
       Treatment of Alcoholism. Ed. E.J. Tongue. Lausanne:
       International Council on Alcohol and Addictions, 1978,
       pages 283-294.

2866. Jenner, C. Dynamisch-Integratives Therapieprogramm Bei
       Aloholkranken Frauen. (Dynamic and Integrated Therapy
       Program for Women Alcoholics.) Wiener Zeitschrift fur
       Suchtforschung, 3(4-5): 11-19, 1980.

2867. Jenny, L. (AKA Jenny, Jennings) and Schwartz, R.H. Adolescent
       Drug Dependency and the Family. Virginia Medical,
       112(11): 711-715, 1985.

2868. Jensen, Gary F. and Brownfield, David. Parents and Drugs.
       Criminology, 21(4): 543-554, 1983.

2869. Jeri, F.R., Carbajal, C. and Sanchez, M.C. Uso De Drogas Y
       Alucinogenos En Adolescents Y Escolares. (Use of Drugs and
       Hallucinogenics in Adolescents and School Children. Revista
       De Neuro Psiquiatria, Lima, 34(4): 243-273, 1971.

2870. Jerntorp, P. and Almer, L.O. Chlorpropamide-Alcohol Flushing in
       Relation to Macroangiopathy and Peripheral Neuropathy in
       Non-Insulin Dependent Diabetes. Acta Medica Scandinavica,
       211(Supplement 656): 33-36, 1981.

2871. Jesse, R.C. Children of Alcoholics: A Clinical Investigation
       of Familial Role Relationships. Doctoral Dissertation.
       (University Microfilms No. 77-32440). San Diego: California
       School of Professional Psychology, 1977. (Also in:
       Dissertation Abstracts International, 38: 5573-5574B, 1978.)

2872. Jesse, Rosalie, McFadd, Adrienne, Gray, Gloria and Bucky, Steven F.
       Interpersonal Effects of Alcohol Abuse. In: The Impact of
       Alcoholism. Center City, MN: Hazelden, 1978, pages 45-68.

2873. Jessor, Richard. Adolescent Problem Drinking: Psychosocial
       Aspects and Developmental Outcomes. In: Proceedings:
       NIAAA-WHO Collaborating Center Designation Meeting and
       Alcohol Research Seminar. Ed. L.H. Towle. Washington,
       D.C.: United States Department HHS, 1984, pages 104-143.

2874. Jessor, Richard, Chase, James A. and Donovan, John E. Psychosocial
       Correlates of Marijuana Use and Problem Drinking in a National
       Sample of Adolescents. American Journal of Public Health,
       70: 604-613, 1980.

2875. Jessor, Richard, Cureton, L.W., Zucher, R.A. and Barron, F.H. Youth.
       In: Preceedings of the First Annual Alcoholism Conference
       of the National Institute on Alcohol Abuse and Alcoholism.
       Ed. M. Chafetz. Rockville, MD: National Institute on Alcohol
       Abuse and Alcoholism, 1974, pages 258-299.

2876. Jessor, S. and Jessor, R. Maternal Ideology and Adolescent Problem
       Behavior. Developmental Psychology, 10(2): 246-254, 1974.

2877. Jimenez, D.R.   A Comparative Analysis of the Support Systems of
         White and Puerto Rican Clients in Drug Treatment Programs.
         Doctoral Dissertation. (University Microfilms No. 77-15271.)
         Bradford, MA: Brandeis University, The Florence Heller Graduate
         School for Advanced Studies in Social Welfare, 1977.

2878. Joffe, J.M. and Soyka, L.F. Paternal Drug Exposure: Effects
         on Reproduction and Progeny. Seminars in Perinatology,
         6(2): 116-124, 1982.

2879. Johannesson, K. Alkohovard i Jugoslavien. (The Treatment of
         Alcoholics in Yugoslavia.) Alkohol och Narkotika, 69:
         253-256, 1975.

2880. Johanson, Eva. Background and Development of Youth-Prison
         Inmates. A Long-Term, Follow-Up Study of 128 Consecutive
         Inmates and of a Control Group. Scandinavian Journal of
         Social Medicine, Stockholm, 9: 1-290, 1974.

2881. Johanson, Eva. Home Conditions, Family Size, Birth Rank.
         Scandinavian Journal of Social Medicine, Stockholm, 9:
         241-264, 1974.

2882. Johanson, Eva. Mental Health and Morbidity in Original and
         Control Subjects and Their Relatives. "Personality."
         Scandinavian Journal of Social Medicine, Stockholm, 9:
         141-175, 1974.

2883. Johanson, Eva. Recidivistic Criminals and Their Families:
         Morbidity, Mortality and Abuse of Alcohol. A Longitudinal
         Study of Earlier Youth Prison Inmates and of a Control
         Group and their Families in Three Generations. Scandinavian
         Journal of Social Medicine, Stockholm, 9(Supplement 27):
         1-101, 1981.

2884. Johanson, Eva. Summary and Conclusions. Scandinavian Journal of
         Social Medicine, Stockholm, 9: 265-273, 1981.

2885. Johns, H. Family Law and Alcohol Problems. In: Alcohol and
         the Family. Eds. J. Orford and J. Harwin. New York:
         St. Martin's Press, 1982, pages 167-179.

2886. Johnson, B.E. Family Intervention: The Beginning of Recovery.
         Paper presented at the 8th Annual Meeting of the Association
         of Labor-Management Administrators and Consultants on Alcoholism
         Inc., Detorit, October, 1979. (Also in: Proceedings of the
         Eighth Annual Meeting of ALMACA. Arlington, VA: ALMACA,
         1980, pages 59-64.)

2887. Johnson, Bruce D. Toward a Theory of Drug Subcultures. In:
         Theories on Drug Abuse: Selected Contemporary Perspectives.
         (NIDA Research Monograph Series 30.) Eds. Dan J. Lettieri,
         Mollie Sayers and Helen Wallenstein Pearson. Washington, D.C.:
         U.S. Government Printing Office, 1980.

2888. Johnson, C. Anderson and Solis, Julie. Comprehensive Community
         Programs for Drug Abuse Prevention: Implications of the
         Community Heart Disease Prevention Programs for Future
         Research. In: Preventing Adolescent Drug Abuse: Intervention
         Strategies. (National Institute on Drug Abuse Research
         Monograph No. 47. A Raus Review Report.) Eds. Thomas J. Glynn,
         Carl G. Leukefeld, Jacqueline P. Ludford. Washington, D.C.:
         U.S. Government Printing Office, 1983, pages 76-114.

2889. Johnson, Craig and Berndt, David J. Preliminary Investigation of
         Bulimia and Life Adjustment. American Journal of Psychiatry,
         140(6): 774-777, 1983.

2890. Johnson, E.L. Alcoholism: The Workplace. In: Alcoholism: New Perspectives. Eds. H.K. Cleminshaw and E.B. Truitt. Akron: University of Akron, 1983, pages 65-78.

2891. Johnson, Elizabeth, J. Family Counseling for Low Income Abusers. In: Drug Abuse from the Family Perspective. Ed. Barbara Gray Ellis. Washington, D.C.: U.S. Government Printing Office, 1980, pages 78-85.

2892. Johnson, F.G. Alcoholism - Disease and Irresponsibility. Canadian Journal of Public Health, 60: 416-421, 1969.

2893. Johnson, Glenn M., Shontz, Franklin G., and Locke, Thomas P. Relationships Between Adolescent Drug Use and Parental Drug Behaviors. Adolescence, 19(74): 295-299, 1984.

2894. Johnson, Gordon F. and Hunt, Glen. Suicidal Behavior in Bipolar Manic-Depressive Patients and Their Families. Comprehensive Psychiatry, 20(2): 159-164, 1979.

2895. Johnson, Gordon F. and Leeman, Marsha M. Analysis of Familial Factors in Bipolar Affective Illness. Archives of General Psychiatry, 34(9): 1074-1083, 1977.

2896. Johnson, Greg. Executive Junkies. Industry Week, 205(2): 52-55, 59-60, 1980.

2897. Johnson, Holly Ellen. A Genetic Study of Hyperactivity. Dissertation Abstracts International, 43(8): 2709B, 1982.

2898. Johnson Institute. Chemical Dependency and Recovery are a Family Affair. Pamphlet. Minneapolis: Johnson Institute, 1979.

2899. Johnson Institute. Recovery of Chemically Dependent Families. Pamphlet. Center City, MN: Hazelden, no date.

2900. Johnson, J.L. Risk and Protective Factors in Children Vulnerable to Alcohol Abuse. Paper presented at the National Council on Alcoholism Forum, Washington, D.C., April, 1985.

2901. Johnson, Kirk Alan. Adolescent Alcohol Use and Social Control. Dissertation Abstracts International, 42(7): 3311-3312A, 1981.

2902. Johnson, M.W., DeVries, J.C. and Houghton, M.I. The Female Alcoholic. Nursing Research, 15: 343-347, 1966.

2903. Johnson, N. Counselor Cites Special Treatment Needs of Alcoholic Adult Children of Alcoholics. Alcohol Health and Research World, 8(4): 26-27, 1984.

2904. Johnson, N. Heredity and Environmental Risk Factors in Alcoholism. Research Reports. Alcohol Health and Research World, 7(2): 51-53, 1982-1983.

2905. Johnson, Nancy. Effects of Family History of Alcoholism. Alcohol Health and Research World, 6(2): 39-40, 1981-1982.

2906. Johnson, Nancy. From Father and Mother to Son and Daughter. Alcohol Health and Research World, 7(2): 51-53, 1982-1983.

2907. Johnson, Nancy. Research Center Probes Etiology of Alcoholism. NIAAA Information and Feature Service, (IFS No. 90): 2, November 30, 1981.

2908. Johnson, Paula B. Sex Differences, Women's Roles and Alcohol Use: Preliminary National Data. Journal of Social Issues, 38(2): 93-116, 1982.

2909.   Johnson, R.C. Further Investigation of Racial/Ethnic Differences
        and of Familial Resemblances in Flushing in Response to
        Alcohol. Behavior Genetics, 14(3): 171-178, 1984.

2910.   Johnson, S.L., Leonard, K.E. and Jacob, T. Children of Alcoholics --
        Drinking, Drinking Attitudes, and Drug-Use. Alcoholism:
        Clinical and Experimental Research, 10(1): 96, 1986.

2911.   Johnson, Sandie and Garzon, Sally Roy. Alcoholism and Women.
        The American Journal of Drug and Alcohol Abuse, 5(1):
        107-122, 1978.

2912.   Johnson, V.E. Changing Concepts in the Treatment of Alcoholism.
        Editorial. Social Casework, 59: 51-52, 1978.

2913.   Johnson, W.D. Tapping the Unconscious: Jungian Techniques for
        ACoA's. Focus on Family and Chemical Dependency, 8(1):
        13-14, 1985.

2914.   Johnston, C., Owerbach, D., Leslie, R.D.G., Pyke, D.A. and Nerup,
        J. Letters to the Editor: Mason-Type Diabetes and DNA
        Insertion Polymorphism. The Lancet, 1(8371): 280, 1984.

2915.   Johnston, Gerald P. "The Pen is Mightier than the Sword": Some
        Dangers of Script Writing. A Report of the Commission on
        Physician Impairment. The Journal of the Indiana State
        Medical Association, 74(7): 428-429, 1981.

2916.   Johnston, J. Alcoholism and the Wastage of Child Life. British
        Journal of Inebriety, 6: 179-185, 1909.

2917.   Johnston, J. Parenthood and Alcohol. British Medical Journal,
        1: 1273, 1912.

2918.   Johnston, L., Bachman, J. and O'Malley, M. Drugs and the Class
        of '78; Behaviors, Attitudes and Recent National Trends.
        DHEW Publciation No. (ADM) 79-877. Rockville, MD: National
        Institute on Drug Abuse, 1979.

2919.   Johnston, Mary Ellen. Influences of the Family Climate. Paper
        presented at the National Institute on Drug Abuse, Program
        for Women's Concerns, Miami Beach, October, 1975. (Also in:
        Drugs, Alcohol and Women; A National Forum Source Book.
        Ed. M. Nellis. Washington, D.C.: National Research and
        Communications Associates, Inc., 1976, pages 71-72.

2920.   Johnston, P.J. Effects of Spouse Counseling on the Treatment
        Outcome of the Problem Drinker. Doctoral Dissertation.
        (University Microfilms No. 80-04431.) Williamsburg, VA:
        The College of William and Mary, 1979.

2921.   Johnston, S.J., Jones, P.F., Kyle, J. and Needham, C.D.
        Epidemiology and Course of Gastrointestinal Haemorrhage
        in North-East Scotland. British Medical Journal, London,
        3(882): 655-660, 1973.

2922.   Jokerst, R. Dominance, Nurturance, and Abasement Needs in the
        Wives of Alcoholics. Doctoral Dissertation. Edwardsville:
        Southern Illinois University, Department of Psychology, 1981.

2923.   Jonas, Doris F. and Jonas, A. David. A Bioanthropological Overview
        of Addiction. Perspectives in Biology and Medicine, 20:
        345-354, 1977. (Also in: Theories on Drug Abuse: Selected
        Contemporary Perspectives. (NIDA Research Monograph Series
        30.) Eds. Dan J. Lettieri, Mollie Sayers and Helen Wallenstein
        Pearson. Washington, D.C.: U.S. Government Printing Office,
        1980, pages 269-277.)

2924. Jones, H. Alcoholic Addiction: A Psycho-Social Approach to Abnormal Drinking. London: Tavistock, 1963.

2925. Jones, I.H. Social Unrest in an Aboriginal Community. The Medical Journal of Australia, Sydney, 1(Supplement 4): 5-7, 1977.

2926. Jones, J. Children are Alcoholism's "Most Unprotected Victims." Magazine of the Texas Commission on Alcoholism, 5(2): 20-21, 1979.

2927. Jones, J.W. Acquisitional Processes Underlying Illicit Alcohol Abuse in Underage Children: An Observational Learning Model. Psychological Reports, 45: 735-740, 1979.

2928. Jones, J.W. Children of Alcoholics Screening Test: Development, Research and Applications. Paper presented at the Children of Alcoholics Conference, Springfield, IL, April, 1983.

2929. Jones, J.W. Children of Alcoholics Screening Test: Test Manual. Chicago: Camelot Unlimited, 1985.

2930. Jones, J.W. Preliminary Test Manual: The Children of Alcoholics Screening Test. Park Ridge, IL: London House Consultants, Inc., 1982.

2931. Jones, J.W. A Screening Test to Identify Children in Alcoholic Families. Paper presented at the 148th Meeting of the American Association for the Advancement of Science, Washington, D.C., January, 1982.

2932. Jones, John W. and Muldoon, Joe. Screening Test for Children of Alcoholics. Community Intervention, (Winter): 5, 15, 1985.

2933. Jones, K.L., Smith, D.W., Streissguth, A.P. and Myrianthopoulos, N.C. Outcome in Offspring of Chronic Alcoholic Women. Lancet, 1: 1076-1078, 1974.

2934. Jones, Kenneth L. Maternal Alcoholism. Paper presented at the National Institute on Drug Abuse, Program for Women's Concerns, Miami Beach, October, 1975. (Also in: Drugs, Alcohol and Women; A National Forum Source Book. Ed. M. Nellis. Washington, D.C.: National Research and Communications Associates, Inc., 1976, pages 172-173.)

2935. Jones, Kenneth L., Smith, David W. and Ulleland, Christy N. Pattern of Malformation in Offspring of Alcoholic Mothers. Lancet, 1(1715): 1267-1271, 1973.

2936. Jones, M.B. and Borland, B.L. Social Mobility and Alcoholism; A Comparison of Alcoholics With Their Fathers and Brothers. Journal of Studies on Alcohol, 36: 62-68, 1975.

2937. Jones, Mary Cover. Personality Correlates and Antecedents of Drinking Patterns in Adult Males. Journal of Consulting and Clinical Psychology, 32(1): 2-12, 1968.

2938. Jones, Robert W. Alcoholism Among Relatives of Alcoholic Patients. Quarterly Journal of Studies on Alcohol, 33: 810, 1972.

2939. Jones-Saumty, Deborah J., Dru, Ralph L. and Zeiner, Arthur R. Causal Attribution of Drinking Antecedents in American Indian and Caucasian Social Drinkers. Advances in Alcohol & Substance Abuse, 4(1): 19-28, 1984.

2940. Jones-Saumty, Deborah J., Hochhaus, Larry, Dru, Ralph and Zeiner, Arthur. Psychological Factors of Familial Alcoholism in American Indians and Caucasians. Journal of Clinical Psychology, 39(5): 783-790, 1983.

2941. Jong, K.E. de. The Effects of Alcoholism on the Offspring.
       Nederlands Maandschrift voor Verloskunde en Vrouwenziekten
       en voor Kindergeneeskundee, 3: 469-510, 1914.

2942. Jonsson, E. and Nilsson, T. Alkoholkonsumtion Hos Monozygota Och
       Dizygota Tvillingpar. (Alcohol Consumption in Monozygotic
       and Dizygotic Pair of Twins.) Nordisk Hygienisk Tidskrift,
       Umea, 49: 21-25, 1968.

2943. Jonsson, G. Delinquent Boys, Their Parents and Grandparents. Acta
       Psychiatrica Scandinavica, Copenhagen, 43(Supplement 195):
       1-264, 1967.

2944. Jorgensen, G. Genetische Determination des Alkoholismus. (Genetic
       Determination of Alcoholism.) Munchener Medizinische
       Wochenschrift, Munich, 123(32/33): 1230-1231, 1981.

2945. Jorgensen, Gary Q., Hammond, D. Corydon and Hardy, Arthur.
       Saturation Marathon Couples' Therapy in Prison: A Rationale.
       International Journal of Group Psychotherapy, 27(1):
       97-103, 1977.

2946. Jorgensen, Jens Peder, Jorgensen, Anna, Jensen, Keld Gammelby,
       Abildgard, Jorger and Andersen, Hans Jorger. Vold Mod
       Kvinder Parforhold. En Prospektiv Opgorelse. (Violence
       to Women by Their Consorts. A Prospective Investigation.)
       Ugeskrift for Laegerforening, 143(36): 2321-2324, 1981.

2947. Jornvall, H., Hempel, J., Vallee, B.L., Bosron, W.F. and Li, T.K.
       Human Liver Alcohol Dehydrogenase. Proceedings of the
       National Academy of Sciences, 81(10): 3024-3028, 1984.

2948. Josita, Mary. Management of the Alcoholic Beyond the Hospital.
       Paper presented at the Symposium: Alcohol and Drugs --
       A Challenge for Education, Melbourne, January, 1971,
       pages 57-60.

2949. Jost, J. Wird Die Gesundheits-, Sozial- und Jegendhilfe den
       Auswirkungen des Erhohten Alkoholmissbrauch und dem Schutz
       der Familie Gerecht? (Are Health Education, Social Help
       and Youth Protection Adequate to Shield Families from
       Increasing Alcohol Abuse?) Gesundheitsfursorge,
       Stuttgrat, 16: 85-86, 1966.

2950. Jost, J. Wenn der Mann Trinkt: Beratungsprobleme Gegenuber
       der Ehefrau des Alkoholikers. (When the Husband Drinks:
       Problems in Counseling the Wife of the Alcoholic.)
       Gesundheitsfursorge, Stuttgart, 18: 25-29, 1968.

2951. Jovanovic, Ljubica. Alkoholizam -- Brak I Porodica. (Alcoholism,
       Marriage and Family.) Sociologija, Belgrade, 7(4): 73-86,
       1965.

2952. Jovicevic, M. Alkoholizam u Porodici i Korelacija sa Nekim
       Sociopatskim Obrascima Ponasanja Licnosti. (Alcoholism
       in the Family and its Correlation with Some Sociopathic
       Behavior Patterns.) Alkoholizam, Belgrade, 14(1-2):
       28-31, 1974.

2953. Jovicevic, M. Epidemiological Approach to the Study of
       Alcoholism, Some Psychopathologic Manifestations in
       Families of Adolescents and the Influence of These
       Phenomena on the Development of Personality. Narodno
       Zdravje, 29(4): 107-109, 1973.

2954. Judd, Lewis L. and Mandell, Arnold L. A "Free Clinic" Patient
       Population and Drug Use Patterns. American Journal of
       Psychiatry, 128(10): 1298-1302, 1972.

2955. Judge Involves Parents in Treatment of Substance-Abusing
      Offenders. Substance Abuse Report, 16(4): 4, 1985.

2956. Juell, Hazel May. A Descriptive Model of the Emotional, Sexual,
      Physical and Relational Effects of Childhood Sexual
      Molestation on Adult Females. Dissertation Abstracts
      International, 44(12): 3936B, 1983.

2957. Julian, Valerie and Mohr, Cynthia. Father-Daughter Incest:
      Profile of the Offender. Report. Denver: National Study
      on Child Neglect and Abuse Reporting, no date. (Also in:
      Victimology, 4(4): 348-360, 1979.)

2958. Julius, Eloise Kates and Papp, Peggy. Family Choreography:
      A Multigenerational View of an Alcoholic Family System.
      In: Family Therapy of Drug and Alcohol Abuse.
      Eds. E. Kaufman and P.N. Kaufmann. New York: Gardner
      Press, 1979, pages 201-213.

2959. Jurich, A.P., Polson, C.J., Jurich, J.A. and Bates, R.A.
      Family Factors in the Lives of Drug Users and Abusers.
      Adolescence, 20(77): 143-159, 1985.

2960. Justice, B. and Justice R. Broken Taboo: Sex in the Family.
      New York: Human Sciences Press, 1979.

K

2961. Kabanov, M.M., Miager, V.K. and Volovik, V.M. Research in Family Psychotherapy as Reported by the Leningrad Bekhterev Psychoneurological Institute. _International Journal of Family Psychiatry_, 1(4): 437-451, 1980.

2962. Kachru, R.B., Proskey, A.J. and Telischi, M. Histocompatibility Antigens and Alcoholic Cardiomyopathy. _Tissue Antigens_, 15: 398-399, 1980.

2963. Kadushin, L.R. Drug Attitudes, Parental Child-Rearing Attitudes, and Youth's Perceptions of Parental Attitude Agreement. Doctoral Dissertation. (University Microfilms No. 72-11362.) University of Texas at Austin, 1971.

2964. Kaflik, R., Kaflik, I. and Sternalski, M. Alkoholik W Rolach Meza I Ojca. (The Alcoholic in the Role of Husband and Father.) _Problemy Alkoholizmu_, Warsaw, 26(5): 5, 1979.

2965. Kahn, A. Biologic Effects of Alcohol. _Journal of the Arkansas Medical Society_, 81(12): 647-649, 1985.

2966. Kahn, A.J. A Generational Drift in Rate of Development of Aversion to Ethanol: Associated Shift in the Sensitive Period. _Growth_, 46: 322-330, 1982.

2967. Kahn, Marvin W. and Delk, John L. Developing a Community Mental Health Clinic on an Indian Reservation. _The International Journal of Social Psychiatry_, London, 19(3-4): 299-306, 1973.

2968. Kahn, Marvin W. and Gingras Terry. Drinking Patterns and Effects: Alcoholics in Treatment Compared to Medical Outpatients. _International Journal of the Addictions_, 18(3): 419-428, 1983.

2969. Kahn, Marvin W., Henry, Joseph and Cawte, John. Mental Health Services by and for Australian Aborigines. _Australian and New Zealand Journal of Psychiatry_, Melbourne, 10(3): 221-228, 1976.

2970. Kahn, Marvin W., Kennedy, Eva V. and Cawte, John. Mental Health Services by and for Aborigines and Islanders: A Follow-Up Report. _Australian & New Zealand Journal of Psychiatry_, Melbourne, 12(1): 39-41, 1978.

2971. Kahn, Michael D. and Bank, Stephen. Therapy with Siblings in Reorganizing Families: II. _International Journal of Family Therapy_, 2(3): 155-158, 1980.

2972. Kaij, H.L. Definitions of Alcoholism and Genetic Research. _Annals of the New York Academy of Sciences_, 197: 110-113, 1972.

2973. Kaij, Lennart. _Alcoholism in Twins. Studies on the Etiology and Sequels of Abuse of Alcohol_. Stockholm: Almqvist and Wiksell, 1960.

2974. Kaij, Lennart. Drinking Habits in Twins. Acta Genetica et Statisticac Medica, Basel, 7: 437-441, 1957.

2975. Kaij, Lennart and Dock, Jan. Grandsons of Alcoholics: A Test of Sex-Linked Transmission of Alcohol Abuse. Archives of General Psychiatry, 32: 1379-1381, 1975.

2976. Kaij, Lennart and McNeil, T.F. Genetic Aspects of Alcoholism. In: Alcoholism: A Multidisciplinary Approach. (Advances in Biological Psychiatry, Vol. 3.) New York: S. Karger, 1979, pages 54-65.

2977. Kalant, Oriana Josseau. Sex Differences in Alcohol and Drug Problems -- Some Highlights. In: Research Advances in Alcohol and Drug Problems, Volume 5: Alcohol and Drug Problems in Women. Ed. O.J. Kalant. New York: Plenum Press, 1980, pages 1-24.

2978. Kalashian, M.M. Working with the Wives of Alcoholics in an Out-Patient Clinic Setting. Journal of Marriage and the Family, 21: 130-133, 1959.

2979. Kalow, W. Ethnic Differences in Drug Metabolism. Clinical Pharmacokinetics, 7: 373-400, 1980.

2980. Kamaryt, J. and Brunecky, Z. Dedicni Cinitele Metabolismu Etanolu A Alkoholismu. (Heredity Factors in the Metabolism of Ethanol and Alcoholism.) In: Vnitrni Lekarstvi, Prague, 21: 689-694, 1975.

2981. Kamback, M.C. The Family and Alcohol Abuse -- A Systems Approach. Baltimore: Johns Hopkins University, no date.

2982. Kamback, M.C. Familial Transmission of Alcoholism Perceived Quality of Parental Pathologies and Family Relationships. Paper presented at the 13th Annual Medical-Scientific Conference of the National Alcoholism Forum on Progress in Alcoholism Research and Treatment, Washington, D.C., April, 1982. (Also in: Alcoholism: Clinical and Experimental Research, 6(1): 146, 1982.)

2983. Kaminski, B. Nieprzystosowanie Pozytywne Dzieci z Rodzin Alkoholikow. (Social Maladjustment of Children from Alcoholic Families.) Problemy Alkoholizmu, Warsaw, 23(12): 5-6, 1976.

2984. Kammeier, Mary Leo. Adolescents From Families With and Without Alcohol Problems. Center City, MN: Hazelden, no date. (Also in: Quarterly Journal of Studies on Alcohol, 32(2): 364-372, 1971.)

2985. Kammeier, Mary Leo. Biographic, Cognitive, Demographic and Personality Differences Between Adolescents From Families With Identifiable Alcohol Problems and From Families Without Identifiable Alcohol Problems. (University Microfilms No. 69-16274.) Doctoral Dissertation. Grand Forks: University of North Dakota, 1969. (Also in: Dissertation Abstracts International, 30: 1398-1399A, 1969.)

2986. Kammerer, T., Singer, L., Gurfein, L. and Wysoki, V. Application d'une Nouvelle Methode d'analyse Mathematique a l'etude des Tentatives de Suicide. (Application of a New Method of Mathematical Analysis to the Study of Suicide Attempts.) Annales Medico-Psychologiques, Paris, 125(2): 296-303, 1967.

2987. Kampfer, Merlin W. Drug Abuse Prevention -- A Community Approach. Preventive Medicine, 2(4): 524-528, 1973.

2988. Kampler, Hyman L. and MacKenna, Pat. Clinical Observations and
       Brief Family Therapy of Drug Abusing Adolescents and Their
       Families. Paper presented at the 52nd Annual Meeting, American
       Orthopsychiatric Association, Washington, D.C., March, 1975.

2989. Kanas, N. Alcoholism and Group Psychotherapy. In: Encyclopedic
       Handbook of Alcoholism. Ed. E. Pattison and E. Kaufman.
       New York: Gardner Press, 1982, pages 1011-1021.

2990. Kandel, Denise B. Developmental Stages in Adolescent Drug Involvement.
       In: Theories on Drug Abuse: Selected Contemporary Perspectives.
       (NIDA Research Monograph Series 30.) Eds. Dan J. Lettieri, Mollie
       Sayers and Helen Wallenstein Pearson. Washington, D.C.: U.S.
       Government Printing Office, 1980, pages 120-127.

2991. Kandel, Denise B. Drug and Drinking Behavior Among Youth.
       Annual Review of Sociology, 6: 235-285, 1980.

2992. Kandel, Denise B. Drug Use By Youth: An Overview. In: Drug
       Abuse and the American Adolescent. Eds. Dan J. Lettieri
       and Jacqueline P. Ludford. NIDA Research Monograph No. 38,
       1981, pages 1-24.

2993. Kandel, Denise B. Inter- and Intra-generational Influences on
       Adolescent Marijuana Use. Journal of Social Issues,
       30(2): 107-135, 1974.

2994. Kandel, Denise B. On Processes of Peer Influences in Adolescent
       Drug Use: A Developmental Perspective. In: Alcohol and
       Substance Abuse in Adolescence. Eds. J. Brook, D. Lettieri,
       D. Brook and B. Stimmel. New York: Haworth Press, 1985,
       pages 139-163. (Also in: Advances in Alcohol and Substance
       Abuse, 4(3/4): 139-163, 1985.)

2995. Kandel, Denise. Reaching the Hard-to-Reach: Illicit Drug Use
       Among High School Absentees. Addictive Diseases, 1(4):
       465-480, 1975.

2996. Kandel, Denise B. Socialization and Adolescent Drinking.
       In: Alcohol and Youth. (Child Health and Development,
       Volume 2.) Ed. O. Jeanneret. Basel: S. Karger, 1983,
       pages 66-75.

2997. Kandel, Denise B., Kessler, Ronald C. and Margulies, Rebecca Z.
       Antecedents of Adolescent Initiation into Stages of Drug
       Use: A Developmental Analysis. In: Longitudinal Research
       on Drug Use. Washington, D.C.: Hemisphere Publishing
       Corp., 1978, pages 73-99.

2998. Kandel, Denise B., Treiman, D., Faust, R. and Single, E.
       Adolescent Involvement in Legal and Illegal Drug Use:
       A Multiple Classification Analysis. In: Drugs and the
       Family. Washington, D.C.: U.S. Government Printing
       Office, 1981, pages 172-174.

2999. Kane, R.A. Family Rituals: The Significance of Subtle Tradition.
       Focus on Family, 8(5): 9, 47, 1985.

3000. Kane, Robert L. and Patterson, Elizabeth. Drinking Attitudes and
       Behavior of High-School Students in Kentucky. Quarterly
       Journal of Studies on Alcohol, 33(3): 635-646, 1972.

3001. Kane, Rosalie A. To Our Health! Social Work and Alcohol
       Problems. Health & Social Work, 4(4): 3-8, 1979.

3002. Kang, S.H. Juvenile Delinquency Associated with Grief Reaction.
       Kyungpook University Medical Journal, 18(2): 222-228, 1977.

3003. Kant, O. Zur Psychobiologie der Trinkerehe. (On the Psychobiology of Marriage to an Alcoholic.) Zeitschrift Fuer Die Gesamte Neurologie Und Psychiatrie, Berlin, 106: 401-410, 1926.

3004. Kaplan, Howard B. Self-Enhancing Functions of Alcohol Abuse Among Male Adolescents. In: Phenomenology and Treatment of Alcoholism. Eds. William E. Fann, Ismet Karacan, Alex D. Pokorny, and Robert L. Williams. Jamaica, NY: Scientific and Medical Books, 1980, pages 151-166.

3005. Kaprio, Jaakko, Koskenvuo, Markku and Sarna, Seppo. Cigarette Smoking, Use of Alcohol, and Leisure-Time Physical Activity Among Same-Sexed Adult Male Twins. In: Twin Research 3: Proceedings of the Third International Congress on Twin Studies, June 16-20, 1980, Jerusalem; Part C: Epidemiological and Clinical Studies. Eds. Luigi Gedda, Paolo Parisi, Walter E. Nance. New York: Alan R. Liss, 1981, pages 37-46.

3006. Kari-Koskinen, O., Hirvonen, L. and Sourander, C. Shelter Home in the Treatment of Severe Alcoholics. Alcoholism, Zagreb, 6: 11, 1970.

3007. Karlen, H. Alcoholism in Conflicted Marriages. American Journal of Orthopsychiatry, 35: 326-327, 1965.

3008. Karlsson, J.L. Academic Achievement of Psychotic or Alcoholic Patients. Hereditas, Lund, 99(1): 69-72, 1983.

3009. Karsikas, Helena, Moren, Riitta, Piirainen, Kaija and Taipale, Vappu. Motives of Excessive Drinking and Psychosocial Background Factors in Alcohol Intoxication Patients Treated in the Department of Pediatrics, Helsinki, University Central Hospital, in 1975-1979. Acta Paedopsychiatrica, Switzerland, 48(5): 221-229, 1982.

3010. Karsikas, Helena, Moren, Riitta, Piirainen, Kaija and Taipale, Vappu. Psychosocial Problems Among Children Intoxicated by Alcohol. Sosiaalilaaketieteellinen Aikakauslehti, 18(1): 4-10, 1981.

3011. Kastler-Maitron and Burckard, Ed. Quelques Considerations Sur L'Alcoolisme Chronique Chez La Femme. (Some Considerations on Chronic Alcoholism in Women.) Cahiers de Psychiatrie, Clermont, 10: 31-44, 1955.

3012. Kastrup, M. Alkoholambulatoriers Klientel. (Clientele of Ambulatory Alcoholism Clinics.) Ugeskrift for Laeger, 140: 2949-2951, 1978.

3013. Kates, Solis L. and Schmolke, Merton F. Self-Related and Parent-Related Verbalizations and Bender-Gestalt Performance of Alcoholics. Quarterly Journal of Studies on Alcohol, 14: 38-48, 1953.

3014. Kato, Akemi. Alcoholics Anonymous Family Groups. Iryo to Fukushi, Tokyo, 6(16): 17-18, 1969.

3015. Kato, Hoichi, Iizuka, Toshifumi, Watanabe, Hiroshi, Hirata, Katsuji, Saito, Takao, Hirashima, Toshio, Itabashi, Masayuki and Hirota, Teruyuki. Esophageal Cancer Associated with Gastric Cancer. Japanese Journal of Clinical Oncology, Tokyo, 11(2): 315-320, 1981.

3016. Kattan, L., Horwitz, J., Caballero, E., Cordua, M. and Marambio, C. Caracteristicas del Alcoholismo en la Mujer y Evaluacion del Resultado de su Tratamiento en Chile. (Characteristics of Alcoholism in Women and Evaluation of its Treatment in Chile.) Acta Psiquiatrica y Psicologica de America Latina, 19: 194-204, 1973.

3017. Katz, Amanda, Morgan, Marsha Y. and Sherlock, Sheila A.
       Alcoholism Treatment in a Medical Setting. Journal
       of Studies on Alcohol, 42(1): 136-143, 1981.

3018. Katz, Barbara J. The Washington Post, 2 July 1978, section 2,
       page 1, column 3. (Alcoholism and Heredity.)

3019. Katz, Judith. Review of You and Your Alcoholic Parent by
       Edith Lynn Hornik. Alcohol Health and Research World,
       Fall: 30, 1974.

3020. Kaufman, Arthur. Gasoline Sniffing Among Children in a Pueblo
       Indian Village. Pediatrics, 51(6): 1060-1064, 1973.

3021. Kaufman, E. The Application of the Basic Principles of Family
       Therapy to the Treatment of Drug and Alcohol Abusers.
       In: Family Therapy of Drug and Alcohol Abuse.
       Eds. E. Kaufman and P.N. Kaufmann. New York: Gardner
       Press, 1979, pages 255-272.

3022. Kaufman, E. Commentary: Variations in the Families of
       Alcoholics. Family Process, 24(3): 377-380, 1985.

3023. Kaufman, E. Current State of Family Intervention in Alcoholism
       Treatment. In: Psychosocial Treatment of Alcoholism.
       Eds. Marc Galanter and E. Mansell Pattison. Washington, D.C.:
       American Psychiatric Press, 1984, pages 1-15.

3024. Kaufman, E. Family Treatment of Substance Abusers. In: Problems
       of the 70's; Solutions for the 80's. Ed. R. Faulkinberry.
       Lafayette, LA: Endac/Print Media, 1980, pages 406-411.

3025. Kaufman, E. Family Who Wouldn't Give Up: Structural-Dynamic Family
       Therapy with a Dry System. In: Power to Change: Family Case
       Studies in the Treatment of Alcoholism. Ed. E. Kaufman.
       New York: Gardner Press, 1984, pages 293-312.

3026. Kaufman, E. Myth and Reality in the Family Patterns and Treatment of
       Substance Abusers. American Journal of Drug and Alcohol Abuse,
       7(3/4): 257-279, 1980.

3027. Kaufman, E. Relationship of Social Class and Ethnicity to Drug
       Abuse. In: Multicultural View of Drug Abuse. Ed. D.E. Smith.
       Cambridge, MA: G.K. Hall/Schenkman, 1978, pages 158-164.

3028. Kaufman, E. A Workable System of Family-Therapy for Drug-Dependence.
       Journal of Psychoactive Drugs, 18(1): 43-50, 1986.

3029. Kaufman, E., Roschmann, J. and Woods, B. A Likable Couple: The
       Use of Interwoven Multiple Family Groups in the Treatment of a
       Blended Alcoholic Family. In: Power to Change: Family Case
       Studies in the Treatment of Alcoholism. Ed. E. Kaufman.
       New York, NY: Gardner Press, 1984, pages 267-291.

3030. Kaufman, Edward. Critical Issues in Family Research in Drug
       Abuse. Journal of Drug Issues, Fall: 463-475, 1985.

3031. Kaufman, Edward. Family Structures of Narcotic Addicts. The
       International Journal of the Addictions, 16: 273-282, 1981.

3032. Kaufman, Edward. Family System Variables in Alcoholism.
       Alcoholism: Clinical and Experimental Research, 8(1):
       4-8, 1984.

3033. Kaufman, Edward. Family Systems and Family Therapy of Substance
       Abuse: An Overview of Two Decades of Research and Clinical
       Experience. International Journal of the Addictions,
       20(6/7): 897-916, 1985.

3034. Kaufman, Edward. Family Therapy: A Treatment Approach with
       Substance Abusers. In: <u>Substance Abuse: Clinical Problems
       and Perspectives</u>. Eds. Joyce H. Lowinson and P. Ruiz.
       Baltimore: Williams and Wilkins, 1981, pages 437-448.

3035. Kaufman, Edward. <u>Family Therapy of Drug & Alcohol Abuse</u>.
       Pamphlet. New York: National Council on Alcoholism, 1979.

3036. Kaufman, Edward (Ed.) <u>Power to Change: Family Case Studies in
       the Treatment of Alcoholism</u>. New York: Gardner Press, 1984.

3037. Kaufman, Edward and Borders, Linda. Adolescent Substance Abuse
       in Anglo-American Families. <u>Journal of Drug Issues</u>,
       <u>14</u>(2): 365-377, 1984.

3038. Kaufman, Edward and Kaufman, Pauline N. <u>Family Therapy of Drug
       and Alcohol Abuse</u>. New York: Gardner Press, 1979.

3039. Kaufman, Edward and Kaufmann, Pauline N. Multiple Family Therapy:
       A New Direction in the Treatment of Drug Abusers. <u>American
       Journal of Drug & Alcohol Abuse</u>, <u>4</u>(4): 467-478, 1977.

3040. Kaufman, Edward and Pattison, E.M. Differential Methods of
       Family Therapy in the Treatment of Alcoholism. <u>Journal of
       Studies on Alcohol</u>, <u>42</u>(11): 951-971, 1981. (Also in:
       <u>Digest of Alcoholism Theory and Application</u>, <u>1</u>(3):
       5-15, 1982.)

3041. Kaufman, Edward and Pattison, E.M. Family and Alcoholism. In:
       <u>Encyclopedic Handbook of Alcoholism</u>. Eds. E. Pattison and
       Edward Kaufman. New York: Gardner Press, 1982, pages 663-672.

3042. Kaufman, Edward and Pattison, E.M. Family and Network Therapy
       in Alcoholism. In: <u>Encyclopedic Handbook of Alcoholism</u>.
       Eds. E. Pattison and Edward Kaufman. New York: Gardner
       Press, 1982, pages 1022-1032.

3043. Kaufman, Irving, Frank, Thomas, Heims, Lora, Herrick, Joan and
       Willer, Lee. Parents of Schizophrenic Children: Workshop,
       1958. 3. Four Types of Defense in Mothers and Fathers
       of Schizophrenic Children. <u>American Journal of
       Orthopsychiatry</u>, <u>29</u>(3): 460-472, 1959.

3044. Kaufmann, Pauline N. Family, Family on the Run, Who is the
       Fastest and the Most Fun? In: <u>Power to Change: Family
       Case Studies in the Treatment of Alcoholism</u>. Ed. Edward
       Kaufman. New York: Gardner Press, 1984, pages 79-97.

3045. Kaufmann, Pauline N. Family Therapy With Adolescent Substance
       Abusers. In: <u>Family Therapy of Drug and Alcohol Abuse</u>.
       Eds. E. Kaufman and P.N. Kaufmann. New York: Gardner Press,
       1979, pages 71-79.

3046. Kaufmann, Pauline and Lilly, M. A Recovering Alcoholic Speaks and
       Her Family Therapist Introduces Her. In: <u>Family Therapy of
       Drug and Alcohol Abuse</u>. Eds. E. Kaufman and P.N. Kaufmann.
       New York: Gardner Press, 1979, pages 243-253.

3047. Kaufmann, Pauline N. and Kaufman, Edward. From Multiple Family
       Therapy to Couples Therapy. In: <u>Family Therapy of Drug
       and Alcohol Abuse</u>. Ed. E. Kaufman. New York: Gardner
       Press, 1979, pages 95-103.

3048. Kaunitz, P. Alcoholism is Not an Illness. <u>Medical World News</u>,
       <u>15</u>(39): 124, 1974.

3049. Kaunitz, Paul E. On the Other Hand. <u>Medical World News</u>,
       <u>15</u>(39): 124, 1974.

3050. Kawakami, F., Fukui, K., Kitabayashi, M., Haga, H., Tani, N., Nabekura, M. and Kato, N. A Survey of Concern for Drinking and Alcoholics 5th Report: The Students of University of Education. Japanese Journal of Alcohol Studies & Drug Dependence, Kyoto, 17(4): 368-376, 1982.

3051. Kay, D.W.K. Assessment of Familial Risks in the Functional Psychoses and Their Application in Genetic Counseling. British Journal of Psychiatry, London, 133: 385-403, 1978.

3052. Kay, D.W.K., Roth, M., Atkinson, M.W., Stephens, D.A. and Garside, R.F. Genetic Hypotheses and Environmental Factors in the Light of Psychiatric Morbidity in the Families of Schizophrenics. British Journal of Psychiatry, 127: 109-118, 1975.

3053. Kaye, Elizabeth. Jason Robards: Recovery from Alcoholism. Loved Backed to Health. Family Health, 10(5): 24-26, 29, 1978.

3054. Keane, A. and Roche, D. Developmental Disorders in the Children of Male Alcoholics. In: Papers Presented at the 20th International Institute on the Prevention and Treatment of Alcoholism, Manchester, England, 1974. Lausanne: International Council on Alcohol and Addictions, 1974, pages 82-90.

3055. Keane, J.S. Factors Related to the Psychological Well-Being of Children of Alcoholics. Paper presented at the National Alcoholism Forum, Houston, April, 1983.

3056. Keane, Jeraldine Spillane. A Study of the Relationships of Perception of Family Environment, Locus of Control, and Quality of Interpersonal Relationships to the Psychological Well-Being of Children of Alcoholics. Dissertation Abstracts International, 43(12): 3848A, 1983.

3057. Keane, T.M., Foy, D.W., Nunn, B. and Tychtarik, R.G. Spouse Contracting to Increase Antabuse Compliance in Alcoholic Veterans. Journal of Clinical Psychology, 40(1): 340-344, 1984.

3058. Kearney, Thomas R. and Taylor, Clarence. Emotionally Disturbed Adolescents with Alcoholic Parents. Acta Paedopsychiatria, Basel, 36: 215-221, 1969.

3059. Keeler, M.H. Alcoholism and Affective Disorder. In: Encyclopedic Handbook of Alcoholism. Eds. E. Pattison and E. Kaufman. New York: Gardner Press, 1982, pages 618-627.

3060. Keene, A. and Roche, D. Developmental Disorders in the Children of Male Alcoholics. Waterford, Ireland: Belmont Park Hospital, 1976.

3061. Kegley, Jeffrey J. Kicking the Booze Blues. Access, 2(4): 34-35, 1979.

3062. Kehoe, J.P. and Abbott, A.P. Suicide and Attempted Suicide in the Yukon Territory. Canadian Psychiatric Association Journal, Ottawa, 20(1): 15-23, 1975.

3063. Keil, T.J. Social Correlates of Female Abstinence from Marijuana: Results of a Household Survey. International Journal of the Addictions, 15: 957-967, 1980.

3064. Keil, T.J., Usui, W.M. and Busch, J.A. Repeat Admissions for Perceived Problem Drinking. A Social Resources Perspective. Journal of Studies on Alcohol, 44(1): 95-108, 1983.

3065. Keil, Thomas J. Sex Role Variations and Women's Drinking: Results from a Household Survey in Pennsylvania. Journal of Studies on Alcohol, 39(5): 859-868, 1978.

3066. Keituri, E. Alkoholistin Isa. (The Fathers of Alcoholics.)
       Alkoholikysymys, Helsinki, 22: 99-123, 1954.

3067. Kellam, Sheppard G., Ensminger, Margaret E. and Simon, Marlene B.
       Mental Health in First Grade and Teenage Drug, Alcohol, and
       Cigarette Use. Drug and Alcohol Dependence, Lausanne,
       5(4): 273-304, 1980.

3068. Keller, C. Alcoholics and Their Families. New Zealand Nursing
       Journal, 69(8): 4-5, 1975.

3069. Keller, J.E. Alcohol, A Family Affair: Help for Families in
       Which There is Alcohol Misuse. Santa Ynez, CA: Kroc
       Foundation, 1977.

3070. Keller, M. Alcohol and Youth. In: Adolescence and Alcohol.
       Eds. J.E. Mayer and W.J. Filstead. Cambridge, MA:
       Ballinger, 1980, pages 245-256.

3071. Kellermann, Joseph L. AA--A Family Affair. Pamphlet.
       Charlotte, NC: Charlotte Council on Alcoholism, 1974.
       (Also in: Addictions, Toronto, 21(1): 20-33, 1974.)

3072. Kellermann, Joseph L. Alcohol is a Family Disease. State Department
       Newsletter, 171(37), 1975.

3073. Kellermann, Joseph L. Alcoholism. A Guide for the Clergy.
       New York: National Council on Alcoholism, 1963.

3074. Kellermann, Joseph L. Alcoholism: How to Help. St. Luke
       Journal, 21(4): 271-279, 1978.

3075. Kellermann, Joseph L. Alcoholism & the Family. A Move from
       Pathology to Process. Center City, MN: Hazelden
       Foundation, 1984.

3076. Kellermann, Joseph L. Focus on the Family. Alcohol Health and
       Research World, Fall: 9-11, 1974.

3077. Kellermann, Joseph L. Guide for the Family of the Alcoholic.
       Long Grove, IL: Kemper Insurance Group, 1972; New York:
       Al-Anon Family Group Headquarters; Center City, MN: Hazelden.

3078. Kellermann, Joseph L. Alcoholism: A Mery-Go-Round Named Denial.
       Addictions, Toronto, 17(4): 1-18, 1970.

3079. Kellermann, Joseph L. A Message of Hope. Pamphlet. Center City,
       MN: Hazelden, no date.

3080. Kellermann, Joseph L. Pastoral Care in Alcoholism. Annals of
       the New York Academy of Sciences, 233: 144-146, 1974.

3081. Kellerman, J. The Souse's Spouse: Victim or Villain? Alcoholism:
       The National Magazine, 3: 26-29, 1981.

3082. Kellermann, Joseph L. and Kellermann, G. The Family in Recovery.
       Recovery Newsletter Magazine in Alcoholism The National
       Magazine, Mar-Apr: 9, 1985.

3083. Kellermann, Joseph L. and Kellermann, G. Family Triangle. Recovery
       Newsletter Magazine in Alcoholism and Addiction Magazine,
       Sept-Oct: 13, 1985.

3084. Kellermann, Joseph L. and Kellerman, G. Make Holidays Holy Days.
       Alcoholism The National Magazine, 5(2): R7, 1984.

3085. Kellett, Peter. Attempted Suicide in Durban: A General Hospital
       Study. South African Medical Journal, Capetown, 40(5):
       90-95, 1966.

3086.   Kelley, C.K. and King. G.D. Behavioral Correlates of the 2-7-8
        MMPI Profile Type in Students at a University Mental Health
        Center. Journal of Consulting and Clinical Psychology,
        47: 679-685, 1979.

3087.   Kelley, D. Alcoholism and the Family. Maryland State Medical
        Journal, 22: 25-30, 1973.

3088.   Kelley, J. USA Today, 19 December 1984. (Drunken-Driving
        Communication Gap?)

3089.   Kellock, Karen Marie. A Systems-Theoretic View of Pathologic
        Interaction: Alcoholism and Al-Anon. Dissertation
        Abstracts International, 37(6): 3151-3152B, 1976.

3090.   Kelly, Dorothy. Alcoholism and the Family. Maryland State Medical
        Journal, 22(1): 25-30, 1973.

3091.   Kelsey, F.D. Early Signs of Mental Illness. 2. Nursing Times,
        London, 63(14): 463-464, 1967.

3092.   Kelsey, Jennifer L., Dwyer, Terence, Holford, Theodore R. and
        Bracken, Michael B. Maternal Smoking and Congenital
        Malformations: An Epidemiological Study. Journal of
        Epidemiology and Community Health, 32: 102-107, 1978.

3093.   Kempler, Hyman L. and MacKenna, Pat. Drug Abusing Adolescents
        and Their Families: A Structural View and Treatment
        Approach. American Journal of Orthopsychiatry, 45(2):
        223-224, 1975.

3094.   Kendall, R.F. The Context and Implications of Drinking and Drug
        Use Among High School and College Students. Doctoral
        Dissertation. (University Microfilms No. 76-19514.)
        New York University, 1976.

3095.   Kendis, J. The Effect of Attitudes in the Therapy of the Alcoholic.
        British Journal of Addiction, Edinburgh, 62: 307-315, 1967.

3096.   Kendler, Kenneth S. A Twin Study of Individuals with Both
        Schizophrenia and Alcoholism. British Journal of Psychiatry,
        147: 48-53, 1985.

3097.   Kendler, Kenneth S., Gruenberg, Alan M. and Tsuang, Ming T.
        Psychiatric Illness in First-Degree Relatives of
        Schizophrenic and Surgical Control Patients. Archives
        of General Psychiatry, 42(8): 770-779, 1985.

3098.   Kennedy, Dennis L. Behavior of Alcoholics and Spouses in a
        Simulation Game Situation. The Journal of Nervous and
        Mental Disease, 162(1): 23-34, 1976.

3099.   Kennedy, Peter and Hird, F. Description and Evaluation of a
        Short-Stay Admission Ward. British Journal of Psychiatry,
        London, 136: 205-215, 1980.

3100.   Kennedy, W.J. and Slater, W.C. A Study of the Application of
        the Sex-Linked Recessive Inheritance Model for Alcoholism
        with Weighted and Unweighted Admission Standards Utilizing
        Genetic Profiles. In: Alcoholism: A Modern Perspective.
        Ed. P. Golding. Lancaster, England: MTP Press, 1982, pages
        503-508.

3101.   Kent, P. An American Woman and Alcohol. New York: Holt,
        Rinehart and Winston, 1967.

3102.   Kenward, K.A. Study of the Impact of an Employee Assistance
        Program on the Medical Care Costs of Employees and Their
        Family Members. Dissertation Abstracts International,

3103. Kenward, Kevin and Rissover, Jean. A Family Systems Approach to the Treatment and Prevention of Alcoholism: A Review. Family Therapy, 7(2): 97-106, 1980.

3104. Kenya, P.R. and Asal, N.R. An Epidemiological Study of Esophageal Carcinoma in Oklahoma City Hospitals 1970-1975. American Journal of Epidemiology, 106(3): 24, 1977.

3105. Kephart, William M. Drinking and Marital Disruption. A Research Note. Quarterly Journal of Studies on Alcohol, 15: 63-73, 1954.

3106. Kepner, Elaine. Application of Learning Theory to the Etiology and Treatment of Alcoholism. Quarterly Journal of Studies on Alcohol, 25: 279-291, 1964.

3107. Kern, Joseph C. County of Nassau, Department of Drug & Alcohol Addiction, Mineola, New York. In: Services for Children of Alcoholics. Symposium Held in September, 1979 at Silver Spring, Maryland. Ed. U.S. National Institute on Alcohol Abuse and Alcoholism. Research Monograph No. 4, DHHS Publication No. ADM 81-1007. Washington, D.C.: U.S. Government Printing Office, 1981, pages 102-109.

3108. Kern, Joseph C., Hassett, Carol, Collipp, Platon, Bridges, Carolyn, Solomon, Miriam and Condren, Raymond. Children of Alcoholics: Locus of control, Mental Age and Zinc Level. Journal of Psychiatric Treatment and Evaluation, 3(2): 169-173, 1981.

3109. Kern, Joseph C., Paul, Stewart R. and Tippman, Joan. Family as the "Primary Client" in Alcoholism Intervention Programs. Paper presented at the Alcohol and Drug Problems Association Conference, San Francisco, December, 1974.

3110. Kern, Joseph C., Schmelter, William and Fanelli, Michael. A Comparison of Three Alcoholism Treatment Populations. Implications for Treatment. Journal of Studies on Alcohol, 39(5): 785-792, 1978.

3111. Kern, Joseph C., Tippman, Joan, Fortgang, Jeffrey and Paul, Stewart R. A Treatment Approach for Children of Alcoholics. Journal of Drug Education, 7(3): 207-218, 1977-1978.

3112. Kessel, N., Hore, B.D., Makenjuola, J.D.A., Redmond, A.D., Rossall, C.J., Rees, D.W., Chand, T.G., Gordon, M., Wallace, P.C. Alcoholism: The Manchester Detoxification Service: Description and Evaluation. The Lancet, 1(8381): 839-842, 1984.

3113. Kesselman, Martin S., Solomon, Joel, Beaudett, Malcolm and Thornton, Barbara. Alcoholism and Schizophrenia. In: Alcoholism and Clinical Psychiatry. Ed. Joel Solomon. New York: Plenum Medical Book Company, 1982, pages 69-80.

3114. Kessler, I.I., Kulcar, Z., Zimolo, A., Grgurevic, M., Strnad, M. and Goodwin, B.J. Cervical Cancer in Yugoslavia. II. Epidemiologic Factors of Possible Etiologic Significance. Journal of the National Cancer Institute, 53(1): 51-60, 1974.

3115. Kesteven, W.H. Discussion on the Report of the Committee on the Society Upon the Heredity of Inebriety. Proceedings of the Society on the Studies of Inebriety, London, 69: 3-4, 1901.

3116. Keynes, J.M. Influence of Parental Alcoholism. Journal of the Royal Statistical Society, London, 73: 114-121, 1910. (Also in: Journal of the Royal Statistical Society, London, 74: 339-345, 1911.)

3117. Keyserlingk, H. Jugendgefahrdung Durch Alkohol. (Youth
       Endangered by Alcohol.) Psychiatrie, Neurologie und
       Medizinische Psychologie, Leipzig, 15: 270-276, 1963.

3118. Khan, M.Z. and Unnitham, N. Prabha. Association of Socio-Economic
       Factors with Drug Use Among College Students in an Indian
       Town. Bulletin on Narcotics, 31(2): 61-69, 1979.

3119. Khantzian, Edward J. Organic Problems in the Aged: Brain
       Syndromes and Alcoholism -- Discussion: On the Nature
       of the Dependency and Denial Problems of Alcoholics.
       Journal of Geriatric Psychiatry, 11(2): 191-202, 1978.

3120. Khwanmitra, S. Thai Alcoholic's Wives. Paper presented at
       the 31st International Congress on Alcoholism and Drug
       Dependence, Bangkok, February, 1975, pages 673-674.

3121. Kielholz, P. Addiction Hazards. Bulletin der Schweizerischen
       Akadenne de Medizinischen Wissenschaften, 26(5): 366-373, 1971.

3122. Kielholz, P. Alcohol and Depression. British Journal of Addiction,
       Edinburgh, 65: 187-193, 1970.

3123. Kielholz, P. and Battegay, R. Vergleichende Untersuchungen Uber
       Die Genese und den Verlauf der Drogenabhangigkeit und des
       Alkoholismus. (Comparative Studies of the Causes and Development
       of Drug Dependence and Alcoholism.) Schweizerische Medizinische
       Wochenschrift, 97: 893-898, 1967.

3124. Kiianmaa, K and Tabakoff, B. Neurochemical Correlates of
       Tolerance and Strain Differences in the Neurochemical
       Effects of Ethanol. Pharmacology, Biochemistry and
       Behavior, 18(Supplement 1): 383-388, 1983.

3125. Kilgus, R.H. Analysis of Prognostic Indicators in an Alcoholic
       Patient Population. Doctoral Dissertation. Northern
       Illinois University, 1978.

3126. Kilibarda, M. and Stojiljkovic, S. Znacaj Psihijatrijske
       Depistaze u Prevenciji Alkoholizma. (The Importance of
       Psychiatric Screening in the Prevention of Alcoholism.)
       Alkoholizam, Beograd, 8(4): 72-79, 1968.

3127. Killorin, Eleanor and Olson, David H. Chaotic Flippers in
       Treatment. In: Power to Change: Family Case Studies
       in the Treatment of Alcoholism. Ed. Edward Kaufman.
       New York: Gardner Press, 1984, pages 99-129.

3128. Kilty, Keith M. Attitudinal and Normative Variables as Predictors
       of Drinking Behavior. Journal of Studies on Alcohol, 39(7):
       1178-1194, 1978.

3129. Kimball, Kerry E., Healey, James C., McIntire, Walter G. and
       Smith, Donald. Families in Alcoholic Transaction: The
       Family Systems Approach to Alcoholism in the Family and
       Family Rehabilitation. International Journal of Family
       Psychiatry, 3(1): 57-67, 1982.

3130. Kimball, Kerry Eugene Kerwin. The Family in Alcoholic Transaction
       an Empirical Test of Family Systems Theory. Dissertation
       Abstracts International, 42(10): 4607A, 1981.

3131. Kimmel, Carol K. A Prevention Program with Punch -- The National
       PTA's Alcohol Education Project. Journal of School Health
       46(4): 208-210, 1976.

3132. Kincannon, J.C. Alcohol Problems in Social Networks: A Phoenix
       Too Frequent. In: Alcoholism: A Modern Perspective.
       Lancaster, England: MTP Press, 1982, pages 53-63.

3133. King, B. Betraying the Alcoholic or Protecting the Child? The Dilemma of Confidentiality. Alcoholism: The National Magazine, 3(7): 59-61, 1983.

3134. King, B., Bissell, L. and Holding, E. The Usefulness of the Disease Concept of Alcoholism in Working With Wives of Alcoholics. Social Work in Health Care, New York, 3: 443-455, 1978.

3135. King, L.J. The Depressine Syndrome: A Follow-Up Study of 130 Professionals Working Overseas. The American Journal of Psychiatry, 132(6): 636-640, 1975.

3136. King, L.J., Murphy, G.E., Robins, L.N. and Darvish, H. Alcohol Abuse: A Crucial Factor in the Social Problems of Negro Men. American Journal of Psychiatry, 125: 1682-1690, 1969.

3137. King, L.J. and Pittman, G.D. A Six-Year Follow-Up Study of 65 Adolescent Patients: Natural History of Affective Disorders in Adolescence. Archives of General Psychiatry, 22(3): 230-236, 1970.

3138. King, Lewis M. Alcoholism: Studies Regarding Black Americans -- 1977-1980. In: Black Alcoholism: Toward a Comprehensive Understanding. Eds. Thomas D. Watts and Roosevelt Wright, Jr. Springfield, IL: Charles C. Thomas, 1983, pages 37-63.

3139. King, Mary-Claire, Lee, Geraldine M., Spinner, Nancy B., Thomson, Glenys and Wrensch, Margaret R. Genetic Epidemiology. In: Annual Review of Public Health, Volume 5. Eds. Lester Breslow, Jonathan E. Fielding and Lester B. Lave. Palo Alto, CA: Annual Reviews Inc., 1984, pages 1-52.

3140. Kinney, Jean and Leaton, Gwen. Effects of Alcohol on Behavior. In: Loosening the Grip: A Handbook of Alcohol Information. St. Louis: C.V. Mosby Co., 1978, pages 116-126.

3141. Kinney, Jean and Leaton, Gwen. Effects of Alcoholism on the Family. In: Loosening the Grip: A Handbook of Alcohol Information. St. Louis: C.V. Mosby Co., 1978, pages 127-131.

3142. Kinney, Jean and Leaton, Gwen. Etiology of Alcoholism. In: Loosening the Grip: A Handbook of Alcohol Information. St. Louis: C.V. Mosby Co., 1978, pages 55-75.

3143. Kinney, Jean and Leaton, Gwen. Special Populations. In: Loosening the Grip: A Handbook of Alcohol Information. St. Louis: C.V. Mosby Co., 1978, pages 217-265.

3144. Kinney, Jean and Leaton, Gwen. Treatment. In: Loosening the Grip: A Handbook of Alcohol Information. St. Louis: C.V. Mosby Co., 1978, pages 132-192.

3145. Kinney, Jean and Leaton, Gwen. Understanding Alcohol. St. Louis: C.V. Mosby, 1982.

3146. Kinney, J.M., Madsen, B., Fleming, T. and Haapala, D.A. Homebuilders: Keeping Families Together. Journal of Consulting and Clinical Psychology, 45: 667-673, 1977.

3147. Kinsella, Samuel B. Family Group Counseling for Alcoholics. Journal of Employment Counseling, 7(2): 46-48, 1970.

3148. Kinsey, B.A. The Female Alcoholic: A Social Psychological Study. Springfield, IL: Charles C. Thomas, 1966.

3149. Kinsey, B.A. Psychological Factors in Alcoholic Women from a State Hospital Sample. American Journal of Psychiatry, 124: 1463-1466, 1968.

3150. Kinsey, B.A. Sociocultural Characteristics of a Group of
       Female Alcoholics. Analysis of Data: 1. Sociocultural
       Characteristics of the Sample. In: The Female Alcoholic:
       A Social Psychological Study. Springfield, IL: Charles C.
       Thomas, 1966, pages 80-111.

3151. Kinsey, B.A. Summary and Implications of a Study of the
       Symbolic-Interaction Approach to Alcoholism. Summary and
       Implications. In: The Female Alcoholic: A Social
       Psychological Study. Springfield, Illinois: Charles C.
       Thomas, 1966, pages 143-186.

3152. Kinsey, Barry A. and Phillips, Lorne. Evaluation of Anomy as a
       Predisposing or Developmental Factor in Alcohol Addiction.
       Quarterly Journal of Studies on Alcohol, 29(4): 892-898,
       1968.

3153. Kirk, J. Alcoholism and Child Welfare. Medical Press and
       Circular, 154: 70-72, 1917.

3154. Kirk, J. Alcoholism and Child Welfare in War Time. British
       Journal of Inebriety, 14: 141-155, 1917.

3155. Kirk, J. The Incidence of Alcoholism in a Family Practice.
       Medical Times, 103(6): 36-40, 1975.

3156. Kirk, Stuart A. and Masi, James. Aftercare for Alcoholics:
       Services of Community Mental Health Centers. Journal of
       Studies on Alcohol, 39(3): 545-547, 1978.

3157. Kirkland, K.D. and Bauer, C.A. MMPI Traits of Incestuous Fathers.
       Journal of Clinical Psychology, 38(3): 645-649, 1982.

3158. Kirkpatrick, J.B. and Pearson, J. Fatal Cerebral Injury in
       the Elderly. Journal of the American Geriatrics Society,
       26: 489-497, 1978.

3159. Kissin, Benjamin. Medical Management of the Alcoholic Patient.
       In: The Biology of Alcoholism. Volume 5. Treatment
       and Rehabilitation of the Chronic Alcoholic. Eds. Benjamin
       Kissin and Henri Begleiter. New York: Plenum Press, 1977,
       pages 53-103.

3160. Kitamura, Akihide. A Comparative Study of Suicide in Children
       and Adolescents: West Germany and Japan. Japanese Journal
       of Child & Adolescent Psychiatry, 23(2): 124-137, 1982.

3161. Kitamura, Toshinori. Family History Questionnaire. Bulletin of
       the Seishin-Igaku Institute, 21: 153-155, 1977/78.

3162. Kittredge, Lee D., Franklin, Jack L., Thrasher, Jean H. and
       Berdiansky, Harold A. Estimating a Population in Need of
       Alcoholism Services: A New Approach. The International
       Journal of the Addictions, 12(2-3): 205-226, 1977.

3163. Kittrell, R.C. and Miller. L.P. Don't Feel Rained On. Pamphlet.
       Raleigh: North Carolina Department of Human Resources, 1981.

3164. Klagsbrun, Micheline and Davis, Donald I. Substance Abuse and
       Family Interaction. Family Process, 16(2): 149-164, 1977.

3165. Klassen, D. and Hornstra, R.K. Prevalence of Problem Drinking
       in a Community Survey. Missouri Medicine: Journal of the
       Missouri State Medical Association, 73(2): 81-84, 1976.

3166. Klein, Dorie A. Can This Marriage Be Saved?: Battery and Sheltering.
       Crime and Social Justice, 12(Winter): 19-33, 1979.

3167. Klein, Dorie A. Drinking and Battering: Alcohol and Gender
       Domination. Paper presented to the Society for the Study
       of Social Problems, 1981.

3168. Klein, R.M. Interaction Processes in Alcoholic and Non-Alcoholic
       Marital Dyads. Doctoral Dissertation. Washington
       University, 1978.

3169. Klerman, Gerald L. Prevention of Alcoholism. In: Alcoholism
       and Clinical Psychiatry. Ed. Joel Solomon. New York:
       Plenum Medical Book Company, 1982, pages 21-33.

3170. Kline, Michael V. Working with the Woman Alcoholic: Emerging
       Awareness and Training Needs of Alcoholism Caregivers.
       In: Women Who Drink: Alcoholic Experience and Psycho-
       therapy. Ed. Vasanti Burtle. Springfield, IL: Charles C.
       Thomas, 1979, pages 175-194.

3171. Klinefelter, Harry Fitch III. Cognitive and Experimental Group
       Counseling for University Students of Alcoholic Parentage.
       Dissertation Abstracts International, 43(10): 3218A, 1982.

3172. Klinge, V. A Comparison of Parental and Adolescent MMPIs as
       Related to Substance Use. International Journal of the
       Addictions, 18(8): 1179-1185, 1983.

3173. Klinge, V. and Vaziri, H. Characteristics of Drug Abusers in
       an Adolescent In-Patient Psychiatric Facility. Diseases
       of the Nervous System, 38: 275-279, 1977.

3174. Kloepper, Howard W., Leonard, Wilbert M. II, and Huang, Lucy
       Jen. A Comparison of the "Only Child" and the Siblings'
       Perceptions of Parental Norms and Sanctions. Adolescence,
       16(63): 641-655, 1981.

3175. Kluge, Karl J. and Strassburg, Barbara. Wollen Jugendliche
       durch Alkoholkonsum Hemmungen Ablegen, Kontakte Knupfen
       bzw ihre Probleme Ertranken? Eine Stellungnahme zu
       Aussagen der Bundesregierung aus der Sicht der Kolner
       Verhaltensauffallingenpauagogik. (Alcohol Abuse in
       Adolescents -- A Means of Discarding Inhibitions, of
       Establishing Contacts, or of Drowning One's Problems.)
       Praxis Der Kinderpsychologie und Kinderpsychiatrie,
       30(1): 24-32, 1981.

3176. Kmoskova, L. and Matejcek, Z. Deti v Alkoholicke Rodine.
       (Children in the Alcoholic Family.) Protialkoholicky
       Obzor, Bratislava, 7: 171-174, 1972.

3177. Knauert, Arthur P. Perspective from a Private Practice:
       The Differential Diagnosis of Alcoholism. Family and
       Community Health, 2(2): 1-12, 1979.

3178. Knight, B.J., Osborn, S.G. and West, D.J. Early Marriage
       and Criminal Tendency in Males. British Journal of
       Criminology, London, 17(4): 348-360, 1977.

3179. Knight, James. Alcoholism and Other Drug Dependencies: The
       Family. Paper presented at the University of Utah School
       of Alcoholism and Other Drug Dependencies, June, 1970.
       (Also as: Manual Supplement. New Orleans, LA, 1971.)

3180. Knight, James A. The Family in the Crisis of Alcoholism.
       In: Alcoholism: A Practical Treatment Guide.
       Eds. Stanley E. Gitglow and Herbert S. Peyser. New York:
       Grune & Stratton, 1980, pages 205-228.

3181. Knitzer, Jane and Olson, Lynn. The Children and Their Families:
       Some Profiles. In: Unclaimed Children: The Failure of
       Public Responsibility to Children and Adolescents in Need
       of Mental Health Services. Washington, D.C.: Children's
       Defense Fund, 1982, pages 2-13.

3182. Knitzer, Jane and Olson, Lynn. The Federal Role: The Shadowy
       Presence. In: Unclaimed Children: The Failure of Public
       Responsibility to Children and Adolescents in Need of Mental
       Health Services. Washington, D.C.: Children's Defense
       Fund, 1982, pages 80-92.

3183. Knitzer, Jane and Olson, Lynn. The Services: Definitions and
       Profiles. In: Unclaimed Children: The Failure of Public
       Responsibility to Children and Adolescents in Need of
       Mental Health Services. Washington, D.C.: Children's
       Defense Fund, 1982, pages 14-41.

3184. Knop, Joachim. Premorbid Assessment of Young Men at High Risk
       for Alcoholism. In: Recent Developments in Alcoholism.
       Volume 3. High-Risk Studies, Prostaglandins and
       Leukotrienes, Cardiovascular Effects, Cerebral Function
       in Social Drinkers. Ed. Marc Galanter. New York, NY:
       Plenum Press, 1985, pages 53-64.

3185. Knop, Joachim. Selection of Variables in a Prospective Study of
       Young Men at High Risk for Alcoholism. Acta Psychiatrica
       Scandinavica, Copenhagen, 285: 347-352, 1980.

3186. Knop, J., Goodwin, D., Teasdale, T.W., Mikkelsen, U. and
       Schulsinger, F. Danish Prospective Study of Young Males
       at High Risk for Alcoholism. In: Longitudinal Research
       in Alcoholism. Eds. Donald E. Goodwin, Katherine Teilmann
       Van Dusen and Sarnoff A. Mednick. Boston: Kluwer Academic
       Publishers, 1984, pages 107-124. (Also in: Journal of
       Studies on Alcohol, 46(4): 273-278, 1985.)

3187. Knott, David H., Fink, Robert D. and Morgan, Jack C. After
       Detoxification -- The Physician's Role in the Initial Treatment
       Phase of Alcoholism. In: Alcoholism: A Practical Treatment
       Guide. Eds. Stanley E. Gitglow and Herbert S. Peyser.
       New York: Grune and Stratton, 1980, pages 89-102.

3188. Knott, David H., Thomson, Mal J. and Beard, James D. The Forgotten
       Addict. American Family Physician, 3(6): 92-95, 1971.

3189. Knowles, Philip, Smith, James W. and Lemere, Frederick. A Longitudinal
       Analysis of Patient Characteristics at a Private Alcoholism
       Hospital. Journal of Studies on Alcohol, 44(3): 524-529, 1983.

3190. Knowlton, J.M. and Chaitin, R.D. Detachment: Seven Simple Steps.
       Pamphlet. Morristown, NJ: PIP, 1985.

3191. Knowlton, J.M. and Chaitin, R.D. Enabling. Pamphlet. Morristown,
       NJ: PIP, 1985.

3192. Knox, Wilma J. Objective Psychological Measurement and Alcoholism:
       Review of Literature. Psychological Reports, 38(3 Pt 2):
       1023-1050, 1976.

3193. Knudson, Doris Gonzalez. Interpersonal Dynamics and Mothers'
       Involvement in Father-Daughter Incest in Puerto Rico.
       Dissertation Abstracts International, 42(7): 3305A, 1981.

3194. Knupfer, G. Epidemiologic Studies and Control Programs in Alcoholism.
       V. The Epidemiology of Problem Drinking. American Journal of
       Public Health and the Nation's Health, 57(6): 973-986, 1967.

3195. Knupfer, G. Problems Associated with Drunkenness in Women:
       Some Research Issues. In: Alcohol and Health Monograph
       No. 4: Special Population Issues. Washington, D.C.:
       U.S. Government Printing Office, 1982, pages 3-39.

3196. Knupfer, G. Reciprocal Percpetion of Personality Traits by
       Married Couples. Working Papers, 2: 15, 1965.

3197. Knutsen, E. Family Therapy with Physicians: A Family Perspective
       on the Etiology and Treatment of Impairment of Physicians.
       Paper presented at a Conference Titled What You Need to Know
       About Alcohol Impairment in Physicians, San Francisco, March,
       1978, pages 29-38.

3198. Koch, Alberta. Family Stress, Personal Resources, & Alcoholism.
       Paper presented at the National Council on Family Relations
       Annual Meeting, St. Paul, MN, October, 1983.

3199. Koebberling, J., Bengsch, N., Brueggeboes, B., Schwarck, H.,
       Tillil, H. and Weber, M. The Chlorpropamide Alcohol Flush
       Lack of Specificity for Familial Noninsulin Dependent
       Diabetes. Diabetologia, 19(4): 359-363, 1980.

3200. Kogan, K.L. and Jackson, J.K. Alcoholism: The Fable of the
       Noxious Wife. Mental Hygiene, 49: 428-437, 1965.

3201. Kogan, K.L. and Jackson, J.K. Conventional Sex Role Stereotypes
       and Actual Perceptions. Psychological Reports, 13:
       27-30, 1963.

3202. Kogan, K.L. and Jackson, J.K. Patterns of Atypical Perceptions of
       Self and Spouse in Wives of Alcoholics. Quarterly Journal of
       Studies on Alcohol, 25(3): 555-557, 1964.

3203. Kogan, K.L. and Jackson, J.K. Personality Adjustment and Childhood
       Experiences. Journal of Health and Human Behavior, 5: 50-54,
       1964.

3204. Kogan, K.L. and Jackson, J.K. Role Perceptions in Wives of Alcoholics
       and of Nonalcoholics. Quarterly Journal of Studies on Alcohol,
       24(4): 627-639, 1963.

3205. Kogan, K.L. and Jackson, J.K. Some Concomitants of Personal
       Difficulties in Wives of Alcoholics and Nonalcoholics.
       Quarterly Journal of Studies on Alcohol, 26(4): 595-604, 1965.

3206. Kogan, K.L. and Jackson, J.K. Some Role Perceptions of Wives of
       Alcoholics. Psychological Reports, 9(1): 119-124, 1961.

3207. Kogan, K.L. and Jackson, J.K. Stress, Personality and Emotional
       Disturbance in Wives of Alcoholics. Quarterly Journal of
       Studies on Alcohol, 26(3): 486-495, 1965.

3208. Kogan, Kate L., Fordyce, Wilbert E. and Jackson, Joan K. Personality
       Disturbance in Wives of Alcoholics. Quarterly Journal of Studies
       on Alcohol, 24: 227-238, 1963.

3209. Kohnlein, G. and Mende, W. Alkoholismus -- Ein Vordringliche
       Aufgabenbereich der Sozialpsychiatrie. (Alcoholism -- An
       Urgent Task for Social Psychiatry.) Munchene Medizinische
       Wochenschr, 112(22): 1050-1053, 1970.

3210. Kok, Jensen A. Insufficiency of Primary Treatment of Pulmonary
       Tuberculosis in Relation to Marriage and Abuse of Alcohol.
       Scandinavian Journal of Respiratory Diseases, 53(5):
       274-279, 1972.

3211. Kolata, G.B. Teratogens Acting Through Males. Science, 202:
       733, 1978.

3212. Kolb, Douglas and Gunderson, E.K. Eric. Antisocial Histories in
      Young Alcoholics. San Diego, CA: Naval Health Research
      Center, 1976.

3213. Kolb, Douglas, Gunderson, E.K. Eric and Bucky, Steven F.
      Outcomes for Recidivists in Navy Alcohol Rehabilitation
      Programs. Military Medicine, 142(6): 435-437, 1977.

3214. Kolb, Douglas, Gunderson, Eric K. and Bucky, Steven. Prognostic
      Indicators for Black and White Alcoholics in the U.S. Navy.
      Journal of Studies on Alcohol, 37(7): 890-899, 1976.

3215. Koljonen, H. Alkoholistien Vaimojen Ryhmatoiminta. (The Group Work
      of the Wives of Alcoholics.) Alkoholikysymys, Helsinki, 26:
      69-93, 1958.

3216. Koller, K.M. and Castanos, J.N. Attempted Suicide and Alcoholism.
      Medical Journal of Australia, 2: 835-837, 1968.

3217. Koller, K.M. and Castanos, J.N. Family Background and Life
      Situation in Alcoholics: A Comparative Study of Parental
      Deprivation and Other Features in Australians. Archives
      of General Psychiatry, 21: 602-610, 1969.

3218. Koller, K.M. and Williams, W.T. Early Prenatal Deprivation and
      Later Behavioural Outcomes: Cluster Analysis Study of
      Normal and Abnormal Groups. Australian & New Zealand
      Journal of Psychiatry, 8(2): 89-96, 1974.

3219. Kolonel, Laurence. Smoking and Drinking Patterns among Different
      Ethnic Groups in Hawaii U.S.A. In: National Cancer
      Institute Monographs, No. 53. Second Symposium on
      Epidemiology and Cancer Registries in the Pacific Basin,
      Maui, Hawaii, U.S.A., January, 1978. Ed. B.E. Henderson.
      Bethesda, MD: National Cancer Institute, 1979, pages 81-88.

3220. Kolonel, Laurence N., Hirohata, Tomio and Nomura, Abraham, M.
      Adequacy of Survey Data Collected from Substitute Respondents.
      American Journal of Epidemiology, 106(6): 476-484, 1977.

3221. Kolonel, Laurence N. and Lee, J. Husband-Wife Correspondence in
      Smoking, Drinking and Dietary Habits. The American Journal
      of Clinical Nutrition, 34: 99-104, 1981.

3222. Kolpakov, M.N. Influence of Alcoholism on Degeneration, Dying
      Out of Posterity, and Its Connection with Mental Disease.
      Voenno-Meditsinkii Zhurnal, 79: 1255-1286, 1901.

3223. Kondek, Jadwiga and Lusina, M. Doniesienia Z Badan. (Research
      Reports.) Problemy Alkoholizmu, Warsaw, 6(297): 1980.

3224. Konieczna, Wanda, Narojek, Lucyna and Siczek, Jadwiga. Wplyw
      Czynnikow Srodowiskowych Na Stan Odzywienia Dzieci I
      Mlodziezy W Wietu Szlcolnym. Czesc. I. Charakterystyka
      Srodowiska Rodzinnego I Ocena Sposobu Zywienia Dzieci I
      Mlodziezy. Influence of Environmental Factors on Nutritional
      Status of School Children and Youth. I. Characteristics of
      Family Environment and Evaluation of Nutrition Habits of
      Children and Youth. Roczniki Panstwowego Zakladu Higieny,
      Warsaw, 19(2): 213-220, 1968.

3225. Konovsky, M. and Wilsnack, S.C. Social Drinking and Self-Esteem
      in Married Couples. Journal of Studies on Alcohol, 43(3):
      319-333, 1982.

3226. Kooi, Ronald Charles Vander. An Analysis of Drinking Practices
      and Problems Among Male Undergraduates at a Midwestern
      University. Master's Thesis, Western Michigan Universtiy.
      Lansing: Michigan State Board of Alcoholism, 1961.

3227.   Koppisch, Arthur. Alcoholism and the Family. Journal of Perth Amboy General Hospital, 3(4): 18-23, 1974.

3228.   Korcok, Milan. Children of Alcoholics Comprise by Share of Society's Future. Focus on Alcohol and Drug Issues, 6(4): 2-3, 1981.

3229.   Korlath, M.J. Alcoholism in Battered Women: A Report of Advocacy Services to Clients in a Detoxification Facility. Victimology, 4(2): 292-299, 1979.

3230.   Kortteinen, M. Turhapuro Syndrooma. (Turhapuro Syndrome.) Alkoholipolitiikka, 48(2): 60-67, 1983.

3231.   Kos, M., Kryspin-Exner, K. and Zapotoczky, H.G. Studies on the Mental Status of Children of Alcoholics. Wiener Zeitschrif fur Nervenheilkunde und deren Grenzebebieten, 26: 197-212, 1968. (Also in: Quarterly Journal of Studies on Alcohol, 31: 1012, 1970.)

3232.   Koslacz, Andrzej, Knyba, Edmund and Kornacki, Lech. (Przyczyny Nawrotow Do Nalogu W Ocenie Pacjentow I Ich Rodzin.) Causes of Relapses into Intoxication as Seen by Patients and Their Families. Problemy Alkoholizmu, Warsaw, 22(9): 9-12, 1974.

3233.   Kosten, T.R., Rounsaville, B.J. and Kleber, H.D. Parental Alcoholism in Opioid Addicts. Journal of Nervous and Mental Disease, 173(8): 461-469, 1985.

3234.   Kostitch, A. Experimental Evidence Bearing Upon Alcoholic Heredity. Scientific Temperance Journal, 30: 206-210, 1922.

3235.   Kosugi, Yoshihiro and Tanaka, Misono. Parental Deprivation, Birth Order and Alcoholism. Japanese Journal of Studies on Alcohol, Kyoto, 10(3): 70-77, 1975.

3236.   Kosviner, Adele, Hawks, David and Webb, M.G.T. Cannabis Use Amongst British University Students. I. Prevalence Rates and Differences Between Students Who Have Tried Cannabis and Those Who Have Never Tried It. British Journal of Addiction, Edinburgh, 69(1): 35-60, 1969.

3237.   Kotis, John P. Initial Sessions of Group Counseling with Alcoholics and Their Spouses. Social Casework, 49(4): 228-232, 1968.

3238.   Kotis, John P. Study of the Verbal Interaction in the Initial Session of Group Counseling with Marital Pairs in Which One Spouse is Alcoholic and the Other is Not. Doctoral Dissertation. Philadelphia: University of Pennsylvania, 1965.

3239.   Koumans, Alfred J.R. and Fleming, Ronald C. A Personal Assistance Program for Troubled Employees at a Large University: Formation, Implementation, and Results. Journal of the American College Health Association, 28(4): 218-221, 1980.

3240.   Kovach, J.A. Relationship Between Treatment Failures of Alcoholic Women and Incestuous Histories with Possible Implications for Post-Traumatic Stress Disorder Symptomatology. Dissertation Abstracts International, 44(3): 710A, 1983.

3241.   Kowalson, Bella. Metabolic Dysperception. The Role of the Family Physician in Its Diagnosis and Management. In: Orthomolecular Psychiatry. Treatment of Schizophrenia. Eds. David Hawkins and Linus Pauling. San Francisco: W.H. Freeman and Co., 1973, 404-410.

3242. Koyake, Daiten. Drinking and Delinquency. Kesu Kenkyu, Tokyo,
       117: 60-64, 1970.

3243. Koznar, Jan, Matijek, Gustav and Uhrova, Alena. Results of
       Retrospective Study of the Family Conditions of Problem
       Children in Counseling. Ceskoslovenska Psychologie,
       23(5): 365-374, 1979.

3244. Kraft, S.P. Typology of Family Social Environments for Families
       of Alcoholics. Doctoral Dissertation (University Microfilms
       No. 77-25112). George Peabody College for Teachers, 1977.

3245. Kraines, S.H. Therapy of the Chronic Depressions. Diseases of
       the Nervous System, 28(9): 577-584, 1967.

3246. Krammeier, M.L. Biographic, Cognitive, Demographic and Personality
       Difference Between Adolescents From Families With Identifiable
       Alcohol Problems and From Families Without Identifiable Alcohol
       Problems. Doctoral Dissertation. (University Microfilms No.
       69-16274.) Grand Forks: University of North Dakota, 1969.

3247. Krampen, Gunter and Nispel, Luise. Zur Effektivitat Stationarer
       Kurzzeitbehandlungen Von Alkoholikern. (Effectiveness of a
       Short-Term Treatment of Alcoholics: A One-Year Follow-Up.)
       Suchtgefahren, 29(4): 345-349, 1983.

3248. Krampen, Gunter and Nispel, Luise. Ein Jahr Danach-Selbst und
       Fremdkatamnestische Befunde Zur Situation Von Patienten Einer
       Gwochigen Alkohol-Entziehungskur. One Year Later--Self and
       Other's Recalled Reports of the Situation of Patients of
       a 6-Week Alcohol Withdrawal Cure. Zeitschrift Fur Klinische
       Psychologie, Forschung und Praxis, 10(1): 13-26, 1981.

3249. Krasner, Barbara R. and Controneo, Margaret. Addiction,
       Alienation and Parenting. The Nursing Clinics of North
       America, 11(3): 517-525, 1976.

3250. Krasojevic-Janjetovic, L., Ilic, A. and Janjetovic, V. Porodica Kao
       Jedan Od Faktora U Rehabilitaciji I Resocijalizaciji Obolelih
       Od Alkoholizma. (The Family as One of the Factors in the
       Rehabilitation and Resocialization of Alcoholics.) Alkoholizam,
       15(1-2): 106-111, 1975.

3251. Krause, Merton S., Breedlove, James L., Bonniface, Kathryn I.
       Evaluation of the Results of Treatment. In: Casework with
       Wives of Alcoholics. Eds. P.C. Cohen and M.S. Krause.
       New York: Family Service Association of America, 1971,
       pages 121-146.

3252. Krause, Merton S., Ransohoff, Daniel J. and Cohen, Pauline.
       Promoting Possible Alcoholism Referrals. Community
       Mental Health Journal, 4(1): 13-16, 1968.

3253. Krauthamer, Carole M. Maternal Attitudes of Alcoholic and
       Nonalcoholic Upper Middle Class Women. The International
       Journal of The Addictions, 14(5): 639-644, 1979.

3254. Krauthamer, Carole M. The Personality of Alcoholic Mothers and
       Their Children: A Study of Their Relationship to Birth Order,
       Mother-Child Attitude, and Socioeconomic Status. Doctoral
       Dissertation. (University Microfilms No. 74-8798.) Rutgers
       University, The State University of New Jersey, 1973. (Also in:
       Dissertation Abstracts International, 34: 5198A, 1974).

3255. Krauweel, H.J. Enige Mededelingen Over Een Poging Tot Een
       Sociale Typologie Van De Alcoholist. (Contributions Toward
       A Social Typology of Alcoholics.) Maandblad Geestelijke
       Volksgezondheid, Netherlands, 7: 113-129, 1952.

3256. Krauweel, H.J. Desarrollo Historico y Administrativo de un
       Programa Nacional Para el Control del Alcoholismo. Archivos
       de Biologia y Medicina Experimentales, Supplement, No. 3:
       328-335, 1969. (Also as: History and Administration of a
       National Alcoholism Program in the Netherlands. In: Alcohol
       and Alcoholism. Ed. R.E. Popham. Toronto: University of
       Toronto Press, 1970, pages 377-384.)

3257. Krebesova, M. Medzirezortna Spolupraca pri Rieseni Socialno-Pravnych
       Problemov Alkoholika A Jeho Rodiny Z Pohladu Sestry Pre Socialnu
       Sluzbu V Psychiatrii. (Interdepartmental Cooperation in the
       Solution of the Social and Legal Problems of an Alcoholic and
       His Family from a Nurse's Viewpoint Performing Social Work in
       Psychiatry.) Protialkoholicky Obzor, Bratislava, 15: 39-41,
       1980.

3258. Kregel, Herman J. Alcoholics Turn to Clergy for Aid. California
       Alcoholism Review, 2(2): 49-50, 61, 1967.

3259. Kreitman, Norman. Married Couples Admitted to Mental Hospital.
       Part I. Diagnostic Similarity and the Relation of Illness
       to Marriage. British Journal of Psychiatry, London,
       114(511): 699-709, 1968.

3260. Kreitman, Norman and Schreiber, M. Parasuicide in Young Edinburgh
       Women, 1968-75. Psychological Medicine, 9(3): 469-479, 1979.

3261. Krell, Robert and Miles, James E. Marital Therapy of Couples in Which
       the Husband is a Physician. American Journal of Psychotherapy,
       20(2): 267-275, 1976.

3262. Krieger, Edith C. The Effects of Therapeutic Community Treatment on
       the Interpersonal Resource Needs and Self Esteem of Drug Addicts.
       Dissertation Abstracts International, 43(3): 913B, 1982.

3263. Krimmel, Herman E. The Alcoholic and His Family. In: Alcoholism:
       Progress in Research and Treatment. Eds. P.G. Bourne and
       R. Fox. New York: Academic Press, 1973, pages 297-310.

3264. Krimmel, Herman E. Alcoholism and the Family. Pamphlet.
       Center City, MN: Hazelden, no date.

3265. Krimmel, Herman E. Alcoholism; Challenge for Social Work Education.
       New York: Council on Social Work Education, 1971.

3266. Krimmel, Herman E. and Spers, Helen R. Effect of Parental
       Alcoholism on Adolescents. Monograph. Ohio: Cleveland
       Center on Alcoholism, no date.

3267. Kritsberg, W. Chronic Shock and Emotional Numbness in Adult
       Children of Alcoholics. Focus on Family and Chemical
       Dependency, 7(6): 24-25, 40, 1984.

3268. Kritzer, R. Needs Assessment for Children of Alcoholic Parents.
       Columbus, OH: Columbus Health Department, Alcoholism and
       Drug Abuse Section, 1985.

3269. Krohn, Marvin D., Akers, Ronald L., Radosevich, Marcia J. and
       Lanza, Kaduce Lonn. Norm Qualities and Adolescent
       Substance Use: The Effects of Norm Source and Quality
       on Using and Abusing Alcohol and Marijuana. Journal of
       Drug Issues, 12: 343-359, 1982.

3270. Kroll, Phillip and Ryan, Colleen. The Schizotypal Personality
       on an Alcohol Treatment Unit. Comprehensive Psychiatry,
       24(3): 262-270, 1983.

3271. Kronfol, Ziad and Tsuang, Ming T. A Family History Study of Drug
       Abuse with Psychosis. Paper presented at the American
       Psychiatric Association, Washington, D.C., 1978. (Also as:
       Continuing Medical Education: Syllabus and Proceedings in
       Summary Form. Washington, D.C.: American Psychiatric
       Association, 1978, pages 143-144.)

3272. Kroon, H.M. Heredity of Alcoholism in a Certain Family. Nederlandsch
       Tijdschrift Voor Geneeskunde, 68: 1855-1862, 1924.

3273. Krstic, S. Simptomatska Epilepsija u Bolesnika sa Alkoholnim
       Encefalopatijama. (Symptomatic Epilepsy in Patients with
       Alcoholic Encephalopathy.) Alkoholizam, Beograd,
       11(3-4): 137-143, 1971.

3274. Krupp, S.L. and Lehmann, N. Incidence of Alcohol-Related
       Domestic Violence: An Assessment. Alcohol Health and
       Research World, 8(2): 23-27, 39, 1984.

3275. Krupski, Ann Marie. Inside the Adolescent Alcoholic. Center
       City, MN: Hazelden, no date.

3276. Kruse, W. Suchtfragen Unter Dem Aspekt Der Gesundheitsberatung:
       Umgang Mit Alkoholkranken Aus Der Sicht Des Hausarztes.
       (Questions of Addiction in Aspects of Health Care: Dealing
       with Alcoholics from the Viewpoint of the General
       Practitioner.) Munchener Medizinische Wochenschrift,
       127(12): 279-281, 1985.

3277. Kryspin-Exner, K. Behandlung des Alkoholismus. (Treatment of
       Alcoholism.) Nervenarzt, 50: 277-285, 1979.

3278. Kubicka, Ludek and Skala, Jaroslav. Three-Year Follow-Up Study
       Comparing 6 Weeks with 13 Week Inpatient Treatment Program
       for Alcoholics. Paper presented at the 23rd International
       Institute on the Prevention and Treatment of Alcoholism,
       Dresden, E. Germany, June, 1977, pages 269-277.

3279. Kubie, L.S. The Reverberating Chain Reaction in Alcoholics.
       Annals of the New York Academy of Sciences, 233:
       78-84, 1974.

3280. Kucek, P. Efekt Psychoterapie Na Manzelskeho Partnera Lieceneho
       Alkoholika. (The Effect of Psychotherapy on the Spouse of
       a Treated Alcoholic.) Protialkoholicky Obzur, Bratislava,
       15: 37-38, 1980.

3281. Kukolwicz, T. Rola Obyczajowosci Rodzinnej W Zapobieganiu
       Alkoholizmowi. (The Role of Family in Prevention of Alcoholism.)
       Problemy Alkoholizmu, Warsaw, 24(3): 5-6, 1977.

3282. Kul'tepina, O.S. and Polezhayeva, I.B. Alkogol'i Deti. (Alcohol
       and Children.) Pamphlet. Moscow: Meditsina, 1976.

3283. Kumasaka, Y. Community-Orientation of Psychiatrists and Its
       Effect on the Mental Hospital Population. Behavioral
       Neuropsychiatry, 1(8): 25-30, 36, 1969.

3284. Kunda, Stanislav and Adamica, Zigmund. (Kazuistiky Aplikovanej
       Psychoterapie Z Protialkoholickych Poradni.) Case Histories of
       Applied Psychotherapy from Antialcoholic Consultation Centers.
       Protialkoholicky Obzor, Bratislava, 6(2): 58-60, 1971.

3285. Kunec, E.J. Preventing Drunk Driving. In: Toward the Prevention
       of Alcohol Problems: Government, Business, and Community Action.
       Ed. Dean Gerstein. Washington, D.C.: National Academy Press,
       1984, pages 124-126.

3286. Kuo, Peter T. Hyperlipoproteinemia and Atherosclerosis: Dietary Intervention. American Journal of Medicine, 74(5A): 15-18, 1983.

3287. Kupetz, Karen, Larosa, Judie, Klagsbrun, Micheline and Davis, Donald I The Family and Drug Abuse Symposium. Family Process, 16(2): 141-147, 1977.

3288. Kurland, J. Realistic Alternative for Employee Assistance Programs. EAP Digest, 1(3): 20-21, 1981.

3289. Kurn, Hans Christoph. Zur Alkoholismusproblematik im Bereich von Partnerwahl und Ehe. (Problems of Alcoholism in the Realm of Choice of Partner and Marriage.) Soziologenkorrespondenz, 6: 147-170, 1979.

3290. Kury, Helmut and Patzschke, Hilmar. Zur Atiologie des Drogenkonsums Jugendlicher. (The Etiology of Juvenile Drug Use.) Praxis der Kinderpsychologie und Kinderpsychiatrie, 28(5): 176-187, 1979.

3291. Kushner, J.P., Barbuto, A.J. and Lee, G.R. An Inherited Enzymatic Defect in Porphyria Cutanea Tarda Decreased Uro Porphyrinogen Decarboxylase Activity. Journal of Clinical Investigation, 58(5): 1089-1097, 1976.

3292. Kushner, J.P., Edwards, C.Q., Dadone, M.M. and Skolnick, M.H. Heterozygosity for HLA-Linked Hemochromatosis as a Likely Cause of the Hepatic Siderosis Associated with Sporadic Porphyria Cutanea Tarda. Gastroenterology, 88(5-1): 1232-1238, 1985.

3293. Kuttner, Robert E. and Lorincz, Albert B. Alcoholism and Addiction in Urbanized Sioux Indians. Mental Hygiene, 51(4): 530-542, 1967.

3294. Kyllerman, M., Aronson, M., Sabel, K.G., Karlberg, E., Sandin, B. and Olegard, R. Children of Alcoholic Mothers. Growth and Motor Performance Compared to Matched Controls. Acta Paediatrica Scandinavica, 74: 20-26, 1985.

L

3295. La Fe Youth Hostel. Alcoholic Beverage Use and Family Drinking Patterns Among Students in Santa Fe High School. Santa Fe, NM, 1975.

3296. LaBundy, J.F. Simulating Family Bonding: Outpatient Group Experience with ACOA's. Focus on Family, 8(5): 22-23, 39, 1985.

3297. LaDine, J., Bradford, B.U., Glassman, E., Forman, D. and Thurman, R.G. The Swift Increase in Alcohol Metabolism in Humans: Comparison Between Individuals with a Positive and Negative Family History for Alcoholism. Chapel Hill: University of North Carolina at Chapel Hill, no date.

3298. Lafferty, Nancy A., Holden, J.M.C. and Klein, Helen E. Norm Qualities and Alcoholism. International Journal of Social Psychiatry, 26(3): 159-165, 1980.

3299. Lagerberg, D. and Sundelin, C. Viktigaste Utmaningen - Att Hitta Metoder Att Hjalpa Dessa Barn. (The Primary Challenge - To Devise a Method of Helping Children of Alcoholic Fathers.) Alkohol och Norkotika, 75(3): 7-9, 1981.

3300. Laignel-Lavastine. Retentissement de l'Alcoolisme sur la Famille et l'enfant. (The Repercussions of Alcoholism on the Family and the Child.) Archives Internationales de Neurologie, Paris, 60: 165-187, 207-211, 1941.

3301. Laitinen, T. Alcohol and Offspring. Medical Temperance Review, 10: 263-264, 1907.

3302. Laitinen, T. A Contribution to the Study of the Influence of Alcohol on the Degeneration of Human Offspring. International Congress Against Alcoholism, 12: 263-270, 1909.

3303. Laitinen, T. The Influence of Alcohol Upon Offspring. National Temperance Quarterly, London, 2: 325-328, no date.

3304. Lamache, A., Davost, H., Chuberre and Delalande. L'activite Genesique des Alcooliques Chroniques. (Genetic Activity of Chronic Alcoholics.) Echos de le Medicine, Paris, 23(23): 1-2, 1952. (Also in: Bulletin de l'Academie Nationale de Medicine, Paris, 136: 530-532, 1952.

3305. Laman, K. Selected Behavioural Characteristics of Alcoholics and Their Spouses. Canadian Journal of Public Health, Ottawa, 65: 221-223, 1974.

3306. La-Marca, Donald. Alcohol and Sexuality: The Myths and Facts Surrounding Alcohol. In: Papers presented at the 24th International Institute on the Prevention and Treatment of Alcoholism. Ed. E.J. Tongue. Lausanne: International Council on Alcohol and Addictions, 1978, pages 399-408.

3307. Lambert, Michael J. The Effects of Psychotherapy: I. In:
       Annual Research Reviews: The Effects of Psychotherapy.
       St. Albans, VT: Eden Medical Research, 1979, pages 1-158.

3308. Lamontagne, Y., Tetreault, L. and Boyer, R. Consommation
       d'Alcool et de Drogues Chez les Etudiants: III. Milieu
       Familial, Secteurs d'Etude Impliques et Comparaison entre
       Etudiants et Etudiantes Alcooliques au Niveau Collegial
       (CEGEP). (Alcohol and Drug Consumption in Students.
       III. Family Environment, Areas of Study and Comparison of
       Men and Women Alcoholics Enrolled in Colleges [CEGEP].)
       Union Medicale du Canada, 108: 573-575, 1979.

3309. Landau, Rita, Harth, Paula, Othnay, Nava and Sharfhertz, Cila.
       The Influence of Psychotic Parents on Their Children's
       Development. American Journal of Psychiatry, 129(1):
       38-43, 1972.

3310. Landau, Stephen G., Neal, David L., Meisner, Marc and Prudic,
       Joan. Depressive Symptomatology among Laid-Off Workers.
       Journal of Psychiatric Treatment and Evaluation, 2(1):
       5-12, 1980.

3311. Landes, S. The Children of Alcoholics: Program Needs and
       Implications Derived from Experience Within the Adolescent
       Alcohol Abuse Treatment Program--The Door, New York City, A
       Multiservice Center for Youth. In: Services for Children
       of Alcoholics. Symposium held in September, 1979 at
       Silver Springs, MD. U.S. National Institute on Alcohol
       Abuse and Alcoholism. Research Monograph No. 4. Washington,
       D.C.: U.S. Government Printing Office, 1981, pages 110-130.
       (DHHS Publication No. ADM 81-1007).

3312. Landesman-Dwyer, S. Relationship of Children's Behavior to
       Maternal Alcohol Consumption. In: Fetal Alcohol Syndrome:
       Volume II. Human Studies. Ed. E.L. Abel. Boca Raton, FL:
       CRC Press, 1982, pages 127-148.

3313. Landesman-Dwyer, S., Ragozin, A.S. and Little, R.E. Behavioral
       Correlates of Prenatal Alcohol Exposure: A Four-Year Follow
       Up Study. Neurobehavioral Toxicology and Teratology, 3:
       187-193, 1981.

3314. Landesman-Dwyer, S., Ragozin, A.S. and Little, R.E. Long-Term
       Behavioral Effects of Prenatal Alcohol Exposure. Alcoholism:
       Clinical and Experimental Research, 4(2): 221, 1980.

3315. Lang, B. Psihoterapija Alkoholicara. (Psychotherapy of
       Alcoholics.) Alali Klinicke Bolnice, Dr. M. Stojanovic,
       Zagreb, 18: 202-206, 1979.

3316. Lange, E. and Trubsbach, G. Entwicklungsbesonderheiten,
       Soziales Bezugsfeld und Familienstruktur bei 100 Jungen,
       Straffallig Gewordenen Gewohnheits-Gesselligkeistrinkern
       der Stadt Dresden. (Developmental Peculiarities, Social
       Environment and Family Structure of 100 Juvenile Delinquent
       Habitual Social Drinkers in Dresden.) Psychiatrie,
       Neurologie und Medizinische Psycholgie, Leipzig, 21:
       311-317, 1969.

3317. Langelier, Regis. French Canadian Families. In: Ethnicity and
       Family Therapy. Eds. Monica McGoldrick, John K. Pearce
       and Joseph Giordano. New York: The Guilford Press, 1982,
       pages 229-246.

3318. Langer, H., Kisiel, B., Bako, W. and Balcerska, A. The Neglected
       Child and its Family Environment (With Particular Reference to
       Alcoholism). Pediatria Polska, Warsaw, 58(1): 57-62, 1983.

3319. Langinvainio, H., Kaprio, J., Koskenvuo, M. and Tarkkonen, L.
       Structural Analysis of Smoking, Alcohol Use, and Personality
       Factors in MZ and DZ Twin Pair Relationships. In: Twin
       Research 3: Epidemiological and Clinical Studies.
       New York: Alan R. Liss, Inc., 1981, pages 23-35.

3320. Langley, Roger and Levy, Richard C. Wife Beating: The Silent
       Crisis. New York: E.P. Dutton, 1977.

3321. Langone, J. and Langone, D. Women Who Drink. Reading, MA:
       Addison-Wesley, 1980.

3322. Lanier, D.C. Familial Alcoholism. Journal of Family Practice,
       18(3): 417-422, 1984.

3323. Lanu, K.E. The Alcoholic and the Family. Katilolehti, 73(1):
       14-22, 1968.

3324. Lanza-Kaduce, Lonn, Akers, Ronald L., Krohn, Marvin D. and
       Radosevich, Marcia. Cessation of Alcohol and Drug Use Among
       Adolescents: A Social Learning Model. Deviant Behavior,
       5: 79-96, 1984.

3325. Lardennois, C. Protection Legale de l'Enfance au Regard de
       l'Alcool. (Legal Protection of Youth from Alcohol.)
       Alcool Ou Sante, Paris, 152(1): 27-32, 1980.

3326. Larkin, E.J. Review of Alcohol and Other Drugs: Perspectives
       on Use, Abuse, Treatment and Prevention, Ed. by Paul C.
       Whitehead, Carl F. Grindstaff and Craig L. Boydell. Canadian
       Psychologist, 15(4): 393, 1974.

3327. Larkin, William Easley. An Examination of Parental Response to
       Adolescent Deviance. Doctoral Dissertation. (University
       Microfilms No. 73-13569.)

3328. Larkin-Cullen, M. Verbal and Nonverbal Communication Patterns in
       Alcoholism-Complicated Marriages. Dissertation Abstracts
       International, 44(11): 3532B, 1984.

3329. Larsen, D.E. and Abu-Laban, B. Norm Qualities and Deviant Drinking
       Behavior. Social Problems, 15: 441-450, 1968.

3330. Larsen, E. Race Against Yesterday: The Ups and Downs of Intimacy
       for ACOAs. Focus on Family and Chemical Dependency, 8(4):
       10-11, 44, 1985.

3331. Larson, David B. and Wilson, William P. Religious Life of Alcoholics.
       Southern Medical Journal, 73(6): 723-727, 1980.

3332. Larson, T.G. Alcoholism and Drugs: Addiction. Minnesota Medicine,
       55(12): 1144-1146, 1170, 1972.

3333. Larsson, G. Prevention of Fetal Alcohol Effects. An Antenatal
       Program for Early Detection of Pregnancies at Risk. Acta
       Obstetrica et Gynecologica Scandinavica, Stockholm,
       62(2): 171-178, 1983.

3334. Larsson, G. and Ekenstein, G. Institutional Care of Infants in
       Sweden: Criteria for Admission in 1970, 1975 and 1980.
       Child Abuse and Neglect, Oxford, 7(1): 11-16, 1983.

3335. Larsson, G. and Larsson, A. Health of Children Whose Parents
       Seek Psychiatric Care. Acta Psychiatrica Scandinavica,
       Copenhagen, 66(2): 154-162.

3336. Laskarzewski, Peter M., Khoury, Philip, Kelly, Kathe, Mellies, Margot, J., Morrison, John A. and Glueck, Charles J. Prevalence of Familial Hyper Lipo Proteinemia and Hypo Lipo Proteinemia in Blacks: The Princeton School District Family Study. Preventive Medicine, 11(2): 142-161, 1982.

3337. Laskarzewski, Peter M., Khoury, Philip, Kelly, Kathe, Mellies, Margot J., Morrison, John A. and Glueck, Charles J. Prevalence of Familial Hypertriglyceridemia: The Princeton School District Family Study. Preventive Medicine, 11(3): 317-345, 1982.

3338. Laskarzewski, Peter M., Khoury, Philip, Morrison, John A., Kelly, Kathe, Mellies, Margot, and Glueck, Charles J. Cancer, Cholesterol, and Lipoprotein Cholesterols. Preventive Medicine, 11(3): 253-268, 1982.

3339. Lassey, Marie L. and Carlson, John E. Drinking Among Rural Youth: The Dynamics of Parental and Peer Influence. The International Journal of the Addictions, 15(1): 61-75, 1980.

3340. Laszlo, Cseh Szombathy. A Devians Magatartasi Formak Elsajatitasa A Csaladban Vegbemeno Szocializalodas Soran. (The Internalization of Deviant Behaviour Patterns During Socialization in the Family.) Demografia, 13(4): 386-393, 1970.

3341. Latcham, R.W. Familial Alcoholism: Evidence from 237 Alcoholics. British Journal of Psychiatry, 147(July): 54-57, 1985.

3342. Laudeman, Kent A. Seventeen Ways to Get Parents Involved in Substance Abuse Education. Journal of Drug Education, 14(4): 307-314, 1984.

3343. Lauderdale, M.L., Anderson, R. and Cramer, S.E. Relationship Between Child Abuse and Neglect and Substance Abuse in a Predominantly Mexican-American Population. In: Child Abuse and Neglect: Issues on Innovation and Implementation. Washington, D.C.: National Center on Child Abuse and Neglect, 1978.

3344. Laudinet, S. and Kohler, C. New Reflections on the Descent of Alcoholic Parents. Psychiatrie De L'Enfant, 13(1): 273-305, 1970.

3345. Laundergan, J.C., Schroeder, M.R. and Barnett, P.J. Family Program Client Changes: A Follow-Up. Alcoholism: Clinical and Experimental Research, 4: 221, 1980.

3346. Laundergan, J. Clark and Williams, Terence. Hazelden: Evaluation of a Residential Family Program. Alcohol Health and Research World, 3(4): 13-16, 1979.

3347. Laverty, S.G. Reported Levels of Ethanol Consumption Related to the Development of Drinking Problems. Addictive Diseases: An International Journal, 2(3): 441-448, 1976.

3348. Lavik, N.J. Forebyggende Arbeid Ma' Loses Innenfor Et Folkehelsperspektiv. (The Problem of Prevention Must Be Solved from a Public Health Perspective.) Alkohol och Narkotika, 75(3): 10-11, 1981.

3349. Lavino, J. Family Members of Alcoholics at Work; Al-Anon as a Treatment Resource. Labor-Management Alcoholism Journal, 10: 133-136, 1981.

3350. Lavino, J. Family Members of Alcoholics in the Workplace: Does
       Anyone Know We're Here? Paper presented at the 8th Annual Meeting
       of ALMACA, Detroit, October, 1979. (Also in: Association of
       Labor-Management Administrators and Consultants on Alcoholism,
       Inc. Compiled by Marsha Moran-Sackett. Arlington, VA: ALMACA,
       1980, pages 672-680.)

3351. Lavino, J.J. Family Members of Alcoholics: The Forgotten People of
       Occupational Alcoholism Programs. Paper Presented at the National
       Council on Alcoholism Forum. St. Louis: May, 1978. (Also in:
       Labor-Management Alcoholism Journal, 7(6): 6-14, 1978.)

3352. Lavino, J.J. Jr and Kane, M.E. Family Members of Alcoholics: The
       Forgotten People of Occupational Alcoholism Programs. Paper
       presented at the 7th Annual Meeting of ALMACA, San Francisco,
       October, 1978. (Also in: Association of Labor-Management
       Administrators and Consultants on Alcoholism, Inc. Arlington,
       VA: ALMACA, 1978, pages 93-102.)

3353. Lawrence, T.S. and Velleman, J.D. Correlates of Student Drug Use
       in a Suburban High School. Psychiatry, 37: 129-136, 1974.

3354. Lawson, A. Alcoholism and the Family. Gaithersburg, MD:
       Aspen Systems Corp., 1983.

3355. Lawson, A.W. Treating the Whole Family: When Intervention and
       Education Aren't Enough. Focus on Family and Chemical
       Dependency, 7(4): 14-16, 1984.

3356. Lawson, D.G. Search Within; The Story of a Family's Struggle
       with Alcoholism. Hicksville, NY: Eposition, 1979.

3357. Lawson, Gary, Peterson, James S. and Lawson, James. Alcoholism
       and the Family: A Guide to Treatment and Prevention.
       Rockville, MD: Aspen Systems Corporation, 1983.

3358. Lawson, J.S. and Blatch, J.C. Early Progress Report of Practical
       Experience with Lifestyle Programmes in a Suburban Population.
       Medical Journal of Australia, Sydney, 2(3): 119-121, 1981.

3359. Lazar, Usher M., Jay, J. and Glass, D. Family Therapy as a
       Treatment Modality for Alcoholism. Journal of Studies on
       Alcohol, 43(9): 927-938, 1982.

3360. Lazare, A. and Klerman, G.L. Hysteria and Depression: The
       Frequency and Significance of Hysterical Personality Features
       in Hospitalized Depressed Women. The American Journal of
       Psychiatry, 124(11): 48-56, 1968.

3361. Lazic, N. General System Theory and the Treatment of Alcoholism.
       Alcoholism, Zagreb, 14(1): 13-18, 1978.

3362. Lazic, Nebojsa. A Systematic Approach to Solving the Problem
       of an "Unending Struggle" Between Marital Partners.
       Psihijatrija Danas, 9(4): 449-457, 1977.

3363. Leach, Barry. "Near Alcoholism": A New Empirically Generated
       Conceptualization for Helping the Families of Problem
       Drinkers. Paper presented at the North American Congress
       on Alcohol and Drug Problems, San Francisco, 1974, pages 1-30.

3364. Leane, A. and Roche, D. Developmental Disorder in the Children
       of Male Alcoholics. In: Papers Presented at the 20th
       International Institute on the Prevention and Treatment of
       Alcoholism, Manchester, England. Ed. B. Hore. Lausanne:
       International Council on Alcohol and Addictions, 1974, pages
       82-91.

3365. Leary, Stephanie. In Defense of Alcoholism Counseling for the
       Family. Alcoholism, 1(2): 47-48, 1980.

3366. Leary, Stephanie A. Family Forum -- When Does Treatment = Prevention?
       Alcoholism: The National Magazine, 2: 15, 1982.

3367. Lebedev, B.A. Alkogol' i Sem'ya. (Alcohol and the Family.)
       Lenigrad: Meditsina, 1974.

3368. Leckman, A. Lane, Umland, Berthold E. and Blay, Maggie. Alcoholism in
       the Families of Family Practice Outpatients. Journal of Family
       Practice, 19(2): 205-207, 1984.

3369. Leckman, A. Lane, Umland, Berthold E. and Blay, Maggie. Prevalence
       of Alcoholism in a Family Practice Center. Journal of Family
       Practice, 18(6): 867-870, 1984.

3370. Leckman, J.F., Weissman, M.M., Merikangas, K.R., Pauls, D.L. and
       Prusoff, B.A. Panic Disorder and Major Depression. Increased
       Risk of Depression, Alcoholism, Panic and Phobic Disorders in
       Families of Depressed Probands with Panic Disorder. Archives of
       General Psychiatry, 40(10): 1055-1060, 1983.

3371. Lecomte, M. Elements d'Heredopathologie. (Elements of
       Heredopathology.) Scalpel, Brussels, 103: 1133-1145, 1950.

3372. Ledwidge, L.   At the End of the Bottle: A Disturbing Account of the
       Alcoholic Parents' Effect on Children. ALK Organization, 1977.

3373. Lee, Essie E. The Counselor's Role in Alcohol Education Programs.
       School Counselor, 23(4): 289-292, 1976.

3374. Lee, Essie E. Survey of Knowledge, Attitudes and Practices
       of Fifth and Eighth Grade Students Regarding Alcoholic
       Beverages in Urban Parochial Schools. Journal of Alcohol
       and Drug Education, 28(2): 73-84, 1983.

3375. Lee, J.C. Families in Transition: Adolescent Alcohol Abuse.
       Focus on Family and Chemical Dependency, 7(3): 22-25, 1984.

3376. Lee, J.P. Clinic for Alcoholics Makes Friends and Influences
       Patients. Modern Hospital, 71(6): 68-69, 1948.

3377. Lee, L.J. Reducing Black Adolescents' Drug Use: Family Revisited.
       In: Adolescent Substance Abuse: A Guide to Prevention and
       Treatment. Eds. R. Isralowitz and M. Singer. New York:
       Haworth Press, 1983, pages 57-69.

3378. Lee, Richard H. Conflict, Efficiency, Flexibility, and Concealment
       in Families of Alcoholics. Doctoral Dissertation. (University
       Microfilms No. 75-04903.) Cambridge: Harvard University, 1975.

3379. LeFager, J. Double Dilemma of Chemically Dependent Parents
       and Substance-Abusing Adolescents. Focus on Family and
       Chemical Dependency, 7(6): 33, 35, 1984.

3380. Leger, J.M. and Daudet, G. L'Appetence a l'Alcool et son Traitment.
       (Craving for Alcohol and Its Treatment.) Annales Medico-
       Psychologiques, Paris, 2(2): 193-217, 1971.

3381. Lehmann, Nannette and Krupp, Steven L. Alcohol-Related Domestic
       Violence: Clinical Implications and Intervention Strategies.
       Alcoholism Treatment Quarterly, 1(4): 111-115, 1984.

3382. Lehmann, Nannette and Krupp, Steven L. Incidence of Alcohol-
       Related Domestic Violence: An Assessment. Alcohol Health
       and Research World, 8(2): 23-27, 39, 1984.

3383. Leighton, Alexander. Is Social Environment A Cause of Psychiatric
       Disorder. In: Psychiatric Research Report No. 22. Eds. Russell
       R. Monroe, Gerald D. Klee and Eugene B. Brody. Washington, D.C.:
       American Psychiatric Association, 1967, pages 337-345.

3384. Leite, Evelyn. To Be Somebody. Center City, MN: Hazelden, 1979.

3385. Leite, Evelyn. Newcomers to Al-Anon. Pamphlet. Center City, MN:
       Hazelden, 1979.

3386. Leite, Evelyn. When Daddy's a Drunk--What to Tell the Kids.
       Pamphlet. Center City, MN: Hazelden, 1979.

3387. Lejosne, M.C. Une Experience Jusqu'a l'Absurde. (Experience to
       an Absurd Degree.) Alcool Ou Sante, 163(4): 6-9, 1982.

3388. Lejosne, M.C. L'entourage de la Personne Ayant un Probleme
       d'Alcool: Quelle Aide Possible? (People Close to One with
       Alcohol Problems: Can They Help?) In: International
       Meeting on Cultures, Drinking Habits and Alcoholism
       Proceedings. Eds. Guy Carlo and Jean-Francoise Lemoine.
       Rennes, 1984, pages 539-541.

3389. Leland, J. Sex Role, Family Organization and Alcohol Abuse.
       In: Alcohol and the Family. Eds. J. Orford and J.
       Harwin. New York: St. Martin's Press, 1982, pages 88-113.

3390. Leland, J. Women and Alcohol in an Indian Settlement. Medical
       Anthropology, 2(4): 85-119, 1978.

3391. Lemay, Diane. The Need for an Awareness of Specialized Issues
       in Counseling Alcoholic Women. Personnel and Guidance
       Journal, 59(2): 103-106, 1980.

3392. Lemere, F., Voegtlin, W.L., Broz, W.R., O'Hollaren, P. and Tupper,
       W.E. Heredity as an Etiologic Factor in Chronic Alcoholism.
       Northwest Medicine, 42: 110-111, 1943.

3393. Lemert, Edwin M. Dependency in Married Alcoholics. Quarterly
       Journal of Studies on Alcohol, 23: 590-609, 1962.

3394. Lemert, Edwin M. The Occurrence and Sequence of Events in the
       Adjustment of Families to Alcoholism. Quarterly Journal of
       Studies on Alcohol, 21: 679-697, 1960.

3395. Lemoine, P., Harousseau, H. and Borteyru, J.P. Les Enfants De
       Parents Alcooliques. Anomalies Observees. A Propos De 127
       Cas. (Children of Alcoholic Parents. Anomalies Observed.
       127 Cases.) Quest-Medical, Paris, 21: 476-482, 1968.

3396. Lengrand, J.P. Contributions a L'etude de l'Alcoolisme Feminin
       Dans le Nord. (Contributions to the Study of Female
       Alcoholism in the North of France.) Baillue, 1964.

3397. Leonard, C.V. Self-ratings of Alienation in Suicidal Patients.
       Journal of Clinical Psychology, 29(4): 423-428, 1973.

3398. Leonard, Kenneth E., Bromet, E.J., Parkinson, D.K., Day, N.L. and Ryan,
       C.M. Patterns of Alcohol Use and Physically Aggressive
       Behavior in Men. Journal of Studies on Alcohol, 46(4):
       279-282, 1985.

3399. Leonard, Kenneth E., Dunn, Nancy Jo and Jacob, Theodore. Drinking
       Problems of Alcoholics: Correspondence Between Self and
       Spouse Reports. Addictive Behaviors, Oxford, 8(4):
       369-373, 1983.

3400. Leonard, Kenneth E. and Jacob, T.   Marital Interactions Among
       Binge and Steady Alcoholics. Alcoholism: Clinical and
       Experimental Research, 10(1): 97, 1986.

3401. Leowski, J., Saplis-Krasowska, L. and Korczak, C.W.   Spozycie Alkoholu
       Przez Mlodziez Szkolna Wojewocztw Warszawskiego. (Alcohol
       Drinking by School Children in the Province of Warsaw.)
       Zdrowie, 79: 153-159, 1968.

3402. Leowski, J., Saplis-Krasowska, L. and Korczak, C.W.   Warunki
       Spoleiznobytowe a Czestosc Picia Napojow Alkoholowych Przez
       Mlodziez Szkolna Wojewodztwa Warszawskiego. (Socioeconomic
       Conditions and the Frequency of Alcohol Drinking among School
       Children in the Province of Warsaw.) Zdrowie, 79: 161-167,
       1968.

3403. Lerner, R.   Co-Dependency: The Swirl of Energy Surrounded by
       Confusion. Focus on Family and Chemical Dependency,
       8(1): 10, 29, 34-36, 1985.

3404. Lerner, Rokelle.   Children of Alcoholics: Their Special Needs.
       In: Alcoholism and the Family: A Book of Readings.
       Eds. Sharon Wegscheider-Cruse and Richard W. Esterly.
       Wernersville, PA: The Caron Institute, 1985, pages 19-24.

3405. Lerner, Rokelle.   Daily Affirmations. Center City, MN:
       Hazelden, no date.

3406. Lerner, Rokelle.   Growing Up in an Alcoholic Home--What's it Like?
       Focus on Alcohol and Drug Issues, 6(4): 12-15, 1981.

3407. Lerner, Rokelle.   Schools Can Provide Drug Abuse Prevention Tools.
       Focus on Alcohol and Drug Issues, 6(2): 22-23, 1983.

3408. Lerner, S.E. and Linder, R.L.   Birth Order and Polydrug Abuse
       among Heroin Addicts. Journal of Drug Education, 5:
       285-291, 1975.

3409. Lesch, O., Rajna, P., Rustenbegovic, A. and Spielhofer, H.
       Catamnestic Study of Alcoholism Patients Receiving
       Disulfiram Therapy Who have been Abstinent for 2 Years.
       Alcoholism, Zagreb, 18(1): 43-49, 1982.

3410. Leslie, R.D.G. and Pyke, D.A.   Chlorpropamide-Alcohol Flushing:
       Dominantly Inherited Trait Associated with Diabetes.
       British Medical Journal, London, 2: 1519-1521, 1978.

3411. Leslie, R.D.G., Pyke, D.A. and Stubbs, W.A.   Sensitivity to
       Enkephalin as a Cause of Noninsulin Dependent Diabetes.
       Lancet, 1(8112): 341-343, 1979.

3412. Leslie, R. Murray.   Alcoholism and Eugenics. British Journal
       of Inebriety, 13: 70-72, 1915.

3413. Lester, D.   A Biological Approach to the Etiology of Alcoholism.
       Quarterly Journal of Studies on Alcohol, 21: 701-703, 1960.

3414. Lester, D.   Self-Selection of Alcohol by Animals, Human Variation,
       and the Etiology of Alcoholism; A Critical Review. Quarterly
       Journal of Studies on Alcohol, 27: 395-438, 1966.

3415. Lester, Lois.   The Special Needs of the Female Alcoholics. Social
       Casework, 63(8): 451-456, 1982.

3416. Let's Pull Together. Alcoholism is a Family Problem. Pamphlet.
       New York: National Council on Alcoholism, 1976. (Also from:
       Rockville, MD: National Institute on Alcohol Abuse and
       Alcoholism, 1976.)

3417. Letter to My Sister. Freedom Fighter From Idaho, 6-7, 51, 1985.

3418. A Letter to Our Alcoholic Dad. Pamphlet. Center City, MN: Hazelden, no date.

3419. Lettieri, Dan J. Suicide in the Aging. Empirical Prediction of Suicidal Risk among the Aging. Journal of Geriatric Psychiatry, 7(1): 7-42, 1973.

3420. Lettieri, Dan J. and Ludford, Jacqueline P. Drug Abuse and the American Adolescent. Research Monograph Series Number 38. National Technical Information Service, 1981.

3421. Leung, Sophia M.R. and Carter, James E. Cross Cultural Study of Child Abuse Among Chinese, Native Indians and Anglo-Canadian Children. Journal of Psychiatric Treatment and Evaluation, 5(1): 37-44, 1983.

3422. Levenberg, Stephen B. Outpatient Treatment of the Problem Drinker: Strategies for Attaining Abstinence. General Hospital Psychiatry, 3(3): 219-225, 1981.

3423. Levendel, L., Mezei, A. Nemes, L. and Mezei-Erdely, F. Some Data Concerning the Personality Structure of Alcoholic Patients. British Journal of Addiction, Edinburgh, 62: 317-330, 1967.

3424. Levine, B.L. Adolescent Substance Abuse: Toward an Integration of Family Systems and Individual Adaptation Theories. American Journal of Family Therapy, 13(2): 3-16, 1985.

3425. Levine, Carol. When Alcoholism is a Family Problem. Parents Magazine and Better Family Living, 46(2): 75-106, 1971.

3426. Levine, Jacob. The Sexual Adjustment of Alcoholics. A Clinical Study of a Selected Sample. Quarterly Journal of Studies on Alcohol, 16: 675-680, 1955.

3427. Levinson, David and Malone, Martin J. Alcoholism. In: Toward Explaining Human Culture: A Critical Review of the Findings of Worldwide Cross-Cultural Research. Eds. David Levinson and Martin J. Malone. New Haven, CT: HRAF Press, 1980, pages 261-266.

3428. Levinson, David and Malone, Martin J. Psychoanalytic Theory. In: Toward Explaining Human Culture: A Critical Review of the Findings of Worldwide Cross-Cultural Research. Eds. David Levinson and Martin J. Malone. New Haven, CT: HRAF Press, 1980, pages 217-228.

3429. Levinson, T. Controlled Drinking in the Alcoholic -- A Search for Common Features. In: Alcoholism and Drug Dependence; A Multidisciplinary Approach. Eds. J.S. Madden, R. Walker and W. Kenyon. New York: Plenum Press, 1977.

3430. Levy, Claude. Caracteristiques Sociales Des Enfants Etudies. (Social Characteristics of the Children Studied.) In: Les Jeunes Handicapes Mentaux. Paris: Presses Universitaires De France, 1970, pages 21-37.

3431. Levy, M. and Green, H. Family Vs. Drink and Drugs. New York: Standard Security Life Insurance Company of New York, Institute for the Study of Drug Misuse, National Council on the Problem of Drug Misuse, 1974.

3432. Levy, S.J. Managing the Drugs in Your Life. A Personal & Family Guide to the Responsible Use of Drugs, Alcohol & Medicine. New York: McGraw-Hill Book Co., 1984.

3433. Levy, Shirley Deborah. Adolescent Drug Users and Their Parents:
      A Study of Their Personality and Family Interactions.
      Dissertation Abstracts International, 41(6): 2330B, 1980.

3434. Lewis, Collins E., Rice, John and Helzer, John E. Diagnostic
      Interactions. Alcoholism and Antisocial Personality. Journal
      of Nervous and Mental Disease, 171(2): 105-113, 1983.

3435. Lewis, David A. and Winokur, George. The Familial Classification of
      Primary Unipolar Depression: Biological Validation of Distinct
      Subtypes. Comprehensive Psychiatry, 24(6): 495-501, 1983.

3436. Lewis, David C. Diagnosis and Management of the Alcoholic Patient
      Rhode Island Medical Journal, 63(1-2): 27-31, 1980.

3437. Lewis, David C. Review of Addictive Drinking: The Road to Recovery
      for Problem Drinkers and Those Who Love Them, by Clark Vaughan.
      New England Journal of Medicine, 308: 728-729, 1983.

3438. Lewis, David C. Review of Medical Disorders of Alcoholism:
      Pathogenesis and Treatment, by Charles S. Lieber.
      New England Journal of Medicine, 308: 728-729, 1983.

3439. Lewis, M. The Initial Contact with Wives of Alcoholics. Social
      Casework, 35: 8-14, 1954.

3440. Lewis, Nolan D.C. Personality Factors in Alcoholic Addiction.
      Quarterly Journal of Studies on Alcohol, 1: 21-44, 1940.

3441. Leyden, J.L. Helping the Families of Alcoholics. Labor-Management
      Alcoholism Journal, 12(4): 125-127, 130-132, 1983. (Also as:
      Paper presented at the National Council on Alcoholism Forum,
      Houston, April, 1983.)

3442. Liakos, A., Madianos, M. and Stefanis, C. Alcohol Consumption
      and Rates of Alcoholism in Greece. Drug and Alcohol
      Dependence, Lausanne, 6(6): 425-430, 1980.

3443. Liban, Carolyn and Smart, Reginald G. Generational and Other
      Differences Between Males and Females in Problem Drinking
      and Its Treatment. Drug and Alcohol Dependence, Lausanne,
      5(3): 207-221, 1980.

3444. Libscom, W.R. and Goddard, L.L. Black Family Features and Drinking
      Behavior. Journal of Drug Issues, 14(2): 337-347, 1984.

3445. Liccione, William James. The Relative Influence of Significant
      Others on Adolescent Drinking: An Exploratory Study. Journal
      of Alcohol and Drug Education, 26:(1): 55-62, 1980.

3446. Lickiss, J.N. Social Deviance in Aboriginal Boys. The Medical
      Journal of Australia, Sydney, 2(9): 460-470, 1971.

3447. Lidberg, L. Social Background Conditions in Young Criminal Drug
      Addicts. Acta Psychiatrica Scandanavica, 27(Supplement 60):
      1970.

3448. Lidkea, Mary Rabb. Counseling as a Factor in the Later Incidence of
      Wife Abuse: A Follow Up Study of the Clients of Brevard Family
      Aid Society, Inc. Dissertation Abstracts International,
      43(12): 4153B, 1982.

3449. Lief, Victor F. Is Alcoholism Just Another Addiction. Drug Forum,
      4(1): 1-2, 1974.

3450. Liepman, M.R. and Tauriainen, M.E. Factors Contributing to Success
      or Failure of Family Coercive Interventions on Alcoholics.
      Alcoholism: Clinical and Experimental Research, 4(2): 222,
      1980.

3451. Liepman, Michael R. Helping Alcoholic Families Recover Through Manipulation of Social Resources. Seminars in Family Medicine, 1(4): 271-281, 1980.

3452. Liepman, Michael R. Some Theoretical Connections Between Family Violence and Substance Abuse. The Catalyst, 1(3): 37-42, 1980.

3453. Liepman, Michael R., Nirenberg, Ted D. and White, William T. Family-Oriented Treatment of Alcoholism. Rhode Island Medical Journal, 68(3): 123-126, 1985.

3454. Lieske, Anna Marie. Incest: An Overview. Perspectives in Psychiatric Care, 19(2): 59-63, 1981.

3455. Life and Health. Del Mar, CA: Ziff-Davis, 1972.

3456. Life with an Alcohol-Abusing Husband: Is There Marriage after Drink? Journal of Psychosocial Nursing and Mental Health Services, 23(3): 30-33, 1985.

3457. Lightfoot, H., Lippman, C. and Suffet, F. Final Report: The Parent and Child Treatment Program. New York: New York Medical College Center for Comprehensive Health Practice, 1983.

3458. Likhtanskii, G.P. Vliyaniye Alkogolizma Na Potomstvo. (The Effect of Alcoholism on Progeny.) Vrachebnoe Delo, Kiev, 2: 138-139, 1975.

3459. Liljestrom, J. Is the Higher Frequency of Alcoholism in Men Genetically Conditioned? Tirfing, 30: 65-74, 1936.

3460. Lille, Mildred L. Drinking and Domestic Relations. In: Toward Prevention: Scientific Studies on Alcohol and Alcoholism. Washington, D.C.: Narcotics Education, Inc., 1971, pages 97-105.

3461. Lindbeck, Vera L. Adjustment of Adolescents to Paternal Alcoholism. Report. Boston: Massachusetts General Hospital, 1971.

3462. Lindbeck, Vera L. Adjustment to Sobriety. In: Casework with Wives of Alcoholics. Eds. P.C. Cohen and M.S. Krause. New York: Family Service Association of America, 1971.

3463. Lindbeck, Vera L. The Woman Alcoholic: A Review of the Literature. The International Journal of the Addictions, 7(3): 567-580, 1972.

3464. Lindelius, R. A Study of Schizophrenia. A Clinical, Prognostic and Family Investigation. Acta Psychiatrica Scandinavica, Copenhagen, 216: 1, 1970.

3465. Linder, Ronald L. and Lerner, Steven E. Self-Medication: An Only Child Syndrome? Journal of Psychedelic Drugs, 5(1): 62-66, 1972.

3466. Lindsay, J.A. Alcoholism and Eugenics. The British Journal of Inebriety, 13: 79-81, 1915.

3467. Linn, Margaret W. Attrition of Older Alcoholics from Treatment. Addictive Diseases, 3(3): 437-447, 1978.

3468. Linn, Margaret W. and Caffey, Eugene M. Jr. Foster Placement for the Older Psychiatric Patient. Journal of Gerontology, 32(3): 340-345, 1977.

3469. Lipp, Douglas Owen. The Development and Validation of an Instrument for Evaluating Mental Health Programs for Adolescents. Dissertation Abstracts International, 43(7): 2344B, 1981.

3470. Lippmann, S. Parenatal Alcohol and Minimal Brain Dysfunction. Southern Medical Journal, 73(9): 1173-1174, 1980.

3471. Lipscomb, Thomas R. The Effects of Familial History of Alcoholism, Drinking Pattern and Tolerance on Blood Alcohol Level Discrimination, Using Internal Cues. Dissertation Abstracts International, 39(2): 987B, 1978.

3472. Lipscomb, Thomas R., Carpenter, J.A. and Nathan, P.E. Static Ataxia: A Predictor of Alcoholism? British Journal of Addictions, 74: 289-294, 1979.

3473. Lipscomb, Thomas R. and Nathan, P.E. Blood Alcohol Level Discrimination; The Effects of Family History of Alcoholism, Drinking Pattern, and Tolerance. Archives of General Psychiatry, 37: 571-576, 1980.

3474. Lipscomb, Wendell R. and Goddard, Lawford L. Black Family Features and Drinking Behavior. Journal of Drug Issues, 14(2): 337-347, 1984.

3475. Liptow, W. Das "Alkoholbehinderte" Kind. (The "Alcohol Handicapped" Child.) Hamburg: Neuland-Verlagsgesellschaft, 1977. (Also in: Papers presented at the 23rd International Institute on the Prevention and Treatment of Alcoholism. Eds. E.J. Tongue and I. Moos. Lausanne, International Council on Alcohol and Addiction, 1977, pages 240-252.)

3476. Lisa, P. Alcoholism: A Family Disease. Australian Journal of Alcoholism and Drug Dependency, 2: 117-119, 1975.

3477. Lisansky, Edith S. Alcoholism in Women: Social and Psychological Concomitants. I. Social History Data. Quarterly Journal of Studies on Alcohol, 18: 588-623, 1957.

3478. Lisansky Gomberg, E.S. and Lisansky, J.M. Alcohol Problems in Women: Antecedents, Consequences, and Intervention. New York: Guilford Press, 1984, pages 233-259.

3479. Lisowska, Jadwiga, Zakowska-Dabrowska, Teresa and Twarowska, Joanna. Ocena Skutecznosci Leczenia Odwykowego Alkoholikow W Warunkach Zamknietych. (Effectiveness of Treatment of Alcoholics Under Closed Conditions.) Problemy Alkoholizmu, Warsaw, 6(225): 7-8, 1973.

3480. Lister, John. By the London Post. The Role of Women in Medicine -- Alcohol and Alcoholism -- Defining an Internist. New England Journal of Medicine, 300(22): 1260-1261, 1979.

3481. Lister, John. Disabled Children -- Free Contraception for All? More Liberal Liquor Laws? New England Journal of Medicine, 288(8): 406-408, 1973.

3482. Lister, L.M. Inpatient Alcoholic Rehabilitation Care. Maryland State Medical Journal, 20(5): 33-35, 1971.

3483. Litman, G.K., Eiser, J.R. and Taylor, C. Dependence, Relapse and Extinction: A Theoretical Critique and a Behavioral Examination. Journal of Clinical Psychiatry, 35: 192-199, 1979.

3484. Little, Ruth E. and Ervin, Cynthia H. Alcohol Use and Reproduction. In: Alcohol Problems in Women: Antecedents, Consequences, and Intervention. Eds. Sharon C. Wilsnack and Linda J. Beckman. New York: The Guilford Press, 1984, pages 155-188.

3485. Little, William T. The Domestic Illness Profile Seen in a Family-Court Setting. Criminologica, 2(2): 3-8, 1964.

3486. Littleton, J.M. The Biological Basis of Alcoholism: Some Recent Experimental Evidence. In: Alcoholism: New Knowledge and New Responses. Eds. G. Edwards and M. Grant. London: Croom Helm, 1977, pages 107-116.

3487. Litz, Jean Elaine. Life Stresses and Alcoholism in Women. Doctoral Dissertation. (University Microfilms No. 7900793.) (Also in: Dissertation Abstracts International, 39(7): 3525B, 1979.)

3488. Liu, M. Peripheral Blood Lymphocyte Chromosome Aberration and the Sister Chromatid Exchange in Patients with Lead Poisoning Caused by Alcohol Drinking. Chung Hua Yu Fang I Hsueh Tsa Chih, 17(1): 43-44, 1983.

3489. Livingston, R., Nugent, H., Rader, L. and Smith, G.R. Family Histories of Depressed and Severely Anxious Children. American Journal of Psychiatry, 142(12): 1497-1499, 1985.

3490. Lloyd, J. and McMahon, M. Loaf of Bread, a Jug of Wine and Thou. Focus on Alcohol and Drug Issues, 6(2): 10-11, 29-30, 1983.

3491. Lobascher, M.E., Kingerlee, P.E. and Gubbay, S.S. Childhood Autism: An Investigation of Aetiological Factors in Twenty-Five Cases. The British Journal of Psychiatry: The Journal of Mental Science, London, 117(540): 525-529, 1970.

3492. Lobos, Roberto. Marital Problems from the Viewpoint of Social Psychiatry. Schweizer Archiv fur Neurologie Neurochirurgie und Psychiatrie, Zurich, 109(2): 367-397, 1971.

3493. Lockett, D.B. Carrier Clinic: Concealed Repetitive Therapy Techniques. In: Alcoholism Rehabilitation; Methods and Experiences of Private Rehabilitation Centers. NIAAA-RUCAS Alcoholism Treatment Series No. 3. Ed. V. Groupe. New Brunswick, NJ: Rutgers Center of Alcohol Studies, 1978, pages 7-17.

3494. Loehlin, J.C. An Analysis of Alcohol-Related Questionnaire Items From the National Merit Twin Study. Annals of the New York Academy of Sciences, 197: 117-120, 1972.

3495. Loescher, D.A. Time Limited Group Therapy for Alcoholic Marriages. Medical Ecology and Clinical Research, 3(1): 30-32, 1970.

3496. Lofgren, B. Behandling av alkoholism -aktiv familjeterapi ger bra resultat. (Treatment of Alcoholism-Active Family Therapy Gets Good Results.) Lakartidningen, Stockholm, 78: 783-786, 1981.

3497. Lofthouse, W.F. Parental Example and Intemperance. British Journal of Inebriety, 11: 67-75, 1913.

3498. Logan, David G. Getting Alcoholics to Treatment by Social Network Intervention. Hospital and Community Psychiatry, 34(4): 360-361, 1983.

3499. Logan, Diane. Marital Adjustment and Interaction Between Recovered Alcoholic Wives and Their Husbands. Dissertation Abstracts International, 41(10): 4510A, 1980.

3500. Lois, W. Lois Remembers; Memoirs of the Co-Founder of Al-Anon and Wife of the Co-Founder of Alcoholics Anonymous. New York: Family Group Headquarters, 1979.

3501. Lolli, G. Assets Outweigh Liabilities. International Journal of Psychiatry, 9: 358-368, 1970-71.

3502. Lolli, Giorgio. Alcohol and the Family. Paper presented at the
2nd Conference on Alcohol Education, Stowe, VT, October, 1961.
(Also in: Community Factors in Alcohol Education, 1961,
pages 27-41.)

3503. Lolli, Giorgio, Schesler, Esther and Golder, Grace M. Choice of
Alcoholic Beverage among 105 Alcoholics in New York. Quarterly
Journal of Studies on Alcohol, 21: 475-482, 1960.

3504. Lomnitz, Larissa. Alcohol and Culture: The Historical Evolution
of Drinking Patterns Among the Mapuche. In: Cross-Cultural
Approaches to the Study of Alcohol: An Interdisciplinary
Perspective. Eds. Michael W. Everett, Jack O. Waddell and
Dwight B. Heath. Paris: Mouton Publishers, 1976, pages 177-198.

3505. London, Ray William. The Impact of the Practice of Hypnosis Upon
the Therapist. Australian Journal of Clinical Hypnotherapy,
2(1): 15-35, 1981.

3506. Long, B.A. The Relationship Between the Physical/Sexual Abuse
and Rape of Women and the Use of Alcohol. M.S. Thesis.
Long Beach: California State University, 1980.

3507. Long, Jancis V.F. and Vallant, George E. Natural History of
Male Psychological Health. XI: Escape from the Underclass.
American Journal of Psychiatry, 141(3): 341-346 1984.

3508. Longclaws, Lyle, Barnes, Gordon E., Grieve, Linda and Dumoff, Ron.
Alcohol and Drug Use Among the Brokenhead Ojibwa. Journal
of Studies on Alcohol, 41(1): 21-36, 1980.

3509. Longmate, N. Alcohol and the Family in History. In: Alcohol
and the Family. Eds. J. Orford and J. Harwin. New York:
St. Martin's Press, 1982, pages 9-24.

3510. Looser, B. Kinder Von Alkoholikerinnen. (The Children of Women
Alcoholics.) Fursorger, 44: 8-10, 1976.

3511. Lopez, Sarah C. Marital Satisfaction and Wife Abuse as Functions
of Sex-Role Identity, Self-Esteem, and Interpersonal Style.
Dissertation Abstracts International, 42(11): 4560B, 1981.

3512. Lopez-Lee, David. Alcoholism Among Third World Women: Research
and Treatment. In: Women Who Drink: Alcoholic Experience
and Psychotherapy. Ed. Vasanti Burtle. Springfield, IL:
Charles C. Thomas, 1979, pages 98-115.

3513. Loranger, Armand W. and Tulis, Elaine H. Family History of
Alcoholism in Borderline Personality Disorder. Archives
of General Psychiatry, 42: 153-157, 1985.

3514. Loranger, Peter DeGaspe. An Analysis of Problem Drinkers Undergoing
Treatment Through Educational Therapy, Group Therapy and Family
Orientation. Doctoral Dissertation. (University Microfilms
No. 73-7028.) (Also in: Dissertation Abstracts International,
33(9): 4350B, 1973.)

3515. Lorch, B.D. and Crawford, L.E. Marriage to a Physician: The
Stress and Responsibilities. A Comparison of the Roles
of Physicians' and Lawyers' Wives. Colorado Medicine,
80(3): 84-86, 1983.

3516. Lord, Daniel Bryer. Differential Impact of Parental Alcoholism
on Children's Apperceptions. Dissertation Abstracts International, 43(10): 3219A, 1982.

3517. Lord, Daniel Bryer. Parental Alcoholism and the Mental Health of
Children: A Bibliography and Brief Observations. Journal
of Alcohol and Drug Education, 29(1): 1-11, 1983.

3518. Lotterhos, Jerry F. Alcoholism Training Program of North Carolina.
       Inventory, 21(4): 10-13, 1972.

3519. Lourie, R.S. Alcoholism in Children. American Journal of
       Orthopsychiatry, 13: 322-338, 1943.

3520. Lovald, Keith and Neuwirth, Gertrud. Exposed and Shielded Drinking:
       Drinking as Role Behavior and Some Consequences for Social
       Control and Self-Concept. Archives of General Psychiatry,
       19(1): 95-103, 1968.

3521. Love, M. Dependency Problems in General Practice (in the N.Z.
       Setting). Paper presented at the 10th Biennial Summer School
       of the National Society on Alcoholism and Drug Dependency,
       Wellington, New Zealand, January, 1983.

3522. Lovern, J.D. and Zohn, J. Indirect Hypnotic Communication in
       Multiple Family Group Therapy with Alcoholics. Report. CA:
       Loma Linda University School of Medicine, 1980.

3523. Lovern, J.D. and Zohn, J. Utilization and Indirect Suggestion in
       Multiple-Family Group Therapy with Alcoholics. Journal of
       Marital and Family Therapy, 8(3): 325-333, 1982.

3524. Lovinfosse, M. Incest Connection. Alcoholism The National
       Magazine, 5(2): 51, 1984.

3525. Lowe, Warren C. and Thomas, Sam D. Assessing Alcoholism Treatment
       Effectiveness. A Comparison of Three Evaluative Measures.
       Journal of Studies on Alcohol, 37(7): 883-889, 1976.

3526. Lowenfish, S.K. Is Alcoholism in Our Genetic Package and are
       Women the Distributors? A Survey of Hereditary Aspects
       of Alcoholism. Focus on Women, 1(1): 1-14, 1980.

3527. Lowman, Cherry. Facts for Planning No. 6: Parental Dimensions
       in Teenage Drinking. Alcohol Health and Research World,
       6(4): 58-63, 1982.

3528. Lowman, Cherry and Johnson, Nancy. Epidemiology Symposium.
       Alcohol Health and Research World, 7(1): 49, 1982.

3529. Lowney, J. Wall Gang: A Study of Interpersonal Process and
       Deviance among Twenty-Three Middle-Class Youths. Adolescence,
       19(75): 527-538, 1984.

3530. Lowry, J.V. and Ebaugh, F.G. A Post-Repeal Study of 300 Chronic
       Alcoholics. American Journal of the Medical Sciences,
       203: 120-124, 1942.

3531. Lozano-Suarez, M., Hernandez-Garcia, P. and Rodriguex-Treceno, M.
       Terapia De Grupo Familiar En La Asociacion De Alcoholicos
       Rehabilitados De Salamanca. (Family Therapy at the
       Salamanca Association of Rehabilitated Alcoholics.)
       Drogalcohol, 5: 65-72, 1980.

3532. Lubin, Bernard, Lubin, Alice W. and Taylor, Audrey. The Group
       Psychotherapy Literature: 1978. International Journal of
       Group Psychotherapy, 29(4): 523-576, 1979.

3533. Lucero, Rubel Joseph, Jensen, Karl F. and Ramsey, Catherine.
       Alcoholism and Teetotalism in Blood Relatives of Abstaining
       Alcoholics. Quarterly Journal of Studies on Alcohol,
       32(1): 183-185, 1971.

3534. Ludwig, A.M. On and Off the Wagon: Reasons for Drinking and
       Abstaining by Alcoholics. Quarterly Journal of Studies on
       Alcohol, 33: 91-96, 1972.

3535. Ludwig, M.J. and Waite, B.J. Growing Concern: How to Provide Services for Children from Alcoholic Families. Report. Rockville, MD: National Institute on Alcohol Abuse and Alcoholism, 1983.

3536. Luisada, Paul V., Peele, Roger and Pittard, Elizabeth A. The Hysterical Personality in Men. American Journal of Psychiatry, 131(5): 518-522, 1974.

3537. Lukash, William M. The Family Physician and Confrontation in Alcoholism. Cancer Research, 39(7 Pt 2): 2834-2835, 1979.

3538. Luks, Allan (Ed.). Having Been There. New York: Charles Scribner's Sons, 1979.

3539. Lund, Charles A. and Landesman-Dwyer, Sharon. Pre-Delinquent and Disturbed Adolescents: The Role of Parental Alcoholism. In: Currents in Alcoholism. Volume 5. Biomedical Issues and Clinical Effects of Alcoholism. Ed. M. Galanter. New York: Grune and Stratton, 1979, pages 339-348.

3540. Lund, D. The Relation Between the Alcoholism of Parents and the Moral Degeneration of the Children. Tirfing: 77-83, 1920.

3541. Lund, M. Omaha Area Council on Alcoholism, Omaha, Nebraska. In: Services for Children of Alcoholics. Symposium held in September, 1979 at Silver Spring, MD. U.S. National Institute on Alcohol Abuse and Alcoholism. Research Monograph No. 4. Washington, D.C.: U.S. Government Printing Office, 1979, pages 131-137. (DHHS Publication No. (ADM) 81-1007).

3542. Lundquist, G. Delirium Tremens. A Comparative Study of Pathogenesis, Course, and Prognosis with Delirium Tremens. Acta Psychiatrica Scandinavica, 36: 443-466, 1961.

3543. Lundquist, G.A.R. Alcohol Dependence. Acta Psychiatrica Scandinavica, 49 332-340, 1973.

3544. Lutz, M., Appelt, H. and Cohen, R. Problems in Families of Alcoholic and Depressive Women as Seen by Their Husbands. Social Psychiatry, 15(3): 137-144, 1980.

3545. Lydic, L. Mr. Lauren "Al" Lydic: American Council on Alcoholism. Paper presented at the Family Awareness Conference, Washington, D.C., December, 1984, pages 15-16.

3546. Lyman, Bill. Camp NaCOAra: Love is What Makes Dreams Come True. COA Newsletter, 2(3): 3, 5, 1984.

3547. Lynn, E.J. Treatment for Alcoholism: Psychotherapy is Still Alive and Well. Hospital and Community Psychiatry, 27(4): 282-283, 1976.

3548. Lyons, William Kenneth Jr. A Police Recruit Family Program for the Anne Arundel County Police Department. Introducing the Problem of Stress and Resultant Anxiety in the Police Officer and the Secular and Faith Resources Available. Disseration Abstracts International, 42(3): 1235B, 1981.

Mc

3549. MacDonald, D.E. Mental Disorders in Wives of Alcoholics. Quarterly Journal of Studies on Alcohol, 17: 282-287, 1956.

3550. MacDonald, Donald E. Group Characteristics of Alcoholics: A Videotape Demonstration. Annals of the New York Academy of Sciences, 233: 128-134, 1974.

3551. MacDonald, Donald E. Group Psychotherapy with Wives of Alcoholics. Quarterly Journal of Studies on Alcohol, 19: 125-132, 1958.

3552. MacDonald, Donald E. Physician Management of Alcoholism. North Carolina Medical Journal, 31(12): 451-453, 1970.

3553. MacDonald, Donald Ian. Drugs, Drinking, and Alcoholics. Chicago: Year Book Medical Publishers, 1984. (Also in: American Journal of Diseases of Children, 138(2): 117-125, 1984.)

3554. MacDonald, Donald I. From the Administrator. ADAMHA News, (Alcohol, Drug Abuse, and Mental Health Administration), 11(2): 2, 1985.

3555. MacDowell, E.C. The Influence of Parental Alcoholism on the Learning Capacity of the Offspring. Anatomical Record, 11: 502-503, 1916.

3556. MacDowell, E.C. The Influence of Parental Alcoholism Upon Habit Formation in Albino Rats. Proceedings of the Society for Experimental Biology and Medicine, 16: 125-126, 1919.

3557. MacKay, James R. Alcohol, Alcoholism, and Youth. Social Work, 10(1): 75-80, 1965.

3558. MacKay, James R. Clinical Observations on Adolescent Problem Drinkers. Quarterly Journal of Studies on Alcohol, 22: 124-134, 1961.

3559. MacKay, James R. Problem Drinking Among Juvenile Delinquents. In: Crime in America. Ed. B. Cohen. Itasca, IL: F.E. Peacock, 1970, pages 197-202.

3560. MacKay, James R., Murray, Andrew E., Hagerty, Thomas J. and Collins, Lawrence J. Juvenile Delinquency and Drinking Behavior. Journal of Health and Social Behavior, 4(4): 276-282, 1963.

3561. MacKay, James R., Phillips, Derek L. and Bryce, Forbes O. Drinking Behavior Among Teen-Agers: A Comparison of Institutionalized and Non-Institutionalized Youth. Journal of Health and Social Behavior, 8(1): 46-54, 1967.

3562. MacMurray, V.D. The Effect and Nature of Alcohol Use in Cases of Child Abuse and Neglect. Victimology, 4: 29-45, 1979. (Also in: International Sociological Association (ISA), 2746, 1978.)

3563. MacNicholl, T.A. Alcohol and Heredity. International Congress Against Alcoholism, 11: 129-131, 1908.

3564. MacPherson, Myra. Joan Kennedy Faces the Music. McCalls, 110: 92, 135, 136, 138, 140, 1983.

3565. Macrory, Boyd E. The Tavern and the Community. Quarterly Journal of Studies on Alcohol, 13: 609-637, 1952.

3566. MacVicar, A.S. Community Psychiatry in the Canadian Air Division, Europe. Canadian Medical Association Journal, Toronto, 95(7): 307-312, 1966.

3567. McAllister, Robert J. The Mental Health of Members of Religious Communities. International Psychiatry Clinics, London, 5(4): 211-222, 1969.

3568. McAndrew, J.A. Children of Alcoholics: School Intervention. Childhood Education, May/June: 343-345, 1985.

3569. McAndrew, M. Alcoholism, the Family and Youth. Paper presented at the 36th Annual Symposium. Cherry Hill, NJ, June, 1984. (Also in: Blue Book, Volume 36, pages 18-27.)

3570. McAndrew, M. Identification of Alcoholism in Pre-Marriage Counselling. Paper presented at Seton Hall University, 1982. (Also in: Blue Book, Volume 34.)

3571. McAuley, T., Longabaugh, R. and Gross, H. Comparative Effectiveness of Self and Family Forms of the Michigan Alcoholism Screening Test. Journal of Studies on Alcohol, 39: 1622-1627, 1978.

3572. McCabe, E. Family and the Alcoholic. South African Medical Journal, 68(7): 451, 1985.

3573. McCabe, John M. Children in Need: Consent Issues in Treatment. Alcohol Health and Research World, 2(1): 2-12, 1977.

3574. McCabe, John M. Child's Consent to Treatment. Report Prepared for NIAAA. Chicago, IL: National Conference of Commissioners on Uniform State Laws, 1977.

3575. McCabe, Thomas R. Victims No More. Center City, MN: Hazelden Foundation, 1978.

3576. McCafferty, Charles, Cline, David and Jordan, James. Issues in the Psychiatric Approach to Substance Abuse in the Adolescent Psychiatric Annals, 11(8): 53-55, 58-59, 1981.

3577. McCall, Cheryl. Tragic Youth. Life, 7(4): 19, 1984.

3578. McCance, C. Aetiological Factors in Alcoholism: Some Areas of Research. Journal of Psychosomatic Research, London, 14(3): 285-294, 1970.

3579. McCance, Kathryn Lee. Nursing Intervention to Promote Primary and Secondary Intervention of Cad in First Degree Relatives of Sudden Cardiac Death Victims. Dissertation Abstracts International, 43(6): 1796B, 1982.

3580. McCann, J.D. The Destructive Element of Perfectionism as Evidenced in Alcoholism. Pastoral Psychology, 22(211): 23-26, 65, 1971.

3581. McCarrick, Helen. Demon Drink. Nursing Times, London, 66(46): 1433, 1970.

3582. McCarthy, John Michael. The Prevalence of Hopelessness in Hospitalized Alcoholics. Dissertation Abstracts International, 41(12): 4676B, 1981. (Also as: University Microfilms No. 8112340.)

3583. McClearn, G.E. Commonalities in Substance Use: A Genetic Perspective. In: Commonalities in Substance Abuse and Habitual Behavior. Eds. P.K. Levison, D.R. Gerstein and D.R. Maloff. Lexington, MA: Lexington Books, D.C. Heath and Company, 1983, pages 323-341.

3584. McClearn, G.E. Genetic Factors in Alcohol Abuse: Animal Models. In: The Pathogenesis of Alcoholism; Biological Factors. Eds. B. Kissin and H. Begleiter. New York, Plenum Press, 1983, pages 1-30.

3585. McClearn, G.E. Genetics and Alcoholism Simulacra. Alcoholism: Clinical and Experimental Research, 3: 255-258, 1979.

3586. McClearn, G.E. Genetics as a Tool in Alcohol Research. Annals of the New York Academy of Sciences, 197: 26-31, 1972.

3587. McClearn, G.E., Wilson, J.R., Petersen, D.R. and Allen, D.L. Selective Breeding in Mice for Severity of the Ethanol Withdrawal Syndrome. Substance and Alcohol Actions/ Misuse, 3(3): 135-144, 1982.

3588. McClearn, Gerald E. The Genetic Aspects of Alcoholism. In: Alcoholism: Progress in Research and Treatment. Ed. Peter G. Bourne and R. Fox. New York: Academic Press, 1973, pages 337-358.

3589. McClearn, Gerald E. The Genetics of Alcohol Preference. In: International Symposium (on the) Biological Aspects of Alcohol Consumption. Eds. Olof Forsander and Kalervo Eriksson. September, 1971, pages 113-119. (Also in: Finnish Foundation for Alcohol Studies, Helsinki, 20, 1972).

3590. McClearn, Gerald E. and Erwin, V. Gene. Mechanisms of Genetic Influence on Alcohol-Related Behaviors. In: Alcohol Consumption and Related Problems. U.S. Department of Health and Human Services, National Institute on Alcohol Abuse and Alcoholism. NIAAA Alcohol and Health Monograph 1. Washington, D.C.: U.S. Government Printing Office, 1982, pages 263-285.

3591. McClellan, Keith. An Overview of Occupational Alcoholism Issues for the 80's. Journal of Drug Education, 12(1): 1-27, 1982.

3592. McClintock, F.H. Criminological Aspects of Family Violence. In: Violence and the Family Ed. J.P. Martin. New York: Wiley, 1978, pages 81-101.

3593. McConville, Brian J., Soudek, D., Sroka, H., Cote, J., Boag, L. and Berry, J. Length of the Y Chromosome and Chromosomal Variants in Inpatient Children with Psychiatric Disorders: Two Studies. Canadian Journal of Psychiatry, Ottawa, 28(1): 8-13, 1983.

3594. McCord, Joan. Alcoholism and Criminality; Confounding and Differentiating Factors. Journal of Studies on Alcohol, 42: 739-748, 1981.

3595. McCord, Joan. Etiological Factors in Alcoholism; Family and Personal Characteristics. Quarterly Journal of Studies on Alcohol, 33: 1020-1027, 1972.

3596. McCord, Joan. A Forty Year Perspective on Effects of Child Abuse
      and Neglect. Child Abuse and Neglect, 7(3): 265-270, 1983.

3597. McCord, Joan. Some Differences in Backgrounds of Alcoholics and
      Criminals. Annals of the New York Academy of Sciences,
      197: 183-187, 1972.

3598. McCord, Joan and McCord, William. The Effects of Parental Role
      Model on Criminality. In: Readings in Juvenile Deliquency.
      Ed. R. Cavan. New York: J.P. Lippincott, 1969, pages 176-186.

3599. McCord, William and McCord, Joan. A Longitudinal Study of the
      Personality of Alcoholics. In: Society, Culture and Drinking
      Patterns. Eds. D.J. Pittman and C.R. Snyder. New York:
      Wiley, 1962, pages 413-430.

3600. McCord, William and McCord, Joan. Origins of Alcoholism.
      Stanford: Stanford University Press, 1960.

3601. McCord, William, McCord, Joan and Gudeman, Jon. Some Current
      Theories of Alcoholism: A Longitudinal Evaluation. Quarterly
      Journal of Studies on Alcohol, 20: 727-749, 1959.

3602. McCrady, B.S. Conjoint Behavioral Treatment of an Alcoholic and
      His Spouse. In: Clinical Case Studies in the Behavioral
      Treatment of Alcoholism. Eds. William H. Hay and P. Nathan.
      New York: Plenum Press, 1982, pages 127-156.

3603. McCrady, B.S. Marital Dysfunction: Alcoholism and Marriage. In:
      Encyclopedic Handbook of Alcoholism. Eds. E. Pattison and
      E. Kaufman. New York: Gardner Press, 1982, pages 673-685.

3604. McCrady, B.S. Relative Effectiveness of Differing Components of
      Spouse-Involved Alcoholism Treatment. Substance Abuse,
      6(1): 12-15, 1985.

3605. McCrady, B.S. Treating the Alcoholic Marriage. American
      Journal of Family Therapy, 9(3): 87-89, 1981.

3606. McCrady, B.S. Women and Alcoholism. In: Behavior Modification
      with Women. Ed. Elaine A. Blechman. New York: Guilford
      Publications, 1984, pages 428-449.

3607. McCrady, B.S. and Hay, W. The Role of the Spouse in the
      Treatment of Alcoholism. Paper presented at the Annual
      Meeting of the American Psychological Association, New York,
      Septemer, 1979. (Eric Document Number ED182623.)

3608. McCrady, B.S., Moreau, J., Paolino, T.J. Jr. and Longabaugh, R.
      Joint Hospitalization and Couples Therapy for Alcoholism;
      a Four-Year Follow-Up. Journal of Studies on Alcohol,
      43: 1244-1250, 1982.

3609. McCrady, B.S., Paolino, T.J. Jr. and Longabaugh, R. Correspondence
      Between Reports of Problem Drinkers and Spouses on Drinking
      Behavior and Impairment. Journal of Studies on Alcohol,
      39(7): 1252-1257, 1978.

3610. McCrady, B.S., Paolino, T.J. Jr., Longabaugh, R. and Rossi, J.
      Effects of Joint Hospital Admission and Couples Treatment
      for Hospitalized Alcoholics: A Pilot Study. Addictive
      Behaviors, Oxford, 4: 155-165, 1979.

3611. McCrady, B.S. and Wiener, J. Verbal and Nonverbal Marital
      Interactions in Male and Female Alcoholics. Paper presented
      at the Annual Meeting of the Association for the Advancement
      of Behavior Therapy, Chicago, November, 1978.

3612. McCready, William C., Greeley, Andrew M. and Thiesen, Gary.
Ethnicity and Nationality in Alcoholism. In: The Biology
of Alcoholism. Volume 6. The Pathogenesis of Alcohol:
Psychosocial Factors. Eds. Benjamin Kissin and Henri
Begleiter. New York: Plenum Press, 1983, pages 309-340.

3613. McCreery, Patrick. The Three Spheres of Alcoholism. Mental
Hygiene, 60(3): 9-11, 1976.

3614. McCullough, William E. A Two-Year Survey of Alcoholic Patients
in a California State Hospital. Quarterly Journal of
Studies on Alcohol, 13: 240-253, 1952.

3615. McDaniel, J.G. Misery Loves Company. Journal of the Medical
Association of Georgia, 65(3): 97-98, 1976.

3616. McDermott, Diane. The Relationship of Parental Drug Use and
Parents' Attitude Concerning Adolescent Drug Use to
Adolescent Drug Use. Adolescence, 19(73): 89-97, 1984.

3617. McDonald, C. A Controlled Study of Crude-Spirits Drinkers.
Medical Journal of Australia, Sidney, 1: 850-852, 1967.

3618. McDonald, D.I. Progressive Stages of Teenage Drug Abuse.
Paper presented at the Southeast Drug Conference, Atlanta,
April, 1980, pages 131-136.

3619. McDonald, Jay C. Montessori Class Aids Children with Needed
Skills, Independence. Magazine of the Texas Commission
on Alcoholism, 3(3): 20-21, 1977.

3620. McDonald, Jay C. Social Work in Family Life Enrichment: The
Children of Alcoholics -- A Montessori Approach. American
Montessori Society Bulletin, 16(1): 1-14, 1978.
(Eric Document Number ED159532.)

3621. McElfresh, Orville H. Supportive Groups for Teenagers of the
Alcoholic Patient: A Preliminary Report. Medical Ecology
and Clinical Research, 3(1): 26-29, 1970. (Also in:
Perspectives on Treatment of Alcoholism. Eds. M.J. Goby
and J.E. Keller. Park Ridge, IL: Lutheran General Hospital,
1978, pages 82-87.)

3622. McElfresh, Orville H. Timing Issues with Alcoholics and Their
Families. In: Perspectives on Treatment of Alcoholism.
Eds. M.J. Goby and J.E. Keller. Park Ridge, IL: Lutheran
General Hospital, 1978, pages 51-53.

3623. McElhearn, Lura. Community Drinking. Report. Dekalb Junction,
NY: c/o Lura McElhearn, Box 167. 1974.

3624. McFadd, Adrienne C. Milton. Rehabilitation of Married Male
Alcohol Abusers and Wives' Level of Participation in
Treatment. Doctoral Dissertation. (University Microfilms
No. 77-32491.) San Diego: California School of Professional
Psychology, 1976.

3625. McGahee, Bernard M. Psychosocial Reinforcement Model of Alcoholism.
Doctoral Dissertation. (Ann Arbor, MI: University Microfilms
No. 75-07418). Lubbock: Texas Technological University, 1975.

3626. McGenty, D. Family Relationships Contributing to Alcoholism.
American Catholic Sociological Review, 19: 13-23, 1958.

3627. McGlannan, Frances. Abstracts: Childhood Hyperactivity Tied
to Risk of Later Alcoholism; Arousal, Activation, and
Effort in the Control of Attention -- Part II: Activation.
Journal of Learning Disabilities, 10(9): 560-563, 1977.

3628. McGlothlin, William H., Arnold, David O. and Rowan, Paul K.
       Marijuana Use Among Young Adults. Psychiatry, 33(4):
       433-443, 1970.

3629. McGoldrick, Monica. Irish Families. In: Ethnicity and Family
       Therapy. Eds. Monica McGoldrick, John K. Pearce, and
       Joseph Giordano. New York: Guilford Press, 1982, pages
       310-339.

3630. McGoldrick, Monica and Pearce, John K. Family Therapy with Irish-
       Americans. Family Process, 20: 223-241, 1981.

3631. McGoldrick Monica, Pearce, John K. and Giordano, Joseph. (Eds.)
       Ethnicity and Family Therapy. New York: Guilford Press, 1982.

3632. McGonegal, J. The Role of Sanction in Drinking Behavior. Quarterly
       Journal of Studies on Alcohol, 33(3): 692-697, 1972.

3633. McGrath, William, Owens, Uriel and Bigge, Robin. Comprehensive
       Approach for the Treatment of Black Families or Individuals
       with Drinking Problems in Wyandotte County, Kansas. Paper
       presented at the Alcohol and Drug Problems Association
       Conference, San Francisco, December, 1974.

3634. McGuffin, Samuel J. Drinking Patterns of Young People in
       Northern Ireland. Ulster Medical Journal, Belfast,
       48(2): 160-165, 1979.

3635. McGuire, Mariann. The Panel for the Impaired Physician.
       Illinois Medical Journal, 151(4): 286-291, 1977.

3636. McHenry, R. and Crabb, D.W. Alcoholism Research: Recent
       Developments. Indiana Medicine, 78(8): 663-668, 1985.

3637. McInerney, James. Al-Anon As an Aid to Professionals in Alcoholism.
       In: Perspectives on Treatment of Alcoholism. Eds. M.J. Goby
       and J.E. Keller. Park Ridge, IL: Lutheran General Hospital,
       1978, pages 112-116.

3638. McKamy, L. Ray. Multiple Family Therapy on an Alcohol Treatment
       Unit. Family Therapy, 3(3): 197-209, 1976.

3639. McKay, A.J., Hawthorne, V.M. and McCartney, H.N. Drug Taking Among
       Medical Students at Glasgow University. British Medical
       Journal, London, 1(852): 540-543, 1973.

3640. McKechnie, R.J. Parents, Children and Learning to Drink. In:
       Alcoholism and Drug Dependence; A Multidisciplinary Approach.
       Eds. J.S. Madden, R. Walker and W.H. Kenyon. New York: Plenum
       Press, 1977, pages 451-456.

3641. McKechnie, R.J., Cameron, D., Cameron, I.A. and Drewery, J.
       Teenage Drinking in South-West Scotland. British Journal
       of Addiction, 72(4): 287-295, 1977.

3642. McKeever, Eric. How to Handle an Alcoholic or a Problem
       Drinker. Baltimore: The American Young Co., 1978.

3643. McKenna, Thomas and Pickens, Roy. Alcoholic Children of Alcoholics.
       Minneapolis: Hazelden Research Services, 1980. (Also in:
       Journal of Studies on Alcohol, 42(1): 1021-1029, 1981.)

3644. McKenna, Thomas and Pickens, Roy. Personality Characteristics
       of Alcoholic Children of Alcoholics. Minneapolis: Hazelden
       Research Services, 1983. (Also in: Journal of Studies on
       Alcohol, 44(4): 688-700, 1983.)

3645. McKenzie, J.C. Social Implications of Alcohol Consumption.
       Proceedings of the Nutrition Society, London, 31(2):
       99-106, 1972.

3646. McKeon, Patricia and Pandina, Robert J. Extent of Drug Use as
       a Function of Number of Risk Factors. Journal of Abnormal
       Psychology, 91(4): 273-279, 1982.

3647. McKnight, A. Family Systems and Alcoholism. Georgetown Family
       Center Report. Arlington, VA: Alcohol Center, 1982.

3648. McKnight, A. Family Systems Theory and Alcoholism. Paper presented
       at the Georgetown University Family Center Conference,
       Washington, D.C., April, 1982.

3649. McLachlan, J.F.C., Walderman, R.L., Birchmore, D.F. and
       Marsden, L.R. Self-Evaluation, Role Satisfaction, and
       Anxiety in the Woman Alcoholic. International Journal
       of the Addictions, 14: 809-832, 1979.

3650. McLachlan, J.F.C., Walderman, R.L. and Thomas, S. A Study of
       Teenagers with Alcoholic Parents. (Monograph No. 3.)
       Toronto: Donwood Institute, 1973.

3651. McLaughlin, Robert J., Baer, Paul E., Burnside, Mary A. and
       Pokorny, Alex D. Psychosocial Correlates of Alcohol Use
       at Two Age Levels During Adolescence. Journal of Studies
       on Alcohol, 46(3): 212-218, 1985.

3652. McLellan, A. Thomas, Erdlen, Frank R., Erdlen, Diane L. and
       O'Brien, Charles P. Psychological Severity and Response
       to Alcoholism Rehabilitation. Drug and Alcohol Dependence,
       Lausanne, 8(1): 23-36, 1981.

3653. McLellan, A. Thomas, Luborsky, Lester, Woody, George E. and O'Brien,
       Charles P. The Generality of Benefits from Alcohol and Drug
       Abuse Treatments. National Institute on Drug Abuse Research
       Monograph Series, No. 34, 1981, pages 373-379.

3654. McLellan, A. Thomas, Luborsky, Lester, Woody, George E. and
       O'Brien, Charles P. An Improved Diagnostic Evaluation
       Instrument for Substance Abuse Patients: The Addiction
       Severity Index. Journal of Nervous and Mental Disease,
       168(1): 26-33, 1980.

3655. McLellan, A. Thomas, Luborsky, Lester, Woody, George E., O'Brien,
       Charles P. and Kron, Ruben. Are the "Addiction-Related"
       Problems of Substance Abusers Really Related. Journal of
       Nervous and Mental Disease, 169(4): 232-239, 1981.

3656. McLellan, A. Thomas, MacGahan, John A., Druley, Keith A. Changes
       in Drug Abuse Clients 1972-77: Implications for Revised
       Treatment. In: Continuing Medical Education: Syllabus and
       Proceedings in Summary Form. Washington, D.C.: American
       Psychiatric Association, 1978, pages 145-146. (Also in:
       American Journal of Drug and Alcohol Abuse, 6(2): 151-162,
       1979.)

3657. McLellan, A. Thomas, O'Brien, Charles P., Woody, George E.,
       Luborsky, Lester and Druley, Keith A. Is Drug Abuse
       Treatment Effective? National Institute on Drug Abuse
       Research Monograph Series No. 41, 1982, pages 223-229.

3658. McNamara, J.H. The Disease Conception of Alcoholism; Its
       Therapeutic Value for the Alcoholic and His Wife.
       Social Casework, 41: 460-465, 1960.

3659. McNichol, Ronald W. Family Circle Therapy Circular Psychodrama.
       In: The Treatment of Delirium Tremens and Related States.
       Springfield, IL: Charles C. Thomas, 1970, pages 105-118.

3660. McNichol, Ronald W. Understanding the Alcoholic Patient.
       In: The Treatment of Delirium Tremens and Related States.
       Springfield, IL: Charles C. Thomas, 1970, pages 5-11.

3661. McPeek, Francis W. Youth, Alcohol and Delinquency. Quarterly
       Journal of Studies on Alcohol, 4: 568-579, 1944.

3662. McWilliams, James J.   Tough Love: A Method of Coping with the
       Alcoholic and Motivating Her/Him to Accept Treatment.
       Pamphlet. Kansas City: National Council on Alcoholism, 1978.

M

3663. M. Anthony. The Al-Anon Program: A Personal Report. Al-Anon.
       Journal of the American Medical Association, 238(10):
       1062-1063, 1977.

3664. M. Mary. Family Denial. Pamphlet. Center City, MN: Hazelden,
       no date.

3665. Machell, D.F. Belongingness: The Critical Variable in the
       Residential Treatment of Alcoholism. Paper presented at
       the 92nd Annual Convention of the American Psychological
       Association, Toronto, August, 1984.

3666. Machover, S. and Puzzo, F.S. Clinical and Objective Studies
       of Personality Variables in Alcoholism. I. Clinical
       Investigation of the "Alcoholic Personaliy." Quarterly
       Journal of Studies on Alcohol, 20: 505-519, 1959.

3667. Machover, S. and Puzzo, F.S. Clinical and Objective Studies of
       Personality Variables in Alcoholism. II. Clinical Study of
       Personality Correlates of Remissison from Active Alcoholism.
       Quarterly Journal of Studies on Alcohol, 20: 520-527, 1959.

3668. Machover, S. and Puzzo, F.S. Clinical and Objective Studies
       of Personality Variables in Alcoholism. III. An Objective
       Study of Homosexuality in Alcoholism. Quarterly Journal of
       Studies on Alcohol, 20: 528-542, 1959.

3669. Macrae, A.K.M., Ratcliff, R.A.W., and Liddle, S.M. Alcoholism
       in Scotland in the 1960's. Health Bulletin, Edinburgh,
       30(1): 16-22, 1972.

3670. Madden, J.S. and Kenyon, W.H. Group Counseling of Alcoholics
       by a Voluntary Agency. British Journal of Psychiatry:
       London, 126: 289-291, 1975.

3671. Maddox, George L. Adolescence and Alcohol. In: Alcohol Education
       for Classroom and Community: A Source Book for Educators.
       Ed. R.G. McCarthy. New York: McGraw-Hill, 1964, pages 32-47.

3672. Maddox, George L. The Domesticated Drug; Drinking Among Collegians.
       New Haven, CT: College and University Press, 1970.

3673. Maddox, George L. and Allen, Bernice. A Comparative Study of
       Social Definitions of Alcohol and Its Uses Among Selected
       Male Negro and White Undergraduates. Quarterly Journal of
       Studies on Alcohol, 22(3): 418-427, 1961.

3674. Maddox, George L. and McCall, Bevode C. Drinking Among Teenagers:
       A Sociological Interpretation of Alcohol Use by High School
       Students. Monograph No. 4. New Brunswick, NJ: Rutgers Center
       of Alcohol Studies, 1964.

3675. Maddux, J.F. and Desmond, D.P. Heroin Addicts and Nonaddicted Brothers. American Journal of Drug and Alcohol Abuse, 10(2): 237-248, 1984.

3676. Madison, Bernice. Family and Child Welfare Services. In: Social Welfare in the Soviet Union. Ed. B. Madison. Stanford, CA: Stanford University Press, 1968, pages 147-176.

3677. Magni, G. Symmetry and Complementarity in the Alcoholic Marriage: A Pilot Study. Drug and Alcohol Dependence, Lausanne, 11(3/4): 373-381, 1983.

3678. Magri, S. Neurobiologic Aspects of Familial Alcoholism. Lavoro Neuropsichiatrico, Rome, 67(3): 53-76, 1980.

3679. Maida, Carl A. Social-Network Considerations in the Alcohol Field. In: Recent Developments in Alcoholism, Volume 2; Learning and Social Models; Alcohol and the Liver; Aging and Alcoholism; Anthropology. Ed. M. Galanter. New York: Plenum Press, 1984, pages 339-353.

3680. Maida, P.R. Parent-Peer Group Relationships and Teenage Drug Use. Rockville, MD: National Institute of Mental Health, 1973.

3681. Mainard, R., De Berranger, P. and Cadudal, J.L. Une Consequence Frequente Et Grave De L'Alcoolisme Parental: Les Sevices Commis Sur Les Enfants. (Frequent and Serious Consequence of Parental Alcoholism: Child Abuse.) Revue De L'Alcoolisme, Paris, 17(1): 21-23, 1971.

3682. Majchrowicz, E. and Hunt, W.A. Neurobiological Correlates of Intoxication and Physical Dependence upon Ethanol: Introductory Remarks. Federation Proceedings, 40(7): 2048-2049, 1981.

3683. Majchrzak, Shirley. At-Home Rehabilitation Program for Families of Women Alcoholics. Paper presented at the Annual Meeting of the Canadian Guidance and Counseling Association, Halifax, 1976. (Eric Document Number ED143960.)

3684. Majumdar, Mahbubon N. and Bhatia, Pritam, S. Effective Family Position and Likelihood of Becoming an Alcoholic. Paper presented at the 104th National Conference on Social Welfare, Chicago, May, 1977. (Also in: Journal of Alcohol and Drug Education, 25(2): 19-31, 1980.)

3685. Malcolm, M.T. and Madden, J.S. The Use of Disulfiram Implantation in Alcoholism. The British Journal of Psychiatry, London, 123(572): 41-45, 1973.

3686. Maletzky, Barry M. The Episodic Dyscontrol Syndrome. Diseases of the Nervous System, 34(3): 178-185, 1973.

3687. Malhotra, M.K. Alkohol Bei Schulern im Kreis Mettmann. (Alcohol Among School Students in the Mettmann Region.) Offentliche Gesundheitswesen, Stuttgart, 38(4): 226-245, 1976.

3688. Malhotra, M.K. Familial and Personal Correlates (Risk Factors) of Drug Consumption Among German Youth. Acta Paedopsychiatrica, 49(5): 199-209, 1983.

3689. Malignac, G. Delinquance Juvenile et Alcoolisme. (Juvenile Delinquency and Alcoholism.) Reeducation, Paris, 8(53): 27-31, 1954.

3690. Malinas, C. and Malinas, Y. Emile Zola and Medical Genetics. Comments about Hereditary Neurosis in the Rougon-Macquart Family. Journal of Genetique Humaine, 29(5): 593-602, 1981.

3691. Mallams, John H., Godley, Mark D., Hall, George M. and Meyers,
       Robert J. A Social-Systems Approach to Resocializing
       Alcoholics in the Community. Journal of Studies on Alcohol,
       43(11): 1115-1123, 1982.

3692. Malloy, Elaine S. Strategies in Sexual Counseling in Alcoholic
       Marriages. Paper presented at the Workshop on Sexual
       Counseling for Persons with Alcohol Problems, Pittsburgh,
       PA, January, 1976, pages, 66-81.

3693. Mally, M.A. A Study of Family Patterns of Alcoholic Marriages.
       American Journal of Orthopsychiatry, 35: 325-326, 1965.

3694. Maltby, K. Children Remembered: Echoes of Parental Alcoholism
       Linger on. Part I. The Journal, 14(4): C1-C4, 1985.

3695. Maltby, K. Children Remembered: Echoes of Parental Alcoholism
       Linger on. Part II. The Journal, 14(5): C1-C4, 1985.

3696. Malzberg, Benjamin. First Admissions with Alcoholic Psychoses
       in New York State, Year Ended March 31, 1984. With a Note on
       First Admissions for Alcoholism Without Psychosis. Quarterly
       Journal of Studies on Alcohol, 10: 461-470, 1949.

3697. Malzberg, Benjamin. A Study of First Admissions with Alcoholic
       Psychoses in New York State, 1943-1944. Quarterly Journal
       of Studies on Alcohol, 8: 274-295, 1947.

3698. Mandel, Jack Sheldon. Epidemiologic Study of Etiologic Factors in
       Prostatic Cancer. Dissertation Abstracts International,
       42(1): 155B, 1981.

3699. Mandel, Jane B. and Marcotte, David B. Teaching Family Practice
       Residents to Identify and Treat Battered Women. Journal of
       Family Practice, 17(4): 708-716, 1983.

3700. Mandell, W. Youthful Alcoholism: Sources, Dynamics and Treatment.
       Alcohol Technical Reports, 12-13: 13-22, 1983-84.

3701. Mandell, Wallace. Types and Phases of Alcohol Dependence Illness.
       In: Recent Developments in Alcoholism, Volume 1, Genetics,
       Behavioral Treatment, Social Mediators and Prevention,
       Current Concepts in Diagnosis. Ed. Marc Galanter.
       New York: Plenum Press, 1983, pages 415-447.

3702. Mandic, N. Difficulties in Alcoholics' Families Reorganizing.
       Alcoholism: Journal on Alcoholism and Related Addictions,
       Zagreb, 18(1): 50-54, 1982.

3703. Mandic, N. Bracni i Obiteljski Zivot Kao Mjerilo Uspjesnosti
       Rehabilitacije Alkoholicara. (Marital and Family Life --
       The Criterion of Success in Alcoholism Rehabilitation.)
       Alkoholizam, Beograd, 19(3-4): 131-138, 1979.

3704. Mandic, N. The Structure of Therapeutic Group of Alcoholics.
       Alcoholism, Zagreb, 14: 158-163, 1978.

3705. Mandic, N. and Ruzic, K. Anxiety in the Alcoholic's Family.
       Alcoholism: Journal of Alcoholism and Related
       Addictions, 12(2): 92-97, 1976.

3706. Mann, G.A. An Alcoholic Treatment Center; An Interim Report
       on the Planning and Implementation Within a Community.
       Minnesota Medicine, 53: 455-457, 1970.

3707. Mann, G.A. An Alcoholic Treatment Center in a Community General
       Hospital. Hospital Progress, 50: 125-128, 1969.

3708. Mann, M. The Family of the Alcoholic. In: Steps for Today
       Toward Better Mental Health. Report of the 1957 National
       Health Forum. Cincinnati: National Health Council, 1957,
       pages 58-61.

3709. Manohar, V., Des-Roches, J. and Ferneau, E.W. Jr. An Education
       Program in Alcoholism for Social Workers: Its Impact on
       Attitudes and Treatment Oriented Behavior. British Journal
       of Addictions, 71: 225-234, 1976.

3710. Man's Drinking May Harm His Offspring. Science News, 107:
       116, 1975.

3711. Mansfield, E. Eating Disorders and Alcoholism: Linking
       Family System Dynamics. Focus on Family and Chemical
       Dependency, 7(4): 22, 27-28, 31, 1984.

3712. Manshadi, Manoochehr, Lippmann, Steven, O'Daniel, Regina G. and
       Blackman, Anita. Alcohol Abuse and Attention Deficit
       Disorder. Journal of Clinical Psychiatry, 44(10):
       379-380, 1983.

3713. Mantek, M. Alcoholism in Women. (STIAR 30.) Rockville, MD:
       National Clearinghouse for Alcohol Information, 1979.

3714. Manzke, H. and Grosse, F.R. Inkomplettes und Komplettes
       "Fetales Alkoholsyndrom" Bei Drei Kindern Einer Trinkerin.
       (Incomplete and Complete "Fetal Alcohol Syndrome" in Three
       Children of an Alcoholic Mother.) Medizinische Welt,
       Stuttgart, 26: 709-712, 1975.

3715. Mapes, B.E., Johnson, R.A. and Sandler, K.R. Alcoholic Family:
       Diagnosis and Treatment. Alcoholism Treatment Quarterly,
       1(4): 67-83, 1984.

3716. Mapother, Edward. Aetiology of Alcoholism. Proceedings of the
       Royal Society of Medicine, 21: 1346-1351, 1928.

3717. Marcelli, D. Suicidal Attempts of the Child: Statistical and
       General Epidemiological Aspects. Acta Paedopsychiatrica,
       43(5-6): 213-221, 1978.

3718. Marcinkowski, W. Los Najbiedniejszych. (The Lot of the Most
       Unfortunate. The Children of Inebriates.) Problemy
       Alkoholizmu, Warsaw, 26(4): 12, 1979.

3719. Marcus, A. and Tisne, S. Correlates of Academic Achievement
       in Children of Alcoholic Mothers. Paper presented at the
       National Council on Alcoholism Forum, Washington, D.C., April,
       1985.

3720. Marcus, A.M. Comparative Study of Maternal Alcoholism and
       Maternal Child-Rearing Attitudes, Child Perception of
       Maternal Behavior, Child's Academic Achievement and School
       Attendance. Doctoral Dissertation. New York: Fordham
       University. Dissertation Abstracts International, 44(7):
       2267B, 1984.

3721. Marcus, S.H. Relationship of Social Support to Remaining
       in Alcoholism Treatment: A Multivariate Approach. Doctoral
       Dissertation. Fort Worth: Texas Christian University.
       Dissertation Abstracts International, 45(8): 2717B, 1985.

3722. Mardones, J. Evidence of Genetic Factors in the Appetite for
       Alcohol and Alcoholism. Annals of the New York Academy
       of Sciences, 197: 138-142, 1972.

3723. Mardones, J. On the Relationship Between Deficiency of B Vitamins and Alcohol Intake in Rats. *Quarterly Journal of Studies on Alcohol*, 12: 563-575, 1951.

3724. Mardones, J., Segovia, N. and Hederra, A. Herencia del Alcoholismo en Ratas. I. Comportamiento de la Primera Generacion de Ratas Bebedoras, Colocadas en Dieta Carenciada en Factor N . (Inheritance of Alcoholism in Rats. I. Behavior of the First Generation of Alcoholic Rats Placed on Factor N -Deficient Diets.) *Revista de Medicina y Alimentacion*, Chile, 9: 61-62, 1950.

3725. Marek, Andrzej E. and Redo, Slawomir. Drug Abuse in Poland. *Bulletin on Narcotics*, 30(1): 43-53, 1978.

3726. Mareth, Thomas Ray. Suicide and the Family Physician: Clinical Assessment of Suicide Risk. *Texas Medicine*, 73(10): 57-63, 1977.

3727. Marg, E. and Busche, P. Ergebnisse der Stationaren Behandlung Chronischer Trinker: Ein Katamnestischer Bericht. (Results of Hospital Treatment of Chronic Drinkers. Case History.) *Psychiatrie, Neurologi und Medizinische Psychologie*, Leipzig, 22(11): 424-427, 1970.

3728. Margolis, M., Krystal, H. and Siegal, S. Psychotherapy with Alcoholic Offenders. *Quarterly Journal of Studies on Alcohol*, 25: 85-99, 1964.

3729. Margulies, Rebecca Z., Kessler, Ronald C. and Kandel, Denise B. A Longitudinal Study of Onset of Drinking Among High-School Students. *Journal of Studies on Alcohol*, 38(5): 897-912, 1977.

3730. Maril, Robert and Zavaleta, Anthony. Drinking Patterns of Low-Income Mexican Women. *Journal of Studies on Alcohol*, 40(5): 480-484, 1979.

3731. Marin, Gerardo. Social-Psychological Correlates of Drug Use Among Colombian University Students. *The International Journal of the Addictions*, 11(2): 199-207, 1976.

3732. Marjot, D.H. Alcohol, Aggression, and Violence. *Practitioner*, London, 226(1364): 287-290, 292, 294, 1982.

3733. Marjot, D.H. Aspects of Alcohol and Service Medicine. *Journal of the Royal Naval Medical Service*, 53: 113-136, 1967.

3734. Markell, W.A. Alcohol Abuse Prevention Through Group Work with Elementary-Age Children and Their Families. *Proceedings of the Fourth Annual Alcoholism Conference, National Institute on Alcohol Abuse and Alcoholism*. Ed. Morris E. Chafetz. Rockville, MD: National Institute on Alcohol Abuse and Alcoholism, 1975, pages 470-475.

3735. Markham, J.E. Alcohol and Food in Health and Disease; Sociological Aspects of Alcohol and Food Deviations. *Annals of the New York Academy of Sciences*, 133(3): 814-819, 1966.

3736. Marmot, M.G., Adelstein, A.M. and Bulusu, L. Epidemiology: Lessons From the Study of Immigrant Mortality. *The Lancet*, 1(8392): 1455-1459, 1984.

3737. Maroncelli, P. La Personalita Premorbosa Nelle Psicosi Alcooliche. (The Premorbid Personality in Alcoholic Psychoses.) *Giornale di Psichiatria e de Neuropatologia*, Ferrara, 85: 151-170, 1957.

3738. Marriott, J.A.S. Family Background and Psychiatric Disorders:
       Experience with Admissions to the University Hospital of
       the West Indies. Canadian Psychiatric Association Journal,
       Ottawa, 18(3): 209-214, 1973.

3739. Marsden, Dennis. Sociological Perspectives on Family Violence.
       In: Violence in the Family. Ed. J.P. Martin. New York:
       Wiley, 1978, pages 103-133.

3740. Marsh, J. You Can Help the Alcoholic: A Christian Plan for
       Intervention. Notre Dame, IN: Ave Maria Press, 1983.

3741. Marsh, Jeanne C., Colten, Mary Ellen and Tucker, M. Belinda.
       Women's Use of Drugs and Alcohol: New Perspectives.
       The Journal of Social Issues, 38(2): 1-8, 1982.

3742. Marshall, H. Daddy, Please Don't Get Drunk! Freedom Fighter
       Wyoming State, 1(1): 6-7, 1985.

3743. Marshall, K. and Milkman, H. Countering Resistance to a
       Community Oriented, Academically Based Alcoholism Family
       Specialist Training Program. Paper presented at the
       National Council on Alcoholism Forum, Washington, D.C., 1982.

3744. Marshall, K.M. Teaching Family Therapy Skills to Alcoholism
       Specialists. Report. Denver: Drug and/or Alcohol Institute
       of Metropolitan State College, no date.

3745. Marson, Stephen M. The Alcoholic Client and the Rehabilitation
       Counselor. Journal of Applied Rehabilitation Counseling,
       9(3): 91-95, 1978.

3746. Marten, Sue, Munoz, Rodrigo A., Gentry, Kathye A. and Robins, Eli.
       Belligerence: Its Frequency and Correlates in a Psychiatric
       Emergency Room Population. Comprehensive Psychiatry,
       13(3): 241-249, 1972.

3747. Marten, Sue A., Cadoret, Remi J., Winokur, George and Ora, Elizabeth.
       Unipolar Depression: A Family History Study. Biological
       Psychiatry, 4(3): 205-213, 1972.

3748. Martensen-Larsen, O. Kann der Unterschied in der Familienkonstellation
       der Alkoholiker, Epileptiker und Schizophrenen Psychodynamisch
       Ursachen Enthullen? (Can the Difference in the Family
       Constellation of Alcoholics, Epileptics and Schizophrenics Reveal
       Psychodynamic Causes?) Acta Psychiatrica Scandinavica,
       Copenhagen, 39(Supplement 169): 193-196, 1963.

3749. Martensen-Larsen, O. Dokumentationsbeispiele Zur Familienanamnese
       Als Zugang Zum Problem Der "Endogenitat." (Documented
       Examples of the Family Asamnesis as an Approach to the
       Problem of Endogeny.) Psychotherapy & Psychosomatics,
       15(1): 44, 1967.

3750. Martensen-Larsen, O. The Family Constellation Analysis and
       Alcoholism. Acta Geneticae et Statistica Medica, 7:
       441-444, 1957.

3751. Martensen-Larsen, O. Family Constellation Analysis and Male
       Alcoholism. Acta Psychiatrica Scandinavica, Copenhagen,
       106(Supplement): 241-247, 1956.

3752. Martensen-Larsen, O. Die Bedeutung der Behandlung Beider Ehegatten,
       Mit Besonderer Berucksichtigung der Gruppentherapie von
       Alkoholikern. (The Importance of Treatment of Both Spouses,
       with Special Reference to Group Therapy of Alcoholics.) Acta
       Psychiatrica Scandinavica, Copenhagen, 39(Supplement 169):
       134-135, 1963.

3753. Martin, Del. Drunkenness and Alcoholism. In: Battered Wives.
       San Francisco: Glide Publications, 1976, pages 55-57.

3754. Martin, I.C.A. Are We Treating the Right Person? Nursing
       Times, London, 73(34): 1332-1333, 1977.

3755. Martin, J. Alcohol and the Family: Three Sure Ways to Solve
       the Problem. Ligouri, MO: Liguori Publications, 1978.

3756. Martin, Joseph C. No Laughing Matter. Center City, MN:
       Hazelden, no date.

3757. Martin, Joseph C. Spiritually and the Family. In: Alcoholism
       and the Family: A Book of Readings. Eds. Sharon
       Wegscheider-Cruse and Richard Esterly. Wernersville, PA:
       Caron Institute, 1985, pages 63-67.

3758. Martin, J.C. With Love and a Blessing. Recovery Newsletter in
       Alcoholism the National Magazine, 5(6): R4, 1985.

3759. Martin, J.P. (Ed.) Violence and the Family. New York: Wiley, 1978.

3760. Martin, M.J. Familial Correlates of Child Abuse and Neglect.
       Doctoral Dissertation. (University Microfilms No. 7923131.)
       Athens: Georgia University, 1979.

3761. Martin, Maurice J. Psychiatric Problems of Physicians and Their
       Families. Mayo Clinic Proceedings, 56(1): 35-44, 1981.

3762. Martin, N.G., Perl, J., Oakeshott, J.G., Gibson, J.B., Starmer,
       G.A. and Wilks, A.V. Twin Study of Ethanol Metabolism.
       Behavior Genetics, 15(2): 93-109, 1985.

3763. Martin, Ronald L., Cloninger, C. Robert and Guze, Samuel B.
       Alcoholism and Female Criminality. Journal of Clinical
       Psychiatry, 43: 400-403, 1982.

3764. Martinez, I. Factors Associated with Cancer of the Esophagus,
       Mouth, and Pharynx in Puerto Rico. Journal of the National
       Cancer Institute, 42(6): 1069-1094, 1969.

3765. Mascari, J.B. and Sanders-Mascari, A. Family Meetings: Prevention
       Begins in the Home. Focus on Family and Chemical Dependency,
       7(3): 17-19, 1984.

3766. Mascia, George V., Bowen, William T. and Goldstein, Gerald.
       Predicting the In-Hospital Responsiveness to Treatment of
       Alcoholics. Social Factors as Predictors of Outcome.
       Brain Damage as a Factor in Treatment of Chronic Alcoholic
       Patients. 1970. (Eric Document Number ED044734.)

3767. Maslach, Christina and Jackson, Susan E. Burned-Out Cops and
       Their Families. Psychology Today, 12(12): 58-62, 1979.

3768. Mason, J.B. and Arnold, J.F. Epidemiological Patterns of
       Alcoholism in Family and General-Practice. Alcoholism:
       Clinical and Experimental Research, 3(2): 185, 1979.

3769. Mason, M. Relationships to Recovery: Sexuality as an Intimacy
       Barrier. In: Alcoholism: A Modern Perspective.
       Ed. P. Golding. Lancaster, England: MTP Press, 1982,
       pages 243-253.

3770. Masserman, J.H. Alcoholism: Disease or Dis-ease? International
       Journal of Mental Health, 5: 3-15, 1976.

3771. Masserman, J.H. and Wigdahl, L.C. The Neuroses. Progress in
       Neurology and Psychiatry, 23: 482-495, 1968.

3772. Massey, E.W. Neurology of the "Nonalcoholic." American Journal of Psychiatry, 134: 328, 1977.

3773. Massot, Hamel J. and Deliry. Alcoolisme Feminin: Donnees Statistiques Et Psychopathologiques. (Alcoholism in Women; Statistical and Psychopathological Data.) Journal de Medicine de Lyon, 37: 265-269, 1956.

3774. Masterson, Patricia Jane. An Exploratory Study of the Effects of Alcoholism on Families that Remain Intact. Doctoral Dissertation. (University Microfilms No. 8011465.) Kent State University, 1979. (Also in: Dissertation Abstracts International, 40(11): 5796A, 1979.)

3775. Masuda, Minoru and Holmes, Thomas H. Life Events: Perceptions and Frequencies. Psychosomatic Medicine, 40(3): 236-261, 1978.

3776. Masur, J. Abordagem Biologica, Psicologica E Social Do Alcoolismo. (Biological, Psychological and Social Approach to Alcoholism.) Ciencia E Cultura, Sao Paulo, 30: 686-696, 1978.

3777. Masur, J., Del-Porto, J.A., Shirakawa, A.J.M. and Gattaz, D. Nonmedical Treatment of Alcoholism with Emetic Drugs and Disulfiram in Brazil. Journal of Studies on Alcohol, 42: 814-817, 1981.

3778. Matakas, F., Koester, H. and Leidner, B. Welche Behandlung Fur Welche Alkoholiker? Eine Ubersicht. (Which Treatment for Which Alcoholics? A Review.) Psychiatrische Praxis, 5: 143-152, 1978.

3779. Matejcek, Zdenek. Deti V Rodinach Alkoholiku. (Children in Families of Alcoholics.) Psychologia A Patopsychologia Dietata, 16(6): 537-560, 1981.

3780. Matejcek, Zdenek. Deti V Rodinach Alkoholiku: 1. Vychovna Situace V Rodinach. (Children in Families of Alcoholics: I. Rearing Situation.) Psychologia A Patopsychologia Dietata, 16(4): 303-318, 1981.

3781. Matejcek, Zdenek. Vyzkum Deti z Rodin Alkoholiku. (Study of Children from Families of Alcoholics. Protialkoholicky Obzor, Bratislava, 13: 201-205, 1978.

3782. Matejcek, Zdenek and Bauerova, N. Health Status of Children from Families of Alcoholics. Ceskoslovenska Pediatrie, Prague, 36(10): 588-592, 1981.

3783. Matejcek, Zdenek, Skala, J. and Kmoskova, L. The Alcoholism Score and the Child Rearing Situation in Families of Alcoholics. Ceskoslovenska Psychiatrie, Prague, 79(6): 380-386, 1983.

3784. Matejcek, Zdenek and Strohbachova, Ingrid. Kresba Zacarovane Rodiny. (The Drawing of an Enchanted Family.) Ceskoslovenska Psychologie, 25(4): 316-329, 1981.

3785. Mathers, G.C. Alcoholism and Drug Addiction in a Small Community. Personal View. British Medical Journal, London, 3(5716): 220, 1970.

3786. Mathews, J.D. Significance of Genetic Factors in Alcohol-Related Diseases. Paper presented at the 1980 Autumn School of Studies on Alcohol and Drugs, Melbourne, 1980, pages 203-213.

3787. Matijevic, I. Alkoholizam U Obiteljima Malodobnih Prijestupnika. (Alcoholism in the Families of Juvenile Delinquents.) Anali Klinicke Bolnice "Dr. M. Stojanovic", Zagreb, 14(4): 98-101, 1975.

3788.   Matsui, R.T. Honorable Robert T. Matsui (D-Calif.). Paper presented
        at the Family Awareness Conference, Washington, D.C.,
        December, 1984, pages 4-7.

3789.   Matter, M.L. and McAllister, W.F. Relationship Enhancement for
        the Recovering Couple: Working with the Intangible.
        Focus on Family and Chemical Dependency, 7(5): 21-23,
        40, 1984.

3790.   Mattera, Gloria, Watson, James, Kunitz, Stephen, Lynch, Robert
        and Morales, Richard. Alcohol Use Among Migrant Laborers.
        Final Report. New York State Health Research Council, 1983.
        (Eric Document Number ED234937.)

3791.   Matthews, R.A. Co-Alcoholism as an Indicator of Family Denial.
        Almacan, 12(8): 8-9, 1982.

3792.   Mattison, Judith. I'm Worried About Your Drinking. Feelings
        of Family & Friends Who Care. Minneapolis: Augsburg
        Publishing House, 1978.

3793.   Matveev, V.F., Kucher, L.D. and Lagovskii, Alu. Development
        and Prognosis of Alcoholism. Sovetskaya Meditsina, 12:
        15-19, 1979.

3794.   Maule, H.G. and Cooper, J. Alcoholism and Crime; A Study of the
        Drinking and Criminal Habits of 50 Discharged Prisoners.
        British Journal of Addiction, Edinburgh, 61: 201-212, 1966.

3795.   Maus, L. Mervin. Alcohol and Racial Degeneracy. Medical Record,
        85: 102-105, 1914.

3796.   Maximy, B. de. Alcoolisme et Comportement Sexuel. (Alcoholism
        and Sexual Behavior.) Alcool ou Sante, Paris, 160(1):
        33-38, 1982.

3797.   Maxwell, Milton A. Drinking Behavior in the State of Washington.
        Quarterly Journal of Studies on Alcohol, 13: 219-239, 1952.

3798.   Maxwell, Ruth. The Booze Battle. New York: Praeger
        Publishers, 1976.

3799.   May, J. Family Unit Clinic; An Attack on Alcoholism. Nursing
        Times, London, 61: 406-407, 1965.

3800.   May, M. Violence in the Family: An Historical Perspective.
        In: Violence and the Family. Ed. J.P. Martin. New York:
        Wiley, 1978, pages 135-167.

3801.   Mayer, John E. Adolescent Alcohol Misuse: A Family Systems
        Perspective. Journal of Alcohol and Drug Education,
        26(1): 1-11, 1980.

3802.   Mayer, John E. and Filstead, William J. (Eds.) Adolescence and
        Alcohol. Cambridge, MA: Ballinger Publishing Company, 1980.

3803.   Mayer, Joseph and Black, Rebecca. Child Abuse and Neglect in
        Families with an Alcohol or Opiate Addicted Parent.
        Boston: Washington Center for Addictions, 1976. (Also in:
        Child Abuse and Neglect, 1: 85-98, 1977; Drugs and the
        Family. Ed. Thomas J. Glynn. Washington, D.C.: U.S.
        Government Printing Office, 1981, pages 116-117.)

3804.   Mayer, Joseph and Black, Rebecca. Child Care Issues in Families
        with Alcoholism. Paper presented at the National Council on
        Alcoholism Annual Forum, Washington, D.C., May, 1976.

3805. Mayer, Joseph and Black, Rebecca. An Investigation of the
       Relationship Between Substance Abuse and Child Abuse and
       Neglect. Boston: National Center on Child Abuse and
       Neglect, 1975.

3806. Mayer, Joseph and Black, Rebecca. The Relationship Between
       Alcoholism and Child Abuse/Neglect. Paper presented at the
       7th Annual Medical-Scientific Session of the National
       Alcoholism Forum, Washington, D.C., May, 1976. (Also in:
       Currents in Alcoholism. Ed. F.A. Seixas, New York:
       Grune and Stratton, 1977, pages 429-444.

3807. Mayer, Joseph, Black, Rebecca and MacDonall, James S. Child-Abuse
       and Neglect in Families with an Alcohol Addicted Parent.
       Alcoholism: Clinical and Experimental Research, 1(2): 176,
       1977.

3808. Mayer, Joseph, Black, Rebecca and MacDonall, James. Child Care
       in Families with an Alcohol-Addicted Parent. In: Currents
       in Alcoholism. Volume 4. Psychiatric, Psychological,
       Social and Epidemiological Studies. Ed. Frank A. Seixas,
       New York: Grune and Stratton, 1978, pages 329-338.

3809. Mayer, Joseph and Green, Monroe. Group Therapy of Alcoholic
       Women Ex-Prisoners. Quarterly Journal of Studies on
       Alcohol, 28: 483-504, 1967.

3810. Mayer, Joseph and Myerson, David J. Characteristics of Outpatient
       Alcoholics in Relation to Change in Drinking, Work and
       Marital Status During Treatment. Quarterly Journal of
       Studies on Alcohol, 31(4): 889-897, 1970.

3811. Maynard, Peter E. and Maynard, Nancy E. Stress in Police
       Families: Some Policy Implications. Journal of Police
       Science & Administration, 10(3): 302-314, 1982.

3812. Mayo, Yolanda Q. Summary and Recommendations. In: Proceedings
       of Puerto Rican Conferences on Human Services. Ed. D.J.
       Curren. Washington, D.C.: National Coalition of Spanish-
       Speaking Mental Health Organizations, 1975, pages 107-110.

3813. Mazalkova, J. Adaptation to Psychological Examination Depending
       on the Family Type and on Age of the Child. Ceskoslovenska
       Psychologie, 18: 308-326, 1974. (Also in: Pediatrics
       and Pediatric Surgery, 33(2323), 1975.)

3814. Mazer, M. Characteristics of Multi-Problem Households. A Study
       in Psychosocial Epidemiology. American Journal of Ortho-
       Psychiatry, 42(5): 792-802, 1972.

3815. Mazza, Nicholas. Poetry: A Therapeutic Tool in the Early Stages
       of Alcoholism Treatment. Journal of Studies on Alcohol,
       40(1): 123-128, 1979.

3816. Meadow, Arnold, Estabridis, Horacio and Batallanos, Elias. La
       Delincuencia Femenina. (Female Delinquency.) Revista De
       Ciencias Psicologicas Y Neurologicas, Lima, 4(2-3):
       145-176, 1967.

3817. Mechkunov, K. Soin De La Famille Et De La Societe Chez Les
       Alcooliques. (Family Care and Society Care of Alcoholics.)
       Alcoholism, Zagreb, 9: 22-25, 1973.

3818. Mecir, J., Meskova, H. and Pihrtova, S. Delinkuenti A Nedelinkuenti
       Evidovani V Protialkoholni Poradne Pro Mladistve V Praze.
       (Delinquents and Non-Delinquents Registered at a Juvenile
       Antialcoholic Clinic in Prague.) Ceskoslovenska Psychiatrie,
       Prague, 72(3): 156-163, 1976.

3819. Meddings, J. Place of Inpatient Treatment in Dealing with Alcoholism. In: Alcoholism: A Modern Perspective. Ed. P. Golding. Lancaster, England: MTP Press, 1982, pages 209-213.

3820. Mednick, S.A. and Gabrielli, W.F. Intellectual Performance in Children of Alcoholics. Journal of Nervous and Mental Disease, 171(7): 444-447, 1983.

3821. Medora, Nilufer Phiroze. Variables Affecting Loneliness Among Individuals Undergoing Treatment in Alcohol Rehabilitation Centers. Dissertation Abstracts International, 44(4): 958A, 1983.

3822. Meehan, Thomas W. The Relationship Between Alcoholism and Child Battering. Smith College Studies in Social Work, 47(1): 34-35, 1976.

3823. Meeks, Donald E. Alcoholism and the Family. Pamphlet. Toronto: Addiction Research Foundation School for Addiction Studies, 1978.

3824. Meeks, Donald E. Family Therapy. In: Alcoholism. Eds. R.E. Tarter and A.A. Sugerman. Reading, MA: Addison-Wesley, 1976, pages 835-852.

3825. Meeks, Donald E. Family Therapy with the Families of Recovering Alcoholics. Pamphlet. New York: National Council on Alcoholism, no date.

3826. Meeks, Donald E. and Kelly, Colleen. Family Therapy with the Families of Recovering Alcoholics. Quarterly Journal of Studies on Alcohol, 31: 399-413, 1970. (Also in: Alcoholism: Introduction to Theory and Treatment. Ed. D.A. Ward. Dubuque, IA: Kendall/Hunt Publishing Co., 1980, pages 373-383.)

3827. Mehl, Duane. You and the Alcoholic in Your Home. Minneapolis, MN: Augsburg Publishing House, 1979.

3828. Mehle, Miran. Mental and Social Prophylaxis of Cardiovascular Diseases. Psihijatrija Danas, 11(3-4): 339-343, 1979.

3829. Meier-Tackmann, D. Untersuchungen zum Polymorphismus der Alkoholdehydrogenase und Aldehyddehydrogen ase in Menschlichen Autopsieproben, Blut und Haarwurzeln. (Polymorphism of Alcohol Dehydrogenase and Aldehyde Dehydrogenase in Human Autopsy Samples, Blood, and Hair Follicles.) Beitrage Zur Gerichtlichen Medizin, Vienna, 39: 287-293, 1981.

3830. Meisch, Richard A. Alcohol Self-Administration by Experimental Animals. In: Research Advances in Alcohol and Drug Problems, Volume 8. Eds. Reginald G. Smart, Howard D. Cappell and Frederick B. Glaser. New York: Plenum Press, 1984, pages 23-45.

3831. Meiselman, K.C. Participants in Father-Daughter Incest. In: Incest: A Psychological Study.... San Francisco: Jossey-Bass, 1979, pages 83-139.

3832. Mele, A. and Beluffi, M. Problemi Essenziali della Riforma Legislativa e Sociale della Tossicomania Alcoolica in Italia. (Fundamental Problems of Legislative and Social Reform Concerning Alcoholism in Italy.) Difesa Sociale, Rome, 45: 229-252, 1966.

3833. Mello, Nancy K. and Mendelson, Jack. The New York Times, 24 June
       1973, Page 46, Column 3. (Genetic Defect and Cirrhosis of the
       Liver.)

3834. Mellor, C.S. The Epidemiology of Alcoholism. British Journal
       of Psychiatry, 9: 252-262, 1975.

3835. Mellsop, G.W. The Effect of Distance in Determining Hospital
       Admission Rates. The Medical Journal of Australia,
       Sydney, 2(16): 814-817, 1969.

3836. Melus, Antonio. Culture and Language in the Treatment of
       Alcoholism: The Hispanic Perspective. Alcohol Health
       and Research World, 4(4): 19-20, 1980.

3837. Melville, Joy. Some Violent Families. In: Violence and
       the Family. Ed. J.P. Martin. New York: Wiley, 1978,
       pages 9-18.

3838. Melville, Joy. Women in Refuges. In: Violence and the Family.
       Ed. J.P. Martin. New York: Wiley, 1978, pages 293-309.

3839. Member of the Community of St. Mary the Virgin. The Moral,
       Mental and Physical Background of Female Inebriates.
       British Journal of Inebriety, 42: 3-20, 1944.

3840. Mendelson, Jack H., Miller, Kenneth D., Mello, Nancy K., Pratt,
       Herbert and Schmitz, Robert. Hospital Treatment of Alcoholism:
       A Profile of Middle Income Americans. Alcoholism: Clinical
       and Experimental Research, 6(3): 377-383, 1982.

3841. Mendelson, Myer, Norris, Weinberg and Stunkard, Albert J.
       Obesity in Men: A Clinical Study of Twenty-Five Cases.
       Annals of Internal Medicine, 54(4): 660-671, 1961.

3842. Mendlewicz, J. Genetic Aspects of Alcoholism. Revue de
       Medecine, Paris, 23(13): 645-648, 1982.

3843. Mendlewicz, J. and Baron, M. Morbidity Risks in Subtypes of
       Unipolar Depressive Illness: Differences Between Early
       and Late Onset Forms. British Journal of Psychiatry,
       139: 463-466, 1981.

3844. Mendlewicz, J., Fieve, R.R., Rainer, J.D. and Fleiss, J.L. Manic-
       Depressive Illness: A Comparative Study of Patients with and
       without a Family History. British Journal of Psychiatry,
       London, 120(558): 523-530, 1972.

3845. Mendonca, M.M. de. L'usage des Boissons Alcooliques Chez
       L'enfant. (Consumption of Alcoholic Beverages by
       Children.) Toxicomanies, Quebec, 5: 255-261, 1972.

3846. Mendonca, M.M. de. Etude Pedopsychiatrique Sur Des Enfants de Pere
       Alcoolique. (Pedopsychiatric Study of Children of Alcoholic
       Fathers.) Revue de Neuropsychiatrie Infantile et d'Hygiene
       Mentale de l'En Fance, Paris, 25(7): 411-428, 1977.

3847. Mendonca, M.M. de. Reflexions d'us Pedopsychiatre Sur Les
       Enfants de Pere Alcoolique. (A Pedopsychiatrist's Thoughts
       Concerning Children of Alcoholic Fathers.) Toxicomanies,
       Quebec, 8: 311-330, 1975.

3848. Mendonca, M.M. de. The Repercussions of Alcoholism on the Family.
       Jornal Do Medico, Porto, 72(1433): 569-576, 1970.

3849. Mendonca, M.M. de, Matos, A.P. and da Costa Motta, A. Contri-
       bution to the Study of the Academic Under-Achievement in
       Children of Alcoholics. Lisbon, Portugal: The Scientific
       Education and Investigation Ministry, 1980.

3850. Mendonca, M.M. de, Matos, A.P. and da Costa Motta, A. Poor
       Scholastic Performance Among Children of Alcoholic Fathers.
       Journal da Sociedade de Ciencias Medicas de Lisboa, 142:
       67-96, 1978.

3851. Mercer, G.W., Hundleby, J.D. and Carpenter, R.A. Adolescent Drug
       Use and Attitudes Toward the Family. Canadian Journal of
       Behavioral Science, Montreal, 10(1): 79-90, 1978.

3852. Mercer, G.W. and Kohn, P.M. Child-Rearing Factors, Authoritarianism,
       Drug Use Attitudes, and Adolescent Drug Use: A Model. Journal
       of Genetic Psychology, 136: 159-171, 1980.

3853. Mercer, M. How to Help an Alcoholic without Making Matters
       Worse. Good Housekeeping, 195(5): 50, 52, 54, 56, 1982.

3854. Merces-de-Mello, M.L., Moreira-Diniz, R. and Frazao-Monteiro,
       M.H. Quelques Reflexions Sur Le Traitement de L'Alcoolique
       et sur sa Promotion. (Some Reflections Concerning the
       Treatment of the Alcoholic and His Improvement.)
       Toxicomanies, Quebec, 5: 243-253, 1972.

3855. Mercuri, G. Gelosia Morbosa e Criminalita; Descrizione di un
       Caso. (Morbid Jealousy and Crime; Description of One Case.)
       Lavoro Neuropsichiatrico, 57(3): 171-182, 1975.

3856. Merikangas, Kathleen Ries. The Relationship of Assortative
       Mating to Social Adjustment and Course of Illness in
       Primary Affective Disorder. Dissertation Abstracts
       International, 42(8): 3190B, 1981.

3857. Merikangas, Kathleen Ries, Leckman, James F., Prusoff, Brigitte A.,
       Pauls, David L. and Weissman, Myrna M. Familial Transmission
       of Depression and Alcoholism. Archives of General Psychiatry,
       42(4): 367-372, 1985.

3858. Merikangas, Kathleen Ries and Spiker, Duane G. Assortative
       Mating among In-Patients with Primary Affective Disorder.
       Psychological Medicine, 12(4): 753-764, 1982.

3859. Merikangas, Kathleen R., Weissman, Myrna M., Prusoff, Brigitte A.,
       Pauls, David L. and Leckman, James F. Depressives with
       Secondary Alcoholism: Psychiatric Disorders in Offspring.
       Journal of Studies on Alcohol, 46(3): 199-204, 1985.

3860. Merker, Jarrold F. Indians of the Great Plains: Issues in
       Counseling and Family Therapy. Paper presented at the
       National Council on Alcoholism Forum, New Orleans, April,
       1981. (Also in: Focus on Alcohol and Drug Issues, 4(4):
       14-16, 1981.)

3861. Merl-Nachinson, Susan. Lifestyle Approaches to Alcoholism.
       In: Lifestyle Counseling for Adjustment to Disability.
       Ed. Warren R. Rule. Rockville, MD: Aspen Systems
       Corporation, 1984, pages 277-287.

3862. Mertz, Audrey W. Plan for Treatment of Alcoholics in Hawaii:
       The Role of Physician and the General Hospital. Hawaii
       Medical Journal, 28(5): 380-383, 1969.

3863. Meryman, R. Broken Promises, Mended Dreams. Toronto, Canada:
       Little, Brown and Company, 1984.

3864. Meskova, H. Zkusenosti Z Tabora Deti Alkoholiku. (Experiences
       from the Summer Camp for Children from Families with
       Alcoholic Problems.) Protialkoholicky Obzor,
       Bratislava, 6(3): 89-91, 1971.

3865. Meskova, H., Mecir, J. and Pihrtova, S. Paternal Element in
      Boys Treated at the Antialcoholic Clinic in Prague.
      Ceskoslovenska Psychiatrie, 74(6): 402-405, 1978.

3866. Mesmer, Roger E.G. and Mishler, Mary. A Community Home Program
      for Patients Attending a Day Treatment Center. Hospital &
      Community Psychiatry, 28(6): 426-427, 1977.

3867. Metaxas, A., Ballis, T., Triantaphyllou M., Hadjishephanou, A.
      and Velissaris, A. Psychopathic Antisocial Patients Treated
      in an Army Hospital. Statistical Hospital. Hellenic Armed
      Forces Medical Review, 13(6): 789-795, 1979.

3868. Metchkounov, K. Soin De La Famille Et De La Societe Chez Les
      Alcooliques. (Family and Public Care with Alcoholics.)
      Alcoholism, Zagreb, 9(1): 22-24, 1973.

3869. Metts, W. Deep River. Denver: Accent Books, 1978.

3870. Metzger, L. The Family's Need to Maintain Drinking. Paper presented
      at the 7th Annual Meeting of the Association of Labor-Management
      Administrators and Consultants on Alcoholism, Inc., San
      Francisco, October, 1978, pages 234-243.

3871. Meyer, J.R. Dispositional Assessment with Alcoholics. Doctoral
      Dissertation. (University Microfilms Number 7918017.) Lincoln:
      The University of Nebraska, 1978.

3872. Meyer, Marie-Louise. Counselling Families of Alcoholics.
      Health Visitor, London, 50: 136-142, 1977.

3873. Meyer, Marie-Louise. Counselling Families of Alcoholics:
      A Guideline for the Helping Professions. Pamphlet.
      London: The London Council on Alcoholism, 1978.

3874. Meyer, Marie-Louise. Drinking Problems - Family Problems:
      Practical Guidelines for the Problem Drinker, the Partner,
      and All Those Involved. Surrey, England: Momenta
      Publishing, 1982.

3875. Meyer, R.M.S. and Morris, D.T. Alcoholic Cardiomyopathy: A
      Nursing Approach. Nursing Research, 26: 422-427, 1977.

3876. Meyer, Roberta. The Parent Connection: How to Communicate With
      Your Child About Alcohol and Other Drugs. New York:
      Franklin Watts, 1984.

3877. Meyer, Roger E., Babor, Thomas F. and Mirkin, Peter M. Typologies
      in Alcoholism: An Overview. International Journal of the
      Addictions, 18(2): 235-249, 1983.

3878. Meyer, S.R. and Hookstead, S.A. Characteristics of Adolescent
      Users and Non-Users of Drugs. Journal of Alcohol and Drug
      Education, 21(3): 47-54, 1976.

3879. Meyers, A.R., Hingson, R. Mucatel, M. and Goldman, E. Social
      and Psychologic Correlates of Problem Drinking in Old Age.
      Journal of the American Geriatrics Society, 30(7):
      452-456, 1982.

3880. Mezei, A. and Levendel, L. Die Personlichkeit des Alkoholikers.
      (The Personality of the Alcoholic.) Medizinische Klinik,
      63: 489-492, 1968.

3881. Michalik, M.A. The Impact of an Alcoholic Father on the Adjustment
      of Adolescent Sons. Doctoral Dissertation. (University
      Microfilms Number 8124678.) San Diego: California School
      of Professional Psychology, 1981. (Also in: Dissertation
      Abstracts International, 42: 2070-2071B, 1981.)

3882. Michaux, P. Alcoolisme et Criminalite. Consequences Familiales --
       Heredite. (Alcoholism and Criminality. Effects on the
       Family -- Heredity.) Quest Medical, Paris, 31: 1265-1269,
       1978.

3883. Midanik, Lorraine. Familial Alcoholism and Problem Drinking in a
       National Drinking Practices Survey. Addictive Behaviors,
       Oxford, 8(2): 133-141, 1983.

3884. Middleton, J.L. Adult Children of Alcoholics Become Parents:
       A "Pioneering" Effort. Focus on Family and Chemical
       Dependency, 8(1): 9, 37, 1985.

3885. Middleton, J.L. Delayed Fuse of Alcoholism. Recovery, Jan-Feb:
       12, 1985.

3886. Middleton, J.L. Double Stigma: Sexual Abuse within the Alcoholic
       Family. Focus on Family and Chemical Dependency, 7(5):
       6, 10-11, 1984.

3887. Mider, Paul Albert. Patient-Treatment Approach Interaction:
       Personality Traits and Cognitive-Perceptual Characteristics
       of Drug Addicts in Methadone Maintenance and in Drug-Free
       Therapeutic Communities. Dissertation Abstracts Inter-
       national, 43(11): 3738B, 1982.

3888. Midgley, J. Drinking and Attitudes Toward Drinking in a Muslim
       Community. Quarterly Journal of Studies on Alcohol, 32:
       148-158, 1971.

3889. Mik, G. Sons of Alcoholic Fathers. British Journal of Addiction,
       65: 305-315, 1970.

3890. Miketic, B. The Influence of Parental Alcoholism in the Development
       of Mental Disturbances in Children. Alcoholism, Zagreb, 8:
       135-139, 1972.

3891. Mikita, M.R. Familial Alcoholism as a Pre-disposing Common Cause
       for Substance Abuse and Sociopathy Among Incarcerated Youthful
       Offenders. Doctoral Dissertation. (University Microfilms
       Number 8026130.) The Florida State University, 1980. (Also
       in: Dissertation Abstracts International, 41: 1923B, 1980.)

3892. Miklasz, M. (Rola Zony W Kryzysie Alkoholowym Rodziny. (The
       Wife's Role in the Alcoholic Crisis of the Family.) Problemy
       Alkoholizmu, Warsaw, 7(7): 12-13, 1972.

3893. Milcinski, L. Family Atmosphere and Suicide. Wiener Medizinische
       Wochenschrift, 121: 220-223, 1971. (Also in: Psychiatry,
       25(902): 1972.)

3894. Miles, J.E., Krell, R. and Lin, T. Doctor's Wife: Mental Illness
       and Marital Patterns. In: Psychiatric Illness in Physicians.
       Ed. S.E. Shortt. Springfield, IL: Charles C. Thomas, 1982,
       pages 126-132. (Also in: The International Journal of
       Psychiatry in Medicine, 6(4): 481-487, 1975.)

3895. Milgram, Gail Gleason. Alcoholism in the Family: Implication
       for the School System. Focus on Alcohol and Drug Issues,
       6(4): 4-5, 22, 1981.

3896. Milgram, Gail Gleason. Coping with Alcohol. New York: Richards
       Rosen Press, 1980.

3897. Milgram, Gail Gleason. What, When, & How to Talk to Children
       About Alcohol and Other Drugs - A Guide for Parents,
       Center City, MN: Hazelden, 1983.

3898. Milgram, Gail Gleason. Youthful Drinking: Past and Present.
       Journal of Drug Education, 12(4): 289-308, 1982.

3899. Milkman, Harvey, Weiner, Scott E. and Sunderwirth, Stanley.
       Addiction Relapse. In: The Addictive Behaviors.
       Eds. H. Shaffer and B. Stimmel. New York: Haworth Press,
       1984, pages 119-134.

3900. Miller, B.A., Pokorny, A.D. and Kanas, T.E. Problems in Treating
       Homeless, Jobless Alcoholics. Hospital and Community
       Psychiatry, 21: 98-99, 1970.

3901. Miller, Byron A. and Kanas, Thomas E. Treatment for the
       Physiological Need for Alcohol. U.S. Medicine,
       7(6): 10-11, 1971.

3902. Miller, D.S. Like Father, Like Son. Freedom Fighter from Idaho,
       24-25, 50, 1985.

3903. Miller, D.S. Tough Love is True Love. Freedom Fighter from
       Idaho: 22-23, 1985.

3904. Miller, Donna. Substance Abuse: The Sick Family. Seminars
       in Family Medicine, 1(4): 299-304, 1980.

3905. Miller, Dorothy. The Alcoholic Family and Larger Systems: A
       Systemic Assessment of Interactional Patterns and Metaphoric
       Communication. Dissertation Abstracts International,
       44(4): 1035A, 1983.

3906. Miller, Dorothy and Barnhouse, Robert C. Married Mental Patients
       in Crisis: A Research Report. The American Journal of
       Psychiatry, 124(3): 364-370, 1967.

3907. Miller, Dorothy and Jang, Michael. Children of Alcoholics:
       A 20-year Longitudinal Study. Social Work Research &
       Abstracts, 13(4): 23-29, 1977.

3908. Miller, Judith Droitcour and Cisin, Ira H. Highlights from
       the National Survey on Drug Abuse, 1982. United States
       Department of Health and Human Services. Public Health
       Service. Alcohol, Drug Abuse, and Mental Health
       Administration. National Institute on Drug Abuse.
       Rockville, MD. U.S. Government Printing Office,
       DHHS Publication No. (ADM) 83-1277. 1983.

3909. Miller, Kenneth D., Lescault, Barbara A., Heller, Joan E. and
       Bernstein, Benjamin. Differences in Demographic
       Characteristics, Drinking History and Response to
       Treatment of Black and White Women Seen at an Alcohol
       Detoxification Center. Focus on Women: Journal of
       Addictions and Health, 1(2): 136-144, 1980.

3910. Miller, Laurence Brent. Reflections on the Merging Training
       Needs of Mental-Health, Alcohol and Drug Service Providers.
       Contemporary Drug Problems, 7(2): 259-263, 1978.

3911. Miller, M. Cooperation of Some Wives in Their Husbands' Suicides.
       Psychological Reports, 44: 39-42, 1979.

3912. Miller, Marlene and Gorski, Terence T. Family Recovery.
       Growing Beyond Addiction. Center City, MN: Hazelden,
       no date.

3913. Miller, Merlene and Gorski, Terence T. Relapse: The Family's
       Involvement. Focus on Family and Chemical Dependency,
       6(5): 17-18, 1983.

3914. Miller, Merlene and Gorski, Terence T. Relapse: The Family's
       Involvement. Part Two: Co-alcoholism and Relapse. Focus
       on Family and Chemical Dependency, 6(6): 10-11, 1983.

3915. Miller, Merlene and Gorski, Terence. Relapse: The Family's
       Involvement. Part Three: Protocol for Long-Term Recovery.
       Focus on Family and Chemical Dependency, 7(1): 13, 36,
       1984.

3916. Miller, P. Alcoholism Recovery for Women and Their Children:
       A New Approach. Paper presented at the 11th Annual National
       Council on Alcoholism Conference, Seattle, May, 1980.

3917. Miller, Peter M. Alternative Skills Training in Alcoholism
       Treatment. Paper presented at the NATO Conference on
       Experimental and Behavioral Approaches to Alcoholism,
       Oslo, Norway, August-September, 1977, pages 119-142.

3918. Miller, Peter M. An Analysis of Chronic Drunkenness Offenders
       with Implications for Behavioral Intervention. Inter-
       national Journal of the Addictions, 10(6): 995-1005, 1975.

3919. Miller, P.M. Behavioral Treatment on Binge Drinking.
       In: Clinical Case Studies in the Behavioral Treatment
       of Alcoholism. Eds. W. Hay and P. Nathan. New York:
       Plenum Press, 1982, pages 3-21.

3920. Miller, Peter M. Behavioral Treatment of Alcoholism. Oxford:
       Pergamon, 1976.

3921. Miller, R.C. Effect of Low Doses of Alcohol on Human Behavior.
       Dissertation Abstracts International, 45(8): 2695B, 1985.

3922. Miller, Sheldon I. and Tuchfeld, Barry S. Adult Children of
       Alcoholics. Hospital and Community Psychiatry, 37(3):
       235-236, 1986.

3923. Miller, T.R. Recovering from Alcoholism: Personal Observations
       Over an 8-Year Period. In: Alcoholism: A Modern
       Perspective. Ed. P. Golding. Lancaster, England,
       MTP Press, 1982, pages 355-359.

3924. Miller, T. Rothrock. My Life as an Alcoholic Doctor. Medical
       Economics, 54(26): 192-208, 1977.

3925. Miller, William R., Crawford, V. Lloyd and Taylor, Cheryl A.
       Significant Others as Corroborative Sources for Problem
       Drinkers. Addictive Behaviors, Oxford, 4: 67-70, 1979.

3926. Miller, William R., Hedrick, Kim E. and Taylor, Cheryl A.
       Addictive Behaviors and Life Problems Before and After
       Behavioral Treatment of Problem Drinkers. Addictive
       Behaviors, 8(4): 403-412, 1983.

3927. Miller, William R. and Hester, R.K. Treating the Problem Drinker:
       Modern Approaches. Addictive Behaviors: Treatment of
       Alcoholism, Drug Abuse, Smoking and Obesity. New York:
       Pergamon Press, 1980, pages 11-141.

3928. Miller, William R. and Joyce, Mark A. Prediction of Abstinence,
       Controlled Drinking, and Heavy Drinking Outcomes Following
       Behavioral Self-Control Training. Journal of Consulting
       and Clinical Psychology, 47(4): 773-775, 1979.

3929. Millman, Doris H. and Su, Wen-Huey. Patterns of Drug Usage Among
       University Students. V. Heavy Use of Marihuana and Alcohol
       by Undergraduates. Journal of the American College Health
       Association, 21: 181-187, 1973.

3930. Millman, Robert B. Adolescent Drug Abuse. In: Treatment
      Aspects of Drug Dependence. Ed. Arnold Schecter.
      West Palm Beach, FL: CRC Press, Inc., 1978, pages 99-108.

3931. Millman, Robert B. Drug and Alcohol Abuse. In: Handbook of
      Treatment of Mental Disorders in Childhood and Adolescence.
      Eds. Benjamin B. Wolman, James Egan and Alan O. Ross.
      Englewood Cliffs, NJ: Prentice-Hall, 1978, pages 238-267.

3932. Millman, Robert B. and Khuri, Elizabeth T. Alcohol and Adolescent
      Psychopathology. In: Alcoholism and Clinical Psychiatry.
      Ed. Joel Solomon. New York: Plenum Medical Book Company,
      1982, pages 163-178.

3933. Milln, Philip and Coppen, Alec. Who Responds to Amitriptyline.
      Lancet, 8171: 763-764, 1980.

3934. Milner, G. Drug Awareness. Drugs and Drink -- Awareness and Action.
      Volume VIII. Melbourne: Perfect Publishing Co., 1979.

3935. Milner, Joel S. and Ayoub, Catherine. Evaluation of "At Risk"
      Parents Using the Child Abuse Potential Inventory. Journal
      of Clinical Psychology, 36(4): 945-948, 1980.

3936. Milosavcevic, V. Vaspitna Zapustenost I Alkoholizam. (Educational
      Neglect and Alcoholism.) Alkoholizam, Belgrade, 15(3):
      193-196, 1975.

3937. Milosavcevic, V. Alkoholizam Roditelja--Uzrok Nastanka Alkoholizma
      Kod Dece. (Parental Alcoholism as the Pathogenic Cause of
      Alcoholism in Children.) Alkoholizam, Belgrade, 14(3-4):
      122-125, 1974.

3938. Milstead, Robin Jane. Systematic Planning for Services to the
      Families of Alcoholics in Rural Areas. Paper presented at the
      22nd International Institute on the Prevention and Treatment of
      Alcoholism. Vigo, Spain, July, 1976. (Also in: The Alcoholism
      Digest Annual, 5: 40-45, 1976-77.)

3939. Milstead-O'Keeffe, R.J. Outpatient Programs for Workers and
      Their Families. Paper presented at the 25th International
      Institute on the Prevention and Treatment of Alcoholism,
      Tours, France, June, 1979, pages 123-132.

3940. Milt, H. Alcoholism, Its Causes and Cure; A New Handbook.
      New York: Scribner, 1976.

3941. Milt, Harry. Methods Used To Treat Alcoholism. Basic Handbook
      on Alcoholism. Fair Haven, NJ: Scientific Aids
      Publications, 1967, pages 64-70.

3942. Milton, P. Den Forandrade Kvinnorollen -- En Orsak Till
      Alkoholmissbruk? (Change in Woman's Role -- A Cause of
      Alcoholism?) Alkohol Och Narkotika, 73(7): 11-13, 1979.

3943. Mindlin, Rowland L. New York Times, 16 September 1975, Page 40,
      Column 5. (Alcoholism and Child Abuse.)

3944. Miner, Jane C. A Day at a Time. Dealing with an Alcoholic.
      Mankato, MN: Crestwood House, 1982.

3945. Minkoff, Howard. The Medical Significance of the Obstetric
      History. American Family Physician, 27(5): 164-166, 1983.

3946. Minor, Marianne. Introduction: A Systems Model for Planning
      Culturally Specific Programs. In: Chicanas and Alcoholism:
      A Socio-Cultural Perspective of Women. Eds. Rodolfo
      Arevalo and Marianne Minor. San Jose: San Jose State
      University, School of Social Work, 1981, pages 1-5.

3947. Mirin, Steven M. Treatment of Opiate Dependence in the Context
       of a Clinical Research Program. McLean Hospital Journal,
       1(3): 167-173, 1976.

3948. Mirone, Leonora. The Effect of Ethyl Alcohol on Growth, Fecundity
       and Voluntary Consumption of Alcohol by Mice. Quarterly
       Journal of Studies on Alcohol, 13: 365-369, 1952.

3949. Missik, T. Vseobecne K Psychopatologii Addikcie So Zvalstnym
       Zretel'om Na Alkoholizmus. (General Ideas on the
       Psychopathology of Addiction, With Special Regard to
       Alcoholism.) Protialkoholicky Obzor, Bratislava, 8:
       169-173, 1973.

3950. Mitchell, E.H. Use of Citrated Calcium Carbimide in Alcoholism.
       Journal of the American Medical Association, 168:
       2008-2009, 1958.

3951. Mitchell, Gust William and Orlin, Malinda B. Service Delivery
       in the Military: Training Issues. Social Casework,
       61(1): 54-57, 1980.

3952. Mitchell, H.E. Alcoholism and the Family: A Social Point of
       View. In: The Legal Issues in Alcoholism and Alcohol
       Usage. Boston: Boston Universtiy Law-Medicine Institute,
       1966, pages 90-100.

3953. Mitchell, H.E. The Interrelatedness of Alcoholism and Marital
       Conflict. Symposium, 1958. 4. Interpersonal Perception
       Theory to Conflicted Marriages in Which Alcoholism is and
       is Not a Problem. American Journal of Orthopsychiatry,
       29: 547-599, 1959.

3954. Mitchell, H.E. and Mudd, E.H. The Development of a Research
       Methodology for Achieving the Cooperation of Alcoholics and
       Their Nonalcoholic Wives. Quarterly Journal of Studies on
       Alcohol, 18: 649-657, 1957.

3955. Mitchell, J.E., Hong, K.M. and Corman, C. Childhood Onset of
       Alcohol Abuse. American Journal of Orthopsychiatry, 49:
       511-513, 1979.

3956. Mitchell, Kenneth R., Kirkby, Robert J. and Mitchell, Daphne M.
       Drug Use by University Freshmen. Journal of College Student
       Personnel, 11(5): 332-336, 1970.

3957. Mitchell, Wayne and Patch, Kenneth. Indian Alcoholism and
       Education. Journal of American Indian Education, 21(1):
       31-33, 1981.

3958. Miyamoto, K. Association of HLA-B40 and DRW9 with Japanese
       Alcoholic Liver Cirrhosis. Pharmacology Biochemistry and
       Behavior, 18(Supplement 1): 467-471, 1983.

3959. Mizoi, Y. Alcohol Sensitivity Related to Polymorphism of Alcohol-
       Metabolizing Enzymes in Japanese. Pharmacology Biochemistry
       and Behavior, 18(Supplement 1): 127-133, 1983.

3960. Mizui, Takemi. A Survey of Family Attitudes Toward Alcoholics.
       Kokoro to Shakai, Tokyo, 6(4): 373-380, 1975.

3961. Moberg, D.P., Krause, W.K. and Klein, P.E. Posttreatment
       Drinking Behavior Among Inpatients from an Industrial
       Alcoholism Program. International Journal of the
       Addictions, 17(3): 549-567, 1982.

3962. Moberg, P. and Hunter, S. PICADA'S Family Education Program: An
        Evaluation Paper. Presented at Madison, WI, February, 1983.
        (Also in: Working with Adolescent Alcohol/Drug Problems:
        Assessment, Intervention and Treatment. pages 55-65.)

3963. Mock, William L., Spiegel, Renee, Gary, Jeffrey D. Family
        Systems Theory Approach to Employee Assistance Programs:
        A Model. Report. Cleveland: Center for Interpersonal
        Development, 1979. (Also in: Labor-Management Alcoholism
        Journal, 9(2): 45-54, 1979.)

3964. Mock, William Leonard. A Study of Certain Psychological
        Processes in Alcoholic Families. Dissertation Abstracts
        International, 43(10): 3369B, 1982.

3965. Moczydlowski, Ken. Predictors of Success in a Correctional
        Halfway House for Youthful and Adult Offenders. Corrective
        & Social Psychiatry & Journal of Behavior Technology,
        Methods & Therapy, 26(2): 59-72, 1980.

3966. Modlin, H.C. and Montes, A. Narcotics Addiction in Physicians.
        In: Psychiatric Illness in Physicians. Ed. S.E. Shortt.
        Springfield IL: Charles C. Thomas, 1982, pages 83-92.

3967. Moffitt, Terrie Edith. Genetic Influence of Parental Psychiatric
        Illness on Violent and Recidivistic Criminal Behavior.
        Dissertation Abstracts International, 45(3): 1025B, 1984.

3968. Mohan, D., Rustagi, P.K., Sundaram, K.R. and Prabhu, G.G. Relative
        Risk of Adolescent Drug Abuse: 1. Socio-Demographic and
        Interpersonal Variables. Bulletin on Narcotics, Geneva,
        33(1): 1-8, 1981.

3969. Molloy, Jane. Alcohol and the OH Role. 1. The Effects of
        Problem Drinking. Occupational Health, London, 35(9):
        409-418, 1983.

3970. Monnelly, Edward P., Hartl, Emil M. and Elderkin, Roland.
        Constitutional Factors Predictive of Alcoholism in a
        Follow-Up of Delinquent Boys. Journal of Studies on
        Alcohol, 44(3): 530-537, 1983.

3971. Monopolis, S. and Savage, C. Substance Abuse, Public Health and
        the Pediatrician. Paediatrician, 11(3-4): 178-196, 1982.

3972. Monroe, N. and Borgman R. Development and Treatment of Pseudo-
        Mental Illness. The American Journal of Psychiatry,
        29(1): 117-127, 1975.

3973. Moon, J.R., Drew, L.R.H. and Buchanan, F.H. Early Detection of
        Drug Dependence. Australian Family Physician, Sydney,
        3: 174-178, 1974.

3974. Mooney, A. John. Alcoholism; A Community Problem, A Medical
        Responsibility. Journal of the Medical Association of
        Georgia, 54: 358-362, 1966.

3975. Moore, M. Alcoholism; Some "Causes" and Treatment. Journal of
        the Tennessee Medical Association, 35: 3-12, 1942.

3976. Moore, Robert A. Treatment of the Alcoholic Patient by the
        Family Physician. Journal of the Michigan State Medical
        Society, 62: 50-53, 1963.

3977. Moore, Robert A. and Ramseur, Freida. A Study of the Background
        of 100 Hospitalized Veterans with Alcoholism. Quarterly
        Journal of Studies on Alcohol, 21: 51-67, 1960.

3978. Moorhead, H.H.   Study of Alcoholism with Onset Forty-Five Years
       or Older. Bulletin of the New York Academy of Medicine,
       34: 99-108, 1958.

3979. Moos, Rudolf H. and Billings, Andrew G. Children of Alcoholics
       During the Recovery Process: Alcoholic and Matched Control
       Families. Addictive Behaviors, Oxford, 7(2): 155-163, 1982.

3980. Moos, Rudolf H. and Billings, Andrew G. Psychosocial Processes
       of Recovery Among Alcoholics and Implications for Clinicians
       and Program Evaluators. Addictive Behaviors, 8(3):
       205-218, 1983.

3981. Moos, Rudolf H., Bromet, E., Tsu, V. and Moos, Bernice S. Family
       Characteristics and the Outcome of Treatment for Alcoholism.
       Journal of Studies on Alcohol, 40: 78-88, 1979.

3982. Moos, Rudolf H. and Finney, J.W. The Expanding Scope of
       Alcoholism Treatment Evaluation. American Psychologist,
       38(10): 1036-1044, 1983.

3983. Moos, Rudolf H., Finney, J.W. and Chan, D.A. The Process of
       Recovery from Alcoholism: I. Comparing Alcoholic Patients
       and Matched Community Controls. Journal of Studies on
       Alcohol, 42: 383-402, 1981.

3984. Moos, Rudolf H., Finney, J.W. and Gamble, W. The Process of
       Recovery from Alcoholism. II. Comparing Spouses of
       Alcoholic Patients and Matched Community Controls.
       Journal of Studies on Alcohol, 43(9): 888-909, 1982.

3985. Moos, Rudolf H. and Moos, Bernice S. The Process of Recovery
       from Alcoholism: III. Comparing Functioning in Families
       of Alcoholics and Matched Control Families. Journal of
       Studies on Alcohol, 45(2): 111-118, 1984.

3986. Moos, Rudolf H. and Moos, Bernice S. A Typology of Family
       Social Environments. Family Process, 15: 357-371, 1976.

3987. Moos, Rudolf H., Moos, Bernice S. and Kulik, James A. College-
       Student Abstainers, Moderate Drinkers, and Heavy Drinkers:
       A Comparative Analysis. Journal of Youth and Adolescence,
       5(4): 349-360, 1976.

3988. Moral, Herbert R. How You Can Help an Alcoholic Stop Drinking.
       Noroton, CT: Noroton Publishing Co., 1951.

3989. Morales, Armando. Substance Abuse and Mexican American Youth:
       An Overview. Journal of Drug Issues, 14(2): 297-311, 1984.

3990. Morawski, J. (Ed.) Alkohol, Alkoholizm I Inne Uzaleznienia. Przejawy,
       Profilaktyka, Terapia. Tom II. (Alcohol, Alcoholism
       and Other Addictions. Symptomatology, Prophylaxis and
       Therapy. Vol. II.) Warsaw: Wydawnictwo Prawnicze, 1977.

3991. Morehouse, E.R. Adolescent COA's: Kids at Highest Risk. Helping
       Adolescent COA's through Student Assistance Programs. NACoA
       Network, 2(1): 1985.

3992. Morehouse, Ellen R. Assessing and Motivating Adolescents Who Have
       Drinking Problems. In: Social Work Treatment of Alcohol
       Problems. Eds. David Cook, Christine Fewell and John Riolo.
       New Brunswick, NJ: Rutgers Center on Alcohol Studies, 1983,
       pages 119-130.

3993. Morehouse, Ellen R. Treating the Alcoholic on Public Assistance.
       Social Casework, 59(1): 36-41, 1978.

3994. Morehouse, Ellen R. Working in the Schools With Children of
        Alcoholic Parents. Health and Social Work, 4(4):
        144-162, 1979.

3995. Morehouse, Ellen R. Working with Alcohol-Abusing Children of
        Alcoholics. Alcohol Health and Research World, 8(4):
        14-19, 1984. (Also in: New Perspectives on Youth Treatment:
        A Book of Readings. Ed. C. Leslie. Rockville, MD: National
        Institute on Alcohol Abuse and Alcoholism, 1982, pages 89-99.)

3996. Morehouse, Ellen R. Working with Children of Alcoholic Parents
        in an Outpatient Alcoholism Treatment Facility and in the
        Schools, Department of Community Mental Health, Westchester
        County, New York. In: Services for Children of Alcoholics.
        Symposium held in September, 1979 at Silver Spring, MD. U.S.
        National Institute on Alcohol Abuse and Alcoholism. Research
        Monograph No. 4. Washington, D.C.: U.S. Government Printing
        Office, 1981, pages 138-151, (DHHS Publication No. ADM 81-1007.)

3997. Morehouse, Ellen R. and Richards, Tarpley. An Examination of
        Dysfunctional Latency Age Children of Alcoholic Parents and
        Problems in Intervention. In: Children of Exceptional Parents.
        Ed. Mary Frank. New York: Haworth Press, 1983, pages 21-33.

3998. Morgado, Anastacio F. Consumo De Drogas Ilicitas-Aspectos Relevantes
        De Insucesso Das Medidas De Controle. (The Consumption of
        Illegal Drugs: Relevant Aspects of the Failure of Control
        Methods.) Jornal Brasileiro De Psiquiatria, 31(6): 377-386,
        1982.

3999. Morgan, D.M. At Sunnybrook Medical Centre: The Human Side of
        Rehabilitation. Canadian Hospital, Toronto, 50(10): 67, 1973.

4000. Morgan, H.G., Burns, Cox C.J., Pocock, H. and Pottle, S. Deliberate
        Self-Harm: Clinical and Socio-Economic Characteristics of 368
        Patients. The British Journal of Psychiatry: The Journal of
        Mental Science, London, 127: 564-574, 1975.

4001. Morgan, P. Overview of the Research in the Area of Alcohol's
        Relationship to Family Violence. Paper presented at the
        Conference on Alcohol and Family Violence, Toronto, November,
        1980.

4002. Morgan, P.A. Leisure, Alcohol and Domestic Violence. Paper presented
        at the 3rd World Congress, Brussels, 1979.

4003. Morgan, P.A. Role of Alcohol in Domestic Violence. Report.
        Berkeley: University of California, School of Public Health,
        Social Research Group, 1980.

4004. Morgan, Patricia A. Alcohol and Family Violence: A Review of
        the Literature. Report. Berkeley: University of California,
        School of Public Health, Social Research Group, 1980. (Also in:
        Alcohol Consumption and Related Problems. United States
        Department of Health and Human Services. NIAAA Alcohol and
        Health Monograph No. 1. Washington, D.C.: U.S. Government
        Printing Office, 1982, pages 223-259.

4005. Mori, T., Aoyama, K. and Kita, Y. Parental Influences on Alcohol
        Drinking Patterns Among College Students. Japanese Journal
        of Alcohol Studies and Drug Dependence, Kyoto, 18(1):
        20-54, 1983.

4006. Moric-Petrovic Slavka and Milosavljevic, P. Alkoholizam U
        Porodicama Bolesnika Iz Shizofrene Grupe. (Alcoholism
        as a Hereditary Factor in Schizophrenia.) Anali Klinicke
        Bolnice "Dr. M. Stojanovic", Zagreb, 6(2-3): 342-347, 1967.
        (Also in: Medicinski Glasnik, Belgrade, 20: 189-191, 1966.)

4007. Moric-Petrovic, Slavka and Petrovic, Dusan. Methodology of
       Treatment and Rehabilitation of Alcoholics. Report.
       Belgrade, Yugoslavia: Institute for Mental Health, 1973.

4008. Morin, T., Feldmann, G., Benhamou, J.-P., Martin, J.P., Rueff, B.
       and Ropartz, C. Heterozygous Alpha -Antitrypsin Deficiency
       and Cirrhosis in Adults, A Fortuitous Association. Lancet,
       1: 250-251, 1975.

4009. Morris, J.B., Kovacs, M., Beck, A.T. and Wolffe, A. Notes
       Toward an Epidemiology of Urban Suicide. Comprehensive
       Psychiatry, 15(6): 537-547, 1974.

4010. Morrison, C. and Schuckit, M.A. Locus of Control in Young Men
       with Alcoholic Relatives and Controls. Journal of Clinical
       Psychiatry, 44(8): 306-307, 1983.

4011. Morrison, J. Adult Psychiatric Disorders in Parents of Hyper-
       active Children. American Journal of Psychiatry, 137:
       825-827, 1980.

4012. Morrison, James R. Early Birth Order in Briquet's Syndrome.
       American Journal of Psychiatry, 140(12): 1596-1598, 1983.

4013. Morrison, James R. The Family Histories of Manic-Depressive
       Patients with and without Alcoholism. Journal of Nervous
       and Mental Disease, 160: 227-229, 1975.

4014. Morrison, James R. Parental Divorce as a Factor in Childhood
       Psychiatric Illness. Comprehensive Psychiatry, 15(2):
       95-102, 1974.

4015. Morrison, James R. Rethinking the Military Family Syndrome.
       American Journal of Psychiatry, 138(3): 354-357, 1981.

4016. Morrison, James R. and Stewart, Mark A. Evidence for Polygenetic
       Inheritance in the Hyperactive Child Syndrome. The American
       Journal of Psychiatry, 130(7): 791-792, 1973.

4017. Morrison, James R. and Stewart, Mark A. A Family Study of the
       Hyper Active Child Syndrome. Biological Psychiatry,
       3(3): 189-195, 1971.

4018. Morrison, James R. and Stewart, Mark A. The Psychiatric Status
       of the Legal Families of Adopted Hyperactive Children.
       Archives of General Psychiatry, 28(6): 888-891, 1973.

4019. Morrissey, Elizabeth R. Alcohol-Related Problems in Adolescents
       and Women. Postgraduate Medicine, 64(6): 111-113, 116,
       118-119, 1978.

4020. Morrissey, Elizabeth Rae. The Role of Life Change in the Development
       of Alcohol-Related Problems: An Investigation of Gender
       Differences. Doctoral Dissertation. (University Microfilms
       No. 8026279.) Seattle: University of Washington, 1980. (Also
       in: Dissertation Abstracts International, 41(5): 2317-2318A,
       1980.)

4021. Morrissey, Elizabeth Rae. The Stress of Children's Births: Gender
       Differences in the Impact on Alcoholics. In: Currents in
       Alcoholism, Volume 8: Recent Advances in Research and Treatment.
       Ed. Marc Galanter. New York: Grune and Stratton, 1981, pages
       301-314.

4022. Morrissey, Elizabeth R. and Schuckit, Marc A. Stressful Life Events
       and Alcohol Problems Among Women Seen at a Detoxication Center.
       Journal of Studies on Alcohol, 39(9): 1559-1576, 1978.

4023. Morse, Robert M. Postoperative Delirium: A Syndrome of Multiple Causation. Psychosomatics, 11(3): 164-168, 1970.

4024. Morse, Robert M. and Hurt, Richard D. Screening for Alcoholism. Journal of the American Medical Association, 242(24): 2688-2690, 1979.

4025. Morse, Robert M. and Swenson, Wendell M. Spouse Response to a Self-Administered Alcoholism Screening Test. Journal of Studies on Alcohol, 36(3): 400-405, 1975.

4026. Mortvedt, Marjory Marvin. Exploration of the Relationship Between Alcoholism and Poverty in Families. Doctoral Dissertation. (University Microfilms No. 72-12576.) Ames: Iowa State University, 1972.

4027. Moser, Joy. Alcohol Problems in Children and Adolescents: A Growing Threat. In: Alcohol and Youth. Ed. O. Jeanneret. Basel: S. Karger, 1983, pages 147-159.

4028. Moses, Donald A. and Burger, Robert E. Are You Driving Your Children to Drink? Coping with Teenage Alcohol and Drug Abuse. New York: Van Nostrand Reinhold Company, 1975.

4029. Moskoff, William. Divorce in the USSR. Journal of Marriage and the Family, 45(2): 419-425, 1983.

4030. Moss, M.C. L'epidemiologie de L'alcoolisme dans un Comte Anglais. (Epidemiology of Alcoholism in an English County.) Toxicomanies, Quebec, 3: 175-191, 1970.

4031. Mowatt, David T., Heard, David B., Steier, Frederick, Stanton, M. Duncan and Todd, Thomas C. Crisis Resolution and the Addiction Cycle. In: The Family Therapy of Drug Abuse and Addiction. Eds. M. Duncan Stanton and Thomas C. Todd. New York: The Guilford Press, 1982, pages 190-202.

4032. Mowatt, David T., VanDeusen, John M. and Wilson, David. Family Therapy and Drug Using Offender. Federal Probation, 48(2): 28-34, 1984.

4033. Mowrer, H.R. Alcoholism and the Family. Journal of Criminal Psychopathology, 3: 90-99, 1941.

4034. Mowrer, Harriet R. A Psychocultural Analysis of the Alcoholic. American Sociological Review, 5: 546-557, 1940.

4035. Mowrer, Harriet, R. and Mowrer, Ernest R. Ecological and Familial Factors Associated with Inebriety. Quarterly Journal of Studies on Alcohol, 6: 36-44, 1945.

4036. Mrazek, P.B. and Kempe, C.H. (Eds.). Sexually Abused Children and Their Families. New York: Pergamon Press, 1981, pages 97-107.

4037. Mrazek, Patricia Beezley. Sexual Abuse of Children. Journal of Child Psychology and Psychiatry and Allied Disciplines, 21(1): 91-95, 1980.

4038. Maucevic, V. Die Heilung Von Alkoholikern im Klub. (The Treatment of Alcoholics in Clubs.) Alcoholism, Zagreb, 5(1): 31-38, 1969.

4039. Muchowski, Patrice M. and Washousky, Richard. Programmatic Approach to Treating the Alcoholic Family. Paper presented at the 28th Annual Meeting of the ADPA, Detroit, September, 1977.

4040. Muchowski-Conley, Patrice M. Assessing the Contributions of
        Involving "Significant Others" in the Treatment of the
        Female Alcoholic. Alcohol Health and Research World,
        6(2): 18-20, 1982.

4041. Muchowski-Conley, Patrice M. Surveying the Need for Significant-
        Other Involvement in the Treatment of Female Alcoholism.
        International Journal of the Addictions, 17(7): 1253-1258,
        1982.

4042. Mueller, John F. Casework with the Family of the Alcoholic.
        Social Work, 17(6): 79-84, 1972.

4043. Muldoon, J. Alcoholism and Domestic Abuse: What's the
        Connection? Community Intervention, 1: 10-11, 1985.

4044. Muldoon, J. Dangerous Misconceptions About Alcohol Abuse and
        Domestic Violence. Community Intervention, Fall, 1, 10-11,
        1985.

4045. Mulford, Harold A. and Miller, Donald E. Public Definitions of
        the Alcoholic. Quarterly Journal of Studies on Alcohol,
        22: 312-320, 1961.

4046. Mulhall, D.J. and Wilson, C. Describing Relationships in Families
        with Alcohol Problems. One Graphic Representation. British
        Journal of Addiction, Edinburgh, 78(2): 181-191, 1983.

4047. Muller, R. Alcohol Consumption in Children and Adolescents
        Description and Explanation of Their Drinking Habits.
        In: Alcohol and Youth. Ed. O. Jeanneret. Basel:
        S. Karger, 1983, pages 54-65.

4048. Muller, R. Solzialtherapeutisches Zentrum Fur Suchtkranke in
        Hamburg--Versuch einer Darstellung der Konzeption und erste
        Erfahrungen. (Sociotherapeutic Center for Addicts in
        Hamburg -- A Description of the Concept and First Experience.)
        Suchtgefahren, Hamburg, 19: 92-99, 1973.

4049. Muller, W. New Directions: Family Center Youth Program. In:
        Services for Children of Alcoholics. Symposium held in
        September, 1979 at Silver Spring, MD. Research Monograph No. 4.
        Washington, D.C.: U.S. Government Printing Office, 1979,
        pages 152-163.

4050. Mulry, James T. Chemical Dependency: A Unified Illness.
        American Family Physician, 29(3): 285-290, 1984.

4051. Multidisciplinary, Multi-Media Approach Makes Possible an Array
        of Teaching Plans. Hospitals, 56(24): 58, 1982.

4052. Mumey, J. Sitting in the Bay Window. Chicago: Contemporary
        Books, Inc., 1984.

4053. Munjack, D.J. and Moss, H.B. Affective Disorder and
        Alcoholism in Families of Agoraphobics. Archives
        of General Psychiatry, 38(8): 869-871, 1981.

4054. Murcia-Valcarcel, E. L'Alcoolisme Chez La Femme. (Alcoholism
        in Women.) Revue de l'Accoolisme, Paris, 15: 285-298, 1969.

4055. Murcia-Valcarcel, Esteban. Rehabilitacion Psiquica, Social, Familiar
        Y Laboral Del Enfermo Alcoholico Por La Psicoterapia De Grupo
        Sin La Reflexoterapia. (Psychological, Social, Familial, and
        Occupational Rehabilitation of the Alcoholic Through Group
        Psychotherapy without Reflex Therapy.) Psychotherapy &
        Psychosomatics, 15(1): 50, 1967.

4056. Murphy, Frank and Helm, Thomas. The Frank Murphy Story: His
       Years in Florida Prisons, His Rehabilitation, and His
       Conquest of Alcoholism. New York: Dodd, Mead & Co., 1968.

4057. Murphy, G.E. Clinical Identification of Suicidal Risk.
       Archives of General Psychiatry, 27(3): 356-359, 1972.

4058. Murphy, G.E., Armstrong, J.W. Jr. and Hermele, S.L. Suicide and
       Alcoholism; Interpersonal Loss Confirmed as a Predictor.
       Archives of General Psychiatry, 36: 65-69, 1979.

4059. Murphy, G.E. and Robins, E. Social Factors in Suicide.
       The Journal of the American Medical Association,
       Chicago, 199(5): 303-308, 1967.

4060. Murphy, G.E. and Wetzel, R.D. Family History of Suicidal
       Behavior Among Suicide Attempters. Journal of
       Nervous and Mental Disease, 170(2): 86-90, 1982.

4061. Murphy, G.E., Wetzel, R.D., Swallow, C.S. and McClure, J.N. Jr.
       Who Calls the Suicide Prevention Center: A Study of 55
       Persons Calling on Their Own Behalf. The American Journal
       of Psychiatry, 126(3): 314-324, 1969.

4062. Murphy, H.B.M. Differences Between Mental Disorders of French
       Canadians and British Canadians. Canadian Psychiatric
       Association Journal, 19: 247-257, 1974.

4063. Murphy, Susan Lyden, Rounsaville, Bruce J., Eyre, Stephen and
       Kleber, Herbert, D. Suicide Attempts in Treated Opiate
       Addicts. Comprehensive Psychiatry, 24(1): 79-89, 1983.

4064. Murray, R.M. Do Personality and Psychiatric Disorders Predispose
       to Alcoholism? In: Pharmacological Treatments for Alcoholism.
       Eds. Griffith Edwards and John Littleton. New York: Methuen,
       1984, pages 445-461.

4065. Murray, Robin M. The Alcoholic Doctor. British Journal of
       Hospital Medicine, London, 18(2): 144, 146-149, 1977.

4066. Murray, Robin M. The Origins of Analgesic Nephropathy. British
       Journal of Psychiatry, London, 123(572): 99-106, 1973.

4067. Murray, Robin M. Persistent Analgesic Abuse in Analgesic
       Nephropathy. Journal of Psychosomatic Research, London,
       16(1): 57-62, 1972.

4068. Murray, Robin M., Clifford, Christine A. and Gurling, Hugh M.D.
       Twin Adoption Studies: How Good is the Evidence for a
       Genetic Role? In: Recent Developments in Alcoholism,
       Volume 1, Genetics, Behavioral Treatment, Social Mediators
       and Prevention, Current Concepts in Diagnosis. Ed. Marc
       Galanter. New York: Plenum Press, 1983, pages 25-48.

4069. Murray, Robin M. and Gurling, Hugh M. Alcoholism: Polygenic
       Influence on a Multifactorial Disorder. British Journal of
       Hospital Medicine, London, 27(4): 328, 331, 333-334, 1982.

4070. Murray, Robin M. and Gurling, Hugh M. Genetic Contributions to
       Normal and Abnormal Drinking. In: Psychopharmacology of
       Alcohol. Ed. M. Sandler. New York: Raven Press, 1980,
       pages 89-105.

4071. Murray, Robin M. and Stabenau, James R. Genetic Factors in
       Alcoholism Predisposition. In: Encyclopedic Handbook of
       Alcoholism. Eds. E. Mansell Pattison and Edward Kaufman.
       New York: Gardner Press, 1982, pages 135-144.

4072. Musello, D. Steady Streams of Double Messages: Adult Children
      of Alcoholics. Focus on Family and Chemical Dependency,
      7(4): 9, 11, 1984.

4073. Mydlarski, J. and Brunowa, M. Anthropologic and Psychiatric
      Studies of Families of Alcoholics. Rocznik
      Psychiatrische, 158-190, 1934.

4074. Myers, M.F. Common Psychiatric Problems in Homosexual Men and
      Women Consulting Family Physicians. Canadian Medical
      Association Journal, Ottawa, 123(5): 359-363, 1980.

4075. Myers, T. Corroboration of Self-Report Alcohol Consumption:
      A Comparison of the Accounts of a Group of Male Prisoners
      and Those of Their Wives/Cohabitees. Alcohol and
      Alcoholism, 18(1): 67-74, 1983.

4076. Myerson, A. Inheritance of Mental Diseases. Baltimore:
      Williams and Wilkins, 1925, pages 33-34, 194-197.

4077. Myerson, David J. An Active Therapeutic Method of Interrupting
      the Dependency Relationship of Certain Male Alcoholics.
      Quarterly Journal of Studies on Alcohol, 14: 419-426, 1953.

4078. Myerson, David J. Organic Problems in the Aged: Brain Syndromes
      and Alcoholism. As the Alcoholic Person Grows Older.
      Journal of Geriatric Psychiatry, 11(2): 175-189, 1978.

4079. Myerson, David J. The "Skid Row" Problem. Further Observations
      on a Group of Alcoholic Patients, with Emphasis on Interpersonal
      Relations and the Therapeutic Approach. New England Journal
      of Medicine, 254: 1168-1173, 1956.

4080. Myerson, David J. A Therapeutic Appraisal of Certain Married
      Alcoholic Women.   International Psychiatry Clinics, 3(2):
      143-157, 1966.

4081. Myerson, David J. and Mayer J. Origins, Treatment and Destiny of
      Skid-Row Alcoholic Men. New England Journal of Medicine,
      275: 419-425, 1966.

N

4082. Nace, Edgar P. Therapeutic Approaches to the Alcoholic Marriage. *Psychiatric Clinics of North America*, 5(3): 543-564, 1982.

4083. Nace, Edgar P., Dephoure, M., Goldberg, M. and Cammarota, C.C. Treatment Priorities in a Family-Oriented Alcoholism Program. *Journal of Marital and Family Therapy*, 8(1): 143-150, 1982.

4084. Nace, Edgar P., Meyers, A.L., O'Brien, C.P., Ream, N.and Mintz, J. Depression in Veterans Two Years After Viet Nam. *American Journal of Psychiatry*, 134(2): 167-170, 1977.

4085. Nace, Edgar P., O'Brien, C.P., Mintz, J., Meyers, A.L. and Ream, N. Follow-Up of Vietnam Veterans: II. Social Adjustment. *Drug and Alcohol Dependence*, 6(4): 209-214, 1980.

4086. Nace, Edgar P., O'Brien, C.P., Mintz, J., Ream, N. and Meyers, A.L. *A Follow-Up Study of Veterans Two Years After Vietnam*. Paper presented at the 84th Annual Convention of the American Psychological Association, Washington, D.C., September, 1976. (Eric Report No. ED 141694.)

4087. Nace, Edgar P., Saxon, James J., Jr. and Shore, Neal. A Comparison of Borderline and Nonborderline Alcoholic Patients. *Archives of General Psychiatry*, 40(1): 54-56, 1983.

4088. Nachin, C. Investigations Preliminaires a une Etude Scientifique de l'alcoolisme Psychiatrique. A Propos de 700 Observations de Buveurs de la Region Lyonnaise. (Preliminary Investigations for the Scientific Study of Psychiatric Alcoholism. Based on 700 Case Histories of Drinkers in the Lyon Region.) Doctoral Dissertation. University of Lyon, 1957.

4089. *The NACoA Network*. *Volume 1*. South Laguna, CA: National Association for Children of Alcoholics, 1984.

4090. Nada, Inada. Alcoholics and Their Families. In: *Alcoholism*. Tokyo: Kinokuniya Shoten, 1971, pages 178-185.

4091. Nadel, Meryl, Petropoulos, Alice W. and Feroe, Nelson. Alcoholism Treatment Resources: Which One When? In: *Social Work Treatment of Alcohol Problems*. Eds. David Cook, Christine Fewell and John Riolo. New Brunswick, NJ: Rutgers Center of Alcohol Studies, 1983, pages 1-15.

4092. Nadelson, Carol C., Polonsky, Derek C. and Mathews, Mary Alice. Marital Stress and Symptom Formation in Mid-Life. *Psychiatric Opinion*, 15(9): 29-32, 1978.

4093. Nagao, S. Clinico-genetic Study of Chronic Alcoholism. *Japanese Journal of Human Genetics*, Tokyo, 9: 111-135, 1964.

4094. Nagaruja, Jaya. The Oral Character and Drug Addiction. Child
       Psychiatry Quarterly, 8(2): 7-12, 1975.

4095. Nagayev, V.V. Nekotoryye Aspekty Sotsial'nogo Podkhoda k
       Izucheniyu Problemy Alkogolizma. (Some Aspects of the
       Social Approach to the Study of the Problem of Alcoholism.)
       Sovetskoe Zdravookhranenie, 31(1): 10-16, 1972.

4096. Naiditch, B. Intervention or Enabling - Where are the Trainers?
       Focus on Alcohol and Drug Issues, 6(2): 23, 27, 1983.

4097. Naiditch, Barbara. Prevention, Intervention & Treatment for
       Grade-School-Aged Children of Alcoholics. In: Changing
       Legacies: Growing Up in an Alcoholic Home. Pompano Beach,
       FL: Health Communications, 1984, pages 13-17.

4098. Nakabayashi, Kemi, Aronson, Sarah C., Siegel, Michael, Sturner,
       William Q. and Aronson, Stanley M. Traffic Fatalities in
       Rhode Island: Part II. The Timing of Accidents and the
       Role of Marital Status, Alcohol, and Psychoactive Drugs.
       Rhode Island Medical Journal, 67(4): 171-178, 1984.

4099. Nale, S. Cry for Help. Philadelphia: Fortress Press, 1982.

4100. Napier, Ted L., Bachtel, Douglas C. and Carter, Michael V.
       Factors Associated with Illegal Drug Use in Rural Georgia.
       Journal of Drug Education, 13(2): 119-140, 1983.

4101. Napier, Ted L., Carter, Timothy J. and Pratt, M. Christine.
       Correlates of Alcohol and Marijuana Use Among Rural High
       School Students. Rural Sociology, 46(2): 319-332, 1981.

4102. Nardi, P.M. Alcohol Abuse and Family Structure. In: Family,
       Self, and Society: Emerging Issues, Alternatives and
       Interventions. Eds. Douglas B. Gutknecht, Edgar W. Butler,
       Larry Criswell and Jerry Meints. Lanham, MD: University
       Press of America, 1983, pages 183-195.

4103. Nardi, P.M. Alcohol and the Family: The Impact on Children.
       Paper presented to the Society for Study of Social Problems,
       1980. (Also in: Sociological Abstracts, 28(Supplement 103):
       104, 1980.)

4104. Nardi, P.M. Alcohol Treatment and the Non-Traditional "Family"
       Structures of Gays and Lesbians. Journal of Alcohol and
       Drug Education, 27(2): 83-89, 1982. (Also in: Grassroots
       Special Populations, 1-4, 1982.)

4105. Nardi, P.M. Children of Alcoholics: A Role-Theoretical Perspective.
       The Journal of Social Psychology, 115: 237-245, 1981.

4106. Nardi, P.M. Children of Alcoholics: An Exploratory Study and
       Proposal. Report. Claremont, CA: Pitzer College, Department
       of Sociology, 1979.

4107. Nardi, P.M. Co-Alcoholism in the Non-Traditional "Family" Structure
       of Gays and Lesbians. Paper presented at the National Council
       on Alcoholism Forum. New Orleans, April, 1981.

4108. Nathan, Peter E. Etiology and Process in the Addictive Behaviors.
       In: The Addictive Behaviors: Treatment of Alcoholism, Drug
       Abuse, Smoking, and Obesity. Ed. William R. Miller.
       New York: Pergamon Press, 1980, pages 241-263.

4109. Nathan, Peter E. and Lipscomb, Thomas R. Behavior Therapy and
       Behavior Modification in the Treatment of Alcoholism.
       In: The Diagnosis and Treatment of Alcoholism.
       Eds. Jack H. Mendelson and Nancy K. Mello. New York:
       McGraw-Hill, 1979, pages 306-357.

4110.   National Center for Alcohol Education Report: November, 1976.
        Arlington, VA: National Center for Alcohol Education, 1976.

4111.   National Clergy Council on Alcoholism and Related Drug Problems,
        Washington, D.C. Blue Book Volume 36: Proceedings from
        the 36th Annual Symposium. Cherry Hill, NJ, 1984.

4112.   National Congress of Parents and Teachers. Alcohol: A Family
        Affair. Chicago, 1974.

4113.   National Council on Alcoholism. 1984 Facts on Alcoholism and
        Alcohol-Related Problems. Pamphlet. New York, 1984.

4114.   National Council on Alcoholism. New York City Affiliate. The
        Rights of Alcoholics and Their Families: A Handbook for
        Social Workers. New York, 1976.

4115.   National Council on Alcoholism Conference Focuses on "Family
        with Alcoholism." NIAAA Information and Feature Service,
        (IFS No. 86): 1, July 30, 1981.

4116.   National Council on Alcoholism, Criteria Committee. Criteria
        for the Diagnosis of Alcoholism. American Journal of
        Psychiatry, 129: 127-135, 1972. (Also in: Annals of
        Internal Medicine, 77: 249-258, 1972; Alcoholism: A
        Practical Treatment Guide. Eds. Stanley E. Gitglow and
        Herbert S. Peyser. New York: Grune and Stratton, 1980,
        pages 247-266.)

4117.   National Council on Alcoholism Speakers Address Family-Related
        Issues in Treatment, Prevention of Alcohol Problems. NIAAA
        Information and Feature Service, (IFS No. 86): 4-5,
        July 30, 1981.

4118.   National Institute on Alcohol Abuse and Alcoholism. Alcohol and
        the Family. Pamphlet. Rockville, MD: National
        Clearinghouse for Alcohol Information, 1980.

4119.   National Institute on Alcohol Abuse and Alcoholism. Children of
        Alcoholics: An Interview with the NIAAA Director. Alcohol
        Health and Research World, 8(4): 3-5, 1984.

4120.   National Institute on Alcohol Abuse and Alcoholism. General
        Conclusions and Recommendations (of the Symposium). In:
        Services for Children of Alcoholics. Symposium held in
        September, 1979 at Silver Spring, MD. U.S. National Institute
        on Alcohol Abuse and Alcoholism. Research Monograph No. 4.
        Washington, D.C.: U.S. Government Printing Office, 1981,
        pages 39-41. (DHHS Publication No. ADM 81-1007).

4121.   National Institute on Alcohol Abuse and Alcoholism. Identification
        (of the Children of Alcoholics). In: Services for Children
        of Alcoholics. Symposium held in September, 1979, Silver
        Spring, MD. U.S. National Institute on Alcohol Abuse and
        Alcoholism. Research Monograph No. 4. Washington, D.C.:
        U.S. Government Printing Office, 1981, pages 7-16. (DHHS
        Publication No. ADM 81-1007).

4122.   National Institute on Alcohol Abuse and Alcoholism. Intervention
        (with the Children of Alcoholics). In: Services for
        Children of Alcoholics. Symposium held in September, 1979,
        Silver Spring, MD. Research Monograph No. 4. Washington, D.C.:
        U.S. Government Printing Office, 1981, pages 17-22. (DHHS
        Publication No. ADM 81-1007).

4123. National Institute on Alcohol Abuse and Alcoholism. Services
        for Children of Alcoholics. Symposium held in September,
        1979 at Silver Spring, MD. Research Monograph No. 4.
        Washington, D.C.: U.S. Government Printing Office, 1981.
        (DHHS Publication No. ADM 81-1007.)

4124. National Institute on Alcohol Abuse and Alcoholism. Someone
        Close Drinks Too Much. Pamphlet. Rockville, MD: National
        Clearinghouse for Alcohol Information, 1974. (Also from:
        Washington, D.C.: U.S. Government Printing Office, 1981;
        DHHS Publication No. (ADM) 81-23.)

4125. National Institute on Alcohol Abuse and Alcoholism. Treatment
        (of the Children of Alcoholics). In: Services for Children
        of Alcoholics. Symposium held in September, 1979 at
        Silver Spring, MD. U.S. National Institute on Alcohol
        Abuse and Alcoholism. Research Monograph No. 4. Washington,
        D.C.: U.S. Government Printing Office, 1981, pages 23-29.
        (DHHS Publication No. ADM 81-1007.)

4126. National Institute on Alcohol Abuse and Alcoholism Prevention.
        Issues Applying to Children of Alcoholics. In: Services
        for Children of Alcoholics. Symposium held on September
        24-26, 1979 at Silver Spring, Maryland. U.S. National
        Institute on Alcohol Abuse and Alcoholism. Research
        Monograph No. 4. Washington, D.C.: U.S. Government
        Printing Office, 1981, pages 30-38. (DHHS Publication
        No. ADM 81-1007.)

4127. National Institute on Drug Abuse. Adolescent Marijuana Abusers
        and Their Families. NIDA Research Monograph No. 40.
        Published in cooperation with the U.S. Department of Health
        and Human Services. Washington, D.C.: U.S. Government
        Printing Office, 1981. (DHHS Publication No. ADM 81-1168).

4128. National Institute on Drug Abuse. Drugs and Family/Peer
        Influence: Family and Peer Influences on Adolescent Drug
        Use. Eds. P. Ferguson, T. Lennox and D. Lettieri.
        Washington, D.C.: U.S. Government Printing Office, 1975.
        (DHEW Publication No. ADM 75-186.)

4129. National Institute on Drug Abuse. A Family Response to the
        Drug Problem: A Family Program for the Prevention of
        Chemical Dependence. Washington, D.C.: U.S. Government
        Printing Office, 1976.

4130. National Institute on Drug Abuse. Division of Resource Development.
        The Use of Family Therapy in Drug Abuse Treatment: A National
        Survey. Washington, D.C.: U.S. Government Printing Office,
        1977. (NO. 78-622.)

4131. National Native Alcohol and Drug Abuse Program. Pamphlet.
        Ottawa: Health and Welfare Canada, Medical Services Branch,
        1982.

4132. Nau, E. Kindesmisshandlung. (Child Abuse.) Monatsschrift fur
        Kinderheilkunde, Berlin, 115: 192-194, 1967.

4133. Navratil, L. Alkoholismus und Geburtennummer. Zur Frage der
        "Konstitution des Letzten Kindes." (Alcoholism and Birth
        Rank. On the Problem of "Constitution of the Last Child.")
        Wiener Klinische Wochenschrift, 68: 158-160, 1956.

4134. Navratil, L. On the Etiology of Alcoholism. Quarterly Journal
        of Studies on Alcohol, 20: 236-244, 1959.

4135. Navratil, L. Die Rolle der Ehefrau in der Pathogenese der
        Trunksucht. (The Role of the Wife in the Pathogenesis
        of Alcoholism.) Wiener Zeitschrfit fur Nervenheilkunde
        und Deren Grenzgehiete, 14: 90-97, 1957.

4136. Naylor, P.R. Alcohol, Alibis and Alateen. Leaflet. New York:
        Al-Anon Family Group Headquarters, 1964.

4137. Nazaryan, S.S. O Nekotorykh Disgarmoniyakh Seksual'noi Zhizni u
        Bol'nykh Alkogolizmom. (Some of the Disorders in the Sex
        Life of Alcoholics.) Zhurnal Eksperimentalnoi I Klinicheskoi
        Meditsiny, 16(2): 88-91, 1976.

4138. Nedoma, K., Mellan, J. and Pondelickova, J. Incestini Pedofilni
        Delinkvence. (Incestuous Pedophilic Delinquency.)
        Ceskoslovenska Psychiatrie, 65(4): 224-229, 1969.

4139. Needle, R., McCubbin, H., Lorence, J. and Hochhauser, M.
        Reliability and Validity of Adolescent Self-Reported Drug
        Use in a Family-Based Study: A Methodological Report.
        International Journal of the Addictions, 18(7): 901-912,
        1983.

4140. Neff, J.A. and Husaini, B.A. Life Events, Drinking Patterns
        and Depressive Symptomatology. The Stress-Buffering Role
        of Alcohol Consumption. Journal of Studies on Alcohol,
        43(3): 301-318, 1982.

4141. Negrete, J.C. Les Attitudes Envers le Comportement des
        Alcooliques; Etude Comparative dans Trois Sous-cultures
        Quebecoises. (Attitudes Toward Behavior of Alcoholics;
        Comparative Study in Three Subcultures of Quebec.)
        Toxicomanies, Quebec, 3: 193-212, 1970.

4142. Negrete, J.C. Cultural Influences on Social Performance of
        Alcoholics. A Comparative Study. Quarterly Journal of
        Studies on Alcohol, 34(3): 905-916, 1973.

4143. Negrete, J.C. and MacPherson, A. Estudio Comparativo Sobre
        La Adaptacion Matrimonial de Alcoholistas "Activos" Y
        "Curados." (Comparative Study of the Marital Adjustment
        of "Active" and "Treated" Alcoholics.) Acta Psiquiatrica
        Y Psicologica De America Latina, Buenos Aires, 12:
        251-256, 1966.

4144. Neidengard, Ted and Yalisove, Daniel. Juvenile Alcoholism and
        Alcohol Abuse. In: Self-Destructive Behavior in Children
        and Adolescents. Eds. Carl F. Wells and Irving R. Stuart.
        New York: Van Nostrand Reinhold Co., 1981, pages 150-162.

4145. Neidig, P.H., Friedman, D.H. and Collins, B.S. Domestic
        Conflict Containment: A Spouse Abuse Treatment Program.
        Social Casework: The Journal of Contemporary Social Work,
        66(4): 195-204, 1985.

4146. Neikirk, J. Experiential Therapy: When Talking is Not Enough.
        In: Alcoholism and the Family: A Book of Readings.
        Eds. Sharon Wegscheider-Cruse and Richard W. Esterly.
        Wernersville, PA: Caron Institute, 1985, pages 41-44.

4147. Neikirk, J.O. Grief, Loss - Constant in Alcoholic Families.
        Focus on Family and Chemical Dependency, 6(5): 13-14, 1983.

4148. Neild, Theodore. Alcoholism and Eugenics. British Journal of
        Inebriety, 13: 84-85, 1915.

4149. Neilsen, N.P., Nava, V. and Drago, C. The Marital Patterns Test
         of Ryle in the Study of Some Aspects of Marital Relationships
         of the Alcoholic; Preliminary Observations. Alcoholism,
         Zagreb, 14: 134-139, 1978. (Also as: Paper presented at the
         Sixth International Congress on Social Psychiatry, Opatija,
         Yugoslavia, October, 1976.)

4150. Nellis, M. (Ed.). Drugs, Alcohol and Women; A National Forum
         Source Book. Washington, D.C.: National Research and
         Communications Associates, Inc., 1976.

4151. Nelson, D.O. A Comparison of Drinking and Alcoholism Between
         Students in Selected High Schools of Utah and in the Utah
         State Industrial School. Journal of Alcohol Education,
         13(4): 17-25, 1968.

4152. Nelson, E.M. Alcoholism is a Disease. Freedom Fighter from
         Idaho: 10-11, 60-62, 1985.

4153. Nelson, G. Therapeutic Communication with the Alcoholic and
         His Family. Canadian Journal of Psychiatric Nursing,
         14(5): 5, 1973.

4154. Nelson, L. Alcoholism in Zuni, New Mexico. Preventive Medicine,
         6(1): 152-166, 1977.

4155. Nelson, Thomas Edwward. A Ministry Intentionally Directed to
         Families of Alcoholics in the Local Church Today. Doctoral
         Dissertation. Nashville, TN: Vanderbilt University Divinity
         School, 1978.

4156. Nemir, S.S. and McDonald C. What is Treatment of Substance
         Abuse? Texas Medicine, 80(6): 55-60, 1984.

4157. Nero, Jack. Drink Like a Lady, Cry Like a Man. Minneapolis:
         Compcare Publications, 1977.

4158. Nesteruk, M. and Lech-Sobczak, C. Czynniki Psychologiczno-
         Srodowiskowe oraz Biologiczne w Przerwaniu Abstynencji
         Alkoholowej. (Psychological, Environmental and Biological
         Factors in Interrupted Alcohol Abstinence.) Psychiatria
         Polska, Warsaw, 12: 626-627, 1978.

4159. Neuberg, Paul. L'alcoolisme Au Grand Duche de Luxembourg.
         Donnees Statistiques et Organisation d'un Service de
         Traitement Specialise. (Alcoholism in the Grand Duchy of
         Luxembourg. Statistical Data and Organization of a
         Specialized Treatment Service. Bulletin de la Societe
         des Sciences Medicales du Grand-Duche de Luxembourg,
         115(2): 89-97, 1978.

4160. Neuberg, Paul. Les Facteurs Socio-Economiques Intervenant dans
         le Traitement des Alcooliques. Description de la Chaine
         Therapeutique. (Socioeconomic Factors Intervening in the
         Treatment of Alcoholics. A Description of the Therapeutic
         Sequence.) Bulletin de las Societe des Sciences Medicales
         du Grand-Duche de Luxembourg, 120(2): 31-36, 1983.

4161. Neumann, H. Moglichkeiten und Schwierigkeiten Bei Der Behandlung
         des Alkoholikers in der Allgemeinpraxis. (Possibilities
         and Limitations in the Treatment of Alcoholics in General
         Practice.) Therapie der Gegenwart, 102: 255-265, 1963.

4162. Neuringer, Charles and Clopton, James R. Use of Psychological
         Tests for the Study of the Identification, Prediction
         and Treatment of Alcoholism. In: Empirical Studies of
         Alcoholism. Eds. G. Goldstein and Charles Neuringer.
         Cambridge, MA: Ballinger, 1976, pages 7-35.

4163. <u>Never Too Early</u>. <u>Never Too Late</u>. Pamphlet. Center City, MN: Hazelden, no date.

4164. Neville, E.C. <u>Garden of Broken Glass</u>. New York: Delacorte, 1975.

4165. Neville, H.J. and Schmidt, A.L. Event-Related Brain Potentials in Subjects at Risk for Alcoholism. In: <u>Early Identification of Alcohol Abuse</u>. (National Institute on Alcohol Abuse and Alcoholism Research Monograph No. 17.) Eds. Norman C. Chang and Helen M. Chao. Washington, D.C.: U.S. Government Printing Office, 1985, pages 228-239.

4166. New Alcoholism Treatment Program. <u>Illinois Medical Journal</u>, <u>135</u>(4): 393, 1969.

4167. New Directions Stresses Family Therapy Approach. <u>NIAAA Information and Feature Service</u>, (IFS No. 67): 5, December 31, 1979.

4168. <u>New Guidebook</u>- Prevention Plus: Involving Schools, Parents, and the Community in Alcohol and Drug Education. <u>ADAMHA News</u>, <u>9</u>(14): 3, 1983.

4169. New Options for Alcoholics. <u>Innovations</u>, <u>5</u>(3): 31-32, 1978.

4170. New Studies of Alcohol and Heredity. <u>Scientific Temperance Journal</u>, <u>26</u>: 6-7, 1916.

4171. Newcomb, Carol Hubbard. An Exploration of the Experience of Parental Deprivation in Low Income Female Alcoholics. Doctoral Dissertation. Washington, D.C.: George Washington University, 1982. (Also in: <u>Dissertation Abstracts International</u>, <u>43</u>(2): 559B, 1962.)

4172. Newcomb, Michael D., Huba, G.J. and Bentler, Peter M. Mothers' Influence on the Drug Use of Their Children: Confirmatory Tests of Direct Modeling and Mediational Theories. <u>Developmental Psychology</u>, <u>19</u>(5): 714-726, 1983.

4173. Newell, M. and Price, J.L. Marital Separation: A Therapeutic Intervention Following Sobriety. <u>Focus on Family and Chemical Dependency</u>, <u>8</u>(6): 14-15, 36, 1985.

4174. Newell, N. Alcoholism and the Father-Image. <u>Quarterly Journal of Studies on Alcohol</u>, <u>11</u>: 92-96, 1950. (Also in: <u>Massachusetts Department of Mental Health</u>, pages 92-96, no date.)

4175. New Light on Some Problems of Involuntary Commitment or Treatment. Drinking as an Element in Custody Cases. <u>Quarterly Journal of Studies on Alcohol</u>, <u>3</u>: 688-679, 1943.

4176. Newman, Joseph (Ed.) <u>Family Treatment Methods in Alcohol Abuse and Alcoholism</u>. <u>Proceeding of a Workshop in Pittsburgh</u>, April, 1975.

4177. Newman, Joseph (Ed.) <u>Marital Counseling in Alcohol Abuse and Alcoholism</u>. <u>Proceedings of a Workshop in Pittsburgh</u>, October, 1975.

4178. Newman, Joseph (Ed.) <u>Sexual Counseling for Persons with Alcohol Problems</u>. <u>Proceedings of a Workshop in Pittsburgh</u>, 1986.

4179. Newman, Stephen. Extended Family Eroding. Seven Characteristics Identify High Risk Adolescents. <u>The U.S. Journal of Drug and Alcohol Dependence</u>, <u>6</u>(8): 38, 1982.

4180. Newman, T.M. Promise Parent Study Groups: A Manual of
       Instruction: Techniques for Enhancing Parenting Skills.
       Chicago: National Congress of Parents and Teachers, 1977.

4181. Nguyen, Lan Dinh, Chabert, Meda and DeGasquet. Enquete
       Alimentaire Chez des Familles de Gros Buveurs de Marseille
       et des Familles Temoins. (Study of Nutrition in Families
       of Heavy Drinkers and Families of a Control Group in
       Marseilles.) Bulletin de l'Institut d'Hygiene, 14:
       575-585, 1959.

4182. Nichols, Beverly B. The Abused Wife Problem. Social Casework,
       57(1): 27-32, 1976.

4183. Nichols, J.R. Alcoholism and Opiate Addiction: Theory and
       Evidence for a Genetic Link Between the Two. Paper presented
       at an International Symposium (on the) Biological Aspects of
       Alcohol Consumption, September, 1971. Eds. Olof Forsander
       and K. Eriksson, pages 131-134. (Finnish Foundation for
       Alcohol Studies, Helsinki, 20, 1972.)

4184. Nichols, J.R. The Children of Addicts: What Do They Inherit?
       Annals of the New York Academy of Sciences, 197: 60-65, 1972.

4185. Nicholson, S.M. Preschoolers from Chemically Dependent Families.
       Focus on Alcohol and Drug Issues, 6(4): 16-17, 1983.

4186. Nicholson, S.M. Teenage Addiction. Alcoholism The National
       Magazine, 5(2): 54, 1984.

4187. Nicholson, Stella. Pre-School-Aged Children from Alcoholic Families.
       In: Changing Leagues: Growing Up in an Alcoholic Home.
       Pompano Beach, FL: Health Communications, 1984, pages 7-11.

4188. Nici, J. Wives of Alcoholics as "Repeaters." Journal of Studies
       on Alcohol, 40: 677-682, 1979.

4189. Nicklin, George. Salvaging the Intractable Alcoholic through
       Positive Intrafamilial Transference. Paper presented at
       the Meeting of the American Academy of Psychoanalysis,
       New York, December, 1972. (Also in: New Hampshire
       Program on Alcohol and Drug Use Bulletin, 20(4): 1975.)

4190. Nielsen, L.A. Sexual Abuse and Chemical Dependency: Assessing
       the Risk for Women Alcoholics and Adult Children. Focus on
       Family and Chemical Dependency, 7(6): 6, 10-11, 37, 1984.

4191. Nielsen, N.P., Nava, V. and Drago, C. The Marital Patterns Test
       of Ryle in the Study of Some Aspects of Marital Relationships
       of the Alcoholic; Preliminary Observations. Alcoholism,
       Zagreb, 14: 134-139, 1978.

4192. Nielsen, N.P., Veneziani, A., Dal Pra, S. and Sammarco, A.M.
       Contributo Allo Studio Della Relazione Coniugale
       Dell'etilista Evidenziata Con il Marital Patterns Test
       Di Ryle. (Contribution to the Study of the Conjugal
       Relationship of the Alcoholic as Evidenced by Ryle's Marital
       Patterns Test.) Rassegna di Studi Psichiatrici, Siena,
       66(1): 47-65, 1977.

4193. Niermeijer, M.F. Erfelijke Factoren Bij Alcoholisme. (Hereditary
       Factors in Alcoholism.) Nederlands Tijdschrift voor
       Geneeskunde, Amsterdam, 123: 1237-1239, 1979.

4194. Nikic, S., Vujosevic, K., Miljanovic, B. and Markovic, M.
       Isolation and Disintegration of the Familiar System of
       Drinkers. Alcoholism, Zagreb, 17(1-2): 34-38, 1982.

4195. Nikkari, J.G. Alcoholic Rehabilitation Unit as a Clinical
          Laboratory for Baccalaureate Nursing Students. Paper
          presented at the Second Spring Conference for Nurse Educators
          in Alcohol and Drug Abuse Nursing, Colorado Springs, May,
          1982, pages 189-197.

4196. Nilsen, Mary Y. When a Bough Breaks. Mending the Family
          Tree. Center City, MN: Hazelden, no date.

4197. Nilson-Giebel, M. Peer Groups Help Prevent Dependence Among Youth
          in the Federal Republic of Germany. International Journal
          of Health Education, Geneva, 23(1): 20-24, 1980.

4198. Niox, Riviere H. and Audouin, D. Regards sur le Fonctionnement
          d'un Service d'Alcoologie en Hopital General. (A Look at
          the Functioning of a Ward of Alcohology in a General
          Hospital.) Psychologie Medicale, Paris, 13(3): 427-430,
          1981.

4199. Nisonoff, Linda and Bitman, Irving. Spouse Abuse: Incidence
          and Relationship to Selected Demographic Variables.
          Victimology, 4(1): 131-140, 1979.

4200. Nitsche, W. Alcoholism. Einteilung, Epidemiologie,
          Entstehungsbedingungen. (Classification, Epidemiology,
          Etiology.) Fortschritte der Medizin, 100(23):
          1111-1115, 1982.

4201. Niven, Robert G. Alcohol and the Family. In: Alcoholism and
          Related Problems: Issues for the American Public.
          Ed. Louis J. West. Englewood Cliffs, NJ: Prentice-Hall,
          1984, pages 91-109.

4202. Niven, Robert G. Note in ADAMHA News, 10: 1a, 1984.

4203. Nixon, P.F. Is There a Genetic Component to the Pathogenesis of
          the Wernicke-Korsakoff Syndrome? Alcohol and Alcoholism,
          19(3): 219-221, 1984.

4204. Noble, E.P., Whipple, S.C., Parker, E.S., Meyers, L. and Poland,
          R.E. Psychological and Biological Studies on Sons of
          Alcoholics. Alcoholism: Clinical and Experimental
          Research, 10(1): 98, 1986.

4205. Noble, Ernest P. Your Role in Alcoholism Detection and Treatment.
          Practical Psychology for Physicians, 3(7): 15-19, 1976.

4206. Nobles, Wade W. Alienation, Human Transformation and Adolescent
          Drug Use: Toward a Reconceptualization of the Problem.
          Journal of Drug Issues, 14(2): 243-252, 1984.

4207. Nocks, J.J. and Bradley, D.L. Self-Esteem in an Alcoholic
          Population. Diseases of the Nervous System, 30(9):
          611-617, 1969.

4208. Noel, N.E. and McCrady, B.S. Behavioral Treatment of an Alcohol
          Abuser with the Spouse Present: Two Case Studies. In: Power
          to Change: Family Case Studies in the Treatment of Alcoholism.
          Ed. Edward Kaufman. New York: Gardner Press, 1984, pages 23-77.

4209. Noll, Robert B. Young Male Offspring of Alcoholic Fathers: Early
          Developmental and Cognitive Differences From the MSU
          Vulnerability Study. Dissertation Abstracts International,
          44(3): 922B, 1983.

4210. Noll, Robert B. and Zucker, Robert A. Developmental Findings from
          an Alcoholic Vulnerability Study: The Preschool Years, 1983.
          (Eric Document Number ED243009.)

4211. Noll, Robert B., Zucker, Robert A., Weil, C. and Greenberg, G.S.
       Cognitive Factors in Substance Abuse: The Case for Early
       Learning. Paper presented at the 92nd Annual Convention of
       the American Psychological Association, Toronto, August, 1984.

4212. Non-Medical Use of Drugs Directorate Research Bureau. Alcohol
       Problems in Canada; A Summary of Current Knowledge.
       Technical Reports Series, Canada, 2: 1976.

4213. Noonan, D.L. Sex-Role Conflict and Drinking Behavior in Children
       of Alcoholic Parents. Doctoral Dissertation. (University
       Microfilms No. 8112393.) Washington, D.C.: George Washington
       University, 1981. (Also in: Dissertation Abstracts
       International, 42: 385B, 1981.)

4214. Nordlicht, Stephen. Effects of Stress on the Police Officer
       and Family. New York State Journal of Medicine, 79(3):
       400-401, 1979.

4215. Noreik, K. Rettspsykiatrisk Observerte Om Streifere.
       (Forensopsychiatric Observations of Male Vagrants.)
       Nordisk Tidsskrift for Kriminalvidenskab, 52: 136-149,
       1964.

4216. Norem-Hebeisen, Ardyth and Hedin, Diane P. Influences on
       Adolescent Problem Behavior: Causes, Connections, and
       Contexts. In: Adolescent Substance Abuse: A Guide to
       Prevention and Treatment. Eds. Richard Isralowitz and
       Mark Singer. New York: The Haworth Press, 1983, pages 35-36.

4217. North, Dorothy B. Skid Row Women. In: Women Who Drink; Alcoholic
       Experience and Psychotherapy. Ed. Vasanti Burtle.
       Springfield, IL: Charles C. Thomas, 1979, pages 81-97.

4218. North, J.W. A Partnership in Intervention. In: Association
       of Labor-Management Administrators and Consultants on
       Alcoholism, Inc. Proceedings of the Seventh Annual Meeting,
       San Francisco, October, 1978. Arlington, VA: ALMACA, 1978.

4219. North, John W. Family Assistance Program: Training Intervention
       Program. Milwaukee, WI: DePaul Rehabilitation Hospital,
       Division of Outpatient Service, 1978.

4220. North, John W. Triangle Approach to Alcoholism. Paper presented
       at the 24th Meeting of Alcohol and Drug Problems Association,
       Bloomington, MN, September, 1973.

4221. North, Robert and Orange, Richard. 25 Myths and Rationalizations
       About Drinking. In: Teenage Drinking: The Number One Drug
       Threat to Young People Today. New York: Macmillan, 1980,
       pages 38-41.

4222. North, Robert and Orange, Richard. Why Are Teens Drinking?
       In: Teenage Drinking: The Number One Drug Threat to Young
       People Today. New York: Macmillan, 1980, pages 14-18.

4223. Novak, D.G. Personality Traits and Family Interaction Patterns
       Associated with Alcoholism. In: Alcoholism: General
       Hospital Issues and Perspectives. Eds. D.G. Novak and
       R.L. Jones. Austin: Texas Hospital Association, 1976,
       pages 33-37.

4224. Novak, V. Antabusoterapiya Alkogolizma V Usloviyakh
       Psikhonevrologicheskogo Dispansera. (Antabus Therapy of
       Alcoholism Under the Conditions of a Psychoneurological
       Dispensary.) Zhurnal Nevropatologii I Psikhiatrii,
       Moscow, 59: 685-692, 1959.

4225. Noyer, Alain. Prisons et Prisonniers. (Prisons and Prisoners.)
Alcool ou Sante, Paris, 131(4): 19-22, 1975.

4226. Noyes, Russell Jr., Clancy, John, Crowe, Raymond, Hoenk, Paul R.
and Slymen, Donald J. The Familial Prevalence of Anxiety
Neurosis. Archives of General Psychiatry, 35: 1057-1059,
1978. (Also in: Advances in Family Psychiatry, 2:
269-277, 1980.)

4227. Nuckols, C.C. and Fares-O'Malley, P. Helping Relationships: A
Family Systems Perspective. Focus on Family and Chemical
Dependency, 7(5): 26, 28, 30, 1984.

4228. Nuckols, Cardwell C. Insight to the Oldest Child from an
Alcoholic Family. In: Changing Legacies: Growing Up
in an Alcoholic Home. Pompano Beach, FL: Health
Communications, 1984, pages 19-23.

4229. Nuller, Yu. L., Ostroumova, M.N. and Berezhnaya, V.A. Nekotoryye
Obshchie Zven'ya v Patogeneze Endogennoy Depressii i
Khronicheskogo Alkogolizma. (Some Common Links in the
Pathogenesis of Endogenous Depression and Chronic Alcoholism.)
Zhurnal Nevropatologii I Psikhiatrii, Moscow, 81(9):
1375-1379, 1981.

4230. Nunes, M.C.P., Sobrinho, L.G., Chalhaz-Jorge, C., Santos, M.A.,
Manricio, J.C. and Sousa, M.F.F. Psychosomatic Factors in
Patients with Hyperprolactinemia and/or Galactorrhea.
Obstetrics and Gynecology, 55: 591-595, 1980.

4231. Nurse, A.R. The Role of Alcoholism in Relationship to Intimacy.
Journal of Psychoactive Drugs, 14(1-2): 159-162, 1982.

4232. Nuttall, Ena V. and Nuttall, Ronald L. Parental Correlates of
Drug Use Among Young Puerto Rican Adults. American Journal
of Drug and Alcohol Abuse, 6(2): 173-188, 1979.

4233. Nuttall, Ena V., Nuttall, Ronald, L., Polit, Denise and Clark,
Karen. Assessing Adolescent Mental Health Needs: The
Views of Consumers, Providers, and Others. Adolescence,
12(46): 277-285, 1977.

4234. Nuttall, Ronald L. and Costa, P.T. Drinking Patterns as Affected
by Age and by Personality Type. Gerontologist, 15(5):
35, 1975.

4235. Nutting, P.A., Price, T.B. and Baty, M.L. Non-Health Professionals
and the School-Age Child: Early Intervention for Behavioral
Problems. The Journal of School Health, 49(2): 73-78, 1979.

4236. Nylander, I. Children of Alcoholic Fathers. Acta Paediatrica
Scandinavica, Stockholm, 49(Supplement 121): 1960.

4237. Nylander, I. A 20-year Prospective Follow-up Study of 2164 Cases
at the Child Guidance Clinics in Stockholm. Acta Pediatrica
Scandanavica, Stockholm, 68(Supplement 276): 1-45, 1979.

4238. Nylander, I. and Rydelius, P.-A. A Comparison Between Children
of Alcoholic Fathers from Excellent Versus Poor Social
Conditions. Acta Paediatrica Scandinavica, Stockholm,
71(5): 809-813, 1982.

4239. Nylander, I. and Rydelius, P.-A. The Relapse of Drunkenness in
Non-Asocial Teen-Age Boys. Acta Psychiatrica Scandinavica,
Copenhagen, 49(4): 435-443, 1973.

4240. Nylander, I. and Zetterstrom, R. Home Environment of Children in a
New Stockholm Suburb. A Prospective Longitudinal Study. Acta
Paediatrica Scandinavica, Stockholm, 72(Supplement 310): 1983.

O

4241. Oakeshott, J.G. and Gibson, J.B. The Genetics of Human Alcoholism:
       A Review. Australian and New Zealand Journal of Psychiatry,
       Melbourne, 11(2): 123-128, 1981.

4242. Oakeshott, J.G. and Gibson, J.B. On the Inheritance of Alcoholism.
       Paper presented at the 1980 Autumn School of Studies on Alcohol
       and Drugs, Melbourne, 1980, pages 193-201.

4243. Obayemi, Ade M.U. Alcohol Usage in an African Society. In: Cross-
       Cultural Approaches to the Study of Alcohol: An Interdisciplinary
       Perspective. Eds. Michael W. Everett, Jack O. Waddell and
       Dwight B. Heath. Paris: Mouton Publishers, 1976, pages 199-208.

4244. Oberst, Byron B. Adolescents and Some of Their Social Problems,
       Including Parenthood. Part I. Nebraska State Medical Journal,
       55(9): 534-537, 1970.

4245. Oberstone, Andrea Kincses. Dimensions of Psychological Adjustment
       and Style of Life in Single Lesbians and Single Heterosexual
       Women. Doctoral Dissertation. (University Microfilms No.
       75-8510.) Los Angeles: California School of Professional
       Psychology, 1974. (Also in: Dissertation Abstracts
       International, 35(10): 5088B, 1974.)

4246. O'Brien, Eugene Michael. Childhood Stress, Situational Factors,
       and Alcohol Drinking Behavior in College. Doctoral
       Dissertation. (University Microfilms No. 8024598.) Kent,
       OH: Kent State University, 1980. (Also in: Dissertation
       Abstracts International 41(5): 1958A, 1980.)

4247. O'Brien, James G. Alcoholism: A Three-Article Symposium.
       Postgraduate Medicine, 74(1): 143-145, 1983.

4248. O'Brien, W.B. Growth and Development of the Therapeutic Community
       Movement in Drug Abuse Treatment. Paper presented at the
       10th Biennial Summer School of the National Society on
       Alcoholism and Drug Dependency, Wellington, New Zealand,
       January, 1983.

4249. Obuchowska, I. Emotional Contact with the Mother as a Social
       Compensatory Factor in Children of Alcoholics. International
       Mental Health Research Newsletter, 16: 2,4, 1974.

4250. Occupational Program Helps Family Members. NIAAA Information
       and Feature Service, (IFS No. 68):1, January 23, 1980.

4251. O'Connell, Alison and Solomon, Miriam. The Coalition for Abused
       Women. COA Newsletter, 3(2): 3, 1985.

4252. O'Connell, Bernard Joseph. Early Family Behavior, Gender
       Differences, and Alcohol Usage in Persons Raised in a Small
       Community. Doctoral Dissertation. University Microfilms
       No. 8025739.) Ann Arbor: University of Michigan, 1980.
       (Also in: Dissertation Abstracts International, 41(5):
       2023A, 1980.)

4253. O'Conner, William J. and Morgan, Donald W. Multidisciplinary
       Treatment of Alcoholism: A Consultation Program for Team
       Coordination. Quarterly Journal of Studies on Alcohol,
       29(4-A): 903-908, 1968.

4254. O'Connor, J.P. and Rosall, J. "Our Vision: A Journey to Better
       Health." Paper presented at the Third National Indian/Alaska
       Native Health Conference, Spokane, July, 1979.

4255. O'Connor, John F. and Stern, Lenore O. Developmental Factors in
       Functional Sexual Disorders. New York State Journal of
       Medicine, 72(4): 1838-1843, 1972.

4256. O'Connor, Joyce. Annotation: Normal and Problem Drinking Among
       Children. Journal of Child Psychology and Psychiatry,
       18(3): 279-284, 1977.

4257. O'Connor, Joyce. Cultural Influences and Drinking Behavior.
       Drinking in Ireland and England: A Tri-Ethnic Study of
       Drinking among Young People and Their Parents. Journal
       of Alcoholism, 10(3): 94-121, 1975.

4258. O'Connor, Joyce. Parental Influences: A Tri-Ethnic Study on the
       Transmission of Drinking Behaviour from Parent to Child --
       Preliminary Communication. Irish Medical Journal, 69:
       152-158, 1976.

4259. O'Connor, Joyce. Social and Cultural Factors Influencing
       Behaviour among Young People: A Cross National Study of
       the Drinking Behaviour and Attitudes Towards Drinking of
       Young People and Their Parents. Volumes 1, 11. Doctoral
       Thesis. National University of Ireland, 1976. (Also as:
       Report to the British Medical Council on Alcoholism, 1976.)

4260. O'Connor, Joyce. The Transmission of Drinking Behaviour from
       Parents to Children: Influences in the Development of
       Drinking Behaviour. Journal of Comparative Family Studies,
       10(2): 253-270, 1979.

4261. O'Donnell, John A. Marital History. In: Narcotics Addicts in
       Kentucky. Ed. J. O'Donnell. Washington, D.C.: U.S. Public
       Health Service Publication No. 1881. 1969, pages 143-160.

4262. O'Farrell, Timothy J. Behavioral Marital Therapy for Alcoholics
       and Spouses: A Comprehensive Annotated Bibliography.
       JSAS/Catalog of Selected Documents in Psychology (APA),
       9(February): 8-9, 1979.

4263. O'Farrell, Timothy J. Marital and Family Therapy for Alcohol
       Problems. Paper presented at the Annual Meeting of the
       American Psychological Association, Washington, D.C.,
       August, 1982.

4264. O'Farrell, Timothy J. Marital Stability Among Wives of Alcoholics:
       Reported Antecedents of a Wife's Decision to Separate from or
       Endure Her Alcoholic Husband. Doctoral Dissertation.
       (University Microfilms No. 75-21006.) Boston University
       Graduate School, 1975.

4265. O'Farrell, Timothy J. and Cutter, Henry S.G. Behavioral Marital
       Therapy Couples Groups for Male Alcoholics and Their Wives.
       Journal of Substance Abuse Treatment, 1(3): 191-204, 1984.

4266. O'Farrell, Timothy J. and Cutter, Henry S.G. Behavioral Marital
       Therapy (BMT) for Alcoholics and Wives: Review of Literature
       and a Proposed Research Program. 1977. Eric Document Number
       ED155531.

4267. O'Farrell, Timothy J. and Cutter, Henry S.G. Behavioral Marital
       Therapy for Male Alcoholics: Clinical Procedures from a
       Treatment Outcome Study in Progress. The American Journal
       of Family Therapy, 12(3): 33-46, 1984.

4268. O'Farrell, Timothy J. and Cutter, Henry S.G. Effects of Adding a
       Behavioral or an Interactional Couples Group to Individual
       Outpatient Alcoholism Counseling. Paper presented at the
       Sixteenth Annual Convention of the Association for the
       Advancement of Behavior Therapy, Los Angeles, November, 1982.

4269. O'Farrell, Timothy J. and Cutter, Henry S.G. Evaluating Behavioral
       Marital Therapy for Male Alcoholics. Paper presented at the
       Annual Meeting of the American Psychological Association,
       Washington, D.C., August, 1982.

4270. O'Farrell, Timothy J. and Cutter, Henry S.G. A Proposed Behavioral
       Couples Group for Male Alcoholics and Their Wives. In:
       Behavioral Group Therapy: An Annual Review. Eds. D. Upper
       and S.M. Ross. Champaign, IL: Research Press, 1979, pages
       279-300.

4271. O'Farrell, Timothy J., Cutter, Henry S.G., Bayog, R.D., Dentch, G.
       and Fortgang, J. Correspondence Between One-Year Retrospective
       Reports of Pretreatment Drinking by Alcoholics and Their Wives.
       Behavioral Assessment, 6(3): 263-274, 1984.

4272. O'Farrell, Timothy J., Cutter, H.S.G. and Floyd, F.J. Evaluating
       Behavioral Marital Therapy for Male Alcoholics: Effects
       on Marital Adjustment and Communication from Before to After
       Treatment. Behavior Therapy, 16(2): 147-167, 1985.

4273. O'Farrell, Timothy J., Harrison, Robert H. and Cutter, Henry S.G.
       Marital Stability Among Wives of Alcoholics: An Evaluation of
       Three Explanations. British Journal of Addiction, 76(2):
       175-190, 1981.

4274. O'Farrell, Timothy J., Harrison, Robert H., Schulmeister, Carolyn A.
       and Cutter, Henry S.G. A Closeness to Divorce Scale for Wives
       of Alcoholics. Drug and Alcohol Dependence, Lausanne, 7(4):
       319-324, 1981.

4275. Offord, David R. and Poushinsky, Mary F. School Performance,
       IQ and Female Delinquency. International Journal of Social
       Psychiatry, 27(1): 53-62, 1981.

4276. Ogden, L.D. The Process and Content of Alcohol Education for
       Nurses in a General Hospital. Journal of Alcohol and Drug
       Education, 22(1): 14-21, 1976.

4277. Oglietti, J.R. and Segal, B. (Eds.) Proceedings of the 1981
       Annual School on Alcohol and Addiction Studies. Anchorage:
       Center for Alcohol and Addiction Studies, 1981.

4278. O'Gorman, P. Primary Prevention for Children of Alcoholics. In:
       Preventing Alcoholism; Primary Prevention. Revised Edition.
       Mill Neck, NY: Christopher D. Smithers Foundation, 1981.

4279. O'Gorman, P.A. Alcoholism: The Family Disease. Urban Health,
       3(5): 27, 38, 1974.

4280. O'Gorman, Patrica. An Historical Look at Children of Alcoholics.
       Focus on Family and Chemical Dependency, 8(1): 5, 43, 1985.

4281. O'Gorman, Patricia and Lacks, Hazel. Aspects of Youthful Drinking.
       Report. New York: National Council on Alcoholism, 1979.

4282. O'Gorman, Patricia and Ross, Robert A. Children of Alcoholics
       in the Juvenile Justice System. Alcohol Health and Research
       World, 8(4): 43-45, 1984.

4283. O'Gorman, Patricia A. Perception of Fathers in Adolescents from
       Alcoholic Homes. Paper presented at 22nd International
       Institute on the Prevention and Treatment of Alcoholism, Vigo,
       Spain, June, 1976.

4284. O'Gorman, Patricia A. Policy Watch: Will We Help the Family?
       Human Ecology Forum, 9(3): 19, 1978.

4285. O'Gorman, Patricia A. Prevention Issues Involving Children of
       Alcoholics. In: Services for Children of Alcoholics.
       Symposium held in September, 1979 at Silver Spring, MD.
       Research Monograph No. 4. Washington, D.C.: U.S. Government
       Printing Office, 1981. (DHHS Publication. No. ADM 81-1007.)

4286. O'Gorman, Patricia A. Proposed Direction for the Mid-America
       Institute on Violence in Families. Report. New York: National
       Council on Alcoholism, 1978.

4287. O'Gorman, Patricia A. Public Policy and the Child of the Alcoholic.
       In: Children of Exceptional Parents. Ed. Mary Frank.
       New York: Haworth Press, 1983, pages 35-41.

4288. O'Gorman, Patricia A. Self-Concept, Focus of Control and Perception
       of Father in Adolescents from Homes with and without Severe
       Drinking Problems. Doctoral Dissertation. (University
       Microfilms No. 76-4189.) New York: Fordham University, 1975.
       (Also in: Dissertation Abstracts International, 36: 5156A,
       1976.)

4289. O'Hagan, Mary. Alcoholism and the Family. In: Notes on Alcohol
       and Alcoholism. Ed. S. Caruana. London: B. Edsall, 1975.

4290. O'Hara, H., Suwaki, H., Yoshida, T. and Hisashige, A. A Study of
       Drinking Habits of Adult Males in Kochi Prefecture Japan.
       Japanese Journal of Alcohol Studies and Drug Dependence,
       Kyoto, 18(2): 170-183, 1983.

4291. O'Hara, Kenshiro, Miyazato, Katsumasa and Honma, Osamu. The
       Addiction of an Entire Family: A Case Study. Clinical
       Psychiatry, Tokyo, 14(10): 929-933, 1972.

4292. Ohira, K. The Genesis and Development of Alcohol-Dependent
       Personality Observed in a Peruvian Shanty Town. Japanese
       Journal of Alcohol Studies and Drug Dependence, Kyoto,
       18(1): 66-73, 1983.

4293. Ohlemacher, Janet. Beloved Alcoholic. What To Do When a Family
       Member Drinks. Grand Rapids, MI: Zondervan Publishing
       House, 1984.

4294. Ohlsson, Arne. Non-Organic Failure to Thrive. Child Abuse and
       Neglect, 3(2): 449-459, 1979.

4295. Ojesjo, L. Long-term Outcome in Alcohol Misuse and Alcoholism
       Among Males in the Lundby General Population, Sweden.
       British Journal of Addiction, 76: 391-400, 1981.

4296. Older Alcoholics Benefit from Family Approach. NIAAA Information
       and Feature Service, (IFS No. 60): 5, June 7, 1979.

4297. O'Leary, D.E., O'Leary, M.R. and Donovan, D.M. Social Skill
        Acquisition and Psychosocial Development of Alcoholics:
        A Review. Addictive Behaviors, 1: 111-120, 1976.

4298. Olejar, Frantisek. Deprivation Syndrome in Children from
        Neglected Families. Studia Psychologica, Bratislava,
        9(4): 292-295, 1967.

4299. Oliver, J.E. and Dewhurst, K.E. Six Generations of Ill-Used
        Children in a Huntington's Pedigree. Postgraduate Medical
        Journal, London, 45(530): 757-760, 1969.

4300. Oliver-Diaz, P. Self Help Groups: Through the Children's Eyes.
        Tempering Commitment with Compassion. Focus on Family
        and Chemical Dependency, 8(2): 28-29, 38, 1985.

4301. Oliver-Diaz, P. Teenage Co-Dependents: The Chemical is Not the
        Issue. Focus on Family and Chemical Dependency, 8(1):
        17-19, 1985.

4302. Ollendick, Duane G. Scores on Three MMPI Alcohol Scales of
        Parents who Receive Child Custody. Psychological Reports,
        55(1): 337-338, 1984.

4303. Ollendick, Duane G. and Otto, B.J. MMPI Characteristics of Parents
        Referred for Child-Custody Studies. Journal of Psychology,
        117(2): 227-232, 1984.

4304. Olson, Cheryl. Dealing with Drug Use. Humanistic Approach
        Works Best. Milwaukee Council on Drug Abuse, 1980.

4305. Olson, David H., Russell, Candyce S. and Sprenkle, Douglas H.
        Marital and Family Therapy: A Decade Review. Journal of
        Marriage and the Family, 42(4): 973-993, 1980.

4306. Oltman, J.E. and Friedman, S. A Consideration of Parental
        Deprivation and Other Factors in Alcohol Addicts. Quarterly
        Journal of Studies on Alcohol, 14: 49-57, 1953.

4307. Oltman, J.E. and Friedman, S. Parental Deprivation in Psychiatric
        Conditions. III. (In Personality Disorders and Other
        Conditions.) Diseases of the Nervous System, 28(5):
        298-303, 1967.

4308. O'Malley A. Heredity and the Medical Treatment. III. (American)
        Ecclesiastical Review, 48: 53-64, 1913.

4309. O'Malley, Stephanie Samples. The Effects of Family Drinking
        History on Responses to Alcohol: Expectancies and the
        Perception of Intoxication (High-Risk, Alcoholism).
        Dissertation Abstracts International, 45(1): 361B, 1983.

4310. O'Malley, Stephanie Samples and Maisto, S.A. Effects of Family
        Drinking History and Expectancies on Responses to Alcohol in
        Men. Journal of Studies on Alcohol, 46(4): 289-297, 1985.

4311. O'Malley, T.A., Everitt, D.E., O'Malley, H.C. and Campion, E.W.
        Identifying and Preventing Family-Mediated Abuse and Neglect
        of Elderly Persons. Annals of Internal Medicine, 98(6):
        998-1005, 1983.

4312. Omeara, E. Warren III. The Family Environment of Depressed
        Recovering Alcoholic Men. Dissertation Abstracts
        International, 43(6): 1994B, 1982.

4313. Omenn, G.S. and Motulsky, A.G. A Biochemical and Genetic Approach
        to Alcoholism. Annals of the New York Academy of Sciences,
        197: 16-23, 1972.

4314.   Omori, Isamu and Imazu, Hiroichi. A Survey of Danshukai (Similar
        to Alcoholics Anonymous in U.S.A.) Throughout Japan. Journal
        of Transportation Medicine, Tokyo, 33(4): 264-271, 1979.

4315.   O'Neill, J. Marriage and Alcoholism. In: Blue Book, Vol. 34.
        South Orange, NJ: Seton Hall University, 1982.

4316.   Only, Mark. High: A Fairwell to the Pain of Alcoholism.
        Englewood Cliffs, NJ: Prentice-Hall, 1974.

4317.   Onnis, Luigi, Aite, Crozzoli, Livia and Menarini, M. Grazia.
        II Sintomo Alcoolico In Una Terapia Di Coppia: Studio
        Di Un Caso Clinico Affrontato Con Un Approccio Relazionale.
        (The Alcoholic Symptom in Couple Therapy: The Study of
        Clinical Case Handled by a Rational Approach.) Rivista
        di Psichiatria, Rome, 13(1): 69-g3, 1978.

4318.   Onstad, Sidgel. Rusmiddelmisbruk Blant Ungdom. I Relasjon Til
        Psykisle Symptomes Hos Den Enkelte Og Foreldrenes Helse.
        (Substance Abuse among Adolescents. In Relation to
        Psychiatric Symptoms in the Individual and the Health of
        the Parents.) Tidsskrift for den Norske Laegeforening,
        103(15): 1246-1248, 1983.

4319.   Operation Threshold. All in the Family - Understanding How We
        Teach and Influence Children About Alcohol. Tulsa:
        U.S. Jaycees, 1975.

4320.   Opinion Research Corporation. Caravan Surveys. Executives'
        Knowledge, Attitudes and Behavior Regarding Alcoholism
        and Alcohol Abuse. Study II. Prepared for U.S. National
        Institute on Alcohol Abuse and Alcoholism. (Report No.
        PB-248-696; NIAAA/NCALI-76/03.) Springfield, VA: U.S.
        National Technical Information Service, 1974.

4321.   Oppenheimer, Audrey. Triumph Over Trauma in the Treatment of
        Child Abuse. Social Casework, 59(6): 352-358, 1978.

4322.   Oppenheimer, Joan L. Francesca, Baby. New York: Scholastic
        Book Services, 1976.

4323.   Orchen, Marla D. A Treatment Efficacy Study Comparing Relaxation
        Training, EMG Biofeedback, and Family Therapy Among Heavy
        Drinkers. Dissertation Abstracts International, 44(8):
        2565B, 1984.

4324.   Orcutt, Ben A. Process Analysis of the First Phase of Treatment.
        In: Casework with Wives of Alcoholics. Eds. P.C. Cohen
        and M.S. Krause. New York: Family Service Association of
        America, 1971, pages 147-164.

4325.   Oreland, Lars. Why Do Alcoholics Have Low Platelet Monoamine
        Oxidase Activity? In: Biological/Genetic Factors in
        Alcoholism. Eds. Victor M. Hesselbrock, Edward G. Shaskan
        and Roger E. Meyer. Washington, D.C.: U.S. Government
        Printing Office, 1983, pages 119-130.

4326.   Orford, Jim. Alcohol and the Family. In: Alcoholism in
        Perspective. Eds. Marcus Grant and Paul Gwinner.
        Baltimore: University Park Press, 1979, pages 77-89.

4327.   Orford, J. Alcohol Problems and the Family. In: Research
        Highlights in Social Work: Approaches to Addiction.
        Ed. Joyce Lishman. New York: St. Martin's Press, 1985,
        pages 62-90.

4328.   Orford, Jim. Alcoholism and Marriage: The Argument Against
        Specialism. Journal of Studies on Alcohol, 36(11):
        1537-1563, 1975.

4329. Orford, Jim. A Comparison of Alcoholics Whose Drinking is
         Totally Uncontrolled and Those Drinking is Mainly Controlled.
         Behaviour Research and Therapy, 11(4): 565-576, 1973.

4330. Orford, Jim. Domestic Context. In: Psychological Problems.
         Eds. P. Feldman and J. Orford. New York: John Wiley & Sons,
         1980, pages 3-38.

4331. Orford, Jim. Impact of Alcoholism on Family and Home.
         In: Alcoholism: New Knowledge and New Responses.
         Eds. Griffith Edwards and Marcus Grant. London: Croom
         Helm, 1977, pages 234-243.

4332. Orford, Jim. The Prevention and Management of Alcohol Problems
         in the Family Setting: A Review of Work Carried Out in
         English-Speaking Countries. Alcohol and Alcoholism,
         19(2): 109-122, 1984.

4333. Orford, Jim. Prevention of Drinking Problems in the Family.
         In: Alcohol and the Family. Eds. J. Orford and J. Harwin.
         New York: St. Martin's Press, 1982, pages 241-259.

4334. Orford, Jim. A Study of the Personalities of Excessive Drinkers
         and Their Wives, Using the Approaches of Leary and Eysenck.
         Journal of Consulting and Clinical Psychology, 44(4):
         534-545, 1976.

4335. Orford, Jim. Understanding Treatment: Controlled Trials and
         Other Strategies. In: Alcoholism Treatment in Transition.
         Eds. G. Edwards and M. Grant. London: Croom Helm, 1980,
         pages, 143-161.

4336. Orford, Jim and Edwards, Griffith. Alcoholism. Oxford: Oxford
         University Press, 1977.

4337. Orford, Jim and Guthrie, Sally. Coping Behavior used by Wives of
         Alcoholics: A Preliminary Investigation. In: Alcohol
         Dependence and Smoking Behavior. Farnborough, Hampshire,
         England: Saxon House, 1976, pages 136-143.

4338. Orford, Jim, Guthrie, Sally and Nicholls, Peter. Self-Reported
         Coping Behavior of Wives of Alcoholics and its Association
         with Drinking Outcome. Journal of Studies on Alcohol,
         36(9): 1254-1267, 1975.

4339. Orford, Jim and Harwin, Judith. Alcohol and the Family.
         London: Croom Helm, 1982. (Also from: St. Martin's Press,
         New York, 1982.)

4340. Orford, Jim, Hawker, Ann and Nicholls, Peter. An Investigation
         of an Alcoholism Rehabilitation Halfway House: I. Types
         of Client and Modes of Discharge. British Journal of
         Addiction, 69: 213-224, 1974.

4341. Orford, Jim, Oppenheimer, Edna and Edwards, Griffith. Abstinence
         or Control: The Outcome for Excessive Drinkers Two Years
         after Consultation. Behaviour Research and Therapy,
         Oxford, 14(6): 409-418, 1976.

4342. Orford, Jim, Oppenheimer, Edna and Egert, Stella. The Cohesiveness
         of Alcoholism-Complicated Marriages and Its Influence on
         Treatment Outcome. British Journal of Psychiatry, London,
         128: 318-339, 1976.

4343. Orford, Jim, Oppenheimer, Edna, Egert, Stella and Hensman, C.
         Role of Excessive Drinking in Alcoholism Complicated
         Marriages. The International Journal of the Addictions,
         12(4): 471-495, 1977.

4344. Orford, Jim, Waller, Seta and Peto, Julian. Drinking Behavior
       and Attitudes and Their Correlates Among University Students
       in England. I. Principal Components in the Drinking Domain.
       II. Personality and Social Influence. III. Sex Differences.
       Quarterly Journal of Studies on Alcohol, 35(4 Pt A):
       1316-1374, 1974.

4345. Orme, T.C. and Rimmer, J. Alcoholism and Child Abuse: A Review.
       Journal of Studies on Alcohol, 42: 273-287, 1981.

4346. O'Rourke, Angus, Gough, Cora and Wilson, Davis Keith. Alcohol --
       A Report on a Study in Dublin Post-Primary Schoolchildren,
       1970. Journal of the Irish Medical Association, 67(13):
       355-358, 1974.

4347. Orr, B. Confront With Love to Break Denial. Magazine of the
       Texas Commission on Alcoholism, 5(2): 8-9, 1979.

4348. Orr, Elizabeth. In Touch With Community. Paper presented at the
       National Institute on Drug Abuse, Program for Women's Concerns.
       Miami Beach, October, 1975. (Also in: Drugs, Alcohol and
       Women; A National Forum Source Book. Ed. M. Nellis.
       Washington, D.C.: National Research and Communications
       Associates, Inc., 1976, pages 142-144.)

4349. Orsel, C.M. The Alcoholic's Family. Revue de Medicine, Paris,
       23(17): 887-890, 1982.

4350. Ortega, Bevia F.J. La Familia de la Mujer Alcoholica. (The Family
       of the Alcoholic Woman.) Actas Luso-Espanolas de Neurologia
       Psiquiatria y Ciencias Afines, Madrid, 4(4): 227-238, 1976.

4351. Orth-Gomer, Kristina and Ahlbom, Anders. Impact of Psychological
       Stress on Ischemic Heart Disease when Controlling for
       Conventional Risk Indicators. Journal of Human Stress,
       6(1): 7-15, 1980.

4352. Ortigues, E. Problemes Poses Par L'etude Sociologique De
       L'Alcoolisme. (Problems Posed by the Sociological Study of
       Alcoholism. Ouest-Medical, Paris, 28(13): 921-923, 1975.

4353. Osborn, S.G. and West, D.J. Do Young Delinquents Really Reform?
       Journal of Adolescence, London, 3(2): 99-114, 1980.

4354. Oshodin, Osayuki Godwin. Alcohol Abuse Among High School Students
       in Benin City, Nigeria. Dissertation Abstracts International,
       41(9): 3894-3895A, 1980. (Also in: Journal of the Royal
       Society of Health, 104(3): 106-107, 1984.)

4355. Osterberg, I. Alcohol Abuse Problem and Families with Children.
       Katilolehti, Helsinki, 86(12): 384-386, 1981.

4356. Osterberg, I. Barn och Fader: En Alkoholpsykologisk Studie.
       (Children and Fathers: An Alcohol-Psychological Study.)
       Alkoholipolitikka, Helsinki, 22: 106-108, 123, 1959.

4357. Osterberg, I. Lapset ja Isat. Alkoholipsykologista Taustaa.
       (Children and Fathers: An Alcohol-Psychological Study.)
       Alkoholipolitiikka, Helsinki, 24: 244-246, 1959.

4358. O'Sullivan, F. A Plea for an Absolute Test, Relative to Cases
       of Drunkenness in Charge of Motorcars. Medical World,
       London, 57: 405-407, 1942.

4359. O'Sullivan, K. Depression and its Treatment in Alcoholics:
       A Review. Canadian Journal of Psychiatry, 29(5):
       379-384, 1984.

4360. O'Sullivan, K., Whillans, P., Daly, M., Carroll, B., Clare, A.
       and Cooney, J. A Comparison of Alcoholics With and Without
       Coexisting Affective Disorder. British Journal of
       Psychiatry, London, 143: 133-138, 1983.

4361. The Other Victims of Alcoholism. Hospital Supervisor's Bulletin,
       474: 3-4, 1983.

4362. Otieno, B., Owola, J.A. and Oduor, P. A Study of Alcoholism in
       a Rural Setting in Kenya. East African Medical Journal,
       56(12): 665-670, 1979.

4363. Ottenberg, Donald J. Combined Treatment of Drug Addicts and
       Alcoholics. Report. Eagleville, PA: Eagleville Hospital
       and Rehabilitation Center, 1973, pages 7, 22-37, 84-89.

4364. Ottenberg, Donald J. and Madden, E.E. Substance Abuse: The Family
       in Trouble. Paper presented at the 13th Annual Eagleville
       Conference, May, 1980.

4365. Ottenheimer, H.M. Marital Dyad and Adolescent Substance Abuse
       Risk. Dissertation Abstracts International, 45(8):
       2698B, 1985.

4366. Otterstrom, Edith. Delinquency and Children from Bad Homes.
       A Study of Their Prognosis from a Social Point of View.
       Acta Paediatrica, Stockholm, 33(Supplement 5), 1946.

4367. Our Greatest Drug Problem--It's an Intensely Personal Thing.
       Listen, 28(5): 2-3, 1975.

4368. Ovenstone, Irene M.K. Spectrum of Suicidal Behaviours in
       Edinburgh. British Journal of Preventive and Social
       Medicine, London, 27(1): 27-35, 1973.

4369. Overall, J.E., Henry, B.W. and Woodward, A. Dependence of Marital
       Problems on Parental Family History. Journal of Abnormal
       Psychology, 83: 446-450, 1974.

4370. Overcoming Alcoholism: How You Can Help. Drug Therapy, 8:
       116-117, 121-123, 126-127, 1978.

4371. Overman, Everett F. The Alcoholic Family: A Psychosocial
       Analysis. American Archives of Rehabilitation Therapy,
       24(2): 25-32, 1976.

4372. Owen, Pat and Hatsukami, Dorothy. Chemical Dependency in Women:
       Course Outline. Curriculum Guide. Minneapolis: University
       of Minnesota, 1979.

4373. Owen, S.M., Rosenberg, J. and Barkley, D. Bottled-Up Children --
       A Group Treatment Approach for Children of Alcoholics.
       Group, 9(3): 31-42, 1985.

4374. Owievczka, J. Psycho-Social Factors in Emergency Admissions
       to a Medical Clinic. Revue Medicale de la Swisse
       Romande, 94(11): 895-902, 1974.

P

4375. P., Lisa. Alcoholism: A Family Disease. *Australian Journal of Alcoholism and Drug Dependence*, 2(4): 117-119, 1975.

4376. Paccalin, J., Mainhagu, P. and Berthon, G. The Alcoholic Therapeutic Strategy in an Internal Medicine Unit. *Semaine des Hopitaux de Paris*, 57(43-44): 1844-1848, 1981.

4377. Paccalin, J., Mainhagu, P. and Berthon, G. Therapeutic Strategy for the Alcoholic Patient in a Department of General Medicine. *Revue de l'Alcoolisme*, Paris, 26(3): 167-174, 1980.

4378. Pacht, Asher R. and Cowden, James E. An Exploratory Study of Five Hundred Sex Offenders. *Criminal Justice and Behavior*, 1(1): 13-20, 1974.

4379. Pacini, Antonella and Martinotti, Antonio. Ordine Di Nascita Ed Alcoolismo. (Order of Birth and Alcoholism.) *Lavoro Neuropsichiatrico*, Rome, 57(1/2): 261-290, 1975.

4380. Pacy, Hanns. The Management of Alcoholism in General Practice. *Medical Journal of Australia*, Sydney, 2(August 17): 712-714, 1968.

4381. Page, A. Counselling. In: *Women and Alcohol*. Volume 13. New York: Tavistock Publications, 1980, pages 159-175.

4382. Page, P. Alateen -- Hope for Children of Alcoholics -- Al-Anon-Family-Group-Headquarters-Inc. *Journal of Studies on Alcohol*, 36(8): 1081-1082, 1975.

4383. Page, Richard C. and Wattenbarger, William. A Comparison of the Problems of the Family Members of Male Prison Inmates with and without Drug Abuse Problems. *The International Journal of the Addictions*, 16(7): 1241-1246, 1981.

4384. Paige, P.E., La-Pointe, W. and Krueger, A. The Marital Dyad as a Diagnostic and Treatment Variable in Alcohol Addiction. *Psychology*, Savannah, 8: 64-73, 1971.

4385. Paillard, M.C., Bergeron, G., Bedoret, J.M. and Blanckaert, D. Les Intoxications Ethyliques Aiques de L'entant. Aspects Cliniques et Sociaux. A Propos de 32 Observations. (Acute Ethylic Intoxications in the Infant. Clinical and Social Aspects. Apropos of 32 Case Reports.) *Larc Medical*, 2(5): 379-380, 382, 385-388, 1982.

4386. Paine, Herbert James. Attitudes and Patterns of Alcohol Use among Mexican Americans: Implications for Service Delivery. *Journal of Studies on Alcohol*, 38(3): 544-553, 1977.

4387. Pajka, S. Spozycie Alkoholu Przez Uczniow Klas VII w Powiecie
       Ostroleckim. (Consumption of Alcohol by 7th-Grade Primary-
       School Pupils and Their Families in the Town of Ostroleka
       and Surrounding Country.) Problemy Alkoholizmu, Warsaw,
       14(3-4): 8-12, 1966.

4388. Palkon, Dennis S. Conjoint Alcohol Family Therapy Services
       for Occupational Alcoholism Programs. Labor-Management
       Alcoholism Journal, 9(2): 55-62, 65-67, 1979.

4389. Palkon, Dennis S. Development and Implementation of Conjoint
       Alcohol Family Therapy Services for Occupational Alcoholism
       Programs. Paper presented at the National Council on
       Alcoholism Annual Conference, Washington, D.C., April, 1979.

4390. Pallett, Alan. Alcoholic Day Treatment Unit Herbert Day Hospital,
       Bournemouth. British Journal of Addiction, Edinburgh,
       71(1): 99-100, 1976.

4391. Pallikkathayil, Leonie and Tweed, Sandra. Substance Abuse:
       Alcohol and Drugs During Adolescence. Nursing Clinics
       of North America, 18(2): 313-321, 1983.

4392. Pallis, D.J., Langley, A.M. and Birtchnell, J. Excessive Use of
       Psychiatric Services by Suicidal Patients. British Medical
       Journal, London, 3(5977): 216-218, 1975.

4393. Palmer, R.D. Parental Perception and Perceived Locus of Control
       in Psychopathology. Journal of Personality, 39(3):
       420-431, 1971.

4394. Palmer, R.H., Ouellete, E.M., Warner, L. and Leichtman, S.R.
       Congenital Malformations in Offspring of a Chronic Alcoholic
       Mother. Pediatrics, 53(4): 490-499, 1974.

4395. Pandina, Robert J., Labouvie, Erich W. and White, Helene Raskin.
       Potential Contributions of the Life Span Developmental
       Approach to the Study of Adolescent Alcohol and Drug Use:
       The Rutgers Health and Human Development Project, a Working
       Model. Journal of Drug Issues, 14(2): 253-268, 1984.

4396. Pandina, Robert J. and Schuele, James A. Psychological and Social
       Features of Alcohol and Drug Use by Adolescents. Digest of
       Alcoholism Theory and Application, 3(3): 62-65, 1984.

4397. Pandina, Robert J. and Schuele, James A. Psychosocial Correlates
       of Alcohol and Drug Use of Adolescent Students and
       Adolescents in Treatment. Journal of Studies on Alcohol,
       44(6): 950-973, 1983.

4398. Panel Workshop: Violence, Crime, Sexual Abuse and Addiction.
       Contemporary Drug Problems, 5(3): 385-440, 1976.

4399. Panepinto, W., Sokolow, L., Forget, D., Cocozza, J. and Burda, R.
       Family Support Systems for the Alcoholic Family: An Inter-
       vention Model for Coping with Parental Role Resumption after
       Hospitalization. Paper presented at the National Council on
       Alcoholism Forum, New Orleans, April, 1981.

4400. Panepinto, William C., Garrett, James A., Williford, William R.
       and Priebe, John A. Short-term Group Treatment Model for
       Problem-Drinking Drivers. In: Social Groupwork and
       Alcoholism. Eds. M. Altman and R. Crocker. New York:
       Haworth Press, 1982, pages 33-40.

4401. Panev, B. La Criminalite et L'Alcoolisme Dans Les Regions de
       Pirdop, Botevgrad et Etropole. (Criminality and Alcoholism
       in the Regions of Pirdop, Botevgrad and Etropole.) Pravna
       Mis'l, Sofia, 8: 80-88, 1964.

4402. Panitz, D.R., McConchie, R.D., Sauber, S.R. and Fonseca, J.A.
       The Role of Machismo and the Hispanic Family in the Etiology
       and Treatment of Alcoholism in Hispanic American Males.
       The American Journal of Family Therapy, 11(1): 31-44, 1983.

4403. Paolino, Thomas J. Jr. A Review and Comparison of the
       Psychoanalytic and Sociological Conceptualizations of
       the Alcoholic Marriage. Rhode Island Medical Journal,
       59(12): 533-558, 1976.

4404. Paolino, Thomas J. Jr. and McCrady, Barbara S. The Alcoholic
       Marriage: Alternative Perspectives. New York: Grune and
       Stratton, 1977.

4405. Paolino, Thomas J. Jr. and McCrady, Barbara S. Joint Admission
       as a Treatment Modality for Problem Drinkers: A Case Report.
       American Journal of Psychiatry, 133(2): 222-224, 1976.

4406. Paolino, Thomas J. Jr., McCrady, Barbara S. and Diamond, Sharon.
       Statistics on Alcoholic Marriages: An Overview. The
       International Journal of the Addictions, 13(8):
       1285-1293, 1978.

4407. Paolino, Thomas J. Jr., McCrady, Barbara S., Diamond, Sharon and
       Longabaugh, R. Psychological Disturbances in Spouses of
       Alcoholics: An Empirical Assessment. Journal of Studies on
       Alcohol, 37: 1600-1608, 1976.

4408. Paolino, Thomas J. Jr., McCrady, Barbara S. and Kogan, Kathryn B.
       Alcoholic Marriages: A Longitudinal Empirical Assessment of
       Alternative Theories. British Journal of Addiction, 73:
       129-138, 1978.

4409. Papanek, M.L. Excessive Drinking, a Factor in Family Disintegration.
       In: International Conference on Alcoholism and Drug Abuse,
       San Juan, Puerto Rico, November, 1973. Lausanne: International
       Council on Alcohol and Addictions, 1974, pages 183-193.

4410. Papas, Arthur N. Questions that Family Doctors Frequently Ask
       About Alcoholism. Medical Times, 105(4): 33D-34D, 36D,
       39D-40D, 1977.

4411. Pardo, Manual P. and Hall, Thomas B. III. Genetic Implications
       of the Alcohol-Induced Flushing Phenomenon in Orientals.
       In: Currents in Alcoholism, Volume 8: Recent Advances in
       Research and Treatment. Ed. Marc Galanter. New York:
       Grune and Stratton, 1981, pages 41-45.

4412. Paredes, A. Denial, Deceptive Maneuvers, and Consistency in the
       Behavior of Alcoholics. Annals of the New York Academy of
       Sciences, 233: 23-33, 1974.

4413. Paredes, Alfonso. Alcoholism Treatment: New Options for Social
       Intervention. Alcoholism: Clinical and Experimental
       Research, 8(2): 165-166, 1984.

4414. Paredes, Alfonso. Marital-Sexual Factors in Alcoholism.
       Medical Aspects of Human Sexuality, 7(4): 98-115, 1973.

4415. Paredes, Alfonso, Hood, William Robert and Gregory, Dick.
       Microecology of Alcoholism: Implications for the Development
       of the Adolescent. In: Current Issues in Adolescent
       Psychiatry. Ed. Joseph C. Schoolar. New York: Brunner/
       Mazel, 1973, pages 158-178.

4416. Parent Drinking Often a Factor in Students' Behavior Problems.
       NIAAA Information and Feature Service, (IFS No. 31): 6,
       December 28, 1976.

4417. Parent Education. In: _Prevention Plus: Involving Schools,_
       Parents, and the Community in Alcohol and Drug Education.
       United States Department of Health and Human Services.
       Rockville, MD: National Institute on Alcohol Abuse and
       Alcoholism, 1983, pages 101-134.

4418. Parental Example: How Important? _Bottom Line on Alcohol in_
       Society, 5(4): 18-19, 1983.

4419. Parental Rights Terminated -- Father's Mental Age -- Drinking
       Problem, etc. Watkins v. Dept. of Human Resources, 237
       S.E.2d 696, Court of Appeals of Georgia. September 7, 1977.
       Mental Health Court Digest, 22(1): 2, 1978.

4420. Parents' Group Initiates Program at Teens' Urging. _NIAAA_
       Information and Feature Service, (IFS No. 38): 1, July 21,
       1977.

4421. Parents and Teenagers: _Discussion of Alcohol Beverage Use._ Report.
       In: _Family Awareness Conference._ Washington, D.C.: Wine
       and Spirits Wholesalers of America, 1984.

4422. Parfrey, P.S. Factors Associated with Undergraduate Alcohol Use.
       British Journal of Preventive and Social Medicine, 28(4):
       252-257, 1974.

4423. Parfrey, P.S. Factors Associated with Undergraduate Marijuana Use
       in Cork. _British Journal of Addiction,_ 72(1): 59-65, 1977.

4424. Park, J.Y. Flushing Response to Alcohol Use Among Koreans and
       Taiwanese. _Journal of Studies on Alcohol,_ 45(6): 481-485,
       1984.

4425. Park, Peter. Problem Drinking and Role Deviation: A Study in
       Incipient Alcoholism. In: _Society, Culture, and Drinking_
       Patterns. Eds. D.J. Pittman and C.R. Snyder. New York:
       John Wiley & Sons, 1962, pages 431-454.

4426. Park, Peter and Whitehead, Paul C. Developmental Sequence and
       Dimensions of Alcoholism. _Quarterly Journal of Studies on_
       Alcohol, 34(3): 887-904, 1973.

4427. Parker, Douglas A. and Parker, Elizabeth E.S. Status and Status
       Inconsistency of Parents on Alcohol Consumption of Teenage
       Children. _The International Journal of the Addictions,_
       15: 1233-1239, 1980.

4428. Parker, Douglas A., Parker, Elizabeth S., Wolz, Michael W. and
       Harford, Thomas C. Sex Roles and Alcohol Consumption: A
       Research Note. _Journal of Health and Social Behavior,_
       21(1): 43-48, 1980.

4429. Parker, Elizabeth S., Parker, Douglas A. and Brody, Jacob A.
       The Impact of Father's Drinking on Cognitive Loss Among
       Social Drinkers. In: _Recent Developments in Alcoholism:_
       Volume 3, High-Risk Studies, Prostaglandins and Leukotrienes,
       Cardiovascular Effects, Cerebral Function in Social Drinkers.
       Ed. Marc Galanter. New York: Plenum Press, 1985, pages 227-240.

4430. Parker, Frederick B. A Comparison of the Sex Temperament of
       Alcoholics and Moderate Drinkers. _American Sociological_
       Review, 24: 366-374, 1959.

4431. Parker, Frederick B. Self-Role Strain and Drinking Disposition
       at a Prealcoholic Age Level. _Journal of Social Psychology,_
       78: 55-61, 1969.

4432. Parker, Frederick B. Sex-Role Adjustment and Drinking Disposition
       of Women College Students. Journal of Studies on Alcohol,
       36(11): 1570-1573, 1975.

4433. Parker, Frederick B. Sex-Role Adjustment in Women Alcoholics.
       Quarterly Journal of Studies on Alcohol, 33: 647-657,
       1972. (Also in: Alcoholism and Women. Ed. C.C. Eddy and
       J.L. Ford. Dubuque, IA: Kendall/Hunt, 1980, pages 6-15.)

4434. Parmee, Rachel. Teenage Drinking Ignored by Adults.
       The New Zealand Nursing Journal, 77(4): 13-15, 1984.

4435. Parnell, Joan. Community Nursing - Anytown Anecdotes. X. One
       for the Road. Nursing Mirror, 154(19): 50-51, 1982.

4436. Parnitzke, K.H. and Prussing, O. Kinder Alkoholsuchtiger Eltern.
       (Children of Chronically Alcoholic Parents.) Psychiatrie,
       Neurologie und Medizinische Psychologie, Leipzig, 18:
       1-5, 1966.

4437. Parr, R.J. Alcoholism and Cruelty to Children. British Journal
       of Inebriety, 6: 77-81, 1908. (Also in: Medical Press
       and Circular, 85: 659, 1908.

4438. Partanen, J. On the Relevance of Twin Studies. Annals of the
       New York Academy of Sciences, 197: 114-116, 1972.

4439. Partanen, Juha, Bruun, Kettil and Markkanen, Touko. Inheritance
       of Drinking Behavior: A Study of Intelligence, Personality
       and Use of Alcohol of Adult Twins. (Finnish Foundation
       for Alcohol Studies, Publication No. 14.) Helsinki, Finland:
       Finnish Foundation for Alcohol Studies, 1966.

4440. Pascal, G.R. and Jenkins, W.O. A Study of the Early Environment
       of Workhouse Inmate Alcoholics and Its Relationship to Adult
       Behavior. Quarterly Journal of Studies on Alcohol, 21:
       40-50, 1960.

4441. Pascalis, G., Chauvot, B. and Dionot, T. Devenir a Sept Ans
       de 43 Enfants et Adolescents Hospitalises en Psychiatrie
       en 1969. (Situation after 7 Years of 43 Children and
       Adolescents Hospitalized for Mental Disorders in 1969.)
       Annales Medico-Psychologiques, 2(3): 449-454, 1977.

4442. Pasciutti, John J. The Role of Parents in Alcohol Problems.
       Leaflet. Montpelier: Vermont Department of Education, 1957.

4443. Pascoe, John M., Hebbert, Virginia, Perl, Trish M. and Loda,
       Frank. Violence in North Carolina Families Referred to a
       Child Protection Team. North Carolina Medical Journal,
       42(1): 35-37, 1981.

4444. Pashchenkov, S.Z. Osobennosti Semeinykh form Alkogolizma.
       (Characteristics of Familial Forms of Alcoholism.)
       Sovetskaya Meditsina, Moscow, 11: 76-79, 1976.

4445. Pashchenkov, S.Z. O Klinicheskom Techenii Alkogolizmu u
       Bol'nykh s Semeinoi Otyagoshchennost'yu. (The Clinical
       Evolution of Alcoholism in Patients with Familial Taints.)
       Klinicheskaia Meditsina, Moscow, 52(3): 93-96, 1974.

4446. Pasnau, R.O. and Russell, A.T. Psychiatric Resident Suicide:
       An Analysis of Five Cases. The American Journal of
       Psychiatry, 132(4): 402-406, 1975.

4447. Paster, S. The Treatment of Chronic Alcoholism. Memphis Medical
       Journal, 23: 88-91, 1948.

4448. Patch, V.D. Human Behavior, Medicine and Social Reform. The New England Journal of Medicine, 280: 1415-1416, 1969.

4449. Patel, A.R., Roy, M. and Wilson, G.M. Self-Poisoning and Alcohol. The Lancet, London, 2(787): 1099-1102, 1972.

4450. Patel, N.S. A Study on Suicide. Medicine, Science and the Law, Bristol, 14(2): 129-136, 1974.

4451. Paton, Ralph T. Review of The Alcoholic and the Help He Needs by Max Glatt. Addictions, 4(5): 15, 1975.

4452. Pattee, James J. Uncovering the Elderly Hidden Alcoholic. Geriatrics, 37(2): 145-146, 1982.

4453. Patterson, E.T., Charles, H.L., Woodward, W.A., Roberts, W.R. and Penk, W.E. Differences in Measures of Personality and Family Environment Among Black and White Alcoholics. Journal of Consulting and Clinical Psychology, 49(1): 1-9, 1981.

4454. Pattison, E.M. Treatment of Alcoholic Families with Nurse Home Visits. Family Process, 4(1): 75-94, 1965.

4455. Pattison, E. Mansell. Management of Alcoholism in Medical Practice. Medical Clinics of North America, 61(4): 797-780, 1977.

4456. Pattison, E. Mansell. The Selection of Treatment Modalities for the Alcoholic Patient. In: The Diagnosis and Treatment of Alcoholism. Eds. Jack H. Mendelson and Nancy K. Mello. New York: McGraw-Hill, 1979, pages 126-227.

4457. Pattison, E. Mansell, Courlas, Peter G., Patti, Rino and Mullen, Dee. Diagnostic-Therapeutic Intake Groups for Wives of Alcoholics. Quarterly Journal of Studies on Alcohol, 26: 605-616, 1965.

4458. Pattison, E. Mansell and Galanter, M. Alcoholism Treatment Through Systems Intervention: A Perspective -- Part I. Introduction to a Symposium. Alcoholism: Clinical and Experimental Research, 8(1): 1-3, 1984.

4459. Pattison, E. Mansell and Kaufman, E. Family Therapy in the Treatment of Alcoholism. In: Family Therapy and Major Psychopathology. Ed. M.W. Lansky. New York: Grune & Stratton, 1981, pages 203-229.

4460. Pauls, David L., Noyes, Russell Jr. and Crowe, Raymond R. The Familial Prevalence in Second-Degree Relatives of Patients with Anxiety Neurosis (Panic Disorder). Journal of Affective Disorders, 1(4): 279-285, 1979.

4461. Pavloff, G. Review of I'll Quit Tomorrow by Vernon E. Johnson. Alcohol Health and Research World, Winter: 30, 1974.

4462. Pavlov, I.S. Kompleksnaya Psikhoterapiya Bol'nykh Khronicheskim Alkogolizmom V Zavisimosti Ot Lichnostnykh Osobennostei. (Alcoholism Psychotherapy Programs Adjusted to Patient Personality Characteristics.) Zhurnal Nevropatologii I Psikhiatrii, Moscow, 80: 597-602, 1980.

4463. Pawlak, Vic. Seniors' Prognosis Good but Family Involvement a Necessity in Treatment Effort. Focus on Alcohol and Drug Issues, 4(3): 26, 1981.

4464. Pawlikowski, Andrzej. Losy Dzieci Z Rodzin Alkoholikow. (Fates of Children from Families of Alcoholics.) Problemy Alkoholizmu, Warsaw, 7(7): 4-6, 1972.

4465. Peacock, P.B., Gelman, A.C. and Lutins, T.A. Preventive Health
       Care Strategies for Health Maintenance Organizations.
       Preventive Medicine, 4: 183-225, 1975.

4466. Pearce, J.M.S. Occasional Survey: Migraine: A Cerebral
       Disorder. The Lancet, 2(8394): 86-89, 1984.

4467. Pearl, A., Buechley, R. and Lipscomb, W.R. Cirrhosis Mortality
       in Three Large Cities: Implications for Alcoholism and
       Intercity Comparisons. In: Society, Culture, and Drinking
       Patterns. Eds. D.J. Pittman and C.R. Snyder. New York:
       John Wiley & Sons, 1962, pages 345-352.

4468. Pearl, R. The Racial Effect of Alcohol. Eugenics Review,
       London, 16: 9-30, 1924.

4469. Pearlman, P. Women in a Residential Setting. In: The Woman
       Next Door. Ed. C. D'Amanda. Hollywood, FL: U.S. Journal
       of Drug and Alcohol Dependence, 1980, pages 49-51.

4470. Pearlman, P., West, M. and Dalton, J. Mothers and Children
       Together: Parenting in a Substance Abuse Program.
       In: Treatment Services for Drug Dependent Women.
       Rockville, MD: NIDA, 1982, pages 532-571.

4471. Pearson, K. Influence of Parental Alcoholism. Journal of the
       Royal Statistical Society, London, 74: 221-229, 1911.

4472. Pearson, Karl and Elderton, Ethelm M. A Second Study of the
       Influence of Parental Alcoholism on the Physique and
       Ability of the Offspring: Being A Reply to Certain Medical
       Critics of the First Memoir and an Examination of the
       Rebuilding Evidence Cited by Them. Eugenics Laboratory
       Memoirs, London, 13: 1-35, 1910.

4473. Pearson, O.A. Pioneer House -- The Minneapolis Project for the
       Rehabilitation of Alcoholics. In: Reports on Government-
       Sponsored Programs. Ed. Ernest A. Shepherd. Quarterly
       Journal of Studies on Alcohol, 11(2): 353-359, 1950.

4474. Peckens, R. and McKenna, T. Personality Characteristics of
       Alcoholic Children of Alcoholics. Journal of Studies on
       Alcohol, 44(4): 688-700, 1983.

4475. Pedersen, Andrew M., Tefft, Bruce M. and Babigian, Haroutun M.
       Risks of Mortality of Suicide Attempters Compared with
       Psychiatric and General Populations. Suicide, 5(3):
       145-157, 1975.

4476. Pedersen, Nancy L. Multivariate Analysis of Familial and
       Non-Familial Influences for Commonality in Drug Use.
       Drug and Alcohol Dependence, 14(1): 67-74, 1984.

4477. Pedersen, Nancy Lee. Genetic and Environmental Factors for
       Usage of Common Drugs. Dissertation Abstracts
       International, 41(4): 1559B, 1980.

4478. Peele, S. Is Alcoholism Different from Other Substance Abuse?
       American Psychologist, 38(8): 963-965, 1983.

4479. Peele, S. Don't Panic!: A Parent's Guide to Understanding and
       Preventing Alcohol and Drug Use. Pamphlet. Minneapolis:
       CompCare Publications, 1983.

4480. Peele, Stanton. The Implications and Limitations of Genetic
       Models of Alcoholism and Other Addictions. Journal of
       Studies on Alcohol, 47(1): 63-73, 1986.

4481. Peele, Stanton. Redefining Addiction. I. Making Addiction a
       Scientifically and Socially Useful Concept. International
       Journal of Health Services, 7(1): 103-124, 1977.

4482. Peitler, E.J. Comparison of the Effectiveness of Group
       Counseling and Alateen on the Psychological Adjustment
       of Two Groups of Adolescent Sons of Alcoholic Fathers.
       Doctoral Dissertation. St. John's University, 1980.

4483. Pela, O.A. The Dynamics of Drug Use in Nigeria. British
       Journal of Addiction, Edinburgh, 77(2): 205-207, 1982.

4484. Pelaez, P., Poblete, L., Montenegro, H., Rego, A.M. and Oritz, L.
       Review of Cases in Center for Adolescents. Revista Chilena
       de Pediatria, Santiago, 41(7): 551-555, 1970.

4485. Pelc, I. Elements Etiopathogeniques de L'alcoolisme.
       (Aetiopathogenic Elements of Alcoholism.) Acta Psychiatrica
       Belgica, 80(2): 138-148, 1980.

4486. Pelka, Slugocka M.D. and Wiercioch, L.R. Zakres Alkoholizmu
       I Naduzywania Alkoholu U Rodzicow Mlodziezy Po Probie
       Samobojczej. (The Range of Alcoholism and Alcohol Abuse
       among Parents of Adolescents Who Attempted Suicide.)
       Zdrowie Psychiczne, Warsaw, 17(4): 90-97, 1976.

4487. Pelton, C.L. Intervention in Family Violence: A Role for the
       Physician and for Society. Postgraduate Medicine, 72(5):
       163-165, 168-170, 1982.

4488. Pelton, L.H. Child Abuse and Neglect and Protective Intervention
       in Mercer County, New Jersey. In: The Social Context of
       Child Abuse and Neglect. Ed. Larry H. Pelton. New York:
       Human Sciences Press, 1981, pages 90-136.

4489. Pelton, L.H. (Ed.). Social Context of Child Abuse and Neglect.
       New York: Human Sciences Press, 1981.

4490. Peltoniemi, T. Alcohol and Family Violence. In: 28th
       International Institute on the Prevention and Treatment
       of Alcoholism. Ed. E.J. Tongue. Lausanne: International
       Council on Alcohol and Addictions, 1982, pages 562-576.

4491. Peltoniemi, T. Begreppet Familjevald; Dess Anknytning Till
       Alkohol Och Andra Sociala Problem. (The Concept of Family
       Violence; Its Connection with Alcohol and Other Social
       Problems.) Alkohol Och Narkotika, 74(5): 21-26, 1980.

4492. Peltoniemi, T. Family Violence: Police House Calls in Helsinki,
       Finland in 1977. Victimology, 5(2-4): 213-224, 1980.

4493. Peltoniemi, T. and Puustinen, M. Familjevald. (Family Violence.)
       Alkoholipolitiikka, Helsinki, 42: 57-66, 1979.

4494. Pemberton, D.A. A Comparison of the Outcome of Treatment in
       Female and Male Alcoholics. The British Journal of
       Psychiatry: The Journal of Mental Science, London,
       113(497): 367-373, 1967.

4495. Pendagast, Eg. In Dealing with Alcoholism--Let's Look at the
       Teetotaling or Passively Alcoholic Generation. The Family,
       8(1): 51, 1980.

4496. Penick, Elizabeth C., Read, Marsha, R., Crowley, Patricia A. and
       Powell, Barbara J. Differentiation of Alcoholics by Family
       History. Journal of Studies on Alcohol, 39(11):
       1944-1948, 1978.

4497. Pentz, Mary Ann. Prevention of Adolescent Substance Abuse Through Social Skill Development. In: Preventing Adolescent Drug Abuse: Intervention Strategies (National Institute on Drug Abuse Research Monograph No. 47. A Rous Review Report). Eds. Thomas J. Glynn, Carl G. Leukefeld and Jacqueline P. Ludford. Washington, D.C.: U.S. Government Printing Office, 1983, pages 195-232.

4498. Perez, Joseph. Coping within the Alcoholic Family. Muncie, IN: Accelerated Development Inc., 1986.

4499. Perez-de-Francisco, C. Alcoholismo; Aspectos Psicologicos Y Psicopatologicos. (Alcoholism; Psychological and Psycho-pathological Aspects.) Actas Luso-Espanolas de Neurologia, Psiquiatria Y Ciencias Afines, Madrid, 2: 169-186, 1974.

4500. Perodeau, Guilleme M. Married Alcoholic Women: A Review. Journal of Drug Issues, 14(4): 703-719, 1984.

4501. Perrin, P. Compagnes de Buveurs. (Companions of Drinkers.) L Revue De L'Alcoolisme, 7: 169-176, 1961.

4502. Perrin, P. Une Classification Simplifiee De L'Alcoolisme A L'Usage Des Generalistes: Etude Critique De Deux Medecins Italiens. (Simplified Classification of Alcoholism for Use by General Practitioners: Clinical Study of Two Italian Doctors.) Revue De L'Alcoolisme, Paris, 20(2): 151-156, 1974.

4503. Perrin, Thomas W. Alcohol and the Parent-Child Relationship. Alcoholism The National Magazine, 5(4): 13, 1985.

4504. Perrin, Thomas W. CoA's Dilemma: Nonexistent Parents. Focus on Family and Chemical Dependency, 6(6): 13, 42-43, 1983.

4505. Perrin, Thomas W. Conference Casualties. Alcoholism The National Magazine, 5(5): 15, 1985.

4506. Perrin, Thomas W. Forgiving Our Parents. Alcoholism The National Magazine, 5(3): 61, 1985.

4507. Perrin, Thomas W. The Genesis Project: Charity Being Formed to Aid Children of Moms in Treatment. Alcoholism and Addiction, 6(3): 49, 1986.

4508. Perrin, Thomas W. Inadequate, Inconsistent...Nonexistent Parenting: A Dilemma for Children From Alcoholic Families. In: Changing Legacies: Growing Up in an Alcoholic Home. Pompano Beach, FL: Health Communications, 1984, pages 57-64.

4509. Perrin, Thomas W. Issues for COA's: The Right to Treatment. COA Review, 5(September/October): 10-11, 1983.

4510. Perrin, Thomas W. Parenting. Alcoholism The National Magazine, 5(2): 23, 1984.

4511. Perrin, Thomas W. When Parents are Alcoholics, Children are in Trouble. COA Review, 2: 4, 1983.

4512. Perrin, Thomas W. Who's on First? What's on Second? COA Review, 7: 4-5, 1984. (Also in: Alcoholism The National Magazine, 5(1): 69, 1984.)

4513. Perrine, M.W. Alcohol Involvement in Highway Crashes: A Review of the Epidemiologic Evidence. Clinics in Plastic Surgery, 2(1): 11-34, 1975.

4514. Perris, C., Perris, H., Ericsson, U. and Von Knorring, L. The
      Genetics of Depression. A Family Study of Uni Polar and
      Neurotic Reactive Depressed Patients. Archiv fur
      Psychiatrie und Nervenkrankheiten, 232(2): 137-156, 1982.

4515. Perris, Hjordis, Eisemann, M., Ericsson, U., von Knorring, L.
      and Perris, C. Attempts to Validate a Classification of
      Unipolar Depression Based on Family Data: Symptomatological
      Aspects. Neuropsychobiology, 9(2-3): 103-107, 1983.

4516. Perry, Sally L., Goldin, George J., Stotsky, Bernard A. and
      Margolin, Reuben J. The Rehabilitation of the Alcohol
      Dependent: An Exploratory Study. Lexington, MA: Heath
      Lexington Books, 1970.

4517. Perspectives. Alcohol Health and Research World, 8(4): 30-36,
      1984.

4518. Persson, Britt. Vuxenpsykiatrin Och Socialvarden Maste Samarbeta
      for Att Skydda Missbrukarnas Barn. (The Adult Psychiatry and
      the Social Care Must Cooperate to Protect the Children of
      the Addicts.) Nordisk Medicin, 97(1): 11-12, 1982.

4519. Pescetto, G. and Simonetti, C. Osservazioni Preliminari Sui
      Fattori Disposizionali Ereditari Nelle Psicosi Alcooliche.
      (Preliminary Observations on Hereditary Predisposing
      Factors in Alcoholic Psychoses.) Rassegna Di Studi
      Psichiatrici, Siena, 49: 631-637, 1960.

4520. Pescor, M.J. and Surgeon, P.A. Suicide Among Hospitalized Drug
      Addicts. Journal of Nervous and Mental Disease, 91(3):
      287-305, 1940.

4521. Pessina, G. Note Sull'alcoolismo Femminile Nella Provincia Di
      Firenze. (Note on Female Alcoholism in the Province of
      Firenze.) Rassegna Di Studi Psichiatrici, Siena, 49:
      532-535, 1960.

4522. Peters, Joseph J. and Sadoff, Robert L. Clinical Observations
      on Child Molesters. Medical Aspects of Human Sexuality,
      4(11): 20-32, 1970.

4523. Petersen, Dennis R. Pharmacogenetic Approaches to the
      Neuropharmacology of Ethanol. In: Recent Developments
      in Alcoholism, Volume 1, Genetics, Behavioral Treatment,
      Social Mediators and Prevention, Current Concepts in
      Diagnosis. Ed. Marc Galanter. New York: Plenum Press,
      1983, pages 49-69.

4524. Petersen, Dennis R., Erwin, V. Gene and Deitrich, Richard A.
      Brain Acetaldehyde Metabolism During Ethanol Consumption.
      In: Biological/Genetic Factors in Alcoholism. (NIAAA
      Research Monograph Series, No. 9.) Eds. Victor M. Hesselbrock,
      Edward G. Shaskan and Roger E. Meyer. Washington, D.C.:
      U.S. Government Printing Office, 1983, pages 93-99.

4525. Petersen-Kelly, Angela. Family Environment and Alateens: A Note
      on Alcohol Abuse Potential. Journal of Community Psychology,
      13: 75-76, 1985.

4526. Petitti, Diana, Wingerd, John, Pellegrin, Frederick and Ramcharan,
      Savitri. Risk of Vascular Disease in Women Smoking, Oral
      Contraceptives, Noncontraceptive Estrogens and Other Factors.
      Journal of the American Medical Association, 242(11):
      1150-1154, 1979.

4527. Petrakis, Peter L. Alcoholism: An Inherited Disease.
      Washington, D.C.: U.S. Government Printing Office, 1985.
      (DHHS Publication No. ADM 85-1426.)

4528. Petrella, Fausto and Barale, Francesco. La Relazione Coniugale
           Dell'etilista. (The Relationship between the Alcoholic and His
           Wife.) Rivista Di Psichiatria, Rome, 9(2): 138-158, 1974.

4529. Petro, J.A., Quann, P.L., Graham, W.P. Wife Abuse: The
           Diagnosis and Its Implications. Journal of the American
           Medical Association, 240(3): 240-241, 1978.

4530. Petropoulos, Alice W. Intake and Referral in an Alcoholism
           Agency. Social Casework, 59(1): 21-26, 1978.

4531. Petroski, Catherine. John Gardner and the Summer Garden.
           In: Having Been There. Ed. A. Luks. New York:
           Charles Scribner's Sons, 1979, pages 36-42.

4532. Petrovan, O. Serdulokoruak Vedelme az Alkoholizmus Veszelyei
           Ellen: Elozetes Megjegyzesek egy Palyazathoz. (The
           Protection of Adolescents Against the Hazards of Alcoholism:
           Preliminary Comments on a Competition.) Alkohologia,
           Budapest, 3: 161-167, 1972.

4533. Petrovic, D., Gacic, B. and Sedmak, T. Evolution De La Conception
           Dans Un Centre De Sante Mentale. (Evolution of Alcoholism
           Concept in a Mental Health Center.) Alcool ou Sante,
           145(2): 14-21, 1978.

4534. Petty, Frederick and Nasrallah, Henry A. Secondary Depression
           in Alcoholism: Implications for Future Research.
           Comprehensive Psychiatry, 22(6): 587-595, 1981.

4535. Petzold, Hilarion. Psychodramatisch Gelenkte Aggression
           In Der Therapie Mit Alkoholikern. (Psychodramatically
           Linked Aggression in Therapy with Alcoholics.)
           Gruppenpsychotherapie Und Gruppendynamik, Gottingen,
           4(3): 268-281, 1971.

4536. Phelps, L.V. Divorces in 1940. Journal of the Medical
           Association of the State of Alabama, 2: 415-416, 1942.

4537. Phillips, H.H. Families of Alcoholics. Editorial. Labor-
           Management Alcoholism Journal, 9: 102-103, 1979.

4538. Phillips, Lorne A. An Application of Anomy Theory to the Study
           of Alcoholism. Journal of Studies on Alcohol, 37(1):
           78-84, 1976. (Also in: Alcoholism: Introduction to
           Theory and Treatment. Ed. David A. Ward. Dubuque, IA:
           Kendall/Hunt, 1980, pages 182-187.)

4539. Phillips, Roland and Kuzma, Jan W. Characteristics of Drinking
           and Nondrinking Mothers and Their Infants II. Paper
           Presented at 104th Annual Meeting of the American Public
           Association, Miami, October, 1976.

4540. Pickens, Roy. Children of Alcoholics. Pamphlet. Center City,
           MN: Hazelden Research Services, no date.

4541. Pickens, Roy W. and Svikis, Dace S. Alcoholic Family Disorders.
           Pamphlet. Center City, MN: Hazelden, no date.

4542. Piety, K.R. Patterns of Parent Perceptions Among Neuropsychiatric
           Patients and Normal Controls. Journal of Clinical Psychology,
           23(4): 428-433, 1967.

4543. Piety, K.R. Perceptual Dissonance and Role Learning. Journal of
           Clinical Psychology, 22(1): 10-14, 1966.

4544. Pilat, J.M. Children of Alcoholics: Identification in a Classroom Setting. In: 28th International Institute on the Prevention and Treatment of Alcoholism. Lausanne: International Council on Alcohol and Addictions, 1982, pages 192-204.

4545. Pilat, J.M. Children of Alcoholics: Needs and Treatment Intervention. Paper presented at the 27th International Institute on the Prevention and Treatment of Alcoholism, Vienna, June, 1981, pages 486-495.

4546. Pilat, J.M. and Jones, J.W. Identification of Children of Alcoholics: Two Empirical Studies. Alcohol Health and Research World, 9(2): 26-33, 36, 1984/85.

4547. Pilat, J.M. and Jones, J.W. Screening Test and Treatment Program for Children in Alcoholic Families. Paper presented at the 30th National Alcoholism Forum, Washington, D.C., April, 1982.

4548. Pilsecker, C. Comments on a Concept. Social Casework, 66(1): 54-57, 1985.

4549. Pincus, J.H. and Tucker, G.J. Violence in Children and Adults: A Neurological View. Journal of the American Academy of Child Psychiatry, 17: 277-288, 1978.

4550. Pinder, L. A Community Agency and the Alcoholic. Addictions, Toronto, 13(3): 11-21, 1966.

4551. Pines, Maya. New York Times. 29 June 1982, Section 3, Page 1, Column 5. (Behavioral Genetics and Alcoholism.)

4552. Pino, R., Kockott, G. and Feuerlein, W. Sechs Jahres Katamnese An Hundert Patienten Mit Suicidversuchen Durch Tabletteneinnahme. (A Six Year Follow-Up Study of 100 Patients Who Attempted Suicide with Drugs.) Archiv Fur Psychiatrie und Nervenkrankheiten, 227(3): 213-226, 1979.

4553. Piree, S., Popa, L. and Borcea, A. Contributii la Studiul Sindroamelor Afective Psihotice in Alcoolismul Cronic (Contribution to the Study of Affectve Psychotic Syndromes in Chronic Alcoholism.) Neurologia, Psihiatria, Neurochirurgia, Bucharest, 14: 179-185, 1969.

4554. Pisani, Vincent D. Rationale for the Process of Familization "In Search of a Family." Paper presented at the International Institute on Alcohol and Drug Dependence, Seville, Spain, 1972.

4555. Pisani, Vincent D. and Catanzaro, R.J. "In Search of a Family": Rationale for the Process of Familization. Paper presented at the 18th International Institute, Prevention and Treatment of Alcoholism Conference. Seville, Spain, 1972, pages 40-46.

4556. Pisani, Vincent D. and Motanky, Guy U. Predictors of Premature Termination of Outpatient Follow-Up Group Psychotherapy Among Male Alcoholics. International Journal of the Addictions, 5(4): 731-737, 1970.

4557. Pittman, David J. Interaction Between Skid Row People and Law Enforcement and Health Professionals. Addictive Diseases, 1(3): 369-388, 1974.

4558. Pittman, David J. Primary Prevention of Alcoholism and Alcoholism Related Damage: New Directions. In: 28th International Institute on the Prevention and Treatment of Alcoholism. Lausanne: International Council on Alcohol and Addictions, 1982, pages 222-234.

4559. Pittman, David J. and Gordon, C. Wayne. Revolving Door -- A Study
       of the Chronic Police Case Inebriate. Glencoe, IL: The Free
       Press, 1958.

4560. Pittman, Frank S. III. Incest. Current Psychiatric Therapies,
       17: 129-134, 1977.

4561. Pitts, F.N. Jr. and Winokur, G. Affective Disorder: VII. Alcoholism
       and Affective Disorder. Journal of Psychiatric Research, 4:
       37-50, 1966.

4562. Pixley, J.M. and Stiefel, J.R. Group Therapy Designed to Meet the
       Needs of the Alcoholic's Wife. Quarterly Journal of Studies
       on Alcohol, 24: 304-314, 1963.

4563. Planansky, K. and Johnston, R. A Survey of Patients Leaving
       a Mental Hospital Against Medical Advice. Hospital and
       Community Psychiatry, 27(12): 865-868, 1976.

4564. Planning Alcoholism Counseling Education (PACE): A Curriculum
       and Instructional Resource Guide. Rockville, MD:
       National Institute on Alcohol Abuse and Alcoholism. 1982.
       (Eric Document Number ED233245.)

4565. Plant, Martin. Occupation and Alcoholism: Cause or Effect?
       A Controlled Study of Recruits to the Drink Trade.
       International Journal of the Addictions, 13(4):
       605-626, 1978.

4566. Plante, G., Cote, H. and Pilic, I. Study on a Group of Inhibited
       Children from a Deprived Urban Area. Canadian Psychiatric
       Association Journal, Ottawa, 18(4): 321-325, 1973.

4567. Plante, Normand. Evaluation and Treatment of the Suicidal
       Patient. L'Union Medicale du Canada, Montreal, 102(11):
       2292-2298, 1973.

4568. Plat, Pierre. Alcool, Biologie et Sante de L'enfant. (Alcohol,
       Biology and Health of the Child. Part IV.) Infirmiere
       Francaise, Paris, 226, 21-26, 1981.

4569. Platt, Nancy V. and Moss, David M. Influence of the Alcoholic
       Parent on Episcopal Seminarians' Ministry to Alcoholics.
       Journal of Pastoral Care, 31(1): 32-37, 1977.

4570. Plaut, Thomas F. Disagreement About Alcohol Use. In: Cooperative
       Commission on the Study of Alcoholism, Alcohol Problems.
       New York: Oxford University Press, 1967, pages 3-29.

4571. Playoust, D., Gentilini, J.L., Macaigne, M. and Zylberberg, G.
       Gamma-glutamyl Transferases: Sociological and Clinical
       Chemistry Approach. Annals de Biologie Clinique, 39(6):
       371-380, 1981.

4572. Plenkovic, J. Influences of Family Deformation on Pupils'
       Behaviour. Alcoholism, Zagreb, 12: 133-137, 1976.

4573. Plenkovic, J. Social Aspect of Alcoholism and Narcomania.
       Alcoholism, Zagreb, 7(2): 169-176, 1971.

4574. Ploscowe, M. Alcoholism and the Family: A Legal Point of View.
       In: The Legal Issues in Alcoholism and Alcohol Usage.
       Boston: Boston University Law-Medicine Institute, 1966,
       pages 84-89.

4575. Podolsky, D.M. NIAAA Laboratory of Clinical Studies. Alcohol
       Health and Research World, 9(3): 22-24, 26-27, 44-45, 1985.

4576. Poikolainen, Kari. Risk of Alcohol-Related Admissions by Marital
       Status and Social Class Among Females. Drug and Alcohol
       Dependence, 10(2-3): 159-164, 1982.

4577. Poikolainen, Kari. Risk of Alcohol-Related Hospital Admissions
       in Men as Predicted by Marital Status and Social Class.
       Journal of Studies on Alcohol, 44(6): 986-995, 1983.

4578. Points de Vue. Newsletter. Lausanne: Swiss Institute for
       Alcoholism Prevention, December 2, 1981.

4579. Pojoga, N., Popovici, I. and Popovici, L. The Influence of
       Parental Alcoholism Upon the School Success and Intelligence
       of Children. Analele de Psihologie, 4: 282-293, 1937.

4580. Pokorny, Alex D. and Kanas, Thomas E. Stages in the Development
       of Alcoholism. In: Phenomenology and Treatment of
       Alcoholism. Eds. William E. Fann, Ismet Karacan, Alex D.
       Pokorny, and Robert L. Williams. Jamaica, NY: Scientific and
       Medical Books, 1980, pages 45-68.

4581. Pokorny, Alex D., Miller, Byron A. and Cleveland, Sidney E.
       Response to Treatment of Alcoholism. A Follow-Up Study.
       Quarterly Journal of Studies on Alcohol, 29(2): 364-381,
       1968.

4582. Polak, Paul. R., Reres, Mary and Fish, Larry. Management of Family
       Crises. In: Emergency Psychiatric Care. Eds. H.L. Rosnik
       and H.L. Ruben. Bowie, MD: Charles Press, 1975, pages 119-142.

4583. Polin, Bonnie Sanders. Variables of Children at Risk for Behavior
       Disorders in the Community. Doctoral Dissertation.
       (University Microfilms No. 8028421.) Washington, D.C.:
       The American University, 1980. (Also in: Dissertation
       Abstracts International, 41(6): 2493A, 1980.)

4584. Pollak, B. The Role of the General Practitioner in Support of
       an Alcoholic Rehabilitation Hostel. British Journal of
       Addiction, London, 65(1): 19-24, 1970.

4585. Pollak, Benno. Two Year Study of Alcoholics in General Practice.
       British Journal on Alcohol and Alcoholism, 13(1): 24-35,
       1978.

4586. Pollak, O. One Therapist or Two? In: Substance Abuse and
       Psychiatric Illness. Eds. E. Gottheil, A.T. McLellan and
       K.A. Druley. New York: Pergamon Press, 1980, pages 115-118.

4587. Pollitt, Ernesto, Eichler, Aviva Weisel and Chan, Chee Khoon.
       Psychosocial Development and Behavior of Mothers of Failure
       to Thrive Children. American Journal of Orthopsychiatry,
       45(4): 525-537, 1975.

4588. Pollock, V.E. The EEG after Alcohol Administration in Men at Risk
       for Alcoholism. Archives of General Psychiatry, 40(8):
       857-861, 1983.

4589. Pollock, V.E. Prospective Study of Alcoholism: Electroencephalo-
       graphic Findings. In: Longitudinal Research in Alcoholism.
       Boston: Kluwer Academic Publishers, 1984, pages 125-145.

4590. Poltavets, V.I. Clinical Manifestations of Alcoholism A Genetic
       Analysis by the Half Sibs Method. Vestnik Akademii
       Meditsinskikh Nauk SSSR, Moscow, 0(1): 46-50, 1982.

4591. Polzella, Sue A. and Selinger, Marilyn. Teacher Intervention for
       the Adolescent Substance Abuser. 1981. (Eric Document Number
       ED204963.)

4592. Pomeranze, J. and Schoen, G. Family Therapy with the Family of an Alcohol Addicted Man. _Journal on Alcoholism and Related Addictions_, 15(1-2): 21-24, 1979.

4593. Ponzetti, James J., Cate, Rodney M. and Koval, James E. Violence Between Couples: Profiling the Male Abuser. _Personnel & Guidance Journal_, 6(14): 222-224, 1982.

4594. Popenoe, P. Heredity and Environment as Related to Alcoholism. _Eugenical News_, 31: 35-38, 1946.

4595. Popler, Lois. Mother-Daughter Relationships in Alcoholic Families. _Smith College Studies in Social Work_, 47(1): 44-45, 1976.

4596. Popova, E.N. Effect of Alcohol on Offspring. _Zhurnal Nevropatologii I Psikhiatrii_, Moscow, 83(2): 275-286, 1983.

4597. Porot, M. and Duboucher, G. Quatre Ans Apres, Ou Les Resultats Eloignes du Traitement des Alcooliques par le Disulfiram (Antabus). (Four Years Later, or Long-Term Results of Treatment of Alcoholics with Disulfiram [Antabus].) _Algerie Medicale_, Algeria, 58: 641-644, 1954. (Also in: _Annales Medico-Psychologiques_, Paris, 112: 439, 1954.)

4598. Porterfield, Kay Marie. _Family Strangers_. _A Guide for Parents in Recovery_. Pamphlet. Center City, MN: Hazelden, no date.

4599. Porterfield, Kay Marie. Single Parent Solutions. _Recovery Newsletter in Alcoholism. The National Magazine_, 5(4): 8, 1985.

4600. Porterfield, Kay Marie. _Under the Same Roof_. _A Guide for Parents in Recovery_. Pamphlet. Center City, MN: Hazelden, no date.

4601. Pospisil, Zavrski K. and Turcin, R. Alkoholizam i cl. 196 kz-Zlostavdijanje i Zapustanje Maloljetnika. (Alcoholism and Paragraph 196 of Criminal Law -- Abuse and Neglect of Minors.) _Neuropsihijatrija_, 16(1): 49-53, 1968.

4602. Post, Felix. Management of Senile Psychiatric Disorders. _British Medical Journal_, London, 5631: 627-630, 1968.

4603. Potosnak, Joseph E. and Illenberger, Terri. Livengrin Foundation: Multiple Family Therapy in Aftercare. In: _Alcoholism Rehabilitation; Methods and Experiences of Private Rehabilitation Centers_. Ed. Vincent Groupe. New Brunswick, NJ: Rutgers Center of Alcohol Studies, 1978, pages 75-85.

4604. Pott, G., Schneider, M., Van Husen, N., von Bassewitz, D.B., Eberhardt, G. and Gerlach, U. Alpha 1-Antitrypsin Phanotypen Bei Patienten Mit Chronischen Leberkrankheiten. (Alpha 1-Antitrypsin Phenotypes in Patients with Chronic Liver Diseases.) _Zeitschrift Fur Gastroenterologie_, Munich, 21(7): 318-323, 1983.

4605. Pottenger, Margaret, McKernon, Janice, Patrie, Lewis E., Weissman, Myrna, M., Ruben, Harvey L. and Newberry, Phyllis. The Frequency and Persistence of Depressive Symptoms in the Alcohol Abuser. _The Journal of Nervous and Mental Disease_, 166(8): 562-570, 1978.

4606. Potter-Efron, R.T. and Potter-Efron, P.S. Family Violence as a Treatment Issue with Chemically Dependent Adolescents. _Alcoholism Treatment Quarterly_, 2(2): 1-15, 1985.

4607. Potvin, Raymond H. and Lee, Che-Fu. Multistage Path Models of Adolescent Alcohol and Drug Use: Age Variations. _Journal of Studies on Alcohol_, 41(5): 531-542, 1980.

4608.   Pouget, R. and Bertier, J.F.   Suicide Apres Sortie de L'Hopital
        Psychiatrique. (Suicide after Release from a Psychiatric
        Hospital.) Annales Medico-Psychologiques, 1(1): 27-57, 1973.

4609.   Povorinskiy, Yu A.   K Voprosu O Patogeneticheski-Obosnovannoy
        Terapii Alkogolizma. (Pathogenetic Basis of Therapy of
        Alcoholism.) Voprosy Psikhiatrii I Nevropatologii,
        Leningrad, 7: 285-292, 1961.

4610.   Powell, B.J. Viamontes, J.A. and Brown, C.S.   Alcohol Effects on
        the Sexual Potency of Alcoholic and Non-alcoholic Males.
        Alcoholism, Zagreb, 10:(1-2): 78-80, 1974.

4611.   Powell, David J.   Counselor Skills and Training Needs: Based on
        Clinical Supervisory Evaluations. Journal of Alcohol and
        Drug Education, 25(2): 15-18, 1980.

4612.   Powell, David J. and Powell, B.B.   Alcohol and Family Violence.
        Human Ecology Forum, 9(3): 20, 1978.

4613.   Powell, G.F., Brasel, J.A. and Blizzard, R.M.   Emotional
        Deprivation and Growth Retardation Simulating Idiopathic
        Hypopituitarism. I. Clinical Evaluation of the Syndrome.
        New England Journal of Medicine, 276(23): 1271-1278, 1967.

4614.   Powell, Keith.   Alcohol and the Adolescent Drinker. Australian
        Family Physician, 7(6): 663-671, 1978.

4615.   Powell, L.W.   Iron Storage in Relatives of Patients with
        Haemochromatosis and in Relatives of Patients with Alcoholic
        Cirrhosis and Haemosiderosis. A Comparative Study of 27
        Families. Quarterly Journal of Medicine, Oxford, 34(136):
        427-442, 1965.

4616.   Powell, S. and Powell, J.   Recovering Couples: Re-Building
        the Marriage after Sobriety. Focus on Family and Chemical
        Dependency, 7(5): 18-19, 1984.

4617.   Powers, J.S. and Spickard, A.   Michigan Alcoholism Screening
        Test to Diagnose Early Alcoholism in a General Practice.
        Southern Medical Journal, 77(7): 852-856, 1984.

4618.   Powers, Robert J., Schlesinger, Louis B. and Benson, Mark.
        Family Violence: Effects of a Film Program for Alcohol
        Dependent Persons. Journal of Drug Education, 13(2):
        153-160, 1983.

4619.   Prager, Kate, Malin, Henry, Spiegler, Danielle, VanNatta, Pearl
        and Placek, Paul J.   Smoking and Drinking Behavior Before
        and During Pregnancy of Married Mothers of Live-Born Infants
        and Stillborn Infants. Public Health Reports, 99(2):
        117-127, 1984.

4620.   Predescu, V. and Christodorescu, D.   Risks in Case of Paternal
        Alcoholism. Revista de Medicina Interna, Neurologie,
        Psihiatrie, Bucharest, 21(2): 145-148, 1976.

4621.   Prendergast, Thomas J. Jr. and Schaefer, Earl S.   Correlates
        of Drinking and Drunkenness among High-School Students.
        Quarterly Journal of Studies on Alcohol, 35(1 pt A):
        232-242, 1974.

4622.   Preschoolers Participants In Alcohol Education Classes.
        NIAAA Information and Feature Service, (IFS No. 72):
        1, June 9, 1980.

4623. Prescott, James. Somatosensory Affectional Deprivation (SAD)
       Theory of Drug and Alcohol Use. In: Theories on Drug
       Abuse: Selected Contemporary Problems. (NIDA Research
       Monograph Series No. 30). U.S. National Institute on Drug
       Abuse. Eds. D. Lettieri, M. Sayers and H. Pearoson.
       Washington, D.C.: U.S. Government Printing Office, 1980,
       pages 286-296. (DHEW Publication No. ADM 80-967.)

4624. Presnall, Lewis F. Alcoholism: The Exposed Family. Salt Lake
       City: Utah Alcoholism Foundation, 1977.

4625. Presnall, Lewis F. Wife of the Alcoholic: A Pattern to Happiness.
       Salt Lake City: Utah Alcoholism Foundation, no date.

4626. Press, Leonard. Treating the Family. Maryland State Medical
       Journal, 24(1): 32-35, 1975.

4627. Press Seminar Spotlights Research. ADAMHA News (Alcohol, Drug
       Abuse, and Mental Health Administration), 11(1): 1, 4-5, 1985.

4628. Preston, Florence Bush. Combined Individual, Joint and Group
       Therapy in the Treatment of Alcoholism. In: Differential
       Diagnosis and Treatment in Social Work. Ed. Francis J.
       Turner. New York: Free Press, 1968, pages 221-228.
       (Also in: Mental Hygiene, 44: 522-528, 1960.)

4629. Preston, James D. Community Norms and Adolescent Drinking
       Behavior: A Comparative Study. Social Science Quarterly,
       49(2): 350-359, 1968.

4630. Preston, John, Schoenfeld, Lawrence, S. and Adams, Russell L.
       Evaluating the Effectiveness of a Telephone Crisis Center
       from the Consumer's Viewpoint. Hospital & Community
       Psychiatry, 26(11): 719-720, 1975.

4631. Prevention Course Stresses Parent-Child Communication. NIAAA
       Information and Feature Service, (IFS No. 37): 1, June 20,
       1977.

4632. Preventive Maintenance for Employees. Modern Office Procedures,
       24(4): 50-53, 1979.

4633. Prewett, M.J., Spence, R. and Chaknis, M. Attribution by Causality
       by Children with Alcoholic Parents. The International Journal
       of the Addictions, 16(2): 367-370, 1981.

4634. Price, Gladys M. Alcoholism. A Family, Community & Nursing
       Problem. Pamphlet. New York: National Council on
       Alcoholism, no date. (Also in: American Journal of
       Nursing, 67(5): 1022-1025, 1967.)

4635. Price, Gladys M. A Study of the Wives of Twenty Alcoholics.
       Quarterly Journal of Studies on Alcohol, 5: 620-627, 1945.

4636. Price, J. and Armstrong, J. Battered Wives: A Controlled Study
       of Predisposition. Australian and New Zealand Journal of
       Psychiatry, Melbourne, 12: 43-47, 1978.

4637. Price, L.H., Nelson, J.C., Charney, D.S. and Quinlan, D.M.
       Clinical Utility of Family History for the Diagnosis of
       Melancholia. Journal of Nervous and Mental Disease,
       172(1): 5-11, 1984.

4638. Price, Richard A. and Vandenberg, Steven G. Spouse Similarity
       in American and Swedish Couples. Behavior Genetics,
       10(1): 59-71, 1980.

4639. Price, Richard H. and Curlee-Salisbury, Joan. Patient-Treatment
      Interactions Among Alcoholics. Journal of Studies on
      Alcohol, 36(5): 659-669, 1975.

4640. Prichep, Leslie S. Psychiatric Evaluation Services to Court
      Referred Drug Users. American Journal of Drug & Alcohol
      Abuse, 2(2): 197-213, 1975.

4641. Priest, Kathryn. Adolescents' Response to Parents' Alcoholism.
      Social Casework, 66(9): 533-539, 1985.

4642. Pringle, W.J. The Alcoholic Family Environment: The Influence
      of the Alcoholic and Nonalcoholic Family of the Origin on
      Present Coping Styles. Doctoral Dissertation. (University
      Microfilms No. 77-10,909.) Fresno: California School of
      Professional Psychology, 1976. (Also in: Dissertation
      Abstracts International, 37: 5847B, 1977.)

4643. Prinsky, Lorraine and Bedell, John. Children's Perceptions of
      Deviance: Labeling Theory and Alcohol Abuse. Journal of
      Drug Issues, 14(3): 509-525, 1984.

4644. A Problem That Won't Go Away. Scholastic Update, 116(4): 1983.

4645. Proceedings of the Seventh World Conference of Therapeutic
      Communities. Chicago, IL, May, 1983.

4646. Promise Parent Study Groups Techniques for Enhancing Parenting
      Skills. Chicago: National Congress of Parents and Teachers,
      1977.

4647. Propping, P. Genetic Influence on the Origins of Alcoholism.
      Therapiewoche, Karlsruhe, 34(21): 3235-3242, 1984.

4648. Propping, P. Influence of Genetic Factors on the Development of
      Alcoholism. Deutsche Apotheker-Zeitung, 121: 1543-1547, 1981.

4649. Propping, P., Krueger, J. and Mark N. Genetic Disposition to
      Alcoholism. An Electro Encephalograph Study in Alcoholics and
      Their Relatives. Human Genetics, Berlin, 59(1): 51-59, 1981.

4650. Prout, C.T., Strongin, E.I. and White, M.A. A Study of Results
      in Hospital Treatment of Alcoholism in Males. American
      Journal of Psychiatry, 107: 14-19, 1950.

4651. Prove, W. Sociologische Aspecten Van Het Alcoholisme; Onderzoek
      Naar Enkele Drinkgewoonten Bij De Gentse Universiteitsstudent.
      (Sociological Aspects of Alcoholism; Investigation into
      Drinking Habits of Ghent University Students.) Archives
      Belges de Medecine Sociale Hygiene, 23: 5-16, 1965.
      (Also in: Revue De L Alcoolisme, Paris, 11: 16-28, 1965.)

4652. Provence, Sally. Unwanted Children: Four Case Studies. In:
      Abortion and the Unwanted Child. Ed. C. Reiterman.
      New York: Springer, 1971, pages 73-76.

4653. Przemysl: Wazne formy ochrony rodziny. (Przemysl: Important Forms
      of Family Protection.) Problemy Alkoholizmu, 27(9): 18, 1980.

4654. Przuntek, H. and Monninger, P. Therapeutic Aspects of
      Kinesiogenic Paroxysmal Choreo Athetosis and Familial
      Paroxysmal Choreo Athetosis of the Mount and Reback Type.
      Journal of Neurology, Berlin, 230(3): 163-170, 1983.

4655. Przuntek, H. and Muhr, H. Essential Familial Myo Clonus.
      Journal of Neurology, Berlin, 230(3): 153-162, 1983.

4656. Psarska, A.D. Jealousy Factor in Homicide in Forensic Psychiatric
      Material. Polish Medical Journal, 9(6): 1504-1510, 1970.

4657. PTA and HEW Act Against Alcoholism. <u>National PTA Bulletin</u>, Summer, 1972.

4658. PTA Produces Alcohol Education Materials Aimed at Teens, Parents and Teachers. <u>NIAAA Information and Feature Service</u>, (IFS No. 61): 6, July 11, 1979.

4659. Ptacek, Pavel. Zkusenosti S Peci O Deti Z Rodin Postizenych Alkoholismem. (Experiences with the Care of Children from Alcoholic Families.) <u>Psychologia A Patopsychologia Dietata</u>, <u>18</u>(3): 245-249, 1983.

4660. <u>Public Information Kit on Al-Anon/Alateen Family Groups</u>. New York: Al-Anon Family Group Headquarters, Inc., 1975.

4661. Puchall, L.B., Coursey, R.D., Buchsbaum, M.S. and Murphy, D.L. Parents of High Risk Subjects Defined by Levels of Monoamin Oxidase Activity. <u>Schizophrenia Bulletin</u>, <u>6</u>(2): 338-346, 1980.

4662. Pugh, Philip F.H. and Schulte, Barbara. Marital Discord Correlated with Sex-Role Identification. <u>South Dakota Journal of Medicine</u>, <u>20</u>: 19-39, 1967.

4663. Puig, Antich Joaquim, Blau, Stephen and Marx, Nola. A Pilot Trial of Imipramine in Prepubertal Depressive Illness. <u>Psychopharmacology Bulletin</u>, <u>14</u>(2): 40-42, 1978.

4664. Pulkkinen, Lea. Youthful Smoking and Drinking in a Longitudinal Perspective. <u>Journal of Youth and Adolescence</u>, <u>12</u>(4): 253-284, 1984.

4665. Purdie, F.R., Honigman, B. and Rosen, P. The Chronic Emergency Department Patient. <u>Annals of Emergency Medicine</u>, <u>10</u>(6): 298-301, 1981.

4666. Pursch, Joseph A. Dear Doc. <u>Alcoholism The National Magazine</u>, <u>5</u>(2): R5, 1984.

4667. Pursch, Joseph A. Dear Doc. <u>Recovery Newsletter in Alcoholism The National Magazine</u>, <u>5</u>(5): R6, 1985.

4668. Pursch, Joseph A. Dear Doc: How Old is Old Enough? <u>Recovery Newsletter in Alcoholism and Addiction Magazine</u>, <u>5</u>(7): R11, 1985.

4669. Pursch, Joseph A. From Quonset Hut to Naval Hospital; The Story of an Alcoholism Rehabilitation Service. <u>Journal of Studies on Alcohol</u>, <u>37</u>: 1655-1665, 1976.

4670. Pursch, Joseph A. Physicians' Attitudinal Changes in Alcoholism. <u>Alcoholism: Clinical and Experimental Research</u>, <u>2</u>(4): 358-361, 1978.

4671. Pursch, Joseph A. Why Johnny Can't Think. <u>Alcoholism The National Magazine</u>, <u>5</u>(2): 13, 1984.

4672. Pushkash, M. and Quereshi, M.Y. Perception of Self and Significant Others by Male and Female Alcoholics. <u>Journal of Clinical Psychology</u>, <u>36</u>: 571-576, 1980.

4673. Pyke, D.A. and Leslie, R.D.G. Chlorpropamide-Alcohol Flushing: Definition of Its Relation to Noninsulin Dependent Diabetes. <u>British Medical Journal</u>, London, <u>2</u>: 1521-1522, 1978.

4674. Pytkowicz, Ann. Introduction: Female Alcoholism: Impacts on Women and Children. In: <u>Currents in Alcoholism</u>. Ed. Marc Galanter. New York: Grune & Stratton, 1979, pages 429-434.

Q

4675. Quast, W. and Anderson, E.E. Young Children in Alcoholic
Families: A Mental Health Needs-Assessment and an
Intervention/Prevention Strategy. Journal of Primary
Prevention, 3(3): 174-187, 1983.

4676. Queen, D. Attitudes and Skills of the Nurse in Working With the
Alcoholic and his Family. Maryland State Medical Journal,
20(6): 83-85, 1971.

4677. Quehl, Thomas M. The M.D. and the Alcoholic. Journal of the
Florida Medical Association, 58(4): 43-46, 1971.

4678. Quemada, N. and Casadebaig, F. Differential Psychiatric Morbidity
According to Socio-Cultural Class. Social Psychiatry,
15(3): 145-155, 1980.

4679. Quershi, M.Y. and Soat, D.M. Perception of Self and Significant
Others by Alcoholics and Nonalcoholics. Journal of Clinical
Psychology, 32: 189-194, 1976.

4680. Quidu, M., Boschi, J.E. and Gautier, R. La Consommation Ethylique
Excessive Chez Les Jeunes De Moins de 25 Ans. (Excessive Alcohol
Drinking in Persons Under 25.) Revue de Neuropsychiatrie
Infantile et D'Hygiene Mentale de L'Enfance, Paris, 20(6):
551-559, 1972.

4681. Quidu, M., Hellaouet, M., Lobrichon, M.C., Soyer, Y. and Gautier, R.
A Propos De Quelques Cas D'Ivresse Publique Chez Des Mineurs
Penaux. (Several Cases of Public Drunkenness in Delinquent
Children.) Revue De Neuropsychiatrie Infantile et D'Hygiene
Mentale de l'Enfance, Paris, 22(12): 737-751, 1974.

R

4682. Rabei Mansour. The Psychological Treatment of the Disease
        of Alcoholism. *Dissertation Abstracts International*,
        41(4): 1522B, 1980.

4683. Rabow, Jerome and Watts, Ronald K. Alcohol Availability
        Alcoholic Beverage Sales and Alcohol Related Problems.
        Journal of Studies on Alcohol, 43(7): 767-801, 1982.

4684. Rachin, Richard L. and Millett, Francis N. (Eds.) Adolescent Drug
        Use. *Journal of Drug Issues*, 14(2): 1984.

4685. Rada, R.T. Alcoholism and the Child Molester. *Annals of
        the New York Academy of Sciences*, 273: 492-496, 1976.

4686. Rada, Richard T., Kellner, Robert, Laws, D.R. and Winslow, Walter
        W. Drinking, Alcoholism and the Mentally Disordered Sex
        Offender. *Bulletin of the American Academy of Psychiatry
        and the Law*, 6: 296-300, 1978.

4687. Rader, William C. The Paradoxical Therapeutic Alliance Between
        Physician and Alcoholic Patient. *Maryland State Medical
        Journal*, 24(7): 78-80, 1975.

4688. Radouco-Thomas, S., Garcin, F. and LaCroix, D. Major Concepts
        and Trends in Alcoholism; Some Issues in Clinical and
        Experimental Biomedical Research. In: *Alcoholism: A
        Multidisciplinary Approach*. Ed. J. Mendlewicz. New York:
        S. Krager, 1979, pages 33-53.

4689. Radouco-Thomas, Simone, Garcin, Francoise, Denver, D., Gaudreault, V.
        and Radouco-Thomas, C. A Possible "Eco-Pharmacogenetic" Model
        in Neuropsychopharmacology Aspects in Alcoholism and Pharmaco-
        dependence. *Progress in Neuro-Psychopharmacology*, 4:
        313-315, 1980.

4690. Radouco-Thomas, Simone, Garcin, Francoise, Laperriere, A., Marquis,
        P.A., Lambert, J., Denver, J., Lacerte, M., Lacroix, Denise and
        Radouco-Thomas C. Genetic Epidemiology and the Prevention of
        Functional Mental Disorders and Alcoholism: Family Study and
        Biological Predictors. *Progress in Neuro-Psychopharmacology*,
        3(1-3): 165-189, 1979.

4691. Radouco-Thomas, Simone, Garcin, Francoise, Radouco-Thomas, C.,
        Marquis, P.A., Lambert, J., LaForge, H., Denver, D., LaPerriere,
        A., LaCroix, D. and Gaudreault, V. Primary and Secondary
        Prevention of Alcoholism: Emerging Trends and Research Strategy.
        Progress in Neuro-Psychopharmacology, 3(5-6): 579-600, 1979.

4692. Radouco-Thomas, Simone, LaForge, H., Bilodeau, D.C. and Gaudet, D.
        Alcoholism Subtyping and Drinking Behavior. Paper presented
        at the First Congress of the International Society for
        Biomedical Research on Alcoholism, Munich, July, 1982.

4693.   Radouco, Thomas S., Laperriere, A. and LaForge, H.   A Family Study
        in Alcoholism.   Some Characteristics of Familial Alcoholism.
        Paper presented at the 4th Annual Meeting of the Canadian
        College of Neuro-Psychopharmacology, Toronto, 1981.   (Also in:
        Progress in Neuro-Psychopharmacology, 5(3): 310, 1981.)

4694.   Rae, Grant and Naomi, I.   Arresting the Vicious Cycle: Care and
        Treatment of Adolescents Displaying the Ovinnik Syndrome.
        Canadian Psychiatric Association Journal, 23: 22-40, 1978.

4695.   Rae, J.B.   The Influence of the Wives on the Treatment Outcome
        of Alcoholics: A Follow-up Study at Two Years.   British
        Journal of Psychiatry, 120(559): 601-613, 1972.

4696.   Rae, J.B. and Drewery, J.   Interpersonal Patterns in Alcoholic
        Marriages.   Paper presented at the Third International
        Conference on Alcoholism and Addictions, Cardiff, Wales,
        1970, pages 175-188.   (Also in: British Journal of
        Psychiatry, 120(559): 615-621, 1972.)

4697.   Rae, J.B. and Forbes, A.R.   Clinical and Psychometric
        Characteristics of the Wives of Alcoholics.   British
        Journal of Psychiatry, 112(483): 197-200, 1966.

4698.   Rae, John Turner.   Alcoholism and Eugenics.   British Journal of
        Inebriety, 13: 85-86, 1915.

4699.   Ragozin, Arlene S., Landesman-Dwyer, Sharon and Streissguth,
        Ann Pytkowicz.   The Relationship Between Mothers' Drinking
        Habits and Children's Home Environments.   In: Currents in
        Alcoholism, Volume 4:   Psychiatric, Psychological, Social
        and Epidemiological Studies.   Ed. Frank A. Seixas.
        New York: Grune and Stratton, 1978, pages 39-49.

4700.   Raiford, William H.   Helping the Hopeless.   Social and
        Rehabilitation Record, 3(5): 28-32, 1976.

4701.   Rainer, John D.   Heredity and Character Disorders.   American
        Journal of Psychotherapy, 33(1): 6-16, 1979.

4702.   Rainsford, George L. and Schuman, Stanley H.   Family in Crisis:
        A Case Study of Overwhelming Illness and Stress.   Journal of
        the American Medical Association, 246(1): 60-63, 1981.

4703.   Rakatansky, H.   Co-Alcoholism.   Annals of Internal Medicine,
        100(6): 921, 1984.

4704.   Rakatansky, H.   Correction: Al Anon for Associates of Alcoholics.
        Annals of Internal Medicine, 101(2): 284, 1984.

4705.   Ramee, F. and Michaux, P.   De Quelques Aspects de la Delinquance
        Sexuelle Dans Un Departement de l'Ouest de la France.   (Some
        Aspects of Sexual Offenses in a Province in Western France.)
        Acta Medicinae Legalis et Socialis, Leige, 19: 79-85, 1966.

4706.   Ramirez, Luis F., McCormick, Richard A., Russo, Angel M. and
        Taber, Julian I.   Patterns of Substance Abuse in Pathological
        Gamblers Undergoing Treatment.   Addictive Behaviors,
        Oxford, 8(4): 425-428, 1983.

4707.   Ramsay, A., Vredenburgh, J. and Gallagher, R.   Recognizing
        Alcoholism among Patients with Psychiatric Problems in a
        Family Practice Clinic.   Digest of Alcoholism Theory and
        Application, 3(3): 59-61, 1984.   (Also in: Journal of
        Family Practice, 17(5): 829-832, 1983.)

4708.   Ramsay, L.E.   Clinical Features of Hypertension in Frequent and
        Heavy Alcohol Drinkers.   Scottish Medical Journal, Glasgow,
        27(3): 207-211, 1982.

4709. Rangaswami, K. Personality, Life Events and Alcoholism. Indian
       Journal of Clinical Psychology, 10(1): 179-182, 1983.

4710. Rao, V. Nandini, Rao, V.V. Prakasa and Benjamin, Rommel.
       Sex, Parental Background, and Drinking Behavior of Black
       Collegians. International Journal of Sociology of the
       Family, 9: 47-66, 1979.

4711. Rapoport, J., Elkins, R., Langer, D.H., Sceery, W., Buchsbaum,
       M.S., Gillin, J.C., Murphy, D.L., Zahn, T.P. and Lake, R.
       Childhood Obsessive-Compulsive Disorder. American Journal
       of Psychiatry, 138: 1545-1554, 1981.

4712. Rappaport, L.J. Role and Context Interaction in Families of
       Alcoholics. Doctoral Dissertation (University Microfilms
       No. 77-9803). Boston College, 1976.

4713. Rardin, Donald R., Lawson, Thomas R. and Kruzich, David J.
       Opiates, Amphetamines, Alcohol: A Comparative Study of
       American Soldiers. The International Journal of the
       Addictions, 9(6): 891-898, 1974.

4714. Rasmussen, F., Gustavson, K.H. and Bille, B. Familial Minor
       Neuro Developmental Disorders. Clinical Genetics,
       Copenhagen, 25(2): 148-154, 1984.

4715. Rasmussen, Gary A. and Deboer, Ronald P. Alcohol and Drug Use
       Among Clients at A Residential Vocational Rehabilitation
       Facility. Alcohol Health and Research World, 5(2):
       48-56, 1981.

4716. Rasmussen, Paul K. and Ferraro, Kathleen J. The Divorce Process.
       Alternative Lifestyles, 2(4): 443-460, 1979.

4717. Rasmussen, R.K. Perceived Family Climate and Interpersonal
       Characteristics of Alcoholic Women and Their Husbands.
       Doctoral Dissertation. (University Microfilms No. 80-00928.)
       Berkeley: California School of Professional Psychology, 1979.

4718. Rathbone-McCuan, Eloise and Triegaardt, Jean. The Older
       Alcoholic and the Family. Alcohol Health and Research
       World, 3(4): 7-12, 1979. (Also as: National Council
       on Alcoholism Conference Paper, St. Louis, 1978; The Older
       Alcoholic and the Family. St. Louis: The George Brown
       School of Social Work, Washington University, no date.)

4719. Rathod, N.H., Gregory, E., Blows, D. and Thomas, G.H. A Two-Year
       Follow-Up Study of Alcoholic Patients. British Journal of
       Psychiatry, London, 112: 683-692, 1966.

4720. Rathod, N.H. and Thomson, I.C. Women Alcoholics; A Clinical
       Study. Quarterly Journal of Studies on Alcohol, 32:
       45-52, 1971.

4721. Rathus, Spencer A., Fichner-Rathus, Lois and Siegel, Larry J.
       Behavioral and Familial Correlates of Episodic Heroin Abuse
       among Suburban Adolescents. The International Journal of
       the Addictions, 12(5): 625-632, 1977.

4722. Rauzy, Alain. Remarques Sur La Personnalite Des Femmes
       D'Alcooliques. (Remarks on the Personality of Alcoholics'
       Wives.) Psychologie Medicale, 13(3): 471-477, 1981.

4723. Ravasini, Carlo, Malvasi, Zenaide and Mangoni, Alfonso.
       Osservazioni Cliniche E Considerazioni Psicopatologiche
       Sull'alcoolismo Femminile. (Clinical Observations and
       Psychopathological Considerations on Alcoholism Among Women.)
       Rivista Di Psichiatria, Rome, 3(1): 69-92, 1968.

4724. Reader, D.H. Alcoholism and Excessive Drinking; A Sociological
       Review. Psychologia Africana, Johannesburg, Monograph
       Supplement No. 3: 1-69, 1967.

4725. Readers Exchange: Children of Alcoholics and the Case for a New
       Diagnostic Category of Co-Dependency. Rockville, MD: National
       Clearinghouse for Alcohol Information, 1984.

4726. Readers Exchange: Children of Alcoholics in the Juvenile Justice
       System. Rockville, MD: National Clearinghouse for Alcohol
       Information, 1984.

4727. Reading, Anthony. Alcoholism Treatment by the Family Physician.
       Alcohol Health & Research World, Fall: 11-14, 1975.
       (Also in: Maryland State Medical Journal, 25(12):
       81-83, 1976.)

4728. Reading List: Alcohol and the Family. NCALI. 1983.

4729. Reckman, Lynne Williams, Babcock, Pamela and O'Bryan, Terry.
       Meeting the Child Care Needs of the Female Alcoholic.
       Child Welfare League of America, 63(6): 541-546, 1984.

4730. Recovering Alcoholic Women, Families Receive Help in Home.
       NIAAA Information and Feature Service, (IFS No. 77): 1,
       October 29, 1980.

4731. Reddy, B. Alcoholism: A Family Illness. In: Perspectives on
       the Treatment of Alcoholism. Eds. M.J. Goby and J.E.
       Keller. Park Ridge, IL: Lutheran General Hospital, Inc.,
       1978, pages 29-36.

4732. Reddy, Betty and McElfresh, Orville H. Detachment and Recovery from
       Alcoholism - A Dilemma. Paper presented at the 28th Annual
       Meeting of the ADPA, Detroit, September, 1977. (Also in:
       Alcohol Health and Research World, 2(3): 28-33, 1978.)

4733. Redfield, C.L. Alcoholism and Heredity. Medical Review of
       Reviews, 26: 305-309, 1920.

4734. Redknap, Stephen. Nursing Care Study. Two Steps to Freedom.
       Nursing Mirror, 157(25): 50-53, 1983.

4735. Redl, M. Sexual Interaction among Recovering Chemically Dependent
       Couples. Journal of Psychoactive Drugs, 14(1-2): 137-141,
       1982.

4736. Reed, B.G., Laird, J., Hartman, A. and Harding, L. Working with
       the Child Welfare System to Obtain Needed Services for Drug
       Dependent Women and Their Children. In: Treatment Services
       for Drug Dependent Women. Rockville, MD: National Institute
       on Drug Abuse, 1982, pages 477-531.

4737. Reed, Celeste S. Resources for the Prevention and Treatment
       of Child Abuse and Neglect (CA/N) Available to People in
       Michigan. The Catalyst, 1(3): 48-53, 1980.

4738. Reed, D., McGee, D. and Yano, K. Biological and Social Correlates
       of Blood Pressure Among Japanese Men in Hawaii USA.
       Hypertension, 4(3): 406-414, 1982.

4739. Reed, Lewis K. Let's Take Another Look at Alcoholism.
       Ohio State Medical Journal, 66(8): 816-818, 1970.

4740. Reed, T. Edward. Three Heritable Responses to Alcohol in a
       Heterogeneous Randomly Mated Mouse Strain Inferences for
       Humans. Journal of Studies on Alcohol, 38(3): 618-632,
       1977.

4741. Reeves, D. Parental Power and Adolescents' Drinking. Psychological
       Reports, 55: 161-162, 1984.

4742. Reeves, D. and Draper, T. Reasons for Limiting Alcohol Intake as
       Seen by Adolescents. Paper presented at the 8th Annual Symposium
       on Alcoholism, Winston-Salem, NC, January, 1982. (Also in:
       Alcoholism: Clinical and Experimental Research, 6(2): 285,
       1982.)

4743. Regalado, Rose. New Approaches for Prevention and Education
       of Alcoholism Among Hispanic Women. In: Chicanas and
       Alcoholism: A Sociocultural Perspective of Women.
       Eds. Rodolfo Arevalo and Marianne Minor. San Jose:
       School of Social Work, San Jose State University, 1981,
       pages 13-16.

4744. Regan, Joseph M. Services to the Families of Alcoholics: An
       Assessment of a Social Support System. Doctoral Dissertation.
       (University Microfilms No. 7821713.) Waltham, MA: Brandeis
       University, 1978.

4745. Regan, Joseph M., Connors, Gerard J., O'Farrell Timothy J. and
       Jones, Wyatt C. Services for the Families of Alcoholics: A
       Survey of Treatment Agencies in Massachusetts. Journal of
       Studies on Alcohol, 44: 1072-1082, 1983.

4746. Regan, R. Alcohol Problems and Family Violence: A Message to
       the Helpers. In: The Many Faces of Family Violence.
       Ed. J.P. Flanzer. Springfield, IL: Charles C. Thomas,
       1982, pages 106-120.

4747. Reich, Theodore, Cloninger, C. Robert, Lewis, Collins and Rice, John.
       Some Recent Findings in the Study of Genotype-Environment
       Interaction in Alcoholism. Paper presented at an Alcoholic
       Conference, Farmington, CT, Ocotber, 1979. (Also in:
       Evaluation of the Alcoholic Conference, pages 145-165.)

4748. Reich, Theodore, Rice, John, Cloninger, C. Robert and Lewis,
       Collins. The Contribution of Affected Parents to the Pool
       of Affected Individuals: Path Analysis of the Segregation
       Distribution for Alcoholism. In: Social Consequences of
       Psychiatric Illness. Eds. L. Robins, P. Clayton and
       J. Wing. New York: Brunner/Mazel, 1980, pages 91-119.

4749. Reich, Theodore, Winokur, George and Mullaney, J. Transmission of
       Alcoholism. Proceedings of the American Psychopathological
       Association, 63: 259-271, 1975.

4750. Reid, Betty. Apathy + Adolescence = Alcoholism. Royal Society
       of Health Journal, London, 97(1): 18-21, 1977.

4751. Reid, G. Archdall. Alcoholism and Eugenics. British Journal of
       Inebriety, 13: 67-68, 1915.

4752. Reid, J.C. and Mununggurr, D. We are Losing Our Brothers:
       Sorcery and Alcohol in an Aboriginal Community. Medical
       Journal of Australia, Sydney, 2(4): 1-15, 1977.

4753. Reilly, D.M. Family Factors in the Etiology and Treatment of Youthful
       Drug Abuse. In: Drugs and the Family. Ed. Thomas J. Glynn.
       Washington, D.C.: U.S. Government Printing Office, 1981. (Also
       in: Family Therapy, 2(2): 149-171, 1976.)

4754. Reilly, D.M. Family Therapy with Adolescent Drug Abusers and Their
       Families: Defying Gravity and Achieving Escape Velocity.
       Journal of Drug Issues, 14(2): 381-391, 1984.

4755. Reilly, Peter P. Efficacy of Lithium Carbonate in Alcoholism: Case
       Studies. Rhode Island Medical Journal, 61(2): 86-91, 1978.

4756. Reilly, R.P. Enabling Behavior of Affected Persons. Paper presented
       at the 36th Annual Symposium, Cherry Hill, NJ, June, 1984.
       (Also in: Blue Book, pages 57-58.)

4757. Reimer, F. Der Sogenannte Primitive Trinker Ein Beitrag Zur
       Typologie Des Alkoholikers. (The So-Called Primitive
       Drinker: A Contribution to the Typology of the Alcoholic.)
       Bibliotheca Psychiatrica et Neurologica, Basel, 142:
       155-164, 1969.

4758. Reiss, David, Steinglass, Peter and Costell, Ronald. Multiple
       Family Group as a Small Society: Fitting Theory and Method,
       1977. (Eric Document Number ED151694.)

4759. Relation Entre Alcoolisme Et Mauvais Traitements A Enfants.
       (Relationship between Alcoholism and Child Abuse.) Bulletin
       d'Information sur l'Alcoolisme, Paris, 144(1): 43-46, 1981.

4760. Remedial Youth Classes Require Parental Role. NIAAA Information
       and Feature Service, (IFS No. 40): 2, October 4, 1977.

4761. Rementeria, Jose L. Drug-Addicted Family (Mother, Father, and
       Infant): Some Sociomedical Factors. In: Drug Abuse in
       Pregnancy and Neonatal Effects. Ed. J.L. Rementeria.
       St. Louis: C.V. Mosby, 1977, pages 245-270.

4762. Remschmidt, H. Kindesmi Bhandlung. Aktuelle Diagnostische und
       Therapeutische Probleme. (Child Abuse. Recent Diagnostic and
       Therapeutic Problems.) Monatsschrift fur Kinderheilkunde,
       Berlin, 131(6): 408-412, 1983.

4763. Renaud, N.W. Recovery as a Family Project: Closing One Door...
       Opening Another. Focus on Family and Chemical Dependency,
       7(5): 32, 34-35, 39, 1984.

4764. Renaud, N.W. and Brown, P. Continuum of Care Essentials. Focus on
       Family and Chemical Dependency, 6(5): 31-32, 1983.

4765. Renson, Gisele J., Adams, John E. and Tinklenberg, Jared R.
       Buss-Durkee Assessment and Validation with Violent
       Versus Nonviolent Chronic Alcohol Abusers. Journal of
       Consulting and Clinical Psychology, 46(2): 360-361, 1978.

4766. Repartition de L'Alcoolisme Dans un Comte D'Angleterre.
       (The Distribution of Alcoholism in an English County.)
       La Revue de L'Alcoolisme, Paris, 15(4): 20-26, 1969.

4767. Report Cites Alcohol as Domestic Violence Factor. NIAAA Information
       and Feature Service, (IFS No. 87): 4, August 28, 1981.

4768. Report of the Conference on Research Needs and Opportunities
       for Children of Alcoholics. New York, NY: Children of
       Alcoholics Foundation, 1984.

4769. Report of the Vermont Commission on Alcohol Education. Quarterly
       Journal of Studies on Alcohol, 12: 342-352, 1951.

4770. Research on Children of Alcoholics: Expanding the Knowledge.
       Alcohol Health and Research World, 8(4): 6-13, 37, 1984.

4771. Researchers Investigating Inherited Alcohol Problems. NIAAA
       Information and Feature Service, (IFS No. 99): 1,
       August 30, 1982.

4772. Resnick, H.L. and Ruben, Harvey L. (Eds.) Emergency Psychiatric
       Care, The Management of Mental Health Crises. Bowie, MD:
       Charles Press, 1975.

4773.   Resnick, H.L.P. and Dizmang, Larry H. Observations on Suicidal
        Behavior among American Indians. The American Journal of
        Psychiatry, 127(7): 882-887, 1971.

4774.   Resolution of the National Committee Against Alcoholism. (Voeu
        Emis Par Le Comite National Contre L'Alcoolisme.) Alcool
        Ou Sante, 129(2): 35, 1975.

4775.   Resource Manual for Helping Families with Alcohol Problems.
        Salt Lake City: Church of Jesus Christ of Latter-Day
        Saints, 1984.

4776.   Reuger, Drue Barrett and Liberman, Robert P. Behavioral Family
        Therapy for Delinquent and Substance-Abusing Adolescents.
        Journal of Drug Issues, 14(2): 403-418, 1984.

4777.   Reus, W. The Influence of Alcoholism on the Child.
        Enkrateia, 65-80, 1934.

4778.   Reveley, Adrianne M. and Reveley, Michael A. The Distinction
        of Primary and Secondary Affective Disorders. Journal of
        Affective Disorders, 3(3): 273-279, 1981.

4779.   Review of The Hidden Alcoholic in General Practice by Rodney H.
        Wilkins. Lancet, March 8, 1975.

4780.   Review of The Psychology of Drunkenness by Albion Roy King.
        Quarterly Journal of Studies on Alcohol, 4: 486-487, 1943.

4781.   Reynolds, F. Douglass, O'Leary, Michael R. and Walker, R. Dale.
        Family Environment As a Predictor of Alcoholism Treatment
        Outcome. The International Journal of the Addictions,
        17(3): 505-512, 1982.

4782.   Rhoads, Joanne. Rainbow Retreat, Inc., Phoenix, Arizona. Services
        for Children of Alcoholics. Washington, D.C.: U.S. Government
        Printing Office, 1979, pages 164-176. (Also in: Services for
        Children of Alcoholics. Ed. S. Matlins. DHHS Publication No.
        (ADM) 81-1007, 1981, pages 164-176.)

4783.   Rhodes, Jennifer P. Differences in Character Roles Between
        Adolescents from Alcoholic and Nonalcoholic Families.
        Dissertation Abstracts International, 45(4): 1077A, 1984.

4784.   Ribstein, M., Certhoux, A. and Lavenaire, A. Alcoolisme au Rhum;
        Etude de la Symptomatologie et Analyse de la Personnalite de
        l'Homme Martiniquais Alcoolique au Rhum. (Alcoholism from
        Rum; Study of the Symptomatology and Personality Analysis of
        the Male "Rum Alcoholic" in Martinique.) Annales Medico-
        Psychologiques, Paris, 125(1): 537-548, 1967.

4785.   Rice, John, Reich, Theodore and Cloninger, C.R. Models for the
        Familial Transmission of Alcoholism: Path Analysis and
        Multifactorial Segregation Analysis. In: Biological/
        Genetic Factors in Alcoholism. (National Institute on
        Alcohol Abuse and Alcoholism Research Monograph Series,
        No. 9.) Eds. Victor M. Hesselbrock, Edward G. Shaskan and
        Roger E. Meyer. Washington, D.C.: U.S. Government Printing
        Office, 1983, pages 1-21.

4786.   Rice, M. Fetal Alcohol Syndrome: A Clinical Study. Journal of
        the American Medical Women's Association, 40(1): 23-27, 1985.

4787.   Rice, M.M. Alcohol Use and Abuse in Children. In: Encyclopedic
        Handbook of Alcoholism. Eds. E. Pattison and E. Kaufman.
        New York: Gardner Press, 1982, pages 759-768.

4788. Richards, T.M. Kolmac Clinic, Silver Spring, Maryland. In: Services for Children of Alcoholics. Symposium held in September, 1979 at Silver Spring, M.D. U.S. National Institute on Alcohol Abuse and Alcoholism. Research Monograph No. 4. Washington, D.C.: U.S. Government Printing Office, 1981. (DHHS Publication No. 81-1007.)

4789. Richards, T.M. Interventions with Adult COAs in the Workplace. ALMACAN, 15(9): 24-26, 1985.

4790. Richards, Tarpley M. Alcohol Education for Young Children of Alcoholic Parents. Addictions, 5(4): 18-21, 1977.

4791. Richards, Tarpley M. Splitting as a Defense Mechanism in Children of Alcoholic Parents. Paper presented at the National Council on Alcoholism, Washington, D.C., 1979. (Also in: Currents in Alcoholism: Recent Advances in Research and Treatment. Volume VII. Ed. M. Galanter. New York: Grune & Stratton, 1980, pages 239-244.)

4792. Richards, Tarpley M. Working with Children of an Alcoholic Mother. Alcohol Health and Research World, 3(3): 22-25, 1979.

4793. Richards, Tarpley M. Working with Disturbed Children of Alcoholic Mothers. In: Currents in Alcoholism. Volume 7. Recent Advances in Research and Treatment. Ed. Marc Galanter. New York: Grune and Stratton, 1980, pages 521-528. (Also as: Working with Disturbed Children of Alcoholic Mothers. Maryland: Kolmac Clinic of Silver Spring, Family Treatment Alcoholism Program, 1979.)

4794. Richards, Tarpley M. and Bascue, Loy O. Emotional Stages in Wives of Alcoholics During the Descent and Recovery Process of Alcoholism. Journal of Alcohol and Drug Education, 23(2): 12-17, 1978.

4795. Richards, Tarpley M., Morehouse, Ellen R., Seixas, Judith S. and Kern, Joseph C. Psychosocial Assessment and Intervention with Children of Alcoholic Parents. In: Social Work Treatment of Alcohol Problems. Eds. David Cook, Christine Fewell and John Riolo. New Brunswick, NJ: Rutgers Center of Alcohol Studies, 1983, pages 131-142.

4796. Richardson, D.C. and Campbell, J.L. Alcohol and Wife Abuse: The Effect of Alcohol on Attributions of Blame for Wife Abuse. Personality and Social Psychology Bulletin, 6(1): 51-56, 1980.

4797. Richardson, H.K. Alcoholism, Its Nature and Prevention. Alcohol Hygiene, 1(5): 23-39, 1945.

4798. Richardson, J.J. A Study of the Relationship of Attitudes of College Students and Their Parents Toward Consumption of Alcoholic Beverages. Doctoral Dissertation. (University Microfilms No. 65-1335.) Southern Illinois University, 1964.

4799. Richette, Lisa Aversa. Death-Dealing Homes. In: The Throwaway Children. Philadelphia: J.B. Lippincott, 1969, pages 58-78.

4800. Richman, Joseph and Rosenbaum, Milton. A Clinical Study of the Role of Hostility and Death Wishes by the Family and Society in Suicidal Attempts. The Israel Annals of Psychiatry and Related Disciplines, Jerusalem, 8(3): 213-231, 1970.

4801. Rickles, Nathan K. The Angry Woman Syndrome. Archives of General Psychiatry, 24(1): 91-94, 1971.

4802. Riech, Theodore, Robins, Lee N., Woodruff, Robert A., Taibleson, Mitchell, Rich, Charles and Cunningham, Lynn. Computer-Assisted Derivation of a Screening Interview for Alcoholism. Archives of General Psychiatry, 32(7): 847-852, 1975.

4803. Riegelman, Richard Kenneth. An Epidemiological Study of Utilization of Health Maintenance and Primary Care Services in a Prepaid Health Plan. Dissertation Abstracts International, 43(4): 1055B, 1982.

4804. Riesel, Petr. Deset Let Pece O Alkoholiky A Jejich Rodiny V Protialkoholni Poradne V Chomutove. (Ten Years of Care for Alcoholics and Their Families in the Antialcoholic Counseling Center at Chomutov.) Protialkoholicky Obzor, Bratislava, 7(3): 96-101, 1972.

4805. Riester, A.E. and Zucker, R.A. Adolescent Social Structure and Drinking Behavior. Personnel and Guidance Journal, 47: 304-312, 1968

4806. Rieth, E. Zur Effektivitatsbeurteilung Von Entziehungskuren. (Estimating the Effectiveness of Treatment of Addiction.) Suchtgefahren, Hamburg, 23: 137-146, 1977.

4807. Rieth, E. Die Personlichkeit des Alkoholikers. (The Personality of the Alcoholic.) Fursorger, 42: 1-13, 1974.

4808. Riffenburgh, R.S. and Shea, J.F. Lack of Association Between Color Blindness and Alcoholism. Eye, Ear, Nose and Throat Monthly, 49: 240-242, 1970.

4809. The Rights of Alcoholics and Their Families. Pamphlet. New York: National Council on Alcoholism, 1970.

4810. Rimmer, John. The Children of Alcoholics: An Exploratory Study. Children and Youth Services Review, 4(4): 365-374, 1982.

4811. Rimmer, John. Psychiatric Illness in Husbands of Alcoholics. Quarterly Journal of Studies on Alcohol, 35(1): 281-283, 1974.

4812. Rimmer, John and Chambers, Donald S. Alcoholism: Methodological Considerations in the Study of Family Illness. American Journal of Orthopsychiatry, 39(5): 760-768, 1969.

4813. Rimmer, John and Jacobsen, B. Alcoholism in Schizophrenics and Their Relatives. Journal of Studies on Alcohol, 38: 1781-1784, 1977.

4814. Rimmer, John, Pitts, F.N., Reich, T. and Winokur, G. Alcoholism II. Sex, Socioeconomic Status and Race in Two Hospitalized Samples. Quarterly Journal of Studies on Alcohol, 32: 942-952, 1971.

4815. Rimmer, John, Reich, T. and Winokur, G. Alcoholism. V. Diagnosis and Clinical Variation Among Alcoholics. Quarterly Journal of Studies on Alcohol, 33: 658-666, 1972.

4816. Rimmer, John and Winokur, George. The Spouses of Alcoholics: An Example of Assortative Mating. Diseases of the Nervous System, 33(8): 509-511, 1972.

4817. Rinella, Vincent J. and Goldstein, Marc R. Family Therapy with Substance Abusers: Legal Considerations Regarding Confidentiality. Journal of Marital and Family Therapy, 6(3): 319-325, 1980.

4818. Ringoet, K. Depth Psychological and Cultural-Ethological Aspects in Connection with Alcoholism. Acta Psychiatrica Belgica, 80(2): 175-182, 1980.

4819. Ritchey, Diane. Marital Interaction of Alcoholic Couples: Changes in Affective Communication During Experimental Drinking. Dissertation Abstracts International, 40(5): 2385B, 1979. (University Microfilms No. 79-24738.)

4820. Ritson, Bruce. ABC of Alcohol. Helping the Problem Drinker. British Medical Journal (Clinical Research Ed.), 284(6312): 327-329, 1982.

4821. Ritson, Bruce. Alcohol and Young People. Journal of Adolescence, 4(1): 93-100, 1981.

4822. Ritson, Bruce. Personality and Prognosis in Alcoholism. The British Journal of Psychiatry: The Journal of Mental Science, London, 118(542): 79-82, 1971.

4823. Ritson, Bruce. The Prognosis of Alcohol Addicts Treated by a Specialized Unit. The British Journal of Psychiatry: The Journal of Mental Science, London, 114(513): 1019-1029, 1968.

4824. Ritson, Bruce. Review: Children and Alcohol. Child: Care, Health and Development, Oxford, 1: 263-269, 1975.

4825. Ritson, Bruce. Treatment and Evolution of Alcohol-Dependent Children and Adolescents. In: Alcohol and Youth. (Child Health and Development, Volume 2.) Ed. O. Jeanneret. Basel: S. Karger, 1983, pages 108-118.

4826. Ritson, E.B. Organization of Services to Families of Alcoholics. In: Alcohol and the Family. Eds. J. Orford and J. Harwin. New York: St. Martin's Press, 1982, pages 180-200.

4827. Ritson, E.B. Psychological Medicine. Treatment of Alcoholism. British Medical Journal, London, 2(5963): 124-127, 1975.

4828. Ritson, E.R. Suicide Amongst Alcoholics. British Journal of Medical Psychology, Letchworth, 41: 235-242, 1968.

4829. Ritzman, Ronald F. and Melchior, Christine L. Age and Development of Tolerance to and Physical Dependence on Alcohol. In: Aging, Volume 25: Alcoholism in the Elderly: Social and Biomedical Issues. Eds. James T. Hartford and T. Samorajski. New York: Raven Press, 1984, pages 117-138.

4830. Rivera-Lopez, H. Family Ties Disruption: An Exploratory Study to Examine Alcohol Abuse among Latino Males. Dissertation Abstracts International, 45(10): 3323B, 1985.

4831. Rivers, P. The Making and Breaking of a Nicotinic Alcoholic Depressive (A Completely True Story). New York: Vantage Press, 1978.

4832. Rivoir, Yvonne. Treatment Approaches and Techniques. In: Casework with Wives of Alcoholics. Eds. P.C. Cohen and M.S. Krause. New York: Family Service Association of America, 1971, pages 79-96.

4833. Rix, K. Alcoholism and the District Nurse. Community Outlook, London, 13: 275-276, 278, 1979.

4834. Rix, Keith J.B. and Rix, Elizabeth M. Lumsden. The Alcohol Withdrawal States: Nursing Care. Nursing Times, London, 74(14): 581-583, 1978.

4835. Rizzola, N. and Rosadini, I. Determinanti Familiari E Sociali
       Dell'alcoolismo Femminile. (Familial and Social
       Determinants of Female Alcoholism.) Neuropsichiatria,
       Genova, 30(1-2): 71-78, 1974.

4836. Robbins, L., Robbins, E., Pearlman, S., Phillip A., Robinson, E.
       and Schmitter, B. College Students' Perceptions of Their
       Parents' Attitudes and Practices Toward Drug Use. Journal
       of Alcohol and Drug Education, 18(2): 6-12, 1973.

4837. Robbins, P.R. and Nugent, J.F., 3D. Perceived Consequences of
       Addiction: A Comparison Between Alcoholics and Heroin-
       Addicted Patients. Journal of Clinical Psychology, 31:
       367-369, 1975.

4838. Robe, Lucy B. Haunted Inheritance. Minneapolis: Compcare
       Publications, 1980.

4839. Robe, Lucy B., Robe, Robert S. Jr. and Wilson, P. Ann. Maternal
       Heavy Drinking Related to Delayed Onset of Daughters'
       Menstruation. In: Currents in Alcoholism. Volume 7.
       Recent Advances in Research and Treatment. Ed. M. Glanter.
       New York: Grune and Stratton, 1980, pages 515-520.

4840. Roberts, H.M. Arithmetic of the Familial Transmission of
       Alcoholism in Canada. Canadian Journal of Public Health,
       61: 179, 1970.

4841. Roberts, K.S. and Brent, E.E. Physician Utilization and Illness
       Patterns in Families of Alcoholics. Journal of Studies on
       Alcohol, 43: 119-128, 1982.

4842. Roberts, Kristi Ann Smith. The Effect of Alcoholism on Physician
       Utilization in Family Members. Doctoral Dissertation.
       (University Microfilms No. 80-24389.) University of Missouri-
       Columbia, 1979. (Also in: Dissertation Abstracts International,
       41(5): 1929B, 1980.)

4843. Roberts, M.C. The Interaction of Alcoholic and Non-Alcoholic
       Husbands and Their Wives on a Decision-Making Task.
       Doctoral Dissertation. (University Microfilms No. 75-21008.)
       Boston University Graduate School, 1975.

4844. Roberts, Marjorie C.F., Floyd, Frank J., O'Farrell, Timothy J.
       and Cutter, Henry S.G. Marital Interactions and the Duration
       of Alcoholic Husbands' Sobriety. American Journal of Drug
       and Alcohol Abuse, 11(3/4): 303-313, 1985.

4845. Roberts, S.M. Older Parents of Male Alcoholics: Where Do They
       Turn? Focus on Family and Chemical Dependency, 8(1):
       32-33, 1985.

4846. Robertson, B.A. and Hayward, M.A. Transcultural Factors in
       Child Abuse. South African Medical Journal, Cape Town,
       50(43): 1765-1767, 1976.

4847. Robertson, B.A. and Robertson F.C. Physically Abused Children
       and Their Families. South African Medical Journal,
       Cape Town, 64(13): 484-488, 1983.

4848. Robertson, Dennis M., Morse, Robert M., Moore, S. Breanndan,
       O'Fallon, William M. and Hurt, Richard D. A Study of HLA
       Antigens in Alcoholism. Mayo Clinic Proceedings, 59(4):
       243-246, 1984.

4849. Robertson, F.W. and Cumming, A.M. Effects of Apoprotein E
       Polymorphism on Serum Lipoprotein Concentration.
       Arteriosclerosis, 5(3): 283-292, 1985.

4850.   Robertson, I. Alcohol and the Family. British Journal of
        Clinical Psychology, 22: 150, 1983.

4851.   Robertson, Joan and Downs, William. Perceived Family Environment
        as a Predictor of Adolescent Alcohol Behavior. Paper presented
        at the National Council on Family Relations, Minneapolis, 1981.

4852.   Robertson, Joan and Moberg, Paul. Parental Role Modeling as a
        Predictor of Adolescent Alcohol Behavior. Paper presented
        at the National Council on Family Relations, Minneapolis, 1981.

4853.   Robertson, Joan, Stephenson, John and Downs, William. A Service
        Delivery Model of Family Systems Approach to Alcohol Use &
        Abuse: Knowledge Guided Intervention Parameters. Paper
        presented at the National Counil on Family Relations,
        Minneapolis, 1981.

4854.   Robertson, N.C. The Relationship between Marital Status and
        the Risk of Psychiatric Referral. The British Journal
        of Psychiatry: The Journal of Mental Science, London,
        124: 191-202, 1974.

4855.   Robinovitch, Louise G. Idiot and Imbecile Children. Various
        Cases of Idiocy and Imbecility. The Relation of Alcoholism
        in the Parent to Idiocy and Imbecility of the Offspring.
        Journal of Mental Pathology, 1: 14-24, 86-95, 1901.

4856.   Robinovitch, Louise G. Rapport Entre la Criminalite des Enfants
        et l'Alcoolisme des Parents. (Relationship between Juvenile
        Delinquency and Parental Alcoholism.) Internationale
        Congress de Medicine, Paris, 541-547, 1901.

4857.   Robins, L.N., Clayton, P.J. and Wing, J.K. (Eds.) Social
        Consequences of Psychiatric Illness. New York:
        Brunner/Mazel, 1980.

4858.   Robins, Lee, Bates, William and O'Neal, Patricia. Adult Drinking
        Patterns of Former Problem Children. In: Society, Culture
        and Drinking Patterns. Eds. D.J. Pittman and C.R. Snyder.
        New York: Wiley, 1962, pages 395-412.

4859.   Robins, Lee N. Alcoholism and Labelling Theory. In: Readings
        in Medical Sociology. Ed. D. Mechanic. New York:
        The Free Press, 1980, pages 188-198.

4860.   Robins, Lee N. Deviant Children Grown Up: A Sociological and
        Psychiatric Study of Sociopathic Personality. Baltimore:
        Williams and Wilkins, 1966.

4861.   Robins, Lee N. The Family Setting of the Young Sociopath. In:
        Deviant Children Grown Up: A Sociological and Psychiatric
        Study. Baltimore: Williams & Wilkins, 1966, pages 159-180.

4862.   Robins, Lee N. The Natural Histories of Other Psychiatric
        Diagnoses: Schizophrenia, Alcoholism, Hysteria, and Other
        Neuroses. In: Deviant Children Grown Up: A Sociological
        and Psychiatric Study. Baltimore: Williams & Wilkins,
        1966, pages 238-262.

4863.   Robins, Lee N. The Natural History of Drug Abuse. In: Theories
        on Drug Abuse: Selected Contemporary Problems. (Research
        Monograph Series No. 30) U.S. National Institute on Drug
        Abuse. Eds. D. Lettieri, M. Sayers and H. Pearson. Rockville,
        MD, 1980, pages 215-224. (DHEW Publication No. (ADM) 80-967.)

4864.   Robins, Lee N. Sturdy Childhood Predictors of Adult Antisocial
        Behaviour: Replications from Longitudinal Studies.
        Psychological Medicine, London, 8: 611-622, 1978.

4865. Robins, Lee N., Murphy, George E. and Breckenridge, Mary B.
       Drinking Behavior of Young Urban Negro Men. Quarterly
       Journal of Studies on Alcohol, 29(3A): 657-684, 1968.

4866. Robins, Lee N. and Smith, Elizabeth M. Longitudinal Studies of
       Alcohol and Drug Problems: Sex Differences. In: Research
       Advances in Alcohol and Drug Problems, Volume 5: Alcohol
       and Drug Problems in Women. Ed. Oriana Josseau Kalant.
       New York: Plenum Press, 1980, pages 203-232.

4867. Robins, Lee N., West, P.A., Ratcliff, K.S. and Herjanic, B.M.
       Father's Alcoholism and Children's Outcome. In: Currents
       in Alcoholism. Volume 4. Psychiatric, Psychological,
       Social and Epidemiological Studies. Ed. F.A. Seixas.
       New York: Grune and Stratton, 1978, pages 313-327.
       (Eric Document Number ED 152892.)

4868. Robinson, G.M. Children of Alcoholics. Social Casework,
       64(3): 178-181, 1983.

4869. Robinson, R.R. On the Rocks. Richmond Hill, Ontario:
       Scholastic-TAB Publications, 1979.

4870. Robinson, S.D. Women and Alcohol Abuse: Factors Involved in
       Successful Interventions. International Journal of the
       Addictions, 19(6): 601-611, 1984.

4871. Robles, Rafaela R., Martinez, Ruth E. and Moscoso, Margarita R.
       Predictors of Adolescent Drug Behavior: The Case of Puerto
       Rico. Youth & Society, 11(4): 415-430, 1980.

4872. Robson, Meredith H., France, Richard and Bland, Martin.
       Practice Observed: Clinical Psychologist in Primary Care:
       Controlled Clinical and Economic Evaluation. The British
       Medical Journal, London, 288(6433): 1805-1808, 1984.

4873. Robson, W. Joan. Alcohol Abuse in Adolescence. Alcohol and
       Alcoholism, 19(2): 177-179, 1984.

4874. Rock, Nicholas L. and Donley, Patrick J. Treatment Program for
       Military Personnel with Alcohol Problems. Part II. The
       Program. International Journal of the Addictions, 10(3):
       467-480, 1975.

4875. Rodgers, D.A. A Psychological Interpretation of Alcoholism.
       Annals of the New York Academy of Sciences, 197:
       222-225, 1972.

4876. Rodgers, Georgine. Review of An Alcoholic in the Family
       by Mary Burton. Addiction, 4(1-2): 12-13, 1975.

4877. Rodgers, Georgine. Review of A Sensitive, Passionate Man by
       Barbara Mahoney. Addictions, 4(1-2): 11-12, 1975.

4878. Rodin, A.E. Infants and Gin Mania in 18th Century London.
       Journal of the American Medical Association, 245(12):
       1237-1239, 1981.

4879. Rodino, Peter W. Initiating a Dialogue. Paper presented at the
       National Institute on Drug Abuse, Program for Women's Concerns,
       Miami Beach, October, 1975. (Also in: Drugs, Alcohol and
       Women; A National Forum Source Book. Ed. M. Nellis.
       Washington, D.C.: National Research and Communications
       Associations, Inc., 1976.)

4880. Rodriguez, L.J., Morgan, D.A. and Rodriguez, A.M. Engagement
       of the Family in the Treatment of the Hispanic Alcoholic:
       Two Miami Programs. Report. Washington, D.C.: National
       Coalition of Hispanic Mental Health & Human Services
       Organization, 1979.

4881. Rodriguez, L.J., Morgan, D.A. and Rodriguez, A.M. Therapeutic
       Involvement of the Family in Treating Hispanic Alcoholics:
       Two Miami Programs. In: Hispanic Report on Families and
       Youth. Washington, D.C.: National Coalition of Hispanic
       Mental Health & Human Services Organization, pages 81-85.

4882. Rodriguez-Martos, A. and Ferrer-Vidal, L. Modificacion De
       Actitudes En Pacientes Alcoholicos Recuperados Asistentes
       A Grupos De Discusion. (Attitude Change in Recovering
       Alcoholics Attending Discussion Groups.) Drogalcohol,
       5: 123-128, 1980.

4883. Rodriguez-Martos-Dauer, A. Sobre la Etiologia del Habito
       Alcoholico. (On the Etiology of Habituation to Alcohol.)
       Drogalcohol, 3: 115-119, 1978.

4884. Rodriguez-Martos-Dauer, A. and Welsch-Pastor, T. Interrelaciones
       Entre Alcoholismo y Dinamica Conyugal: Repercusion Sobre
       los Hijos. (Interconnections between Alcoholism and
       Marital Dynamics: Their Repercussions on the Children.)
       Drogalcohol, 4: 13-22, 1979.

4885. Rodzinie i Dziecku w Trudnej Sytuacji. (Child and Family Aid in
       Alcohol-Related Crises.) Problemy Alkoholizmu, Warsaw,
       26(4): 1, 1979.

4886. Roe, Anne. The Adjustment of Children of Alcoholic Parents
       Raised in Foster-Homes. Quarterly Journal of Studies on
       Alcohol, 5: 378-393, 1944.

4887. Roe, Anne. Alcohol and Creative Work. Part I. Painters. Quarterly
       Journal of Studies on Alcohol, 6: 415-467, 1946.

4888. Roe, Anne. Children of Alcoholic Parents Raised in Foster Homes.
       In: Alcohol, Science and Society. Westport, CT: Greenwood
       Press, 1945, pages 115-128.

4889. Roe, Anne and Burks, Barbara. Adult Adjustment of Foster
       Children of Alcoholic and Psychotic Parentage and the
       Influence of the Foster Home. Quarterly Journal of
       Studies on Alcohol, 6: 563, 1945.

4890. Roeske, Nancy C. Stress and the Physician. The Journal of the
       Indiana State Medical Association, 75(2): 108-119, 1982.
       (Also in: Psychiatric Annals, 11(7): 10-12, 14-15,
       19-22, 28-30, 32, 1981.)

4891. Roff, J.D. Adolescent Development and Family Characteristics
       Associated with a Diagnosis of Schizophrenia. Journal of
       Consulting and Clinical Psychology, 44: 933-939, 1976.

4892. Roffe, Michael W. Factorial Structure of the Tennessee Self-
       Concept Scale. Psychological Reports, 48(2): 455-462, 1981.

4893. Rogan, Arleen. Domestic Violence and Alcohol: Barriers to
       Cooperation. Alcohol Health & Research World, 10(2):
       22-27, 1985/86.

4894. Roger, H. La Physionomie de Pheredo-Alcoolique. (People
       with Alcoholic Heredity.) Sud Medical et Chirurgical,
       Marseille, 77: 295-307, 1945.

4895. Roghmann, Klaus. Alcoholics' Versus Nonalcoholics' Use of
      Services of a Health Maintenance Organization. _Journal
      of Studies on Alcohol_, 42(3): 312-322, 1981.

4896. Rogowski, E. W Sprawie Pomocy Dla Rodzin Alkoholikow. (About
      Welfare for the Families of Alcoholics.) _Problemy
      Alkoholiznu_, Warsaw, 22(9): 13-14, 1974.

4897. Rohan, W.P. Follow-Up Study of Problem Drinkers. _Diseases of
      the Nervous System_, 33(3): 196-199, 1972.

4898. Roiter, William Alan. Community Caregivers' and Residents'
      Perceptions and Attitudes Toward Teenage Alcohol Problems.
      Dissertation Abstracts International, 42(7): 3001B, 1981.

4899. The Role of the Public Health Service in Dealing with the Problems
      of Alcoholism. _The Journal of Alcoholism_, London, 5:
      133-135, 1970.

4900. Roman, Paul M. The Impact of Alcoholism on the Family.
      A Sociological View. In: _Health and the Family:
      A Medical-Sociological Analysis_. Ed. C.O. Crawford.
      New York: Macmillan, 1971, pages 217-241.

4901. Room, Robin. _Alcohol as an Instrument of Intimate Domination_.
      Berkeley: University of California, School of Public
      Health, Social Research Group, 1979.

4902. Room, Robin. Cultural Contingencies of Alcoholism: Variations
      between and within Nineteenth-Century Urban Ethnic Groups
      in Alcohol-Related Death Rates. _Journal of Health and
      Social Behavior_, 9(2): 99-113, 1968.

4903. Room, Robin. _Marital Concordance on Personality Traits in a
      General Population_. Report. Washington, D.C.: George
      Washington University, Social Research Group, 1970.

4904. Room, Robin. Scope and Definition of Alcohol-Related Problems.
      Working Paper, F-58. Berkeley: University of
      California at Berkeley, School of Public Health, 1977.

4905. Root, L. Family of the Alcoholic. Paper presented at the
      _15th International Institute on the Prevention and Treatment
      of Alcoholism_, Budapest, June, 1969, pages 145-149.

4906. Root, Laura E. The Role of the Social Worker in the Treatment
      of Alcoholics. In: _Opportunities and Limitations in the
      Treatment of Alcoholics_. Ed. Joseph Hirsh. Springfield,
      IL: Charles C. Thomas, 1967, pages 85-94.

4907. Root, Laura E. _Social Casework with the Alcoholic and His Family_.
      Springfield, IL: Charles C. Thomas, 1974. (Also in:
      Alcoholism: The Total Treatment Approach. Ed. Ronald J.
      Catanzaro. Springfield, IL: Charles C. Thomas, 1977, pages
      208-222.)

4908. Root, Laura E. Treatment of the Alcoholic Family. _Journal of
      Psychoactive Drugs_, 18(1): 51-56, 1986.

4909. Rorsman, B. Mortality Among Psychiatric Patients. _Acta
      Psychiatrica Scandinavica_, Copenhagen, 50(3): 354-375, 1974.

4910. Rosen, Anita L. Wife Abuse in Rural Areas: Some Social, Legal,
      Medical and Service Delivery Issues, 1981. (Eric Document
      Number ED222318).

4911. Rosenbaum, Alan and O'Leary, K. Daniel. Marital Violence:
      Characteristics of Abusive Couples. _Journal of Consulting
      and Clinical Psychology_, 49(1): 63-71, 1981.

4912. Rosenbaum, Bernice. Married Women Alcoholics at the Washingtonian Hospital. Quarterly Journal of Studies on Alcohol, 19: 79-89, 1958.

4913. Rosenbaum, C.P., Adams, J.E., Scott, K.L., Renson, G.J., Tinklenberg, J.R. and Hanks, S.E. Alcohol and Violence: A Clinical Study. In: Biobehavioral Aspects of Aggression. Eds. D.A. Hamburg and M.B. Trudeau. New York: Alan R. Liss, 1981, pages 169-226.

4914. Rosenberg, C.M. Determinants of Psychiatric Illness in Young People. British Journal of Psychiatry, 115: 907-915, 1969.

4915. Rosenberg, C.M. The Young Addict and His Family. British Journal of Psychiatry, 118: 469-470, 1971.

4916. Rosenberg, C.M. Young Alcoholics. British Journal of Psychiatry, 115: 181-188, 1969.

4917. Rosenberg, C.M. Young Drug Addicts: Background and Personality. Journal of Nervous and Mental Disease, 148: 65-73, 1969.

4918. Rosenberg, Donald N. Holistic Therapy with "Alcoholism Families." Alcohol Health and Research World, 6(2): 30-32, 1981-1982.

4919. Rosenblatt, S.M., Gross, M.M. and Chartoff, S. Marital Status and Multiple Psychiatric Admissions for Alcoholism. Quarterly Journal of Studies on Alcohol, 30(2): 445-447, 1969.

4920. Rosenblatt, S.M., Gross, M.M., Malenowski, B., Broman, M. and Lewis, E. Marital Status and Multiple Psychiatric Admissions for Alcoholism: A Cross-Validation. Quarterly Journal of Studies on Alcohol, 32(4): 1092-1096, 1971.

4921. Rosenfeld, Elaine S. Systemic Family Therapy and the Treatment of Intoxication, Abstinence and Recovery. In: Social Work Treatment of Alcohol Problems. Eds. David Cook, Christine Fewell and John Riolo. New Brunswick, NJ: Rutgers Center of Alcohol Studies, 1983, pages 60-67.

4922. Rosenfield, C. Family, Violence and Alcohol: Networking in Action. Paper presented at the National Alcoholism Forum, Houston, April, 1983.

4923. Rosenthal, N.E., Davenport, Y., Cowdry, R.W., Webster, M.H. and Goodwin, F.K. Monoamine Metabolites in Cerebrospinal Fluid of Depressive Subgroups. Psychiatry Research, 2(1): 113-119, 1980.

4924. Rosenthal, Ted L., Akiskal, Hagop S., Scott-Strauss, Alice, Rosenthal, Renate H. and David, Mary. Familial and Developmental Factors in Characterological Depressions. Journal of Affective Disorders, Amsterdam, 3(2): 183-192, 1981.

4925. Rosett, H.L. Letter: Maternal Alcoholism and Intellectual Development of Offspring. Lancet, 2(874): 218, 1974.

4926. Rosett, H.L., Ouellette, E.M. and Weiner, L. A Pilot Prospective Study of the Fetal Alcohol Syndrome at the Boston City Hospital. Part I. Maternal Drinking. Annals of the New York Academy of Sciences, 273: 118-122, 1976.

4927. Rosett, H.L., Snyder, P., Sander, L.W., Lee, A., Cook, P., Weiner, L. and Gould, J. Effects of Maternal Drinking on Neonate State Regulation. Developmental Medicine and Child Neurology, 21(4): 464-473, 1979.

4928. Rosett, Henry L. Effects of Maternal Drinking on Child Development: An Introductory Review. *Annals of the New York Academy of Sciences*, <u>273</u>: 115-117, 1976.

4929. Rosin, Arnold J. and Glatt, M.M. Alcohol Excess in the Elderly. *Quarterly Journal of Studies on Alcohol*, <u>32</u>(1): 53-59, 1971.

4930. Roslund, Barbro and Larson, Carl A. Mental Disturbed Violent Offenders in Sweden. *Neuropsychobiology*, Basel, <u>2</u>(4): 221-232, 1976.

4931. Rosner, Bernard. Family Problem. *The Catalyst*, <u>1</u>(3): 45-47, 1980.

4932. Rosonke, Jerome R. and Pelton, Charles L. Community and Professional Perceptions of Child Abuse and Neglect. *South Dakota Journal of Medicine*, <u>35</u>(2): 7-12, 1982.

4933. Ross, A.B. Al-Anon Help Alcoholics' Wives. *Hospital Progress*, <u>40</u>(4): 70-72, 131, 1959.

4934. Ross, C.F. Comparison of Hospital and Prison Alcoholics. *The British Journal of Psychiatry: The Journal of Mental Science*, London, <u>118</u>(542): 75-78, 1971.

4935. Ross, Matthew. The Impaired Psychiatrist. Continuing Medical Education: Syllabus and Proceedings in Summary Form. Paper presented to the *American Psychiatric Association*, Washington, D.C., 1978, pages 152-153.

4936. Rostow, E.V. Drinking as an Element in Custody Cases. *Quarterly Journal of Studies on Alcohol*, <u>3</u>: 675-676, 1943.

4937. Roth, R. Alcoholism and the Family: Putting the Pieces Together. *Alcoholism: The National Magazine*, <u>1</u>(3): 19-22, 1981.

4938. Rothenbach, Marion. Considerations Actuelles sur le Developpement de L'Action Communautaire en Suisse Romande. (Actual Considerations on the Development of Community Action in the French-Speaking Part of Switzerland. *Revue De L'Alcoolisme*, Paris, <u>20</u>(2): 137-140, 1974.

4939. Rothman, Jack and Kay, Terrence. Community Mental Health Centers and Family Service Agencies. *Social Work Research and Abstracts*, <u>13</u>: 10-16, 1977.

4940. Rotman, D.B. Alcoholism, A Social Disease. *Journal of the American Medical Association*, <u>127</u>: 564-567, 1945.

4941. Rotunno, Marie and McGoldrick, Monica. Italian Families. In: *Ethnicity and Family Therapy*. Eds. Monica McGoldrick, John K. Pearce and Joseph Giordano. New York: The Guilford Press, 1982, pages 340-363.

4942. Roubik, Elaine Ardis Hoveland. Community Leaders' and Service Providers' Perceptions of Mental Health: A Macro Level Comparative Study. *Dissertation Abstracts International*, <u>41</u>(2): 516B, 1980.

4943. Roue, R., Larrouque, P., Farret, O. LeBarbu, M., Favre, J.D., Mansour, C. and Cristau, P. Causes and Motivations of Alcoholism in the Army. *Revue International des Services Sante Armees Terre Mer Air*, <u>54</u>(1): 39-43, 1981.

4944. Round Table: Dependence, Relapse. (Table Ronde: La Dependance, les Rechutes.) In: *Mieux Connaitre L'Alcoolique*. Eds. J.P. Bader and J.J. Tourteau. Paris: La Documentation Francaise, 1979, pages 121-135.

4945.   Rounsaville, Bruce J. Theories in Marital Violence: Evidence
        From a Study of Battered Women. Victimology, 3(1-2):
        11-31, 1978.

4946.   Rounsaville, Bruce J., Kleber, Herbert D., Wilber, Charles,
        Rosenberger, Dale and Rosenberger, Patricia. Comparison
        of Opiate Addicts Reports of Psychiatric History with
        Reports of Significant Other Informants. American Journal
        of Drug and Alcohol Abuse, 8(1): 51-70, 1981.

4947.   Rounsaville, Bruce J., Weissman, Myrna M. and Kleber, Herbert D.
        The Significance of Alcoholism in Treated Opiate Addicts.
        Journal of Nervous and Mental Disease, 170(8): 479-488, 1982.

4948.   Rouse, B.A. Spouse Agreement on Drinking and Indices of Family
        Difficulties. Paper presented at the 13th Annual Medical-
        Scientific Conference of the National Alcoholism Forum on
        Progress in Alcoholism Research and Treatment, Washington,
        D.C., April, 1982. (Also in: Alcoholism: Clinical and
        Experimental Research, 6(1): 152, 1982.)

4949.   Rouse, B.A. Stressful Stages in the Family-Life Cycle and Ethanol
        Intake of Husbands and Wives. Alcoholism: Clinical and
        Experimental Research, 5(1): 166, 1981.

4950.   Rouse, Beatrice A. A Longitudinal Study of Conjugal Family
        Factors and Alcohol Intake in a Framingham Cohort. Doctoral
        Dissertation. (University Microfilms No. 81-04420.) University
        of North Carolina at Chapel Hill, 1981. (Also in: Dissertation
        Abstracts International, 41(8): 2983B, 1981.)

4951.   Rouse, Beatrice A., Waller, Patricia F. and Ewing, John A. Adolescent
        Stress Levels, Coping Activities, and Father's Drinking Behaviors.
        Proceedings of the 81st Annual Conference of the American
        Psychological Association, 8: 681-682, 1973.

4952.   Rouse, Gary A. Dyad Problem Solving with Alcoholics: An Investigation
        of Family Organization Using Consensus Rorschach. Doctoral
        Dissertation. Fresno: California School of Professional
        Psychology, 1980.

4953.   Roy, Maria (Ed.). Battered Women: A Psychosociological Study
        of Domestic Violence. New York: Van Nostrand Reinhold, 1977.

4954.   Roy, Tom and Shields, Richard. Alcohol Education in School Social
        Work. Social Work in Education, 1(3): 43-53, 1979.

4955.   Royce, J.E. The Spouse and Family of the Alcoholic. In: Alcohol
        Problems and Alcoholism; A Comprehensive Survey. New York:
        The Free Press, 1981, pages 119-139.

4956.   Roza, Janos. La Vittima Della Violenza Carnale. (The Victim of
        Carnal Violence.) Quaderni di Criminologia Clinica, Rome,
        19: 445-465, 1977.

4957.   Rozoy, J.G. L'Eradication De L'Alcoolisme En France: Est-elle
        Possible? (Eradication of Alcoholism in France: Is it
        Possible?) Revue De L'Alcoolisme, 20(2): 141-144, 1974.

4958.   Rubington, Earl. The First Year of Abstinence: Notes on an
        Exploratory Study. Journal of Studies on Alcohol, 41(5):
        577-582, 1980.

4959.   Rubington, Earl. The Future of the Halfway House. Quarterly
        Journal of Studies on Alcohol, 31(1) 167-174, 1970.

4960.   Rudestam, K.E. Physical and Psychological Responses to Suicide
        in the Family. Journal of Consulting and Clinical
        Psychology, 45: 162-170, 1977.

4961. Rudestam, Kjell Erik. Demographic Factors in Suicide in Sweden
       and the United States. _International Journal of Social
       Psychiatry_, London, 18(2): 79-90, 1972.

4962. Rudman, Michael S. Suicide in Lancaster County, 1974-75.
       Pennsylvania Medicine, 80(3): 56-58, 1977.

4963. Rudzinska, Wanda. Zaburzenia Zachowania U Dzieci -- Pacjentow
       Poradni Zdrowia Psychicznego A Postawy Rodzicielskie.
       (Behavioral Disturbances of Children Treated in a Mental
       Health Clinic and Parental Attitudes.) _Zagadnienia
       Wychowawcze A Zdrowie Psychiczne_, Warsaw, 10(2): 44-58, 1974.

4964. Rueger, Drue Barrett and Liberman, Robert P. Behavioral Family
       Therapy for Delinquent and Substance-Abusing Adolescents.
       Journal of Drug Issues, 14(2):403-418, 1984.

4965. Rukiewicz, Jan, Swiecicki, Andrzej and Falewicz, Jan Karol. _Social
       Welfare for the Children from Families of Alcoholics_. Warsaw:
       Center of Studies, Social Committee on Alcoholism, 1966.

4966. Rummer, C.A. Building Block of Parenting: Trust in the Alcoholic
       Family. _Focus on Family and Chemical Dependency_, 8(6):
       27, 30, 1985.

4967. Rungelj, V. Teoreticna in Practicna Izrodisca za Skupinsko
       Druzinsko Zdravljenije Alkoholikov ob Delu. (Theoretical
       and Practical Prerequisites of Group and Family Therapy
       for Working Alcoholics.) _Zdravstveni Vestnik_, Ljubljana,
       48(1): 37-41, 1979.

4968. Runyan, D.K., Gould, C.L., Trost, D.C. and Loda, F.A. Determinants
       of Foster Care Placement for the Maltreated Child. _American
       Journal of Public Health_, 71(7): 706-711, 1981.

4969. Rushing, William A. Alcoholism and Suicide Rates by Status Set
       and Occupation. _Quarterly Journal of Studies on Alcohol_,
       29(2): 399-412, 1968.

4970. Russell, A., Russell, L. and Waring, E.M. Cognitive Family
       Therapy: A Preliminary Report. _Canadian Journal of
       Psychiatry_, 25(1): 64-67, 1980.

4971. Russell, Andrew T., Pasnau, Robert O. and Taintor, Zebulom C.
       The Emotionally Disturbed Psychiatric Resident. _American
       Journal of Psychiatry_, 134(1): 59-62, 1977.

4972. Russell, D.H. and Hardman, G.L. Juvenile Delinquency and the
       Quality of Life: The 17-year Depression. _Journal of
       Forensic Sciences_, 25(4): 908-911, 1980.

4973. Russell, M., Henderson, C. and Blume, S.B. _Children of Alcoholics:
       A Review of the Literature_. New York: Children of Alcoholics
       Foundation, 1984.

4974. Russell, Marcia. Intrauterine Growth in Infants Born to Women
       with Alcohol-Related Psychiatric Diagnoses. _Alcoholism:
       Clinical and Experimental Research_, 1(3): 225-231, 1977.

4975. Russell, Marcia and Bigler, L. Screening for Alcohol-Related
       Problems in an Outpatient Obstetric-Gynecologic Clinic.
       American Journal of Obstetrics and Gynecology, 134(1):
       4-12, 1979.

4976. Russell, Robert D. What Constitutes Use and Misuse of Alcohol in
       the Home? _Journal of Alcohol Education_, 15(2): 11-16, 1970.

4977. Rutherford, D. Adolescence and Alcohol. _Royal Society of Health
       Journal_, London, 97(1): 14-17, 1977.

4978. Rutkiewicz, J. and Swiecicki, A. Social Welfare for Children from Families of Alcoholics: Findings of Studies Performed from June 1966 to June 1969. Warsaw: Social Committee on Alcoholism Center of Studies, 1969.

4979. Rutkiewicz, Jan, Swiecicki, Andrezej, Falewicz, Jan Karol, Ciapala, I. and Majewska, A. Social Welfare for Children from Families of Alcoholics. Warsaw: Social Committee on Alcoholism Center of Studies, 1966. (NTIS No. PB-220282/8.)

4980. Rutstein, D.D. and Veech, R.L. Genetics and Addiction to Alcohol. (Editorial) The New England Journal of Medicine, 298: 1140-1141, 1978.

4981. Rutt, C.N. and Offord, D.R. Prenatal and Perinatal Complications in Childhood Schizophrenics and Their Siblings. The Journal of Nervous and Mental Disease, 152(5): 324-331, 1971.

4982. Ryan, Charlotte, Siegel, Freyda and Williams, Carol. How to Talk with Children About Drinking: A Parenting Guide to Alcohol Education. MA: Parent-Teacher-Student Association, 1977.

4983. Ryan, Michael. Some Social Influences on Workers' Morbidity. British Medical Journal (Clinical Research Ed.), 283(6290): 546-547, 1981.

4984. Ryan, N.J. Internal Space Odyssey of a Co-Dependent. Voice: Valuing the Alcoholic, 20(1): 58-61, 1984.

4985. Ryback, R.S. Self-Mutilation During Alcohol Amnesia: Report of a Case. The British Journal of Psychiatry: The Journal of Mental Science, London, 118(546): 533-534, 1971.

4986. Ryback, R.S. Teen-Age Alcoholism and Drug Abuse. The New England Journal of Medicine, 294: 56, 1976.

4987. Rybakov, F.Y. Heredity and Alcoholism; Statistical Investigation Based on 2,000 Cases. Zhurnal Neuropatologii i Psikhiatrii, Moscow, 10: 338-348, 1910.

4988. Rybakova, T.G. Semeinaya Psikhoterapiya Pri Alkogolizme. (Family Psychotherapy in Alcoholism Treatment.) Trudy Instituta-Leningradskii Nauchno-Issledovatelskii Psikhonevrologicheskii Institut Imeni V.M. Bekhtereva, 84: 37-43, 1977.

4989. Rydelius, Per-Anders. Alcohol and Family Life. In: Child Health and Development, Volume 2. Alcohol and Youth. Ed. O. Jeanneret. Basel: S. Karger, 1983, pages 76-85.

4990. Rydelius, Per-Anders. Alcohol-Abusing Teenage Boys. Testing a Hypothesis on the Relationship Between Alcohol Abuse and Social Background Factors, Criminality and Personality in Teenage Boys. Acta Psychiatrica Scandinavica, Copenhagen, 68(5): 368-380, 1983.

4991. Rydelius, Per-Anders. Children of Alcoholic Fathers: A Longitudinal Prospective Study. In: Longitudinal Research in Alcoholism. Eds. Donald E. Goodwin, Katherine Teilmann Van Dusen, and Sarnoff A. Mednick. Boston: Kluwer Academic Publishers, 1984, pages 27-37.

4992. Rydelius, Per-Anders. Barn Till Aalkoholiserade Fader: Deras Sociala Anpassning Och Halsotillsta'nd Under En 20-A'Rig Observationstid. (Children of Alcoholic Fathers: Their Social Adjustment and State of Health Throughout a 20-Year Observation Period. Alkohol Och Narkotika, Stockholm, 75(3): 2-6, 1981.

4993. Rydelius, Per-Anders. Drug Abuse and Alcoholism Among Children
         and Youth in Sweden. In: The Child in His Family:
         Children in Turmoil: Tomorrow's Parents. Volume 7.
         Eds. E. James Anthony and Colette Chiland. New York:
         John Wiley & Sons, 1982, pages 153-161.

4994. Rydelius, Per-Anders. Yesterday's Children in Turmoil -- Today's
         Parents. In: The Child in His Family: Children in Turmoil:
         Tomorrow's Parents. Volume 7. Eds. E. James Anthony and
         Colette Chiland. New York: John Wiley & Sons, 1982, pages 35-42.

4995. Ryerson, Eric. When Your Parent Drinks Too Much: A Book for
         Teenagers. New York: Facts on File Publications, 1985.

4996. Ryle, R.J. The Galton Laboratory Memoir on the Influence of Parental
         Alcoholism. The British Medical Journal, 2: 558, 1910.

S

4997. Saban, J., Ordonez, A., Navascues, I., Suarez, Terry R. and Serrano,
Rios, M. El Sofoco O Flush Inducido Por Clorpropamida-Alcohol
(CAF): Un Marcador Genetico De La Diabetes Mellitus O Un
Effecto Indeseable De La Medication? (Chlorpropamide-Alcohol
Flush (CAF): A Genetic Marker for Diabetes Mellitus or an
Undesirable Effect of Medication?) Revista Clinica Espanola,
176(3): 107-111, 1985.

4998. Sabbah, A. and Toullec, M. Etude Epidemiologique et Prevention
De L'Alcoolisme Dans Un Service Du Centre Psychotherapique
Departemental De Maine-et-Loire. (Epidemiological Study and
Prevention of Alcoholism in a Service of the Psychotherapeutic
Departmental Center of Maine-et-Loire.) Revue De L'Alcoolisme,
Paris, 19(3):166-178, 1973.

4999. Sadoun, Roland and Lolli, Giorgio. Choice of Alcoholic Beverage
among 120 Alcoholics in France. Quarterly Journal of Studies
on Alcohol, 23: 449-458, 1962.

5000. Sainsbury, Peter. Clinical Aspects of Suicide and Its Prevention.
British Journal of Hospital Medicine, London, 19(2):
156, 158, 161-162, 1978.

5001. Saint, E.G., Joske, R.A., MacKay, M.A. and Turner, C.N. Studies
in Chronic Alcoholism. IV. Treatment and Management.
Medical Journal of Australia, Sydney, 39: 742-746, 1952.

5002. Saito, Toshikazu, Murayama, Tohei, Mitamura, Akira, Yuasa, Hiroo,
Ogata, Motoi, Takahata, Noohiko and Nomiya, Tomeo. A
Possible Role of Alcohol on Convulsive Seizures in a Case
of Idiopathic Epilepsy. Japanese Journal of Studies on
Alcohol, Kyoto, 15(3): 175-186, 1980.

5003. Saleeby, Caleb Williams. Alcoholism and Eugenics. British
Journal of Inebriety, 13: 77-79, 1915.

5004. Saleeby, Caleb Williams. The Discussion of Alcoholism at the
Eugenics Congress. The British Journal of Inebriety,
10: 58-65, 1912.

5005. Saleeby, Caleb Williams. The Dysgenics of War and Alcohol.
The British Journal of Inebriety, 13: 23-26, 1915.

5006. Saleeby, Caleb Williams. Eugenics and Dysgenics in Relation to
Alcohol. British Journal of Inebriety, 11: 1-8, 1913.

5007. Saleeby, Caleb Williams. Professor Karl Pearson on Alcoholism and
Offspring. British Journal of Inebriety, 8: 53-66, 1910.

5008. Saleeby, Caleb Williams. The Social Protection of Youth and the
Race. International Review Against Alcoholism, Lausanne,
30: 31-34, 1922.

5009. Salgado, A. El Alcoholismo Paterno y la Delincuencia Juvenil.
       (Paternal Alcoholism and Juvenile Delinquency.) Archivos
       Venezolanos Puericultura y Pediatria, 8: 1711-1783, 1946.

5010. Salonen, S. and Panelius, M. Personlighetsdisintegration Och
       Fortvivlan Vid Sjalvmord Hos Alkoholister. (Personality
       Disintegration and Despair in Suicides of Alcoholics.)
       Nordisk Psykiatrisk Tidsskrift, Copenhagen, 21: 292-299, 1967.

5011. Salvadorini, F., Cioni, P., Parrini, G., Poli, E. and Bartalozzi, G.
       Morbidity Perception and Intervention Request from a Group
       Indication for a Therapeutic Strategy. In: 28th International
       Institute on the Prevention and Treatment of Alcoholism. Ed.
       E.J. Tongue. Lausanne: ICAA, 1982, pages 334-342.

5012. Salzberger, Gideon and Laury, Gabriel V. A Hidden Affair --
       Women and Alcohol: Five Major Therapeutic Considerations
       in Treating Female Alcoholism. Behavioral Medicine,
       8(10): 14-15, 19-20, 1981.

5013. Samkova, M. Vliv Rodinneho Prostredi na Vznik Alkoholismu:
       Pokus o Rozbor Zivotopisu Lecenych Alkoholiku. (The
       Influence of Family Environment on the Development of
       Alcoholism: Life History Analysis of Treated Alcoholics.)
       Protialkoholicky Obzor, Bratislava, 14: 177-182, 1979.

5014. Sanchez-Dirks, Ruth. Reflections on Family Violence. Alcohol
       Health and Research World, 4(1): 12-16, 1979.

5015. Sanders-Phillips, K. and Shultz, S.L. Recognizing the Suicidal
       Child: Age, Sex and Racial Differences. Clinical
       Research, 31(1): 101A, 1983.

5016. Sandmaier, Marian. Women Helping Women: Opening the Door to
       Treatment. Alcohol Health and Research World, 2(1):
       17-23, 1977.

5017. Sandmann, G. Die Einbeziehung Angehoriger in Die Therapie
       Suchtkranker. (The Inclusion of Family Members in the Therapy
       of Addicts.) Suchtgefahren, Hamburg, 20: 152-156, 1974.

5018. Sands, P.M. and Hanson, P.G. Psychotherapeutic Groups for Alcoholics
       and Relatives in an Outpatient Setting. International Journal
       of Group Psychotherapy, 21: 23-33, 1971.

5019. Sands, P.M., Hanson, P.G. and Sheldon, Robert B. Recurring Themes
       in Group Psychotherapy with Alcoholics. Psychiatric Quarterly,
       41(3): 474-482, 1967.

5020. Sanok, M. Alkoholizm Srodowiska Rodzinnego Jako Jedna z Przczyn
       Drugorocznosci i Niedostosowania Spolecznego Mlodziezy.
       (Alcoholism in the Family Environment as One of the Causes of
       Youngsters' Failure at School and Social Lag.) Problemy
       Alkoholizmu, Warsaw, 26(10): 9-10, 1979.

5021. Sans, P. and Besancon, G. L'alcoolique et la Separation. (The
       Alcoholic and Separation.) La Revue de L'alcoolisme, 21:
       236-240, 1975.

5022. Santamaria, J.N. The Social Implications of Alcoholism. Medical
       Journal of Australia, Sydney, 2(10): 523-528, 1972.

5023. Sapir, J.V. The A.A. Story in Connecticut. Connecticut Review
       on Alcoholism, 8: 25-28, 1957.

5024. Sapir, J.V. The Alcoholic as an Agency Client. Social Casework,
       38: 355-361, 1957.

5025. Sapir, J.V. When the Wife of an Alcoholic Comes for Help.
       Connecticut Review on Alcoholism, 6: 1-3, 1954.

5026. Sapp, J.S. Family's Reaction to an Alcoholic: An Application of
       Kubler-Ross's Five Stages. Alcoholism Treatment Quarterly,
       2(2): 49-60, 1985.

5027. Sarett, M., Cheek, F. and Osmond, H. Reports of Wives of Alcoholics
       of Effects of LSD-25 Treatment of Their Husbands. Archives of
       General Psychiatry, 14(2): 171-178, 1966.

5028. Sassoon, Humphrey F., Wise, James B. and Watson, Julia J. Alcoholism
       and Colour-Vision: Are There Familial Links. Lancet, London,
       7668: 367-368, 1970.

5029. Satkova, V. and Brauerova, E. Deti S Nocnim Pomocovanim Z Rodin
       Alkoholiku. (Nocturnal Enuresis in Children From Alcoholic
       Families.) Protialkoholicky Obzur, Bratislava, 14:
       133-138, 1979.

5030. Saucier, Jean-Francois and Ambert, Anne-Marie. Parental Marital
       Status and Adolescents' Health-risk Behavior. Adolescence,
       18 (70): 403-411, 1983.

5031. Sauer, Joan. The Neglected Majority. Pamphlet. Milwaukee, WI:
       DePaul Rehabilitation Hospital, 1976. (Also as: Paper
       presented to the National Council on Alcoholism, Milwaukee,
       WI, May, 1975.)

5032. Saugy, D. de L'alcoolique et sa Femme; Etude Psycho-Sociale
       et Statistique Sur Les Conditions de Leur Developpement
       Individuel et de Leur Vie En Commun. (The Alcoholic and
       His Wife; Psychosocial and Statistical Study of Their
       Individual Development and Their Life in Common.) Hygiene
       Mentale, Paris, 51: 81-128, 145-201, 1962. (Summarized
       by Deniker, P., Saugy, D. de and Ropert, M. The Alcoholic
       and His Wife. Comprehensive Psychiatry, 5: 374-383, 1964.)

5033. Saunders, D.N. Review of Another Chance -- Hope and Health for
       the Alcoholic Family by S. Wegscheider. Social Work,
       28(3): 250-251, 1983.

5034. Saunders, G.R. and Schuckit, Marc A. MMPI Scores in Young Men
       with Alcoholic Relatives and Controls. Journal of Nervous
       and Mental Disease, 169(7): 456-458, 1981.

5035. Saunders, J.B. Alcoholism: New Evidence for a Genetic
       Contribution. British Medical Journal, (Clinical Research
       ed.), London, 284(6323): 1137-1138, 1982.

5036. Saunders, J.B. Genetic and Environmental Determinants
       of Susceptibility to Alcohol-Induced Liver Disease.
       Australian Alcohol/Drug Review, 2(2): 53-64, 1983.

5037. Saunders, J.B. and Williams R. The Genetics of Alcoholism:
       Is There an Inherited Susceptibility to Alcohol-Related
       Problems? Alcohol and Alcoholism, Oxford, 18(3):
       189-217, 1983.

5038. Sausser, G.J., Fishburne, S.B. Jr. and Everett, V.D. Outpatient
       Detoxification of the Alcoholic. Journal of Family
       Practice, 14(5): 863-867, 1982.

5039. Savitz, S. Alan and Kolodner, George F. Day Hospital Treatment of
       Alcoholism. Current Psychiatric Therapies, 17: 257-263,
       1977.

5040. Sazhin, I.V. Alcohol and Heredity. Russkago Vracha, 9: 560-565,
       1910.

5041. Sazhin, I.V. Alcoholic Heredity and the Influence of Alcohol
       on the Developing Organism. Trudy Komissii po Voprosu ob
       Al'kogolizme, 9(1): 658-661, 1908.

5042. Sazhin, I.V. Heredity and Alcoholic Beverages. Trudy Komissii
       po Voprosu ob Al'kogolizme, 9(2): 1109, 1908.

5043. Sbarbori, F. and Maffezzoni, G. Le Psicosi Alcooliche
       Nell'Ospedale Psichiatrico di Castiglione delle Stiviere.
       (Alcoholic Psychoses in the Castiglione delle Stiviere
       Psychiatric Hospital.) Rassegna di Neuropsichiatria e
       Scienze Affini, Salerno, 3: 138-151, 1949.

5044. Schachter, M. Examen Comparativo de las Perturbaciones
       Neuro-Psiquicas Observadas en los Ninos de Padres
       Tuberculosos, Sifiliticos, Paludicos o Alcoholicos.
       (Comparative Analysis of Neuropsychiatric Disturbances
       in Children of Tubercular, Syphilitic, Malarial and
       Alcoholic Fathers.) Revista Espanola de Pediatria,
       Zaragoza, 6: 823-826, 1950.

5045. Schachter, M. De L'Enfant Maltraite Au "Syndrome De L'Enfant
       Battu'." A Propos De La Soi-Disant "Actualite" D'Un Vieux
       Probleme. (Maltreated Child with Battered Child Syndrome:
       The So-Called "Reality" of an Old Problem.) Praxis,
       Zagreb, 64(39): 1248-1253, 1975.

5046. Schachter, M. and Cotte, S. Maladies Sociales et Niveau Mental
       de la Descendance. Alcoolisme, Syphilis, Tuberculose,
       Paludisme. (Social Disease and Intelligence of Offspring.
       Alcoholism, Syphilis, Tuberculosis, Paludism.) Paediatria
       Practica, San Paulo, 21: 215-220, 1950.

5047. Schachter, M.G. Contribution a l'Etude Clinico-Psychologique
       des Enfants Maltraites: Sevices Physiques et Moraux.
       (Contribution to the Clincopsychological Study of
       Mistreated Children: Physical and Moral Cruelty.)
       Giornale di Psichiatria e di Neuropatologia, Ferrarra,
       80: 311-317, 1952.

5048. Schaefer, James M. Drunkenness and Culture Stress: A Holocultural
       Test. In: Cross-Cultural Approaches to the Study of Alcohol;
       An Interdisciplinary Perspective. Eds. Michael W. Everett,
       Jack O. Waddell and Dwight B. Heath. Paris: Mouton, 1976,
       pages 287-321.

5049. Schaefer, James M. Firewater Myths Revisited. Review of Findings
       and Some New Directions. Journal of Studies on Alcohol,
       42(Supplement 9): 99-117, 1981.

5050. Schaefer, James M. A Hologeistic Study of Family Structure and
       Sentiment, Supernatural Beliefs, and Drunkenness.
       Dissertation Abstracts International, 34(6): 2434B, 1973.

5051. Schaeffer, Kim Walter, Parsons, Oscar A. and Yohman, J. Robert.
       Neuropsychological Differences between Male Familial and
       Nonfamilial Alcoholics and Nonalcoholics. Alcoholism:
       Clinical and Experimental Research, 8(4): 347-351, 1984.

5052. Schaffer, Jack B. The Relationship Between Degree of Sobriety
       in Male Alcoholics and Coping Styles Used by Their Wives.
       Doctoral Dissertation. (University Microfilms Number 7810319.)
       (Also in: Dissertation Abstracts International, 39(1):
       397B, 1978.)

5053. Schaffer, Jack B. and Tyler, John D. Degree of Sobriety in Male
       Alcoholics and Coping Styles Used by Their Wives. British
       Journal of Psychiatry, London, 135: 431-437, 1979.

5054.   Schaller, Joseph. A Critical Note on the Conventional Use of
        the Birth Order Variable. *Journal of Genetic Psychology*,
        133(1): 91-96, 1978.

5055.   Scharbach. Lutte Contre L'Alcoolisme Et Prise En Charge
        Psychiatrique. (Fight Against Alcoholism and Taking
        Psychiatric Responsibility.) *Alcool Ou Sante*, Paris,
        123(2): 32-34, 1974.

5056.   Scharbach, H. and Boucard, C. Children of Alcoholic Parents.
        Statistical Study on Its Impact at the Psychopathologic
        and Criminologic Levels. *Annales Medico-Psychologiques*,
        Paris, 140(7): 783-792, 1982.

5057.   Scharffenberg, J. Alcohol and Heredity. Answer to Dr. Gyllensward.
        Tirfing, 18: 47-49, 1924.

5058.   Scharffenberg, J. Curt Gyllensward: "Contribution a La Question
        De L'heredite De L'action De L'alcool." *Internationale
        Zeitschrift gegen den Alkoholismus*, 32: 49-61, 1924.

5059.   Scharffenberg, J. Curt Gyllensward's: A Contribution to the
        Question of the Hereditary Effects of Alcohol. Lecture and
        Criticism. *Tirfing*, 17: 118-126, 1923.

5060.   Scharlieb, M. Alcohol and the Children. *Medical Temperance
        Review*, 10: 227-234, 1907.

5061.   Scharlieb, M. Alcohol and the Children of the Nation. *British
        Journal of Inebriety*, 5: 59-71, 1907.

5062.   Scharlieb, M. Alcoholism in Relation to Women and Children.
        In: *The Drink Problem of Today in Its Medico-Sociological
        Aspects*. Revised. Ed. T.N. Keylnack. London: Methuen &
        Co., Ltd., 1916, pages 128-156.

5063.   Scharlieb, M. The Relation of Alcohol and Alcoholism to Maternity
        and Child Welfare. *British Journal of Inebriety*, 17:
        91-139, 1920. (Also in: *Child*, 10: 97-107, 1919.)

5064.   Schecter, A.J. *Drug Dependence and Alcoholism. Volume 1:
        Biomedical Issues*. New York: Plenum Press, 1981.

5065.   Scheideman, J. Student Nurses Lead Family Groups. *Hospital
        and Community Psychiatry*, 22(12): 378-380, 1971.

5066.   Scheinberg, I.H. The Genetics of Hemo Chromatosis. *Archives
        of Internal Medicine*, 132(1): 126-128, 1973.

5067.   Scheller, Reinhold and Balkenhol, Petra. Einflusse des
        Elternhauses als Determinanten der Alkoholabhangigkeit
        bei Frauen. (The Influence of Family as Determinants
        of Alcohol Dependency in Women.) *Zeitschrift fur Klinische
        Psychologie-Forschung und Praxis*, 15(1): 34-36, 1986.

5068.   Scheller-Gilkey, Geraldine, Gomberg, Edith and Clay, Margaret.
        College Students and Alcohol: An Exploration of Observations.
        and Opinions. *Journal of Alcohol and Drug Education*,
        24(3): 30-41, 1979.

5069.   Scherer, Shawn E. Hard and Soft Hallucinogenic Drug Users: Their
        Drug Taking Patterns and Objectives. *The International
        Journal of the Addictions*, 8(5): 755-766, 1973.

5070.   Scherer, Shawn E. Self-Reported Parent and Child Drug Use.
        British Journal of Addiction, 68(4): 363-364, 1973.

5071. Scherer, Shawn E. and Mukherjee, B.N. "Moderate" and Hard Drug
        Users among College Students: A Study of Their Drug Use
        Patterns and Characteristics. British Journal of Addiction,
        66: 315-328, 1971.

5072. Schlesinger, S.E. Alcohol Abuse and Marital Therapy: Some Cognitive
        Components of Treatment. Cognitive Behaviorist, 5(1):
        10-13, 1983.

5073. Schmeising, E. Invisible Family: Some Considerations in Therapy
        with the Gay Victims of Alcoholism. New York: National
        Association of Gay Alcoholism Professionals, no date.

5074. Schmid, H. Review of Alcoholism in Youth - A Family Sociological
        Study on the Genesis of Alcohol Dependency in Male Youths
        by F. Stimmer. Zeitschrift Fur Klinische Psychologie und
        Psychotherapie, 29(3): 273-274, 1943.

5075. Schmidt, C.W. and Tolle, R. Familienkonstellationen von
        Psychisch Kranken; Ergebnisse und Methoden Statistischer
        Untersuchungen der Familiengrosse, Geburtenfolge und
        Geschwisterposition. (Family Constellations of Mental Patients;
        Results and Methods of Statistical Studies of Family Size,
        Birth Order and Sibling Posititon.) Fortochritte der
        Neurologie - Psychiatrie, 45: 20-52, 1977.

5076. Schmidt, F. Untersuchung Zur Erfassung Und Betreuung
        Sozialgefahrdeter Personengruppen In Einem Kries.
        (Studies on the Registration and Care of Socially
        Endangered Groups of Persons in a District.)
        Medizinische Soziologie, 19: 378-384, 1973.

5077. Schmidt, L. Importance of the Family. Paper presented at the
        Fourth World Congress for the Prevention of Alcoholism and
        Drug Dependency, Nairobi, Kenya, 1983, pages 421-423.

5078. Schmidt, L. Modell az Alkoholistak Kozepes Ideig Tarto Korhazi
        Gyogykezelesere. (A Model for Medium-Term Hospital Treatment
        of Alcoholics.) Alkohologia, Budapest, 3: 1-3, 1972.

5079. Schmidt, William E. New York Times, 16 December 1981, Column 1,
        Page 20. (Unemployment of American Indians and Increase in
        Alcoholism and Child Abuse.)

5080. Schminda, Rajmund. Zmiany Pneumoencefalograficzne W Przebiegu
        Alkoholizmu Przewleklego Wystepujacego Rodzinnie.
        (Pneumoencephalographic Changes in the Course of Chronic
        Alcoholism Occurring Historically in the Family.) Psychiatria
        Polska, Warsaw, 7(10): 583-586, 1973.

5081. Schmitz-Moormann, K. Die Behandlung Von Alkoholkranken Im Centre
        'Louis Sevestre' in La Membrolle-Sur-Choisille; Unter Besonderer
        Berucksichtigung Der Sozio-Therapie. (Treatment of Alcoholics
        in the 'Louis Sevestre' Center at La Membrolle-Sur-Choisille;
        With Special Emphasis on Social Therapy.) Suchtgefahren,
        Hamburg, 25: 180-185, 1979.

5082. Schneidemuhl, A.M. Group Psychotherapy Program at the Spring
        Grove State Hospital. Group Psychotherapy, 4: 41-55, 1951.

5083. Schneider, K. Alcoholism -- A Family Affair. Bond, 50(12):
        14-17, 1974.

5084. Schneider, Karl A. Developing a Training and Educational
        Program for Clergy and Laity for Intervention, Aftercare
        and Prevention of Alcoholism and Addiction. Paper presented
        at the National Drug Abuse Conference. Seattle, April, 1978.

5085.   Schneider, Robert J., Kojak, George Jr. and Ressdorf, Horst.
        Father-Distance and Drug Abuse in Young Men. Journal of
        Nervous and Mental Diseases, 165(4): 269-274, 1977.
        (Also in: Drugs and the Family. Ed. Thomas J. Glynn.
        Washington, D.C.: U.S. Government Printing Office, 1981.)

5086.   Schneiderman, I. Family Approaches to Prevention of Alcoholism.
        Part III: From Society to Family. CAFC News, 8(4):
        15, 22, 1981.

5087.   Schneiderman, I. Family Thinking in Prevention of Alcoholism.
        Preventine Medicine, 4: 296-309, 1975.

5088.   Schnurr, Sonya E. Alcoholic Professional. Family and Community
        Health, 2(1): 33-59, 1979.

5089.   Scholz, H., Demel, I., Fleischhacker, W., Kryspin-Exner, K.,
        Schubert, H. and Zingerle, H. Ergebnisse Einer Vergleichenden
        Halbstandardisierten Befragung von Alkohoholkranken und
        Bezugspersonen Uber Krankheitsentwicklung und Prognose.
        (Results of a Semi-Standardized Interview with Alcoholics and
        Their Relatives Concerning the Development of the Illness
        and Prognosis: A Comparative Study.) Suchtgefahren,
        Hamburg, 27: 23-32, 1981.

5090.   Scholz, H., Demel, I. and Kryspin, Exner, K. Behavior Patterns and
        Problems of Alcoholics and Relatives During the Treatment Phase.
        Therapiewoche, 32(19): 2559-2571, 1982.

5091.   Schonfield, Jacob. Differences in Smoking, Drinking, and Social
        Behavior by Race and Delinquency Status in Adolescent Males.
        Adolescence, 1(4): 367-380, 1966-67.

5092.   Schreiber, Mary Delia. The Phenomenological World of the
        Child Abused Rapist: Six Case Studies (Volumes I-II).
        Dissertation Abstracts International, 39(5): 2762A,
        1978. (University Microfilms No. 7819275.)

5093.   Schroeder, Dwight and Nasrallah, Henry A. High Alcoholism
        Rate in Patients with Essential Tremor. American
        Journal of Psychiatry, 139(11): 1471-1473, 1982.

5094.   Schroeder, Emily. Reorganization of the Family after Aftercare.
        In: Alcoholism and the Family: A Book of Readings.
        Eds. Sharon Wegscheider-Cruse and Richard W. Esterly.
        Wernersville, PA: The Caron Institute, 1985, pages 53-62.

5095.   Schroeder, Oliver C. Jr. Suicide: A Dilemma for Medicine, Law,
        and Society. Postgraduate Medicine, 53(1): 55-57, 1973.

5096.   Schucard, M.K. Parent's Network. In: Fourth World Congress
        for the Prevention of Alcoholism and Drug Dependency.
        Nairobi, Kenya: 1983, pages 457-461.

5097.   Schuckit, Marc A. Acetaldehyde and Alcoholism: Methodology.
        In: Biological/Genetic Factors in Alcoholism. National
        Institute on Alcohol Abuse and Alcoholism Research
        Monograph Series, No. 9. Eds. Victor M. Hesselbrock,
        Edward G. Shaskan and Roger E. Meyer. Washington, D.C.:
        U.S. Government Printing Office, 1983, pages 23-48.

5098.   Schuckit, Marc A. Alcoholic Men with No Alcoholic First-Degree
        Relatives. American Journal of Psychiatry, 140(4):
        439-443, 1983.

5099.   Schuckit, Marc A. Alcoholic Patients with Secondary Depression.
        American Journal of Psychiatry, 140(6): 711-714, 1983.

5100. Schuckit, Marc A. The Alcoholic Woman: A Literature Review.
      Psychiatry in Medicine, 3(1): 37-43, 1972.

5101. Schuckit, Marc A. Alcoholism and Affective Disorder: Diagnostic
      Confusion. In: Alcoholism and Affective Disorders; Clinical,
      Genetic, and Biochemical Studies. Eds. D.W. Goodwin and
      C.K. Erickson. New York: SP Medical & Scientific Books, 1979,
      pages 9-19.

5102. Schuckit, Marc A. Alcoholism and Genetics: Possible Biological
      Mediators. Biological Psychiatry, 15(3): 437-447, 1980.

5103. Schuckit, Marc A. Anxiety and Assertiveness in the Relatives of
      Alcoholics and Controls. Journal of Clinical Psychiatry,
      43(6): 238-239, 1982.

5104. Schuckit, Marc A. Behavioral Effects of Alcohol in Sons of
      Alcoholics. In: Recent Developments in Alcoholism:
      Volume 3, High-Risk Studies, Prostaglandins and Leukotrienes,
      Cardiovascular Effects, Cerebral Function in Social Drinkers.
      Ed. Marc Galanter. New York: Plenum Press, 1985, pages 11-19.

5105. Schuckit, Marc A. Biological Markers: Metabolism and Acute
      Reactions to Alcohol in Sons of Alcoholics. Pharmacology
      Biochemisty and Behavior, 13(Supplement 1): 9-16, 1980.
      (Also in: Drug and Alcohol Dependence, Lausanne, 6: 5,
      1980.)

5106. Schuckit, Marc A. Ethanol-Induced Changes in Body Sway in Men
      at High Alcoholism Risk. Archives of General Psychiatry,
      42(4): 375-379, 1985.

5107. Schuckit, Marc A. Extroversion and Neuroticism in Young Men at
      Higher or Lower Risk for Alcoholism. American Journal of
      Psychiatry, 140(9): 1223-1224, 1983.

5108. Schuckit, Marc A. Family History and Half-Sibling Research in
      Alcoholism. Annals of the New York Academy of Sciences,
      197: 121-125, 1972.

5109. Schuckit, Marc A. Genetic Factors in Alcoholism. Advances in
      Alcoholism, 1(7): 1-3, 1979.

5110. Schuckit, Marc A. Genetics and the Risk for Alcoholism. Journal of
      the American Medical Association, 254(18): 2614-2617, 1985.

5111. Schuckit, Marc A. Genetics of Alcoholism. In: Medical and Social
      Aspects of Alcohol Abuse. Eds. Boris Tabakoff, Patricia B.
      Sutker and Carrie L. Randall. New York: Plenum Press, 1983,
      pages 31-46.

5112. Schuckit, Marc A. The Importance of Family History of Affective
      Disorder in a Group of Young Men. Journal of Nervous and
      Mental Disease, 170(9): 530-535, 1982.

5113. Schuckit, Marc A. Psychology/Psychiatry and the Alcoholic.
      In: Currents in Alcoholism. Volume 4. Ed. F.A. Seixas.
      New York: Grune and Stratton, 1978, pages 1-13.

5114. Schuckit, Marc A. Prospective Markers for Alcoholism. In:
      Longitudinal Research in Alcoholism. Eds. Donald E. Goodwin,
      Katherine Teilmann VanHusen and Sarnoff A. Mednick. Boston:
      Kluwer Academic Publishers, 1984, pages 147-163.

5115. Schuckit, Marc A. Relationship between the Course of Primary
      Alcoholism in Men and Family History. Journal of Studies
      on Alcohol, 45(4): 334-338, 1984.

5116. Schuckit, Marc A. Self-Rating of Alcohol Intoxication by Young
       Men with and without Family Histories of Alcoholism.
       Journal of Studies on Alcohol, 41(3): 242-249, 1980.

5117. Schuckit, Marc A. Sexual Disturbance in the Woman Alcoholic.
       Medical Aspects of Human Sexuality, 6(9): 44, 48-49,
       53, 57, 60-61, 65 1972.

5118. Schuckit, Marc A. Studies of Men At High Risk for Future
       Alcoholism. Paper presented at an International Symposium,
       Lausanne, 1983. (Also in: Currents in Alcohol Research and
       the Prevention of Alcohol Problems. Eds. Jean-Pierre von
       Wartburg, Pierre Magnenat, Richard Muller and Sonja Wyss.
       Berne: Hans Huber Publishers, 1985, pages 45-51.

5119. Schuckit, Marc A. Studies of Populations at High Risk for
       Alcoholism. Psychiatric Developments, 3(1): 31-63, 1985.

5120. Schuckit, Marc A. A Study of Young Men with Alcoholic Close
       Relatives. American Journal of Psychiatry, 139(6):
       791-794, 1982.

5121. Schuckit, Marc A. Subjective Responses to Alcohol in Sons
       of Alcoholics and Control Subjects. Archives of General
       Psychiatry, 41(9): 879-884, 1984.

5122. Schuckit, Marc A. A Theory of Alcohol and Drug Abuse: A Genetic
       Approach. In: Theories on Drug Abuse: Selected Contemporary
       Problems. National Institute on Drug Abuse. Research
       Monograph Series, No. 30. Eds. Dan Lettieri, Mollie Sayers
       and Helen Wallenstein Pearson. Washington, D.C.: U.S.
       Government Printing Office, 1980, pages 297-302. (DHEW
       Publication No. ADM 80-967).

5123. Schuckit, Marc A. and Bernstein, L.I. Sleep Time and Drinking
       History: A Hypothesis. American Journal of Psychiatry,
       138(4): 528-530, 1981.

5124. Schuckit, Marc A. and Chiles, John A. Family History as a
       Diagnostic Aid in Two Samples of Adolescents. Journal of
       Nervous and Mental Disease, 166(3): 165-176, 1978.

5125. Schuckit, Marc A. and Duby, Jane. Alcohol-Related Flushing and
       the Risk for Alcoholism in Sons of Alcoholics. Journal of
       Clinical Psychiatry, 43(10): 415-418, 1982.

5126. Schuckit, Marc A. and Duby, Jane. Alcoholism in Women. In: The
       Biology of Alcoholism, Vol. 6, The Pathogenesis of Alcoholism:
       Psychosocial Factors. Eds. Benjamin Kissin and Henri Begleiter.
       New York: Plenum Press, 1983, pages 215-241.

5127. Schuckit, Marc A., Engstrom, D., Alpert, R. and Duby, Jane.
       Differences in Muscle-Tension Response to Ethanol in Young
       Men with and without Family Histories of Alcoholism.
       Journal of Studies on Alcohol, 42(11): 918-924, 1981.

5128. Schuckit, Marc A., Goodwin, Donald W. and Winokur, George.
       Genetic Investigation in Alcoholism -- The Half-Sibling
       Approach. In: Biological Aspects of Alcohol Consumption.
       Ed. O. Forsander. Helsinki: Finnish Foundation for Alcohol
       Studies, 1972, pages 163-167.

5129. Schuckit, Marc A., Goodwin, D.W. and Winokur, George. The Half
       Sibling Approach in a Genetic Study of Alcoholism.
       In: Life History Research in Psychopathology, 2.
       Eds. M. Roff, L.N. Robins and M. Pollack. Minneapolis:
       University of Minnesota Press, 1972, pages 120-127.

5130. Schuckit, Marc A., Goodwin, Donald W. and Winokur, George.
       A Study of Alcoholism in Half Siblings. American Journal
       of Psychiatry, 128(9): 1132-1136, 1972.

5131. Schuckit, Marc A. and Gunderson, Eric K. Alcoholism in Young
       Men. American Journal of Drug and Alcohol Abuse, 4(4):
       581-592, 1977.

5132. Schuckit, Marc A. and Gunderson, Eric K. Early Identification of
       Alcoholism in Navy Psychiatric Outpatients. Diseases of
       the Nervous System, 38(6): 397-400, 1977.

5133. Schuckit, Marc A., Gunderson, Eric K., Heckman, Norma A. and
       Kolb, D. Family History as a Predictor of Alcoholism in
       U.S. Navy Personnel. Journal of Studies on Alcohol,
       37(11): 1678-1685, 1976.

5134. Schuckit, Marc A. and Haglund, Robert M.J. An Overview of the
       Etiological Theories on Alcoholism. In: Alcoholism:
       Development, Consequences, and Interventions. Eds. Nada J.
       Estes and M. Edith Heinemann. St. Louis: The C.V. Mosby
       Company, 1977, pages 15-27.

5135. Schuckit, Marc A., Herrman, G. and Schuckit, J.J. The Importance
       of Psychiatric Illness in Newly Arrested Prisoners. Journal
       of Nervous and Mental Diseases, 165: 118-125, 1977.

5136. Schuckit, Marc A. and Morrison, C. Locus of Control in Young
       Men with Alcoholic Relatives and Controls. Journal of
       Clinical Psychiatry, 44(8): 306-307, 1983.

5137. Schuckit, Marc A. and Morrissey, Elizabeth R. Alcoholism in
       Women: Some Clinical and Social Perspectives with an
       Emphasis on Possible Subtypes. In: Alcoholism Problems
       in Women and Children. Eds. M. Greenblatt and M.A.
       Schuckit. New York: Grune and Stratton, 1976, pages 5-35.

5138. Schuckit, Marc A. and Morrissey, Elizabeth R. Psychiatric
       Problems in Women Admitted to an Alcoholic Detoxification
       Center. American Journal of Psychiatry, 136: 611-617, 1979.

5139. Schuckit, Marc A., O'Connor, Daniel T., Duby, Jane, Vega, Ralph
       and Moss, Melissa. Dopamine-Beta-Hydroxylase Activity
       Levels in Men at High Risk for Alcoholism and Controls.
       Biological Psychiatry, 16(11): 1067-1075, 1981.

5140. Schuckit, Marc A., Parker, Donal C., and Rossman, Larry R.
       Ethanol-Related Prolactin Responses and Risk for Alcoholism.
       Biological Psychiatry, 18(10): 1153-1159, 1983.

5141. Schuckit, Marc A., Pitts F.N., Jr., Reich, T., King, L.J. and
       Winokur, George. Alcoholism. I. Two Types of Alcoholism
       in Women. Archives of General Psychiatry, 20: 301-306, 1969.

5142. Schuckit, Marc A. and Rayses, Vidamantas. Ethanol Ingestion:
       Differences in Blood Acetaldehyde Concentrations in Relatives
       of Alcoholics and Controls. Science, 203(4375): 54-55, 1979.

5143. Schuckit, Marc A., Rimmer, J. and Winokur, George. Alcoholism:
       The Influence of Parental Illness. British Journal of
       Psychiatry, London, 119: 663-665, 1971.

5144. Schuckit, Marc A., Rimmer, J., Reich, T. and Winokur, George.
       The Bender Alcoholic. British Journal of Psychiatry,
       London, 119: 183-184, 1971.

5145. Schuckit, Marc A., Shaskan, E., Duby, Jane, Vega, R. and Moss, M.
        Platelet Monoamine Oxidase Activity in Relatives of
        Alcoholics. Preliminary Study with Matched Control Subjects.
        Archives of General Psychiatry, 39(2): 137-140, 1982.

5146. Schuckit, Marc A. and Winokur, George. Alcoholic Hallucinosis
        and Schizophrenia: A Negative Study. British Journal of
        Psychiatry: The Journal of Mental Science, London,
        119(552): 549-550, 1971.

5147. Schuckit, Marc A. and Winokur, George. A Short Term Follow Up
        of Women Alcoholics. Diseases of the Nervous System,
        33(10): 672-678, 1972.

5148. Schulsinger, F. Biological Psychopathology. Annual Review of
        Psychology, 31: 583-606, 1980.

5149. Schulte, Karen and Blume, Shelia B. A Day Treatment Center for
        Alcoholic Women. Health & Social Work, 4(4): 222-231, 1979.

5150. Schultz, D. Alcoholism: All In the Family. Science Digest,
        85: 79, 1979.

5151. Schultz, Harriet Taran. Childhood Depression: A Cognitive,
        Behavioral and Family Perspective. Dissertation Abstracts
        International, 44(3): 926B, 1982.

5152. Schultz, S. Social and Psychological Correlates of Intergenerational
        Acceptance in Male Alcoholism. Ed.D. Dissertation. (University
        Microfilms No. 69-16,792.) New York: Columbia University, 1969.

5153. Schulz, Wolfgang. Alcoholism as a Learned Behavior. In: Currents
        in Alcohol Research and the Prevention of Alcohol Problems.
        Eds. Jean-Pierre von Wartburg, Pierre Magnenat, Richard Muller
        and Sonja Wyss. Berne: Hans Huber Publishers, 1985, pages 57-62.

5154. Schut, J. Philadelphia's Community Based Drug Abuse Program.
        Broader Medical and Social Concepts. International Journal
        of Clinical Pharmacology and Biopharmacy, Munich, 11(4):
        286-329, 1975.

5155. Schwam, Jeffrey S., Stein, Jack I. and Winn, Frank J. A Drug-
        Abuse Program at a U.S. Army Post. Comprehensive
        Psychiatry, 17(1): 125-133, 1976.

5156. Schwartzman, John. Alcoholics Anonymous and the Family: A Systemic
        Perspective. American Journal of Drug and Alcohol Abuse,
        11(1-2): 69-89, 1985.

5157. Schwartzman, John. Under the Influence: The Alcoholic and His
        Family. Drug Forum, 6(2): 117-185, 1977.

5158. Schwitters, Sylvia Y., Johnson, Ronald C., Johnson, Steven B. and
        Ahern, Frank M. Familial Resemblances in Flushing Following
        Alcohol Use. Behavior Genetics, 12(3): 349-352, 1982.

5159. Schwitters, Sylvia Y., Johnson, R.C., McClearn, G.E. and Wilson, J.R.
        Alcohol Use and the Flushing Response in Different Racial-Ethnic
        Groups. Journal of Studies on Alcohol, 43: 1259-1262, 1982.

5160. Sclare, A.B. The Problem of Self-Poisoning. Scottish Medical
        Journal, Glasgow, 19(6): 249-250, 1974.

5161. Sclare, A. Balfour. Drinking Habits in Scotland. International
        Journal of Offender Therapy and Comparative Criminology,
        London, 19(3): 241-249, 1975.

5162. Sclare, A. Balfour. The Female Alcoholic. British Journal of
        the Addictions, 65(2): 99-107, 1970.

5163. Sclare, A. Balfour. Treatment of Alcoholism in Scotland.
       International Journal of Offender Therapy and Comparative
       Criminology, 21(2): 153-165, 1977.

5164. Scott, E.M. A Suggested Treatment Plan for the Hostile Alcoholic.
       International Journal of Group Psychotherapy, 13: 93-100,
       1963.

5165. Scott, Edward M. Alcoholic Group: Formation and Beginnings.
       Group Process, 7: 95-116, 1976.

5166. Scott, Edward M. Disturbed Adolescents. International Journal
       of Offender Therapy and Comparative Criminology, 24(3):
       201-212, 1980.

5167. Scott, Edward M. Joint and Group Treatment for Married Alcoholics
       and Their Spouses. Psychological Reports, 5: 725-728, 1959.

5168. Scott, Edward M. Struggles in an Alcoholic Family. Springfield,
       Il: Charles C. Thomas, 1970. (Also in: Journal of Alcoholism,
       7(3): 110, 1972.)

5169. Scott, Edward M., Keener, Jack and Manaugh, Thomas S. Treatment of
       Alcoholism in an Out-Patient Clinic in Oregon. International
       Journal of Offender Therapy & Comparative Criminology, 21(2):
       141-152, 1977.

5170. Scott, Edward M. and Manaugh, Thomas S. Territorial Struggles in the
       Marriages of Alcoholics. Journal of Marriage and the Family
       Counseling, 2(4): 341-346, 1976.

5171. Scott, Edward M. and Scott, Kathy L. Healthy Families.
       International Journal of Offender Therapy and Comparative
       Criminology, 27(1): 71-78, 1983.

5172. Scott, P.D. Battered Wives. British Journal of Psychiatry:
       The Journal of Mental Sciences, London, 125: 433-441, 1974.

5173. Scott, Samuel M. and Van Deusen, John M. Detoxification at Home:
       A Family Approach. In: The Family Therapy of Drug Abuse
       and Addiction. Eds. M. Duncan Stanton and Thomas C. Todd.
       New York: The Guilford Press, 1983, pages 310-334.

5174. Scriver, C.R. Window Panes of Eternity. Health, Disease, and
       Inherited Risk. Yale Journal of Biology and Medicine,
       55(5-6): 487-513, 1982.

5175. Scutt, J.A. Alcoholic Imperative: A Sexist Rationalization of
       Rape and Domestic Violence. Paper presented at the First
       Pan-Pacific Conference on Drugs and Alcohol, Canberra,
       Australia, 1980, pages 86-94.

5176. Seabaugh, Michael O.L. The Vulnerable Self of the Adult Child
       of an Alcoholic: A Phenomenologically Derived Theory.
       Dissertation Abstracts International, 45(2): 686B, 1984.

5177. Seabrooke, B. Home is Where They Take You In. New York:
       William Morrow, 1980.

5178. Seale, F.E. Starlite Village Hospital: Evolution of a Texas
       Hill Country Hospital. In: Alcoholism Rehabilitation:
       Methods and Experiences of Private Rehabilitation Centers.
       Ed. Vincent Groupe. New Brunswick, NJ: Rutgers University
       Center of Alcohol Studies, 1978, pages 106-113.

5179. Seaman, F.J. Problem Drinking among American Railroad Workers.
       In: Alcohol Problems in Employment. Eds. B.D. Hore and
       M.A. Plant. London: Croom Helm, 1981, pages 118-128.

5180. Searle, Maureen. Obsessive-Compulsive Behaviour in American
        Medicine. Social Science & Medicine, 15E(3): 185-193, 1981.

5181. Sedlacek, D.A. Childhood: Setting the Stage for Addiction.
        In: Adolescent Substance Abuse: A Guide to Prevention
        and Treatment. Eds. R. Isralowitz and M. Singer.
        New York: Haworth Press, 1983, pages 23-34.

5182. Sedlackova, J. and Widermannova, L. The Influence of the Alcoholic
        Family Environment of the Neuropsychic Development of the Child.
        Ceskoslovenska Psychiatrie, Praha, 52: 272-277, 1956.

5183. Sedmak, T. and Dordevic-Bankovic, V. Grupna I Transferna
        Zavisnost Lecenih Alkoholicara. (Group and Transference
        Dependency of Treated Alcoholics.) Psihijatrija Danas,
        10: 317-339, 1978.

5184. Sedmak, T., Gacic, Branko and Kacarevic, Radmila. Ucesce Socijalne
        Grupe U Lecenju Alkoholicara. (Participation of the Social
        Group in the Treatment of Alcoholics.) Alkoholizam,
        Beograd, 19(3-4): 45-53, 1979.

5185. Sedmak, T., Kastel, Pavle, Gacic, Branko and Grcic, Radmila.
        Treatment and Dependency of Alcoholics. Socijalna
        Psihijatrija, 7(4): 415-427, 1979.

5186. Seedat, Y.K., Seedat, M.A. and Hackland, D.B.T. Bio Social
        Factors and Hypertension in Urban and Rural Zulus.
        South African Medical Journal, Cape Town, 61(26):
        999-1002, 1982.

5187. Seelye, E.E. Review of Families, Alcoholism and Therapy, by
        Barnard, CP. American Journal of Psychotherapy, 36(4):
        570-571, 1982.

5188. Segal, B.M. The Crisis of the Family System and Alcoholism.
        Paper presented at the 13th Annual Medical-Scientific
        Conference of the National Alcoholism Forum on Progress in
        Alcoholism Research and Treatment, Washington, D.C., April,
        1982. (Also as: Alcoholism: Clinical and Experimental
        Research, 6(1): 153, 1982.)

5189. Segal, B.M. Rol' Nevrozov V Genese Alkogolizma; Analiz
        Psikhodinamicheskikn Kontseptsii. (The Role of
        Neuroses in the Genesis of Alcoholism; Analysis of
        Psychodynamic Conceptions.) Zhurnal Neuropatologii I
        Psikhiatrii Imeni S.S. Korsakova, 67: 246-253, 1967.

5190. Segal, Bernard. Family Background, Personality Characteristics
        and Use of Drugs, Alcohol or Non-Use of Either among College
        Students. In: Papers Presented at the 20th International
        Institute on the Prevention and Treatment of Alcoholism,
        Manchester, England. Ed. B. Hore. Lausanne: International
        Council on Alcohol and Addiction, 1974, pages 165-170.

5191. Seidenberg, R. Corporate Wives, Corporate Casualties: Why Women
        Are Challenging American Business. New York: AMACOM, 1973.

5192. Seidenberg, Robert. Moving on to What? Mental Hygiene,
        59(1): 6-11, 1975.

5193. Seidenschnur, P.-P.T. Exploring the Relationship of Alcohol
        Abuse and Adolescent Abuse/Neglect. Paper presented at the
        Fourth National Conference on Child Abuse and Neglect,
        Los Angeles, October, 1979, pages 234-235.

5194. Seidler, Gary Alcoholism or Not, Its Still Battering: Helping
        Abused Families. Focus on Alcohol and Drug Issues, 4(3):
        21-22, 1981.

5195. Seidler, Gary. Day Care Pays Off: Keeping Family Intact a Key
          to Women's Recovery. Focus on Alcohol and Drug Issues,
          4(3): 12-13, 1981.

5196. Seidler, Gary. Solve Drug Problems on Home Turf. Don't Look
          to Governments to Do the Job. Focus on Alcohol and Drug
          Issues, 2(5): 8, 1979.

5197. Seifert, M.H., Jr. Alcohol Treatment Center; Problems and
          Recommendations. Minnesota Medicine, 56: 803-804, 1973.

5198. Seifert, M.H., Jr. Treating Alcoholism, A Family Disease.
          American Family Physician, 8:(4), 150-153, 1973.

5199. Seilhame, R., Blane, H., McGinnis, C., Rubin, R., Schweibi., J.
          and Leonard, K. Neuropsychological Performance in Male-
          Adult Children of Alcoholics. Alcoholism: Clinical and
          Experimental Research, 10(1): 100, 1986.

5200. Seixas, Frank A. Better Treatment of Alcoholism. Annals of
          Internal Medicine, 81: 396-398, 1974.

5201. Seixas, Frank A. The Course of Alcoholism. In: Alcoholism:
          Development, Consequences, and Interventions. Eds. Nada J.
          Estes and M. Edith Heinemann. St. Louis: The C.V. Mosby
          Company, 1977, pages 59-66.

5202. Seixas, Frank A., Cardoret, Remi and Eggleston, Suzie (Eds.) The
          Person with Alcoholism. Annals of the New York Academy of
          Sciences, 223: 1974.

5203. Seixas, Frank A., Omenn, G.S., Burk, E.D. and Eggleston, S. (Eds.)
          Nature and Nurture in Alcoholism. Annals of the New York
          Academy of Sciences, 197: 1972.

5204. Seixas, Judith. Children from Alcoholic Families. In:
          Alcoholism: Development, Consequences and Interventions.
          Eds. Nada J. Estes and M. Edith Heinemann. St. Louis:
          The C.V. Mosby Company, 1977, pages 153-161.

5205. Seixas, Judith E. Alcohol: What It Is, What It Does.
          New York: Greenwillow Books, 1977.

5206. Seixas, Judith S. Living with a Parent Who Drinks Too Much.
          New York: Greenwillow Books, 1979.

5207. Seixas, Judith S. and Youcha, Geraldine. Children of Alcoholism:
          A Survivor's Manual. New York: Crown Publishers, 1985.

5208. Selby, James W., Calhoun, Lawrence G., Bass, Anthony E. and
          Floyd, W. Russell. Sex Differences among Clients of an
          Emergency Care Unit for Alcoholism. Journal of Clinical
          Psychology, 34(2): 567-568, 1978.

5209. Seldin, Nathan E. The Family of the Addict A Review of the
          Literature. International Journal of the Addictions,
          7(1): 97-107, 1972.

5210. Selective News Summaries. Newsletter. Rockville, MD: National
          Institute on Alcohol Abuse and Alcoholism, January 31, 1980.

5211. Selective News Summaries. Newsletter. Rockville, MD: National
          Institute on Alcohol Abuse and Alcoholism, SNS Number 10,
          February 23, 1979.

5212. Selective News Summaries. Newsletter. Rockville, MD: National
          Institute on Alcohol Abuse and Alcoholism, SNS Number 6,
          December 16, 1978.

5213. Selig, Andrew L. Program Planning, Evaluation, and the Problem
       of Alcoholism. American Journal of Public Health, 65(1):
       72-75, 1975.

5214. Selzer, Melvin L. The Michigan Alcoholism Screening Test: The
       Quest for a New Diagnostic Instrument. In: Alcoholism:
       Introduction to Theory and Treatment. Ed. David A. Ward.
       Dubuque, IA: Kendall/Hunt, 1980, pages 242-251.

5215. Selzer, Melvin L., Vinokur, Amiram, Wilson, Timothy D. A Psycho
       Social Comparison of Drunken Drivers and Alcoholics.
       Journal of Studies on Alcohol, 38(7): 1294-1312, 1977.

5216. Senseman, Laurence A. Alcohol and Traffic Safety: Measures
       Required to Awaken Apathetic Public to Critical Problem.
       Rhode Island Medical Journal, 56(4): 158-159, 167, 1973.

5217. Senseman, Laurence A. Housewife's Secret Illness: How to
       Recognize the Female Alcoholic. Rhode Island Medical
       Journal, 49: 40-42, 1966.

5218. Sentilhes, N. and Brule, C. Rencontre Avec Les Parents de
       Toxicomanes. (Meeting with Parents of an Addict.) Paper
       presented at the 6th International Institute on the
       Prevention & Treatment of Drug Dependence, Hamburg,
       June-July, 1976, pages 228-239.

5219. Seratlic, B. Neki Socio-Medicinski Aspekti Alkoholizma Kod
       Crnogoraca U SAP Vojvodini. (Some Socio-Medical Aspects
       of Alcoholism in Montenegrins in the Socialistic Autonomous
       Region of Vojvodina.) Alkoholizam, Beograd, 18(3-4):
       69-75, 1978.

5220. Seratlic, B. and Dragnic, P. Motivi Za Lecenje Alkoholicara I
       Duzina Trajanja Apstinencije U Odnosu Na Pojedine Od Tih
       Motive. (Treatment Motives of Alcoholics and the Duration
       of Abstinence in Relation to Some of These Motives.)
       Alkoholizam, Beograd, 17(1-2): 85-91, 1977.

5221. Serban, George. Stress in Schizophrenics and Normals. British
       Journal of Psychiatry, 126: 397-407, 1975.

5222. Server, Judith Cohen and Janzen, Curtis. Contraindications
       to Reconstitution of Sexually Abusive Families. Child
       Welfare, 61(5): 279-288, 1982.

5223. Services for Children of Alcoholics. Symposium held in September,
       1979 at Silver Spring, MD. U.S. National Institute on Alcohol
       Abuse and Alcoholism. Research Monograph No. 4. Washington,
       D.C.: U.S. Government Printing Office, 1981. (DHHS Publication
       No. 81-1007).

5224. Sessions, Percy M. Problem of Relating Therapeutically to the
       Addict's Family. In: University of Utah School of
       Alcoholism and Other Drug Dependencies. Washington, D.C.:
       Rehabilitation Center for Alcoholics, 1971.

5225. Sethi, B.B., Gupta, S.C., Sinha, P.K. and Gupta, O.P. Pattern
       of Crime, Alcoholism and Parental Deprivation. Indian
       Journal of Psychiatry, Madura, 13(4): 275-281, 1971.

5226. Sex, Booze and Marriage. Recovery Newsletter in Alcoholism
       The National Magazine, 5(5): R8, 1985.

5227. Sexton, L.D. Social and Economic Impact of the Colonial Intro-
       duction of Alcohol into Highland Papua New Guinea. Paper
       presented at the Conference of the Social History of Alcohol:
       Drinking and Culture in Modern Society, Berkeley, January, 1984.

5228. Sexuality and Substance Abuse. In: United Appeal Agency.
       Cincinnati: Social Health Association, 1978.

5229. Shadravan, F. Fresh Look at the Myth of Alcohol Adaption in
       Drosophila Melanogaster. Dissertation Abstracts Inter-
       national, 44(6): 1719-1720B, 1983.

5230. Shain, Martin. Cannabis, Alcohol, and the Family. In: Sociological
       Aspects of Drug Dependence. Ed. C. Winick. Cleveland:
       Chemical Rubber Company Press, 1974, pages 133-153.

5231. Shain, Martin, Riddell, William and Kilty, Heather. Influence,
       Choice and Drugs. Lexington, MA: Lexington Books, 1977.

5232. Shain, Martin, Suurvali, Helen and Kilty, Heather Lee.
       The Parent Communication Project; A Longitudinal Study
       of the Effects of Parenting Skills on Children's Use of
       Alcohol. Toronto: Addiction Research Foundation, 1980.

5233. Shainess, Natalie. Psychological Aspects of Wife Battering.
       In: Battered Women. Ed. M. Roy. New York: Van Nostrand
       Reinhold, 1977, pages 111-119.

5234. Shanahan, Patricia Mayer. Older Alcoholics: Professional, Family
       Education Programs Aid Treatment. Hospital Progress,
       65(2): 58-63, 1984.

5235. Shankle, R.J. Suicide, Divorce, and Alcoholism among Dentists,
       Fact or Myth? North Carolina Dental Journal, 60(2):
       12-15, 1977.

5236. Shanlkin, M. Choices for the Future: Alcohol and Pregnancy.
       Leaflet. Madison, WI: Clearinghouse for Alcohol and
       Other Drug Information, 1979.

5237. Shannon, Kelly. The Legacy of Andy: A Multi-Dimensional
       Examination of a Disturbed Appalachian Family. Doctoral
       Dissertation. (University Microfilms No. 8004365). (Also in:
       Dissertation Abstracts International, 40(9): 4509B, 1980.)

5238. Shapiro, Abby and Gross, Susan. Preliminary Follow-Up Evaluation
       of Participants in the Phoenix School: A Pilot Drug Program.
       Rockville, MD: Department of Educational Accountability,
       Montgomery County Public Schools, 1981. (Eric Document Number
       ED 223942.)

5239. Shapiro, D. and Goldstein, I.B. Biobehavioral Perspectives
       on Hypertension. Journal of Consulting and Clinical
       Psychology, 50(6): 841-858, 1982.

5240. Shapiro, Rodney, J. Clinical Approaches to Family Violence:
       V. Alcohol and Family Violence. Family Therapy
       Collections, 3: 69-89, 1982.

5241. Shapiro, Rodney, J. Family Therapy Approach to Alcoholism.
       Journal of Marriage and Family Counseling, 3(4): 71-78,
       1977.

5242. Shaskan, Edward G. Assessment of Platelet Monoamine Oxidase
       Activity as a Risk Factor in Epidemiologic Research.
       In: Biological/Genetic Factors in Alcoholism. (National
       Institute on Alcohol Abuse and Alcoholism Research Monograph
       Series No. 9.) Eds. Victor M. Hesselbrock, Edward G. Shaskan
       and Roger E. Meyer. Washington, D.C.: U.S. Government
       Printing Office, 1983, pages 101-118.

5243. Shaw, Ian A. The Treatment of Alcoholism with Tetraethylthiuram
       Disulfied in a State Mental Hospital. Quarterly Journal of
       Studies on Alcohol, 12: 576-586, 1951.

5244.   Shaw, K. and Fougere, D. Case studies: A Female Alcoholic
        in the Work Place. In: Human Services in Industry. Ed.
        D.A. Masi. Baltimore: Sheppard Pratt Div., Professional
        and Public Ed., 1982, pages 188-192.

5245.   Shaw, S. Social Influences on the Use of Alcohol in the Family.
        In: Alcohol and the Family. Eds. J. Orford and J. Harwin.
        New York: St. Martin's Press, 1982, pages 56-72.

5246.   Shaw, Spencer, Stimmel, Barry and Lieber, Charles S. Plasma
        Alpha-Amino-n-Butyric Acid/Leucine; A Biochemical Marker
        of Alcohol Consumption. Application for the Detection and
        Assessment of Alcoholism. In: Currents in Alcoholism,
        Volume 1. Ed. Frank A. Seixas. New York: Grune and
        Stratton, 1977, pages 17-32.

5247.   Shaw, T.C. Alcoholism and Eugenics. British Journal of
        Inebriety, 13: 81-83, 1915.

5248.   Shaywitz, S.E., Cohen, D.J. and Shaywitz, B.A. Behavior and
        Learning Difficulties in Children of Normal Intelligence
        Born to Alcoholic Mothers. Journal of Pediatrics, 96(6):
        978-982, 1980.

5249.   Shenkman, M. The Family Physician and Alcoholism. Maryland
        State Medical Journal, 17(7): 87-88, 1968.

5250.   Shepherd, D.M. and Barraclough, B.M. The Aftermath of Parental
        Suicide for Children. The British Journal of Psychiatry,
        129: 267-276, 1976.

5251.   Shepherd, Ernest A. Alcoholism. A Family Guide to Understanding
        the Illness and What to Do About it. New Hamsphire State
        Department of Health, 1950.

5252.   Sher, Kenneth J. and Descutner, Carol. Reports of Paternal
        Alcoholism: Reliability Across Siblings. Addictive
        Behaviors, 11(1): 25-30, 1986.

5253.   Sher, Kenneth J. and McCrady, B.S. Alcoholism Treatment Approaches:
        Patient Variables: Treatment Variables. In: Medical and
        Social Aspects of Alcohol Abuse. Eds. Boris Tabakoff,
        Patricia B. Sutker and Carrie L. Randall. New York:
        Plenum Press, 1983, pages 309-373.

5254.   Sher, Kenneth J. and McCrady, Barbara S. The MacAndrew
        Alcoholism Scale: Severity of Alcohol Abuse and Parental
        Alcoholism. Addictive Behaviors, Oxford, 9: 99-102, 1984.

5255.   Sherbini, I.H. Islam and the Alcohol Question. Paper presented
        at the Fourth World Congress for the Prevention of Alcoholism
        and Drug Dependency, Nairobi, August-September, 1982, pages
        161-165.

5256.   Sherburne, Zoa. Jennifer. New York: William Morow and Company,
        1959.

5257.   Sherfey, M.J. Psychopathology and Character Structure in Chronic
        Alcoholism. In: Etiology of Chronic Alcoholism. Ed. O.
        Diethelm. Springfield, IL: Charles C. Thomas, 1955, pages
        16-42.

5258.   Sherlock, S. Current Problems in Alcoholic Liver Disease.
        Alcohol and Alcoholism, Oxford, 18(2): 99-118, 1983.

5259.   Sherlock, Sheila. Nutrition: The Changing Scene: Nutrition
        and the Alcoholic. The Lancet, 1(8374): 436-439, 1984.

5260. Sherman, Scott L. Drug Abuse Rehabilitation: A Participant Observer Description of the Family A Self Help Program. Drug Forum, 1(4): 335-355, 1972.

5261. Sherouse, D.L. Professional's Handbook on Geriatric Alcoholism. Springfield, IL: Charles C. Thomas, 1983.

5262. Sherwin, D. and Mead, B. Delirium Tremens in a Nine-Year-Old Child. American Journal of Psychiatry, 132: 1210-1212, 1975.

5263. Shibata, Y., Masuda, T. and Aoki, I. An Investigation on Women Alcoholic Inpatients. Japanese Journal of Studies on Alcohol, Kyoto, 13: 123-134, 1978.

5264. Shields, J. Genetics and Alcoholism. In: Alcoholism. New Knowledge and New Responses. Eds. G. Edwards and M. Grant. London: Croom Helm, 1977, Pages 117-135.

5265. Shields, J. Some Recent Developments in Psychiatric Genetics. Archiv fur Psychiatrie and Nervenkrankheiten, 220(4): 347-360, 1976.

5266. Shields, P.K. Relationship Between Problem Identification Consensus and Marital Adjustment in Alcohol-Complicated Marriages. Dissertation Abstracts International, 45(11): 3312A, 1985.

5267. Shields, Patrick Edward. Marital Interaction, Drinking Behavior, and Life Adjustment Following Treatment in Alcoholism. Doctoral Dissertation. (University Microfilms No. 76-24459.) Chicago: Loyola University, 1976.

5268. Shilling, Sharon and Lalich, Nina R. Maternal Occupation and Industry and the Pregnancy Outcome of U.S. Married Women, 1980. Public Health Reports, 99(2): 152-161, 1984.

5269. Shimizu, T., Kawahara, R., Amemiya, T., Shinjo, T., Omori, Y. and Hirata, Y. Gross Hyper Tri Glyceridemia Induced by Alcohol Intake in a Female Insulin Independent Diabetic Patient with Familial Hyper Lipo Proteinemia Who Type IIB. Journal of the Japan Diabetic Society, Tonyobo, 23(12): 1131-1136, 1981.

5270. Shipp, T.J. Helping the Alcoholic and His Family. Philadelphia: Fortress Press, 1966.

5271. Shirley, K. Natural, Nonconfrontive Process of Guided Intervention through the Family or Close Associate of the Alcohol Individual. Paper presented at the 1979 National Alcoholism Forum of the National Council on Alcoholism, Washington, D.C., April.

5272. Shirly, C.E. and Shirley, K. Process of Recovery for the Alcoholic and the Family. New York: National Council on Alcoholism, New York City Affiliate, 1981.

5273. Shishkov, A.T. and Peneva, M. Alkokhol I Prest"pnost Pri Nep"Lnoletnite. (Alcohol and Juvenile Delinquency.) Nevrologiya, Psikhiatriya I Nevrokhirurgiya, Sofia, 14(2): 116-120, 1975.

5274. Shoham, S. Giora, Rahav, G., Esformes Y., Markovski, R., Chard, F. and Kaplinsky, N. Some Parameters of the Use of Alcohol by Israeli Youth and Its Relationship to Their Involvement with Cannabis and Tobacco. Drug and Alcohol Dependence, Lausanne, 6(5): 263-272, 1981.

5275. Shontz, F.C. and Spotts, J.V. Psychopathology and Chronic Drug Use: A Methodological Paradigm. International Journal of the Addictions, 18(5): 633-680, 1983.

5276. Shore, E.R. Alcohol Consumption Rates among Managers and
       Professionals. Journal of Studies on Alcohol, 46(2):
       153-156, 1985.

5277. Shore, J.H. American Indian Suicide -- Fact and Fantasy.
       Psychiatry, 38(1): 87-91, 1975.

5278. Shore, James H. The Impaired Physician. Four Years After
       Probation. Journal of the American Medical Association,
       248(23): 3127-3130, 1982.

5279. Shore, James H. Suicide and Suicide Attempts Among American
       Indians of the Pacific Northwest. The International
       Journal of Social Psychiatry, London, 18(2): 91-96, 1972.

5280. Shore, James H. and Nicholls, William M. Indian Children and
       Tribal Group Homes: New Interpretations of the Whipper Man.
       American Journal of Psychiatry, 132(4): 454-456, 1975.

5281. Shortt, S.E. (Ed.) Psychiatric Illness in Physicians.
       Springfield, IL: Charles C. Thomas, 1982.

5282. Shortt, S.E. Psychiatric Illness in Physicians. Canadian
       Medical Association Journal, Ottawa, 121(3): 283-288, 1979.

5283. Shostak, Arthur B. Psychiatry Issues and Organized Labor.
       Journal of Occupational Medicine, 21(1): 48-51, 1979.

5284. Shruygin, G.I. Ob Osobennostyakh Psikhicheskogo Razvitiya Detei
       ot Materei, Stradayushchikh Khronicheskim Alkogolizmom.
       (Characteristics of the Mental Development of Children of
       Alcoholic Mothers.) Pediatriya, Moscow, 53: 71-73, 1974.

5285. Shruygin, G.I. Concerning a Psychogenic Pathological Personality
       Formation in Children and Adolescents in Families with Fathers
       Suffering from Alcoholism. Zhurnal Nervopatologii i Psikhiatrii
       im S.S. Korsakova, Moscow, 78: 1566-1569, 1978. (Also in:
       Pediatrics and Pediatric Surgery, 41(1142), 1979.)

5286. Shubin, Seymour. Where the Violent Go for Help. SK&F Psychiatric
       Reporter, 45: 22-24, 1969.

5287. Shulamith, L., Straussner, A., Weinstein, D.L. and Hernandez, R.
       Effects of Alcoholism on the Family System. Health and
       Social Work, 4(4): 111-127, 1979.

5288. Shulman, A.J. Alcohol Addiction. University of Toronto Medical
       Journal, 28: 219-229, 1951.

5289. Shulman, G.D. Residential Family Treatment -- Why Should Insurers
       Reimburse? Paper presented at the National Council on
       Alcoholism Forum, Houston, April, 1983.

5290. Shulman, G.D. Selection of Alcoholism Treatment for Clients of
       an Employee Assistance Program. Paper presented at the 8th
       Annual Meeting of the Association of Labor Management
       Administrators and Consultants on Alcoholism. Inc., Detroit,
       October, 1979. (Also in: ALMACA, compiled by Marcia
       Moran-Sackett. Arlington, VA: ALMACA, 1980, pages 381-415.)

5291. Shulman, Gerald D. and O'Connor, Robert D. The Rehabilitation
       of the Alcoholic. In: Alcoholism: A Practical Treatment
       Guide. Eds. Stanley E. Gitglow and Herbert S. Peyser.
       New York: Grune and Stratton, 1980, pages 103-129.

5292. Shumkov, G. Hereditary Alcoholic Toxicosis in Children.
       Permskii Meditsinskii Zhurnal, Perm, 7: 90-98, 1929.

5293. Shuval, R. and Krasilowsky, D. A Study of Hospitalized Male
       Alcoholics. Israel Annals of Psychiatry and Related
       Disciplines, 1: 277-292, 1964.

5294. Siassi, Irauj and Alston, Dominick C. Methadone Maintenance
       and the Problem with Alcohol. The American Journal of Drug
       and Alcohol Abuse, 3(2): 267-277, 1976.

5295. Sibert, J.R. Hereditary Pancreatitis in England and Wales
       Journal of Medical Genetics, London, 15(3): 189-201, 1978.

5296. Siddons, R. Treatment Profiles of Concerned Others: Enhancing
       Family Therapy Effectiveness. Focus on Family and
       Chemical Dependency, 8(2): 5-6, 43, 1985.

5297. Sieber, Martin F. Social Background, Attitudes and Personality in
       a Three-Year Follow-Up Study of Alcohol Consumers. Drug and
       Alcohol Dependence, 4(5): 407-417, 1979.

5298. Sieck, Patricia. New Life. In: Having Been There.
       Ed. A. Luks. New York: Charles Scribner's Sons, 1979.

5299. Siegal, Harvey A. and Faryna, Alice F. Strategies for Early
       Intervention with the Alcoholic Patients. Urban Health,
       9(9): 42-45, 1980.

5300. Siegelman, Marvin. Family Background of Alcoholics: Some
       Research Considerations. Annals of the New York Academy
       of Science, 197: 226-229, 1972.

5301. Siegler, Miriam, Osmond, Humphry and Newell, Stephens. Models
       of Alcoholism. Quarterly Journal of Studies on Alcohol,
       29: 571-591, 1968.

5302. Sierra-Terradez, E. Estudio Observacional Sobre Grupos De
       Discusion En Enfermos Alcoholicos. (Observational Study
       of Group Therapy in the Treatment of Alcoholics.)
       Drogalcohol, 3: 193-203, 1978.

5303. Sights, Judith Randolph. Parental Antecedents of Bulimia.
       Dissertation Abstracts International, 43(7): 2357B, 1982.

5304. Sigvardsson, S., von Knorrins, A.L., Bohman, M. and Cloninger,
       C.R. Adoption Study of Somatization Disorders: I. The
       Relationship of Somatization of Psychiatric Disability.
       Archives of General Psychiatry, 41(9): 853-59, 1984.

5305. Sikic, Branimi Ivan, Walker, Roger Dale and Peterson, Dennis R.
       An Evaluation of a Program for the Treatment of Alcoholism
       in Croatia. International Journal of Social Psychiatry,
       18(3): 171-182, 1972.

5306. Sikorska-Godwod, C. O Niektorych Zespolach Schizofrenopodobnych
       W Przebiegu Alkoholizmu Przewleklego Wczesnego. (On Some
       Schizophrenialike Syndromes in Early Chronic Alcoholism.)
       Neurologia, Neurochirurgia I Psychiatria Polska, Warsaw,
       6: 923-932, 1956.

5307. Sila, A. Psihopatoloska Obiljezja Pocinitelja Krivicnog Djela
       Ubojstva. (Psychopathologic Traits of Homicide Perpetrators.)
       Socijalna Psihijatrija, Zagreb, 5: 3-87, 1977.

5308. Silber, A. An Addendum to the Technique of Psychotherapy
       with Alcoholics. Journal of Nervous and Mental Disease,
       150(6): 423-437, 1970.

5309. Silber, A. Rationale for the Technique of Psychotherapy with
       Alcoholics. International Journal of Psychoanalytic
       Psychotherapy, 3(1): 28-47, 1974.

5310. Silber, Austin. The Alcohol Induced Hypnoid State and Its
        Analytic Corollary. International Journal of Psycho-
        analytic Psychotherapy, 6: 253-267, 1977.

5311. Silber, Austin. The Contribution of Psychoanalysis to the
        Treatment of Alcoholism. In: Alcoholism and Clinical
        Psychiatry. Ed. Joel Solomon. New York: Plenum Medical
        Book Company, 1982, pages 195-211.

5312. Silberberg, C.G. An Investigation of Family Interaction Patterns:
        Similarities and Differences Among Families with Adolescents
        Designated Normal, Emotionally Disturbed or Drug Abusing.
        Doctoral Dissertation. (University Microfilms No. 77-6537.)
        Bryn Mawr, PA: Bryn Mawr College, 1976.

5313. Silbert, M.H., Pines, A.M. and Lynch, T. Substance Abuse and
        Prostitution. Journal of Psychoactive Drugs, 14(3):
        193-198, 1982.

5314. Silfverskiold, B. Vitamintillsats Till Spritdrycker. (Adding
        Vitamins to Alcoholic Beverages.) Lakartidningen, 75:
        4011-4012, 1978.

5315. Silkworth, William D. New Approach to Psychotherapy in Chronic
        Alcoholism. Lancet, 59: 312-315, 1939.

5316. Silkworth, William D. Psychological Rehabilitation of Alcoholics.
        Medical Record, 150: 65-66, 1939.

5317. Sillman, L.R. Chronic Alcoholism. Journal of Nervous and Mental
        Disease, 107: 127-149, 1948.

5318. Silver, Larry B., Dublin, Christina C. and Lourie, Reginald S.
        Child Abuse Syndrome: The "Gray Areas" in Establishing
        a Diagnosis. Pediatrics, 44(4): 594-600, 1969.

5319. Silver, Richard. Reaching Out to the Alcoholic and the Family.
        (Professional Education Series, No. 6.) Center City, MN:
        Hazelden, 1977.

5320. Simmel, E. Alcoholism and Addiction. Psychoanalytic Quarterly,
        17: 6-31, 1948.

5321. Simon, M. Double Impact on the Aboriginal Family. Aboriginal
        Health Worker, 4(2): 11-15, 1983.

5322. Simon, Marcel, Alexandre, Jean-Luc, Bourel, Michael and Le
        Marec, Bernard. Heredity of Idiopathic Hemochromatosis:
        A Study of 106 Families. Clinical Genetics, Copenhagen,
        11: 327-341, 1977.

5323. Simon, R.I. Type A, AB, B Murderers: Their Relationship to
        the Victims and to the Criminal Justice System. Bulletin
        of the American Academy of Psychiatry and the Law, 5(3):
        344-362, 1977.

5324. Simon, Werner. Drug Addiction. Minnesota Medicine, 47(5):
        541, 543, 1964.

5325. Simonovic, R. and Fligic, M. Lecenje Alkoholicara I Zavisnost
        Rezultata Lecenja Od Vrste Terapije I Drugih Cinilaca.
        (Treatment of Alcoholics and the Dependence of Its Outcome
        on the Kind of Therapy and Other Factors.) Alkoholizam,
        Beograd, 17(1-2): 109-118, 1977.

5326. Simons, Betty, Down, Elinor F. and Hurster, Madeline M. Child
        Abuse: Epidemiologic Study of Medically Reported Cases.
        New York State Journal of Medicine, 67: 2783-2788, 1966.

5327. Simpson, Cynthia A. An Exploratory Study of Self-Mutilation.
        Dissertation Abstracts International, 42(7): 3003B, 1981.

5328. Simpson, Cynthia A. and Porter, Garry L. Self-Mutilation in
        Children and Adolescents. Bulletin of the Menninger Clinic,
        45(5): 428-441, 1982.

5329. Simpson, Michael A. Self-Mutilation. British Journal of
        Hospital Medicine, London, 16(4): 430-438, 1976.

5330. Simpson, W.S. and Webber, P.W. A Field Program in the Treatment
        of Alcoholism. Hospital and Community Psychiatry, 22:
        170-173, 1971.

5331. Simpson, Walter. An Alcoholic Wife. British Medical Journal,
        London, 2: 1345-1346, 1951.

5332. Singer, K. The Choice of Intoxicant Among the Chinese. British
        Journal of Addiction, Edinburgh, 69(3): 257-268, 1974.

5333. Singer, K. and Wong, M. Alcoholic Psychoses and Alcoholism in
        the Chinese. Quarterly Journal of Studies on Alcohol,
        34(3): 878-886, 1973.

5334. Singer, Merrill. Family Comes First: An Examination of the
        Social Networks of Skid Row Men. Human Organization,
        44(2): 137-142, 1985.

5335. Singer, Merrill. Spiritual Healing and Family Therapy: Common
        Approaches to the Treatment of Alcoholism. Family Therapy,
        11(2): 155-162, 1984.

5336. Singewald, M.L. Shelley, H.E., Smoot, R.T., Bosma, W., Beacham,
        E.G., Klinefelter, H.F., Young, R.K., H., D. and Mrs S.
        Treatment of the Alcoholic and the Family. Maryland State
        Medical Journal, 21(1): 67-82, 1972.

5337. Singh, Gurmeet, and Agarwal, M.L. A Family and Genetic Study of
        Primary Affective Disorders. Indian Journal of Psychiatry,
        22(1): 39-50, 1980.

5338. Singh, Ram N. and Haddy, Loretta E. Alcohol Consumption and
        the Students' Use of Hallucinogenic Drugs. West Virginia
        Medical Journal, 69(4): 88-90, 1973.

5339. Singh, Sewa and Broota, K.D. Family-History in Relation
        to Students' Drug Abuse. Indian Journal of Clinical
        Psychology, New Delhi, 5(2): 139-143, 1978.

5340. Sipchen, B. Los Angeles Times, 24 September 1985, Page 2.
        (Children of Alcoholics Battle Trauma.)

5341. Sipova, I. and Nedoma, K. Family Background and Childhood
        in Promiscuous Women and Prostitutes. Ceskoslovenska
        Psychiatrie, Praha, 68(3): 150-153, 1972.

5342. Sisco, Carol B. Uncovering the "Hidden Alcoholic": Identification
        and Treatment of the Female Inebriate. Paper presented at the
        National Institute on Social Work in Rural Areas, Beaufort
        County, SC, July, 1981.

5343. Sisco, Carol B. What if Mom is the Alcoholic? Special Concerns
        and Issues. Focus on Family and Chemical Dependency,
        8(2): 20-21, 37, 40, 1985.

5344. Sisk, Mack. Houston Chronicle, 19 September 1982, Section 1,
        Page 15, Column 2. (Psychogenetic Theory on cause of Alcoholism.)

5345. Sisk, R.D., Fields, T., Higgins, R., White, R. and Knecht, J.
       Alcohol Awareness: A Guide for Teenagers and Their
       Parents. Curriculum Guide. Nashville: Christian
       Life Commission of the Southern Baptist Convention, 1983.

5346. Sisson, R.W. and Azrin, N.H. Family-Member Involvement to Initiate
       and Promote Treatment of Problem Drinkers. *Journal of Behavior*
       Therapy and Experimental Psychiatry, 17(1): 15-21, 1986.

5347. Sjostrom, K. Gruppverksamhet Med Alkoholister I Oppen Vard.
       (Group Activity with Alcoholics in an Open Ward.)
       Socialmedicinsk Tidskrift, Stockholm, 38: 329-333, 1961.

5348. Skala, J. Organizacion de la Asistencia Antialcoholica en
       Praga. (The Organization of Anti-Alcoholic Treatment in
       Prague). *Archivos de Biologia y Medicina Experimentales*,
       Chile, Supplement (3): 323-327, 1969. (Also in: *Alcohol and*
       Alcoholism. Ed. R.E. Popham. Toronto: University of Toronto
       Press, 1970, pages 372-376.)

5349. Skiffington, E.W. and Brown, P.M. Personal, Home and School Factors
       Related to Eleventh Graders' Drug Attitudes. *International*
       Journal of the Addictions, 16(5): 879-892, 1981.

5350. Skinner, Harvey A. and Holt, Stephen. Early Intervention for
       Alcohol Problems. *Journal of the Royal College of General*
       Practitioners, 33(257): 787-791, 1983.

5351. Skinner, Harvey A., Holt, Stephen and Israel, Yedy. Early
       Identification of Alcohol Abuse: I. Critical Issues and
       Psychosocial Indicators for a Composite Index. *Canadian*
       Medical Association Journal, 124(9): 1141-1152, 1981.

5352. Skolnick, J.H. The Stumbling Block: A Sociological Study of the
       Relationship between Selected Religious Norms and Drinking
       Behavior. Doctoral Dissertation. Yale University, 1957.

5353. Skoloda, T.E., Alterman, A.I. and Cornelison, F.S., Jr. and
       Gottheil E. Treatment Outcome in a Drinking-Decisions Program.
       Journal of Studies on Alcohol, 36(3): 365-380, 1975.

5354. Skopkova, Helena. Catamnestic Study of 366 Voluntary and Constrained
       Patients Admitted to the Antialcoholic Ward. *British Journal*
       of Addiction, 62: 13-14, 1967. (Also in: *Anali Klinicke*
       Bolnice Dr. M. Stojanov, Zagreb, 6(2-3): 275-286, 1967.)

5355. Slater, A.D. A Follow-Up Study of Sixty-Three Alcoholics Who Received
       Treatment in Utah Under the Kendall Act. *Utah Alcoholism Review*,
       2(2): 1-8, 1951.

5356. Slater, Elisa J. and Linn, Margaret W. Predictors of Rehospitalization
       in a Male Alcoholic Population. *American Journal of Drug and*
       Alcohol Abuse, 9(2): 211-220, 1982-83.

5357. Slater, Victor, Linn, Margaret W., Harris, Rachel and Odutola, Adedeji
       Ayodele. A Retrospective Review of Relapse. *Journal of*
       Psychiatric Treatment and Evaluation, 3(6): 515-521, 1981.

5358. Slavney, P.R. and Grau, J.G. Fetal Alcohol Damage and Schizophrenia.
       Journal of Clinical Psychiatry, 39(10): 782-783, 1978.

5359. Slavney, Phillip R. and McHugh, Paul R. The Hysterical Personality:
       A Controlled Study. *Archives of General Psychiatry*, 30(3):
       325-329, 1974.

5360. Sloboda, Sharon B. The Children of Alcoholics: A Neglected Problem.
       Hospital and Community Psychiatry, 25(9): 605-606, 1974.

5361. Small, Edward J., Jr. and Leach, Barry. Counseling Homosexual
       Alcoholics; Ten Case Histories. Journal of Studies on
       Alcohol, 38: 2077-2086, 1977.

5362. Small, I.F., Small, J.G., Assue, C.M. and Moore, D.F. The Fate of
       the Mentally Ill Physician. American Journal of Psychiatry,
       125(10): 1333-1342, 1969.

5363. Small, John. Adult Children of Alcoholics Need Intervention.
       ADAMHA News, 10(1): 6A-7A, 1984.

5364. Small, John. Family Systems Theory Explored at Conference.
       NIAAA Information and Feature Service, (IFS No. 100): 5,
       September 29, 1982.

5365. Small, John. Future Directions in Family Research Discussed.
       Alcohol Health and Research World, 6(1): 43-44, 1981.

5366. Small, John. The McKenzie Area Prevention Project. NIAAA
       Information and Feature Service, (IFS No. 96): 4-5, June 1,
       1982.

5367. Small, John. Parent Groups Seen as New Prevention Resource.
       NIAAA Information and Feature Service, (IFS No. 94): 1,
       April 1, 1982.

5368. Smalley, S. Treating Co-Dependency: Shifting the Focus to
       Individual Autonomy. Focus on Family and Chemical
       Dependency, 7(6): 13-15, 1984.

5369. Smart, R.G. Alcoholism, Birth Order and Family Size. Journal of
       Abnormal and Social Psychology, 66: 17-23, 1963.

5370. Smart, R.G. Importance of Birth Order in the Etiology of
       Addictions. Psychiatry Digest, 27(7): 39-44, 1966.

5371. Smart, R.G. Some Current Studies of Psychoactive and Hallucinogenic
       Drug Use. Canadian Journal of Behavioral Science, 2: 232-245,
       1970.

5372. Smart, R.G. and Fejer, D. Drug Use Among Adolescents and Their
       Parents: Closing the Generation Gap in Mood Modification.
       Journal of Abnormal Psychology, 79(2): 153-160, 1972.
       (Also in: Drugs and the Family. Ed. Thomas J. Glynn.
       Washington, D.C.: U.S. Government Printing Office, 1981.)

5373. Smart, R.G. and Fejer, D. Recent Trends in Illicit Drug Use
       Among Adolescents. Canada's Mental Health Supplement,
       68, 1-13, 1971.

5374. Smart, R.G. and Fejer, D. Relationships Between Parental and
       Adolescent Drug Use. In: Drug Abuse: Current Concepts
       and Research. Ed. W. Keup. Springfield, Illinois:
       Charles C. Thomas, 1972, pages 146-153.

5375. Smart, R.G. and Whitehead, P.C. The Uses of an Epidemiology of
       Drug Use: The Canadian Scene. International Journal of
       the Addictions, 9(3): 373-388, 1974.

5376. Smart, Reginald G. Employed Alcoholics Treated Voluntarily
       and Under Constructive Coercion. A Follow-Up Study.
       Quarterly Journal of Studies on Alcohol, 35(1 pt A):
       196-209, 1974.

5377. Smart, Reginald G. A Response to Sprott's 'Use of Chi Square.'
       Journal of Abnormal and Social Psychology, 69(1):
       103-105, 1964.

5378. Smart, Reginald G. and Gray, Gaye. Parental and Peer Influences
       as Correlates of Problem Drinking Among High School Students.
       Toronto: Addiction Research Foundation, 1977. (Also in: The
       International Journal of the Addictions, 14(7): 905-917, 1979.

5379. Smart, Reginald G., Gray, Gaye and Bennett Clif. Predictors of
       Drinking and Signs of Heavy Drinking among High School Students.
       International Journal of the Addictions, 13(7): 1079-1094,
       1978.

5380. Smeraldi, E., Negri, F. and Melica, A.M. A Genetic Study of
       Affective Disorders. Acta Psychiatrica Scandinavica,
       Copenhagen, 56(5): 382-398, 1977.

5381. Smerdon, G. and Paton, A. ABC of Alcohol: Detection in General
       Practice. British Medical Journal (Clinical Research
       Edition), 284(6311): 255-257, 1982.

5382. Smith, Ann. The Dynamics of Abuse and Domestic Violence.
       In: Alcoholism and the Family: A Book of Readings.
       Eds. Sharon Wegscheider-Cruse and Richard Esterly.
       Wernersville, PA: Caron Institute, 1985, pages 25-30.

5383. Smith, A.W. Treatment Issues for Addicted Adult Children from
       Alcoholic Families. Focus on Family and Chemical Dependency,
       8(2): 15, 17, 35, 1985.

5384. Smith, B.E. and Panepinto, W.C. Multi-Generational Family
       Interactions: Implications for Prevention, Intervention
       and Treatment. Paper presented at the National Council on
       Alcoholism, New Orleans, April, 1981.

5385. Smith, C.G. Alcoholics: Their Treatment and Their Wives.
       British Journal of Psychiatry, 115: 1039-1042, 1969.

5386. Smith, C.G. Marital Influences on Treatment Outcome in
       Alcoholism. Journal of the Irish Medical Association,
       Dublin, 60(365): 433-434, 1967.

5387. Smith, C.M. Family Size in Alcoholism. Journal of Abnormal
       Psychology, 70: 230, 1965.

5388. Smith, Cedric M. Overview of Personality, Behavior, and Parental
       Alcoholism. In: Currents in Alcoholism, Volume 5:
       Biomedical Issues and Clinical Effects of Alcoholism.
       Ed. Marc Galanter. New York: Grune and Stratton, 1979,
       pages 297-299.

5389. Smith, Colin M. Measuring Some Effects of Mental Illness on the
       Home. Canadian Psychiatric Association Journal, 14(2):
       97-104, 1969.

5390. Smith, E.J. Adolescent Drug Abuse and Alcoholism -- Directions
       for the School and the Family. Urban Education, 16(3):
       311, 1981.

5391. Smith, J.A. The Social Alcoholic. Diseases of the Nervous
       System, 33(11): 749-751, 1972.

5392. Smith, J.W. Color Vision in Alcoholics. Annals of the New York
       Academy of Sciences, 197: 143-147, 1972.

5393. Smith, James W. Rehabilitation for Alcoholics. Postgraduate
       Medicine, 64(6): 143-148, 152, 1978.

5394. Smith, J.W. and Layden, T.A. Color Vision Defects in Alcoholism.
       British Journal of Addiction, Edinburgh, 66: 31-37, 1971.

5395. Smith, M. The Genetics of Alcoholism. *Advances in Alcohol and Substance Abuse*, 1(3-4): 127-146, 1982.

5396. Smith, Moyra. Occurrence of Alcohol Dehydrogenase in Tissues Other Than Liver and Developmental Changes in Alcohol Dehydrogenase Gene Activity. In: *Biological Approach to Alcoholism*. Ed. Charles S. Lieber. Washington, D.C.: U.S. Government Printing Office, 1983, pages 24-26.

5397. Smith, Sona and Deasy, Patrick. Child Abuse in Ireland: Why Does It Occur? - II. *Journal of the Irish Medical Association*, Dublin, 70(3): 70-74, 1977.

5398. Smith, W.G. Critical Life-Events and Prevention Strategies in Mental Health. *Archives of General Psychiatry*, 25: 103-109, 1971.

5399. Smith, W.R., Varvel, W.A., LeUnes, A.D., Christensen, L.B., Crouch, B.M. and Shaw, R.M. Rural Alcohol Abuse. *Annals of the New York Academy of Sciences*, 273: 659-664, 1976.

5400. Smithers, Christopher D. Foundation. *Alcoholism: A Family Illness*. New York, 1969.

5401. Smithers, Christopher D. Foundation. *Understanding Alcoholism: For the Patient, the Family and the Employer*. New York: Charles Scribner and Sons, 1968. (Also as: Pamphlet. New York: National Council on Alcoholism, 1968.)

5402. Smithurst, B.A. and Armstrong, J.L. Social Background of 171 Women Attending a Female Venereal Disease Clinic in Brisbane. *The Medical Journal of Australia*, Sydney, 1(11): 339-343, 1975.

5403. Smoot, N.L. Teen-age Alcoholism. *Maryland State Medical Journal*, 31(5): 34, 1982.

5404. Smoyak, Shirley A. Therapeutic Approaches to Alcoholism Based on Systems Theories. *Occupational Health Nursing*, 21(4): 27-30, 1973.

5405. Snyder, Anne. *First Step*. New York: Holt, Rinehart and Winston, 1975.

5406. Sobel, R. and Underhill, R.N. Family Disorganization and Teenage Auto Accidents. *Journal of Safety Research*, 8: 8-18, 1976.

5407. *Social Groupwork and Alcoholism*. New York: Haworth Press, 1982.

5408. Social Implications of Alcohol Abuse. *Fourth Special Report to the U.S. Congress on Alcohol and Health from the Secretary of Health and Human Services*. Washington, D.C.: U.S. Government Printing Office, 1981, pages 80-101.

5409. *Socio-Economic Model of the Family with Alcohol Abuse*. Boston: Policy Analysis, Inc., 1975.

5410. Soden, Edward W. The "Team" Approach in the Treatment of Alcoholics. *Federal Probation*, 32(2): 47-49, 1968.

5411. Soleau, J.E. and Works, D.A. *Pastoral Care of Families: Including Alcoholics and Problem Drinkers*. Pamphlet. Boston: North Conway Institute, 1985.

5412. Solms, H. La Rehabilitation Medico-Psycho-Sociale des Alcooliques: Un Effort Auridisciplinaire. (Medico-Psycho-Social Rehabilitation of Alcoholics: A Multidisciplinary Approach.) *Bulletin Der Schweizerischen Akademie Der Medizinischen Wissenschaften*, Basel, 35(1-3): 213-220, 1979.

5413. Solms, Hugo. Synthesis. In: Currents in Alcohol Research and
       the Prevention of Alcohol Problems. Eds. Jean-Pierre von
       Wartburg, Pierre Magnenat, Richard Muller and Sonja Wyss.
       Berne: Hans Huber Publishers, 1985, pages 52-56.

5414. Solomon, Joel. Psychiatric Characteristics of Alcoholics.
       In: The Biology of Alcoholism, Vol. 6, The Pathogenesis of
       Alcoholism: Psychosocial Factors. Eds. Benjamin Kissin
       and Henri Begleiter. New York: Plenum Press, 1983, pages
       67-112.

5415. Solomon, Joel and Hanson, Meredith. Alcoholism and Sociopathy.
       In: Alcoholism and Clinical Psychiatry. Ed. Joel Solomon.
       New York: Plenum Medical Book Company, 1982, pages 111-127.

5416. Somervill, Charles E. The Influence of U.S. Family Social
       Characteristics on Alcoholism. Paper presented to the
       Mid-South Sociological Association, 1977.

5417. Sommer, Conrad. Current Notes: A State Hospital for Alcoholics
       in Illinois. Quarterly Journal of Studies on Alcohol, 4:
       136-139, 1943.

5418. Sommers, Lorin David. Bulimia: A Critical Review of the
       Literature with Reference to Descriptive Data, Etiology
       and Treatment. Dissertation Abstracts International,
       44(3): 928B, 1983.

5419. Sonkin, Nathan. The Hidden Faces of Alcoholism. Rhode Island
       Medical Journal, 56(4): 160-163, 1973.

5420. Sonnenreich, Carol and Goes, Josaphat Ferreira. Maconha E
       Disturbios Psiquicos. (Marihuana and Psychic Disturbances.)
       Neurobiologia, Recife, 25: 69-91, 1962.

5421. Sorenson, D.D. The Art of Preserving Human Resources. Omaha:
       National Publications, 1978.

5422. Sorosiak, Florence M., Thomas, L. Eugene and Balet, Fred N.
       Adolescent Drug Use: An Analysis. Psychological Reports,
       38(1): 211-222, 1976.

5423. Sorrells, James M. Kids Who Kill. Crime and Delinquency,
       23(3): 312-320, 1977.

5424. Southwick, William. Children of Alcoholics. In: Papers
       Presented at the 6th International Institute on the
       Prevention and Treatment of Drug Dependence, Hamburg,
       Germany, June 28-July 2, 1976. Eds. E.J. Tongue and
       L. Graz. Lausanne: International Council on Alcohol and
       Addictions, 1979, pages 455-459. (Also in: Psicodeia,
       Madrid, November: 51-54, 1974.)

5425. Southworth, N. The Relation of Problem Drinking to Current
       Marriage: Comparisons Between Alcoholics and Their
       Wives. Doctoral Dissertation. (University Microfilms
       No. DA8219261.) New York: Fordham University, 1982.

5426. Sovner, Robert D. The Clinical Characteristics and Treatment
       of Atypical Depression. Journal of Clinical Psychiatry,
       42(7): 285-289, 1981.

5427. Sowder, Barbara, Dickey, Susan, Glynn, Thomas J. and Burt
       Associates Inc. Family Therapy: A Summary of Selected
       Literature. (National Institute on Drug Abuse. Services
       Research Monograph Series.) Washington, D.C.: U.S.
       Government Printing Office, 1980. (DHHS Publication No.
       ADM 81-944).

5428. So You Love an Alcoholic? Pamphlet. New York: Al-Anon Family
        Group Headquarters, 1979.

5429. Soyster, Cynthia. Adult Children of Alcoholics: Heirs of Shame.
        Paper presented at 92nd Annual Convention of the American
        Psychological Association, Toronto, August, 1984.

5430. Spaans, C. and Verspreet, F.A.M. Fetal Alcohol Syndrome: Four
        Cases in One Family. Nederlands Tijdschrift Voor
        Geneeskunde, Amsterdam, 125(12): 452-454, 1981.

5431. Spalt, L. Alcoholism; Evidence of an X-Linked Recessive Genetic
        Characteristic. Journal of the American Medical
        Association, 241: 2543-2544, 1979.

5432. Spalt, L. Demorgraphic Characteristics in Affective Disorders.
        Diseases of the Nervous System, 36(4): 209-214, 1975.

5433. Spazzapan, B. and DeVanna M. Cultural Aspects in Alcoholic Habits
        of Secondary School Students. Minerva Psichiatrica,
        22(4): 177-182, 1981.

5434. Spears, Robert and Lawlis, G. Frank. Marriage Relationships
        Shown by Male Alcoholics. Psychological Reports, 34(3):
        946, 1974.

5435. Special Focus: Children of Alcoholics. Alcohol Health and
        Research World, 8(4): 1-62, 1984.

5436. Special Population Groups. In: Alcohol and Health: Third
        Special Report to the United States Congress. Ed. Ernest
        P. Noble. Rockville, MD: National Institute on Alcohol
        Abuse and Alcoholism, 1978, pages 17-24.

5437. Spencer, Christopher and Agahi, Cyrus. Social Background, Personal
        Relationships and Self Descriptions as Predictors of Drug
        User Status A Study of Adolescents in Post Revoluntionary
        Iran. Drug and Alcohol Dependence, 10(1): 77-84, 1982.

5438. Spevack, Michael and Pihl, R.O. Nonmedical Drug Use by High School
        Students: A 3-Year Survey Study. International Journal of
        the Addictions, 11(5): 755-792, 1977.

5439. Spiegel, Marcia Cohn. Profile of the Alcoholic Jew. British
        Journal on Alcohol and Alcoholism, 16(3): 141-149, 1981.

5440. Spiegel, Renee and Mock, William L. A Model for a Family Systems
        Theory Approach to Prevention and Treatment of Alcohol Abusing
        Youth. Paper presented at the National Council on Alcoholism
        Meeting, St. Louis, May, 1978. (Eric Document Number ED 166624.)

5441. Spieker, G. Epilogue. In: The Many Faces of Family Violence.
        Ed. J.P. Flanzer. Springfield, IL: Charles C. Thomas,
        1982, pages 121-129.

5442. Spieker, G. Family Violence and Alcohol Abuse. In: Papers
        Presented at the 24th International Congress on the
        Prevention and Treatment of Alcoholism, Zurich, June, 1978.
        Lausanne: International Council on Alcohol and Addictions,
        1978, pages 335-342. (Also in: Toxicomanies, Quebec, 13(1):
        31-42, 1980.)

5443. Spieker, G. What is the Linkage Between Alcohol Abuse and Violence?
        In: Alcohol, Drug Abuse and Aggression. Ed. E. Gottheil.
        Springfield, IL: Charles C. Thomas, 1983, pages 125-136.

5444. Spieker, G. and Mouzakitis, C.M. Alcohol Abuse and Child Abuse and
       Neglect: An Inquiry Into Alcohol Abusers' Behavior Toward
       Children. Paper presented at the 27th Annual Meeting of the
       Alcohol and Drug Problems Association of North America, New
       Orleans, September, 1976.

5445. Spira, Henry. The Meal Ticket Syndrome. Journal of the Medical
       Association of the State of Alabama, 39(1): 37-39, 1969.

5446. Spisiakova, A. Vyvin Osobnosti Dietata So Znizenym Intelektom
       V Alkoholickej Rodine. (Personality Development of a
       Child with Subnormal Intellect in an Alcoholic Family.)
       Psychologia A Patopsychologia Dietata, Bratislva, 5(4):
       361-365, 1970.

5447. Spitz, Henry I. Group Approaches to Treating Marital Problems.
       Psychiatric Annals, 9(6): 50-70, 1979.

5448. Spotts, J.V. and Shontz, F.C. Psychopathology and Chronic Drug
       Use: A Methodological Paradigm. International Journal of
       the Addictions, 18(5): 633-680, 1983.

5449. Spouses of Alcoholic Persons. Bibliography. Alcohol Health
       and Research World, 1975, pages 31-32.

5450. Spradlin, W.W. The Family and the Alcoholic. West Virginia
       Medical Journal, 66(3): 89-91, 1970.

5451. Spranger, J., Kahn, E. and Shaywitz, S.E. Attention Deficit
       Syndrome in Children Born to Alcoholic Mothers. Journal
       of Pediatrics, 98: 670-671, 1981.

5452. Spreng, M. Vom Einfluss der Trunksucht der Eltern auf die
       Entwicklung der Kinder. Aus dem Blickfeld Fursorgerin
       Gesehen. (Concerning the Influence of Parental Alcoholism
       on Children's Development. From the Viewpoint of the Social
       Caseworker.) Bern: Schule fur Soziale Arbeit, 1958.

5453. Spring, G.K. and Rothsery, J.M. Link Between Alcoholism and
       Affective Disorders. Hospital and Community Psychiatry,
       35(8): 820-823, 1984.

5454. Sreenivasan, U. Anorexia Nervosa in Boys. Canadian Psychiatric
       Association Journal, Ottawa, 23(3): 159-162, 1978.

5455. Stabenau, James R. Family Pedigree of Alcoholic and Control
       Patients. Paper presented at the meeting of the Psychiatric
       Research Society, Boston, September, 1980. (Also in:
       Journal of Psychiatric Research, 16(2): 142, 1981.)

5456. Stabenau, James R. Implications of Family History of
       Alcoholism, Antisocial Personality, and Sex Differences
       in Alcohol Dependence. American Journal of Psychiatry,
       141(10): 1178-1182, 1984.

5457. Stabenau, James R. and Hesselbrock, V.M. Clinical Study:
       Assortative Mating, Family Pedigree and Alcoholism.
       Substance and Alcohol Actions/Misuse, 1: 375-382, 1980.

5458. Stabenau, James R. and Hesselbrock, V.M. Family Pedigree of
       Alcoholic and Control Patients. International Journal of
       the Addictions, 18(3): 351-363, 1983.

5459. Stabenau, James R. and Hesselbrock, V.M. Family Pedigree Typologies
       in Alcoholism (Abstract). Alcoholism: Clinical and
       Experimental Research, 7(1): 122, 1983.

5460. Stacey, B. and Davies, J. Drinking Behaviour in Childhood and
       Adolescence: An Evaluative Review. British Journal of
       Addiction, Edinburgh, 65(3): 203-212, 1970.

5461. Stacey, B. and Davies, J. Teenagers and Alcohol. Health
       Bulletin, Edinburgh, 31(6): 318-319, 1973.

5462. Stafford, Ruth A. and Petway, Judy M. Stigmatization of Men and
       Women Problem Drinkers and Their Spouses: Differential
       Perception and Leveling of Sex Differences. Journal of
       Studies on Alcohol, 38(11): 2109-2121, 1977.

5463. Stamas, D. Breaking Through the Family's Denial. Focus on
       Family and Chemical Dependency, 6(6): 30-31, 44, 1983.

5464. Stamatoyannopoulos, G., Chen, S.-H. and Fukui, M. Liver Alcohol
       Dehydrogenase in Japanese: High Population Frequency of
       Atypicl Form and Its Possible Role in Alcohol Sensitivity.
       American Journal of Human Genetics, 27: 789-796, 1975.

5465. Stanetti, Fedor. Alcoholism Relapses: Relationship and
       Prognostic Significance of the Patient's Personality,
       Social Factors, and Course of Treatment. Socijalna
       Psihijatrija, 4(4): 347-406, 1976.

5466. Stankovic, Zoran and Timotijevic, Ivana. Porodica Alkoholicara
       U Toku Lecenja Alkoholizma. (Family of the Alcoholic During
       Treatment of Alcoholism.) Psihijatrija Danas, Belgrade,
       12(3): 287-291, 1980.

5467. Stankushev, T., Gerdjikov, I., Girginova, V. and Vulcinov, V.
       Alcoholism Among Workers and Employees in the Industry of
       the Town of Vratza. Khigiena I Zdraveopazne, Sofia,
       19(4): 327-334, 1976.

5468. Stankusev, T., Hinova, L. and Razboynikova, E. Peculiarities
       in the Psychic Development and Behavior of Children from
       Alcoholic Parents. Pediatriia, 14: 25-29, 1975.
       (Also in: Psychiatry, 34(737), 1976.)

5469. Stanojevic, Natasa and Djukic, Tatjana. Psychiatric Aspects
       of Juvenile Delinquents. Srpski Arhiv Za Celokupno
       Lekarstvo, Beograd, 94(7): 693-701, 1966.

5470. Stanton, M. Duncan. Breaking Away: The Use of Strategic and
       Bowenian Techniques in Treating an Alcoholic Family through
       One Member. In: Power to Change: Family Case Studies in the
       Treatment of Alcoholism. Ed. Edward Kaufman. New York:
       Gardner Press, 1984, pages 253-266.

5471. Stanton, M. Duncan. A Critique of Kaufman's "Myth and Reality
       in the Family Patterns and Treatment of Substance Abusers."
       American Journal of Drug and Alcohol Abuse, 7(3&4):
       281-290, 1980.

5472. Stanton, M. Duncan. Drugs and the Family: A Review of the Recent
       Literature. Marriage and Family Review, 2: 1-10, 1979.

5473. Stanton, M. Duncan. Drug Misuse and the Family. Focus on Women,
       3(3): 124-151, 1982.

5474. Stanton, M. Duncan. The Family and Drug Misuse: A Bibliography.
       American Journal of Drug and Alcohol Abuse, 5(2):
       151-170, 1978.

5475. Stanton, M. Duncan. Family Treatment Approaches to Drug Abuse
       Problems: A Review. Family Process, Baltimore,
       18: 251-280, 1979.

5476. Stanton, M. Duncan. Family Treatment of Drug Problems: A Review.
       In: Handbook on Drug Abuse. Eds. R.L. Dupont, A. Goldstein
       and J. O'Donnell. Washington, D.C.: U.S. Government Printing
       Office, 1979, pages 133-150.

5477. Stanton, M. Duncan. Marital Therapy From a Structural/Strategic
       Viewpoint. In: Marriage is a Family Affair: A Textbook
       of Marriage and Marital Therapy. Ed. G.P. Sholevar.
       Jamaica, NY: S.P. Medical and Scientific Books, 1981.

5478. Stanton, M. Duncan. Review of Alcoholic Marriage - Alternative
       Perspectives by T.J. Paolino and B.S. McCrady. Journal of
       Marital and Family Therapy, 5(2): 108-109, 1979.

5479. Stanton, M. Duncan. Some Overlooked Aspects of the Family and
       Drug Abuse. In: Drug Abuse From the Family Perspective.
       Ed. Barbara Gray Ellis. Washington, D.C.: U.S. Government
       Printing Office, 1980, pages 1-17.

5480. Stanton, M. Duncan. The Woman Substance Abuser within a Family
       Concept. In: The Woman Next Door. Summary Proceedings
       of a Symposium on the Subject of Drugs and the Modern
       Woman Held at the Institute of Pennsylvania Hospital,
       February 15-16, 1980. Eds. C. D'Amanda and M. Korcok.
       Hollywood, FL: U.S. Journal of Alcohol and Drug
       Dependence, 1980, pages 21-26.

5481. Stanton, M. Duncan and Todd, Thomas C. Principles and Techniques
       for Getting "Resistant" Families into Treatment. In: The
       Family Therapy of Drug Abuse and Addiction. Eds. M. Duncan
       Stanton and Thomas C. Todd. New York: The Guilford Press,
       1983, pages 71-106.

5482. Stanton, M. Duncan and Todd, Thomas C. The Therapy Model.
       In: The Family Therapy of Drug Abuse and Addiction.
       Eds. M. Duncan Stanton and Thomas C. Todd. New York:
       The Guilford Press, 1983, pages 109-153.

5483. Stanton, M. Duncan., Todd, Thomas C., Heard, D., Kirschner, S.,
       Kleiman, J.I., Mowatt, D.T., Riley, P., Scott, S.M. and
       Van Deusen, J.M. Heroin Addiction as a Family Phenomenon:
       A New Conceptual Model. American Journal of Drug and
       Alcohol Abuse, 5(2): 125-150, 1978.

5484. Stanton, M. Duncan, Todd, Thomas C., Heard, David B., Kirschner,
       Sam, Kleiman, Jerry I., Mowatl, David T., Riley, Paul, Scott,
       Samuel M. and Van Deusen, John M. A Conceptual Model.
       In: The Family Therapy of Drug Abuse and Addiction.
       Eds. M. Duncan Stanton and Thomas C. Todd. New York:
       The Guilford Press, 1983, pages 7-30.

5485. Stanton, M. Duncan, Todd, Thomas C. and Steier, F. Outcome for
       Structural Family Therapy with Drug Addicts. In: Problems of
       Drug Dependence. Proceedings of the 41st Annual Scientific
       Meeting, The Committee on Problems of Drug Dependence, Inc.
       (NIDA Research Monograph Series No. 27.) Ed. L.S. Harris.
       Washington, D.C.: U.S. Government Printing Office, 1979,
       pages 415-421.

5486. Star, B. Characteristics of Family Violence. In: The Many Faces
       of Family Violence. Ed. J.P. Flanzer. Springfield, IL:
       Charles C. Thomas, 1982, pages 14-23.

5487. Stark, E.D. Battering Syndrome: Social Knowledge, Social
       Therapy and the Abuse of Women. Dissertation Abstracts
       International, 45(1): 307A, 1984.

5488. Stary, Monica. Teenage Use and Abuse of Alcohol. Education
       Canada, 21(4): 10-13, 48, 1981.

5489. Statewide Task Force on Women and Substance Abuse. <u>Advance</u>, <u>31</u>(3): 20-21, 1981.

5490. Statistical Notes. Newsletter. Lincoln: Nebraska Division on Alcoholism, October, 1979.

5491. Staulcup, H., Kenward, K. and Frigo, D. A Review of Federal Primary Alcoholism Prevention Projects. <u>Journal of Studies on Alcohol</u>, <u>40</u>: 943-968, 1979.

5492. Staver, S. Impaired MD's Ragged Road to Recovery. <u>American Medical News</u>, <u>26</u>: 7, 18, 1982.

5493. Stead, Peter and Viders, Judith. A "SHARP" Approach to Treating Alcoholism. <u>Social Work</u>, <u>24</u>(2): 144-149, 1979.

5494. Steel, R. Personal Continuing Care. <u>Journal of Alcoholism</u>, London, <u>6</u>: 11-14, 1971.

5495. Steer, R.A., Fine, E.W. and Scoles, P.E. Classification of Men Arrested for Driving While Intoxicated, and Treatment Implications. A Cluster-Analytic Study. <u>Journal of Studies on Alcohol</u>, <u>40</u>(3): 222-229, 1979.

5496. Stefanovic, V. Alcoholism and Offenses Against Marriage and the Family in the Borough of Savski Venac, Belgrade. Paper presented at the <u>27th International Institute on the Prevention and Treatment of Alcoholism</u>, Vienna, June, 1981, pages 461-472.

5497. Steffen, J.J. Social Competence, Family Violence, and Problem Drinking. In: <u>The Many Faces of Family Violence</u>. Ed. J.P. Flanzer. Springfield, IL: Charles C. Thomas, 1982, pages 51-65. (Also as: Paper presented to the Mid-America Institute on Violence in Families, Hot Springs, AZ, July, 1978.)

5498. Steffen, John J., Steffen, Veronica B. and Nathan, Peter E. Behavioral Approaches to Alcohol Abuse. In: <u>Alcoholism: Development, Consequences, and Interventions</u>. Eds. Nada J. Estes and M. Edith Heinemann. St. Louis: The C.V. Mosby Company, 1977, pages 283-292.

5499. Stein, Ann and Kahn, Malcolm. <u>Attitudes and Characteristics of Nonusers</u>. 1972. (Eric Document Number ED070007.)

5500. Stein, Leonard I., Niles, Dolores and Ludwig, Arnold M. The Loss of Control Phenomenon in Alcoholics. <u>Quarterly Journal of Studies on Alcohol</u>, <u>29</u>(3): 598-602, 1968.

5501. Stein, Maurice R. The Drifters. Children of Disorganized Lower-Class Families. Sociocultural Perspectives on the Neighborhood and the Families. <u>International Psychiatry Clinics</u>, London, <u>4</u>(4): 299-320, 1967.

5502. Steinglass, Peter. The Alcoholic Family at Home; Patterns of Interaction in Dry, Wet and Transitional Stages of Alcoholism. <u>Archives of General Psychiatry</u>, <u>38</u>(5): 578-584, 1981.

5503. Steinglass, Peter. The Alcoholic Family in the Interaction Laboratory. <u>Journal of Nervous and Mental Disease</u>, <u>167</u>: 428-436, 1979.

5504. Steinglass, Peter. La Famille Alcoolique: Realite Ou Fiction? (Alcoholic Family: Reality or Fiction?) <u>Alcool Ou Sante</u>, <u>173</u>(2): 23-28, 1985.

5505. Steinglass, Peter. Alcoholism and the Family. In: <u>Alcohol,</u>
      <u>Science and Society Revisited</u>. Eds. E.L. Gomberg,
      H.R. White and J.A. Carpenter. Ann Arbor: University
      of Michigan Press, 1982, pages 306-321.

5506. Steinglass, Peter. Assessing Families in Their Own Homes.
      <u>American Journal of Psychiatry</u>, <u>137</u>(12): 1523-1529, 1980.

5507. Steinglass, Peter. An Experimental Treatment Program for Alcoholic
      Couples. <u>Journal of Studies on Alcohol</u>, <u>40</u>: 159-182, 1979.

5508. Steinglass, Peter. Experimenting with Family Treatment Approaches
      to Alcoholism, 1950-1975: A Review. <u>Family Process</u>, <u>15</u>(1):
      97-123, 1976.

5509. Steinglass, Peter. Family Therapy in Alcoholism. In: <u>The</u>
      <u>Biology of Alcoholism</u>. <u>Volume 5</u>. <u>Treatment and</u>
      <u>Rehabilitation of the Chronic Alcoholic</u>. Eds. Benjamin
      Kissin and Henri Begleiter. New York: Plenum Press, 1977,
      pages 259-299.

5510. Steinglass, Peter. Family Therapy with Alcoholics: A Review.
      In: <u>Family Therapy of Drug and Alcohol Abuse</u>. Eds. E.
      Kaufman, and P.N. Kaufmann. New York: Gardner Press, 1979,
      pages 147-186.

5511. Steinglass, Peter. The Impact of Alcoholism on the Family:
      Relationship Between Degree of Alcoholism and Psychiatric
      Symptomatology. <u>Journal of Studies on Alcohol</u>, <u>42</u>(3):
      288-303, 1981.

5512. Steinglass, Peter. A Life History Model of the Alcoholic Family.
      <u>Family Process</u>, <u>19</u>: 211-226, 1980.

5513. Steinglass, Peter. Longitudinal Study of Interactional Behavior
      in Alcoholic Families. <u>Alcoholism: Clinical and</u>
      <u>Experimental Research</u>, <u>3</u>(2): 196, 1979.

5514. Steinglass, Peter. Rejoinder: The Clinician Versus the Statistician.
      <u>Family Process</u>, <u>24</u>(3): 380-383, 1985.

5515. Steinglass, Peter. Research in Family Behavior Related to
      Alcoholism. <u>Substance Abuse</u>, <u>6</u>(1): 16-26, 1985.

5516. Steinglass, Peter. Research: Alcohol as a Member of the Family.
      <u>Human Ecology Forum</u>, <u>9</u>(3): 9-11, 1978.

5517. Steinglass, Peter. Roles of Alcohol in Family Systems. In: <u>Alcohol</u>
      <u>and the Family</u>. Eds. J. Orford and J. Harwin. New York:
      St. Martin's Press, 1982, pages 127-150.

5518. Steinglass, Peter, Davis, Donald and Berenson, David. In-Hospital
      Treatment of Alcoholic Groups. In: <u>Scientific Proceedings in</u>
      <u>Summary Form</u> (of the 128th Annual Meeting, Anaheim, CA, May, 1975).
      Washington, D.C.: American Psychiatric Association, 1975.

5519. Steinglass, Peter, Davis, Donald I. and Berenson, David.
      Observations of Conjointly Hospitalized "Alcoholic Couples"
      During Sobriety and Intoxication: Implications for Theory
      and Therapy. <u>Family Process</u>, <u>16</u>(1): 1-16, 1977.

5520. Steinglass, Peter and Moyer, Janet K. Assessing Alcohol Use in
      Family Life: A Necessary But Neglected Area For Clinical
      Research. <u>The Family Coordinator</u>, <u>26</u>(1): 53-60, 1977.

5521. Steinglass, Peter and Robertson, Anne. The Alcoholic Family.
      In: <u>Biology of Alcoholism; Volume 6 - The Pathogenesis of</u>
      <u>Alcoholism: Psychosocial Factors</u>. Eds. Benjamin Kissin and
      Henri Begleiter. New York: Plenum Press, 1983, pages 243-307.

5522. Steinglass, Peter, Tislenko, Lydia and Reiss, David. Stability/
        Instability in the Alcoholic Marriage: The Interrelationships
        Between Course of Alcoholism, Family Process, and Marital
        Outcome. Family Process, 24(3): 365-376, 1985.

5523. Steinglass, Peter, Weiner, Sheldon and Mendelson, Jack H.
        Interactional Issues as Determinants of Alcoholism.
        American Journal of Psychiatry, 128(3): 275-280, 1971.

5524. Steinglass, Peter, Weiner, Sheldon and Mendelson, Jack H.
        Systems Approach to Alcoholism. Archives of General
        Psychiatry, 24: 401-408, 1971.

5525. Steinhart, Clara. The Unidentified Problem of Alcoholism Among
        Hispanic Women. In: Chicanas and Alcoholism: A Socio-
        Cultural Perspective of Women. Eds. Rodolto Arevalo and
        Marianne Minor. San Jose, CA: School of Social Work,
        San Jose State University, 1981, pages 7-11.

5526. Steinhausen, Hans-Christoph, Gobel, Dietmar and Nestler, Veronica.
        Psychopathology in the Offspring of Alcoholic Parents.
        Journal of the American Academy of Child Psychiatry,
        23(4): 465-471, 1984.

5527. Steinhausen, Hans-Christoph, Nestler, Veronica and Huth, H.
        Psychopathology and Mental Functions in the Offspring of
        Alcoholic and Epileptic Mothers. Journal of the American
        Academy of Child Psychiatry, 21(3): 268-273, 1982.

5528. Steinhausen, Hans-Christoph, Nestler, Veronica and Spohr,
        Hans-Ludwig. Development and Psychopathology of Children
        with the Fetal Alcohol Syndrome. Developmental and
        Behavioral Pediatrics, 3(2): 49-54, 1982.

5529. Steinmetz, S.K. Review of the Literature: Violence between
        Family Members. Marriage and Family Review, 1(3):
        1-16, 1978.

5530. Steinmetz, S.K. Violence-Prone Families. Annals of the
        New York Academy of Sciences, 347: 251-265, 1980.

5531. Stenmark, D.E., Wackwitz, J.H., Pelfrey, M.C. and Dougherty, F.
        Substance Use Among Juvenile Offenders: Relationships to
        Parental Substance Use and Demographic Characteristics.
        Addictive Diseases, 1(1): 43-54, 1974.

5532. Stephens, D.A. Atkinson, M.W., Kay, D.W.K., Roth, M. and
        Garside, R.F. Psychiatric Morbidity in Parents and Sibs
        of Schizophrenics and Non-Schizophrenics. British Journal
        of Psychiatry, 127: 97-108, 1975.

5533. Stephenson, N.L., Boudenwyns, P.A. and Lessing, R.A. Long-Term
        Effects of Peer Group Confrontation Therapy Used with Polydrug
        Abusers. Journal of Drug Issues, 7: 135-149, 1977.

5534. Stern, Douglas Roger. The Role of Conflict in Alcoholic and
        Normal Couples. Doctoral Dissertation. (University
        Microfilms No. 78-12243.) 1978.

5535. Stern, Marilyn, Northman, John E. and Van Slyck, Michael R.
        Father Absence and Adolescent "Problem Behaviors": Alcohol
        Consumption, Drug Use and Sexual Activity. Adolescence,
        19(74): 302-312, 1984.

5536. Sterne, A.E. Effect of Alcohol on the Nervous System, the Mind,
        and Heredity. Journal of the American Medical Association,
        36: 788-790, 1901.

5537. Sterne, A.E. The Effect of Alcohol Upon the Nervous System,
         the Mind and Heredity. Quarterly Journal of Inebriety,
         Hartford, 25: 56-64, 1903.

5538. Sterne, Muriel W. and Pittman, David J. Alcohol Abuse and the
         Black Family. In: Alcohol Abuse and Black America.
         Ed. F.D. Harper. Alexandria, VA: Douglass Publishers,
         Inc., 1976, pages 177-185.

5539. Sternlieb, Jack J. and Munan, Louis. A Survey of Health Problems,
         Practices, and Needs of Youth. Pediatrics, 49(2):
         177-186, 1972.

5540. Stertzer, Joanne C. The Double Blind. COA Newsletter, 3(2):
         4, 1985.

5541. Steuer, Joanne and Austin, Elizabeth. Family Abuse of the
         Elderly. Journal of the American Geriatrics Society,
         28(8): 372-376, 1980.

5542. Stevens, Donald M. Some Adjustment Characteristics of the
         Adolescent Children of Alcoholic Parents. Doctoral
         Dissertation. (University Microfilms No. 689336.)
         Washington: University of Washington, 1967. (Also in:
         Dissertation Abstracts International, 29: 156A, 1968.)

5543. Stevens, S. and Young, R. Co-Dependency and Compulsive-Addictive
         Behavior: Obstacles to Recovery for Adult Children. Focus
         on Family and Chemical Dependency, 8(4): 18-19, 1985.

5544. Stevenson, G.S. Education and the Control of Alcoholism.
         Diseases of the Nervous System, 3: 238-243, 1942.

5545. Stewart, Donald E. Violence and the Family. (Institute of
         Family Studies, Discussion Paper Number 7.) Melbourne:
         Institute of Family Studies, 1982. (Eric Document Number
         ED 224590.)

5546. Stewart, Mark A. and DeBlois, C. Susan. Is Alcoholism Related
         to Physical Abuse of Wives and Children? Paper presented
         at the Annual Meeting of the National Council on Alcoholism,
         St. Louis, April, 1978.

5547. Stewart, Mark A. and DeBlois, C. Susan. Marital Histories of
         Women Whose First Husbands were Alcoholic or Antisocial.
         British Journal of Addiction, Edinburgh, 78(2): 205-213,
         1983.

5548. Stewart, Mark A. and DeBlois, C. Susan. Wife Abuse Among
         Families Attending a Child Psychiatry Clinic. Journal
         of the American Academy of Child Psychiatry, 20(4):
         845-862, 1981.

5549. Stewart, Mark A., DeBlois, C. Susan and Adams, C. Alcoholism
         in Parents of Aggressive and Antisocial Boys. Alcoholism:
         Clinical and Experimental Research, 2: 206, 1978.

5550. Stewart, Mark A., DeBlois, C. Susan and Cummings, Claudette.
         Psychiatric Disorder in the Parents of Hyperactive Boys
         and Those with Conduct Disorder. Journal of Child
         Psychology and Psychiatry and Allied Disciplines,
         New York, 21(4): 283-292, 1980.

5551. Stewart, Mark A., DeBlois, C. Susan and Singer, Sandra.
         Alcoholism and Hyperactivity Revisited: A Preliminary
         Report. In: Currents in Alcoholism, Volume 5,
         Biomedical Issues and Clinical Effects of Alcoholism.
         Ed. M. Galanter. New York: Grune & Stratton, 1979,
         pages 349-357.

5552. Stewart, Mark A., Gath, A. and Hierowski, E. Differences
       between Girls and Boys Admitted to a Child Psychiatry
       Ward. Journal of Clinical Psychiatry, 42: 386-388, 1981.

5553. Stewart, Mark A. and Leone, Loida. A Family Study of Unsocialized
       Aggressive Boys. Biological Psychiatry, 13(1): 107-117, 1978.

5554. Stewart, W.F.R. Drink, Drugs and the Family. London: National
       Society for the Prevention of Cruelty to Children, Developments
       Department, 1971.

5555. Stewart, W.R. Infant Neglect and Cruelty. Paper presented at the
       Third International Conference on Alcoholism and Addictions.
       Cardiff, Wales, September, 1970, pages 215-222.

5556. Stewart, W. Wayne. Establishing A Preventive Program to Identify
       Behavioral Problems in Industry. Industrial Medicine,
       39(12): 41-45, 1970.

5557. Stimmel, Barry. Editorial: The Role of Ethnography in Alcoholism
       and Substance Abuse: The Nature Versus Nurture Controversy.
       Advances in Alcohol & Substance Abuse, 4(1): 1-8, 1984.

5558. Stimmer, F. Jugendalkoholismus; Eine Familiensoziologische
       Untersuchung Zur Genese der Alkoholabhangigkeit Mannlicher
       Jugendlicher. (Alcoholism among Youth; a Sociological
       Family Study on the Development of Alcohol Dependence among
       Young Men.) In: Sozialwissenschaftliche Abhandlungen der
       Gorres-Gesellschaft. Band 2. Berlin: Duncker and Humblot,
       1978.

5559. Stimmer, F. Familiensoziologische Aspekte der Alkoholismusgenese
       Bei Jugendlichen. (Aspects of Family Sociology in the Genesis
       of Alcoholism Among Youths.) Soziologenkorrespondenz, 6:
       171-194, 1979.

5560. Stimmer, F. Zur Genese des Jugendalkoholismus; Eine Studie
       Aus Dem Bereich Der Psychiatrischen Familiensoziologie.
       (Genetic of Juvenile Alcoholism; A Study in the Field of
       Psychiatric Family Sociology.) Fortschritte der Medizin,
       Leipzig, 97(40): 1767-1768, 1824, 1979.

5561. Stimmer, F. Ein Drei-Phasen-Modell zur Soziogenese der
       Alkoholabhangigkeit Mannlicher Jugendlicher: Ein Beitrag
       zur Psychiatrischen Familiensoziologie. (A Three-Phase
       Model for Sociogenesis of Alcohol Dependence Among Young
       Men: A Contribution to Psychiatric Sociology of the Family.)
       In: Jugend und Alkohol: Trinkmuster, Suchtentwicklung
       und Therapie. (Youth and Alcohol: Drinking Patterns,
       Addiction Development and Therapy.) Eds. H. Berger,
       A. Legnaro and K.H. Reuband. Stuttgart: W. Kohlhammer,
       1980, pages 94-114.

5562. Stitzer, M.L., Bigelow, G.E., Liebson, I.A. and McCaul, M.E.
       Contingency Management of Supplemental Drug Use During
       Methadone Treatment. In: Behavioral Intervention
       Techniques in Drug Abuse Treatment. (NIDA Research
       Monograph Series 46.) Eds. J. Grabowski, M. Stitzer and
       J. Henningfield. Washington, D.C.: U.S. Government Printing
       Office, 1984, pages 84-103.

5563. Stivers, R. A Hair of the Dog; Irish Drinking and American
       Stereotype. University Park: Pennsylvania State
       University Press, 1976.

5564. Stockard, C.R. The Effect on the Offspring of Intoxicating
       the Male Parent and the Transmission of the Defects to
       Subsequent Generations. American Naturalist, 47:
       641-682, 1913.

5565.   Stockard, C.R.   The Effects of Alcohol in Development and Heredity.
        In: Alcohol and Man; The Effects of Alcohol on Man in Health
        and Disease.   Ed. H. Emerson.   New York: MacMillan and Co.,
        1932, pages 103-119.

5566.   Stockard, C.R.   The Hereditary Transmission of Degeneracy and
        Deformities by the Descendants of Alcoholized Mammals.
        Interstate Medical Journal, 23: 385-403, 1916.

5567.   Stockard, C.R.   The Influence of Alcoholism on the Offspring.
        Proceedings of the Society for Experimental Biology and
        Medicine, 9: 71-72, 1912.

5568.   Stockard, C.R.   A Study of Further Generations of Mammals from
        Ancestors Treated with Alcohol.   Proceedings of the Society
        for Experimental Biology and Medicine, 11: 136-139, 1914.

5569.   Stockard, C.R. and Papanicolaou, G.   A Further Analysis of
        the Hereditary Transmission of Degeneracy and Deformities
        by the Descendants of Alcoholized Mammals.   American
        Naturalist, 50: 65-88, 144-177, 1916.

5570.   Stoddard, C.   The Elderton Studies of the Influence of Parental
        Alcoholism.   Journal of Inebriety, 34: 1-5, 1912.

5571.   Stoeffler, Victor R.   Physicians Should Identify Teenage
        Alcoholism.   Michigan Medicine, 75(8): 443-444, 1976.

5572.   Stojiljkovic, Srboljub.   Frequency, Causes, Social and Economic
        Consequences, and Prevention of Alcoholism in Families with
        Low Incomes.   Belgrade: Institute of Alcoholism, 1967.

5573.   Stojiljkovic, Srboljub and Kilibarda, Momcilo.   The Role of
        Therapy in Solving the Social Problems of Alcoholism.
        Report on Alcohol, 28(3): 15-25, 1970.

5574.   Stojiljkovic, Srboljub. Kilibarda, Momcilo. and Despotovic, A.
        Epidemiology of Alcoholism in Families with Low Income.
        In: Summaries, Volume 1 - 3rd International Congress of
        Social Psychiatry.   Zagreb, 1970, pages 164-165.

5575.   Stoker, David H. and Meadow, Arnold.   Cultural Differences in
        Child Guidance Clinic Patients.   The International Journal
        of Social Psychiatry, London, 20(3-4): 186-202, 1974.

5576.   Stone, M.H., Kahn, E. and Flye, B.   Psychiatrically Ill Relatives
        of Borderline Patients: A Family Study.   Psychiatric
        Quarterly, 53: 71-84, 1981.

5577.   Storz, M.L.   Effects of Official Labelling on Husbands'
        Perceptions of Their Wives: A Study of Mental Illness.
        Australian and New Zealand Journal of Sociology, 14:
        46-50, 1978.

5578.   Stosberg, K.   Sucht Und Missbrauch-Beurteilung Aus Soziologischer
        Sicht.   Konsequenzen Fur Eine Sozialanamnese.   (Drug Addiction
        and Misuse from a Sociological Point of View.   Results with
        Regard to Social Anamnesis.)   Monatskurse Fur Nie Arztliche
        Fortbildung, Munich, 28: 143-146, 1978.

5579.   Stosberg, K.   Normorientiertheit Suchtiger - Ein
        Sozialisationstheoretischer Angatz.   (Social Theory
        Approach to Standard Trends in the Development of
        Addiction.)   In: Values and Standards in Assistance
        to Addicts.   Ed. U. Kuypers.   Freiburg im Bresgau,
        W. Germany: Lambertus-Verlag, 1984, pages 43-59.

5580.   Strachan, J. George.   Alcoholics Anonymous.   Alcoholism: Treatable
        Illness.   Vancouver, B.C.:   Mitchell Press, 1968, pages 245-269.

5581.   Strachan, J. George. Alcoholism: Treatable Illness, An Update for
        the 80's. Center City, MN: Hazelden Foundation, 1982.

5582.   Strachan, J. George. Treating the Family. In: Alcoholism:
        Treatable Illness. An Honorable Approach to Man's Alcoholism
        Problem. Vancouver, B.C.: Mitchell Press, 1968, pages 177-194.

5583.   Strada-Bello, O., Perez-Alfaro-Calvo, C., Martinez-Gomez, R.
        Experiencia Sobre Tratamiento Sociocomunitario De
        Alcoholicos En El Hospital Psiquiatrico Provincial "Roman
        Alberca", De Murcia. (Experience with Socio-Communicative
        Treatment of Alcoholics at the Provincial Psychiatric
        Hospital "Roman Alberca" at Murcia.) Drogalcohol, 5:
        35-46, 1980.

5584.   Stratton, John G. and Wroe, Brian. Alcoholism and the Policeman:
        Identifying and Dealing With the Problem. FBI Law
        Enforcement Bulletin, 48(3): 20-23, 1979.

5585.   Straus, P. Les Parents Maltraitants: Abord Psychologique, Abord
        Sociologique. (Child-Abusing Parents: Psychological and
        Sociological Approach.) Soins, Paris, 23: 13-17, 1978.

5586.   Straus, Patricia Lawrence. A Study of the Recurrence of
        Father-Daughter Incest Across Generations. Dissertation
        Abstracts International, 42(11): 4564B, 1981.

5587.   Straus, R. Excessive Drinking and Its Relationship to Marriage.
        Marriage and Family Living, 12: 79-82, 94, 1950.

5588.   Straus, Robert. Alcohol and the Homeless Man. Quarterly Journal
        of Studies on Alcohol, 7: 360-404, 1946.

5589.   Straus, Robert. The Life Record of an Alcoholic. Quarterly
        Journal of Studies on Alcohol, 34(4): 1212-1219, 1973.

5590.   Straus, Robert and Bacon, Selden D. Alcoholism and Social
        Stability. A Study of Occupational Integration in 2,023
        Male Clinic Patients. Quarterly Journal of Studies on
        Alcohol, 12: 231-260, 1951.

5591.   Straus, Robert and McCarthy, Raymond G. Nonaddictive Pathological
        Drinking Patterns of Homeless Men. Quarterly Journal of
        Studies on Alcohol, 12: 601-611, 1951.

5592.   Straus, Robert and Winterbottom, Miriam T. Drinking Patterns
        of an Occupational Group: Domestic Servants. Quarterly
        Journal of Studies on Alcohol, 10: 441-460, 1949.

5593.   Strauss, L. Las Toxicofrenias Alcoholicas En La Republica de
        Panama. (Alcoholic Psychoses in the Republic of Panama.)
        Boletin de la Asociacion Medica Nacional de Panama, 13:
        65-90, 1950.

5594.   Straussner, S.L.A., Weinstein, D.L. and Hernandez, R. Effects
        of Alcoholism on the Family System. Health and Social
        Work, 4(4): 111-127, 1979.

5595.   Strayer, Robert. The Social Worker's Role in Handling the
        Resistances of the Alcoholic. In: Differential Diagnosis
        and Treatment in Social Work. Ed. Francis J. Turner.
        New York: Free Press, 1968, pages 215-221.

5596.   Strayer, Robert. A Study of the Negro Alcoholic. Quarterly
        Journal of Studies on Alcohol, 22: 111-123, 1961.

5597.   Strayer, Robert. Treatment of Client and Spouse by the Same
        Caseworker. Quarterly Journal of Studies on Alcohol,
        20: 86-102, 1959.

5598. Strecker, E.A. Psychotherapy in Pathological Drinking. Journal of the American Medical Association, 147: 813-815, 1951.

5599. Streissguth, Ann Pytkowicz. Alcohol and Pregnancy: An Overview and an Update. Substance and Alcohol Actions/Misuse, 4 (2/3): 149-171, 1983.

5600. Streissguth, Ann Pytkowicz. Psychologic Handicaps in Children with the Fetal Alcohol Syndrome. Annals of the New York Academy of Sciences, 273: 140-145, 1976.

5601. Streissguth, Ann Pytkowicz. Maternal Alcoholism and the Outcome of Pregnancy: A Review of the Fetal Alcohol Syndrome. In: Alcoholism Problems In Women and Children. Eds. M. Greenblatt and M.A. Schuckit. 1976, pages 251-274.

5602. Streissguth, Ann Pytkowicz. Maternal Drinking and the Outcome of Pregnancy: Implications for Child Mental Health. American Journal of Orthopsychiatry, 47(3): 422-431, 1977.

5603. Streissguth, Ann Pytkowicz. Clarren, S.K. and Jones, K.L. Natural History of the Fetal Alcohol Syndrome: A 10-Year Follow-Up of Eleven Patients. Lancet, 2(8446): 85-91, 1985.

5604. Streissguth, Ann Pytkowicz, Herman, C.S. and Smith, D.W. Intelligence, Behavior, and Dysmorphogenesis in the Fetal Alcohol Syndrome: A Report on 20 Patients. Journal of Pediatrics, 92: 363-367, 1978.

5605. Streit, F. and Nicolich, M.J. Myths Versus Data on American Indian Drug Abuse. Journal of Drug Education, 7: 117-122, 1977.

5606. Streit, Fred, Halsted, Donald L. and Pascale, Pietro J. Differences Among Youthful Users and Nonusers of Drugs Based on Their Perceptions of Parental Behavior. International Journal of the Addictions, 9(5): 749-755, 1974.

5607. Streit, Fred and Oliver, Hilory, G. Jr. The Child's Perception of His Family and Its Relationship to Drug Use. Drug Forum, 1(3): 283-289, 1972.

5608. Strelnick, A.H. Multiple Family Group Therapy: A Review of the Literature. Family Process, 16(3): 307-325, 1977.

5609. Strickland, D.E. and Pittman, D.J. Social Learning and Teenage Alcohol Use: Interpersonal and Observational Influences within the Sociocultural Environment. Journal of Drug Issues, 14(1): 137-150, 1984.

5610. Stricklin, A.B. and Austad, C.S. Perceptions of Neglected Children and Negligent Parents About Causes for Removal from Parental Homes. Psychological Reports, 51(3, Part 2): 1103-1108, 1982.

5611. Strober, Michael. The Significance of Bulimia in Juvenile Anorexia Nervosa: An Exploration of Possible Etiologic Factors. International Journal of Eating Disorders, 1(1): 28-43, 1981.

5612. Strober, Michael, Salkin, Barbara, Burroughs, Jane and Morrell, Wendy. Validity of the Bulimia-Restricter Distinction in Anorexia Nervosa. Parental Personality Characteristics and Family Psychiatric Morbidity. Journal of Nervous and Mental Disease, 170(6): 345-351, 1982.

5613. Stromgren, E. Genetic Implications of Alcoholism. Acta Geneticae Medicae et Gemellologiae, Rome, 11: 333-337, 1962.

5614. Strug, David L. and Hyman, Merton M. Social Networks of Alcoholics. Journal of Studies on Alcohol, 42: 855-884, 1981.

5615. Strzembosz, A. Dzieci Z 200 Rodzin Alkoholikow I Alkoholiczek.
       (Children From 200 Families of Alcoholic Mothers and
       Fathers.) Archiv fur Kryminologie, 7: 265-286, 1976.

5616. Strzembosz, A. Stopien Przystosowania Spolecznego Dzieci
       Alkoholikow Z Warszawy Objetych Przed 10 Laty Postepowaniem
       Opiekunczym. (Degree of Social Adjustment in Children of
       Warsaw Alcoholics 10 Years After They Had Been Placed in
       Guardianship.) Problemy Alkoholizmu, Warsaw, 26(10):
       11, 14, 1979.

5617. Stuart, J. Families of Alcohol and Drug Dependent Persons.
       In: 1982 Autumn School of Studies on Alcohol and
       Drugs. Melbourne, 1982, pages 129-133.

5618. Stubblefield, Robert L. Synopsis: Multidimensional Problems
       of Alcoholism. Journal: National Association of Private
       Psychiatric Hospitals, 9(4): 31-32, 1978.

5619. Stuckey, R.F. Daughters of Alcoholics and the Women's Movement.
       The U.S. Journal of Drug and Alcohol Dependence, 9(7):
       7, 1985. (Also in: Focus on Family and Chemical Dependency,
       8(3): 30-31, 37, 1985.)

5620. Stuckey, R.F. and Harrison, J.S. Alcoholism Rehabilitation
       Center. In: Encyclopedic Handbook of Alcoholism.
       Eds. E. Pattison and E. Kaufman. New York: Gardner
       Press, 1982, pages 865-873.

5621. Stucki, A. Mania Begins in Childhood. Praxis, Bern, 66(8):
       238-239, 1977.

5622. Student, V. and Matova, A. Vyvoj Psychickych Poruch u
       Manzelek Alkoholiku. (Development of Mental Disorders
       in Wives of Alcoholics.) Ceskoslovenska Psychiatrie,
       65: 23-29, 1969.

5623. Studies Indicate Teen Drinking Behavior Influenced by Parents.
       NIAAA Information and Feature Service. (Experimental Issue):
       April, 1974, page 5.

5624. Study: Alcoholism Treatment Costs. ADAMHA News (Alcohol, Drug
       Abuse, and Mental Health Administration), 11(3):1, 7, 1985.

5625. Study Examines Parents' Drinking Patterns. NIAAA Information
       and Feature Service, (No. 86): 9, July 30, 1981.

5626. Stumphauzer, Jerome S. and Perez Philip Jr. Learning to Drink:
       II. Peer Survey of Normal Adolescents. International
       Journal of the Addictions, 17(8): 1363-1372, 1982.

5627. Sturge, M.D. and Horsley, V. On Some of the Biological and
       Statistical Errors in the Work on Parental Alcoholism by
       Miss Elderton and Professor Karl Pearson. British Medical
       Journal, 1: 72-82, 1911.

5628. Sturkie, D. Kinly and Flanzer, Jerry P. An Examination of Two
       Social Work Treatment Models with Abusive Families. In:
       Family Treatment in Social Work. University Centennial
       Edition. Ed. Elizabeth McBroom. Los Angeles: School of
       Social Work, University of Southern California, 1981.
       (Eric Document Number ED225644.) (Also in: Social Work
       Papers, 16: 53-62, 1981.)

5629. Subby, Robert. Chemically Dependent Marriage. Focus on Alcohol
       and Drug Issues, 6(2): 19-21, 1983.

5630. Subby, Robert. Co-Dependency: Family Process Outcome. Focus on
       Family and Chemical Dependency, 6(6): 21, 36, 1983.

5631. Subby, Robert. The Dynamics of the Family Illness. In: Alcoholism and the Family: A Book of Readings. Eds. Sharon Wegscheider-Cruse and Richard W. Esterly. Wernersville, PA: The Caron Institute, 1985, pages 9-18.

5632. Sudia, C.E. What Services Do Abusive and Neglecting Families Need? In: Social Context of Child Abuse and Neglect. Ed. L.H. Pelton. New York: Human Sciences Press, 1981, pages 268-290.

5633. Sudduth, W.H. The Role of Bacteria and Enterotoxemia in Physical Addiction to Alcohol. Journal of the International Academy of Preventive Medicine, 4(2): 23-46, 1977.

5634. Sue, Stanley and Nakamura, Charles Y. An Integrative Model of Physiological and Social/Psychological Factors in Alcohol Consumption Among Chinese and Japanese Americans. Journal of Drug Issues, 14(2): 349-364, 1984.

5635. Suhre, M.P. Family Members of Alcoholics at Work; Al-Anon as a Treatment Resource. Labor-Management Alcoholism Journal 10: 177-178, 1981.

5636. Suliman, Hassaba. Alcohol and Islamic Faith. Drug and Alcohol Dependence, 11(1): 63-66, 1983.

5637. Sulkunen, Pekka. The Wet Generation, Living Conditions and Drinking Patterns in Finland. Continuities in a Reanalysis of Finnish Drinking Survey Data. (Reports from the Social Research Institute of Alcohol Studies, No. 155, December 1981.) Helsinki: The State Alcohol Monopolis, Social Research Institute of Alcohol Studies, 1981.

5638. Sullivan, A.C., Targum, S.D. and Advani, M.T. Variables Related to Outcome of Treatment for Inpatient Alcoholics. Alcohol Health and Research World, 6(1): 58-60, 1981.

5639. Sullivan, Daniel J. Putting the Relationship on the Shelf. Focus on Family and Chemical Dependency, 8(4): 22-23, 30, 1985.

5640. Sullivan, J.L., Cavenar, J.O., Jr., Maltbie, A.A., Lister, P. and Zung, W.W.K. Familial Biochemical and Clinical Correlates of Alcoholics with Low Platelet Momoamine Oxidase Activity. Biological Psychiatry, 14: 385-394, 1979.

5641. Sullivan, John L., Sullivan, Paula D., Davidson, Jonathan, Coffey, C. Edward, Mahorney, Steven, Taska, Ronald J. and Cavenar, Jesse O. Predictive Value of Platelek Monoamine Oxidase Activity in the Treatment of Depressed Alcoholics With Lithium. In: Biological/Genetic Factors in Alcoholism. (National Institute on Alcohol and Alcohol Abuse Research Monograph Series, No. 9.) Eds. Victor M. Hesselbrock, Edward G. Shaskan and Roger E. Meyer. Washington, D.C.: U.S. Government Printing Office, 1983, pages 131-143.

5642. Sullivan, W.C. The Causes of Inebriety in the Female, and the Effects of Alcoholism on Racial Degeneration. British Journal of Inebriety, Edinburgh, 1: 61-64, 1903.

5643. Sullivan, William C. Alcoholism and Eugenics. The British Journal of Inebriety, Edinburgh; 13: 75-77, 1915.

5644. Summary of Group Discussions. In: What Family Agencies Can Do to Help Alcoholics and Families. Ed. A. Kuhn. Illinois Division of Alcoholism, 1962, pages 62-67.

5645. Summary Report on Short Term Family Therapy for Alcoholics: A Research and Evaluation Study. Washington, D.C.: North American Association of Alcoholism Programs, 1970.

5646. Sumrak, D. Poremecaji Ponasanja I Teskoce Ucenja Kod Djece
      I Omladine Ciji Roditelji Imaju Neuropsihijatrijske
      Poremecaje. (Behavior Disorders and Learning Difficulties
      of Children and Adolescents with Parents Suffering from
      Neuropsychiatric Disorders.) Alkoholizam, Beograd,
      19:(3-4), 118-122, 1979.

5647. Sundgren, Ann Shea. Sex Differences in Adjustment to an
      Alcoholic Spouse. Doctoral Dissertation. (University
      Microfilms No. 7917644.) Washington: University of
      Washington, 1978. (Also in: Dissertation Abstracts
      International, 40(2):1111A, 1979.)

5648. Surawicz, Frida G. Alcoholic Hallucinosis: A Missed Diagnosis.
      Differential Diagnosis and Management. Canadian Journal of
      Psychiatry, 25(1): 57-63, 1980.

5649. Survey of A.A. Members. Public Health Reports, 84(2): 120,
      1969.

5650. Suslak, Lorraine, Shopsin, Baron, Silbey, Esther, Mendlewicz,
      Julien and Gersbon, Samuel. Genetics of Affective Disorders:
      I. Familial Incidence Study of Bipolar, Unipolar and Schizo-
      Affective Illnesses. Neuropsychobiology, 2(1): 18-27, 1976.

5651. Sutherland, Ediwn H., Schroeder, H.G. and Tordella, C.L. Personality
      Traits and the Alcoholic. A Critique of Existing Studies.
      Quarterly Journal of Studies on Alcohol, 11: 547-561, 1950.

5652. Sutherland, Mary S. Relevant Curriculum Planning in Health
      Education: A Methodology. Journal of School Health,
      49(7): 387-389, 1979.

5653. Suwaki, H. Alcoholism and Affective Disorder. International
      Journal of Rehabilitation Research, 2(4): 531-532, 1979.

5654. Suwaki, H. Japan: Culturally Based Treatment of Alcoholism. In:
      Drug Problems in the Sociocultural Context. Eds. G. Edwards
      and A. Arif. Geneva: World Health Organization, 1980, pages
      139-143.

5655. Suwaki, H., Horii, S., Ikeda, H., Otsuki, S., Nishii, Y. and
      Takahashi, S. and Fujimoto, A. A Survey of In Patient
      Alcoholics in Okayama Prefecture Japan. Okayama Igakkai
      Zasshi, Okayama, 92(1-2): 85-92, 1980.

5656. Suwaki, H. Naikan and Danshukai for the Treatment of Japanese
      Alcoholic Patients. The British Journal of Addiction,
      74(1): 15-20, 1979.

5657. Suwaki, H., Nishii, Y., Ikeda, H. and Ohara, H. A Survey of
      Inpatient Alcoholics in Kochi Prefecture. Japanese Journal
      of Studies on Alcohol, 15:304-316, 1980.

5658. Suwaki, H., Nishi, Y., Yoshida, T. and Ohara, H. Backgrounds
      and Prognosis of Adolescents with Glue Sniffing. Japanese
      Journal of Alcohol Studies and Drug Dependence, Kyoto,
      17(1): 74-86, 1982.

5659. Suzuki, S., Suzuki, Y., Sugita, T., Funakoshi, A., Ohara, K. and
      Hattori, S. On the Alcoholics Under 35 Years Old in Contrast
      with Alcoholics in Their Forties. Japanese Journal of Alcohol
      Studies and Drug Dependenc, Kyoto, 19(1): 63-73, 1984.

5660. Svanstrom L. and Urwitz, V. Sociomedical Development Work at a
      Social Welfare Office in a Metropolitan Area. A Preliminary
      Report. Scandanavian Journal of Social Medicine, Stockholm,
      1(3): 91-95, 1973.

5661.   Swanson, D.W. Adult Sexual Abuse of Children: The Man and
        Circumstances. Diseases of the Nervous System, 29:
        677-683, 1968.

5662.   Swanson, D.W., Moore, G.L. and Nobrega, F.T. Family History
        of Alcoholism in Patients with Chronic Fatigue. Journal
        of Clinical Psychiatry, 39(10): 754-755, 1978.

5663.   Swanson, D.W., Weddige, R.L. and Morse, R.M. Abuse of
        Prescription Drugs. Mayo Clinic Proceedings, 48(5):
        359-367, 1973.

5664.   Swanson, David W., Bratrude, Amos P. and Brown, Edward M.
        Alcohol Abuse in a Population of Indian Children.
        Diseases of the Nervous System, 32(12): 835-842, 1971.

5665.   Swanson, David W., Brown, Edward M. and Beuret, Lawrence J.
        A Family with Five Schizophrenic Children. Diseases of
        the Nervous System, 30(3): 189-193, 1969.

5666.   Swanson, R.W. Battered Wife Syndrome. Canadian Medical
        Association Journal, Ottawa, 130(6): 709-712, 1984.

5667.   'Sweet Seventeen' From the Child of an Alcoholic. COA Newsletter,
        3(2): 5, 1985.

5668.   Swegan, W.E. Alcoholism: The Family Disorder. Pamphlet.
        Oakland, CA: Occupational Health Services, 1978.

5669.   Swensen, Clifford H. and Davis, Hugh C. Types of Workhouse Inmate
        Alcoholics. Quarterly Journal of Studies on Alcohol, 20:
        757-766, 1959.

5670.   Swenson, W.M. and Morse, R.M. The Use of a Self-Administered
        Alcoholism Screening Test (SAAST) in a Medical Center.
        Mayo Clinic Proceedings, 50: 204-208, 1975.

5671.   Swiecicki, A. Przystosowanie Spoleczne Doroslych Dzieci z Rodzin
        Alkoholikow i nie Alkoholikow: Badania Retrospektywne
        Obejmujace Okres 10 Lat. (Adult Adjustment of Children from
        Alcoholic and Nonalcoholic Families: A 10-Year Follow-Up Study.)
        Problemy Alkoholizmu, Warsaw, 17(2): 1-7, 1969.

5672.   Swiecicki, A. Dzieci i Pomoc Udzielana Dzieciom z Rodzin
        Alkoholikow i Rodzin Grupy Kontrolnej. (Children and
        Assistance Given to Children from Alcoholic Families
        and Control Families.) Problemy Alkoholizmu, Warsaw,
        15(8): 1-4, 1967.

5673.   Swift, Harold A. and Williams, Terence. Recovery for the Whole
        Family. Pamphlet. Center City, MN: Hazelden Educational
        Services, 1975.

5674.   Swihart, J.J., Borek, T. and Schumm, W.R. Psycho Social Factors
        Associated with the Adjustment of Basic Trainees in the USA
        Army. Psychological Reports, 52(3): 757-758, 1983.

5675.   Swinson, R.P. Colour Vision Defects in Alcoholism. British
        Journal of Physiological Optics, 27: 43-50, 1972.

5676.   Swinson, R.P. Genetic Polymorphism and Alcoholism. Annals of
        the New York Academy of Sciences, 197: 129-133, 1972.

5677.   Swinson, Richard P. Sex Differences in the Inheritance of
        Alcoholism. In: Research Advances in Alcohol and Drug
        Problems, Volume 5: Alcohol and Drug Problems in Women.
        Ed. Oriana Josseau Kalant. New York: Plenum Press, 1980,
        pages 233-262.

5678. Swinson, Richard P. and Eaves, Derek. Alcoholism and Addiction. Totowa, NJ: Woburn Press, 1978.

5679. Swinson, Richard P. and Eaves, Derek. Individual Factors in the Causation of Alcoholism and Drug Dependence. In: Alcoholism and Addiction. Totowa, NJ: Woburn Press, 1978, pages 100-132.

5680. Swinson, Richard P. and Eaves, Derek. Medical Management of Alcoholism and Drug Dependence. In: Alcoholism and Addiction. Totowa, NJ: Woburn Press, 1978, pages 199-232.

5681. Swinson, Richard P. and Eaves, Derek. Normal Drinking and Drug-Taking. In: Alcoholism and Addiction. Totowa, NJ: Woburn Press, 1978, pages 1-15.

5682. Swinson, Richard P. and Eaves, Derek. Outcome of Treatment. In: Alcoholism and Addiction. Totowa, NJ: Woburn Press, 1978, pages 261-294.

5683. Swinson, Richard P. and Eaves Derek. Social Complications of Alcoholism and Drug Abuse. In: Alcoholism and Addiction. Totowa, NJ: Woburn Press, 1978, pages 158-198.

5684. Swinson, Richard P. and Eaves, Derek. Social Influences in the Causation of Alcoholism and Drug Dependence. In: Alcoholism and Addiction. Totowa, NJ: Woburn Press, 1978, pages 74-99.

5685. Swinson, Richard P. and Eaves, Derek. The Social Management of Alcoholism and Addiction. In: Alcoholism and Addiction. Totowa, NJ: Woburn Press, 1978, pages 233-260.

5686. Swinson, Robert P. Genetic Markers and Alcoholism. In: Recent Developments in Alcoholism, Volume 1, Genetics, Behavioral Treatment, Social Mediators and Prevention, Current Concepts in Diagnosis. Ed. Marc Galanter. New York: Plenum Press, 1983, pages 9-24.

5687. Swint, J. Michael and Lairson, David R. Economic Evaluation of Occupation-Based Programs: Conflicting Criteria and the Case for Government Subsidy. Journal of Studies on Alcohol, 46(2): 157-160, 1985.

5688. Synol, Kathryn M. Family Mapping: Toward an Understanding of the Interactional Dynamic of the Alcoholic Marital Dyad. International Journal of the Addictions, 19(7): 743-752, 1984.

5689. Sytinsky, I.A. and Boyko, V.V. Training of the Students of Medical and Pedagogical Institutions of Higher Education for Preventive Antialcohol Work. Paper presented at the 25th International Institute on the Prevention and Treatment of Alcoholism, Tours, France, June 1979, pages 45-46.

5690. Szakacs, F., Fargo, K. and Molnar, I. Alkoholista Esnem Alkoholista Apak Csaladjaban Elo Gyermekek Szocialis-Moralis Fejlettsege Es Mentalis Szinvonala. (The Social-Moral Maturity and Mental Level of Children Living in Families with an Alcoholic and a Nonalcoholic Father.) Alkohologia, Budapest, 5: 4-24, 1974.

5691. Szamosi, J. A Gyermekkori Alkoholmergezes es Therapiaja. (Alcohol Intoxication in Childhood and its Treatment.) Gyermekgyogyaszat, Budapest, 14: 81-88, 1963.

5692. Szapocznik, Jose, Lasaga, Jose I. and Scopetta, Mercedes A. Culture Specific Approaches to the Treatment of Latin Multiple Substance Abusers: Family and Ecological Intervention Models. Rockville, MD: National Institute on Alcohol Abuse and Alcoholism, 1976.

5693. Szapocznik, Jose, Scopetta, Mercedes, A. and De Los Angeles
       Aranalde, Maria. The Characteristics of Cuban Immigrant
       Inhalant Abusers. American Journal of Drug and Alcohol
       Abuse, 4(3): 377-389, 1977.

5694. Szilagyi, Pagowska I. Development of Children of Alcoholic
       Parents Assessed on the Basis of Some Somatic Features.
       Pediatria Polska, 48(11): 1421-1428, 1972.

5695. Szymanowska, A. Sytuacja Bytowa Rodzin Alkoholikoow. (Living
       Conditions in Families of Alcoholics.) Problemy Alkoholiznu,
       Warsaw, 21(10): 1-2, 1973.

T

5696. Tabakoff, B., Sutker, P.B. and Randall, C.L. (Eds.) Medical and Social Aspects of Alcohol Abuse. New York: Plenum Press, 1983.

5697. Tableman, B. Commonalities in Prevention Programming to Reduce Alcohol, Drug Abuse and Mental Health Problems Among Children and Youth. Paper Presented at the First Annual Alcohol, Drug Abuse and Mental Health Administration Conference on Prevention, Silver Spring, MD, September, 1979.

5698. Tableman, B. Overview of Programs to Prevent Mental Health Problems of Children. Public Health Reports, 96(1): 38-44, 1981.

5699. Tagliavini, F., Pietrini, V., Pilleri, G., Trabattoni, G. and Lechi, A. Adult Meta Chromatic Leuko Dystrophy Clinico Pathological Report of Two Familial Cases with Slow Course. Neuropathology and Applied Neurobiology, Oxford, 5(3): 233-244, 1979.

5700. Tahka, Jorma. Alcoholism as a Disorder of Self-Esteem. Duodecim, Helsinki, 98(4): 243-250, 1982.

5701. Tahka, V. The Alcoholic Personality; a Clinical Study. Helsinki: Finnish Foundation for Alcohol Studies (Publication Number 13), 1966.

5702. Tahka, V. Juoppouden Psykodynaamisesta Etiologiasta. (On the Psychodynamic Etiology of Drunkenness.) Alkoholipolitiikka, Helsinki, (6): 175-182, 1954.

5703. Tahka, V. Om Drychenskapens Psykodynamiska Etiologi. (On the Psychodynamic Etiology of Drunkenness.) Alkoholipolitiikka, Helsinki, (4): 103-110, 1954.

5704. Takach, G. and Flam, A. Die Rolle Und Die Bedeutung Von Ehepaargruppen Beim Verlauf Der Rehabilitation Von Alkoholkranken. (Role and Significance of Groups of Married Couples for Progressive Rehabilitation of Alcoholic Patients.) Paper presented at the 27th International Institute on the Prevention and Treatment of Alcoholism, Vienna, 1981, pages 361-373.

5705. Takahashi, S., Fujimoto, A., Suwaki, H., Horii, S. and Nishii, Y. A Survey of Danshukai Members in Okayama Prefecture (Japan). Okayama Igakkai Zasshi, Okayama, 93(7-8): 729-738, 1981.

5706. Takman, J. Thinner-, Alkohol- ock Tablettmissbruk Bland Barn Och Ungdom: Socialmedicinska Synpunkter. (Thinner, Alcohol and Drug Misuse in Children and Adolescents: Sociomedical Aspects.) Nordisk Medicin, Copenhagen, 70: 899-903, 1963.

5707. Talbott, Evelyn, Kuller, Lewis H., Detre, Katherine and Perper, Joshua. Biologic and Psychosocial Risk Factors of Sudden Death From Coronary Disease in White Women. American Journal of Cardiology, 39(6): 858-864, 1977.

5708. Talbott, G.D., Severinsen, D., Townshend, P. and Duren, R. Beginning. In: Courage to Change. Ed. D. Wholey. Boston: Houghton Mifflin Company, 1984, pages 15-43.

5709. Talbott, G. Douglas and Benson, Earl B. Impaired Physicians. The Dilemma of Identification. Postgraduate Medicine, 68(6): 56-64, 1980.

5710. Talbott, G. Douglas and Cooney, M. Today's Disease: Alcohol and Drug Dependence. Springfield, IL: Charles C. Thomas, 1982.

5711. Talbott, G. Douglas and Martin, Carolyn A. Family Factors in Treating Impaired Health Professionals. Focus on Family and Chemical Dependency, 8(3): 12-13, 36, 1985.

5712. Talcott, G.W. Familial and Nonfamilial Alcoholism Among Inpatient Alcoholic Males: A Multivariate Analysis Using the MMPI. Dissertation Abstracts International, 45(8): 2460A, 1985.

5713. Taleghani, M. Quelques Regles d'Epistemologie en Alcoologie. (Some Epistemological Principles in the Study of Alcoholism.) La Revue de l'Alcoolisme, Paris, 29(4): 238-240, 1983.

5714. Tamerin, J.S. and Neumann, C.P. Prognostic Factors in the Evaluation of Addicted Individuals. International Pharmacopsychiatry, 6(2): 69-76, 1971.

5715. Tamerin, J.S., Tolor, A., DeWolfe, J., Packer, L. and Neumann, C.P. Spouses' Perceptions of Their Alcoholic Partners: A Retrospective View of Alcoholics by Themselves and Their Spouses. Paper presented at the Third Annual Alcoholism Conference of the National Institute on Alcohol Abuse and Alcoholism, Washington, D.C., June, 1973. (Also in: Proceedings of the Third Annual Alcoholism Conference of the NIAAA. Ed. Morris E. Chafetz. Washington, D.C.: U.S. Government Printing Office, 1974.)

5716. Tamerin, John S. Alcoholism and Family Discord. Medical Aspects of Human Sexuality, 13(2): 143-144, 1978.

5717. Tamerin, John S. and Neumann, Charles P. Psychological Aspects of Treating Alcoholism. Alcohol Health and Research World, (Spring): 14-18, 1974.

5718. Tamerin, John S., Tolor, Alexander and Harrington, Betsy. Sex Differences in Alcoholics: A Comparison of Male and Female Alcoholics' Self and Spouse Perceptions. American Journal of Drug and Alcohol Abuse, 3(3): 457-472, 1976.

5719. Tamerin, John S., Tolor, Alexander and Harrington, Betsy. Sex Differences in Alcoholics: A Comparison of Self and Spouse Perceptions. Paper Presented at Alcohol and Drug Problems Association Conference, San Francisco, December, 1974.

5720. Tanabe, K. What Drove My Husband to Drinking. Kango, 30(3): 81-85, 1978.

5721. Tanna, Vasantkumar L., Go, Rodney, C.P., Winokur, George and Elston, Robert C. Possible Linkage Between Alpha-Haptoglobin (Hp) and Depression Spectrum Disease. Neuropsychobiology, Basel, 5: 102-113, 1979.

5722. Tanna, Vasantkumar L., Go, Rodney C.P., Winokur, George and
        Elston, Robert C. Possible Linkage Between Group-Specific
        Component (Gc Protein) and Pure Depressive Disease. Acta
        Psychiatrica Scandinavica, Stockholm, 55(2): 111-115, 1977.

5723. Tanna, Vasantkumar L., Winokur, George, Elston, Robert C. and
        Go, Rodney C. Blood Markers and Depressive Disorders:
        An Association Study. Comprehensive Psychiatry, 18(3):
        263-269, 1977.

5724. Tanna, Vasantkumar L., Winokur, George, Elston, Robert C. and Go, Rodney
        C. A Linkage Study of Depression Spectrum Disease: The Use of the
        Sib-Pair Method. Neuropsychobiology, Basel, 2(1): 52-62, 1976.

5725. Tapia-P. I., Gaete-A. J., Munoz-L. C., Sescovitch, S., Miranda, I.,
        Minguell-I. J., Perez-P. G. and Orellana-A.G. Patrones Socio-
        Culturales de la Ingestion de Alcohol en Chiloe; Informe
        Preliminar: Algunos Problemas Metodologicos. (Sociocultural
        Patterns of Drinking on the Isle of Chiloe; Preliminary Report:
        Some Methodological Problems.) Acta Psiquiatrica Y Psicologica
        De America Latina, Buenos Aires, 12: 232-240, 1966.

5726. Targum, S.D., Byrnes, S.M. and Sullivan, A.C. Subtypes of Unipolar
        Depression Distinguished by the Dexamethasone Suppression Test.
        Journal of Affective Disorders, Amsterdam, 4(1): 21-27, 1982.

5727. Tarnower, S.M. and Toole, H.M. Evaluation of Patients in Alcoholism
        Clinic for More Than Ten Years. Diseases of the Nervous System,
        29(1): 28-31, 1968.

5728. Tarter, Ralph E. The Causes of Alcoholism: A Biopsychological
        Analysis. In: Etiologic Aspects of Alcohol and Drug Abuse.
        Eds. Edward Gottheil, Keith A. Druley, Thomas E. Skoloda and
        Howard M. Waxman. Springfield, IL: Charles C. Thomas, 1983,
        pages 173-201.

5729. Tarter, Ralph E. Etiology of Alcoholism: Interdisciplinary
        Integration. Paper presented at the NATO Conference on
        Experimental and Behavioral Approaches to Alcoholism,
        Oslo, August-September, 1977, pages 41-70.

5730. Tarter, Ralph E. Personality of Wives of Alcoholics. Journal of
        Clinical Psychology, 32(3): 741-743, 1976.

5731. Tarter, Ralph E. and Alterman, Arthur I. Neuropsychological
        Deficits in Alcoholics: Etiological Considerations.
        Journal of Studies on Alcohol, 45(1): 1-9, 1984.

5732. Tarter, Ralph E., Alterman, Arthur I. and Edwards, Kathleen L.
        Vulnerability to Alcoholism in Men: A Behavior-Genetic
        Perspective. Journal of Studies on Alcohol, 46(4):
        329-356, 1985.

5733. Tarter, Ralph E., Hegedus, Andrea M. and Gavaler, Joan S.
        Hyperactivity in Sons of Alcoholics. Journal of Studies
        on Alcohol, 46(3): 259-261, 1985.

5734. Tarter, Ralph E., Hegedus, Andrea M., Goldstein, G., Shelly, C.
        and Alterman, A.I. Adolescent Sons of Alcoholics: Neuro-
        psychological and Personality Characteristics. Alcoholism:
        Clinical and Experimental Research, 8(2): 216-222, 1984.

5735. Tarter, Ralph E., McBride, Herbert, Buonpane, Nancy and Schneider,
        Dorothea U. Differentiation of Alcoholics: Childhood History of
        Minimal Brain Dysfunction, Family History, and Drinking Pattern.
        Archives of General Psychiatry, 34(7): 761-768, 1977.

5736. Tarter, Ralph E. and Schneider, D.U. Blackouts; Relationship
       with Memory Capacity and Alcoholism History. Archives of
       General Psychiatry, 33: 1492-1496, 1976.

5737. Tarter, Ralph E. and Sugerman, A.A. (Eds.) Alcoholism;
       Interdisciplinary Approaches to an Enduring Problem.
       Reading, MA: Addison-Wesley, 1976.

5738. TASC to Serve Mentally Ill, Spouse Abusers. U.S. Law Enforcement
       Assistance Administration. LEAA Newsletter, 2(4): 6-7, 1981.

5739. Tate, J.B. Aftercare: Protecting Your Investment. EAP Digest,
       4(2): 24-26, 1984.

5740. Tavarone, Antonia Regina. The Role of Family Members in the Treatment
       of Women Alcoholics. Dissertation Abstracts International,
       44(10): 3175A, 1984.

5741. Taylor, John R. and Helzer, John E. The Natural History of Alcoholism.
       In: The Biology of Alcoholism, Vol. 6, The Pathogenesis of
       Alcoholism: Psychosocial Factors. Eds. Benjamin Kissin and
       Henri Begleiter. New York: Plenum Press, 1983, pages 17-65.

5742. Taylor, Michael A. and Abrams, Richard. Acute Mania: Clinical and
       Genetic Study of Responders and Nonresponders to Treatments.
       Archives of General Psychiatry, 32(7): 863-865, 1975.

5743. Taylor, Michael A. and Abrams, Richard. Early- and Late-Onset
       Bipolar Illness. Archives of General Psychiatry, 38(1):
       58-61, 1981.

5744. Taylor, Michael A. and Abrams, Richard. Manic States: A Genetic
       Study of Early and Late Onset Affective Disorders. Archives of
       General Psychiatry, 28(5): 656-658, 1973.

5745. Taylor, Michael A., Gaztanaga, Pedro and Abrams, Richard. Manic-
       Depressive Illness and Acute Schizophrenia: A Clinical, Family
       History, and Treatment-Response Study. American Journal of
       Psychiatry, 131(6): 678-682, 1974.

5746. Taylor, N. Alcohol Abuse Prevention Among Women: A Community
       Approach. Paper Presented at the 30th National Alcoholism
       Forum, Washington, D.C., April, 1982.

5747. Taylor, Nancy. Structural Family Therapy: The Sanchez Family.
       In: Chicanas and Alcoholism: A Sociocultural Perspective
       of Women. Eds. Rodolfo Arevalo and Marianne Minor. San Jose:
       School of Social Work, San Jose State University, 1981, pages
       45-55.

5748. Taylor, P. and Bell, P. Alcoholism and Black Families: Cultural
       Barriers...Cultural Diversity. Focus on Family and Chemical
       Dependency, 7(2): 34-35, 1984.

5749. Taylor, Robert B., Camp, Larry, Rogers, Jack M., Updike, Jan and
       Lyle, Carolyn. A Third-Year Family Medicine Clerkship Based
       in an Academic Family Practice Center. Journal of Medical
       Education, 59(1): 39-44, 1984.

5750. Taylor, Thomas R. Psychological Illness in Medical Outpatients.
       Postgraduate Medical Journal, London, 45(521): 173-179, 1969.

5751. Tec, Leon. Family Therapy and Drug Abuse. International
       Pharmacopsychiatry, 7(1-4): 53-55, 1972.

5752. Tec, Nechama. Parent-Child Drug Abuse: Generational Continuity or
       Adolescent Deviancy? Adolescence, 9(35): 351-364, 1974.

5753. Techniques for Enhancing Parenting Skills. Chicago: National Parent Teacher Association, 1977.

5754. Tedder, I.R. and Sidorov, P.I. Influence of the Family on the Attitudes of Children to the Demand for Alcoholic Drinks. Zdravookhranenie Rossiiskoi Federatsii, 7: 10-12, 1976.

5755. Teenage Drinking in Ontario. Information Review. Toronto: Addiction Research Foundation, 1978.

5756. Teich, J. Alcoholic Physician: Issues in Diagnosis and Treatment. In: Alcoholism: Treatment and Recovery. Ed. Marshall Goby. St. Louis, MO: Catholic Health Association, 1984, pages 185-196.

5757. Teicher, Joseph D., Sinay, Ruth D. and Stumphauzer, Jerome S. Behavior Therapy and Alcohol Abuse in Adolescents. In: Scientific Proceedings in Summary Form: 128th Annual Meeting of the American Psychological Association. Washington: American Psychiatric Association, 1975, pages 36-37.

5758. Teicher, Joseph D., Sinay, Ruth D. and Stumphauzer, Jerome S. Training Community-Based Paraprofessionals as Behavior Therapists with Families of Alcohol-Abusing Adolescents. American Journal of Psychiatry, 133(7): 847-850, 1976.

5759. Teja, Jagdish S. Mental Illness and the Family in America and India. International Journal of Social Psychiatry, London, 24(3): 225-231, 1978.

5760. Templer, D.I., Ruff, C.F. and Ayers, J. Essential Alcoholism and Family History of Alcoholism. Quarterly Journal of Studies on Alcohol, 35: 655-657, 1974.

5761. Tennant, F. Dependency Traits Among Parents of Drug Abusers. Journal of Drug Education, 6(1): 83-88, 1976.

5762. Tennant, Forest S. Jr. Childhood Antecendents of Alcohol and Drug Abuse. Doctoral Dissertation. (University Microfilms Number 75-2005.) Los Angeles: University of California, 1974. (Also as: Paper presented at the Thirty-Seventh Annual Scientific Meeting, Committee on Problems of Drug Dependence, Washington, D.C., May, 1975.)

5763. Tennant, Forest S. Jr. Treatment of Alcoholism by the Family Physician. Seminars in Family Medicine, 1(4): 265-270, 1980.

5764. Tennant, Forest S., Jr. and Detels, Roger. Relationship of Alcohol, Cigarette, and Drug Abuse in Adulthood with Alcohol, Cigarette and Coffee Consumption in Childhood. Preventive Medicine, 5: 70-77, 1976.

5765. Tennant, Forest S. Jr., Detels, Roger and Clark, Virginia. Some Childhood Antecedents of Drug and Alcohol Abuse. American Journal of Epidemiology, 102(5): 377-385, 1975.

5766. Tennant, Forest S. Jr. and La-Cour, J. Children at High Risk for Addiction and Alcoholism: Identification and Intervention. Pediatric Nursing, 6: 26-27, 1980.

5767. Tennes, K. and Blackard, C. Maternal Alcohol Consumption, Birth Weight and Minor Physical Anomalies. American Journal of Obstetrics and Gynecology, 138(7): 774-780, 1980.

5768. Terkelsen, K.G. Review of Families, Alcoholism and Therapy by C.P. Barnard. Family Process, 21(4): 490-492, 1982.

5769. Terman, S.A. Varied Problems of the Newly Sober Couple: Strategic
       Approaches in Couples Group. In: Power to Change: Family
       Case Studies in the Treatment of Alcoholism. Ed. Edward Kaufman.
       New York: Gardner Press, 1984, pages 237-251.

5770. Termansen, Paul E. and Bywater, Cathryn. S.A.F.E.R.: A Follow-Up
       Service for Attempted Suicide in Vancouver. Canadian Psychiatric
       Association Journal, Ottawa, 20(1): 29-34, 1975.

5771. Thacher, F.J., Esmiol, P., Ives, H.R. and Mandelkorn, Barbara.
       Can On-Site Counseling Programs Aid Workers, Reduce Health
       Costs. Occupational Health and Safety, 46(6): 48-50, 1977.

5772. Thacker, S.B., Veech, R.L., Vernon, A.A. and Rutstein, D.D. Genetic
       and Biochemical Factors Relevant to Alcoholism. Alcoholism:
       Clinical and Experimental Research, 8(4): 375-383, 1984.

5773. Thacore, V.R., Gupta, S.C. and Suraiya, M. Psychiatric Morbidity
       in a North Indian Community. British Medical Journal: The
       Journal of Mental Science, London, 126: 365-369, 1975.

5774. Thematic Section: Children of Alcoholics. Rockville, MD:
       National Clearinghouse for Alcohol Information, 1984.

5775. Therapeutic Issues of Adult Children of Alcoholics. Rockville, MD:
       National Clearinghouse for Alcohol Information, 1984.

5776. Thimann, J. Constructive Teamwork in the Treatment of Alcoholism.
       Quarterly Journal of Studies on Alcohol, 8: 569-579, 1948.

5777. Thirty-five Year Study: Alcoholic Children Mimic Parents.
       Medical World News, 18(16): 24-25, 1977.

5778. Thomas, Beryl. Social Worker Role in the Treatment of Alcohol
       Dependency. Paper presented at Canterbury University, Christ
       Church, New Zealand, 1974, pages 54-62.

5779. Thomas, Caroline Bedell. Precursors of Premature Disease and
       Death: The Predictive Potential of Habits and Family Attitudes.
       Annals of Internal Medicine, 85(5): 653-658, 1976.

5780. Thomas, David Arthur. A Study of Selected Factors on Successfully
       and Unsuccessfully Treated Alcoholic Women. Dissertation
       Abstracts International, 32(3): 1862-1863B, 1971.

5781. Thomas, Edwin J. and Santa, Cathleen A. Unilateral Family
       Therapy for Alcohol Abuse: A Working Conception. American
       Journal of Family Therapy, 10(3): 49-58, 1982.

5782. Thomas, J.L. Marital Failure and Duration. Social Order, 3:
       24-29, 1953.

5783. Thomas, R. Buckland, Luber, Shula A. and Smith, Jackson A.
       A Survey of Alcohol and Drug Use in Medical Students.
       Diseases of the Nervous System, 38(1): 41-43, 1977.

5784. Thomas, Robert E., Gilliam, J.H., and Walker, D.R. Casework
       Services for Alcoholics in a Magistrate's Court. Social
       Work, 5(1): 39-45, 1960.

5785. Thomas, Robert E., Gliedman, Lester H., Freund, Julia, Imber,
       Stanley D. and Stone, Anthony R. Favorable Response in the
       Clinical Treatment of Chronic Alcoholism. Journal of the
       American Medical Association, 169: 1994-1997, 1959.

5786. Thomas, Robert E., Gliedman, Lester H., Imber, Stanley D.,
       Stone, Anthony R. and Freund, Julia. Evaluation of the
       Maryland Alcoholic Rehabilitation Clinics. Quarterly
       Journal of Studies on Alcohol, 20: 71-76, 1959.

5787. Thomas, Ronald Edward. Alcohol Abuse Among Black Males in
       a Detoxification Center: A Study of Stress and Social
       Supports. Doctoral Dissertation. Boston University
       Graduate School, 1982. (Also in: Dissertation Abstracts
       International, 43(4): 1271B, 1982.)

5788. Thompson, Kevin M. and Wilsnack, Richard W. Drinking and
       Drinking Problems Among Female Adolescents: Patterns and
       Influences. In: Alcohol Problems in Women -- Antecedents,
       Consequences and Intervention. Eds. S.C. Wilsnack and
       L.J. Beckman. New York: Guilford Press, 1984, pages 37-65.

5789. Thompson, L. Role of Alcoholism in Families of the Incarcerated.
       Paper presented at the National Council on Alcoholism Forum,
       New Orleans, April, 1981.

5790. Thompson, L.L. and Zander, T.A. Treating Children of Alcoholics:
       A Cognitive-Behavioral Approach. Paper presented at the
       92nd Annual Convention of the American Psychological,
       Association, Toronto, August, 1984.

5791. Thompson, Robert J. Jr. Effects of Maternal Alcohol Consumption
       on Offspring: Review, Critical Assessment, and Future
       Directions. Journal of Pediatric Psychology, 4(3):
       265-276, 1979.

5792. Thompson, W. Douglas, Orvaschel, Helen, Prusoff, Brigitte A.
       and Kidd, Kenneth K. An Evaluation of the Family History
       Method for Ascertaining Psychiatric Disorders. Archives
       of General Psychiatry, 39(1): 53-58, 1982.

5793. Thorne, Daniel R. Techniques for Use in Intervention. Journal
       of Alcohol and Drug Education, 28(2): 46-50, 1983.

5794. Thornton, Shirley Ann. An Evaluation Study of Women, Incorporated --
       A Substance Abuse Treatment Program for Females. Dissertation
       Abstracts International, 42(9): 3924A, 1982.

5795. Thorvall, Kerstin. And Leffe was Instead of a Dad. Scarsdale,
       NY: Bradbury Press, 1974.

5796. Three-Day Therapy Offered Family of Alcoholic. NIAAA Information
       and Feature Service, (IFS No. 36): 3, May 24, 1977.

5797. Thuline, H.C. Considerations in Regard to a Proposed Association
       of Alcoholism and Color Blindness. Annals of the New York
       Academy of Sciences, 197: 148-151, 1972.

5798. Tillman, Debbie. Personal Perspectives: 'Alice's Wonderland.'
       NACoA Newsletter, 2(3): 7, 1985.

5799. Tillotson, Kenneth J. and Fleming Robert. Personality and
       Sociologic Factors in the Prognosis and Treatment of Chronic
       Alcoholism. The New England Journal of Medicine, 217:
       611-615, 1937.

5800. Timsit, M., Sabatier, J., Mees, P., Degossely, M. and Binot, E.
       L'emploi des Ordinateurs en Clinique Psychiatrique. Etude
       Statistique d'un Population d'Alcooliques Traites. (Use of
       Computers in Clinical Psychiatry. Statistical Study of a
       Population of Treated Alcoholics.) Acta Psychiatrica Belgica,
       75(2): 133-159, 1975.

5801. Tindale, Joseph. The Management of Self Among Old Men on Skid
       Row. Essence, Downsview, 2(1): 49-58, 1977.

5802. Tindel, M., Lavillaureix, J. and Singer, L. Mental Hygiene and
       Habitat. Problem of Large Developments in Relation to an
       Epidemiological Study Carried out at Mulhouse. Annales
       Medico-Psychologiques, Paris, 2(1): 31-63, 1975.

5803. Tishler, Carl L. and McKenry, Patrick C. Parental Negative Self
       and Adolescent Suicide Attempts. Journal of the American
       Academy of Child Psychiatry, 21(4): 404-408, 1982.

5804. Tittmar, H.A. FAS: A Misnomer? Paper presented at the
       International Congress on Applied Psychology, Edinburgh,
       July, 1982. (Also in: Advanced Concepts in Alcoholism.
       Oxford: Pergamon Press, 1984, pages 35-38.)

5805. Tkachevskiy, Yu.M. Alkogolizm I Sem'ya. (Alcoholism and the
       Family.) In: Bibliotechka Narodnogo Druzhinnika.
       Moscow: Yuridicheskaya Literatura, 1976, pages 10-12.

5806. Tobias, Jerry J. and Wax, Judy. Youthful Drinking Patterns in
       the Suburbs. Adolescence, 8(29): 113-118, 1973.

5807. Todd, J.W. Born to Drink? Lancet, 1: 216, 1979.

5808. Todd, Thomas C. Contingency Analysis of Family Treatment and Drug
       Abuse. In: Behavioral Intervention Techniques in Drug
       Abuse Treatment. (NIDA Research Monograph Series 46.)
       Eds. J. Grabowski, M. Stitzer and J. Henningfield. Washington,
       D.C.: Government Printing Office, 1984, pages 104-113.

5809. Todd, Thomas C. and Stanton, M. Duncan. Comment on Strategies
       and Techniques. In: The Family Therapy of Drug Abuse and
       Addiction. Eds. M. Duncan Stanton and Thomas C. Todd.
       New York: The Guilford Press, 1982, pages 377-389.

5810. Tolle, R. Family Constellations of Alcoholics. Suchtgefahren,
       Hamburg, 29(4): 350-354, 1983.

5811. Tolone, William L. and Dermott, Diane. Some Correlates of Drug
       Use Among High School Youth in a Midwestern Rural Community.
       The International Journal of the Addictions, 10(5):
       761-777, 1975.

5812. Tolor, A. and Tamerin, J.S. The Question of a Genetic Basis for
       Alcoholism: Comment on the Study by Goodwin, et al. and a
       Response. Quarterly Journal of Studies on Alcohol, 34:
       1341-1347, 1973. (Also in: Alcoholism: Introduction to
       Theory and Treatment. Ed. David A. Ward. Dubuque:
       Kendall/Hunt, 1980, pages 153-158.)

5813. Tomelleri, C.J., Herjanic, M., Herjanic, B. and Wetzel, R.D. Wife of
       the Alcoholic. In: Currents in Alcoholism, Vol. 4. Ed.
       F.A. Seixas. New York: Grune and Stratton, 1978, pages 29-38.

5814. Tomorug, E., Diacicov, S. and Rodin, Z. Der Alkoholeinfluss Auf
       Die Entwicklung Der Familie. (Effect of Alcohol on Family
       Development.) Alcoholism, Zagreb, 13: 18-22, 1977.

5815. Toomingas, K. Alcoholics in Schizophrenic Families. Eesti
       Arstideseltside Liit, 5: 121-127, 1926.

5816. Topiar, A. and Satkova, V. Chouani Opjektu Incestnich Delinkuentu.
       (Behaviour of Objects of Incest Delinquents.) Ceskoslovenska
       Psychiatrie, 70(1): 55-58, 1974.

5817. Torda, Clara. Comments on the Character Structure and Psychodynamic
       Processes of Heroin Addicts. Perceptual and Motor Skills,
       27(1): 143-146, 1968. (Also in: Drugs and the Family.
       Ed. Thomas J. Glynn. Rockville, MD: National Institute on
       Drug Abuse, 1981, pages 141-142.)

5818. Torok, D. de. Chromosomal Aberrations in Alcoholics; Cause or
       Consequence? In: International Symposium (on the) Biological
       Aspects of Alcohol Consumption 27-29th September 1971. Eds.
       Olof Forsander and Kalerro Eriksson. Helsinki: Finnish
       Foundation for Alcohol Studies, 20, pages 135-143, 1972.

5819. Torok, D. de. Chromosomal Irregularities in Alcoholics. Annals
       of the New York Academy of Sciences, 197: 90-100, 1972.

5820. Towell, J.F., Townsend, W.F., Wang, R.I.H. and Barboria., J.J.
       A Biochemical Marker of Alcohol-Abuse -- Erythrocyte Aldehyde
       Dehydrogenase -- Normal Values from 375 Healthy-Subjects.
       Alcoholism: Clinical and Experimental Research, 10(1):
       102, 1986.

5821. Towle, L.H. (Ed.) Proceedings: NIAAA-WHO Collaborating Center
       Designation Meeting and Alcohol Research Seminar.
       Washington, D.C.: U.S. Government Printing Office, 1985.

5822. Toyoda, K. Drinking Patterns of Students and Their Families,
       and the Interrelationship Among Them. Japanese Journal
       of Studies on Alcohol, Kyoto, 11(1-2): 67-72, 1976.

5823. Trachtenberg, D. Public Health Responsibility for the Alcoholic.
       Maryland State Medical Journal, 16(8): 90-94, 1967.
       (Also in: Maryland State Medical Journal, 16(9):
       99-104, 1967.)

5824. Tracy, Don. What You Should Know About Alcoholism. New York:
       Dodd, Mead and Company, 1975.

5825. Tracy, K.B. and Wanck, B. Inpatient Treatment for Adolescent
       Drug Abusers: The Relationship Between Family Variables
       and Abstinence Following Discharge. Paper presented at the
       112th Annual Meeting of the American Public Health Association,
       Annaheim, CA, November, 1984.

5826. Trafford-Abigail. New Health Hazard: Being Out of Work; Family
       Discord, Alcoholism, High Blood Pressure, Stomach Ailments --
       These and a Host of Other Problems Tend to Rise in Hand with
       Joblessness. U.S. News and World Report, 92: 81-82, 1982.

5827. Trainor, D. Father's Drinking Disturbs Family Harmony. The Journal,
       2(10): 4, 1973.

5828. Trama, J.A. Comparison of the Impact of an Alcohol Education
       Program with Al-Anon on Knowledge and Attitudes About
       Alcoholism and Perceptions of the Family Environment.
       Dissertation Abstracts International, 45(8): 2668A, 1985.

5829. Tramer, M. Psychohygiene des Alkoholismus. (Psychohygiene of
       Alcoholism.) Schweizerische Medizinische Wochenschrift
       Journal Suisse de Medecine, Basel, 72: 15-17, 1942.

5830. Tramm, Madeleine. Employee Assistance Programs. In: Alcoholism
       and the Family: A Book of Readings. Eds. Sharon
       Wegscheider-Cruse and Richard W. Esterly. Wernersville, PA:
       The Caron Institute, 1985, pages 49-50.

5831. Transeau. E.L. Stockard's Contributions to the Study of Heredity.
       Scientific Temperance Journal, 30: 23-35, 1921.

5832. Travers, D.J. Alcoholism and the Social Worker. Paper presented
       at the Victorian Foundation on Alcoholism and Drug Dependence,
       Melbourne, March, 1976.

5833. Travis, Robert. Suicide in Northwest Alaska. White Cloud Journal,
       3(1): 23-30, 1983.

5834. Trawinska, M. Alkoholizm Patologia Rodzinna. (Family Pathology in
       Alcoholism.) Problemy Alkoholizmu, Warsaw, 27(9): 5, 1980.

5835. Trbovic, M. Dinamska Obiljezja Kronicnih Alkoholicara Mladih Od
       Supruge. (Dynamic Traits of Chronic Alcoholics Younger Than Their
       Wives.) Socijalna Psihijatrtija, Zagreb, 1: 179-186, 1973.

5836. Treacher, D.E. Family Therapy in the Treatment of Alcoholism. In:
       29th International Congress on Alcoholism and Drug Dependence.
       Ed. L. Kiloh. Sydney: Butterworth, 1971, pages 440-444.

5837. Treadway, David. Who's on First? Mapping the Terrain For Family
       Systems Therapy. Focus on Family and Chemical Dependency,
       8(5): 14-15, 34-35, 1985.

5838. Treanor, William and Vanhouten, Therese. Survey of Alcohol Related
       Problems Among Runaway Youth Seen in Runaway Centers.
       Washington, D.C.: National Youth Alternatives Project, Inc.,
       1976.

5839. Treatment and Rehabilitation. Alcohol Health and Research World,
       5(3): 48-58, 1981.

5840. Treatment and Rehabilitation. In: United States Department of
       Health and and Human Services. National Institute on Alcohol
       Abuse and Alcoholism. Fourth Special Report to the U.S. Congress
       on Alcohol and Health from the Secretary of Health and Human
       Services. Washington, D.C.: U.S. Government Printing Office,
       1981, pages 136-167.

5841. Treatment Center for Women Allows Mothers to Keep Children with Them.
       NIAAA Information and Feature Service, (IFS No. 34): 1, March 30,
       1977.

5842. Treatment: Emerging Trends in Research and Practice. In: Alcohol
       and Health: Fifth Special Report to the United States Congress.
       Rockville, MD: National Institute on Alcohol Abuse and Alcoholism,
       1983, pages 100-121.

5843. Treatment of Alcoholism. In: United States Department of
       Health, Education, and Welfare. National Institute on
       Alcohol Abuse and Alcoholism. First Special Report to the
       U.S. Congress on Alcohol and Health from the Secretary of
       Health, Education, and Welfare. Washington, D.C.:
       U.S. Government Printing Office, 1971, pages 71-84.

5844. Treatment of the Alcoholic and the Family. A Panel-Symposium
       Sponsored by the Committee on Medicine and Religion of the
       Medical and Chirurgical Faculty. Maryland State Medical
       Journal, 21(1): 67-82, 1972.

5845. Treger, H. The Alcoholic and the Probation Officer: A New
       Relationship. Federal Probation, 26(4): 23-25, 1962.

5846. Treml, Vladimir G. Production and Consumption of Alcoholic
       Beverages in the USSR: A Statistical Study. Journal of
       Studies on Alcohol, 36(3): 285-320, 1975.

5847. Trends in Treatment of Alcoholism. In: United States Department
       of Health, Education, and Welfare. National Institute on
       Alcohol Abuse and Alcoholism. Second Special Report to the
       U.S. Congress on Alcohol and Health from the Secretary of
       Health, Education, and Welfare. Washington, D.C.: U.S.
       Government Printing Office, 1974, pages 111-127.

5848. Trial and Error: The Wife of an Alcoholic Speaks. Pamphlet.
       Toronto: Addiction Research Foundation, no date.

5849. Trice, Harrison M. Alcoholics: Vulnerable Personalities and Drinking Groups. In: Alcoholism in America. New York: McGraw-Hill, 1966, pages 42-61.

5850. Trice, Harrison M. Impact on Family and Work Life. Alcoholism: in America. New York: McGraw-Hill, 1966, pages 62-79.

5851. Tridon, P. L'enfant et L'alcool. (Children and Alcohol.) In: Alcoologie. Riom: Riom Laboratories, 1984, pages 197-201.

5852. Trierweiler, D. Betreuung Von Drogenabhangigen. Hilfen Des Gesundheitsamtes. (Care for Drug Addicts. Assistance Offered by the Public Health Office.) Zeitschrift fur Allgemeinmedizin, 55: 943-948, 1979.

5853. Tripkovic, Dobrosav. Problem Drinkers in the Penitentiary at Stremska Mitrovica. Quarterly Journal of Studies on Alcohol, 28: 738-741, 1967.

5854. Triplett, June L. and Arneson, Sara W. Children of Alcoholic Parents: A Neglected Issue. Journal of School Health, 48(10): 596-599, 1978.

5855. Triplett, June L. and Arneson, Sara W. Working with Children of Alcoholics. Pediatric Nursing, 9(5): 317-320, 1983.

5856. Troncale, J.A. Endocrine Effects of Alcoholism. Journal of Family Practice, 19(1): 17-32, 1984.

5857. Troszynski, Michal. Alcohol and Progeny. (Information about Some Scientific and Other Publications.) Warsaw: Governing Board of the Civil Committee to Fight Alcoholism, 1970.

5858. Troszynski, Michal. Wplyw Alkoholizmu Rodzicow na Rozwoj ich Potpmstwa. (The Influence of Parental Alcoholism on the Development of Progeny.) Problemy Alkoholizmu, Warsaw, 23(3): 5,18, 1976.

5859. Trotter, A.B., Gozali, J. and Cunningham, L.J. Family Participation in the Treatment of Alcoholism. Personnel and Guidance Journal, 48(2): 140-143, 1969.

5860. Trotter, R.T., 2d. Evidence of an Ethnomedical Form of Aversion Therapy on the United States-Mexico Border. Journal of Ethnopharmacology, 1: 279-284, 1979.

5861. Trout, Michael D. Diagnosis of Infant Abuse and Neglect by Alcohol Abuse Counselors: An Observational Model. The Catalyst, 1(3): 28-34, 1980.

5862. Trube-Becker, Elisabeth. The Death of Children Following Negligence: Social Aspects. Forensic Science, Lausanne, 9(2): 111-115, 1977. (Also in: Child Abuse and Neglect: The International Journal, 1(1): 25-30, 1977.)

5863. Truckenbrodt, H. Die Kindesmisshandlung und ihre Folgen. (Child Abuse and Its Consequences.) Offentliche Gesundheitswenson, Stuttgart, 41: 835-838, 1979.

5864. Truitt, E.B. (Ed.) and Cleminshaw, H.K. Alcoholism: New Perspectives. Akron: University of Akron Center for Urban Studies, 1983.

5865. Tryfan, B. Alkoholizm A Dezintegracja Rodziny Wiejskiej. (Alcoholism and Disintegration of the Rural Family.) Problemy Alkoholizmu, Warsaw, 24(11): 3-4, 1977.

5866.   Tseng, Wen Shing and Hsu, Jing. Chinese Culture, Personality
        Formation and Mental Illness. The International Journal
        of Social Psychiatry, London, 16(1): 5-14, 1969.

5867.   Tsuang, M.T. Birth Order and Maternal Age of Psychiatric In-Patients.
        The British Journal of Psychiatry: The Journal of Mental
        Science, London, 112(492): 1131-1141, 1966.

5868.   Tsuang, M.T. Genetic Counseling for Psychiatric Patients and
        Their Families. American Journal of Psychiatry, 135(12):
        1465-1475, 1978.

5869.   Tsuang, M.T. Genetic Factors in Suicide. Diseases of the
        Nervous System, 38: 498-501, 1977.

5870.   Tsuang, Ming T. and Vandermey, Randall. Alcoholism. In: Genes
        and the Mind: Inheritance of Mental Illness. New York:
        Oxford University Press, 1980, pages 115-129.

5871.   Tsukamoto, S. Study on Fluctuating Factors in Alcohol Metabolism:
        Differences in Ethanol Level and Acetaldehyde Level Among Mouse
        Strains. Japanese Journal of Alcohol Studies and Drug
        Dependence, Kyoto, 18(2): 218-235, 1983.

5872.   Tuason, V.B. The Psychiatrist and the Violent Patient.
        Diseases of the Nervous System, 32(11): 764-768, 1971.

5873.   Tudor, Cynthia G., Petersen, David M. and Elifson, Kirk W. An
        Examination of the Relationship Between Peer and Parental
        Influences and Adolescent Drug Use. Adolescence, 15(60):
        783-798, 1980.

5874.   Tuerk, I. Factors in the Treatment and Management of the Alcoholic
        and His Family. Modern Treatment, 6(4): 760-766, 1969.

5875.   Tupin, J.P., Mahar, D. and Smith, D. Two Types of Violent
        Offenders with Psychosocial Descriptors. Diseases of
        the Nervous System, 34(7): 356-363, 1973.

5876.   Turner, Carol and Willis, Robert. The Relationship of College
        Students' Use of Marijuana to Parental Attitudes and
        Drug-Taking Behavior. International Journal of the
        Addictions, 15(7): 1103-1112, 1980.

5877.   Turner, G. The Fetal Alcohol Syndrome. Medical Journal of
        Australia, 1(1): 18-19, 1978.

5878.   Turner, W.J. Alcoholism, Homosexuality, and Bipolar Affective
        Disorder. American Journal of Psychiatry, 138: 262-263, 1981.

5879.   Twemlow, S.W. and Bowen, W.T. Socio Cultural Predictors of Self
        Actualization in Electro Encephalograph Bio Feedback Treated
        Alcoholics. Psychological Reports, 40(2): 591-598, 1977.

5880.   Twerski, Abraham J. Caution: "Kindness" Can Be Dangerous to the
        Alcoholic. Englewood Cliffs, NJ: Prentice-Hall, Inc., 1981.

5881.   Tyler, A.J. Comment on Alcoholism as Stage Phenomena: A Frame
        of Reference for Counselors. Personnel and Guidance Journal,
        61: 69, 1982.

5882.   Typpo, M.H. and Hastings, J.M. Elephant in the Living Room: The
        Children's Book. Minneapolis: CompCare Publications, 1984.

5883.   Tyson, Charles A. Counseling the Alcoholic Family. Military
        Chaplins' Review, 12(3): 33-43, 1983.

U

5884. Uchtenhagen, A., Zimmer, D. and Widmer, A. Characteristics and Relevance of Treatment of the Family in Heroin Addicts. Paper presented at the Second International Symposium on the Current Status of the Treatment of Those Dependent Upon Drugs and Alcohol, Basel, September, 1981. (Also in: Drogen und Alkohol 2: Erfahrungen und Ergebnisse in der Behandlung Drogen-und Alkoholabhaengiger. (Drugs and Alcohol: 2. Experiences and Results in Treating Those Dependent Upon Drugs and Alcohol.) Basel: S. Karger, 1982.)

5885. Ueprus, V. Study of the Effects of Alcoholism on Offspring. Eesh Arst, 10: 117-123, 1932.

5886. Ugarte, G., Cruz-Coke, R., Rivera, L., Altschiller, H. and Mardones, J. Relationship of Color Blindness to Alcoholic Liver Damage. Pharmacology, Basel, 4: 297-308, 1970.

5887. Uglesic, B., Luksic, P., Kovacevic, K. and Cizmic, A. Possibilita E Risultati Nel Trattamento Degli Alcoolisti Con Approccio Psichiatrico-Sociale, Durante Degenze Brevi. (Possibility and Results of Treatment of Alcoholism Through Brief Hospitalization and Concomitant Sociopsychiatric Approach.) Alcoholism, Zabreb, 8(1): 15-19, 1972.

5888. Uhlig, George E. Personality Interaction in the Alcoholic Marriage. Psychology: A Quarterly Journal of Human Behavior, 19(2/3): 28-36, 1982.

5889. Ullman, A.D., Demone, H.W. and Stearns, A.W. Does Failure Run in Families? A Further Study of One Thousand Unsuccessful Careers. American Journal of Psychiatry, 107: 667-676, 1951.

5890. Ulvedal, Susan K. and Feeg, Veronica D. Pregnant Teens Who Choose Childbirth. Journal of School Health, 53(4): 229-233, 1983.

5891. Understanding the Experiences of Wive's of Recuperating Alcoholics. (Conocimientos Del Alcoholismo De La Experiencias De La Esposas De Alcoholicos En Recuperacion.) Pamphlet. Milwaukee: Inner City Council on Alcoholism, no date.

5892. Underwood, Charles Calvin. Wives of Recovering Alcoholics: Their Personal Concerns During Their Husbands' First Eighteen Months of Sobriety. Dissertation Abstracts International, 43(3): 930A, 1982.

5893. Ungaro, S.K. Teen Alcoholics Speak Out: What Every Parent Must Know. Family Circle, October, 34, 36, 38-39, 62-63, 1984.

5894. Unger, Robert A. The Treatment of Adolescent Alcoholism. Social Casework, 59(1): 27-35, 1978.

5895.   United States Congress and House. Committee on Education and
        Labor. Subcommittee on Select Education. Domestic Violence:
        Hearings Before the Subcommittee on Select Education of the
        Committee on Education and Labor on H.R. 7927 and H.R. 8948.
        House of Representatives, Ninety-Fifth Congress, 2nd Session.
        Washington, D.C.: U.S. Government Printing Office, March, 1978.

5896.   United States Congress and Senate. Committee on Armed Services.
        Subcommittee on Drug Abuse in the Military. Staff Report
        on Drug and Alcohol Abuse Among U.S. Military Personnel and
        Dependents in Germany for the Information of the Subcommittee
        on Drug Abuse in the Military of the Committee on Armed Services,
        United States Senate, Ninety-Second Congress, Second Session.
        Washington, D.C.: U.S. Government Printing Office, 1972.

5897.   United States Congress and Senate. Committee on Human Resources.
        Subcommittee on Alcoholism and Drug Abuse. Impact of
        Alcoholism on the Family, 1977: Hearing Before the
        Subcommittee on Alcoholism and Drug Abuse of the Committee
        on Human Resources, United States Senate, Ninety-Fifth
        Congress, First Session. June 20, 1977, Salt Lake City,
        Washington, D.C.: U.S. Government Printing Office, 1978.

5898.   United States Congress and Senate. Committee on Labor and Human
        Resources. Subcommittee on Alcoholism and Drug Abuse.
        Comprehensive Alcohol Abuse and Alcoholism Prevention,
        Treatment, and Rehabilitation Act Amendments of 1979.
        Hearings Before the Subcommittee on Alcoholism and Drug
        Abuse of the Committee on Labor and Human Resources, United
        States Senate, Ninety-sixth Congress, First Session on S.440.
        Washington, D.C.: U.S. Government Printing Office, 1979.

5899.   United States Congress and Senate. Committee on Labor and Human
        Resources. Subcommittee on Alcoholism and Drug Abuse. Drug
        Abuse Prevention, Treatment, and Rehabilitation Act of 1979.
        Hearings Before the Subcommittee on Alcoholism and Drug Abuse
        of the Committee on Labor and Human Resources, United States
        Senate, Ninety-Sixth Congress, First Session on S.525.
        Washington, D.C.: U.S. Government Printing Office, 1979.

5900.   United States Congress and Senate. Committee on Labor and Human
        Resources. Subcommittee on Investigations and General Oversight.
        Drug Abuse in the American School System. Hearing Before the
        Subcommittee on Labor and Human Resources, United States Senate.
        Ninety-Seventh Congress, Second Session. Washington, D.C.:
        U.S. Government Printing Office, 1982. (Eric Document Number
        ED220783.)

5901.   United States Department of the Air Force. A Guide for Family
        Support: Assistance to Families of Alcoholics in Treatment.
        Washington: Department of the Air Force, 1977.

5902.   United States Department of Health, Education and Welfare. National
        Institute on Alcohol Abuse and Alcoholism. Alcohol -- A Family
        Affair. Rockville, MD: Public Health Service, Alcohol, Drug
        Abuse, and Mental Health Administration, 1974.

5903.   United States Department of Health, Education and Welfare. Social
        Welfare and Alcoholism. Conference Proceedings of the
        Secretary's Conference on Social Welfare and Alcoholism,
        June, 1967. Washington, D.C.: U.S. Government Printing Office,
        1968.

5904.   United States Department of Health and Human Services. National
        Institute on Alcohol Abuse and Alcoholism. Alcohol and
        the Family Reading List. Rockville, MD: National
        Clearinghouse for Alcohol Information, May, 1983.

5905. United States Department of Health and Human Services. National
       Institute on Alcohol Abuse and Alcoholism. General Conclusions
       and Recommendations (of the Symposium). In: Services for
       Children of Alcoholics. U.S. Department of Health and Human
       Services. National Institute on Alcohol Abuse and Alcoholism.
       Washington, D.C.: U.S. Government Printing Office, 1979, pages
       39-41.

5906. United States Department of Health and Human Services. National
       Institute on Alcohol Abuse and Alcoholism. Prevention Plus:
       Involving Schools, Parents and Community in Alcohol and Drug
       Education. Washington, D.C.: U.S. Government Printing Office,
       1983.

5907. United States Department of Health and Human Services. National
       Institute on Drug Abuse. Communities: What You Can Do
       About Drug and Alcohol Abuse. Washington, D.C.:
       U.S. Government Printing Office, 1983, (DHHS Publication
       No. (ADM) 84-1310).

5908. United States Jaycees. All in the Family: Understanding How We
       Teach and Influence Children About Alcohol. Pamphlet.
       Tulsa, 1975.

5909. University of Melbourne, Department of Medicine, St. Vincent's
       Hospital. Symposium: Alcohol and the Family. Presented
       at the Third Summer School of Alcohol Studies, January 26,
       1968. Melbourne, 1968.

5910. University of Tennessee Develops Program for Medical Students.
       AMA Impaired Physician Newsletter, February, 1, 1985.

5911. Urbanski, M.J. Relationship of Self-Esteem and Locus of Control
       to Drinking Behavior in Adolescents. Doctoral Dissertation.
       Dekalb: Northern Illinois University. Dissertation Abstracts
       International, 45(9): 2828A, 1985.

5912. Urton, G. and Kaplan, H.M. Marriage Counseling with Alcoholics
       and Their Spouses: II. The Correlation of Excessive Drinking
       Behavior with Family Pathology and Social Deterioration.
       British Journal of Addiction, 63: 161-170, 1968.

5913. Usher, Marion L., Jay, Jeffrey and Glass, David Jr. Family-Therapy
       Approach to Restricted Emotional Interaction Following Initial
       Sobriety. Alcoholism: Clinical and Experimental Research,
       3(2): 199, 1979.

5914. Usher, Marion L., Jay, Jeffrey and Glass, David R. Jr. Family
       Therapy as a Treatment Modality for Alcoholism. Journal of
       Studies on Alcohol, 43(9): 927-938, 1982.

5915. Usher, M.L. and Steinglass, P.J. Responding to Presenting
       Complaints in an Alcoholic Family. In: Questions & Answers
       in the Practice of Family Therapy. Ed. A.S. Gurman.
       New York: Brunner/Mazel, 1981, pages 265-268.

5916. Utne, H.E., Hansen, F. Vallo, Winkler, K. and Schulsinger, F.
       Alcohol Elimination Rates in Adoptees With and Without
       Alcoholic Parents. Journal of Studies on Alcohol, 38(7):
       1219-1223, 1977.

V

5917. Vaglum, P. and Fossheim, I. Results of Different Institutional Treatment Programs: Are They Different in Groups of Drug Abusers?
Acta Psychiatrica Scandinavica, 62(284): 21-28, 1980.

5918. Vaillant, George. Can Alcoholics Go Back to "Social" Drinking?
Harvard Medical School Health Letter, 8(3): 3, 1983.

5919. Vaillant, George E. The Contribution of Prospective Studies to the
Understanding of Etiologic Factors in Alcoholism. In: _Research
Advances in Alcohol and Drug Problems, Volume 8_. Eds. Reginald
G. Smart, Howard D. Coppell and Frederick B. Glaser. New York:
Plenum Press, 1984 pages 265-289.

5920. Vaillant, Geroge E. Dangers of Psychotherapy in the Treatment of
Alcoholism. In: _Dynamic Approaches to the Understanding and
Treatment of Alcoholism_. Eds. Margaret H. Bean and Norman E.
Zinberg. New York: The Free Press, 1981.

5921. Vaillant, George E. _The Natural History of Alcoholism_. Cambridge,
MA: Harvard University Press, 1983.

5922. Vaillant, George E. Why Men Seek Psychotherapy. I. Results of
a Survey of College Graduates. _The American Journal of
Psychiatry_, 129(6): 645-651, 1972.

5923. Vaillant, George E., Gale, L. and Milofsky, E.S. Natural History
of Male Alcoholism. II. The Relationship Between Different
Diagnostic Dimensions. _Journal of Studies on Alcohol_,
43: 216-232, 1982.

5924. Vaillant, George E. and Milofsky, Eva S. The Etiology of Alcoholism:
A Prospective Viewpoint. _American Psychologist_, 37(5):
494-503, 1982.

5925. Vaillant, George E., Sobowale, N.C. and McArthur, C. Some
Psychologic Vulnerabilities of Physicians. _New England
Journal of Medicine_, 287: 372-375, 1972.

5926. Valentich, Mary. Women and Drug Dependence. _Journal of Alcohol
and Drug Education_, 28(1): 12-17, 1982.

5927. Valle, Stephen K. Consumer Involvement in Community Alcoholism
Programs: The Taunton Model. _Alcohol Health & Research
World_, Winter Issue: 20-24, 1975-76.

5928. Valle, Stephen K. Consumer Involvement: A Critical Variable
in Community Alcohol Programming. Paper presented at the
North American Congress on Alcohol and Drug Problems,
San Francisco, December, 1974.

5929. Valles, J. _Alcoholismo; El Alcoholico Y Su Familia_. (_Alcoholism;
The Alcoholic and His Family_.) Mexico: B. Costa-Amic, 1973.

5930. Valles, Jorge. How to Live With an Alcoholic. New York: Simon & Schuster, 1967.

5931. Valles, Jorge and Sikes, Melvin P. A Program for the Treatment and Study of Alcoholism in a Veterans Administration Hospital. Quarterly Journal of Studies on Alcohol, 25: 100-107, 1964.

5932. Vallet, R., Deschamps, G., Beauseigneur, T. and Leviet, M.Q. A Propos de Quelques Femmes d'Alcooliques; Etude Relationnelle du Couple. (Some Wives of Alcoholics; A Family Study of Married Couples.) La Revue de l'Alcoolisme, 11: 29-44, 1965.

5933. Vallet, R., Deschamps, G., Leviet, M.Q., Beauseigneur, T. and Chelkowsky, D. Observations on a Special Type of Wives of Alcoholics: The Women as the Family Head. Evolution Psychiatrique, 30(3): 525-539, 1965.

5934. Van Amberg, R.J. A Study of Fifty Women Patients Hospitalized for Alcohol Addiction. Diseases of the Nervous System, 4: 246-251, 1943.

5935. Van Damme, L. Alcoholism, Pregnancy and Offspring. Vlaams Diergeneeskundig Tijdschrift, 20: 925-930, 1939.

5936. Vande Creek, Larry, Zachrich, Richard L., Scherger, William E. The Use of Standardized Screening Tests in Family Practice. Family Practice Research Journal, 2(1): 11-17, 1982.

5937. Van Der Kolk, Bessel A. Organic Problems in the Aged: Brain Syndromes and Alcoholism: Introductory Remarks on Alcoholism. Journal of Geriatric Psychiatry, 11(2): 171-173, 1978.

5938. Vander Veldt, Albert J. and McAllister, Robert J. Psychiatric Illness in Hospitalized Clergy: Alcoholism. Quarterly Journal of Studies on Alcohol, 23: 124-130, 1962.

5939. Van Fleet, Charles. Help for the Hospitalized Alcoholic. Journal of Rehabilitation, 33(2): 22-25, 1967.

5940. Van Gee, Susan J. Alcoholism and the Family: A Psychodrama Approach. Journal of Psychiatric Nursing, 17(8): 9-12, 1979.

5941. Van Harte, E.L. Services Available for Coloured Alcoholics and the Problems Encountered: Work Done at Sanca Western Cape Society, Althlone Office. Paper presented at the South African National Council on Alcoholism and Drug Dependence, July, 1973, Number 4, pages 30-31.

5942. Van Hasselt, Vincent, B., Morrison, Randell L. and Bellack, Alan S. Alcohol Use in Wife Abusers and Their Spouses. Addictive Behaviors, 10(2): 127-135, 1985.

5943. Van Houten, Therese and Golembiewski, Gary. Adolescent Life Stress as a Predictor of Alcohol Abuse and/or Runaway Behavior. Washington, D.C.: National Youth Alternatives Project, 1978.

5944. Vannicelli, M.L. Treatment Outcome of Alcoholic Women: The State of the Art. Paper presented at the Third Annual National Conference for Nurse Educators on Alcohol and Drug Abuse, Washington, D.C., May, 1983. (Also in: Current Issues in Alcohol and Drug Abuse Nursing; Research, Education and Clinical Practice. Belmont, MA, pages 17-31, 1983.)

5945. Vannicelli, Marsha, Gingerich, Susan and Ryback, Ralph. Family
       Problems Related to the Treatment and Outcome of Alcoholic
       Patients. British Journal of Addiction, Edinburgh,
       78(2): 193-204, 1983.

5946. VanValkenburg, C., Winokur, G., Lowry, M., Behar, D. and
       VanValkenburg, D. Depression Occurring in Chronically
       Anxious Persons. Comprehensive Psychiatry, 24(3):
       285-289, 1983.

5947. VanValkenburg, Charles, Akiskal, Hagop, S. and Puzantian, Vahe.
       Depression Spectrum Disease or Character Spectrum Disorder?
       A Clinical Study of Major Depressives with Familial Alcoholism
       or Sociopathy. Comprehensive Psychiatry, 24(6): 589-595, 1983.

5948. Vardy, Michael M. and Kay, Stanley R. LSD Psychosis or LSD-Induced
       Schizophrenia? A Multimethod Inquiry. Archives of General
       Psychiatry, 40(8): 877-883, 1983.

5949. Varela, A., Rivera, L., Mardones, J. and Cruz-Coke, R. Color
       Vision Defects in Non-Alcoholic Relatives of Alcoholic
       Patients. British Journal of Addiction, Edinburgh, 64:
       67-73, 1969.

5950. Vartabedian, Laurel C. Klinger and Vartabedian, Robert A.
       The Alcoholic Family: A Communication Perspective.
       U.S. Oklahoma, 1980. Eric Document Number ED197411.

5951. Vasev, C. and Petrovic, D. Alkoholizam-Uzrok Deficitnih Licnih
       Dohodaka i Socijalnih Posledica u Porodicama Alkoholicara.
       (Alcoholism-Cause of Low Incomes and Social Difficulties in
       the Families of Alcoholics.) Alkoholizam, Beograd, 9(2):
       77-89, 1969.

5952. Vat, Dan Van Der. Times of London, 19 August 1981, p. 3, col. 1.
       (Genetic Marker and Liver Diseases Including Alcoholic Hepatitis
       and Cirrhosis.)

5953. Vaughn, Susan M. The Normative Structures of College Students
       and Patterns of Drinking Behavior. Sociological Focus,
       16(3): 181-193, 1983.

5954. Vaux, Alan Charles. Adolescent Life Change, Work Stress, and
       Social Support. Dissertation Abstracts International,
       42(9): 3846B, 1981.

5955. Vaziri, H. Frequence De L'Oligophrenie, De La Psychopathie Et
       De L'Alcoolisme Dans 79 Familles De Schizophrenes. (The
       Incidence of Oligophrenia, Psychopathy and Alcoholism in 79
       Families of Schizophrenics.) Schweizer Archiv Fur Neurologie,
       Neurochirurgie and Psychiatrie, 87: 160-177, 1961.

5956. Veenstra, S. Peter Pan Syndrome: Can Adult Children of
       Alcoholics Ever Grow Up? Paper presened at the National
       Council on Alcoholism Forum, Washington, D.C., April, 1985.

5957. Vejnas, Jill. Transmission of Alcohol Problems Combination of
       Nature and Nurture. ADAMHA News, 10(1): 5a, 1984.

5958. Vejnoska, J. Research on Children of Alcoholics: Expanding the
       Knowledge. NIAAA Clinical Center Conducts Family Research.
       Alcohol Health and Research World, 8(4): 6, 8-9, 1984.

5959. Velleman, Jim and Lawrence, Ted. Do Drinking Parents Make Teen
       Addicts? Survey by Students Turns Up a Shocker. Science
       Digest: Adventure in Science and Discovery, 47-56, 1970.

5960. Velleman, R. Drinking Problems -- Family Problems. Alcohol and
       Alcoholism, 18(3): 279, 1983.

5961. Velleman, R. and Orford, J. Intergenerational Transmission of Alcohol Problems: Hypothesis to be Tested. In: Alcohol Related Problems: Room for Manoeuvre. Eds. Neville Krasner, J.S. Madden and Robin J. Walker. New York: John Wiley and Sons, 1984, pages 97-113.

5962. Verdery, E.A. Pastoral Care of the Alcoholic's Family after Sobriety. Pastoral Psychology, 13(123): 30-38, 1962.

5963. Verinis, J.S. Agreement Between Alcoholics and Relatives When Reporting Follow-Up Status. International Journal of the Addictions, 18(6): 891-894, 1983.

5964. Vermont Department of Education. The Role of Parents in Alcohol Problems. Pamphlet. Montpelier, VT, 1957.

5965. Vernon, J. Children of Alcoholics. Kiwanis Magazine, April, 1985.

5966. Veyrat, J.G., Renouardiere, R. and Lebourges, J. Etude Psychopathogique De 200 Cas De Spasmophilie Chez L'Adulte. (Psycho-Pathological Study of 200 Cases of Adult Spasmophilia.) Annales Medico-Psychologiques, Paris, 136: 1224-1235, 1979.

5967. Viamontes, Jorge A. and Powell, Barbara J. Demographic Characteristics of Black and White Male Alcoholics. International Journal of the Addictions, 9(3): 489-494, 1974.

5968. Videotape Effect. Potomac (Washington Post), 4 November 1973, pages 20, 24.

5969. Vidojkovic, P. Sociomedicinski Aspekt Alkoholizma Sreza Leskovac Za Period Od 1962. Do 1965. Godine. (Sociomedical Aspects of Alcoholism in the District of Leskovac from 1962 to 1965.) Anali Bolnice "Dr. M. Stojanovic", Zagreb, 6(2-3): 160-166, 1967.

5970. Viguie, F. Alcoolisme ou Alcoolismes? (Alcoholism or Alcoholisms?) Union Medicale du Canada, 106: 1127-1134, 1977.

5971. Viken, Richard M. Family Violence: Aids to Recognition. Postgraduate Medicine, 71(5): 115-117, 120-122, 1982.

5972. Villanueva, C., F.P. de. Anomalias Congenitas Fisicas y Psiquicas de Origen Alcoholica. (Congenital Physical and Psychological Abnormalities of Alcoholic Origin.) Revista de Medicina y Cirugia, Colombia, 13(12a): 77-86, 1946.

5973. Vincent, M.O. Doctor and Mrs. -- Their Mental Health. Canadian Psychiatric Association Journal, Ottawa, 14(5): 509-515, 1969.

5974. Vincent, M.O. The Doctor's Marriage and Family. Nova Scotia Medical Bulletin, 50(6): 143-146, 1971.

5975. Vincent, M.O. Female Physicians as Psychiatric Patients. Canadian Psychiatric Association Journal, Ottawa, 21(7): 461-465, 1976.

5976. Vincent, M.O. Some Sequelae of Stress in Physicians. Psychiatric Journal of the University of Ottawa, 8(3): 120-124, 1983.

5977. Vincent, M.O., Robinson, E.A. and Latt, L. Physicians as Patients: Private Psychiatric Hospital Experience. Canadian Medical Association Journal, Toronto, 100(9): 403-412, 1969.

5978. Violence in the Family. Lancet, London, 1799: 1348-1349, 1976.

5979. The Violent Reality of Alcoholism. World Medicine, 16(19): 36, 1981.

5980. Virkkunen, M. Alcoholism and Antisocial Personality.
       Acta Psychiatrica Scandinavica, 59: 493-501, 1979.

5981. Virkkunen, M. Insesti (Sukurutasaus) Rikokset Ja Alkoholismi.
       (Incest Offenses and Alcoholism.) Alkoholikysymys, 41:
       92-97, 1973. (Also in: Medical Science and the Law, 14(2):
       124-128, 1974.)

5982. Viskum, K. Mind and Ulcer. Acta Psychiatrica Scandinavica,
       Copenhagen, 51(3): 182-200, 1975.

5983. Vitez, M., Koranyi, G., Gonczy, E., Rudas, T. and Czeizel, A.
       A Semiquantitative Score System for Epidemiologic
       Studies of Fetal Alcohol Syndrome. American Journal of
       Epidemiology, 119(3): 301-308, 1984.

5984. Vitols, M.M. Culture Patterns of Drinking in Negro and White
       Alcoholics. Diseases of the Nervous System, 29:
       391-394, 1968.

5985. Vivaldo, Juan Carlos. Alcoholismo Y Dipsomania En Un Debil Mental
       Congenito. Algunas Consideraciones. (Alcoholism and Dipsomania
       in a Mentally Retarded Person. Some Considerations.) Prensa
       Medica Argentia, 27: 1587-1594, 1940.

5986. Vocational Training, Physical Exercise, and Family Therapy at an
       Open-Treatment Center for Alcoholics. (Yrkesopplring, Fysisk
       Trening Og Familie Behandling i Behandlingstilbudet for
       Alkoholister.) Norsk Tidsskrift om Edruskapsspdrsma, Oslo,
       27: 11-14, 1975.

5987. Vodrazka, R. Uzus a Abuzus Allcoholu Mezi Skolni Maadezi. (Use
       and Abuse of Alcohol in School Children.) Ceskoslovenska
       Pediatrie, 36(7): 402-404, 1981.

5988. Vogel-Sprott, M., Chipperfield, B. and Hart, D.M. Family History
       of Problem Drinking Among Young Male Social Drinkers:
       Reliability of the Family Tree Questionnaire. Drug and
       Alcohol Dependence, 16: 251-256, 1985.

5989. Vogt, I. Zum Klinischen Bild Der Alkoholikerin: Kritische
       Anmerkungen Zur Reduzierten Beschreibung Eines Komplexen
       Krankheitsbildes. (Clinical Picture of Alcoholic Women:
       Critical Remarks on the Reduced Description of a Complex
       Disease Picture.) Wiener Zeitshcrift fur Suchtforschung,
       7(1-2): 47-54, 1984.

5990. Vogt, Irmgard. Jugendlicher Alkoholkonsum und Familienmilieu.
       (Drinking By Adolescents and the Family Environment.)
       In: Papers presented at the 24th International Congress
       on the Prevention and Treatment of Alcoholism, Zurich,
       June, 1978. Ed. E.J. Tongue. Lausanne, Switzerland:
       International Council on Alcohol and Addictions, 1978,
       pages 203-216.

5991. Volavka, Jan, Pollock, Vicki, Gabrielli, William F. Jr. and
       Mednick, Sarnoff A. EEG in Persons at Risk for Alcoholism.
       In: Recent Developments in Alcoholism, Volume 3, High-Risk
       Studies, Prostaglandins and Leukotrienes, Cardiovascular
       Effects, Cerebral Function in Social Drinkers. Ed. Marc
       Galanter. New York: Plenum Press, 1985, pages 21-36.

5992. Volicer, Beverly J., Cahill, Mary H. and Smith, Janice L. Sex
       Differences in Correlates of Problem Drinking Among Employed
       Males and Females. Drug and Alcohol Dependence, 8(3):
       175-187, 1981.

5993. Volicer, Beverly J., Volicer, Ladislav and D'Angelo, Nestore.
       Variation in Length of Time to Development of Alcoholism
       by Family History of Problem Drinking. Drug and Alcohol
       Dependence, Lausanne, 12(1): 69-83, 1983.

5994. Volicer, Ladislav, Volicer, Beverly J. and D'Angelo, Nestore.
       Assessment of Genetic Predisposition to Alcoholism in Male
       Alcoholics. Alcohol and Alcoholism: International Journal
       of the Medical Council on Alcoholism, 20(1): 63-68, 1985.

5995. Volicer, Ladislav, Volicer, Beverly J. and D'Angelo, Nestore.
       Relationship of Family History of Alcoholism to Patterns of
       Drinking and Physical Dependence in Male Alcoholics. Drug
       and Alcohol Dependence, Lausanne, 13(3): 215-223, 1984.

5996. Volpe, Joan. Links to Sobriety. Alcohol Health and Research
       World, 4(2): 39-44, 1979-80.

5997. Vorster, C. An Investigation Into the Effect of Relationship
       Orientated Therapy on the Drinking Behaviour of Alcoholics.
       Doctoral Disseration. Pretoria: University of South Africa,
       1978.

5998. Vourakis, Christine. Homosexuals in Substance Abuse Treatment.
       In: Substance Abuse: Pharmacologic, Developmental, and
       Clinical Perspectives. Eds. G. Bennett, C. Vourakis and
       D.S. Woolf. New York: John Wiley and Sons, 1983, pages 400-419.

5999. Vujosevic, K. and Marcetic, V. Chronic Alcoholism of the Father
       and Its Effect on a Person's Adaptability to a Military
       Setting. Alkoholizam, 14: 32-37, 1974. (Also in:
       Journal of Studies on Alcohol, 36(652): 1975.)

W

6000. W. Carolyn. Detaching with Love. Pamphlet. Center City, MN: Hazelden, no date.

6001. Waal, Helge. Treatment of Juvenile Drug Abusers in a Specialized Treatment Center for Drug Addicts: Three Years of Experience -- Evaluation According to a Follow-Up Study. Acta Psychiatrica Scandinavica, Copenhagen, 217: 37-38, 1970.

6002. Wachter, R. Om Fortjusningen I Det Sjuka. (Fascination with the Ill.) Alkohol Och Narkotika, 75(3): 12-13, 1981.

6003. Waddell, Jack O. For Individual Power and Social Credit: The Use of Alcohol Among Tucson Papagos. Human Organization, 34(1): 9-15, 1975.

6004. Waddy, N. and Gilling, B. Alcohol and the Family. In: Alcohol in Australia: Problems and Programmes. Eds. A.P. Diehm, R.F. Seaborn and G.C. Wilson. New York: McGraw-Hill, 1978, pages 122-133.

6005. Wadsworth, Allen P., Barker, Harry A. Jr. and Wilson, Warner. Differential Perceptions of Alcoholic Males and Their Wives of Factors Contributing to Marital Happiness and Unhappiness. Newsletter for Research in Mental Health and Behavioral Sciences, 17(4): 19-26, 1975.

6006. Wadsworth, Allen P., Wilson, Warner and Barker, Harry R. Determinants of Marital Happiness and Unhappiness Rated by Alcoholics and Their Wives. Journal of Studies on Alcohol, 36(5): 634-644, 1975.

6007. Wagner, Claudia. Zur Entstenhung Weiblicher Alkoholabhangigkeit Unter Besonderer Berucksichtigung der Situation der Frau in Familie und Gesellschaft. (The Origins of Alcohol Dependency among Women, with Particular Reference to the Situation of the Woman in the Family and Society.) Soziologenkorrespondenz, 6: 121-146, 1979.

6008. Wahl, C.W. Some Antecedent Factors in the Family Histories of 109 Alcoholics. Quarterly Journal of Studies on Alcohol, 17(4): 643-654, 1956.

6009. Waite, Barbara J. and Ludwig, Meredith J. A Growing Concern: How to Provide Services for Children from Alcoholic Families. (DHHS Publication No. (ADM) 83-1257.) Rockville, MD: National Institute on Alcohol Abuse and Alcoholism, 1983.

6010. Waite, Barbara J. and Ludwig, Meredith J. Issues and Strategies in the Provision of Services to Children of Alcoholics. Arlington, VA: Evaluation Technologies Incorporated, 1982.

6011. Wakasugi, Choei, Nishi, Katsuji, Hamaguchi, Asnyo and Yamada, Tadashi. Statistical Study of Medico-Legal Cases in Osaka Prefecture. _Japanese Journal of Legal Medicine_, Tokyo, 35(5): 312-339, 1981.

6012. Wakefield, Mary L. Effects of Length of Abstinence, Age of Onset, Amount Consumed, Drinking Pattern, Family History, and Duration of Neuropsychological Performance of Male Chronic Alcoholics. _Dissertation Abstracts International_, 42(6): 2554B, 1981.

6013. Walcott, Esther P. and Straus, Robert. Use of a Hospital Facility in Conjunction with Outpatient Clinics in the Treatment of Alcoholics. _Quarterly Journal of Studies on Alcohol_, 13: 60-77, 1952.

6014. Waldo, Michael and Guerney, Bernard G. _Dyadic Marital Relationship Enhancement Therapy in the Treatment of Alcoholism_. Report. Rockville, MD: National Clearinghouse for Alcohol Information, no date.

6015. Waldo, Michael and Guerney, Bernard G. Marital Relationship Enhancement Therapy in the Treatment of Alcoholism. _Journal of Marital and Family Therapy_, 9(3): 321-323, 1983.

6016. Waldorf, Dan. Life Without Heroin: Some Social Adjustments During Long-Term Periods of Voluntary Abstention. In: _Drug Use and Social Policy_. Ed. J. Susman. New York: AMS Press, 1972, pages 471-486.

6017. Waldron, I. and Eyer, J. Socioeconomic Causes of the Recent Rise in Death Rates for 15-24-Year-Olds. _Social Science and Medicine_, Oxford, 9(7): 383-396, 1975.

6018. Waldum, Shirley Joan. Relationships Between White Middle-Class Drug-Abusing Adolescent Girls and Their Mothers. _Dissertation Abstracts International_, 44(8): 2572B, 1983.

6019. Walker, C.G. Influence of Parental Drinking Behavior on that of Adolescent Native Americans. M.A. Thesis. University of Washington, Seattle, 1976.

6020. Walker, L.E. _The Battered Woman_. New York: Harper & Row, 1979.

6021. Walker-Weber, J. Aiding the Adolescent's Search for "Self." _Alcoholism: The National Magazine_, 44(1): 27-28, 1983.

6022. Wall, J.H. and Allen, E.B. Results of Hospital Treatment of Alcoholism. _American Journal of Psychiatry_, 100: 474-479, 1944.

6023. Wallace, B. All in the Family. _Connecticut_, June: 71-73, 172, 1985.

6024. Wallace, D.C. Huntington's Chorea in Queensland. A Not Uncommon Disease. _The Medical Journal of Australia_, Sydney, 1(7): 299-307, 1972.

6025. Wallace, J. After Hospitalization: Treatment Support of Alcoholics. _Bulletin of the New York Academy of Medicine_, 59(2): 250-254, 1983.

6026. Wallace, J. Alcoholism Controversy. _American Psychologist_, 40(3): 372-373, 1985.

6027. Wallace, J. Careful Look at Families in Pain and in Recovery. _Human Ecology Forum_, 9(3): 12-15, 1978.

6028. Wallace, J. Personality Disturbances Before...After Onset of Alcoholism. <u>Focus on Family and Chemical Dependency</u>, <u>7</u>(3): 14-15, 1984.

6029. Waller, Suzan and Lorch (Day), Barbara. Social and Psychological Characteristics of Alcoholics: A Male-Female Comparison. <u>International Journal of the Addictions</u>, <u>13</u>(2): 201-212, 1978.

6030. Wallis, G.G. Stress in Service Families. <u>Proceedings of the Royal Society of Medicine</u>, London, <u>61</u>(10): 976-978, 1968.

6031. Wallner, C.J. and Godlaski, T.M. Alcohol Abuse and Domestic Violence, A Problem in Interdisciplinary Communication: One Community's Solution. Paper presented at National Council on Alcoholism Forum. Seattle, May, 1980.

6032. Walonick, David. Endangered Children and the Misuse of Intoxication by Controlling Adults. Minneapolis, MN: St. Mary's Junior College, 1977.

6033. Walpole, I.R. and Hockey, A. Fetal Alcohol Syndrome: Implications to Family and Society in Australia. <u>Australian Paediatric Journal</u>, Parkville, <u>16</u>(2): 101-105, 1980.

6034. Walsh, Arthur and Lukas, Emma. Alcoholic Brain Damage: Anticoagulant Therapy. <u>Journal of American Geriatrics Society</u>, <u>22</u>(12): 555-556, 1974.

6035. Walsh, Joanne and Cohen, Pauline C. Theoretical Framework. In: <u>Casework with Wives of Alcoholics</u>. Eds. P.C. Cohen and M.S. Krause. New York: Family Service Association of America, 1971, pages 17-32.

6036. Walsh, Noel. Psychiatry in the People's Republic of China. <u>Psychiatric Annals</u>, <u>8</u>(6): 42, 51, 55-56, 59, 63, 1978.

6037. Walshe, Brennan K.S. An Analysis of Homicide by Young Persons in England and Wales. <u>Acta Psychiatrica Scandinavica</u>, Munksgaard, <u>54</u>(2): 92-98, 1976.

6038. Walshe, Brennan K.S. The Roots of Child Crime. <u>Nursing Mirror and Midwives Journal</u>, London, <u>143</u>(9): 66-68, 1976.

6039. Walte, B.J. and Ludwig, M.J. <u>Issues and Strategies in the Provision of Services to Children of Alcoholics</u>. Report. Arlington, VA: Evaluation Technologies Incorporated, 1982.

6040. Walters, Orville S. The Religious Background of Fifty Alcoholics. <u>Quarterly Journal of Studies on Alcohol</u>, <u>18</u>: 405-415, 1957.

6041. Walton, R. Mancare Community: The Salvation Army Bridge Program. Paper presented at Second Pan Pacific Conference on Drugs and Alcohol, Hong Kong, November-December, 1983.

6042. Wanberg, Kenneth W. and Horn, John L. Alcoholism Symptom Patterns of Men and Women; A Comparative Study. <u>Quarterly Journal of Studies on Alcohol</u>, <u>31</u>(1): 40-61, 1970.

6043. Wanberg, Kenneth W. and Horn, John L. Alcoholism Syndromes Related to Sociological Classifications. <u>International Journal of the Addictions</u>, <u>8</u>(1): 99-120, 1973.

6044. Wanberg, Kenneth W. Lewis, Ron and Foster, F. Mark. Alcoholism and Ethnicity: A Comparative Study of Alcohol Use Patterns Across Ethnic Groups. <u>International Journal of the Addictions</u>, <u>13</u>(8): 1245-1262, 1978.

6045. Wang, Richard P. A Study of Alcoholism in Chinatown. International
       Journal of Social Psychiatry, London, 14(4): 260-267, 1968.

6046. Ward, David A. Conceptions of Alcoholism. In: Alcoholism:
       Introduction to Theory and Treatment. Ed. David A. Ward.
       Dubuque, IA: Kendall/Hunt, 1980, pages 4-12.

6047. Ward, David A. Evidence for Controlled Drinking in Diagnosed
       Alcoholics: A Critical Analysis of the Goodwin et al.
       Adoption Study. Journal of Drug Issues, 8: 373-378, 1978.

6048. Ward, David A. Family Therapy; Introduction. In: Alcoholism:
       Introduction to Theory and Treatment. Ed. David A. Ward.
       Dubuque, IA: Kendall/Hunt, 1980.

6049. Ward, David A. The Influence of Family Relationships on Social
       and Psychological Functioning: A Follow-Up Study. Journal
       of Marriage and the Family, 43(4): 807-815, 1981.

6050. Ward, David A. (Ed.) Labeling Theory and the Development of
       Alcoholism. In: Alcoholism: Introduction to Theory and
       Development. Dubuque, IA: Kendall/Hunt, 1980, pages
       188-197.

6051. Ward, David A., Bendel, Robert B. and Lange, Donald. A
       Reconsideration of Environmental Resources and the
       Posttreatment Functioning of Alcoholic Patients. Journal
       of Health and Social Behavior, 23(4): 310-317, 1982.

6052. Ward, Elizabeth Mary. A Case-Control Study of the Etiology of
       Neuroblastoma. Dissertation Abstracts International,
       44(12): 3732B, 1983.

6053. Ward, J.A. and Fox, Joseph. A Suicide Epidemic on an Indian
       Reserve. Canadian Psychiatric Association Journal,
       22(8): 423-426, 1977.

6054. Ward, Kevin, Weir, Donald G., McCrodden, John M., Tipton, Keith F.
       Blood Acetaldehyde Levels in Relatives of Alcoholics Following
       Ethanol Ingestion. IRCS Medical Science, 11: 950, 1983.

6055. Ward, N.G. and Schuckit, M.A. Factors Associated with Suicidal
       Behavior in Polydrug Abusers. Journal of Clinical
       Psychiatry, 41: 379-385, 1980.

6056. Ward, Robert F. and Faillace, Louis A. The Alcoholic and His
       Helpers; A Systems View. Quarterly Journal of Studies on
       Alcohol, 31: 684-691, 1970.

6057. Ward, S.D., Melin, J.R. and Lloyd, F.P. Determinants of Plasma
       Cholesterol in Children-A Family Study. American Journal
       of Clinical Nutrition, 33: 63-70, 1980.

6058. Warder, J. and Ross, C.J. Age and Alcoholism. The British
       Journal of Addiction, 66(1): 45-51, 1971.

6059. Warmington, R. Female Alcoholism: A Pilot Study of Women in
       Treatment. Australian Family Physician, Sydney, 10(11):
       887-891, 1981.

6060. Warner, J.S. and Hinchman, M. Personality Patterns in Adult
       Children of Alcoholics (ACOAs): A Pilot Study. Paper
       presented at National Council on Alcoholism Forum,
       Washington, D.C., April, 1985.

6061. Warner, M.D. and Bernard, J.M. Pastoral Counseling with
       Alcoholics and Their Families. Pastoral Psychology,
       31(1): 26-39, 1982.

6062. Warner, R.H. and Rosett, H.L. The Effects of Drinking on Offspring:
       An Historical Survey of the American and British Literature.
       Journal of Studies on Alcohol, 36(11): 1395-1420, 1975.

6063. Warren, Glenda Annette. A Survey of the Drinking Patterns
       of Never Married College Women. Dissertation Abstracts
       International, 40(6): 3136A, 1979.

6064. Wartburg, J.P. von. Polymorphism of Human Alcohol and
       Aldehyde Dehydrogenase. In: Biological Approach to
       Alcoholism. Ed. Charles S. Lieber. Proceedings of a
       Conference, September 30-October 1, 1980. Sponsored by
       National Research Centers Branch, NIAAA; Veterans Adminis-
       tration; and Mt. Sinai School of Medicine. U.S. Department
       of Health and Human Services. National Institute on Alcohol
       Abuse and Alcoholism. Research Monograph No. 11.
       Washington, D.C.: U.S. Government Printing Office, 1983.

6065. Wartburg, J.P. von. Variability of Human Alcohol Metabolism.
       In: Ethanol Tolerance and Dependence: Endocrinological
       Aspects. Rockville, MD: National Institute on Alcohol
       Abuse and Alcoholism, 1983, pages 168-177.

6066. Wartburg, J.P. von and Buhler, R. Biology of Disease: Alcoholism
       and Aldehydism: New Biomedical Concepts. Laboratory
       Investigation, 50(1): 5-15, 1984.

6067. Wartburg, J.P. von, Buhler, R., Maring, J.-A. and Pestalozzi, D.
       Polymorphisms of Alcohol and Aldehyde Dehydrogenase and
       Their Significance for Acetaldehyde Toxicity. Pharmacology,
       Biochemistry and Behavior, 18(Supplement 1): 123-125, 1983.

6068. Wasileski, Maryann, Callaghan-Chaffee, Martha E. and Chaffee, R.
       Blake. Spousal Violence in Military Homes: An Initial
       Survey. Military Medicine, 147(9): 761-765, 1982.

6069. Waters, F.E. and Twaite, J.A. ACOA Personality Profile: An
       Empirical Test. Paper presented at National Council on
       Alcoholism Forum, Washington, D.C., April, 1985.

6070. Waters, W.E., Cochrane, A.L. and Collins, J. Evaluation of Social
       Therapy in Chronic Alcoholism. British Journal of Preventive
       and Social Medicine, London, 26(1): 57-58, 1972.

6071. Watson, F. and Dick, M. Distribution and Inheritance of Low
       Serum Thyroxine-Binding Globulin Levels in Australian
       Aborigines. A New Genetic Variation. Medical Journal of
       Australia, Sydney, 1(7): 385-387, 1980.

6072. Watson, Nicholas R. New Council in N. Ireland. (Letter to
       the Editor.) British Journal on Alcohol and Alcoholism,
       12(1): 10-11, 1977.

6073. Watters, Trina S. and Theimer, William. Children of Alcoholics:
       A Critical Review of Some Literature. Contemporary Drug
       Problems, 7(2): 195-201, 1978.

6074. Watterson, Donald J. Psychiatric Illness in the Medical
       Profession: Incidence in Relation to Sex and Field of
       Practice. Canadian Medical Association Journal,
       Ottawa, 115(4): 311-317, 1976.

6075. Wattis, John P. Alcohol Problems in the Elderly. Journal of
       the American Geriatrics Society, 29(3): 131-134, 1981.

6076. Watts, Thomas D. and Wright, Roosevelt Jr. Discussion. In:
       Black Alcoholism: Toward a Comprehensive Understanding.
       Eds. Thomas D. Watts and Roosevelt Wright, Jr. Springfield,
       IL: Charles C. Thomas, 1983, pages 5-18.

6077. Weathers, Brenda. Alcoholism and the Lesbian Community. In: Alcoholism in Women. Eds. Cristen C. Eddy and John L. Ford. Dubuque, IA: Kendall/Hunt, 1980, pages 142-149.

6078. Weathers, Caislin and Billingsley, Donna. Body Image and Sex-Role Stereotype as Features of Addiction in Women. International Journal of the Addictions, 17: 343-347, 1982.

6079. Webb, L.F. Is Crisis in the Alcoholic Black Family Different from the Crisis in the Average Alcoholic White Family? Paper presented at the Nassau County Department of Drug and Alcohol Addiction, Mineola, NY. (Also in: Critical Concerns in the Field of Drug Abuse. New York: Marcel Dekker, 1978, pages 857-861.)

6080. Webb, N.L., Pratt, T.C., Linn, M.W. and Carmichael, J.S. Focus on the Family as a Factor in Differential Treatment Outcome. In: Drugs and the Family. Ed. Thomas J. Glynn. Washington, D.C.: U.S. Government Printing Office, 1981, pages 269-271. (Also in: International Journal of the Addictions, 13: 783-795, 1978.)

6081. Webb, R. The Forgotten Victims. Treating the Alcoholic's Family. Texas Hospitals, 39(8): 11-12, 1984.

6082. Webb, R.A.J. and Bruen, W.J. Multiple Child-Parent Therapy in a Family Therapeutic Community. International Journal of Social Psychiatry, London, 14(1): 50-55, 1967.

6083. Weber, W. Gefahrdung Durch Alkohol Bei 10- Bis 14 Jahrigen Jungen. (Risk of Problem Drinking in Youths Aged 10-14.) Suchtgefahren, Hamburg, 25: 136-139, 1979.

6084. Wechsler, Henry and Thum, Denise. Alcohol and Drug Use Among Teenagers: A Questionnaire Study. In: Psychological and Social Factors in Drinking and Treatment Evaluation. Ed. M.E. Chafetz. Washington, D.C.: U.S. Government Printing Office, 1973, pages 33-46. (Also as: Proceedings of the Second Annual Alcoholism Conference of the NIAAA. Ed. M. Chafetz. Rockville, MD: NIAAA, 1973, pages 33-46.)

6085. Wechsler, Henry and Thum, Denise. Teen-Age Drinking, Drug Use, and Social Correlates. Quarterly Journal of Studies on Alcohol, 34(4): 1220-1227, 1973.

6086. Wechsler, Henry, Thum, Denise, Demone, Harold W. Jr. and Dwinnell, Joanne. Social Characteristics and Blood Alcohol Level. Measurements of Subgroup Differences. Quarterly Journal of Studies on Alcohol, 33(1): 132-147, 1972.

6087. Wegner, Marwood E. Surviving Sobriety. Pamphlet. Center City, MN: Hazelden, no date.

6088. Wegscheider, D. From Survival to Living: A Look at Aftercare. The Forgotten Part of Treatment. Focus on Family and Chemical Dependency, 7(6): 27-28, 39, 1984.

6089. Wegscheider, D. and Wegscheider, S. Family Illness: Chemical Dependency. Mattituck, NY: TFL Press, 1978.

6090. Wegscheider, Sharon. Another Chance: Hope and Health for the Alcoholic Family. Palo Alto, CA: Science and Behavior Books, 1981.

6091. Wegscheider, Sharon. Chemical Dependency: A System Illness. Focus on Alcohol and Drug Issues, 6(2): 2-3, 30, 1983.

6092. Wegscheider, Sharon. Family Trap. In: Another Chance. Palo Alto, CA: Science and Behavior Books, 1979.

6093. Wegscheider, Sharon. The Family Trap: No One Escapes from a Chemically Dependent Family. Second Edition. Crystal, MN: Nurturing Networks, 1979. (Also as: Pamphlet. Minneapolis: Johnson Institute, 1976.)

6094. Wegscheider, Sharon. From the Family Trap to Family Freedom. Alcoholism: The National Magazine, 1(3): 36-39, 1981.

6095. Wegscheider, Sharon. Inside Structured Intervention. Alcoholism: The National Magazine, 2(6): 35-36, 1982.

6096. Wegscheider-Cruse, Sharon. Choicemaking: For Co-Dependents, Adult Children and Spirituality Seekers. Pompano Beach, FL: Health Communications Inc., 1985.

6097. Wegscheider-Cruse, Sharon. The Thirst for Freedom. In: Alcoholism and the Family: A Book of Readings. Eds. Sharon Wegscheider-Cruse and Richard W. Esterly. Wernersville, PA: The Caron Institute, 1985, pages 69-70.

6098. Wegscheider-Cruse, Sharon and Esterly, Richard W. (Eds.). Alcoholism and the Family: A Book of Readings. Wernersville, PA: The Caron Institute, 1985.

6099. Weibel-Orlando, Joan. Substance Abuse Among American Indian Youth: A Continuing Crisis. Journal of Drug Issues, 14(2): 313-335, 1984.

6100. Weidman, Arthur. The Compulsive Adolescent Substance Abuser: Psychological Differentiation and Family Process. Journal of Drug Education, 13(2): 161-172, 1983.

6101. Weidman, Arthur A. Engaging the Families of Substance Abusing Adolescents in Family Therapy. Journal of Substance Abuse Treatment, 2(2): 97-105, 1985.

6102. Weidmann, M., Ladewig, D., Faust, V., Gastpar, M., Heise, H., Hobi, V., Mayer, Boss, Sybille and Wyss, P. Drug Consumption by Basel School Children -- An Epidemiologic Study. Schweizerische Medizinische Wochenschrift, 103(4): 121-126, 1973.

6103. Weijl, Simon. Theoretical and Practical Aspects of Psychoanalytic Therapy of Problem Drinkers. Quarterly Journal of Studies on Alcohol, 5: 200-211, 1944.

6104. Weil, C. Alcohol Problems and the Family. In: Impact of Alcohol on the People of Michigan: Volume 1. East Lansing: Michigan State University, 1985, pages 8-1 - 8-26.

6105. Weil, M.W., Jones, J. and Weil, P.E. Alcoholism and the Impact of Intra-Familial Discord. In: Sociological Perspectives in Marriage and the Family: Concepts and Readings, 2d ed. Ed. M.W. Weil. Danville, Il: Interstate Printers and Publishers, Inc., 1979, pages 261-272. (Also as: Eric Document Number ED 141664.)

6106. Weinberg, J.R. Alcoholism; Why Do Alcoholics Deny Their Problem? Minnesota Medicine, 56: 709-711, 1973.

6107. Weinberg, J.R. Assessing Drinking Problems By History. Postgraduate Medicine, 59(4): 87-90, 1976.

6108. Weinberg, J.R. Interview Techniques for Diagnosing Alcoholism. American Family Physician, 9(3): 107-115, 1974.

6109. Weiner, H. and Fisher, D. Substance Abuse: A Family Tradition
       Through Three Generations. Paper presented at the 7th
       World Conference of Therapeutic Communities, Chicago,
       May, 1983, pages 49-52.

6110. Weiner, Sheldon, Tamerin, John S., Steinglass, Peter and Mendelson,
       J.H. Familial Patterns in Chronic Alcoholism: A Study of a
       Father and Son During Experimental Intoxication. American
       Journal of Psychiatry, 127: 1646-1651, 1971. (Also in:
       American Journal of Orthopsychiatry, 40: 356-357, 1970.)

6111. Weingarten, Helen Ruth. The Impact of Remarriage on Social and
       Psychological Well Being: Evidence from a National Survey.
       Dissertation Abstracts International, 42(6): 2512B, 1981.

6112. Weingarten, Nicholes. Treating Adolescent Drug Abuse as a Symptom
       of Dysfunction in the Family. In: Drug Abuse from the
       Family Perspective. Ed. Barbara Gray Ellis. Washington,
       D.C.: U.S. Government Printing Office, 1980, pages 57-62.

6113. Weinstein, Luis. Alcoholism as a Political Problem in Chile.
       Mental Health and Society, Basel, 3(1-2): 72-76, 1976.

6114. Weir, W.R. Counseling Youth Whose Parents are Alcoholic: A Means
       to an End as Well as an End in Itself. Journal of Alcohol
       Education, 16(1): 13-19, 1970.

6115. Weir, W.R. Needs of Students with an Alcohol Problem in
       Their Family, 1968. (Eric Document Number ED 020538).

6116. Weir, W.R. A Program of Alcohol Education and Counseling for
       High School Students with and without a Family Alcohol
       Problem. Doctoral Dissertation. (University Microfilms
       No. 68-6797.) Grand Forks: The University of North Dakota,
       1967.

6117. Weir, William and Gade, Eldon. An Approach to Counseling
       Alcoholics. Rehabilitation Counseling Bulletin, 12(4):
       227-229, 1969.

6118. Weisner, T.S., Weibel-Orlando, J.C. and Long, J. "Serious
       Drinking," "White Man's Drinking" and "Teetotaling":
       Drinking Levels in Styles in an Urban Indian Population.
       Journal of Studies on Alcohol, 45(3): 237-250, 1984.

6119. Weiss, Kenneth M. The Evolutionary Basis of Alcoholism:
       A Question of the Neocortex. In: Aging, Volume 25:
       Alcoholism in the Elderly: Social and Biomedical Issues.
       Eds. James T. Hartford and T. Samorajski. New York:
       Raven Press, 1984, pages 5-23.

6120. Weiss, Robert W. and Russakoff, Sheldon. The Sex Role Identity
       of Male Drug Abusers. Journal of Clinical Psychology,
       34(4): 1010-1013, 1978.

6121. Weissman, Andrew. A Social Service Strategy in Industry.
       Social Work, 20(5): 401-402, 1975.

6122. Weissman, M.M., Gershon, E.S. and Kidd, K.K. Psychiatric
       Disorders in the Relatives of Probands with Affective
       Disorders. Archives of General Psychiatry, 41(1):
       13-21, 1984.

6123. Wellisch, D.K. Family Considerations in Drug Abuse Problems.
       Paper presented at the Third Annual Symposium on Alcoholism
       and Drug Abuse, Houston, May, 1980.

6124. Wellisch, David K. Drug Problems in Children of the Wealthy and
       Famous. Journal of Drug Issues, 14(2): 233-242, 1984.

6125. Wellisch, David, DeAngelis, G.G. and Bond, Doug. Family
       Treatment of the Homosexual Adolescent Drug Abuser:
       On Being Gay in a Sad Family. In: Family Therapy of
       Drug and Alcohol Abuse. Eds. E. Kaufman and P.N. Kaufman.
       New York: Gardner Press, 1979, pages 105-114.

6126. Wellman, M. Fatigue During the Second Six Months of Abstinence.
       Canadian Medical Association Journal, 72: 338-342, 1955.

6127. Wellman, M. Towards an Etiology of Alcoholism: Why Young Men
       Drink Too Much. Canadian Medical Association Journal,
       73: 717-725, 1955.

6128. Wells, S. Adolescent Alcohol and Drug Abuse. Voices: Valuing
       the Alcoholic, 20(1): 52-54, 1984.

6129. Welner, A., Liss, J.L. and Robins, E. Personality Disorder:
       II. Follow-up. The British Journal of Psychiatry: The
       Journal of Mental Science, London, 124(0): 359-366, 1974.

6130. Welsh, Tina. The Washington Star News, 7 April 1974, Teen
       Section. (Alateens Talk about their Problems.)

6131. Wender, Paul H. Psychiatric Genetics and the Primary Prevention
       of Psychiatric Disorders. Biblioteca Psychiatrica, 160:
       7-14, 1981.

6132. Wenger, P. History of a Drinking Habit in 400 Inmates of a Penal
       Institution. New York State Journal of Medicine, 44:
       1898-1904, 1944.

6133. Weninger, Marvin E. and Leeper, Edna. A Treatment Program for
       Alcoholics. Journal of the Tennessee Medical Association,
       69(12): 849-850, 1976.

6134. Werner, Barbara. Management of the Alcoholic Beyond the Hospital.
       Paper presented at the Symposium on Alcohol and Drugs -- A
       Challenge for Education. Melbourne, January 1971, pages
       55-56.

6135. Werner, Emmy E. Resilient Offspring of Alcoholics: A Longitudinal
       Study from Birth to Age 18. Journal of Studies on Alcohol,
       47(1): 34-40, 1986.

6136. Wertham, F. Battered Children and Baffled Adults. Bulletin of
       the New York Academy of Medicine, 48(7): 887-898, 1972.

6137. Wessely, P. and Pernhaupt, G. Female Alcoholism in Comparison to
       the Male Control Group. Wiener Medizinsche Wochenschrift,
       123(28): 473-478, 1973.

6138. West, J.A. Prince Charming Syndrome in Alcoholic Women.
       Dissertation Abstracts International, 44(8): 2544B, 1984.

6139. West, James W. Little Company of Mary Hospital: The Role of
       a General Hospital in the Alcoholism Treatment Network.
       In: Alcoholism Rehabilitation: Methods and Experiences
       of Private Rehabilitation Centers. Ed. Vincent Groupe.
       New Brunswick, NJ: Rutgers University Center of Alcohol
       Studies, 1978, pages 56-63.

6140. West, Malcolm, Frankel, Barbara and Dalton, Jeanne. Treatment
       Progress of Substance Dependent Mothers and Their Children
       at Family House. In: Drug Dependence and Alcoholism,
       Volume 1: Biomedical Issues. Ed. A.J. Schecter.
       New York: Plenum Press, 1981, pages 789-799.

6141. Westcott, W.W. and Campbell, H. Report of the Committee Upon the Heredity of Inebriety. Proceedings of the Society on the Studies of Inebriety, London, 68: 2-10, 1902.

6142. Westermeyer, Joseph. Alcoholism from the Cross Cultural Perspective: A Review and Critique of Clinical Studies. American Journal of Drug and Alcohol Abuse, 1: 89-105, 1974.

6143. Westermeyer, Joseph. A Comparison of Amok and Other Homicide in Laos. American Journal of Psychiatry, 129(6): 703-709, 1972.

6144. Westermeyer, Joseph. Cross-Racial Foster Home Placement Among Native American Psychiatric Patients. Journal of the National Medical Association, 69(4): 231-236, 1977.

6145. Westermeyer, Joseph. Introduction to Alcoholism and Women. In: Currents in Alcoholism: Volume 6. Ed. M. Galanter. New York: Grune and Stratton, 1979, pages 197-199.

6146. Westermeyer, Joseph. Opium Smoking in Laos: A Survey of 40 Addicts. American Journal of Psychiatry, 131(2): 165-170, 1974.

6147. Westermeyer, Joseph. Options Regarding Alcohol Use Among the Chippewa. American Journal of Orthopsychiatry, 42(3): 398-403, 1972.

6148. Westermeyer, Joesph. The Role of Ethnicity in Substance Abuse. Advances in Alcohol & Substance Abuse, 4(1): 9-18, 1984.

6149. Westermeyer, Joseph. Role of the Family Physician in the Diagnosis and Treatment of Substance Abuse. Seminars in Family Medicine, 1(4): 237-247, 1980.

6150. Westermeyer, Joseph. Treatment of Alcohol Abuse: Psychotherapies and Sociotherapies. In: Treatment Aspects of Drug Dependence. Ed. Arnold Schecter. West Palm Beach: CRC Press, Inc., 1978, pages 223-234.

6151. Westermeyer, Joseph and Lang, Gretchen. Ethnic Differences in Use of Alcoholism Facilities. The International Journal of the Addictions, 10(3): 513-520, 1975.

6152. Westermeyer, Joseph and Neider, John. Predicting Treatment Outcome After 10 Years Among American Indian Alcoholics. Alcoholism: Clinical and Experimental Research, 8(2): 179-184, 1984.

6153. Westermeyer, Joseph and Peake, E. A Ten-year Follow-Up of Alcoholic Native Americans in Minnesota. American Journal of Psychiatry, 140(2): 189-194, 1983.

6154. Westfield, D.R. Two Years' Experience of Group Methods in the Treatment of Male Alcoholics in a Scottish Mental Hospital. British Journal of Addiction, Edinburgh, 67: 267-276, 1972.

6155. Wexberg, L.E. A Critique of Physiopathological Theories of the Etiology of Alcoholism. Quarterly Journal of Studies on Alcohol, 11: 113-118, 1950.

6156. Whalen, Thelma. Wives of Alcoholics: Four Types Observed in a Family Service Agency. Quarterly Journal of Studies on Alcohol, 14: 632-641, 1953.

6157. Whalley, L.J. Social and Biological Variables in Alcoholism: A Selective Review. In: Psychopharmacology of Alcohol. Ed. M. Sandler. New York: Raven Press, 1980.

6158.   Whalley, Lawrence J., Robinson, T.J., McIsaac, Mary and Wolff, Sula.
        Psychiatric Referrals from Scottish Children's Hearings: A
        Comparative Study. Journal of Child Psychology and Psychiatry
        and Allied Disciplines, 19(3): 269-278, 1978.

6159.   What Does "Drunken" Mean, Mom?? (Ques es "Borracho" Mamma?)
        Pamphlet. New York: Al-Anon Family Group Headquarters,
        Inc., no date.

6160.   What Kids Should Know About Parents and Drinking. South
        Deerfield, MA: Channing L. Bete, 1984.

6161.   What You Need to Know About Impairment in Physicians. Paper
        presented at the California Medical Association, Committee
        on the Well-Being of Physicians, San Francisco, March, 1978.

6162.   Wheat, P. and Novak, T. You're Not Alone: Kids' Book on Alcoholism
        and Child Abuse. Chicago, IL: National Committee for
        Prevention of Child Abuse (NCPCA) Publishing Department, 1985.

6163.   When Someone Close Drinks Too Much. Pamphlet. Center City, MN:
        Hazelden, no date.

6164.   Whipple, S.C., Berka, C., Poland, R.E. and Noble, E.P. Electro-
        physiological and Neuroendocrine Measures in Male Alcoholics
        and Their Sons. Paper presented at the Society for
        Neuroscience Meeting, Anaheim, October, 1984.

6165.   Whitcroft, Cannon Thomas H. Alcoholism: A Terminal Illness.
        Canada's Mental Health, 29(1): 23-25, 1981.

6166.   White, W.L. Taking Care of the Treatment Family. Focus on
        Alcohol and Drug Issues, 6(4): 4, 31, 1983.

6167.   White, W.T. Remembering Young Children of Alcoholics: A New
        Family Therapy Approach. Paper presented at National
        Council on Alcoholism Forum, Houston, April, 1983.

6168.   Whitehead, Paul C. Drug Use Among Adolescent Students in
        Halifax. Nova Scotia: Halifax Youth Agency, 1969.

6169.   Whitehead, Paul C. Notes on the Association Between Alcoholism
        and Suicide. The International Journal of the Addictions,
        7(3): 525-532, 1972.

6170.   Whitehead, Paul C. Social Dimensions of Alcoholism; A Correlational
        and Typological Analysis. Doctoral Dissertation. (University
        Microfilms No. 69-19158.) University of Massachusetts, 1969.

6171.   Whitehead, Paul C. and Ferrence, Roberta G. Women and Children
        Last: Implications of Trends in Consumption for Women and
        Young People. In: Alcoholism Problems in Women and
        Children. Eds. Milton Greenblatt and Marc A. Schuckit.
        New York: Grune and Stratton, 1976, pages 163-196.

6172.   White House Conference on Families: Summary of State Reports.
        Volume One, 1980. (Eric Document Number ED194194.)

6173.   White House Conference on Families: Summary of State Reports.
        Volume Two, 1980. (Eric Document Number ED194195.)

6174.   White House Conference on Families: Summary of State Reports.
        Volume Three, 1980. (Eric Document Number ED194196.)

6175.   Whitfield, Charles L. Alcoholism, Other Drug Problems &
        Spirituality: A Transpersonal Approach. Report.
        Baltimore: The Resource Group, 1984.

6176. Whitfield, Charles L. Children of Alcoholics: Treatment Issues.
      Maryland State Medical Journal, 29(6): 86-91, 1981. (Also
      in: Services for Children of Alcoholics. U.S. Department of
      Health and Human Resources. National Institute on Alcohol Abuse
      and Alcoholism. Washington, D.C.: U.S. Government Printing
      Office, 1981.)

6177. Whitfield, Charles L. Co-Dependency -- An Emerging Illness Among
      Professionals. Part I: Recognition and Identification.
      Focus on Alcohol and Drug Issues, 6(3): 10-11, 13, 29,
      31, 1983.

6178. Whitfield, Charles L. Outpatient Management of the Alcoholic
      Patient. Psychiatric Annals, 12(4): 447-451, 455-456,
      458, 1982.

6179. Whitfield, J.B. and Martin, N.G. Individual Differences in Plasma
      ALT, AST and GGT: Contributions of Genetic and Environmental
      Factors, Including Alcohol Consumption. Enzyme, 33(2):
      61-69, 1985.

6180. Whitfield, J.B. and Martin, N.G. Inheritance and Alcohol as
      Factors Influencing Plasma Uric Acid Levels. Acta Geneticae
      Medicae et Gemellologiae, Rome, 32(2): 117-126, 1983.

6181. Whitlock, F.A. Alcoholism: A Genetic Disorder? Australian and
      New Zealand Journal of Psychiatry, 9: 3-7, 1975.

6182. Whitlock, F.A., Price, J. and Weston, M.J. Inheritance of
      Alcoholism. British Journal of Psychiatry, 133: 286, 1978.

6183. Whitney, D.D. The Effects of Alcohol Not Inherited in Hydatina
      Senta. American Nation, 46: 41-56, 1912.

6184. Whitney, G., McClearn, G.E. and DeFries, J.C. Heritability of
      Alcohol Preference in Laboratory Mice and Rats: Erroneous
      Estimates. Behavior Genetics, 12: 543-546, 1982.

6185. Whitney, S. Ties that Bind: Strategies for Counseling the Gay
      Male Co-Alcoholic. New York: National Association of Gay
      Alcoholism Professionals, no date.

6186. W.H.O. and a New Perspective on Alcoholism. Lancet, London,
      8021: 1087-1088, 1977.

6187. Wholey, C.C. Alcohol and Heredity. West Virginia Medical
      Journal, 7: 260-264, 1912.

6188. Wholey, Dennis. The Courage to Change. Hope & Help for Alcoholics &
      Their Families. Boston: Houghton Mifflin Co., 1984.

6189. Wholey, Dennis. I'm Dennis, and I'm an Alcoholic. In: Courage
      to Change. Boston: Houghton Mifflin Co., 1984, pages 1-13.

6190. Whorley, L.W. Social Recovery and Therapeutic Mission. International
      Journal of the Addictions, 19(7): 753-765, 1984.

6191. Widespread "Prejudice" Against Female Alcoholics. Nursing Times,
      London, 72(16): 602, 1976.

6192. Widseth, Jane C. Reported Dependent Behaviors Toward Mother and
      Use of Alcohol in Delinquent Girls. Doctoral Disseration
      (University Microfilms No. 72-25354.) Boston University
      Graduate School, 1972.

6193. Widseth, Jane C. and Mayer, Joseph. Drinking Behavior and
      Attitudes Toward Alcohol in Delinquent Girls. International
      Journal of the Addictions, 6(3): 453-461, 1971.

6194. Wiens, Arthur N., Menustik, Carole E., Miller, Sheldon, I. and
       Schmitz, Robert E. Medical-Behavioral Treatment of the
       Older Alcohol Patient. _American Journal of Drug and Alcohol
       Abuse_, _9_(4): 461-475, 1982.

6195. Wieser, S. Uber Das Trinkverhalten Der Allgemeinen Bevolkerung
       Und Stereotype Des Abstinenten Und Trinkers: Eine Empirische
       Sozio-Psychiatrische Studie Im Bundesland Bremen. (The
       Drinking Practices of the General Population, and Stereotype
       of the Abstainer and of the Drinker: An Empirical
       Sociopsychiatric Study in Federal District of Bremen.)
       _Forschritte Der Neurologie, Psychiatrie & Ihrer
       Grenzgebiete_, Stuttgart, _36_(9): 485-509, 1968.

6196. _Wife of the Alcoholic_. _Journal of Alcoholism_, London, _9_(2):
       41, 1974.

6197. _Wife of the Alcoholic: A Pattern to Happiness_. Salt Lake City:
       Utah Alcoholism Foundation, 1971.

6198. Wijnhoven, Petronella. _Special Services to Families of Problem
       Drinkers_. Northampton, MA: Children's Aid and Family
       Service, 1977.

6199. Wilcox, J.A. Adolescent Alcoholism. _Journal of Psychoactive
       Drugs_, _17_(2): 77-85, 1985.

6200. Wilkerson, D. _Fast Track to Nowhere_. Old Tappan, NJ: Spire
       Books, 1979.

6201. Wilkes, E. The Co-ordination of Care in the Field of Alcoholism.
       In: _Alcoholism and Drug Dependence; A Multidisciplinary
       Approach_. Eds. J.S. Madden, R. Walker and W.H. Kenyon.
       New York: Plenum, 1977, pages 395-398.

6202. Wilkins, J. Suicide Calls and Identification of Suicidal Callers.
       The Medical Journal of Australia, Sydney, _2_(17): 923-929,
       1972.

6203. Wilkins, R.H. The Community Nurse and the Alcoholic. _Nursing Times_,
       London, _69_(33): 1071-1072, 1973.

6204. Wilkinson, Rupert. _The Prevention of Drinking Problems: Alcohol
       Control and Cultural Influences_. New York: Oxford University
       Press, 1970.

6205. Wilks, Jeffrey and Callan, Victor J. Similarity of University
       Students' and Their Parents' Attitudes Toward Alcohol.
       Journal of Studies on Alcohol, _45_(4): 326-333, 1984.

6206. Willette, Joanne Lightle. Family Socialization and High School
       Social Climate Effects on Adolescent Alcohol and Marijuana Use.
       Dissertation Abstracts International, _39_(2): 1151A, 1978.

6207. Williams, Allan F., McCourt, William F. and Schneider, Laurence.
       Personality Self-Descriptions of Alcoholics and Heavy Drinkers.
       Quarterly Journal of Studies on Alcohol, _32_: 310-317, 1971.

6208. Williams, Andrew. Inborn Alcoholism. _Lancet_, _2_(8446): 96-97,
       1985.

6209. Williams, Art. There But for the Grace of God. _Saturday Evening
       Post_, _255_(September): 93-112, 1983.

6210. Williams, Carol N. Differences in Child Care Practices Among
       Families with Alcoholic Fathers, Alcoholic Mothers, and Two
       Alcoholic Parents. Doctoral Dissertation. Waltham, MA:
       Brandeis University, 1983. (Also in: _Dissertation Abstracts
       International_, _44_(1):299A, 1983.)

6211.   Williams, Carol N. and Klerman, Lorraine V. Female Alcohol Abuse:
         Its Effects on the Family. In: Alcohol Problems in Women:
         Antecedents, Consequences, and Intervention. Eds. S. Wilsnack
         and L. Beckman. New York: Guilford Press, 1984, pages 280-312.

6212.   Williams, Etta B. Assessment and Identification of the Problem.
         In: The Community Health Nurse and Alcohol-Related Problems.
         Rockville, MD: National Institute on Alcohol Abuse and
         Alcoholism, 1978, pages 53-64.

6213.   Williams, Harold L., Rundell, O.H., Galloway, Dan C., Bayles,
         Richard L. and Hyman, Fred. Relationships Among Cognitive,
         Somnographic and CT Scan Variables in Alcoholics. Alcohol
         Technical Reports, 12-13: 47-57, 1983-84.

6214.   Williams, J.W. Heredity; Eugenics; Hereditary Alcoholism an
         Undeniable Fact. Virginia Medical Semi-Monthly, 18:
         460-463, 1913.

6215.   Williams, James H., Van Lewen, Alan and Bowers, Edwin C. Final
         Report: Short Term Family Therapy for Alcoholics; A
         Research and Evaluation Study. Tallahassee, FL: Bureau
         of Alcoholic Rehabilitation, Department of Health and
         Rehabilitative Services, 1972.

6216.   Williams, James H., Van Lewen, Alan and Bowers, Edwin C. Short
         Term Family Therapy for Alcoholics: A Research and Evaluation
         Study. Southern Sociological Society, 324, 1971.

6217.   Williams, James H., Van Lewen, Alan and Breen, Tessa. Evaluation
         of a 6-Day Course in Alcoholism Education and Orientation.
         The International Journal of the Addictions, 9(5): 673-699,
         1974.

6218.   Williams, Juan. The Washington Post, 27 October 1976, section 2,
         page 1, column 4. (Alcohol and Adolescent Abuse by Parents.)

6219.   Williams, K.H. Children and Family of the Alcoholic. Audio
         Recording from the 1st Annual Seminar for Advanced Studies
         on Alcoholism, Dallas/Houston, October, 1981.

6220.   Williams, K.H. Children of Alcoholics. Paper presented at the
         5th Annual Conference, Alcoholism: Handicaps on the Road
         to Recovery, Livonia, MI, May, 1981.

6221.   Williams, K.H. Intervention with Children of Alcoholics. Paper
         presented at the NIAAA Symposium, Silver Springs, MD,
         September, 1979. (Also in: Services to Children of Alcoholics.
         Washington, D.C.: U.S. Government Printing Office, 1979, pages
         60-65.)

6222.   Williams, K.H. The Medical Model of Alcoholism: The Disease Concept.
         In: Time for Change in Alcoholism Treatment? Traditional and
         Emerging Concepts. Ed. J. Newman. University of Pittsburgh:
         Western Pennsylvania Institute of Alcohol Studies, 1979, pages
         1-26.

6223.   Williams, Millree. County Program Initiates "Co-Alcoholic" Groups.
         NIAAA Information and Feature Service, (IFS No. 105): 1,
         March 3, 1983.

6224.   Williams, Millree. Latino Alcoholism Program Stresses Family
         Counseling. NIAAA Information and Feature Service,
         (IFS No. 107): 3, May 3, 1983.

6225.   Williams, Millree. Research on Children of Alcoholics: Expanding
         the Knowledge. GWU Researchers Focus on Family Environment.
         Alcohol Health and Research World, 8(4): 6-7, 10-11, 1984.

6226. Williams, Millree. Senior Program Stresses Peer, Family Involvement.
       NIAAA Information and Feature Service, (IFS No. 106): 1,
       April 1, 1983.

6227. Williams, Millree. Young Children of Alcoholics Target of
       Prevention Program. ADAMHA News, 10(1): 2A-3A, 1984.

6228. Williams, Millree and Decosta, Marc. New Investigators: Frank
       George, Ph.D., Kenneth Sher, Ph.D., Stella Hughes, Ph.D.
       Alcohol Health and Research World, 9(3): 28-33, 1985.

6229. Williams, Paul. Psychotropic Drug Use and the Family. Inter-
       national Journal of Family Psychiatry, 2(1-2): 55-63, 1981.

6230. Williams, R.B. Jr., Overlan, E.M., Ryzewski, J.H., Beach, M.J.
       and Willard, H.N. The Use of a Therapeutic Milieu on a
       Continuing Care Unit in a General Hospital. Annals of
       Internal Medicine, 73(6): 957-962, 1970.

6231. Williams, R.J., Berry, L.J. and Beerstecher, E. Jr. Individual
       Metabolic Patterns, Alcoholism, Genetotrophic Diseases.
       Science, 109: 441, 1949. (Also in: Proceedings of
       the National Academy of Sciences, Washington, D.C., 35:
       265-271, 1949.)

6232. Williams, Robert John. Social Stability on Admission and Success
       of In-Patient Treatment for Alcoholism. Drug and Alcohol
       Dependence, Lausanne, 2(2): 81-90, 1977.

6233. Williams, Roger J. The Etiology of Alcoholism: A Working Hypothesis
       Involving the Interplay of Hereditary and Environmental Factors.
       Quarterly Journal of Studies on Alcohol, 7: 567-587, 1947.

6234. Williams, Roger J., Pelton, Richard B. and Rogers, Lorene L.
       Dietary Deficiencies in Animals in Relation to Voluntary
       Alcohol and Sugar Consumption. Quarterly Journal of Studies
       on Alcohol, 16: 234-244, 1955.

6235. Williams, S. Child Abuse: Its Association with Drugs and Alcohol.
       Paper presented at the First Pan-Pacific Conference on Drugs
       and Alcohol, Canberra, Australia, February-March, 1980, pages
       188-190.

6236. Williams, Stephen G. and Baron, Jason. Effects of Short-Term
       Intensive Hospital Psychotherapy on Youthful Drug Abusers
       I. Preliminary Minnesota Multiphasic Personality Inventory
       Data. Psychological Reports, 50(1): 79-82, 1982.

6237. Williams, Terrence. Hazelden Family Program. Paper presented
       at the 24th Annual Meeting of Alcohol and Drug Problems
       Association, Bloomington, September, 1973.

6238. Williams, Wade H. Red Flags of Alcoholism. People, Human
       Resources in North Carolina. Raleigh: 30-32, 1974.

6239. Willoughby, Alan. The Alcohol Troubled Person; Known and
       Unknown. Chicago: Nelson-Hall Publishers, 1979.

6240. Wilmes, D. Fostering Children from Chemically Dependent
       Environments: Instructor Manual. Curriculum Guide.
       Minneapolis: University of Minnesota, Continuing Education
       in Social Work, Foster Care Education Program, 1981.

6241. Wilmes, D. Fostering Children from Chemically Dependent
       Environments: Participant Manual. Curriculum Guide.
       Minneapolis: University of Minnesota, Continuing Education
       in Social Work, Foster Care Education Program, 1981.

6242. Wilsnack, Richard W. and Wilsnack, Sharon C. Drinking and
       Denial of Social Obligations Among Adolescent Boys.
       Journal of Studies on Alcohol, 41(11): 1118-1133, 1980.

6243. Wilsnack, Richard W., Wilsnack, Sharon C. and Klassen, Albert D.
       Women's Drinking and Drinking Problems: Patterns From a
       1981 National Survey. American Journal of Public Health,
       74(11): 1231-1238, 1984.

6244. Wilsnack, Sharon C. Drinking, Sexuality, and Sexual Dysfunction
       in Women. In: Alcohol Problems in Women: Antecedents,
       Consequences, and Intervention. Eds. Sharon C. Wilsnack
       and Linda J. Beckman. New York: Guilford Press, 1984,
       pages 189-227.

6245. Wilsnack, Sharon C. The Impact of Sex Roles on Women's Alcohol
       Use and Abuse. In: Alcoholism Problems in Women and
       Children. Eds. Milton Greenblatt and Marc A. Schuckit.
       New York: Grune and Stratton, 1976, pages 37-63.

6246. Wilsnack, Sharon C. Sex Role Identity in Female Alcoholism.
       Journal of Abnormal Psychology, 82: 253-261, 1973.

6247. Wilsnack, Sharon C. and Beckman, Linda J. (Eds.). Alcohol
       Problems in Women: Antecedents, Consequences, and
       Intervention. New York: Guilford Press, 1984.

6248. Wilsnack, Sharon C., Wilsnack, Richard W. and Klassen, Albert D.
       Drinking and Drinking Problems Among Women in a U.S. National
       Survey. Alcohol Health & Research World, 9(2): 3-13, 1985.

6249. Wilson, A. Towards a Three-Process Learning Theory of Alcoholism.
       British Journal of Addiction, 72: 99-108, 1977.

6250. Wilson, C.A., Trammel, S. and Greer, B.G. Exploratory Study of the
       Relationship Between Child Abuse/Neglect and Alcohol/Drug Abuse.
       Memphis: Department of Human and Social Services, 1977.

6251. Wilson, Clare. The Family. In: Women and Alcohol. New York:
       Tavistock Publications, 1980, pages 101-132.

6252. Wilson, Clare. Impact on Children. In: Alcohol and the Family.
       Eds. J. Orford and J. Harwin. New York: St. Martin's Press,
       1982, pages 151-166.

6253. Wilson, Clare and Mulhall, David, J. Describing Relationships in
       Families with Alcohol Problems. The Family Relations Index:
       1 Graphic Representation. British Journal of Addiction,
       78(2): 181-191, 1983.

6254. Wilson, Clare and Orford, Jim. Children of Alcoholics. Report
       of a Preliminary Study and Comments on the Literature.
       Journal of Studies on Alcohol, 39(1): 121-142, 1978.
       (Also in: International Journal of Rehabilitation
       Research, 3(1): 94-96, 1980.)

6255. Wilson, E. Domiciliary Family Planning Service in Glasgow.
       British Medical Journal, London, 4(789): 731-733, 1971.

6256. Wilson, G.C. Aftercare. Paper presented at First Pan-Pacific
       Conference on Drugs and Alcohol, Canberra, Australia,
       February-March, 1980, pages 443-446.

6257. Wilson, G.C. Alcoholism in Industry Programmes Involving the
       Private Practitioner. Medical Journal of Australia,
       Sydney, 1(11): 559-561, 1981.

6258. Wilson, J.B. Family Communication, Interpersonal Influence and
       Teenage Alcohol Consumption. Dissertation Abstracts
       International, 46(3): 800A, 1985.

6259. Wilson, J.R., Erwin, V.G., McClearn, G.E., Plomin, R., Johnson,
       R.C., Ahern, F.M. and Cole, R.E. Effects of Ethanol:
       II. Behavioral Sensitivity and Acute Behavioral Tolerance.
       Alcoholism: Clinical and Experimental Research, 8(4):
       366-374, 1984.

6260. Wilson, J.R., Plomin, R., Erwin, V.G., Gabrielli, W.F. and
       Rhea, S.A. Effects of Positive Family History (FHP) for
       Heavy Alcohol Use. Alcoholism: Clinical and Experimental
       Research, 9(2): 186, 1985.

6261. Wilson, J.S. Pancreatitis, Alcohol and Lipid Metabolism.
       Dissertation Abstracts International, 44(12): 3726-3727B,
       1984.

6262. Wilson, J.S., Gossat, D., Tait, A., Rouse, S., Juan, X.J. and
       Pivola, R.C. Evidence for an Inherited Predisposition to
       Alcoholic Pancreatitis: A Controlled HLA Typing Study.
       Digestive Diseases and Sciences, 29(8): 727-730, 1984.

6263. Wilson, M.S. Do College Girls Confrom to the Standards of Their
       Parents? Marriage and Family, 15: 207-208, 1953.

6264. Wilson, Patti. The Whole Family Must Be Involved (Model
       Therapeutic Program, New Choice, Inc; Drugs, Alcohol,
       Family Violence.) E/SA, 10: 24-28, 1982.

6265. Wilson, S. Should You Offer Teenagers Drinks in Your Home?
       Leaflet. Harrisburg: Pennsylvania Council on Alcohol Problems,
       no date. (Also in: Reader's Digest, December, 1964.)

6266. Wilson, Wayne M. and Helm, Stanley T. An Alcoholism Program
       Tailored to Community Needs. Hospital and Community
       Psychiatry, 21(12): 406-408, 1970.

6267. Wiltse, F.L. Sr. Exploring Alcohol and Alcoholism: Instructor's
       Manual and Student Workbook. Curriculum Guide. Sycamore,
       IL: Kishwaukee Publishing Co., 1978.

6268. The Wine and Spirits Wholesalers of America. "Let's Talk About
       Drinking." A Guide for Families. Washington, D.C.:
       The Wine and Spirits Wholesalers of America, 1983.

6269. The Wine and Spirits Wholesalers of America. Proceedings of Family
       Awareness Conference, Washington, D.C., December, 1984.

6270. Winkler, Allan M. Drinking on the American Frontier. Quarterly
       Journal of Studies on Alcohol, 29(2A): 413-445, 1968.

6271. Winkler, Emil Guenther, Weissman, Max and McDermaid, Gladys.
       Alcoholism and Anti-Social Behavior: Statistical Analysis.
       Psychiatric Quarterly, 28(Supplement 2): 242-254, 1954.

6272. Winokur, George. Alcoholism and Depression. Paper presented at the
       International Symposium on the Psychobiology of Alcoholism,
       Beverly Hills, January, 1983. (Also in: Substance and Alcohol
       Actions/Misuse, 4(2-3): 111-119, 1983.)

6273. Winokur, George. Alcoholism and Depression in the Same Family.
       In: Alcoholism and Affective Disorders; Clincial, Genetic,
       and Biochemical Studies. Eds. D.W. Goodwin and C.K. Erickson.
       New York: SP Medical & Scientific Books, 1979, pages 49-56.

6274. Winokur, George. Alcoholism in Adoptees Raised Apart from
        Biological Alcoholic Parents. In: Alcoholism Problems in
        Women and Children. Eds. Milton Greenblatt and Marc A.
        Schuckit, New York: Grune and Stratton, 1976, pages 239-249.

6275. Winokur, George. Depression Spectrum Disease: Description and
        Family Study. Comprehensive Psychiatry, 13(1): 3-8, 1972.

6276. Winokur, George. Diagnostic and Genetic Aspects of Affective
        Illness. Psychiatric Annals, 3(2): 6-15, 1973.

6277. Winokur, George. The Division of Psychiatric Illness into
        Depressive Spectrum Disease and Pure Depressive Illness.
        International Pharmacopsychiatry, 9: 5-13, 1974.

6278. Winokur, George. Duration of Illness Prior to Hospitalization
        Onset in the Affective Disorders. Neuropsychobiology,
        Basel, 2(2-3): 87-93, 1976.

6279. Winokur, George. Family History Studies. VIII. Secondary
        Depression is Alive and Well. Diseases of the Nervous
        System, 32(2): 94-99, 1972.

6280. Winokur, George. Genetic Aspects of Depression. Paper presented
        at the American Association for the Advancement of Science,
        Chicago, December, 1970. (Also in: Separation and Depression,
        Clinical and Research Aspects. Eds. John Paul Scott and
        Edward C. Senay. Washington, D.C.: American Association for
        the Advancement of Science, 1973; pages 125-137.)

6281. Winokur, George. Genetic Markers in Depressive Disorders. Progress
        in Neuro-Psychopharmacology, 3(5-6): 625-630, 1979.

6282. Winokur, George. Types of Depressive Illness. British Journal
        of Psychiatry, London, 120(556): 265-266, 1972.

6283. Winokur, George. Unipolar Depression: Is It Devisible Into
        Autonomous Subtypes? Archives of General Psychiatry, 36:
        47-52, 1979.

6284. Winokur, George. The Validity of Familial Subtypes in Unipolar
        Depression. McLean Hospital Journal, 8(1): 17-37, 1983.

6285. Winokur, George, Behar, David, Vanvalkenburg, Charles and Lowry,
        Michael. Is a Familial Definition of Depression Both
        Feasible and Valid. Journal of Nervous and Mental Disease,
        166(11): 764-768, 1978.

6286. Winokur, George, Cadoret, R., Baker, M. and Dorzab, J. Depression
        Spectrum Disease Versus Pure Depressive Disease: Some Further
        Data. British Journal of Psychiatry, 127: 75-77, 1975.

6287. Winokur, George, Cadoret, R., Dorzab, J. and Baker, M. Depressive
        Disease: A Genetic Study. Archives of General Psychiatry,
        24: 135-144, 1971.

6288. Winokur, George and Clayton, C. Family History Studies. II. Sex
        Differences and Alcoholism in Primary Affective Illness.
        The British Journal of Psychiatry, London, 113: 973-979, 1967.

6289. Winokur, George and Clayton, P.J. Family History Studies.
        IV. Comparison of Male and Female Alcoholics. Quarterly
        Journal of Studies on Alcohol, 29: 885-891, 1968.

6290. Winokur, George, Morrison, James, Clancy, John and Crowe, Raymond.
        The Iowa 500: Familial and Clinical Findings Favor Two Kinds
        of Depressive Illness. Comprehensive Psychiatry, 14(2):
        99-106, 1973.

6291. Winokur, George and Reich, Theodore. Two Genetic Factors in
        Manic-Depressive Disease. Comprehensive Psychiatry,
        11(2): 93-99, 1970.

6292. Winokur, George, Reich, Theodore and Rimmer, John. Alcoholism.
        III. Diagnosis and Familial Psychiatric Illness in 259
        Alcoholic Probands. Archives of General Psychiatry, 23:
        104-111, 1970.

6293. Winokur, George, Rimmer, John and Reich, Theodore. Alcoholism.
        IV. Is There More Than One Type of Alcoholism? British
        Journal of Psychiatry, London, 118: 525-531, 1971.

6294. Winokur, George, Tanna, V., Elston, R. and Go, R. Lack of
        Association of Genetic Traits with Alcoholism; C3, SS and
        ABO Systems. Journal of Studies on Alcohol, 37(9):
        1313-1315, 1976.

6295. Winokur, George and Tsuang, M.T. Expectancy of Alcoholism in
        a Midwestern Population. Journal of Studies on Alcohol,
        39(11): 1964-1967, 1978.

6296. Wintemute, Ginger and Messer, Bonnie (Eds.) Social Work
        Practice with Native American Families: A Handbook.
        1980. (Eric Document Number ED239812.)

6297. Wintrob, R.M. and Diamen, S. The Impact of Culture Change on
        Mistassini Cree Youth. Canadian Psychiatric Association,
        Ottawa, 19(4): 331-342, 1974.

6298. Wise, Frederick. Mental Health and Support Systems Among Urban
        Native Americans. Dissertation Abstracts International,
        42(8): 3450B, 1981.

6299. Wiseman, Jacqueline P. Alcohol, Eroticism and Sexual Performance:
        A Social Interactionist Perspective. Journal of Drug Issues,
        15(2): 291-308, 1985.

6300. Wiseman, Jacqueline P. An Alternative Role for the Wife of an
        Alcoholic in Finland. Journal of Marriage and the Family,
        37(1): 172-179, 1975. (Also in: Toxicomanies, Quebec,
        8: 179-194, 1975.)

6301. Wiseman, Jacqueline P. The "Home Treatment": The First Step
        in Trying to Cope with an Alcoholic Husband. Family
        Relations, 29(4): 541-549, 1980.

6302. Wiseman, Jacqueline P. Spouses of Alcoholics. Paper presented
        to the National Institute on Drug Abuse, Program for Womens
        Concerns, Miami Beach, October, 1975. (Also in: Drugs,
        Alcohol and Women; a National Forum Source Book. Ed.
        M. Nellis. Washington, D.C.: National Research and
        Communications Associates, 1976.)

6303. Wiseman, Jacqueline P. Sober Comportment; Patterns and
        Perspectives on Alcohol Addiction. Journal of Studies on
        Alcohol, 42: 106-126, 1981.

6304. Wiseman, Jacqueline P. Sober Time: The Neglected Variable in
        the Recidivism of Alcoholic Persons. In: Psychological
        and Social Factors in Drinking and Treatment Evaluation.
        Ed. M.E. Chafetz. Proceedings of the Second Annual
        Conference of the National Institute on Alcohol Abuse and
        Alcoholism. Washington, D.C.: U.S. Government Printing
        Office, 1973, pages 165-184.

6305. Wiseman, Jacqueline P. Social Forces and the Politics of Research
       Approaches-Studying the Wives of Alcoholics. Paper presented
       at the University of California, San Francisco, August, 1975.
       (Also in: Women and Their Health: Research Implications for
       a New Era. Ed. V. Olesen. Washington, D.C.: Public Health
       Service, Health Resources Association, 1977.)

6306. Wiseman, Jacqueline P. Alkoholistien Vaimot I. Alkoholismin
       Maaritteleminien Ja Kasittelystrategiat Perhepiirissa.
       (The Wives of Alcoholics. Part I. Diagnosis of
       Alcoholism and Treatment Strategy Involving the Family.)
       Alkoholipolitiikka, 41: 62-72, 1976.

6307. Wiseman, Jacqueline P. Alkoholistien Vaimot II. Elaminen
       Alkoholistin Kanssa. (Wives of Alcoholics. Part II.
       Living with an Alcoholic.) Alkoholipolitiikka, 41:
       109-117, 1976.

6308. Wisner, Jean Shorb. Adult Women Physically Abused as Children.
       Dissertation Abstracts International, 44(2): 620B, 1982.

6309. Wisniewski, Nadine M., Glenwick, David S. and Graham, John R.
       MacAndrew Scale and Sociodemographic Correlates of Adolescent
       Alcohol and Drug Use. Addictive Behaviors, 10(1): 55-67,
       1985.

6310. Wittman, Mary Phyllis. Developmental Characteristics and
       Personalities of Chronic Alcoholics. Journal of Abnormal
       and Social Psychology, 34: 361-377, 1939. (Also in:
       Elgin State Hospital Papers, 3: 77-84, 1939.)

6311. Wives of Alcohlics: The "Forgotten Patients." Journal of
       Psychosocial Nursing and Mental Health Services, 20(10):
       35-38, 1982.

6312. Woerner, Philip I. and Guze, Samuel B. A Family and Marital Study
       of Hysteria. British Journal of Psychiatry: The Journal of
       Mental Science, London, 114(507): 161-168, 1968.

6313. Woititz, Janet G. Adult Children of Alcoholics. Hollywood, FL:
       Health Communications, 1983. (Also in: Alcoholism Treatment
       Quarterly, 1(1): 71-99, 1984.)

6314. Woititz, Janet G. Adult Children of Alcoholics: A Treatment
       Issue. Focus on Alcohol and Drug Issues, 6(4): 10-11, 1981.

6315. Woititz, Janet G. Alcoholism and the Family: A Survey of
       the Literature. Journal of Alcohol and Drug Education,
       23: 18-23, 1978.

6316. Woititz, Janet G. The Educational Aspects of Servicing the Children
       of Alcoholics. Paper presented at the NIAAA Symposium, Silver
       Springs, MD, September, 1979. (Also in: Services to Children
       of Alcoholics. U.S. Department of Health and Human Services.
       National Institute on Alcohol Abuse and Alcoholism. Washington,
       D.C.: U.S. Government Printing Office, 1979, pages 186-191.)

6317. Woititz, Janet G. For Better or Worse, Richer or Poorer:
       The Insidious Invader of Intimacy. Focus on Alcohol and
       Drug Issues, 6(2): 16-17, 25, 1983.

6318. Woititz, Janet G. Marriage on the Rocks: Learning to Live with
       Yourself and an Alcoholic. New York: Delacorte Press, 1979.

6319. Woititz, Janet G. (Ed.) Struggle for Intimacy. Pompano Beach,
       FL: Health Communications Inc., 1985.

6320. Woititz, Janet G. A Study of Self-Esteem in Children of Alcoholics.
       Doctoral Dissertation. (University Microfilms No. 77-13299.)
       Rutgers University, The State University of New Jersey, 1976.
       (Also in: Dissertation Abstracts International, 37: 7554A,
       1977.)

6321. Wolf, Evelyne Roberts. Evaluation of the Lawyers and Judges
       Assistance Program: A Diagnostic, Referral and Outreach
       Program of the Michigan State Bar Association. Dissertation
       Abstracts International, 43(3): 860B, 1982.

6322. Wolf, Jean Karen. A Study of Two Models for the Prediction
       of Outcome in Family Treatment for Chemical Dependency.
       Dissertation Abstracts International, 43(8): 2721B, 1982.

6323. Wolfe, Janet L. A Cognitive/Behavioral Approach to Working with
       Women Alcoholics. In: Women Who Drink: Alcoholic Experience
       and Psychotherapy. Ed. Vasanti Burtle. Springfield, IL:
       Charles C. Thomas, 1979, pages 197-216.

6324. Wolfe, Mary and Taylor, Roy. Aftercare Recovery Plan and Program.
       Maryland State Medical Journal, 27(6): 62-66, 1978.

6325. Wolfgang, Marvin. Violence in the Family. In: Violence.
       Eds. I.L. Kutash, S.B. Kutash and L.B. Schlesinger.
       San Francisco: Jossey Bass, 1978, pages 238-253.

6326. Wolin, Steven J. Family Rituals and the Recurrence of Alcoholism
       Over Generations. American Journal of Psychiatry, 136(4):
       589-593B, 1979.

6327. Wolin, Steven J. Some Characteristics of Families with Alcohol
       Abuse. Advances in Alcoholism, 2(14): 1-3, 1982.

6328. Wolin, Steven J. and Bennett, Linda A. Heritage Continuity Among
       the Children of Alcoholics. In: Etiologic Aspects of Alcohol
       and Drug Abuse. Eds. Edward Gottheil, Keith A. Druley,
       Thomas E. Skoloda and Howard W. Waxman. Springfield, IL:
       Charles C. Thomas, 1983, 271-284.

6329. Wolin, Steven J., Bennett, Linda A. and Noonan, Denise L.
       Alcoholism Continuity and Family Interaction. Alcoholism:
       Clinical and Experimental Research, 2(2): 214, 1978.

6330. Wolin, Steven J., Bennett, Linda A. and Noonan, Denise L. Family
       Rituals and the Recurrence of Alcoholism Over Generations.
       American Journal of Psychiatry, 136: 589-593, 1979.

6331. Wolin, Steven J., Bennett, Linda A., Noonan, Denise L. and
       Teitelbaum, Martha A. Disrupted Family Rituals; A Factor
       in the Intergenerational Transmission of Alcoholism.
       Journal of Studies on Alcohol, 41: 199-214, 1980.

6332. Wolin, Steven J., Bennett, Linda A., Noonan, Denise L. and
       Teitebaum, Martha A. Family Rituals and the Transmission
       of Alcoholism. Digest of Alcoholism Theory and
       Application, 1(1): 7-17, 1981.

6333. Wolin, Steven J., Steinglass, Peter, Sendroff, Paula, Davis, D.
       and Berenson, D. Marital Interaction During Experimental
       Intoxication and the Relationship to Family History.
       In: Alcohol Intoxication and Withdrawal; Experimental
       Studies II, Vol. 59. Ed. M. Gross. New York: Plenum
       Press, 1975, pages 645-654.

6334. Wolniewicz-Grzelak, B. Relationship Between Childhood Experiences
       and Neurosis in Adulthood. Psychiatria Polska, 11:
       65-72, 1977.

6335. Wolowitz, Howard M. and Barker, Michael J. Alcoholism and Oral
       Passivity. Quarterly Journal of Studies on Alcohol,
       29(3A): 592-597, 1968.

6336. Wolper, B. and Scheiner, Z. Family Therapy Approaches and Drug
       Dependent Women. In: Treatment Services for Drug Dependent
       Women. Ed. G.M. Beschner. Washington, D.C.: U.S. Government
       Printing Office, 1981, pages 343-407.

6337. Women Alcoholics in New Jersey. Alcohol Technical Reports, 5:
       64-69, 1976.

6338. Women in Crisis Conference Told: Much Like Alcoholism, Heroin
       Abuse a Family Problem. U.S. Journal of Drug and Alcohol
       Dependence, 5(7): 11, 1981.

6339. Women's Treatment Program Adds Component for Children. NIAAA
       Information and Feature Service, (IFS No. 78): 3,
       December 1, 1980.

6340. Wood, A.J. 1. The World of Drug Dependence. Pharmaceutical
       Journal, London, 200(5452): 473-478, 1968.

6341. Wood, Abigail. My Parents Drink Too Much. Seventeen, 30(4):
       168-170, 1971.

6342. Wood, B.L. Children of Alcoholics: Patterns of Dysfunction
       in Adult Life. Paper presented at the American Psychological
       Association Convention, Toronto, 1984.

6343. Wood, B.L. COA Therapist: When the Family Hero Turns Pro.
       Paper presented at the American Psychological Association
       Convention, Toronto, 1984.

6344. Wood, Howard P. and Duffy, Edward L. Psychological Factors in
       Alcoholic Women. American Journal of Psychiatry, 123(3):
       341-345, 1966.

6345. Woodruff, Robert A. Jr., Guze, Samuel B. and Clayton, Paula J.
       Alcoholics Who See a Psychiatrist Compared with Those Who
       Do Not. Quarterly Journal of Studies on Alcohol, 34(4):
       1162-1171, 1973.

6346. Woodruff, Robert A. Jr., Guze, Samuel B. and Clayton, Paula J.
       Anxiety Neurosis Among Psychiatric Outpatients. Comprehensive
       Psychiatry, 13(2): 165-170, 1972.

6347. Woodruff, Robert A. Jr., Guze, Samuel B. and Clayton, Paula J.
       Divorce Among Psychiatric Out-Patients. British Journal
       of Psychiatry, 121(562): 289-292, 1972.

6348. Woodruff, Robert A. Jr., Clayton, Paula J. and Guze, Samuel B.
       Suicide Attempts and Psychiatric Diagnosis. Diseases of the
       Nervous System, 33: 617-621, 1972.

6349. Woodruff, Robert A. Jr., Guze, Samuel B., Clayton, Paula J. and
       Carr, Dianne. Alcoholism and Depression. Archives of
       General Psychiatry, 28(1): 97-100, 1973.

6350. Woods, A. Family Life and Alcoholism. Proceedings of the
       National Conference on Social Work, 44: 491-494, 1917.

6351. Woods, M. Intoxication in the Parent Producing Epilepsy in the
       Child. Journal of Inebriety, 32: 85-90, 1910.

6352. Woodside, M. Women Drinkers Admitted to Holloway Prison During
       February 1960: A Pilot Survey. British Journal of
       Criminology, 1: 221-235, 1961.

6353. Woodside, Migs. Children of Alcoholic Parents: Inherited and
        Psycho-Social Influences. Journal of Psychiatric Treatment
        and Evaluation, 5: 531-537, 1983.

6354. Woodside, Migs. Children of Alcoholics. Albany: New York
        State Division of Alcoholism and Alcohol Abuse, 1982.

6355. Woodward, B.S. Assessment of a Prevention Program for Children
        of Alcoholics. Dissertation Abstracts International,
        45(7): 2324B, 1985.

6356. Woodward, Nancy Hyden. If Your Child is Drinking. What You Can
        Do to Fight Alcohol Abuse at Home, at School, and in the
        Community. New York: Academic Press, Inc., 1981.

6357. Woon, T.H. and George, Shirley. A Battered Wife. Medical
        Journal of Malaysia, 34(3): 281-284, 1980.

6358. Worden, M. Family as Patient: Implications of a Paradigm Shift.
        Focus on Family, 8(5): 6-7, 46, 1985.

6359. Worden, M. Happily Ever After: Family Treatment of Chemical
        Dependency. Focus on Family and Chemical Dependency,
        8(4): 6-7, 38-39, 1985.

6360. Worden, M. Outpatient Alternative. Alcoholism: The National
        Magazine, 2(6): 59-60, 1982.

6361. Worden, M. Stigma Alive and Well for Women Alcoholics.
        The U.S. Journal of Drug and Alcohol Dependence, 9(2):
        22, 1985.

6362. Worker with Alcoholic Kin Needs Help. NIAAA Information and
        Feature Service, (IFS No. 49): 2, July 11, 1978.

6363. Working with Abusive/Neglectful Indian Parents. Revised.
        Washington, D.C.: National Center on Child Abuse and
        Neglect (DHEW/OHD), 1980. (Eric Document Number ED229191.)

6364. Works, David A. Statement on 18 Year Old Drinking. Journal of
        Alcohol Education, 18(3): 14-15, 1973.

6365. Works, David A. Alcoholism: Spiritual Illness. Paper presented
        at National Alcoholism Forum, Washington, D.C., April, 1979.

6366. Worrell, D. Frank. The Child, School, Alcohol, and Abuse.
        School Guidance Worker, 32(2): 43-47, 1976.

6367. Wright, Barbara S. A Comparative Study of the Psychosocial
        Network of the Acute and Recovered Alcoholic. Doctoral
        Dissertation. (University Microfilms No 76-20977.)
        San Diego: United States International University, 1976.

6368. Wright, David. 1981-82 Iowa Study of Alcohol and Drug Attitudes
        and Behaviors Among Youth. Report 1: Normative and Trend
        Data. February, 1982. (Eric Document Number ED229672.)

6369. Wright, J. and Popham, J. Alcohol and Battering: The Double
        Bind. Aegis, 36: 53-59, 1982.

6370. Wright, Janet M. Fetal Alcohol Syndrome: The Social Work
        Connection. Health and Social Work, 6(1): 5-10, 1981.

6371. Wright, K.D. and Scott, T.B. The Relationship of Wives'
        Treatment to the Drinking Status of Alcoholics. Journal
        of Studies on Alcohol, 39(9): 1577-1581, 1978.

6372.   Wright, Katherine Dodd. Current Drinking Status of Alcoholic
         Men and the Treatment Received by Their Non-Alcoholic Wives.
         Doctoral Dissertation. (University Microfilms No. 76-18156.)
         Grand Forks: University of North Dakota, 1975.

6373.   Wright, Lloyd S. Correlates of Reported Drinking Problems Among
         Male and Female College Students. Journal of Alcohol and
         Drug Education, 28(3): 47-57, 1983.

6374.   Wright, Lloyd S. Parental Permission to Date and Its Relationship
         to Drug Use and Suicidal Thoughts Among Adolescents.
         Adolescence, 17(66): 409-418, 1982.

6375.   Wright, Lloyd S. and Moore, R. Correlates of Reported Drug Abuse
         Problems Among College Undergraduates. Journal of Drug
         Education, 12(1): 65-73, 1982.

6376.   Wuthrich, P. Social Problems of Alcoholics. Journal of Studies
         on Alcohol, 38(5): 881-890, 1977.

6377.   Wye, P. Once an Alcoholic, Always an Alcoholic. British Medical
         Journal, London, 2(6205): 1665-1666, 1979.

6378.   Wynder, Ernst L., Hertzberg, Sidney and Parker, Ellen (Eds.)
         The Book of Health. New York: Franklin Watts, 1981.

Y

6379. Yakichuk, Albert J. A Study of the Self-Concept Evaluations of Alcoholics and Non-Alcoholics. Journal of Drug Education, 8(1): 41-49, 1978.

6380. Yamamoto, J. Optimal Treatment for Patients of All Races and Social Classes in a Los Angeles Clinic. International Psychiatry Clinics, 8(2): 143-166, 1971.

6381. Yamane, H., Katoh, N. and Fujita, T. Characteristics of Three Groups of Men Alcoholics Differentiated by Age at First Admission for Alcoholism Treatment in Japan. Journal of Studies on Alcohol, 41: 100-104, 1980.

6382. Yamazaki, S., Tsuwaga, K. and Odagiri, Y. Prognosis of Alcohol-Dependent Patients and Their Families. Kango Gijutsu, Tokyo, 26(16): 2145-2150, 1980.

6383. Yang, Chung S., Miao, Jian, Yang, Wenkian, Huang, Mei, Wang, Tianyuan, Xue, Hongji, You, Shuhong, Lu, Jianbang, Wu, Jinming. Diet and Vitamin Nutrition of the High Esophageal Cancer Risk Population in Linxian, China. In: Nutrition and Cancer. Volume 4. Philadelphia: Franklin Institute Press, 1982, pages 154-164.

6384. Yang, Martin M.C. Child Training and Child Behavior in Varying Family Patterns in a Changing Chinese Society. Kuo Li Tai-wan Ta Hsueh She Hui Hsueh K'an, 3: 77-83, 1967.

6385. Yates, Richard. Disturbing the Peace. New York: Delacorte Press, 1975.

6386. Yavkin, V.M. Anomalies in Children of Alcoholic Parents. Alcoholism, Zagreb, 10: 13-23, 1974.

6387. Yavkin, V.M. Anomalies of Development in Children of Chronic Alcoholics. Alcoholism: Journal on Alcoholism and Related Addictions, 10(1-2): 13-23, 1974.

6388. Yavkin, V.M. Effects of Parental Alcoholism on the Clinical Manifestations of Mental Retardation in Children. Alcoholism, Zagreb, 14: 97-106, 1978.

6389. Yearwood, Alma C. Smithers Alcoholism Center. American Journal of Nursing, 76(11): 1775, 1976.

6390. Yesavage, J.A. and Widrow, L. Early Parental Discipline and Adult Self-Destructive Acts. Journal of Nervous and Mental Disease, 173(2): 74-77, 1985.

6391.   Yesavage, Jerome A., Benezech, Michel, Ceccaldi, Phillipe,
            Bourgeois, Marc and Addad, Moise. Arson in Mentally Ill
            and Criminal Populations. Journal of Clinical Psychiatry,
            44(4): 128-130, 1983.

6392.   Yoham, Joseph Robert. Verbal Abilities in Alcoholics. Dissertation
            Abstracts International, 43(10): 3403B, 1982.

6393.   Young Alcoholics. The Medical Journal of Australia, Sydney,
            1(24): 1251, 1969.

6394.   Young, H.T.P. Parental Alcoholism as a Factor in Adolescent
            Crime. British Journal of Inebriety, 35: 93-113, 1938.

6395.   Young, Martha Drake. Needs Assessment for Services and Programs
            for Children and Families in a Rural County. Dissertation
            Abstracts International, 41(11): 4249B, 1980.

6396.   Young, Rebecca. Washington Post Health, 13 March 1985, p. 7.
            (When Mom and Dad Drink: Grown Children of Alcoholics Meet
            to Discuss the Scars that Remain.)

6397.   Youth and Drugs. Report of a WHO Study Group. World Health
            Organization Technical Report Series, Geneva, 516: 1-45, 1973.

6398.   Youth Hostel Stresses Family Involvement. NIAAA Information and
            Feature Service, (IFS No. 12): 2, May 20, 1975.

6399.   Youth Screened for Parental Alcoholism. NIAAA Information and
            Feature Service, (IFS No. 67): 6, December 31, 1979.

6400.   Yvonneau, M. and Vigneaux, H. Alcoolisme et Amines Biogenes.
            (Alcoholism and Biogenic Amines.) Revue de l'Alcoolisme,
            Paris, 19: 195-212, 1973.

Z

6401. Zaccaria, Joseph S. and Weir, William R.   A Comparison of Alcoholics
and Selected Samples of Nonalcoholics in Terms of a Positive
Concept of Mental Health.   Journal of Social Psychology,
71(1): 151-157, 1967.

6402. Zacker, Joseph and Bard, Morton.   Further Findings on Assaultiveness
and Alcohol Use in Interpersonal Disputes.   American Journal of
Community Psychology, 5(4): 373-383, 1977.

6403. Zahourek, R., Scheffler, C., Chetrick, C. and Hamm, F.B.   Letters
to the Editor: Marriage After Drink?   Journal of Psychosocial
Nursing, 23(8): 5, 37, 1985.

6404. Zakrzewski, P.   Mlodociani Alkoholicy.   (Adolescent Alcoholics.)
Problemy Alkoholizmu, Warsaw, 26(2): 9-10, 16, 1979.

6405. Zakrzewski, P.   Zawarcie Malzenstwa Przez Mlodych Alkoholikow.
(The End of Marriages of Young Alcoholics.)   Problemy
Alkoholizmu, Warsaw, 22(10): 4-7, 1974.

6406. Zamami, M.   Study on Alcoholism and Family Dynamics: On the Focus
of Father-Son Relationship.   Japanese Journal of Alcohol Studies
and Drug Dependence, Kyoto, 18(1): 74-84, 1983.

6407. Zamami, M. and Hayaski, N.   Paternal Loss and Birth Order of Alcoholics:
From the Investigation of Alcoholics and Schizophrenics.   Japanese
Journal of Alcohol Studies and Drug Dependence, Kyoto, 18(3):
316-324, 1983.

6408. Zeiner, Arthur R., Paredes, Alfonso, Musicant, Robert A. and Cowden,
Lawrence.   Racial Differences in Psychophysiological Responses to
Ethanol and Placebo.   In: Currents in Alcoholism, Volume 1.
Ed. Frank A. Seixas. New York: Grune and Stratton, 1977, page
271-286.

6409. Zenevich, G.V.   O Nozologicheskoi Samostoyatel'nosti Khronicheskogo
Alkogolizma.   (On the Nosological Independence of Chronic
Alcoholism.)   Zhurnal Neuropatologii I Psikhiatrii Imeni S.S.
Korsakova, 67: 239-246, 1967.

6410. Zerbin, Rudin Edith.   Genetische Aspekte Des Suchtproblems.   (Genetic
Aspects of Addiction Problems.)   Suchtgefahren, 23: 1-9, 1977.

6411. Ziegler-Driscoll, Genevra.   Family Research Study at Eagleville
Hospital and Rehabilitation Center.   Family Process, 16:
175-189, 1977.

6412. Ziegler-Driscoll, Genevra. Family Treatment with Parent Addict
       Families. In: Drugs and the Family. Ed. Thomas J. Glynn.
       Washington, D.C.: U.S. Government Printing Office, 1981,
       pages 281-282. (Also in: A Multicultural View of Drug Abuse:
       Proceedings of the National Drug Abuse Conference, 1977.
       Eds. D.E. Smith, S.M. Anderson, M. Buxton, N. Gottlieb, W. Harvey
       and T. Chung. Cambridge, MA: Schenkman, 1978, pages 389-396.)

6413. Ziegler-Driscoll, Genevra. The Similarities in Families of Drug
       Dependents and Alcoholics. In: Drugs and the Family.
       Eds. Thomas J. Glynn. Washington, D.C.: U.S. Government
       Printing Office, 1981, pages 278-280. (Also in: Family
       Therapy of Drug and Alcohol Abuse. Eds. E. Kaufman and
       P.N. Kaufman. New York: Gardner Press, 1979, pages 19-39.)

6414. Zimberg, Sheldon. Alcoholics Anonymous and Al-Anon. In: The
       Clinical Management of Alcoholism. New York: Brunner/
       Mazel, 1982, pages 117-124.

6415. Zimberg, Sheldon. Clinical Evaluation of Alcoholism Treatment.
       In: The Clinical Management of Alcoholism. New York:
       Brunner/Mazel, 1982, pages 177-201.

6416. Zimberg, Sheldon. Evaluation of Alcoholism Treatment in Harlem.
       Quarterly Journal of Studies on Alcohol, 35: 550-557, 1974.

6417. Zimberg, Sheldon. Family Therapy. In: The Clinical Management
       of Alcoholism. New York: Brunner/Mazel, 1982, pages 88-95.

6418. Zimberg, Sheldon. Individual Therapy. In: The Clinical Management
       of Alcoholism. New York: Brunner/Mazel, 1982, pages 70-80.

6419. Zimberg, Sheldon. Interviewing the Alcoholic. In: The Clinical
       Management of Alcoholism. New York: Brunner/Mazel, 1982,
       pages 45-49.

6420. Zimberg, Sheldon. Interviewing the Significant Other. In: The
       Clinical Management of Alcoholism. New York: Brunner/
       Mazel, 1982, pages 50-54.

6421. Zimberg, Sheldon. Is Abstinence the Only Way? In: The Clinical
       Management of Alcoholism. New York: Brunner/Mazel, 1982,
       pages 145-156.

6422. Zimberg, Sheldon. New York State Task Force on Alcohol Problems:
       Position Paper on Treatment. New York State Journal of
       Medicine, 75(10): 1794-1798, 1975.

6423. Zimberg, Sheldon. Office Psychotherapy of Alcoholism. In: Alcoholism
       and Clinical Psychiatry. Ed. Joel Solomon. New York: Plenum
       Medical Book Company, 1982, pages 213-229.

6424. Zimberg, Sheldon. Psychotherapy in the Treatment of Alcoholism.
       In: Encyclopedic Handbook of Alcoholism. Eds. E. Pattison
       and E. Kaufman. New York: Gardner Press, 1982, pages 999-1010.

6425. Zimberg, Sheldon. Psychotherapy with Alcoholics. In: Specialized
       Techniques in Individual Psychotherapy. New York: Brunner/
       Mazel, 1980, pages 382-399.

6426. Zimberg, Sheldon. Role of Psychiatry in Alcoholism. In: The
       Clinical Management of Alcoholism. New York: Brunner/Mazel,
       1982, pages 19-29.

6427. Zimberg, Sheldon. Special Approaches for Subpopulations of Alcoholics.
       In: The Clinical Management of Alcoholism. New York: Brunner/
       Mazel, 1982, pages 157-176.

6428. Zimberg, Sheldon. Understanding Alcoholism as a Disease. In: The
        Clinical Management of Alcoholism. New York: Brunner/Mazel,
        1982, pages 3-18.

6429. Zimmerman, M. Diagnosing the Alcoholic in the Doctor's Office.
        Alcoholism Treatment Digest, 14(1): 4-6, 1969.

6430. Zimmermann, M. Pastoral Counseling of Alcoholics. Alcoholism
        Treatment Digest, 14(1): 11-13, 1969.

6431. Zinberg, Norman E. Alcohol Addiction: Toward a More Comprehensive
        Definition. In: Dynamic Approaches to the Understanding and
        Treatment of Alcoholism. Eds. Margaret H. Bean and Norman E.
        Zinberg. New York: The Free Press, 1981, pages 97-127.

6432. Zinberg, Norman E. and Bean, Margaret H. (Eds.) Introduction:
        Alcohol Use, Alcoholism, and the Problems of Treatment.
        In: Dynamic Approaches to the Understanding and Treatment of
        Alcoholism. New York, NY: The Free Press, 1981, pages 1-35.

6433. Zourbas, J. Alcoholism in Young People. La Semaine Des Hopitaux
        de Paris, 58(14): 881-885, 1982.

6434. Zourbas, J. and Couturier, C. Alcoholism and Youth. Revue du
        Praticien, 30(37): 2449-2452, 1980.

6435. Zourbas, J., Senecal, J. and Touffet, R. Alcoholization of
        Adolescents and Information at School. Toxicomanies,
        Quebec, 12(3-4): 331-347, 1979.

6436. Zucker, Martine and Snoddy, James E. Needs, Attitudes and Behaviors
        of Teachers Relative to Stress Situations of Children. Journal
        of Alcohol and Drug Education, 28(1): 32-42, 1982.

6437. Zucker, Robert A. Developmental Aspects of Drinking Through the
        Young Adult Years. In: Youth, Alcohol and Social Policy.
        Eds. H.T. Blane and M.E. Chafetz. New York: Plenum Press, 1979.

6438. Zucker, Robert A. Heavy Drinking and Affiliative Motivation Among
        Adolescents. Paper presented at the 1970 Southwestern
        Psychological Association Meetings, St. Louis, April, 1970.

6439. Zucker, Robert A. Parental Influences Upon the Drinking Patterns
        of Their Children. In: Alcoholism Problems in Women and
        Children. Eds. Milton Greenblatt and Marc A. Schuckit.
        New York: Grune & Stratton, 1976, pages 211-238.

6440. Zucker, Robert A. and Barron, Frank H. Do Wives Drive Husbands
        To Drink? Paper presented at the Meeting of Southwestern
        Psychological Association, San Antonio, April, 1971.

6441. Zucker, Robert A. and Barron, Frank H. Parental Behaviors
        Associated with Problem Drinking and Antisocial Behavior
        Among Adolescent Males. In: Research on Alcoholism:
        Clinical Problems and Special Populations, Proceedings of
        the First Annual Alcoholism Conference of the National
        Institute on Alcohol Abuse and Alcoholism, June 25-26, 1971.
        Ed. Morris E. Chafetz. Washington, D.C.: U.S. Government
        Printing Office, 1973, pages 276-296.

6442. Zucker, Robert A. and Devoe, C.I. Life History Characteristics
        Associated with Problem Drinking and Antisocial Behavior
        in Adolescent Girls: A Comparison with Male Findings.
        In: Life History Research in Psychopathology. 4.
        Eds. R.D. Wirt, G. Winokur and M. Roff. Minneapolis:
        The University of Minnesota Press, 1975, pages 109-134.

6443.   Zucker, Robert A. and Van Horn, H. Sibling Social Structure and
        Oral Behavior: Drinking and Smoking in Adolescence. Quarterly
        Journal of Studies on Alcohol, 33: 193-197, 1972.

6444.   Zuckerman, Marvin. Sensation Seeking: The Initial Motive for Drug
        Abuse. In: Etiologic Aspects of Alcohol and Drug Abuse. Eds.
        Edward Gottheil, Keith A. Druley, Thomas E. Skoloda and Howard W.
        Waxman. Springfield, IL: Charles C. Thomas, 1983, pages 202-220.

6445.   Zuk, Gerald H. Critical Incidents in the Context of Family Therapy.
        Critical Incident No. 2. International Psychiatry Clinics,
        London, 7(4): 273-289, 1970.

6446.   Zuska, Joseph J. and Pursch, Joseph A. Long-Term Management. In:
        Alcoholism: A Practical Treatment Guide. Eds. Stanley E. Gitlow
        and Herbert S. Peyser. New York: Grune and Stratton, 1980, pages
        131-163.

6447.   Zvidrins, P.P. A Hazassagfelbomlasok Okainak Tanulmanyozasa A Lett
        Szovjet Szocialista Koztarsasagban. (Study of the Dissolution of
        Marriages in the Latvian Soviet Socialist Republic.) Demografia,
        Budapest, 14(4): 332-342, 1971.

6448.   Zweben, Allen. Problem Drinking and Marital Adjustment. Journal of
        Studies on Alcohol, 47: 167-172, 1986.

6449.   Zweben, Allen and Pearlman, Shelly. Evaluating the Effectiveness of
        Conjoint Treatment of Alcohol-Complicated Marriages: Clinical
        and Methodological Issues. Journal of Marital and Family
        Therapy, 9(1): 61-72, 1983.

6450.   Zweben, Allen, Pearlman, Shelly and Li, Selina. Reducing Attrition
        from Conjoint Therapy with Alcoholic Couples. Drug and Alcohol
        Dependence, Lausanne, 11(3/4): 321-331, 1983.

6451.   Zylman, Richard. Accidents, Alcohol and Single-Cause Explanations.
        Lessons from the Grand Rapids Study. Quarterly Journal of
        Studies on Alcohol, Supplement, 4: 212-233, 1968.

6452.   Zylman, Richard. Drinking Practices Among Youth Are Changing
        Regardless of Legal Drinking Age. Journal of Traffic Safety
        Education, 24(1): 31-32, 37, 1976.

Index

(continued on next page)

Alabama   4536

Al-Anon   10, 12, 22-23, 27, 61, 63-64, 83-93, 95, 97-99, 102, 104, 107-111,
     113, 115-118, 122, 139, 147, 168, 200, 211, 245, 307, 309, 345-346, 353,
     533, 535, 592, 615, 814, 857, 956, 962, 1002, 1007, 1192, 1213, 1251,
     1276, 1338, 1498, 1526, 1748, 1926-1927, 1961, 2066, 2267-2268, 2344-2345,
     2444, 2765, 3071, 3079, 3089, 3349, 3384-3386, 3437, 3482, 3500, 3637,
     3663, 3758, 3827, 3872, 3896, 3950, 4156-4157, 4300, 4375, 4625, 4660,
     4703-4704, 4732, 4933, 5023-5024, 5031, 5205, 5473, 5492, 5580, 5635,
     5685, 5739, 5809, 5828, 5893, 5898, 6000, 6025, 6027, 6056, 6090, 6159,
     6267, 6371, 6373, 6414

     See also Alateen
             Alcoholics Anonymous

Alaska - Alaskan Natives   295, 1858, 2473, 5833

Alateen   12, 27, 61, 86, 94-96, 100-101, 103, 105-106, 110, 114, 118, 121, 139,
     211, 307, 309, 345-346, 592, 962, 1213, 1276, 1498, 1926-1927, 1961, 2066,
     2692, 2750, 3827, 3896, 4136, 4382, 4482, 4525, 4660, 5205, 5405, 5580,
     5685, 5739, 5882, 6025, 6056, 6090, 6130, 6159, 6267, 6414

     See also Al-Anon
             Alcoholics Anonymous

Alcoholics Anonymous   75, 83, 139, 149, 169, 180, 211, 369, 533, 535, 592, 770,
     857, 861, 925, 956, 1192, 1201, 1213, 1337-1338, 1508, 1748, 1926-1927,
     1961, 2066, 2124, 2504, 2811, 2847, 3437, 3757-3758, 4156-4157, 4300,
     4599, 4625, 4666, 5156, 5205, 5649, 5685, 5893, 6088, 6090, 6159, 6322

     See also Al-Anon
             Alateen

Alienation   7, 244, 422, 1208, 3249, 3397, 6043, 6085

     See also Deviant Behavior

American Indians   124, 295, 464, 1788-1790, 1859, 1987, 2362, 2413-2414, 2421,
     2489, 2655, 2657, 2792-2793, 2939-2940, 2967, 3020, 3293, 3390, 3508,
     3860, 3957, 4131, 4154, 4235, 4773, 5079, 5262, 5277, 5279-5280, 5605,
     6019, 6044, 6053, 6099, 6118, 6144, 6147, 6152-6153, 6296-6298, 6363

Anorexia Nervosa

     See Eating Disorders

Antabuse   3057, 3409, 3777

Anthropological Factors   25, 28-29, 206, 2413, 4073

Anti-Social Behavior

     See Delinquent Youth
             Deviant Behavior

Anxiety

     See Stress

Arizona   1380, 4782

Arkansas   1889

Armenians   1998-1999

Art Therapy   3357

Artists   4887

Behavioral Therapy (continued)

    general   3607, 3917-3920, 3926, 4109, 4265, 4267-4270, 4272, 4776, 4964, 6194

    reviews 4262, 4266

Bereavement 38, 435, 495, 503, 511, 590, 650, 761, 796, 1078, 1148-1149, 1399, 1850, 2012, 4147, 4929

    See also Death
           Suicide

Biological Markers 72, 79, 311, 486, 525, 1502, 1622, 2528-2529, 2664, 3776, 4204, 4424, 4527, 4848, 4997, 5105, 5109, 5111, 5246, 5686, 5820, 5952, 6281, 6283

Birth Order 337, 359, 420-421, 423-424, 630-631, 1166-1167, 1247, 1377-1378, 2317, 2351, 2500, 2881, 2911, 3235, 3254-3255, 3408, 3465, 3477, 3597, 3684, 3748, 3750-3751, 4012, 4024, 4133-4134, 4228, 4354, 4379, 4445, 4483, 5054, 5075, 5132, 5351, 5369-5370, 5377, 5651, 5867, 6407

Blacks 49, 261, 512-513, 735-736, 784-787, 825, 1243, 1310, 1355, 1861, 2398, 2451-2452, 2456, 2544, 2597, 2804, 2832, 3067, 3136, 3138, 3163, 3214, 3377, 3444, 3474, 3633, 3673, 3909, 4453, 4710, 4749, 4847, 4865, 5399, 5538, 5596, 5748, 5787, 5941, 5967, 5984, 6044, 6076, 6079, 6109, 6132, 6416

Blood Alcohol Level 3471, 3473, 4588, 5116, 5121, 5871, 6086

Blood Groups 2613, 5640-5641, 6294

Blood Pressure

    See Hypertension

Brain Functions 480, 483, 525, 2067, 2588, 3470, 3678, 4588-4589, 4627, 4649, 5080, 5600, 5729, 5735, 5991, 6034

    See also Evoked Potentials
           Neuropsychological Aspects

Brazil - Brazilians 1301, 3777

Breast-Feeding 880

Burnout 522, 1995

California 488, 1223, 1298, 1351, 1467, 1644, 1758, 3393-3394, 3614, 4049, 4539, 5135, 5758, 6380

Canada 672, 881, 911, 963, 975, 1191, 1652, 3062, 3317, 3851, 4062, 4141, 4143, 4212, 4840, 5375-5376, 5755, 5770, 6168

Cancer 2832, 3015, 3104, 3114, 3338, 3698, 3764, 6383

Cardiovascular System 1991, 2422, 2962, 3579, 3828, 3875, 4351

Case Histories 83, 96, 151, 165, 258, 188, 342, 524, 781-782, 1199, 1281, 1896, 2042, 2287, 2289, 2924, 3044, 3263, 3267, 3284, 3569, 3715, 4088, 4405, 4550, 5361, 5512, 5558, 5629

Case Studies 30, 207-208, 362, 430, 518, 660, 879, 887, 985, 1183, 1227, 1276, 1424, 1592, 1603, 2052, 2312, 2390, 2453, 2519, 2867, 3029, 3036, 3127, 4291, 4652, 4702, 5244, 5470, 5595, 5688, 6109

CAST

    See Children of Alcoholics Screening Test

        (continued on next page)

     (continued on next page)

(continued on next page)

(continued on next page)

Marital Relationships

(continued on next page)

Psychiatric Disorders (continued)   5101, 5107, 5112-5113, 5118, 5120, 5124,
5132, 5141, 5143-5144, 5146, 5182, 5189, 5221, 5257, 5281-5282, 5304, 5306,
5337, 5358, 5380, 5415, 5420, 5426, 5432, 5453, 5458, 5468, 5506, 5511, 5532,
5560-5561, 5593, 5622, 5648, 5650, 5662-5663, 5742-5745, 5750, 5800, 5829,
5872, 5955, 5969, 6122, 6134, 6292, 6312, 6347, 6390

> See also Children of Alcoholics - psychiatric disorders
>   Parental Mental Illness

Psychiatric Hospitals

> See Mental Hospitals

Psychiatrists 4935

Psychological Factors 55, 59, 75, 135, 174, 197, 266, 271, 288, 303, 304, 343,
420, 442, 458, 461, 521, 687-688, 710, 839, 846, 871, 873, 920, 951, 1157,
1199, 1361, 1412, 1501, 1804, 2068, 2188-2189, 2465-2466, 2473, 2900, 2913,
2940, 3055-3056, 3058, 3149, 3152, 3192, 3813, 3886, 3964, 4093, 4204, 4230,
4245, 4356-4357, 4396, 4403-4404, 4407, 4499, 4548, 4623, 4818, 5113, 5176,
5316, 5320, 5344, 5965, 5972, 6028, 6100, 6318, 6345

> See also Psychosocial Factors
>   Social Factors

Psychological Tests 4, 2051, 2383, 2420, 2533, 2639, 2768, 3013, 3935, 4149,
4162, 4191-4192, 4334, 4892, 4952, 5275, 5297, 5399, 5659

> See also Questionnaires

Psychosocial Factors 57, 381, 517, 578, 701, 760, 805, 901, 1136, 1700, 1770,
1772, 1906, 2052, 2288, 2640, 2663, 2841, 2873-2874, 3009-3010, 3148, 3625,
3814, 3969, 3980, 4297, 4371, 4397, 4554-4555, 4689, 4795, 4905, 4953, 5032,
5909, 6353, 6367

> See also Psychological Factors
>   Social Factors

Psychotherapy 529, 543, 642, 713, 743, 772, 937, 984, 1012, 1090, 1172, 1241,
1245, 1304, 1376, 1655, 1673, 1704, 1965, 2037, 2042, 2050, 2281, 2782, 2961,
2989, 3280, 3284, 3307, 3532, 3551, 4462, 4988, 5082, 5309, 5315, 5598, 5920,
5922, 5940, 6103

> See also Counseling
>   Family Therapy
>   Group Therapy
>   Treatment

Public Policy 83, 1083, 4284, 4286-4287, 4517

Puerto Rico - Puerto Ricans 8, 972, 1406, 1432, 1545, 2056, 2877, 3193, 3812,
4232, 4871

> See also Hispanics

Puerto Rico 3193, 4871

Questionnaires 19, 125, 174-175, 200, 259, 383, 399, 403, 503, 507, 559, 626,
638, 686, 712, 853, 854, 864, 866, 874, 879, 907, 945-947, 1152, 1212, 1251,
1273, 1430, 1436, 1579, 1592, 1641, 1828, 1867, 1991, 2052-2053, 2180, 2191,
2348, 2514, 2526, 2553, 2640, 2643, 2698, 2847, 2876, 3054, 3063, 3065, 3088,
3126, 3161, 3165, 3220, 3363, 3369, 3374, 3469, 3494, 3614, 3623, 3625, 3646,
3851, 3883, 3908, 3960, 3981, 4030, 4130, 4139, 4141, 4151, 4158, 4186, 4233,
4314, 4337-4338, 4383, 4396, 4421, 4423, 4427, 4490, 4563, 4569, 4651, 4692,
4744-4745, 5120, 5217, 5230, 5276, 5297, 5406, 5434, 5438, 5539, 5605, 5626,
5637, 5657, 5725, 5760, 5783, 5786, 5838, 5853, 5922, 5959, 5988, 6063, 6068,
6078, 6084, 6111, 6146, 6168, 6170, 6177, 6195, 6243-6244, 6248, 6300, 6352,
6372, 6375, 6404, 6440

> See also Psychological Test

Race 882, 2544, 3795, 4468, 5091, 5159, 6380

    See also names of specific groups

Railroad Workers 5179

Rape 396, 1897, 2331, 3506, 5175

    See also Child Abuse
           Incest
           Sexual Abuse
           Spouse Abuse

Reasons for Drinking

    See Motivation for Drinking

Rebellion

    See Delinquent Youth

Recovery 70, 76, 110, 168, 170, 259, 442, 578, 606, 615, 664, 669, 810, 831,
917, 987, 1050, 1058, 1176, 1274, 1294, 1342, 1351-1353, 1380, 1424, 1472,
1482, 1507, 1546, 1616, 1808, 1867, 1929, 2004, 2199, 2285, 2295, 2297-2298,
2322-2323, 2502, 2526, 2632, 2886, 2898, 2899, 2999, 3046, 3053, 3082, 3084,
3119, 3437, 3451, 3499, 3769, 3789, 3825-3826, 3863, 3868, 3912, 3916, 3923,
3979-3980, 3983-3985, 4312, 4598-4600, 4616, 4624, 4634, 4682 4730, 4732, 4735,
4763-4764, 4794, 4882, 4984, 5195, 5272, 5428, 5543, 5673, 5891-5893, 5945,
6021, 6027, 6087-6088, 6096, 6098, 6138, 6164, 6190, 6219, 6367

Referral to Treatment

    See Treatment - referral

Rehabilitation 75, 149, 177, 286, 318, 325, 391, 456, 501, 721, 750, 823,
964-965, 967, 1061, 1092, 1298, 1351-1353, 1381, 1388, 1412, 1641, 1655, 1960,
1978, 2013, 2107, 2133, 2260, 2463, 2605, 2650, 2652, 2825, 3041, 3129, 3213,
3250, 3298, 3482, 3493, 3624, 3683, 3821, 3952, 4056, 4340, 4399, 4473, 4516,
4669, 4715, 4905, 5195, 5260, 5614, 5786, 6041, 6134

    See also Treatment

Relapse 2271-2273, 3232, 3899, 3913-3915, 3980, 3983-3985, 4158, 4239, 5357,
5465, 5618

    See also Treatment - outcome

Religion/Religious Factors 61, 94, 174-175, 222, 388, 465, 605, 652, 695, 778,
818, 854, 945-946, 1060, 1096-1099, 1522, 1869, 1903, 1998-1999, 2787, 2913,
3269, 3298, 3331, 3740, 3757-3758, 4111, 4155, 4315, 4666, 4775, 5335, 5352,
6040, 6096, 6098, 6175, 6200, 6364-6365

    See also Clergy
           Nuns
           names of specific religious groups

Research 3030, 4517, 5365, 5520

Retirement 2265

Reviews (General) 24, 26, 367, 969, 1211, 1845, 1849, 2837, 2959, 3103, 3322,
5209, 5504-5505, 6032, 6315

    See also Behavioral Therapy - reviews   Genetic Influences - reviews
           Child Abuse - reviews   Marital Relationships - review
           Children of Alcoholics - reviews   Wife Abuse - reviews
           Family Therapy - reviews   Wives' Drinking - reviews
                              Wives of Drinkers - reviews

(continued on next page)

Treatment (continued)

motivation   644, 2713, 3265, 3662, 4452, 5220, 5346, 5614

outcome   180, 435, 467, 492, 508, 565, 756, 1071, 1153, 1526, 1590, 1852, 1907, 1980, 2106, 2484-2486, 3016, 3125, 3247-3248, 3251, 3278, 3479, 3525, 3657, 3981, 4342, 4695, 4781, 5185, 5353, 5386, 5780, 5879, 6001, 6080, 6152-6153, 6322

See also Relapse

outpatient   132, 172, 335, 479, 566, 772, 848, 1785, 2092, 2170, 2197, 2978, 3296, 3810, 3996, 5169, 6360

prognosis   2116, 2170, 2649, 3543, 3871, 4295, 4463, 4719, 6232

referral   3012, 3252, 3498, 4169, 4380, 4640, 5208, 5346, 5417

residential programs   75, 807, 845, 3665, 4469-4470, 6041, 6100, 6140

See also Al-Anon   Counseling
        Alateen   Family Therapy
        Alcoholics Anonymous   Group Therapy
        Behavioral Therapy   Psychotherapy
        Children of Alcoholics - treatment   Rehabilitation

Twins   13, 701, 1093, 2021-2022, 2211, 2225, 2227, 2242, 2354, 2356-2357, 2812, 2942, 2973-2974, 3005, 3096, 3142, 3319, 3494, 3762, 3776, 3877, 4068, 4438-4439, 4527, 4589, 5105, 5109-5111, 5119, 5148, 5265, 6179, 6260, 6428

See also Genetic Influences

Unemployment   47, 132, 503, 711, 1548, 3310, 3900, 5079, 5826

United Kingdom

See England
    Ireland
    Scotland
    Wales

United States   322, 331, 378, 621-622, 640, 994, 2109, 2874, 2908, 2918-2919, 2934, 3121, 3420, 3735, 3840, 3908, 4130, 4150, 4348, 4638, 4951, 4961, 5179-5180, 5268, 5416, 5759, 6243, 6248

Urban Factors   1389, 1396, 1413, 1570, 1582, 3374, 4009, 4566, 4865, 4902, 5186, 6118, 6298

Uruguay   558

Utah   4151, 5355

Vermont   281

Veterans   38, 414, 507, 546, 779, 2765, 3057, 3977, 4085-4086, 4188, 5931, 6040, 6390

See also Military

Vietnamese   3829

Violent Behavior   387, 1293, 2114, 2407, 2946, 3158, 3592, 3739, 3967, 4311, 4398, 4930, 5423, 5628, 5875, 5980, 6402

See also Aggression   Husband Abuse
        Child Abuse   Spouse Abuse
        Crime   Suicide
                                     Wife Abuse